YOUNG CHINESE ARTISTS
THE NEXT GENERATION

CHRISTOPH NOE
CORDELIA NOE
XENIA PIËCH

YOUNG

CHINESE

THE NEXT GENERATION

ARTISTS

PRESTEL
MUNICH · BERLIN · LONDON · NEW YORK

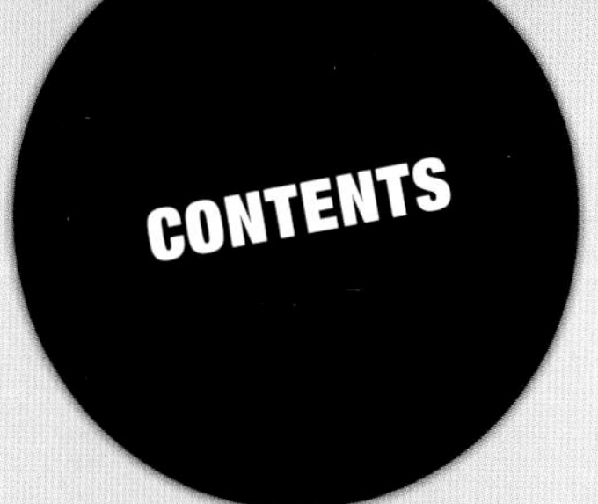
CONTENTS

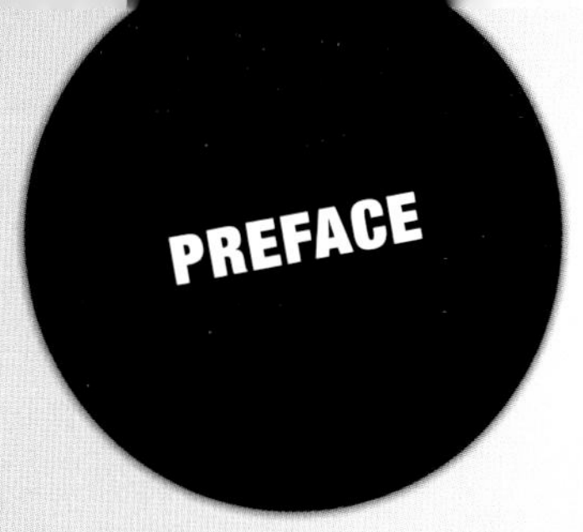

PREFACE TO THE SECOND EDITION

When the first edition of Young Chinese Artists was released in 2008 it was our wish that a wider audience would read and appreciate the publication. The publisher and the contributors to this book are pleased and honored that their expectations were exceeded and the second, revised edition has been released much earlier than expected. We are excited and grateful that the book has already become a standard reference around the current happenings in the young Chinese art scene, not only for a professional audience worldwide but also for those wanting to learn more about emerging artists from China.

There have been many interesting and exciting developments along with new challenges in the Chinese art scene since the release of the first edition. While we have noticed that the exotic factor of Chinese contemporary art is diminishing, we are happy to see a shift towards a deeper engagement with the individual artists, their ideas and work. At the same time, we are seeing some overall challenges in the global art market with the Chinese market being no exception. Therefore we believe that discussions about the art itself, the ideas behind it, and content should be the primary focus.

To support this content-based discussion it is only appropriate to revise portions of this book and to update the works of the artists. The emerging artists featured here are filled with new ideas and impulses which has made an updated version so necessary.

The selection of artists featured has not changed and we would like to emphasize that the book should not be understood as a top list of young Chinese artists. Its aim is to provide an overview of the variety of artists and art being created in China and to introduce artists that also function as their generation's representatives.

Besides expressing our thanks to our readers, we would like to thank Prestel Publishing and in particular Jürgen Krieger for supporting this new edition of the book.

Christoph Noe
Cordelia Noe
Beijing, May 2010

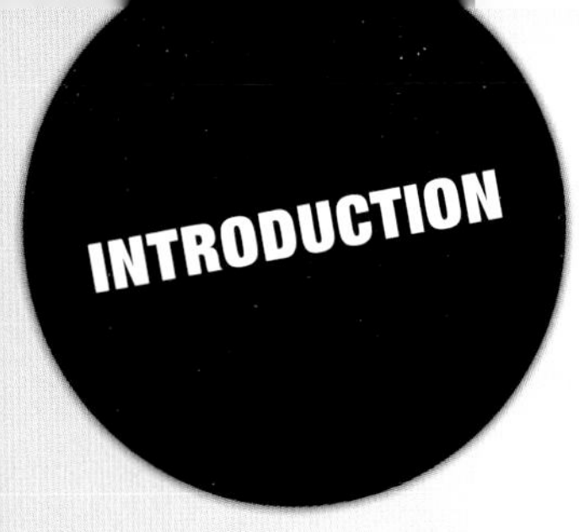

INTRODUCTION

1. WHAT IS THE CONCEPT BEHIND YOUNG CHINESE ARTISTS?

In China's contemporary art scene, artists born after the middle of the 1970s not only focus on a different range of themes than earlier generations of artists, they have also developed a new visual style in which to express them. The progressive opening of China that began with Deng Xiaoping's reforms and Open-Door Policy in the late 1970s, and the resulting, monumental change produced in Chinese society, is largely responsible for this development.

In the past thirty years, the speed of China's development has been breathtaking. Today's China consists of an endless number of skyscrapers and newly created urban landscapes, of an open-market economy home to both national and multinational companies. China holds a dominant position in the world economy in not only production, but also consumption, and has benefited generously from the effects of globalization. The New China is the Internet and text messages, fitness clubs and Diet Coke; it is the creation of new opportunities, yet the loss of others. Young people's lifestyles – the clothes they wear, the food they eat, the homes they live in, the level of education they have, and the way they spend their leisure time – have undergone radical transformation. This combination of factors affects one's perception, one's thinking; it creates new values and an estrangement from older ones; it has shaped the attitudes of today's young adults – and among them, the artists and the art they create.

The coming of age of people born in the 1970s – the so-called Post-70s generation – coincides with the period of China's reform and modernization. From the day they were born, the Post-70s generation has lived this transformation. Often growing up as only-children, they were at times spoon-fed and pampered, but also paid dearly for a lack of company. They were born in an age when the collectivist environment provided families with work and accommodation and the security of a big socialist family. Economic improvement meant the transition from an agrarian society to an industrial one, and the emergence of a materialistic consumer culture. Technological advancement brought with it the availability of a vast amount of new information, and the unprecedented challenge of basing one's life decisions on this information.

The usage of the expression Post-70s[1] might sound unfamiliar to the non-Chinese reader. As it coincides with historical milestones and changes within China, sociologists, political scientists, and psychologists alike use this term for the people born in this decade. Grouping people based on the criteria of the years in which they were born is not China-specific and can be found in Western popular culture, social sciences, and modern history, with the term "Generation X" perhaps the most prominent example.[2]

It is a logical step to apply this Post-70s categorization to the Chinese contemporary art scene, and exhibitions such as *After 70s: The Generation Changed by Market*,[3] and *Next Station, Cartoon?: Paintings from the Post-70s Generation*,[4] as well as art publications, make frequent reference to it.

Ultimately, it is tricky to group all artists born from the beginning to the end of the 1970s and refer to them together as Post-70s. By adopting a more nuanced approach, one can discern quite considerable differences in style, visual taste, themes, and ideology of those artists born in the latter half of the seventies. Consequently, the sociological definition of Post-70s is only applicable in a limited fashion. This book looks at a rather narrower grouping of artists born between 1975 and 1981 who are representative of China's young art scene, and seeks to expose them and their amazingly diverse artistic perspectives to a wider audience.

As we appraise the featured artists and their work, we of course expect to find some commonalities and an unavoidable similitude in themes. But though they share a common background and have lived through thirty years of an incredibly unique period in their nation's history, this book's intention is to introduce each artist on his or her own – as individuals with unique ways of expressing their ideas and with distinct trajectories in developing their forms of visual expression – and thus avoid the risk that they be seen under a reductionist, geographical "Made in China" label.

2. WHAT IS THE COMPOSITION OF THE BOOK?

The greater part of *Young Chinese Artists: The Next Generation* takes up, as the title suggests, young Chinese artists and their art. Nevertheless, we consider it invaluable when discussing artistic creation to also provide the context and environment from which it springs. Since birth, this generation of artists has experienced a China in constant transformation, a reality that influenced their education, their personality, their attitude, and, finally, their art. Given this unprecedented historical reality, we believe it indispensable to offer insight into the factors that shaped their lives as we analyze and draw conclusions about their artistic output. Therefore, included is a historical overview on major milestones from the 1970s to today covering state affairs, popular culture, and lifestyle. In addition, we have invited experts to share their views, experiences, and findings on different topics such as urbanization, business, relationships, love and sex, lifestyle, status symbols and brands, communication and media, as well as sports and health.

In the following section, a selection of thirty artists, six of whom work as duos, are introduced. Each chapter, one for each artist/artist duo, gives an overview of their work and an introduction to their ideas, written by an international team of art critics. An interview conducted with each artist/artist duo, either face-to-face, in a phone call, as a chat, or via questionnaire, is also part of each chapter. This interview was designed not only to offer insight into the personality of the artist as an artist, but also as a representative of a generation. Thus, in addition to typical "art" questions related to their artistic approach, more general questions are posed, such as, "What does your ideal living environment look like?" or "How would you describe your generation?"

3. WHAT CRITERIA WERE USED FOR THE SELECTION PROCESS OF THE ARTISTS?

Though the selection of included artists was based on a set of distinct criteria, any selection process is always to a certain extent subjective, and thus subject to the criticism of being non-inclusive. While some of the featured artists are really not so "young" in the sense that they are established figures in the art scene and have been previously featured in other publications, we think their inclusion in this volume is appropriate. Alongside these more established artists are those who are "emerging" and perhaps not yet well known outside of China.

Age

A book about young Chinese artists obviously uses age as a predominant criterion in the selection process. Taking into account that contemporary art history in China only began some thirty years ago – 1979 is widely considered the starting point[5] – it is amazing to see how much has transpired in this short period, and just how many shifts have occurred in contemporary Chinese art. Running parallel to China's radical transformation in social, political, and economic matters, the Chinese art world has been compressed from ten-year to five-year cycles, if not shorter[6] – a phenomena not specific to contemporary art but also to modern life itself. Given the frenetic pace at which change occurs in China, we thought it unsuitable to cover the entire ten-year span of Post-70s artists; we decided to make this period shorter.

Why did we start with artists born in 1975? Our original idea was to start our overview from 1976, linking it with the birth of the post-Mao era. However, we realized that there are some artists who were born just months before then whom we consider part of that group. Therefore, starting in the year 1976 would have been more a theoretical cut-off rather than one based on our own visual experience, and we thus set the starting point to artists born in 1975.[7]

A similar approach applies to the upper limit, which we concluded with an artist born in 1981. Again, this is based on observation of the commonality of topics and visual expression among the artists. Furthermore, the artists should have had the time to work on their own, and to establish an ample body of work after having graduated from university.

Though a rather short period of time was chosen, namely from 1975 to 1981,[8] upon review of the art scene some three hundred artists met this criterion. However, it was not our intention to provide a comprehensive lexicon of artists, but rather to give an exemplary overview of different artistic positions.

Representing the Generation

As this publication also seeks to offer insight into the life and culture of young adults in today's China, the personality and the topics of the portrayed artists should in some way represent their generation – their themes and ideas should to a certain extent reflect the mindset and ideals of their peers.

Origins in Mainland China

The dramatic changes in Mainland China that began in the middle of the 1970s brought upheaval to the lives of its citizens, thus we felt that the selected artists should have been born and raised there. Wishing to stress the common experiences in child- and adulthood and their influence on artistic creation, having one's origins in Mainland Chinese is a logical starting point as the artists were all exposed to and absorbed the last decades' developments and subsequent transformations.

Media

In the past several years, outside of China, a number of contemporary art exhibitions featuring young Chinese artists showcased artistic forms such as video, multimedia, and installation, which gave the impression that painting was passé and only those mentioned forms contemporary. In contrast, while we have also observed that the employment of these "new" media is indeed widespread (quite a few artists work in more than one discipline), painting is very much a driving force in the contemporary art scene. Our selection attempts to mirror the variety of media used by the artists, as photography, video, animation, performance, installation, sculpture, and painting all play a vital role in the young Chinese art scene.

Additional factors

Local and/or international exposure, as well as the existence of a certain body of work that reflects a discernable artistic development, also figured into the selection process. And, finally, the selection attempted to pay tribute to artists who demonstrate a unique and independent way of thinking, possess coherent artistic personalities, and who, we feel, work in an authentic fashion.

The market value of the artists was not taken under consideration. While it may be true that market forces can influence an artist's way of thinking or even of working, we believe that artists who will endure the test of time will not be dependent upon short-term market trends.

4. WHAT THEMES DO THE "YOUNG CHINESE ARTISTS" EXPLORE IN THEIR ARTWORKS, AND IN WHAT MEDIA DO THEY WORK?

A study conducted by Grey advertising agency and the British Council looked at the basic values of young Chinese adults, revealing that individualism, a craving for a better life, career ambition, more freedom for women, a thirst for knowledge, and a search for enjoyment appeared among the most important.[9] It is clear that self-expression is crucially important to this generation. More self-centered and concerned with their own lives in comparison to the previous generation, this generation has known only peace and an ever-growing economy in which this very growth takes precedence over democratic reforms. Mass consumerism is widespread, and a socialist system has been replaced with a capitalist one that diverges from the collectivist ideology and ideals of the past. Taken together with the frenetic urban expansion within China, these changes represent a deep influence on individual experience and perception.

The young artists chosen portray, in an endless variety of ways, the economic and social transformations China is experiencing, managing to condense their era's special characteristics and what it means for the nation and the individual. Their works can be characterized as less resistant to the system, less preoccupied with social ideals and values of collectivism, and much more attentive to the mainstream. Less concerned with criticizing the current government or politic trends, the artists' works exemplify the social ideals of the new China – commercialism and individualism.

Individualism, self-exploration, and existential issues can be seen as the most prevalent themes in these young artists' works – a reflection and visualization of the increasing awareness of the individual and his or her personal concerns. For example, an image of a little boy crying and extending his arms to preserve his last few feet of his privacy, or another in which he holds a sharp knife, exemplifies this self-centered focus, an unveiling of the personal conflicts and inner struggles typical of this generation.

A constantly altered landscape produces a feeling of loss; continuous political and social change and the cult of the perpetually "new" deny a sense of security. Solitary figures – on top of a hill, astride a pony, or on a Ferris wheel – are visual metaphors that encapsulate these sensations, made stronger still for a generation of only-children who, alone, assume the enormous responsibility for the family – and their family's aspirations. As a consequence, the artists at times look backward, often nostalgically recalling the "old times," as when, for example, a cartoon aesthetic from childhood is employed as an artistic language, or memories of a long-gone past – ranging from school vocabulary charts to abandoned rides in an amusement park fallen in disuse – are depicted with contemporary themes.

The topic of insecurity is often closely linked to that of growing up. The transition from youth to adulthood, with the new responsibilities this entails, can be seen in a literal work showing a girl crying as she grows out of her clothes. Growing up also means developing one's identity – a personal identity, but also an identity of society as a whole. A car with two front ends objectifies the question of "forward" and "backward," apparently asking: "Where do we go?" In other works, staged scenes feature young people dressed as computer game characters situated in normal environments – they are images that represent the struggle of forging one's own identity and pose the questions: "Who am I?" and "Who are you?"

The omnipresent urban environment is another recurring theme. The transformation of the urban landscape – the deconstruction of the traditional and construction of the modern environment – carries implicit with it the alteration of personal space. Urbanization is reflected both realistically and meditatively, such as in images of the smashed remains of half-demolished houses or the city's glamorous lights, and at times in the form of a critical examination, such as a work invoking the human sacrifice involved in the Three Gorges Dam project.

Other representative topics include the relationship between the sexes, the evolving identity of women, and sexuality. In some works, the female body, which in the Mao era (and after) was de-emphasized, is depicted very explicitly; in others, sexuality is flirted with in a more disguised and ironic fashion, such as with the depiction of mating pandas.

The young artists adopt themes taken directly from their daily lives or that have their origins in popular culture. Lifestyle-oriented topics mix with symbols of Western brands, at times contemplatively, at times provokingly. With the normalization of art – understood not only by the intellectual elite, but also accessible to a wider audience – consumer society and a post-ideological reality have received greater attention.

While among the chosen artists painting is the dominant medium used – a reality certainly due in no small part to Chinese artistic tradition and the ubiquity of the medium in early art education – the use of a cartoon-esque visual style deserves special mention. Though opinions differ on its stylistic origins, it is clear that Chinese artists utilize the cartoon or comic language in a novel fashion, using it to express sensations such as pain or vanity, or to explore a whole range of mature and sophisticated themes far removed from the childlike associations the form evokes.

And though we still find the application of traditional techniques, for example in painting with the use of multiple perspectives in contrast to the Western artistic tradition's central perspective, the artists wholly embrace new technologies such as LED displays, lasers, and Flash animations. In between the extremes of the most traditional and the most innovative, lies a broad range of media, from digitally processed photography to video, performance, sculpture, and artworks that exist solely in virtual form on the Internet. Whichever the media employed, the selected young artists have in common a highly developed technical ability and precise craftsmanship, a trait that no doubt finds its origins in their academic training.

China's development continues at a vertiginous pace, generating in the process a series of contradictions often hard to describe in words. The importance of the young Chinese artists lies in their ability to visualize and make patent in their work otherwise inexpressible sentiments about today's China and the way their generation lives and feels, using art to draw connections between the most seemingly irreconcilable contrasts. Their artwork expresses a common feeling about their unique cultural moment, an understanding and acute perception about their world, and in so doing imbues the contemporary art scene with their generation's most pressing concerns.

5. FROM WHAT TRADITION DO THE POST-'75 ARTISTS COME?

China's young artists manifest a far greater concern about quotidian issues than they do about politics. In contrast to the New Wave generation of the 1980s or the Political Pop painters of the 1990s, this younger generation of artists tackles political themes far less in their works. However, no longer having to be political can also be regarded as a new form of freedom. Their attention is focused on the new and endlessly diverse lifestyle choices of their time, a cultural reality which represents a distancing from the collective, and that influences their work as they explore the emotions and questions pertaining to the individual. This generation's seeming indifference to politics and social concerns is, however, more complex, and can perhaps be traced to a background with an incredibly fragmented history.[10]

Though there exists this strong need for self-expression among the young artists, one should not regard this development as superficial. Indeed, the opposite seems to be the case, as this generation openly exhibits their personal thoughts and fears. With hardly any historical baggage to carry, art becomes a personal dialogue with a disentangled and diversified society.[11] A rapidly growing China confronts new struggles and growing pains, and this generation's potential lies in their response to the shifting ideological layers as they witness them first hand. The increasing significance and popular appeal of this generation's unique visual style, their sensibility, naivety, paradoxical approach, and melancholy – qualities absent from the artwork of the previous generation – have an inevitable affect on the emerging generation of artists.

Though there is a lack of overt commitment to political content, the strong emphasis on the individual biography and a strong focus on their time and its specific issues reveals on the part of many of the artists a profound knowledge and intense relation with their own history and tradition. (In China, history is defined as a continuum of three to five thousand years.) A well-preserved traditional artistic spirit manifests itself – to greater or lesser degrees – in newly combined artistic creations which demonstrate that the contemporary and the traditional need not be oppositional.

6. WHAT ARE THE SPECIAL CHARACTERISTICS OF THE ART SCENE FOR THE YOUNG CHINESE ARTISTS?

China is arguably experiencing a cultural explosion comparable to New York and London of decades past, and the art scene has changed dramatically within the last couple of years. While the first commercial gallery in Beijing's major art district, 798, only opened in 2002, today a new art space opens almost weekly and there are now over two hundred galleries. While there were hardly any museums exhibiting contemporary art in the 1990s, today dozens have opened and many more are to follow. And while a couple of years ago there was still no market for Chinese contemporary art, nowadays prices skyrocket as local and international collectors bid for the work. Newly launched art magazines and a growing number of Chinese art critics represent an emancipation from the hegemony of Western interpretation. These changes in the art scene influence all Chinese artists, the Post-'75 artists being no exception. While the structures of the art scene continue to mature and an exact overview would be precipitated, some conclusions about the young Chinese artists can be drawn.

Firstly, there seems to be a strong symbiotic relationship between the universities and the artists. Each university has its own personality and reputation for a particular artistic direction that attracts particular artists, who in turn bolster this tendency through their own production. Shanghai's universities, for example, are more oriented towards new media, particularly video and photography, while the Sichuan Academy of Fine Arts in Chongqing is renowned for their painting department. The China Academy of Fine Art in Hangzhou offers the most exhaustive historical foundation, and is also home to some of the most innovative artists working in video or animation.

Another identifiable trait among the young artists is the tendency to move to major art centers, namely Beijing or Shanghai, after graduating from university – or indeed before entering. While Shanghai seems to attract particularly those artists working with new media, those attracted to Beijing do not exhibit a similar unifying quality. Drawn by the proximity to institutions, art spaces, museums, galleries, curators, and critics, many artists settle permanently in these cities, or for a certain period of time live and work in them. Beijing in particular has generated a certain buzz, and young artists faced with rising studio rents have been pushed to the outskirts where they find more tranquil surroundings and lower rents. It is a phenomenon similar to that of 1980s New York or modern-day Berlin, as national and international artists flocked to these global art meccas.

A third characteristic common to these young artists is a precocious entry into the art market when compared to their predecessors. The art market, being both locally and internationally driven, has seen an increasingly high demand for young, undiscovered artists. Artists cooperating with galleries or exhibition centers while still in the middle of their studies (or just after graduation) are no exception. While this provides new opportunities, it also represents a risk, as an artist often does not have the time to elaborate a personal style nor the possibility to exchange ideas or reflect upon their work before being fully integrated into the market.

It is clear that the art world in China – undoubtedly a reflection of the society as a whole – produces a unique set of circumstances in which young Chinese artists live and work, and which, while certainly similar in some regards to the Western art scene, possesses its own exciting, vital dynamism of constant development and renewal.

7. WHOM DO WE WISH TO THANK FOR CONTRIBUTING TO THIS PUBLICATION?

We want to thank all who supported the realization of this book project:

- First and foremost, we wish to thank our co-editor Xenia Piëch for her passionate and professional work, who engaged us with her expertise throughout this entire project.
- All the artists, their assistants, and their galleries for their time and support providing us with information and picture material.
- Our authors Huang Du, Martina Köppel-Yang, Carol Lu, John Millichap, Ulrike Münter, Song Yi, Philip Tinari, Azure (Wei) Wu, Pauline J. Yao and Mia Yu for contributing the artist portraits, but also for their engagement in the overall concept.
- Our authors and interview partners James Chau, Dirk Jehmlich, Naudia Lou and Christian Taeubert, Rock, Xia Juan, and Zhong Yu for sharing their insights and expertise in the introductory essays.
- Eveline Chao, Jiang Jun, Wolfgang Kohl, Anu Leinonen, Fabijan Tadic, and Trendbüro Asia-Pacific.
- Our project staff Zhao Chong and Li Man for their highly efficient and hard work, which went far beyond standard project support.
- The team of Prestel for their continuous feedback and support.
- Finally, we want to express our thanks to Felix Hoffmann, who from the very beginning acted as advisor and sparring partner.

Christoph Noe
Cordelia Noe
Beijing, July 2008

1 Analogous terms like Post-50s, Post-60s, and Post-80s are also in use.
2 The term was first used in popular culture in the book *Generation X* by Charles Hamblett and Jane Deverson, and later expanded on by Douglas Coupland as he described the generation of people born between the 1960s and 70s. Other terms include Generation Y or Generation Golf, the latter referring to the first German generation of carefree, affluent youth, born between 1965 and 1975 in Germany, who generally drove the Golf model from Volkswagen.
3 Name of a 2005 exhibition at Today Art Gallery, Beijing.
4 Name of a 2005 exhibition at He Xiangning Art Museum, Shenzhen, and Star Gallery, Beijing.
5 The exhibition of the Chinese contemporary art "Star" group in Beijing.
6 See also the catalogue of the exhibit *Infantization*, Shanghai Art Museum, 2007.
7 The artist Li Yu, born in 1973, being an exception, as he works together with Liu Bo as an artist team.
8 Of course there are artists born outside this range of years who share affinities with and could be considered part of the defined group.
9 The study collected data of 70,000 Chinese, ages 16 to 39, living in 30 big cities.
10 See Carol Lu, "Collective Amnesia: A Comparative Study of Chinese Conceptual Art Practices between the 1980s and after 2000," 2008.
11 Ibid.

WITH ESSAYS BY XIA JUAN, NAUDIA LOU AND CHRISTIAN TAEUBERT, CORDELIA NOE, LILY ZHONG, DIRK JEHMLICH, JAMES CHAU AND ROCK

THOUGHTS ON THE NEW CHINA

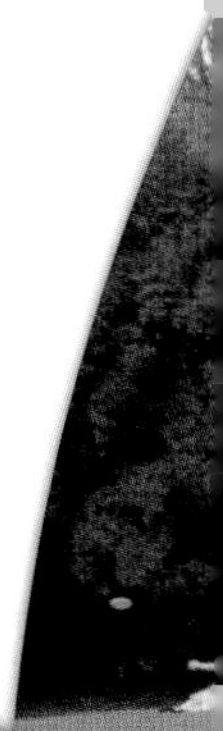

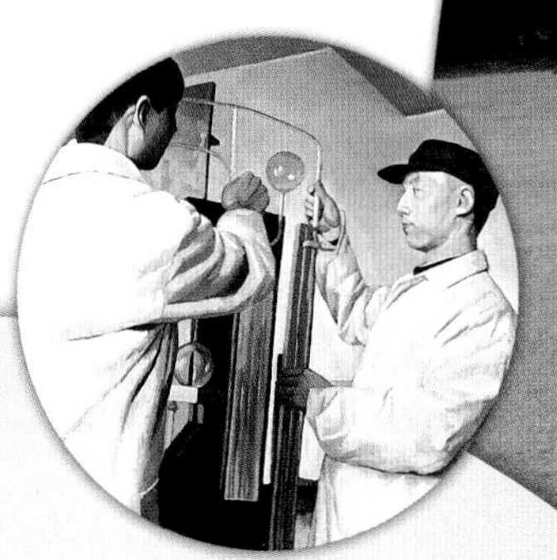

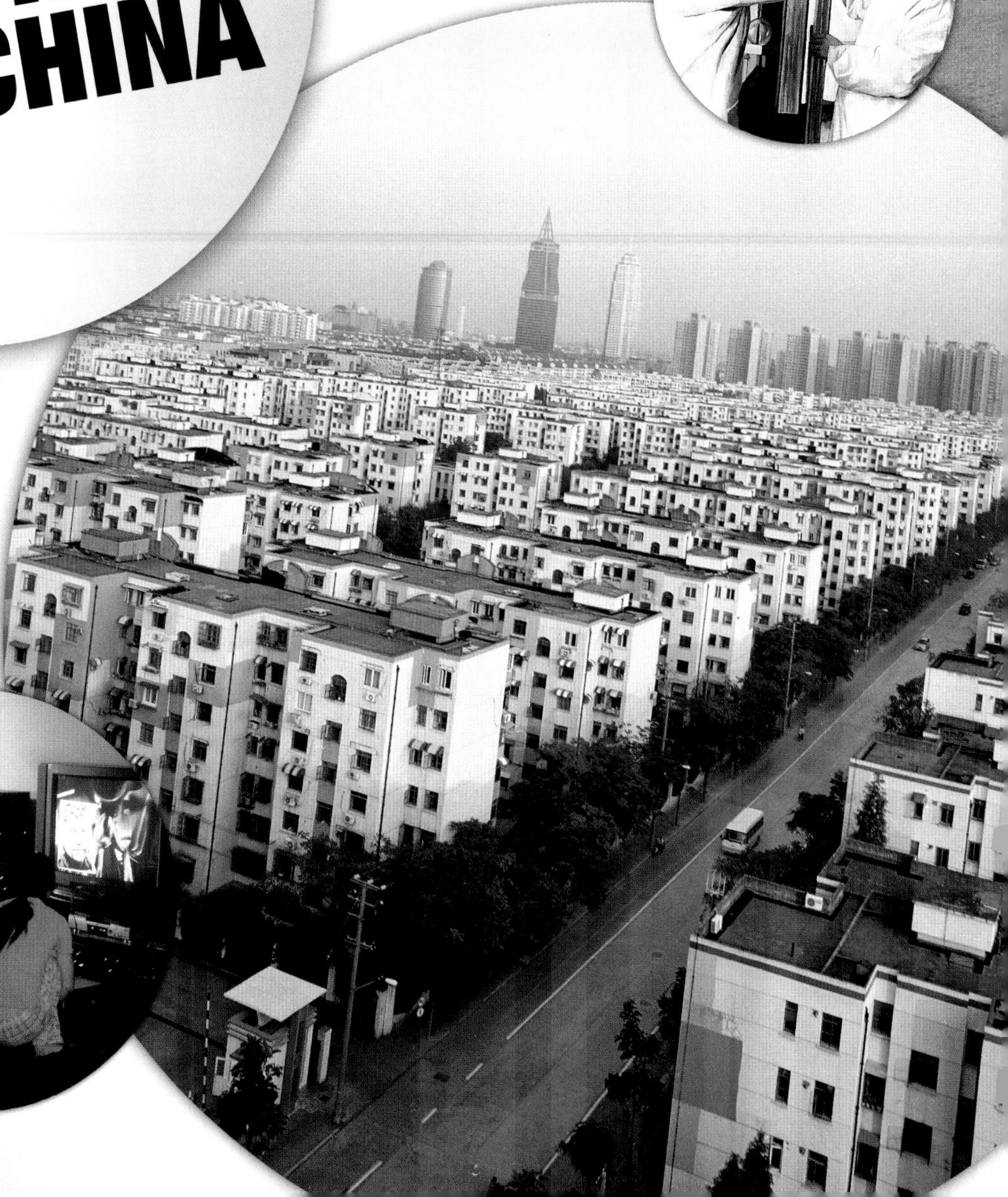

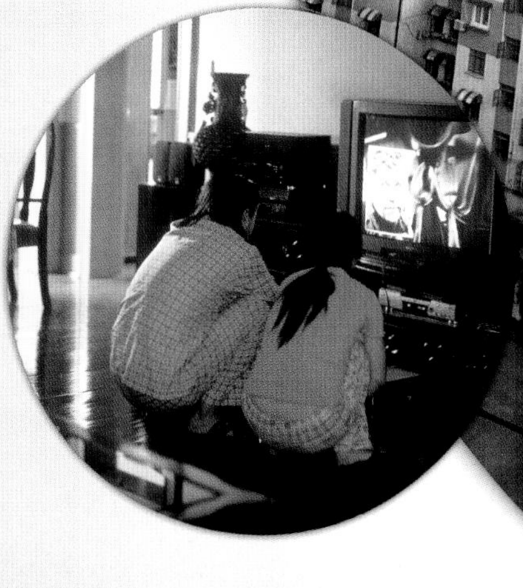

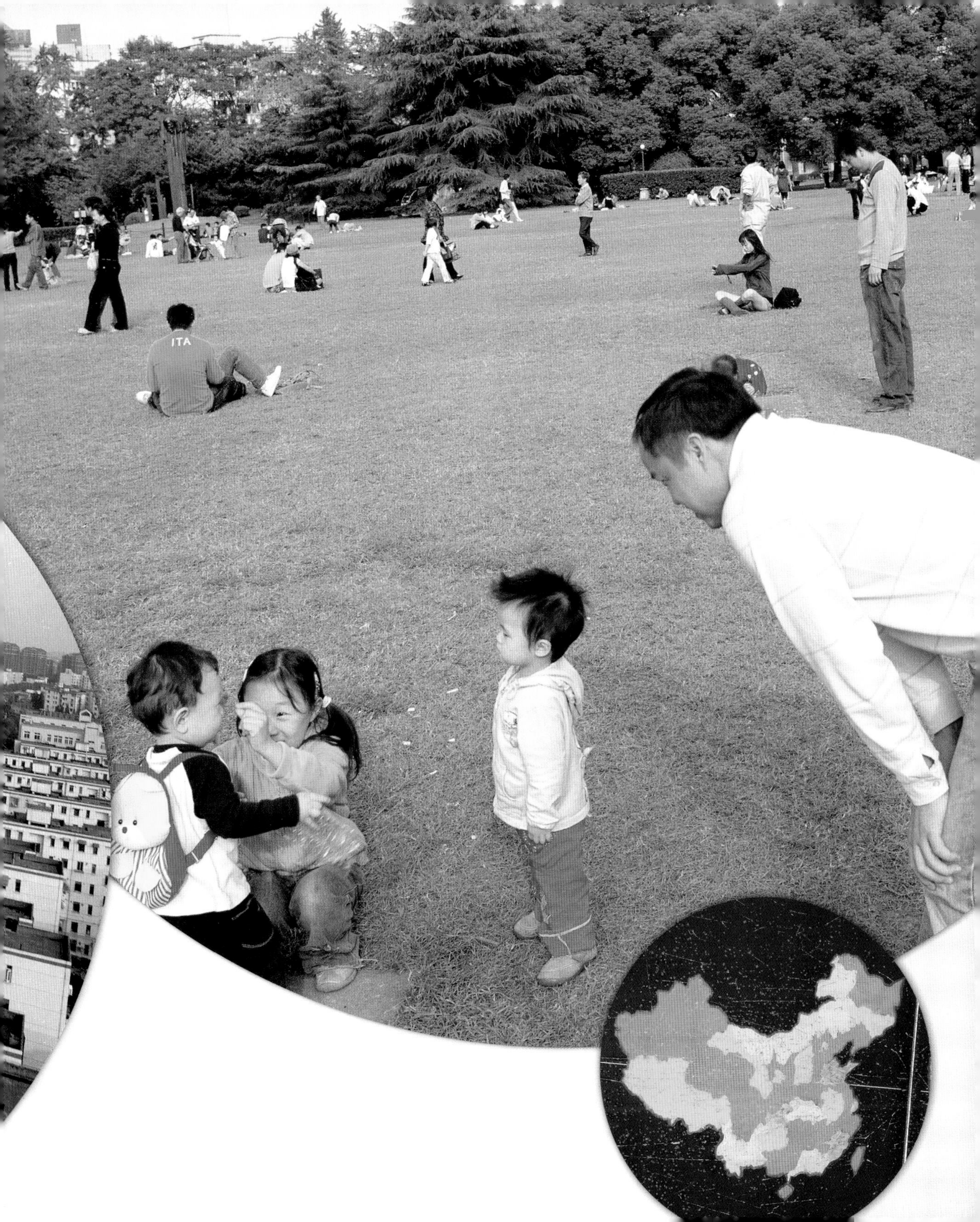
ITA

COLLECTIVE MEMORY - MILESTONES FROM THE 70s TO TODAY

BY XIAJUAN

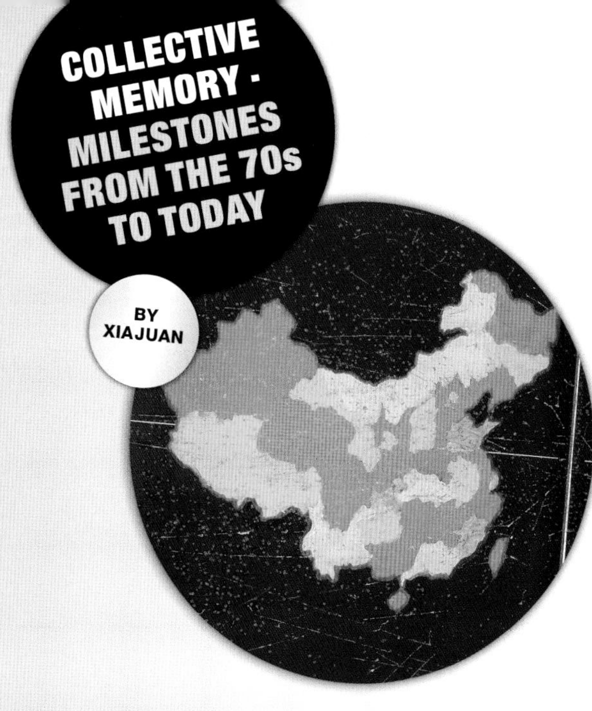

STATE AFFAIRS

END OF THE 70s TO THE END OF THE 80s

1976: THE END OF THE "CULTURAL REVOLUTION"

An unusual year for modern Chinese history. From the death of Mao Zedong on September 9th to the Tangshan earthquake, followed by the arrest of the famous "Gang of Four" on October 6th, it marked the end of a long-lasting era. Everything in China was dated and poised for renewal.

1978: THE IMPLEMENTATION OF THE OPEN-DOOR POLICY

The third plenum of the 11th Party Congress was convened, symbolizing China's entry into a brand-new historical era. By focusing on economic construction, China ended its ultra-left stance, and the macroperspective of focusing on the people's livelihood and economic development was established.

1984: THE BANNER "HELLO, XIAOPING"

Lots of people saw this banner in the media. It was unfolded by the students at Peking University during the National Day Holiday. Via TV broadcasts, the whole world saw this famous slogan. Deng Xiaoping was called the "main architect of reform and opening up" by several generations of Chinese people.

STATE AFFAIRS

END OF THE 80s TO THE END OF THE 90s

1993: THE TREND OF "DIVING INTO THE SEA"

After Deng Xiaoping's speech during his tour of southern China, the second post-1980s wave of "diving into the sea" – meaning going into business – took place, and a lot of intellectuals gave up their studies. Of course, there were a lot of "trend followers" who did not know how to swim and inevitably drowned.

1994: BMW ENTERS THE CHINESE MARKET

BMW established its first office in Beijing, and people started dreaming of becoming rich. After this, car brands from all over the world followed, opening showrooms in China.

1997: HANDOVER OF HONG KONG

The whole nation celebrated the handover of Hong Kong.

POPULAR CULTURE
THE END OF THE 70s TO THE END OF THE 80s

CARTOONS

In addition to books and parents, cartoons also became a part of children's basic education. Among domestically produced cartoons, this generation would remember *Black Cat Police Chief* and *The Story of Afanti*. In the 1980s, Japanese and American cartoons were introduced to China's youth, and characters such as the Ninja Turtles, Mickey Mouse, and Donald Duck became instant classics.

IDOLS

The young idols were mainly singers from Hong Kong and Taiwan; songs such as "Small Town Story," "Orchid Grass," "Childhood," among others, were sung throughout the country.

MARTIAL ARTS MOVIES

The movie *Shaolin Temple*, released in 1982, was a smash hit, and shaving your head and learning martial arts became very popular among young men. In the ten years that followed, studios in Hong Kong and Taiwan produced countless martial arts movies.

LIFESTYLE
THE END OF THE 70s TO THE END OF THE 80s

"CHICKEN NEST" – PERMED HAIRSTYLE

In 1978, the most popular hair styles in the cities were curly hair and permed hair styles. For quite a long time, this was called "petite bourgeoisie sentiment."

COCA-COLA

In 1979, Coca-Cola entered the Chinese market.

AEROBICS

In the middle of the eighties, aerobics became popular. At this time, big cities like Beijing and Shanghai started setting up the country's first aerobics classes.

WESTERN-STYLE FAST FOOD RESTAURANTS

In the middle of the eighties, hamburgers, French fries, ice cream, and other Western food appeared, enriching and endangering the eating and drinking habits of the Chinese people. In 1987, Kentucky Fried Chicken opened its first restaurant in Beijing.

BIKINIS

In 1986, girls dressed in bikinis appeared in national aerobics competitions for the first time, and Chinese people conducted a big discussion on how to judge beauty.

POPULAR CULTURE
END OF THE 80s TO THE END OF THE 90s

POP MUSIC IN MAINLAND CHINA

Around 1993, there was an upsurge of pop music from the mainland, such as "Big China" or "Smiling Face," while at the same time "campus folk songs," such as "You, Who Share My Desk" and "The Brother Who Sleeps in the Bed Above Me," were widely sung on university campuses.

A CRAZE FOR HONG KONG AND TAIWANESE STARS

Hong Kong's four big stars, Alan Tam, Leslie Cheung, The Band Beyond, and Lin Qingxia became the idols of the masses. The movie *Wulitou* by Zhou Xingchi was very popular, while movies such as *Secret Investigations in China* and *Stories from the Journey to the West* were anointed as classics by fans.

"THE FIFTH GENERATION" PHENOMENA

Zhang Yimou, Chen Kaige, and Tian Zhuangzhuang; these fifth-generation directors had a great and immediate impact. *Raise the Red Lantern*, *The Story of Qiu Ju*, and *Farewell My Concubine* won praise for Chinese cinema from all over the world.

LIFESTYLE
END OF THE 80s TO THE END OF THE 90s

HULA HOOPS

At the beginning of the nineties, young and old were swinging hula hoops in streets and alleys all over China. A wave of healthcare spread over the nation. There were lots of different ways of using the hula hoop in those days.

KARAOKE

Karaoke first became popular in the city of Guangzhou. This type of self-entertainment and recreation became very popular at that time, and has continued to this day. Under the influence of this trend, in the beginning of the nineties the first night clubs appeared in China.

"DA GE DA" MOBILE PHONES

The first mobile phones were called "Da Ge Da," and as thick and heavy as building bricks. At the beginning of the 1990s, this communication tool was more of a symbol of status and wealth, and most of its users were the "newly rich people."

TOP INTERNATIONAL FASHION BRANDS

The phrase "fashion" started to be used by an increasing number of Chinese people, and top international fashion brands went to China. Chinese people became familiar with Louis Vuitton, Armani, and Chanel – just to name a few.

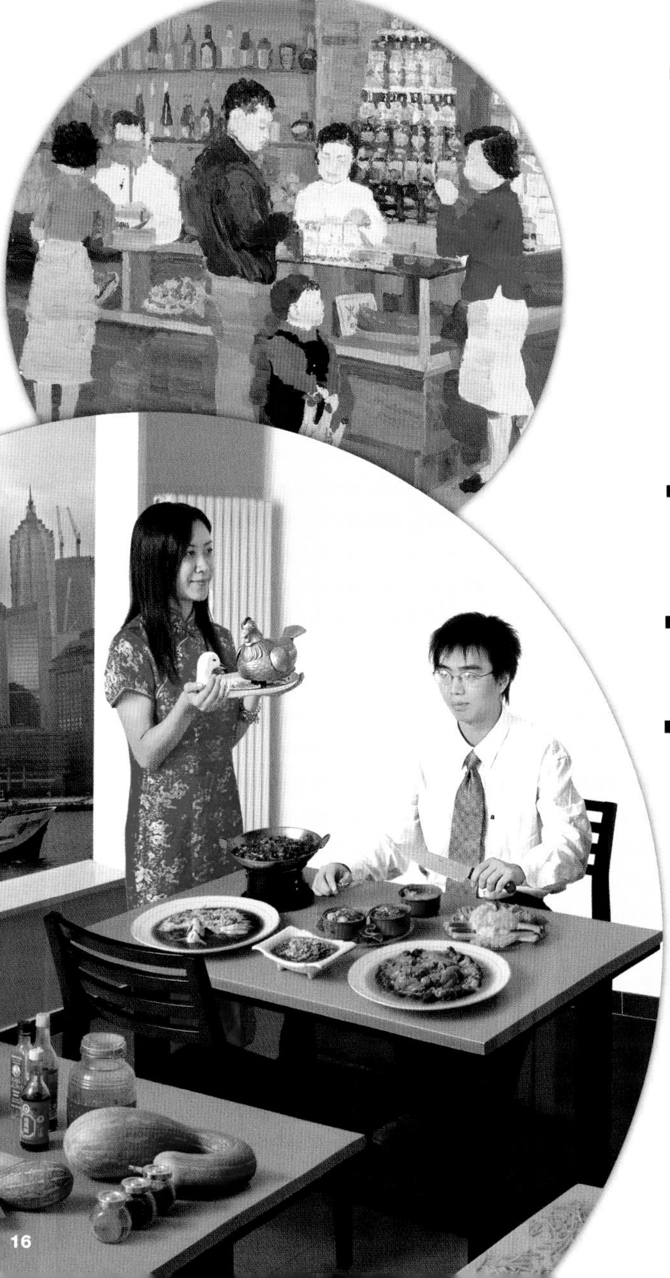

STATE AFFAIRS

END OF THE 80s TO THE END OF THE 90s (CONTINUED)

1998: FIGHT THE FLOOD

The floodwaters during that summer submerged many people's homes, but when facing this gigantic catastrophe, the people's national cohesion and fighting spirit served as an inspiration for everybody.

STATE AFFAIRS

THE BEGINNING OF THE 21ST CENTURY

2001: CHINA ENTERS THE WTO

China joined the WTO. But this was not the only good news in 2001. Also, Beijing was successful in its bid to host the 2008 Olympics, and the Chinese men's soccer team emerged out of Asia for the first time, qualifying for the World Cup.

2003: SARS

The fear of an atypical pneumonia struck every Chinese person, and provided a severe test of the whole nation's public health prevention and protection mechanisms.

2006: THE QINGHAI-TIBET RAILROAD OPENS

The undertaking of "piercing the sky and traversing the top of the world" drew attention from the whole world.

POPULAR CULTURE
END OF THE 80s TO THE END OF THE 90s (CONTINUED)

THE ARRIVAL OF IMPORTED BLOCKBUSTERS

In 1994, the first imported blockbuster, *The Fugitive*, was shown in China. After this, big Hollywood movies were shown one after the other, such as *True Lies*, *Forrest Gump*, and *The Bridges of Madison County*. The 1998 movie *Titanic* earned both the money and the tears of the Chinese masses.

THE EXPLOSION OF TV ENTERTAINMENT PROGRAMS

With the *Big Happy Camp* by Hunan's TV satellite station as the prelude, programs such as *Meeting of the Roses* appeared in succession, and had a strong influence on State TV, which produced *The Dictionary of Happiness* and other programs to fight back. This set off a "Blooming of One Hundred Flowers" among China's TV entertainment programs.

LIFESTYLE
END OF THE 80s TO THE END OF THE 90s (CONTINUED)

SUPERMARKETS

In 1994, the Malaysian Baisheng was the first supermarket to enter China. Subsequently, Carrefour and others swarmed in, making supermarkets the Chinese people's favorite, trendiest venue for buying all kinds of goods.

MBA CRAZE

In 1997, Chinese companies took a shine to the MBA (Master of Business Administration), and the degree became a hot commodity on the market for human resources. At the time, going abroad in order to get an MBA was more of a fashion than an actual way to acquire knowledge. All kinds of MBA books sold like hotcakes.

POPULAR CULTURE
THE BEGINNING OF THE 21ST CENTURY

THE "KOREA TREND" ATTACKS

The "Korea Trend" blew in from the music stage to the world of TV, as well as from Korea's high-tech products, clothes, and food. First, the popular band H.O.T. created a sensation in China in 2000, and their big "barrel pants" and gleaming earrings were copied by young people from all over China. Following this, Korean dramas became popular, and dramas such as *My Wife is the Boss* and *My Crazy Girlfriend* made Korean stars very popular in China.

INTERNET STARS

The popularity of the Internet created a batch of "stars": From Muzimei to Big Sister Furong, Little Sister Tianxian, and today's Chinese Spice Girls – we don't even know their real names.

THE EXPLOSION OF TV CONTESTS

In 2005, *Super Girl* spread across the whole country. Some academics called it the "resurgence of the grassroots spirit." In 2006, there were many new TV contest programs, and more and more "stars" were created by these programs, although many people began to wonder how long their fame would last.

LIFESTYLE
THE BEGINNING OF THE 21ST CENTURY

MP3, MP4

Light and handy, convenient and stylish MP3s and MP4s gradually replaced Walkmans and CD players and became the most popular way of listening to music among the young generation.

BEAUTY CONTESTS

An increasing number of all kinds of beauty contests also entered China. In 2002, for the first time a Chinese girl came in third in the Miss World contest.

SMS

It has been called the fifth media, and is already an indispensable part of the lives of everyone. People use SMS to send New Year greetings, birthday wishes, and love messages – approximately 560 billion SMS messages were sent in 2007.

BLOGS

In 2004, the "Muzimei Case" (the blog of a Chinese girl) gave the Chinese masses an understanding of blogs, but Internet users did not really become acquainted with blogs until 2005, when all the big websites established their own blog channels. Blogs use the Internet as their carrier, and play a special role by swiftly disseminating individual sentiments.

This article was first published in *Nanfang Ren Wu (Southern People's Weekly)* in December 2006 under the title "1976 to 2006: 30 Years of Collective Memory."

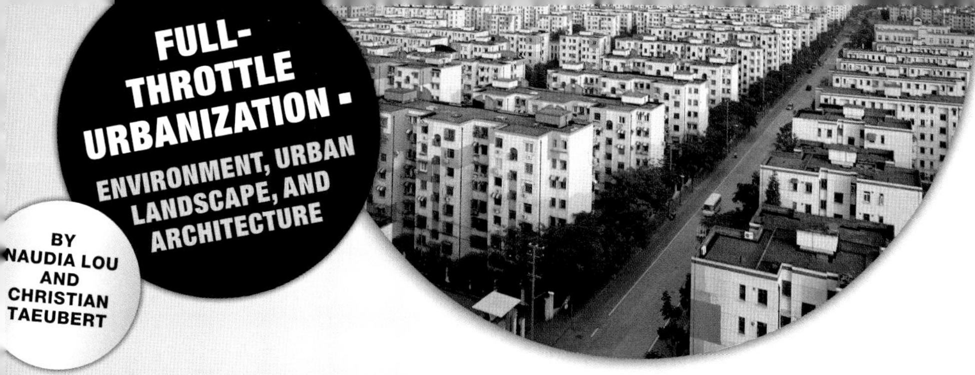

FULL-THROTTLE URBANIZATION - ENVIRONMENT, URBAN LANDSCAPE, AND ARCHITECTURE

BY NAUDIA LOU AND CHRISTIAN TAEUBERT

A little more than a half century ago China was an agrarian society. Now, in the twenty-first century, millions of rural dwellers are moving to cities at an unprecedented pace, and in so doing forming a new empire of urbanites. Urbanization, however, consists not only of creation on a massive scale, but also destruction on an equally massive one. When Chairman Mao said in 1940, "There is no construction without destruction" *[Bu po bu li]*, he could not have imagined that his words would describe the ideological transformation of China as well as the physical one. China's Open Door policy, introduced in the late 1970s by Deng Xiaoping, brought with it a cult of consumerism and a yearning for modernization in both the ideology of the Party and among average citizens. The subsequent introduction of joint ventures, foreign direct investment (FDI), and privatization exponentially increased the speed of urbanization and development. With the close of the Mao era, capitalism was deemed good and the entrepreneurial spirit was equated with patriotism; communists and capitalists joined hands to work towards the betterment of China.

Though having adopted a market economy, China still remains a society in which the government meticulously controls population growth, resource allocation, and the direction of economic development. This control extends to what is materially and spatially available to its citizens, ranging from restrictions on construction to the setting of precise parameters for living conditions. In 1980, for instance, most of China's urbanites lived in low-rise buildings of no more than eight-stories; in older districts, people shared a common cooking space, showers, and bathrooms. In Guangzhou, a city that modernized early on, average living space was slightly less than four square meters per person.[1] The façades of most buildings, constructed to accommodate rapid economic growth, were poorly maintained. As a result, buildings looked dilapidated soon after they were finished. Green space and landscaping for residential compounds was all but nonexistent; individual units were little more than bare concrete boxes furnished with the essentials for daily life and a few family portraits. Since most housing was provided to the individual by his or her *danwei*[2] or work unit, residents were restricted to a specific site, which would become the universe where they would live, raise a family, and grow old. *Danwei*-provided housing was heavily subsidized and thus very basic, as a consequence of which most people's monthly utility bills were actually higher than their rent. At the time, no one anticipated the change that would transform the urban landscape in which the Post-70's generation was to grow up.

In the twenty-first century, after the realization of massive commercial and residential development under the auspices of ambitious urban-planning agendas, many Chinese cities are unrecognizable from what they were just a decade ago. According to Chinese law, urban land in China is owned by the State; however, an amendment in 1988 allowed individuals to acquire a lease to use the land for a period of time, allowing them to build and own commercial buildings, apartments, and other structures. The "privatization" of land use, along with the average citizens' desire to live more comfortably, has opened the floodgates for the private residential housing market. By 2004, average living space per person grew to almost fourteen square meters in the city of Guangzhou – more than triple what it was twenty years prior.[3] On the national level, per capita living space quadrupled from the early 1980s to the beginning of the twenty-first century.[4] The upward and outward expansion of existing cities – and the founding of entirely new cities – is largely responsible for the creation of this new living space. As incomes rose and mortgages became available to average citizens, people started to move out of their *danwei*-provided cubatures and into their own apartments.

Since the 1980s, not only has average living space significantly increased, so too has the range of residential and commercial buildings. Even the most basic apartment units available today are better equipped than the ones built during the Maoist era. White-collar and migrant workers alike are bombarded with advertisements of luxury residential developments or gated communities of stand-alone houses. Double-income households now have the option of taking out large mortgages for their dream house. Major Chinese cities, and even many second- and third-tier cities, are teeming with housing options which include high-end options ranging from Victorian-esque villas to recreations reminiscent of quiet American suburbia. However, the flipside of creation is destruction. In every Chinese city, historical structures make way for eight-lane highways and enormous residential compounds; far-from-old commercial buildings are torn down so new ones can be erected in their place. The urge to preserve has not grown nearly as quickly as the urge to build. With the destruction of traditional architecture and historically significant structures, one can already hear the older generations bemoaning the loss of cultural identity. Those who have witnessed China's fast-paced urbanization are left to question: Where is the line between positive urban growth and negative urban destruction?

A larger proportion of Beijing's old city has been torn down for new development in the last thirty years than in any other historical period. Shanghai on the other hand, even given its high level of exposure to the West and history of western colonialism, had virtually no high-rise office buildings in 1980; now, it has more than double that of New York City. The race to be bigger and faster is evident in China: one need only look toward the city skyline. China is home to the world's largest shopping mall, automobile showroom, gated community, bowling alley, and skate park. In 2008, China also became home to the world's largest airport. Chinese cities are growing at an astronomical rate. As much as half the Chinese urbanites are living in buildings built after 1980.[5]

In 1970, China's urban population constituted slightly more than 17 percent of the total population. That number grew to slightly more than 40 percent by 2005. China's urban population is projected to reach approximately 60 percent of the total population – that's more than 1 billion people – by 2030.[6] Taking into account that China is home to the world's largest population, this move from rural to urban areas constitutes the largest migration of people in the history of mankind. Never before have so many Chinese citizens had so much mobility. And yet, many social and familial bonds formed by rural villages, smaller local towns, and even *danweis* have disintegrated with this newfound mobility and urbanization. Many rural villages are home only to those too old or too young to move to large cities.

Conventional city planning was and still is inadequate when faced with the frantic pace of development in most Chinese cities. Despite the City Planning Act of 1989, master plans formulated by city governments are too broad, and zoning restrictions often go unheeded. The modern-day reality is that construction in cities is commercially driven, and corporate enterprises often marginalize public space. Chinese cities today are the result of both regional governmental planning and local commercial interests, but also derive some of their character from the fact that urbanites seem to always find ad hoc ways to reclaim personal space – such as adding attachments for storage or building makeshift living quarters out of whatever is available.

This mass urbanization spawned new realities that hadn't previously existed. For China's Post-70s generation, everyday life transpires amidst a seemingly never-ending cycle of destruction and reconstruction. Scattered amidst the skyline of many of China's cities, one can see everything ranging from the new and shiny to the ill-conceived or borrowed. This new urban reality, along with the constant shifting of the material, spatial, and ideological, has lead many of those in the Post-70s generation to question what is truly *Chinese*. There is a materialism that exists in Chinese cities today that did not exist in the 1970s. Some see this transformation as a sign of the deterioration of ideals and thoughtless adoption of Western consumerism. Thus, some long for the past, nostalgic for the world sketched in the stories of their parents and grandparents. Some search for the ideals from their own childhoods – a time when becoming a white-collar consumer was the only respectable aspiration.

The creation and destruction of personal space – both in reality and virtually – has a major effect on the Post-70s generation. Everything from modern-day isolation and materialism to hope, creation, and new possibilities were spawned in China's growing urban centers. The end of the 1990s and the beginning of the twenty-first century is perhaps one of the most ideologically confusing times in Chinese history. Having witnessed massive social change, in adulthood the Post-70s generation is witnessing the implications of a society based on mass consumerism and the loss of traditionalism and identity. And yet, this generation seems infused with an undeniable optimism, a reflection of the increased standard of living for millions and the budding of a new and modern Chinese identity. Indeed the riches and possibilities of today were unimaginable for the Post-70s generation in their youth. Through their optimism, one also senses the personal and social liberation of a generation who lived through their parents' stories of the Cultural Revolution, food subsidies, Tiananmen Square, and, now, the hosting of the Olympic games in Beijing.

1 Charlotte Ikels, "The Impact of Housing Policy on China's Urban Elderly," *Urban Anthropology & Studies of Cultural Systems & World Economic Development*, vol. 33, June 22, 2004.
2 Name given to a place of employment in the People's Republic of China. While the term *danwei* remains in use today, it originally referred to a person's place of employment during the period when the Chinese economy was entirely socialist and everyone worked for state-owned enterprises. At the time, *danwei* housing was considered a social welfare benefit and thus complied only with minimum housing standards. http://en.wikipedia.org/wiki/Danwei (accessed June 26, 2008).
3 Ikels, "The Impact of Housing Policy on China's Urban Elderly."
4 Ibid.
5 Daniela Fabricius, "China: New Architectures of Scale," Lecture given at the Centre of Architecture, New York, December 3, 2005. Available at www.peoplesarchitecture.org.
6 UN Global Common Database (UN Population Division Estimates, 2005).

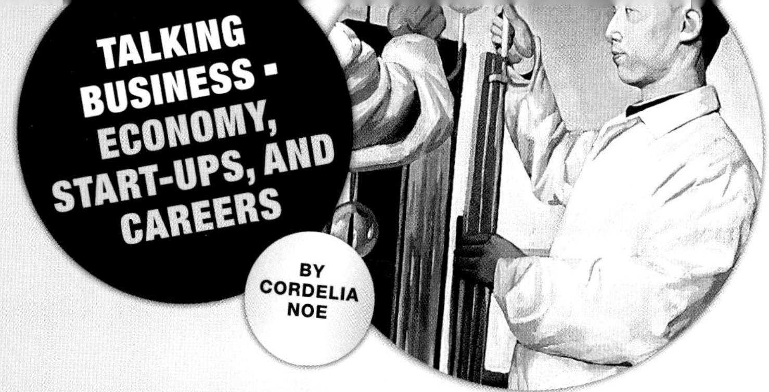

According to Professor Zhou Xiaozheng, sociologist at Renmin University of China, the mantra of China's youth is Deng Xiaoping's famous 1980s slogan: "some people must get rich first." Zhou said the identity of this generation as builders of society is conspicuously different from older generations whose lives were characterized by wars or political campaigns: "The ones born in China in the late 70s or early 80s now constitute the main group of people who want to get rich. They have a strong motivation and drive for making money and society has given them plenty of opportunities."[1]

This marks a profound change. In the 1980s, most young people aspired to an "iron rice bowl," or a guaranteed job with steady income and benefits at a state-owned enterprise. By the 1990s, young graduates were aiming for well-paid jobs in multinational corporations, and now more and more young people are bold enough to establish start-ups and become their own bosses.[2] China's young entrepreneurs have the advantage of overthrowing traditions and challenging traditional patterns. In addition to new sets of modern values, today's China offers a very motivating and dynamic environment. There are plenty of new business opportunities and it is a good time to start one's own business – something hard to imagine only a decade ago.

It still, however, isn't a common occurrence to start one's own business. "Many people value things like a nice car, holidays at the beach, or a spacious apartment. As long as they earn enough money to reach and maintain that desired lifestyle they are risk averse and prefer having a secure income, even if their employment situation does not make them particularly happy and fulfilled," says Tony Chen, one of China's young entrepreneurs who started his own travel service company in early 2006.

People's reactions to someone founding their own business are quite diverse. While some share this new business spirit, there are others who can't understand giving up a secure environment in order to realize a dream. "There were some people that I felt very comfortable talking to because I knew that we shared the same ideas and feelings. But there were also those who did not really understand my decision. One has to understand that for my generation it was and often still is hard to develop ideas because parents have expectations about the sort of career their son or daughter should have," says Chen. "When I came up with my own idea, my parents were surprised, but more in terms of the progress China has made towards entrepreneurship and how things have changed. What we can afford now or what we earn can sometimes be quite confusing for them. For example, if we all go to a nice restaurant and they realize how much one dish costs, they would always calculate how many days they could cook or buy food for the cost of that one dish."

Jason Wang, a twenty-eight-year-old co-partner of ACE Auto – a garage specializing in luxury cars near Beijing – shares Tony Chen's entrepreneurial vision.[3] "Even though many ideas start as a unique idea, competitors are awake and smart. Keeping the prices competitive of course is important, but not the main selling point," explains Wang. "Many of our customers regularly drive from as far away as Shanxi and Tianjin. When I ask why they repeatedly come back over such a long time, they would tell me that they do it because I am trustworthy and they know that I don't cheat them." Asked about his strategy for dealing with competition, Chen says he is "sure that many people already do a similar business and more will follow over the years." He recommends, "Trying to be clear about where to go and not to get lost in too many details."

To constantly challenge oneself and the services one offers seems crucial for young entrepreneurs in order to stay ahead of the competition. Jane Zhu, twenty-eight, whose company specializes in traditional Chinese couture dresses, had to change her initial business model after starting out on her own.[4] "Originally my business was supposed to have a fulfillment side," Zhou said, "But my first experiences brought up that this was too dispiriting. I never got to meet any of my customers and only needed to focus on cutting the costs."

In China's atmosphere of unbridled opportunities, there are many young people having smart ideas at the right moment.

1 "The 'Me Generation'," *Beijing Review*, March 5, 2008.

2 According to the Global Entrepreneurship Monitor (GEM), a research program studying the annual assessment of the national level of entrepreneurial activity globally, China got a rating of 13.7 in the Total Entrepreneurial Activity (TEA) index in 2007. The index indicates the percentage of the labor force actively involved in setting up a company, or being the owner/manager of a company which is less than 42 months old. That means 13.7 out of every 100 Chinese people are involved in start-ups.

3 An article on Jason Wang was first published in *China Business Journal*, no. 244, as "Pimp My Ride," by Eveline Chao.

4 An article on Jane Zhu was first published in *China Business Journal*, no. 244, as "Made to Measure," by Mina Choi.

LISTED BELOW ARE THREE ENTREPRENEURS WHO WERE CHOSEN TO DEPICT THE VARIETY OF THE BUILDERS OF CHINA'S FUTURE.

CUSTOMIZED TOURS

Tony Chen, born in Beijing in 1979, started his career as a bellboy at a Beijing hotel in 1996. At the same time, he started to study English, sensing that it would be key for his future. "Since I was a boy it was my biggest wish to stand on my own two feet. Already my father was a very independent person, which impressed me a lot. Back in 1985, when everybody was happy to have any kind of job, he quit his position in a factory and started his own business selling vegetables.

After two years working in the hotel, Tony Chen quit his job in order to study for a tour guide license in Beijing. In 1999, he started working in the tourist business, mainly guiding around Beijing's tourist attractions. Over the years he got promoted to being in charge of biking and hiking tours for visitors from all over the world, and touring with them all over China. In 2004, after traveling with a group of New Zealand seniors, he was invited to spend some time in New Zealand. There he realized that there were many things in the tourism sector that were not yet available in China and came up with the idea to transfer some of those ideas to Beijing.

At that time, the tourism market was already well established, with many guides competing for the lowest prices but all offering the same trips. This is where he found his niche, offering new kinds of tours tailor-made to special interests. Since early 2006, his travel service business, Stretch-a-Leg, arranges customized trips ranging from motorcycle tours to Inner Mongolia and Buddhist-themed tours across China, to hiking tours in the countryside outside of Beijing.

PIMP MY RIDE

For as long as he can remember, Jason Wang has been obsessed with cars. "When I was little, my mother was always yelling at me because whenever we got on the bus, I would run to the front to watch the driver," Wang recalled. Initially, Wang's passion and his working life didn't fit together. He majored in IT and then worked in software development at a local bank for five years. At that time he already had his own car, which was what brought him to his partner Yuan Wen's garage a couple of years ago. Yuan's garage was well known because during the nineties it was the only shop able to fix BMWs and Mercedes-Benzes, the only luxury car brands in China back then. Combining Wang's business sense and Yuan's experience in repairing cars, they decided to partner up last year. Right after joining the garage, Wang introduced a new component to the business. In addition to repairing luxury cars – such as Jaguars, Porsches, and Audis – the garage started to install custom accessories. After luxury cars are imported to China, there is a big need among buyers to adapt them to the new environment; for example, new GPS systems need to be installed or upgraded with Chinese language features in order to be more user-friendly.

But what Wang never wants to happen is ACE becoming too exclusive. "I don't like this tacky VIP idea in China. Our new garage will be a very open place, where people love their cars, but also understand a car is just a tool."

MADE TO MEASURE

Jane Zhu, born in 1979 in Shanghai, studied abroad and was working as an investment banker before turning her passion into a profession – creating hand tailored Chinese *qipao*s (traditional dresses). At the age of seven, she first tried on her mother's wedding *qipao* and has been in love with these special dresses ever since. Later, when she got a *qipao* tailored for herself, she was excited about the love of detail that went into the process. "It was the most amazing experience I ever had," she said, "I was able to pick the colors, the lining, the stitching – every little thing." Zhu decided to share this amazing experience with other women and came up with the idea to start her own business. She realized that it is not impossible to start one's own business, "it's just about the willingness to risk failure."

Jane Zhu spent three months training with a specialized *qipao*-maker and gathering ideas for her brand name. In 2006, she finally took the plunge. Besides loving the process of selecting patterns and buttons to create the perfect match, she is able to balance her inspiration and creativity with a business strategy. After some initial obstacles, such as calculating the right amount of fabric needed, Zhu reached her goal of expanding her network into global cities such as New York and London, where she successfully collaborates with partner shops. Asked if she would ever think of giving up her business, Zhu said that she "would only give it up if she got tired, if it wasn't fun anymore, or if she started to receive negative feedback from her environment." So far, Zhu is optimistic. "If I had wanted to make a lot of money, I would have stayed an investment banker."

The careers of these three entrepreneurs are a testament to the dynamic environment in which we live. Of course not everyone has entrepreneurial blood running through their veins, but these three examples clearly show that much has changed in the past few decades and that, increasingly, "anything is possible" in today's China.

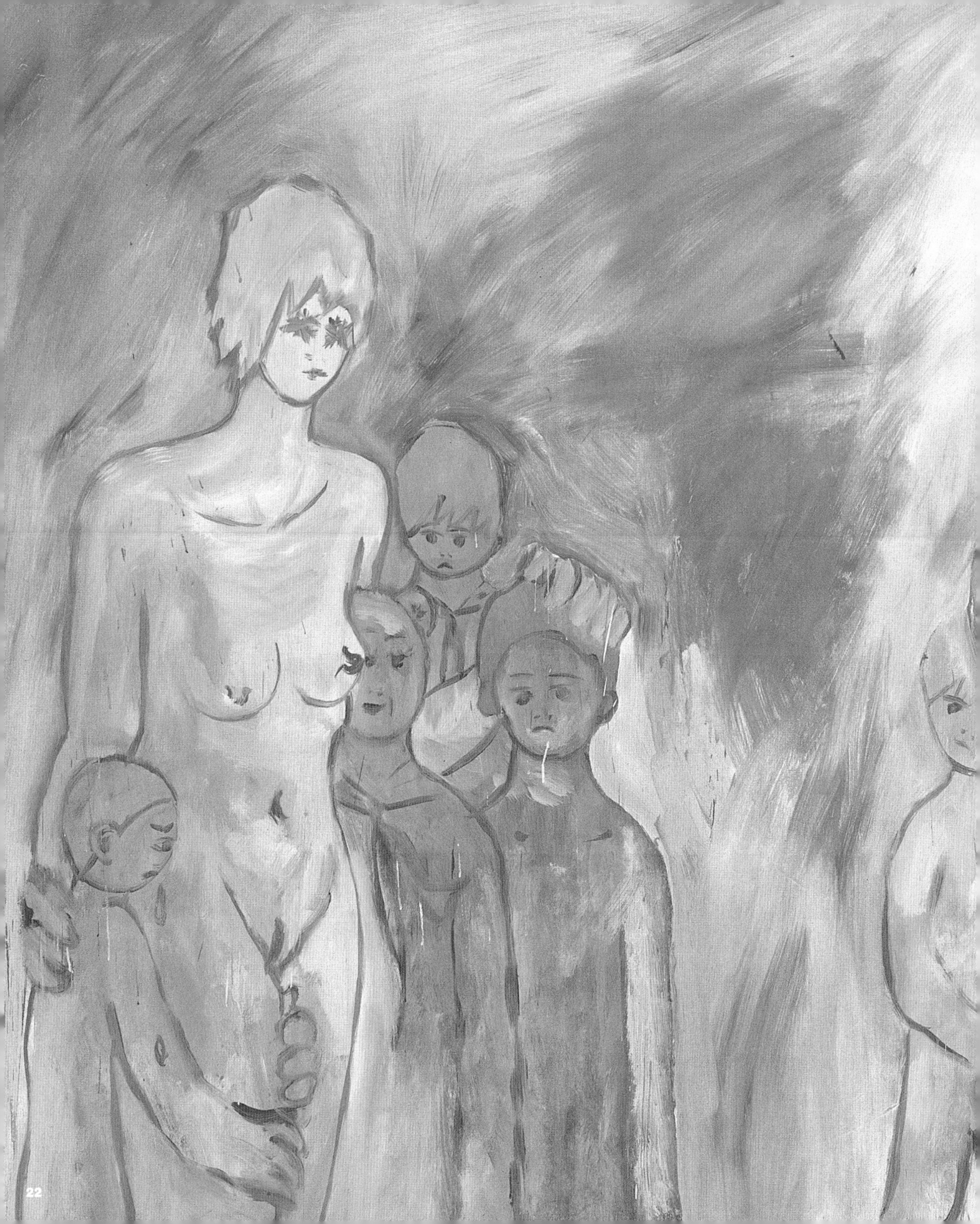

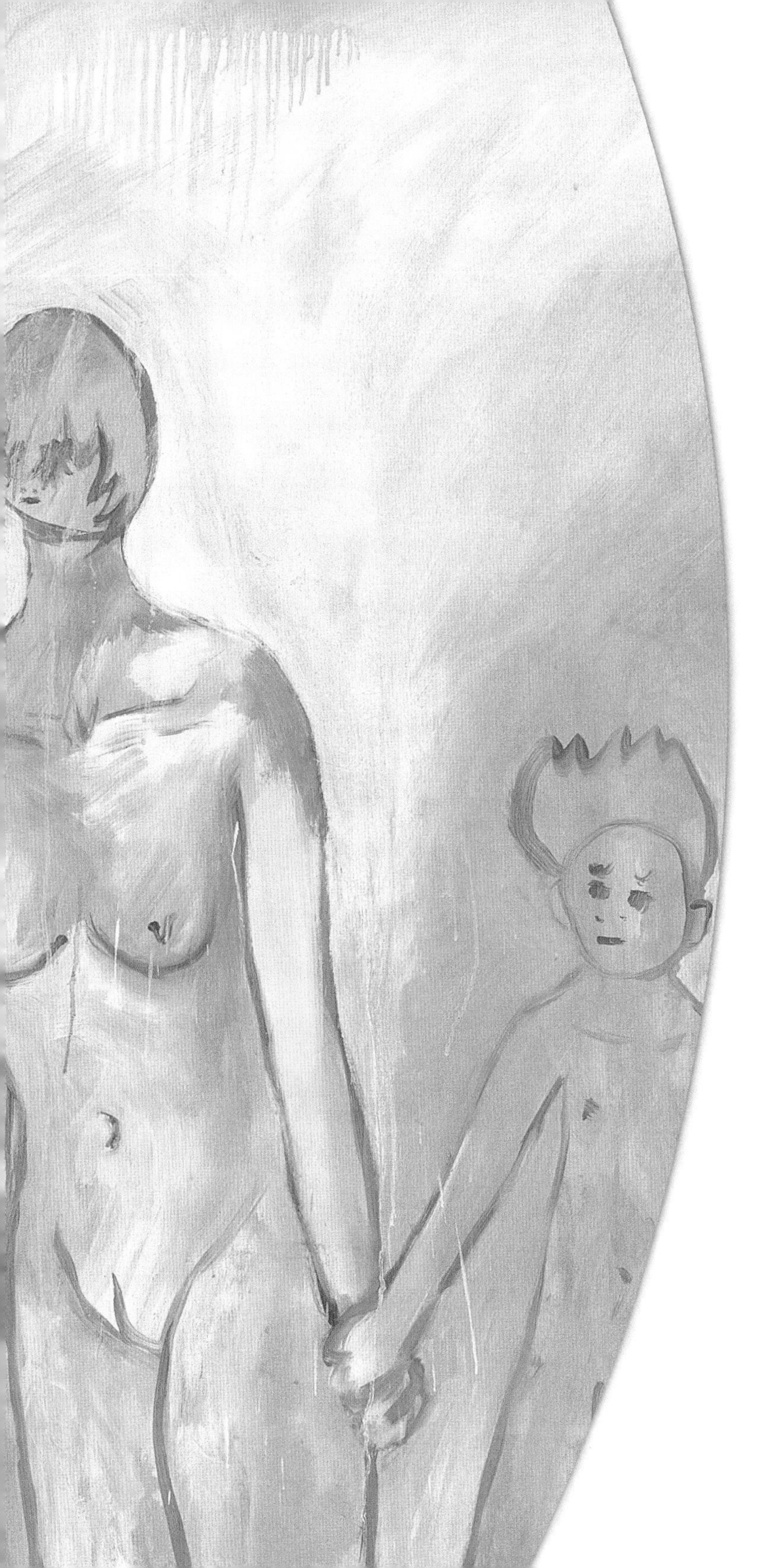

ME AND YOU – LOVE, SEX, AND RELATIONSHIPS

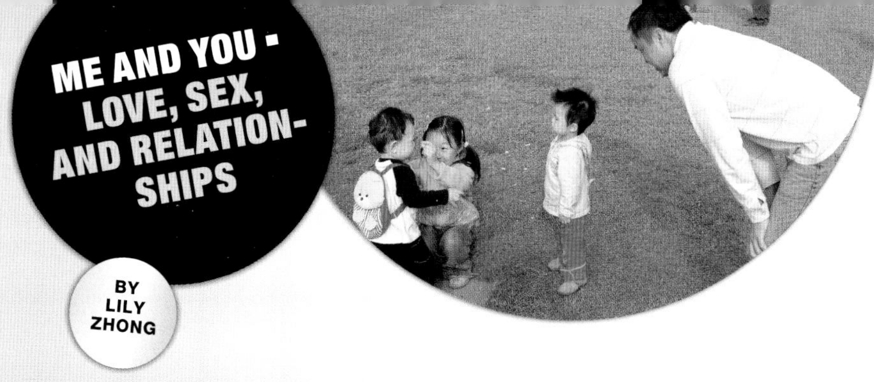

BY LILY ZHONG

China's one-child policy and phenomenal economic growth has created a generation of young adults who not only lived through many social and political developments, but also experienced new trends in the areas of sexuality, family matters, and parenthood, particularly in the big cities. Having their own styles of life, they are now altering by-and-by the traditional concepts of love and family patterns, and start to deal with issues of marriage and parenthood in their own way.

ABOUT LOVE

From the late 1980s to the mid 1990s, when the Post-'75 generation was in their teenage years, romantic relationships were prohibited at high schools and a public kiss would have consequences. While some teachers declined to enforce this prohibition, others worked hard to keep boyfriends and girlfriends from spending time together and informed parents about their children's forbidden romantic involvements. Most teachers and parents, who never had this kind of experience in their youth, claimed that romantic relationships would distract the kids from their studies.[1] First serious relationships often started only after having moved away from home, as privacy was hard to find in the parents' house. Nevertheless, the parents' influence was still present, especially in terms of partner selection. Parents would slip in their ideas and recommendations for the ideal candidate – mainly based on the husband's economic expectations as well as the social background of the potential wife – but it was not common for them to actually pick out a specific partner.

While the life of the Post-'75 generation has largely changed, traditional ideas such as the responsibility of the husband-to-be to buy an apartment as well as financing the marriage have remained intact. As a result, many women who would now have the chance to base their decision on their feelings and emotions have become more and more rational when it comes to choosing a potential husband. Emotions are a significant factor, but other aspects – especially financial circumstances – also play a decisive role. At the same time, men are focusing less on women's incomes than on their outer appearance and social background.

However, due to increasing financial independence of Chinese working women, the age for getting married in the urban environment has increased to an average age of around twenty-eight years in the last decade.[2] This combined with other factors such as working most of the week and having little leisure time, has also led to an increasing amount of women staying single. Living alone or sharing an apartment with people of the same age group is a well-established pattern in the big cities. Many parents are unhappy with this situation and nag their kids or even go as far as to look for a suitable candidate.[3]

ABOUT MARRIAGE AND DIVORCE

For the parents of the Post-'75 generation, getting married was not a choice but an obligation. Marriage was very often arranged by their parents based on different criteria. In order to have a family you had to be married and the idea of becoming a single mom was unacceptable; and whoever did not found a family before his early twenties would have been taken as "eccentric." If someone did not feel happy in his marriage, it was nearly impossible to get a divorce, as this also would have been a disgrace for the whole family. So couples often remained married until the end of their lives. In recent years, marriage and divorce became a more casual issue, and the attitude generally changed from "staying together until the rest of our lives" to "staying together as long as we are happy." This new lifestyle contrasts sharply to that of their parents, who viewed marriage as a duty and divorce a shame. As a result of growing up as single children this generation is weak in horizontal bonding. This makes partnerships challenging. During their adolescence, they were seldom confronted with having to adapt to other points of view, and simply focused on themselves. Looking at the increasing divorce rates, which at a national level rose from 341,000 couples being divorced in 1980, to 800,000 couples in 1990, and to an annual number of 1,870,000 couples officially separating by 2006,[4] the correlation seems to be confirmed.[5] Of course, there are also additional factors such as an increasing financial and spiritual independence of women that support this development. It would be misleading, however, to assume that the increasing divorce rate reflects a decrease in the importance of feelings and emotions. On the contrary, feelings gained in importance and satisfying one's emotional needs is a high priority.

Besides changes in facts and figures, in terms of the wedding ceremony one will also notice a different mindset. Holding a grand banquet for the wedding seems more and more old-fashioned, and exciting happenings, such as an extravagant honeymoon, attract growing attention. While in the sixties the typical wedding ceremony came along with a bowl of peanuts and two rolls of bedding, now having an apartment or at least owning a car is required for urban newlyweds.

ABOUT SEXUALITY

When the Post-'75 generation grew up, it was very difficult for them to get access to information on sexual issues. The respective literature was not yet available on the market, parents were too conservative to touch on the topic, and the Internet was not yet available. Although sex education was part of the curriculum, instead of giving insights into sexual practice it was rather conservative and predominantly based on physical development. Imported DVDs and sharing experiences with friends were often the only way to expand one's knowledge, but hardly offered trustworthy facts in terms of birth control and other related issues. Nowadays, information, even on very intimate topics, is much easier to access. Apart from being able to speak more openly, there are many new sources – the Internet in particular – to expand one's knowledge.[6] An international woman's magazine even published a little booklet on "How to Enjoy Having Sex" in their Chinese edition, aimed at their late-twenties to early-thirties female readership.[7]

ABOUT PARENTHOOD

While for their parents' generation it was normal to have a child without being especially prepared for parenthood, the mindset of the Post-'75 generation towards starting their own family has changed. Starting their own family is still a priority for the majority of young couples. But, compared to their parents, most of them "do not happen to become parents", but "choose to become parents." Although they are often pushed by their parents to start a family, young couples consciously postpone plans for their first baby until they achieve more stability in their life, job, and relationship. This generation grew up as single children,[8] and knows the disadvantages – such as loneliness – of that structure, so most wish to have more than one kid.

Once decided on, the steps towards parenthood are planned in detail. Healthier nutrition before conception and saving for the education of their kids are just some of the concerns, as parents want to offer their offspring the best possible start in life.

Some new parents are very nervous when it comes to choosing the right way to educate their children, despite their rather open-minded upbringing. It is common for new moms to get supported by their own parents, who give them advice on more traditional ideas and values. But at the same time, parents of the Post-'75 generation also have a variety of new sources from which to gather information such as the Internet, specialized books, etc. The outcome is a new mix of values in education.

However, it is very difficult to draw a whole and clear picture of the Post-'75 generation. They spent their childhood and even their youth in a quite traditional environment, and got their first ideas about life and their environment from their parents. But while growing up, they were faced with a changing society and hit by different values and ideas from the media, Internet, friends from abroad, and from their own experiences. Most people of this generation have "mixed minds": their ideas towards love and life are a mix of what they were taught, and what they choose for themselves.

1 Vanessa L. Fong, "Social and Cultural Prohibitions against Sexual Activity among Teenagers in a Chinese City," paper prepared for the annual meeting of the Population Association of America, Harvard University, 2004.
2 Based on *Parents* magazine research.
3 In recent years, public parks became popular for parents to scout a spouse by advertising their single kid's "qualifications." Job and income details are discussed, photos and contact details are exchanged, and a "coincidently" blind date is arranged for the adult kids by both parents.
4 According to the Chinese Civil Affairs Bureau.
5 Since October 2003, simplified divorce procedures have been adopted in China, which are widely regarded as a main reason for the increase. Whereas previously the whole process could take up to one month, nowadays within ten minutes and for the equivalent of around US$1.40 one can get divorced. Surveys revealed that about 70 percent of divorces in the country were initiated by women.
6 Muzimei, born in 1978, is the alias of a young female journalist and blogger from Guangzhou, who became a notorious household name in China in late 2003. Her blog contained detailed descriptions of her sexual encounters with various men, which was a first for China. Since then, she and her blog have been the topic of heated discussions and controversy in print media, bulletin boards, and chat rooms across China.
7 *Marie Claire*, 2007.
8 Almost 100 million single children had been born since the official initiation of the One-Child Policy in the late 1970s. Today's young adults in their late twenties were the first generation to grow up under these new conditions. Experts estimate that China's population of 1.3 billion would be more than 1.7 billion without the family planning policy.

MY CAR, MY HANDBAG, MY MOBILE – LIFESTYLE, STATUS, AND BRANDS

BY DIRK JEHMLICH

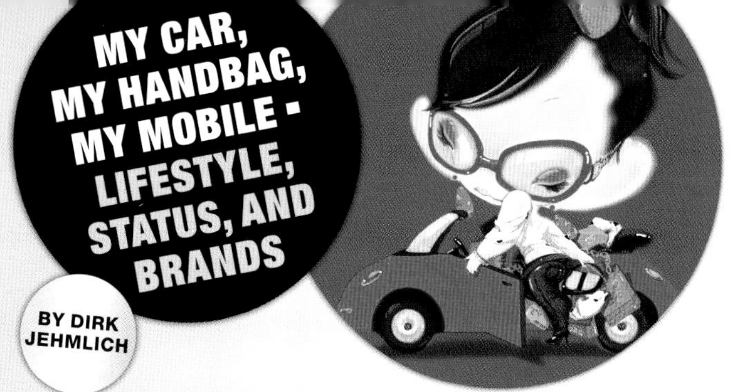

They are drinking Starbucks coffee, wearing Nikes, and blogging obsessively on the Internet. The young generation is better educated, more lifestyle-oriented, and tech-savvy than their parents' generation. They believe much less in politics than in brands, celebrities, and their own success. As the first grown-up generation since the One-Child Policy, their parents and grandparents pampered them like little emperors. Resignation and self-discipline are unknown attitudes to them. Their increasing self-centrism as well as their hedonistic lifestyles unleashes a generation of demanding pleasure hunters and comfort junkies who are convinced that they deserve at least everything. What may sound frightening at first glance turns out to be not too different from young generations of other countries. But what differentiates these young adults from their European or American counterparts? They grew up in transition – in a system where trends replace tradition. Insights into lifestyle, status symbols, and brands are reflected in the following statements that were compiled in consumer surveys and expert interviews emphasizing different positions, but also similarities among the young generation.

LIFESTYLE – FROM COMMUNISM TO CAPITALISM TO CONSUMERISM

To describe the lifestyle of China's young adults would be as difficult as characterizing young adults from Oslo, Brighton, Warsaw, and Madrid at the same time. Different regions reflect different lifestyles. The three largest cities of China exemplify the diversity of the Middle Kingdom. Beijing is functional and independent, Shanghai represents glamorous chic, and Guangzhou is known for its streetwear style. However, they share the major value shift that occurred during the last decades. Three decades of communism were followed by three decades of capitalism. Today, the transition is one from capitalism into consumerism. While Chinese youth still possess a Chinese mindset, they engage in a global lifestyle shaped by McDonald's, Google, and MBAs.

"Today's young adults are the first generation to be given a lifestyle choice." **Veronique Saunier, WGSN**

"We are more self-centered. We live for ourselves, and that's good." **Wang Ning, snowboarder, owner of an advertising company**

"On the wish list of young Chinese, a Nintendo Wii comes way ahead of democracy." **Hung Huang, CEO of CIMG**

"Every Chinese youth wants to be a dragon, but a tame one." **Tom Doctoroff, Greater China CEO of JWT**

"Cool in China is less cool than elsewhere. It is black and white with a dash of color." **Tom Doctoroff, Greater China CEO of JWT**

"In terms of individualism, China is still a developing country." **Yan Jun, 33, journalist**

"I got some old drum machines and stay up until four in the morning working on beats. And maybe take some mushrooms and smoke a bit." **Kirby Lee, rapper**

"Young people rely on the internet to express their thoughts and emotions because they feel it's unsafe to do so in the real world." **Tom Doctoroff, Greater China CEO of JWT**

"I care about my rights when it comes to the quality of a waitress in a restaurant or a product I buy. When it comes to democracy and all that, well ... That doesn't play a role in my life." **Vicky Yang, 29, consultant**

"The web is also used as a way to relieve the pressure of modern life in China." **Jon Briggs, Regional Director, TNS**

"The more we eat, the more we taste and see the more we want." **Maria Zhang, 27, Membership Manager in one of the most exclusive sports clubs, Beijing**

"Chinese people seem to be way ahead of Americans in living a digital life." **Barry Diller, IAC Chairman and CEO**

"Family is important but not as important as it was some decades ago." **Suzy Zhai, 27, working in the creative industry**

"Family orientation is still significant. But people have to focus on career to afford it." **Wei Weng, Trendbüro Asia-Pacific**

"Chinese consumers stick to their key values but give them a new interpretation – from collectivism to membership." **Stefanie Bierbaum, Trendbüro Asia-Pacific**

"Marriage is the most important thing for a girl. Because it is the most beautiful moment for all girls, I want it to be perfect. I need money." **Wei, student, Shanghai**

"The winner is king. The loser is slave. If you win, you are alive. You lose, you die." **Fan Lu, graduate student, Xian**

"I try to earn money. Money is almost everything. If you don't have it, you have nothing." **Wang Jia, 31, white-collar worker**

STATUS SYMBOLS – CORNER PILLAR OF A CONFUCIAN SOCIETY

Status symbols have always been and will remain to be of extraordinary importance for Chinese consumers. They indicate one's social position, a substantial part of a Confucian and, as a result, hierarchy-driven society. The self-perception of Chinese consumers depends most of all on how they are perceived by their environment. One is successful if other people consider one successful. Consequently, and as it is believed that wealth is the adequate result of cleverness and hard work, it is accepted to flaunt newly-obtained wealth. Understatement is a concept that doesn't fit the Chinese mentality. Even people that seem to hide their status end up showing it in a subtle way, the signals being understood in their "peer group."

Status symbols change from generation to generation. While the parents of the young adults were striving for money and power, the generation born after China's reformation is discovering independence, knowledge, and mobility as new forms of self-expression.

"Chinese youth switch phones more often due to the weight placed on the mobile phone as a symbol." **Shaun Rein, China Market Research Group (CMR)**

"Chinese youth don't buy an iPhone because it indicates a certain status. They buy it because it's cool, because it's a peer pressure. The process of creating one's identity with certain symbols happens subconsciously and intuitively, as it does everywhere else." **Elaine Ho, Trendbüro Asia-Pacific**

"I feel naked if I leave the house without my mobile phone." **Xiao Yu, 28, fashion designer**

"Every child of the Chinese only-child generation wants to be unique, and everyone thinks that he or she has to be a celebrity." **Hung Huang, CEO of China Interactive Media Group (CIMG)**

"The classical five status symbols – cash, car, credit card, condominium, and country club – are extended by certificate, community, and charity. In China, where 80 percent of women work, men have to offer more than financial security." **From a lifestyle trend report by Trendbüro Asia-Pacific, 2008**

"Green behavior is an expression of sophistication rather than a statement of ecological responsibility." **Green Luxury, WWF, 2007**

"The struggle to both 'fit-in' and be an individual affects how they dress as well as communicate. Asian youth are brand conscious and image driven. They want products that appear offbeat and unique, but instantly identifiable as a luxury brand. This generation of only-children equates success with money and status." **Allison Mooney, "Engaging China's 'Me Generation'"**

"Chinese luxury consumers are the youngest in the world to enter the luxury market, and they are entering in droves. Correspondingly, BMW's tag as the 'luxury design car' already makes it a favorite in China, and we will continue to see younger and more sporty design tastes as we move forward." **Elaine Ho, Trendbüro Asia-Pacific**

BRANDS – THE NEW DECORATIONS OF CHINA

Brands are the new decorations for Chinese youth and provide orientation in a jungle of unlimited choice. While consumers from developed countries buy brands to manifest their lifestyle, Chinese youth buy to discover their identity, which is still "under construction." Although the young generation is curious and already very confident, brands in China have the possibility to lead consumers. They want to be part of the brand creation and become brand ambassadors. Overall, China is too diverse to generalize brand preferences.

"My father differentiates brands only in two dimensions – from cheap to expensive and from functional to impractical. But my generation expects not only value for money. We are looking for brands that give us something special – personality." **Wang Xi, 27, customer account manager**

"Asian youth are brand conscious and image driven. The right clothes help them to gain respect and approval." **Allison Mooney, "Engaging China's 'Me Generation'"**

"Indulgent luxury goods have to offer more than a brand and price tag. The experiential, authentic, and enjoyable side equally matters." **Hung Huang, CEO of China Interactive Media Group (CIMG)**

"Chinese youth want brands to be their friends. They want to be involved in their creativity process." **Li Bing, CTR Markets Manager of Media & Brand Research**

"Tattoos, fashion design, cartoons, and mobile phones are perceived as cool, but so are big and successful companies such as IBM and Microsoft." **Veronique Saunier, WGSN**

"Louis Vuitton is for girls from second-tier cities now." **Wendy Ye, 28, evening-wear designer**

"This generation hates fakes of their favorite brands. Regarding brands, they are more sophisticated than the generation of their parents." **Dr. Karl Rohde, Cultural Anthropologist at the University of Utrecht**

"There is a small, sophisticated group of affluent Chinese who go for Asian brands. They decline Westernization and rediscover their own values." **Amit Kekre, Planning Director, Grey Worldwide**

"Brand comes first. Big logos sell better than great style." **Elaine Ho, Trendbüro Asia-Pacific**

"Asians are aware of who they are and what they want. This encourages new forms of interaction between the East and West and new degrees of how the 'foreign' must be actively engaged and challenged." **From a lifestyle trend report by Trendbüro Asia-Pacific, 2008**

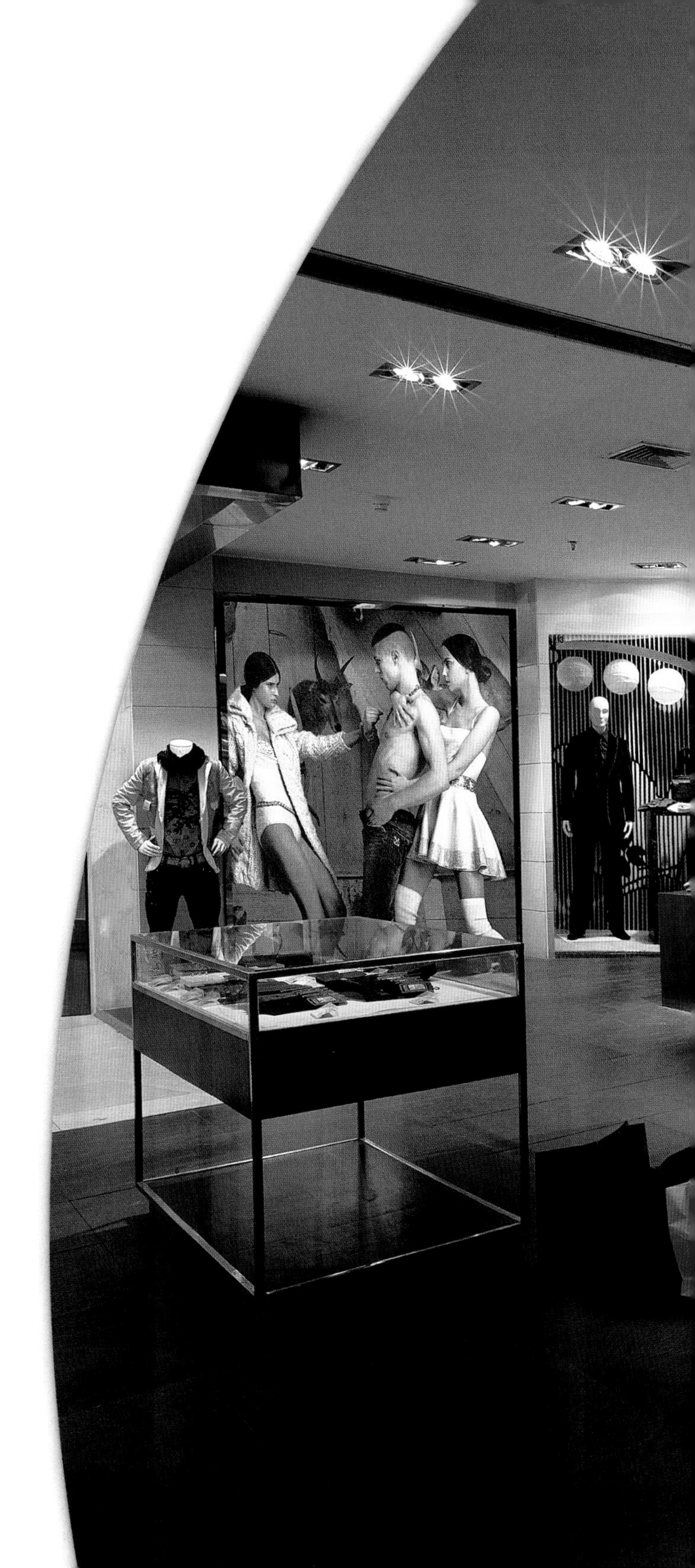

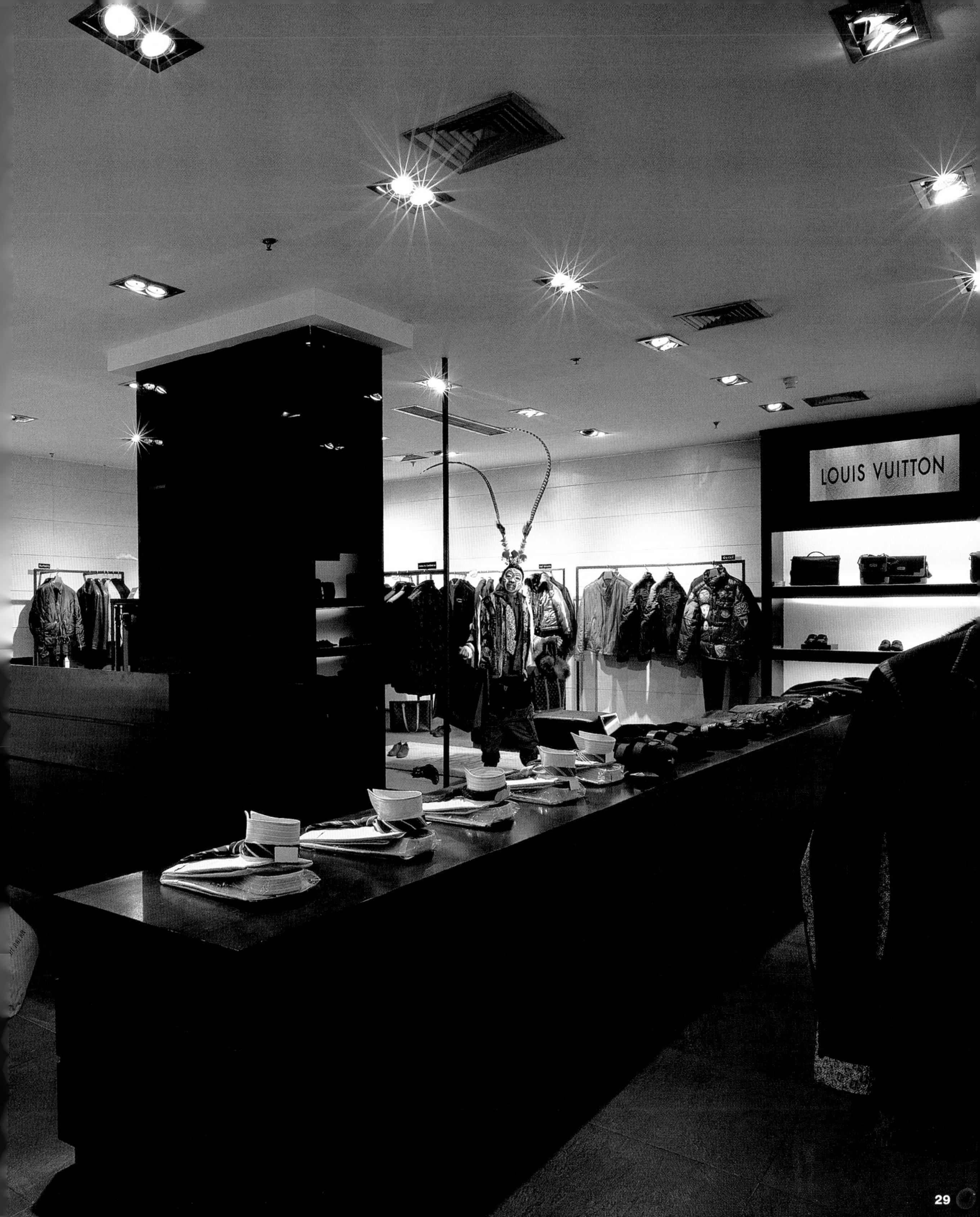
LOUIS VUITTON

AVATAR AND SUPERSTAR – TV, INTERNET, AND SMS

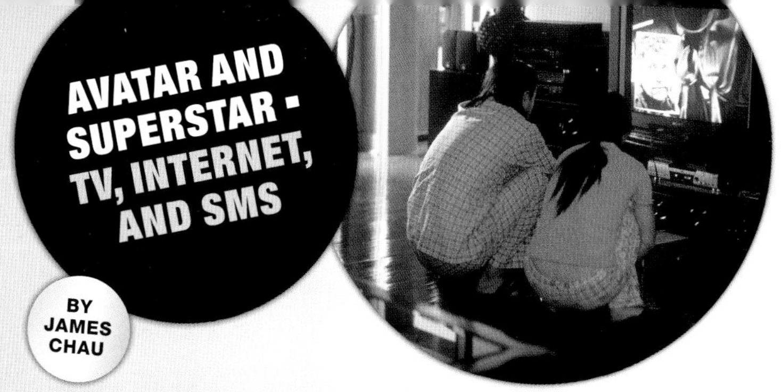

BY JAMES CHAU

I'm part of a dying breed.

I was a precocious ten-year-old when I first appeared on television, beaming away at the cameras and thirsting for my close-up on *Splash*, a daytime children's program which aired on Britain's ITN network. All of my family saw it. So did my friends. And enough people ignored me at school the next day to nicely confirm that I had finally tasted what Andy Warhol described as the "fifteen minutes of fame."

Fortunately, my own "fifteen minutes" have lasted slightly longer, turning into a career as a presenter in Beijing for the state broadcaster, China Central Television (CCTV). But while I love my job and the opportunities it brings, I can't help but notice that television doesn't command the same awe and wonder it perhaps once did.

Here's why.

China is a huge country, and every New Year's Eve its 1.3 billion people sit in front of their television sets to watch the *Spring Festival Gala*. It's a four-hour entertainment show packed full with pop singers, sports stars, and military heroes – the very people whose celebrity and success are shaping and coloring the next generation of Chinese. Indeed, it's such a tried-and-tested ratings winner that people haggle all year round just for tickets to the studio rehearsal. So, here's my question: if the show is such a guaranteed success with audiences and advertisers alike, why are its producers coming under growing pressure?

Welcome to the "New China," where every town, city, and province is switching off its television sets and clicking on their favorite websites as the country continues the "opening-up" reforms that kicked off in the late 1970s. That's when former leader Deng Xiaoping threw off the dust clothes and reintroduced the ancient Middle Kingdom to the modern world outside. Nowadays, everyone from school students to senior citizens are glued not to their television screens, but to their computer monitors – shopping, blogging, and e-mailing their way through the World Wide Web and turning words like "Yahoo" and "MSN" into household names in far-flung villages most of us have never heard of.

It's also official. A recent report in *The Times* of London says China has gone past the U.S. to become the world's biggest Internet user, hitting 221 million in early 2008. It's a phenomenon with every reason to continue. For a start, the Internet is cheap. In China, a basic computer costs upwards of 3,000 RMB, which, despite the number of zeroes, is a figure affordable to many. It's accessible, too, with a wireless connection in what seems like every other coffee shop and, at less than US$20 per month for unlimited use, costs around the same as two or three people going out for dinner. My Chinese friends agree. One of them, Wu Ning, is part of the twenty-something-year-old generation that emerged in the era of the One-Child Policy that's largely defined by a privileged youth who grew up on a diet of McDonalds and Diet Coke. Wu Ning spends more time checking his e-mail than he does the office spreadsheets and, by his own estimate, spends eight hours a day on his home computer. Add to that a typical twelve hours at work, and I'm not sure where he squeezes in his eating, sleeping, and girlfriend in the four hours that remain. He also admits to watching less and less television, and has even stopped buying pirated DVDs because, he says, downloading the newest Hollywood films is not only free but they sometimes come out quicker online than they do in the cinema.

He's not the exception. In fact, he's the rule.

Liang Xin, Lu Chenwei, and Guo Xiaozhang are three friends who work together in Beijing. They're from different parts of the country, all in their late twenties and, like more and more Chinese today, are educated to university level. They also all have QQ accounts. QQ, like MSN, is an instant messaging service that allows users to communicate in "real time" with bonus features such as QQ Mail, QQ Game, and QQ Coin (virtual currency you can trade online). It's owned by the Hong Kong-listed Tencent Holdings, which in 2005 reported earnings four times that of the Facebook social networking site to become the world's third biggest instant messaging service.

It's also a fast way to mobilize any community from your local school to the entire country – in one example, a twenty-nine-year-old woman got twenty million people to sign her online petition. She told a major American newspaper that she prefers instant messaging to conventional e-mailing because it reaches "a lot more people." Research institute BDA China predicts that Internet usage is skyrocketing at 30 percent a year. Likewise, QQ has roughly 160 million customers. I say "roughly" because many of them are known to have more than one account each.

Guo Xiaozhang agrees. One of her university classmates has no less than three separate accounts – one for each of his two girlfriends and a third for "everyone else." But the more sophisticated say they prefer MSN, if only to avoid the chat rooms and mass online groups that make QQ a magnet for the socially lonely. Indeed, the point is made that instant messaging is so popular because it is exactly that – "instant." It's quick, it's happening, and you can communicate and interact with as many as nine million members online at any one time.

The same is true of cell phone text messaging. I've read recently that up to 98 percent of China's 400 million subscribers regularly SMS, so, naturally, I put those figures to the test. Based on my own social network, I discovered that friends and colleagues alike send and receive more than seventy messages each day. We're talking a staggering 2,000-plus a month/per user, but at about two U.S. cents per message it's cheaper than making a local call. Everybody wants to feel connected, "up-to-date," and "in-the-know," and SMS makes that possible. But that's not all.

Also keeping people "in-the-know" are the huge number of celebrity blogs that clog up China's online traffic. All of my colleagues read one, though, unfortunately, it's rarely mine. I churn out a post at least once a month, if only to remind everyone that even if I haven't been on television in the last week, I am, indeed, alive and well. A quick click on Google tells the story. Type in the keywords "China" and "blog," and you'll get 42.7 million search hits. In comparison, "USA" and "blog" generates 39.2 million, with India (whose population is catching up with that of China's) just 21.9 million.

One of my best-known television colleagues once used his blog to decry the presence of a Starbucks outlet inside the historic Forbidden City. Within days, his post generated more than half a million hits and so strongly stirred debate throughout the country that news of the reaction made it into every major world newspaper. I dryly told the *International Herald Tribune* that I would've done the same for the "free" publicity. By far, my most successful blog was a post on Zhang Zilin winning the Miss World beauty pageant. It was so short (I only wrote a title) and had so few photographs (downloaded from my company website), that I was surprised by its number of hits (more than 12,000). It was a reminder once again of China's celebrity-driven society.

True, the same can be said of almost any other country, but we, the Chinese, have an unending curiosity about even Olympic champions in sports as obscure as synchronized diving and rifle shooting. To underline their fame, the ones who come away every four years with a gold medal around their neck are plastered on billboards nationwide, endorsing everything from nutritious diet drinks to bottles of white-wine spirits. It's not just the rich and famous – lots of people have one. A straw poll of the eight people who happened to be in my office the other day was met by a show of five hands when I asked who in the room wrote their own web journal.

For the writers, it's a way to share their feelings and, for the readers, it's a valuable way to interact. It's usually anonymous and, if you're not famous already, maybe a blog will change all that? One example are the "Back Dorm Boys," who didn't find fame as artists (they studied at the Guangzhou Academy of Fine Arts), but for their low-quality web videos in which they lip-synched to songs by the Backstreet Boys. They are now cyber celebrities.

It's a way of getting noticed in a country so big and so vast that one major city can have a population larger than that of a small European state. And it's more an indicator than it is a coincidence that English-language words such as "blog," "IM," and "e-mail" are more ingrained in the everyday vernacular than simple phrases such as "sorry," "please," and "thank you." Indeed, sixty some years after the founding of the People's Republic of China, and its people are as much "netizens" as they are "citizens." While Facebook hasn't taken off in China the same way it has in countries in Europe and North America (though a Chinese-language version could easily change all that), there are already a number of locally-targeted alternatives that come courtesy of the country's biggest online brands – sina.com, baidu.com, and 163.com.

Meanwhile, the Fox-owned MySpace has come to China, where it's headed by Rupert Murdoch's Chinese-born wife, Wendi Deng, and, if you're not interested in interacting, you can hole up in your room and shop twenty-four hours a day through Taobao.com, which has long overtaken eBay China. The Internet is a follow-up to the revolution in the cell phone market. All this talk *doesn't* mean that the television industry is anywhere near expired. If advertisers are in any doubt of the power of visual entertainment, they need only look to *Supergirl*, an *American Idol*-esque talent contest.

Guo Xiaozhang is no big fan of reality shows, but even she admits to withdrawal symptoms whenever each season comes to an end. By this time, she would have become attached to the triumphs and failures of each contestant and, in her everyday life, learnt how to dress like them, talk like them, and, yes, even sing like them. It combines cut-throat competition and unrivaled glamour, and one *Supergirl* contestant has famously gone on to marry Tian Liang, a former Olympic diving champion, as they begin to establish themselves as a celebrity power couple in the mold of Posh Spice and David Beckham.

So, yes – the Internet *is* cutting into the media market, but television brings you the news and provides you the drama in a way that a website, newspaper, or radio simply can't.

I'm part of a dying breed. But not just yet.

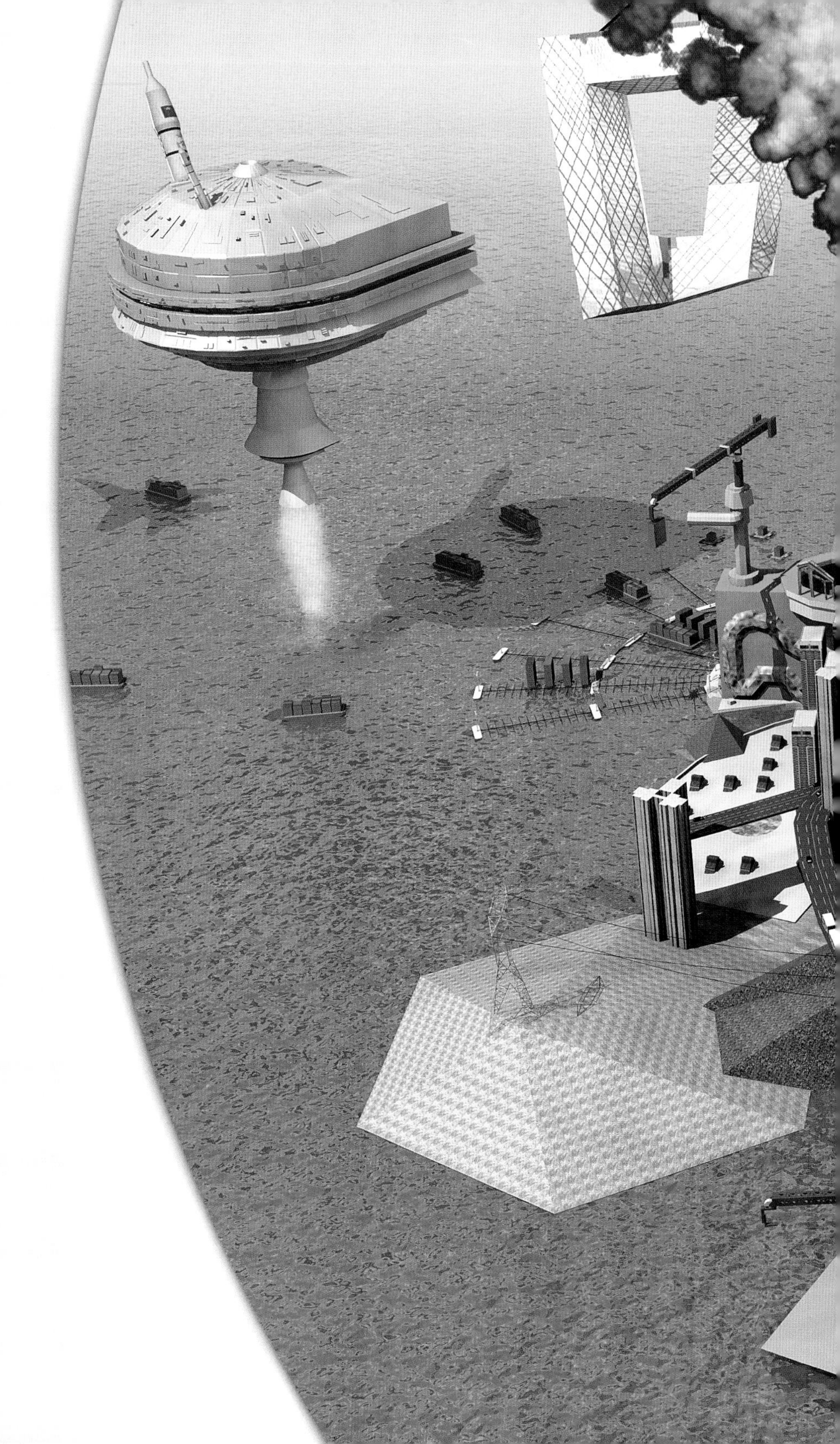

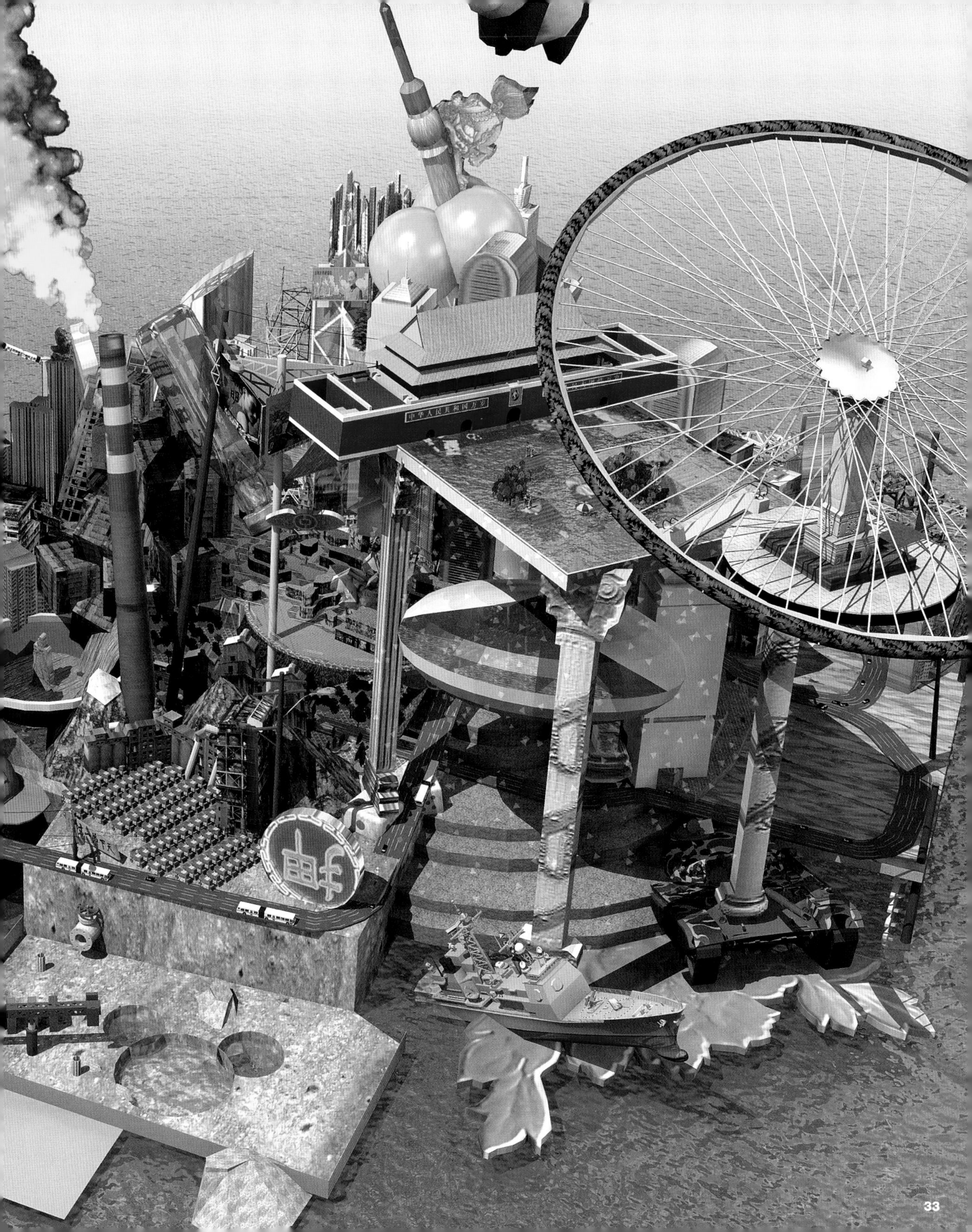
中华人民共和国万岁

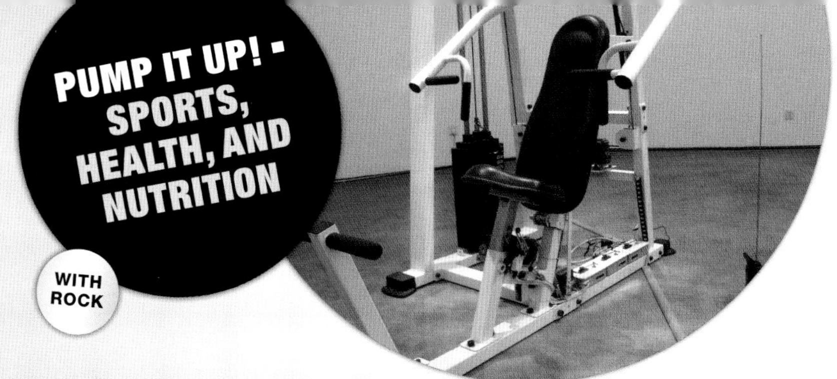

PUMP IT UP! - SPORTS, HEALTH, AND NUTRITION

WITH ROCK

"Hi, I am Rock! Welcome to the Fitness Club. The next class is Spinning, which will start at 6:30 p.m. in the Fly Wheels Studio. Please come and join us."

**INTERVIEW WITH FITNESS INSTRUCTOR ROCK
AT A FITNESS CENTER JUICE BAR
DOWNTOWN BEIJING**

How did you end up in the fitness business?
Being a fitness instructor is a completely new profession in China, but I have been working for ten years in this field. Since I was a kid I was crazy about sports and started taking kung fu classes. At the time there were no special schools to learn kung fu, only some old kung fu masters. You had to audition, and only then might they teach you. Of course, it had never occurred to me that I would become a fitness instructor. However, for me this is a very pleasant surprise, as I feel being a fitness instructor is quite close to my original dream job. Also, the fitness market has huge potential and is developing rapidly. I see many opportunities for my own development.
So what was your dream job when you were a kid?
Wrestling Champion! This was definitely not a profession for making money, but I had a strong desire. Most other kids at my age wanted to become scientists.
What do your parents think about your profession? Do they know what a Spinning class is?
In the beginning my parents were not too happy with my decision, as to them it did not seem to be a stable job. They call it "work of the rising sun," meaning a profession that you can only do while you are young. In the meantime, their attitude has changed and now they respect my job. They don't know exactly what I am doing, but then again we do not talk too much about jobs.
What do your friends think about your job? Do they envy you?
Most of my friends are really jealous and think I have a dream job. They think I have fun all day, and stay in shape while being adored by beautiful women.
What motivates you to work in this job?
I guess it is a combination of different factors. First of all, doing sports is something I really love. Second, it allows me to help other people to stay in shape and be healthy. And finally, it is well paid.
Ten years ago, even three years ago, Beijing was full of bicycles but there were only a few gyms available. Today it is the opposite: there are fewer bicycles, and gyms are full of people exercising on bikes or joining a Spinning class.
Indeed, if you look at it this way it seems quiet awkward. This is due to the increasing standard of living in China, and a good example of the new wealth.
When walking through parks in Beijing you see a lot of elderly people doing Qi Gong, Tai Chi, or ballroom dancing. Then again, you can also observe some younger people exercising in the gym. But what is in between? Does the general population exercise?
Generally, I do not think that the average person does sports just for the fun of doing it, but rather he has a certain goal in mind. Elderly people do it to stay healthy, as they did not have the time or possibilities to take care of their health when they were younger. For younger people, it is often a way to show off: being a member in a fancy gym represents a certain lifestyle. If they are in the end actually working out, or just showing off their membership card, is a different issue.
In that case, is a muscular body and big biceps also a status symbol?
Of course, and we as fitness instructors hope that our members can reach this goal with our help.
To what point can you observe that the beauty ideal is changing?
Since ancient times, a well-toned muscular body and rosy skin has been the male beauty ideal. And this has not changed today. Strength means beauty. And a man who has strength and muscles is considered beautiful.
But there must be more than that?
No doubt, there is an increasing awareness to stay fit and live healthy. Nevertheless, a lot of people are not aware what it means to lead a healthy life. They do not know what factors to consider, and many think that going to the gym is enough – an automatic guarantee of a healthy life. If a personal trainer suggested that there were many more factors involved in leading a healthy lifestyle than just going to the gym, the customers would lose their belief, and stop going.
If a personal trainer gave his clients not only tips on how to work out but also advice on other issues regarding their health, such as nutrition, how would the clients react?
Only a few would follow such advice. Many clients are not very disciplined and forget about my recommendations; and as a trainer you can't watch the client's nutrition, sleeping, and other habits twenty-four hours a day. This can sometimes be frustrating, because they only make little progress and thus see few results. In addition, Chinese clients can easily become pessimistic when they do not see fast results, and then they give up.

You just mentioned nutrition. How do you see the development in the field of nutrition, especially with the rapid introduction of fast-food chains?
Generally, the consciousness about healthy and balanced nutrition has increased, not only among the upper class, but also among ordinary families. Years ago, the most important thing was not to be hungry, and it did not matter which vitamins or nutrients you consumed as long as you had enough. The most important thing for my mom was to prepare us some meat. When we sit together now, you realize that a lot of things have changed; for example, we don't eat chicken skin any more because it is too fatty. This would never have happened in the past. Fast food, which for me does not only include the Western fast-food restaurants but also unhealthy local noodle shacks, is often favored by people who do not have enough time for a proper meal. People are somewhat aware that it is not very healthy, but sometimes there are few alternatives. It is fast and quite cheap. What I consider a major challenge is fast food in children's diets. Kids really love it. As parents and grandparents want to make their kids happy, they take them there, often a couple of times per week.
With your background, could you give your friends who have kids some advice on nutrition?
Although I have a profound knowledge of nutrition, I would not dare to give other parents advice. It would be considered interfering with their family affairs and cause outrage. Due to the One-Child Policy, parents focus on this one kid, and then they spoil them quiet a bit.
How do you evaluate the development of holistic health awareness?
China has developed rapidly in the last years. The urban lifestyle, the environment, the standard of living, and, of course, the mindset of the people has changed dramatically. Not everything is good and not everyone is happy with this rapid change. However, many new topics – health awareness being one example – attract interest, and as this continues knowledge will spread.
How do sport stars influence the attitude towards sports in the general population?
I would say that role models are generally helpful. With a role model you have a certain ideal in mind, an example you would like to follow. And this is important because success requires having an ideal.
Wearing sports brands has became quite popular in the last years. You can see that these big sports brands have obviously established themselves in China in many areas of life beyond the sports market, such as the general lifestyle and outfit sectors. Years ago, it did not matter which brand you were wearing; today, your brand shows your status.
Coming back to fitness clubs, there are some sport brands that cooperate with clubs. Their reasons are twofold: first, they hope to get feedback from their potential customers and understand the demand; second, it is a good platform for them to promote their products. Fitness trainers often serve as testimonials for these brands.
A fitness trainer is not only a testimonial but – at least in the Western world – the profession also has high sex appeal. How is it in China?
The trainer has to be a role model. He has to look healthy and needs a well-toned body in order to motivate others. Therefore, the attractiveness of the profession correlates directly with a person's physical appearance. If the trainer is too slim or overweight, he loses credibility in offering effective training methods. Finally, it is important that a trainer reflects both women's and men's beauty ideals equally.

FITNESS CLUB MEMBERSHIP OF THE URBAN POPULATION IN THE US: 16%
FITNESS CLUB MEMBERSHIP OF THE URBAN POPULATION IN CHINA: 0.6%

AROUND 67% OF CHINESE MEN AND 4% OF CHINESE WOMEN SMOKE

CHINESE SMOKERS CONSUME 3 MILLION CIGARETTES EVERY MINUTE

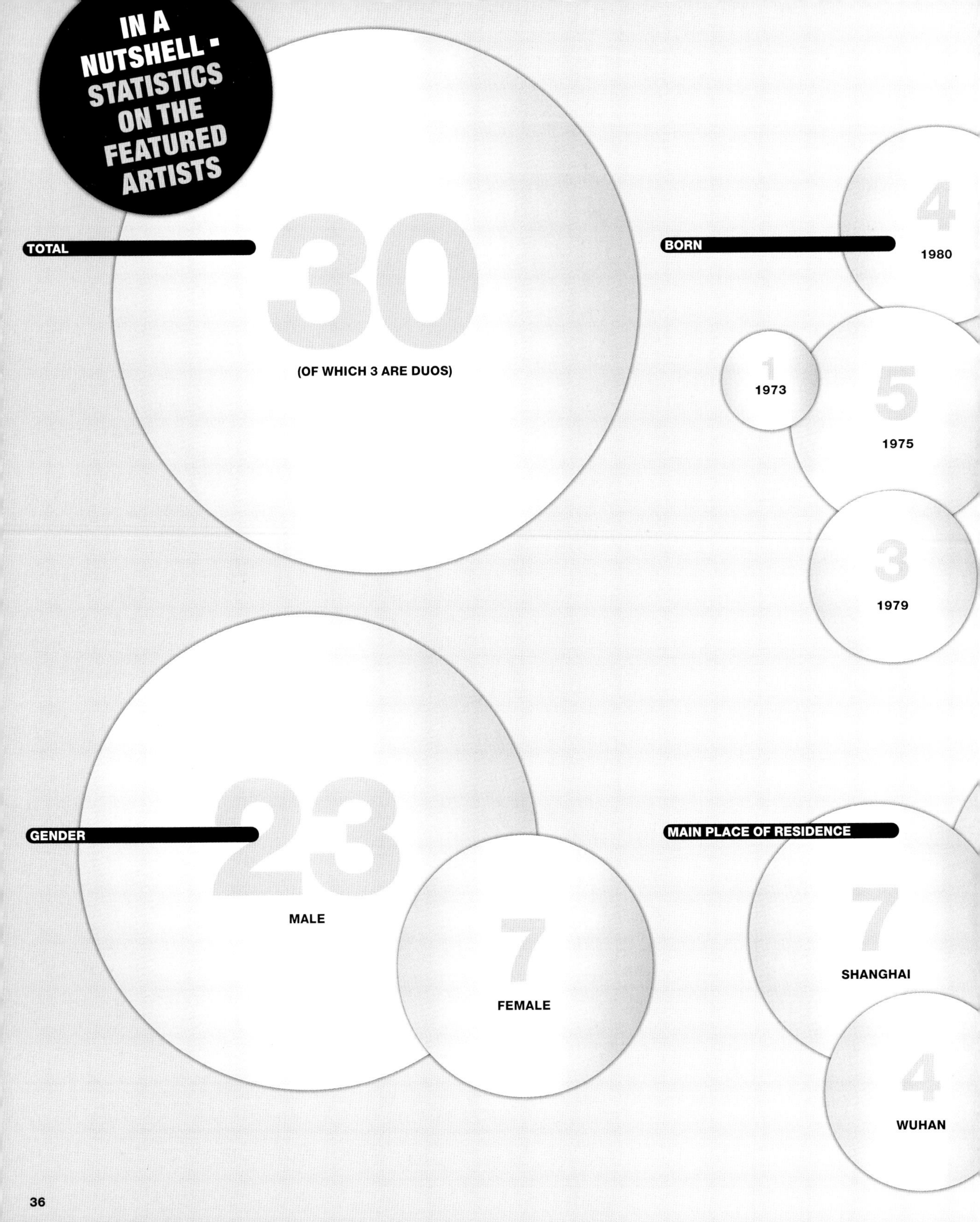
IN A NUTSHELL - STATISTICS ON THE FEATURED ARTISTS
TOTAL
30
(OF WHICH 3 ARE DUOS)
BORN
4
1980
1
1973
5
1975
3
1979
GENDER
23
MALE
7
FEMALE
MAIN PLACE OF RESIDENCE
7
SHANGHAI
4
WUHAN

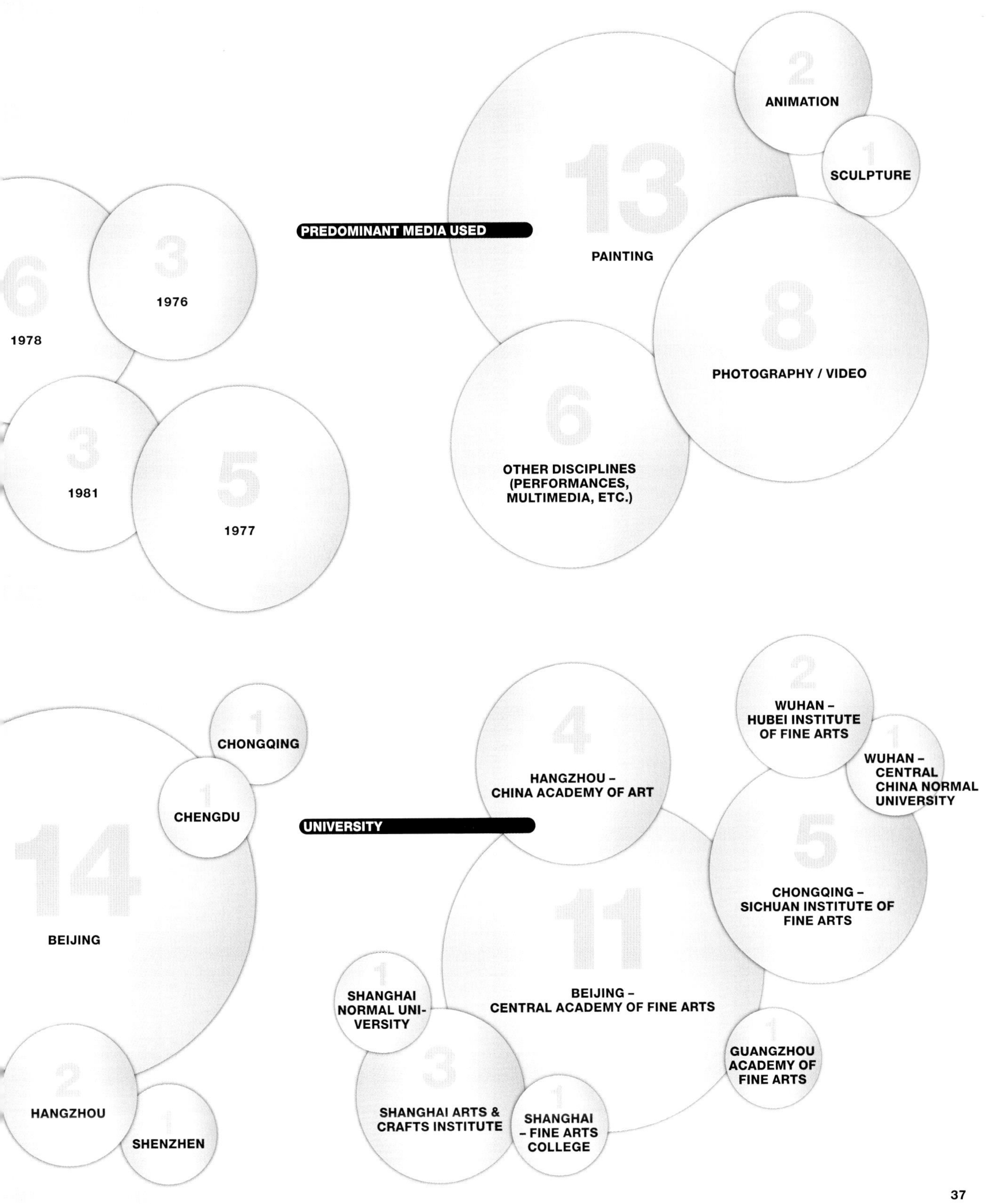

6
1978
3
1976
3
1981
5
1977
PREDOMINANT MEDIA USED
13
PAINTING
2
ANIMATION
1
SCULPTURE
8
PHOTOGRAPHY / VIDEO
6
OTHER DISCIPLINES
(PERFORMANCES,
MULTIMEDIA, ETC.)
14
BEIJING
1
CHONGQING
1
CHENGDU
2
HANGZHOU
1
SHENZHEN
UNIVERSITY
4
HANGZHOU –
CHINA ACADEMY OF ART
2
WUHAN –
HUBEI INSTITUTE
OF FINE ARTS
1
WUHAN –
CENTRAL
CHINA NORMAL
UNIVERSITY
5
CHONGQING –
SICHUAN INSTITUTE OF
FINE ARTS
11
BEIJING –
CENTRAL ACADEMY OF FINE ARTS
1
SHANGHAI
NORMAL UNI-
VERSITY
3
SHANGHAI ARTS &
CRAFTS INSTITUTE
1
SHANGHAI
– FINE ARTS
COLLEGE
1
GUANGZHOU
ACADEMY OF
FINE ARTS

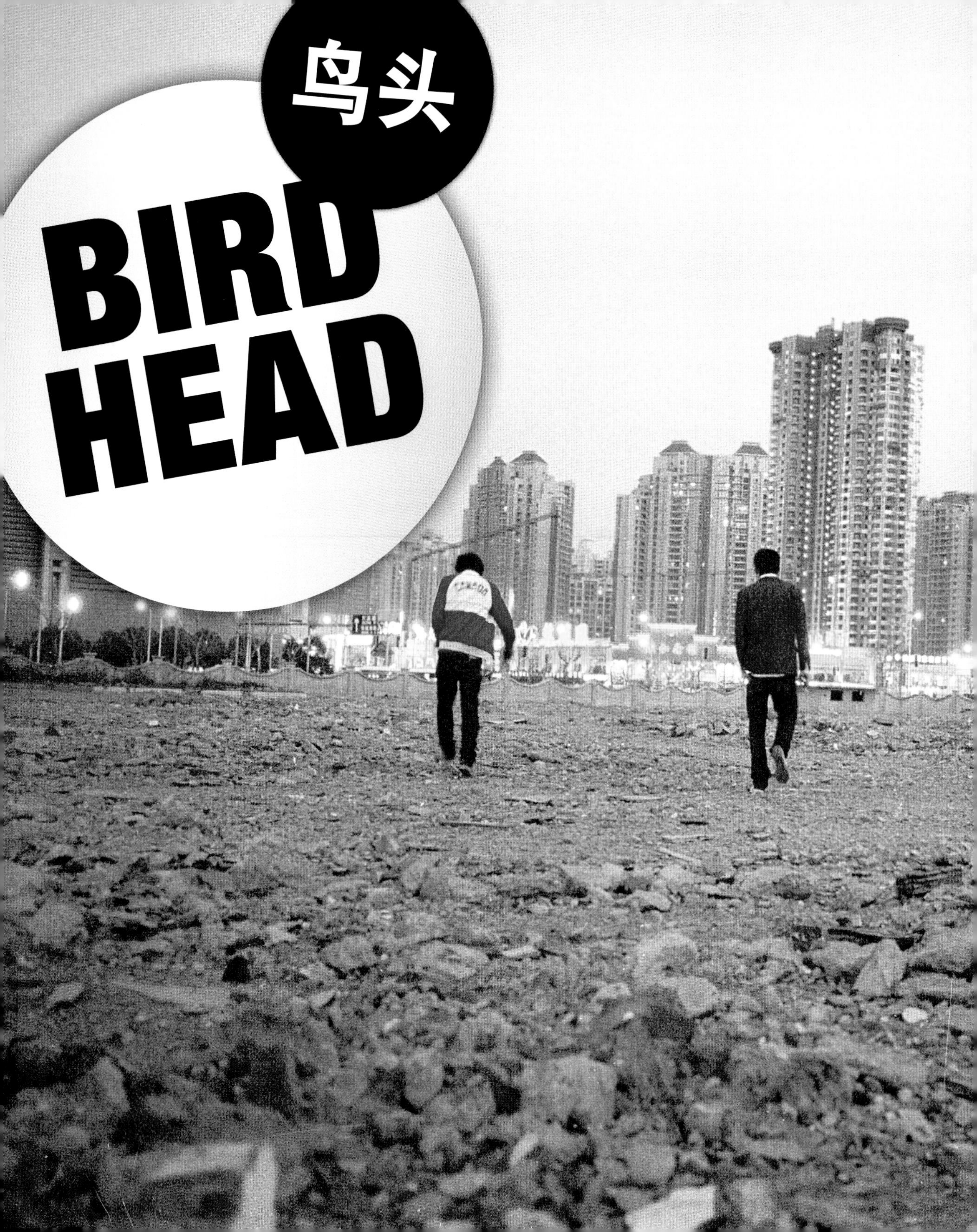
鸟头
BIRD
HEAD

GROUP
BIRDHEAD

NAME	SONG TAO	JI WEIYU
BORN IN	1979, SHANGHAI	1980, SHANGHAI
LIVES IN	SHANGHAI	SHANGHAI

STUDY
SHANGHAI ARTS & CRAFTS INSTITUTE, SHANGHAI

MEDIA
PHOTOGRAPHY

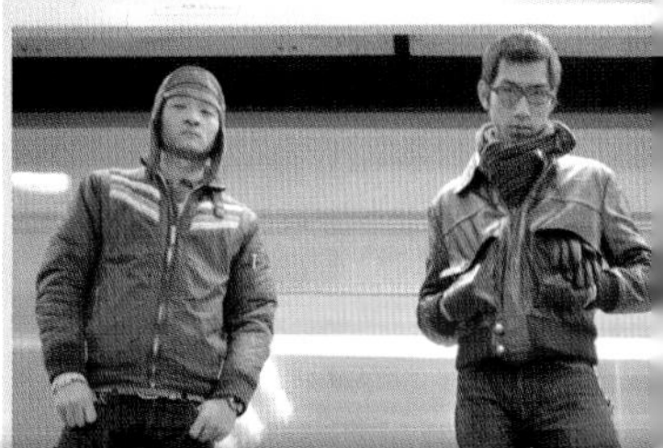

HEADGAMES

Just near the end of Nanjing Road West, or "Shanghai's Oxford Street" as it used to be called, is the construction site for the brand new Shangri-La hotel. The site stands just a few yards across the road from the neon lights and designer boutiques of the city's Jing An Temple retail district, and the jarring mix of thumping pile drivers and shoppers neatly captures the full-throttle pace of China's most dynamic city. The scene has not yet become a subject for Birdhead, the Shanghai-based photo duo comprising Song Tao and Ji Weiyu, but it might seem to have all the necessary qualities.

Song Tao and Ji Weiyu have known each other since kindergarten and began working together after Ji returned from the U.K. in 2004 having completed a four-year course in graphic design at London's Central Saint Martin's College of Art and Design. During this time Song Tao remained in Shanghai and began his career as a video artist and photographer. "He came to meet me at the airport and that evening we discussed what we were going to do. The next day we began taking pictures," says Ji Weiyu, who claims the Birdhead name was born by randomly tapping keys on the computer and searching online for the result.

The resulting first series – entitled *Birdhead 2004* and comprising 400 to 500 images – took just two weeks to complete and according to Ji was intended purely as a personal project. A book of the collected photos includes two front covers that roughly correspond to two series of portraits: one of Song Tao on the right-hand side and an upside down series of Ji Weiyu on the left – or visa versa depending on which cover you begin with. A scattering of street scenes and still lifes point the way to successive collections: *Birdhead 2005 Half Year* project and *Birdhead "Xin Cun"* (2006), which linger on the city's least glamorous aspects: all-night convenience stores, concrete overpasses, and street litter.

In *Birdhead 2005 Half Year* (2005–6), the pair based numerous images on the then redevelopment of Pudong not far from Jinmao Tower, China's tallest building and surely one of the most astonishing areas of urban redevelopment in the world. Characteristically, the photographers place themselves in the scene: clambering over chewed-up piles of concrete and broken bricks, or scaling the smashed remains of a half-demolished house.

In one of the most powerful images of this collection, which comprises approximately 600 photographs taken over six months in locations all over Shanghai, the viewer sees Jinmao itself. The black-and-white shot taken one overcast night looks up at the tower's eighty-eight stories towards the Sky Lounge near the very top, whose lights flare like an erupting volcano. With typical nonchalance, the pair shrugs off the image as just another photo and claim they can't even remember who took it. Yet few of their pictures so succinctly capture the prescient dichotomy of beauty and terrifying energy that characterizes their city.

The works, which are also presented in book form, have a snapshot feel, as if determined to avoid the conventions of professional photography. However, a gradual shift in trajectory is unmistakable. The 2006 series entitled *Birdhead "Xin Cun"* retains much of the original spontaneity of their early works, yet includes fewer self-portraits and is deliberately focused on the city's vanishing "xin cun," or "new villages," a form of bald, mass housing in which both artist's grew up. The series shows a growing maturity and a desire to move away from the informality of the preceding years to explore the potential of Birdhead as an "art" entity.

This view is enforced in their most recent multi-part *Landscape* series (2007–8), which for the first time breaks with the book format. This includes *Landscape Garden* (2007), a series of typical Birdhead images of knick-knacks and bric-a-brac scattered around a back garden, the two-part photo piece *July 14, 3.30 in the afternoon at Zhongshan Park* (2007), and *Birdhead City, Birdhead Jeep* (2007), a kind of road trip photo journal.

The final work of this series, entitled *Landscape*, was completed early in 2008 while Birdhead were artists-in-resident at Nottingham University, in the U.K. The piece comprises a video and photography component that are based on fifty-eight portraits of different people standing in front of a white board bearing the two Chinese characters "feng" and "jing," which make up the word "landscape." The work suggests a reflective attempt to test deeper conceptual waters and has more in common with Song Tao's solo video projects than the hit-and-run tone of much of their earlier work together.

However, a current project to produce one hundred zinc-alloy mini-figurines featuring the pair in photographic action mode and inscribed with the legend "We Will Shoot You" is a more satisfying and characteristically laconic Birdhead gesture. Moreover, the launch of a mass-produced Birdhead product – they originally envisaged 1,000 units – and its branding has strong resonance in Shanghai, a city that pays close attention to such things and which remains the artists' greatest ally. Song Tao says he can never imagine leaving. "Shanghai is our space. We love it. It is where we grew up; our friends and family are here and we know it very well. But it is always changing, especially now. It's what guides our work."

By John Millichap

1
A B

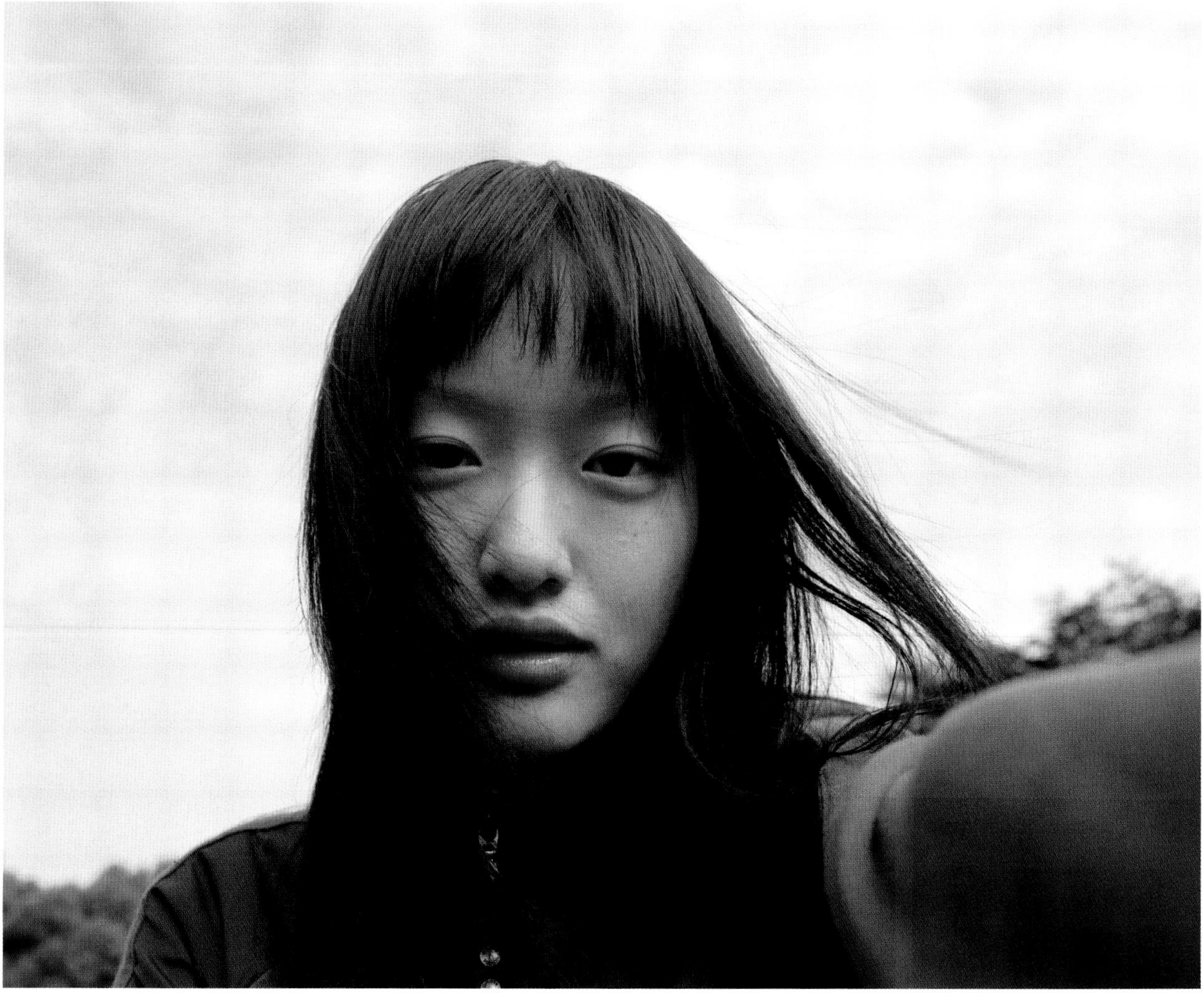

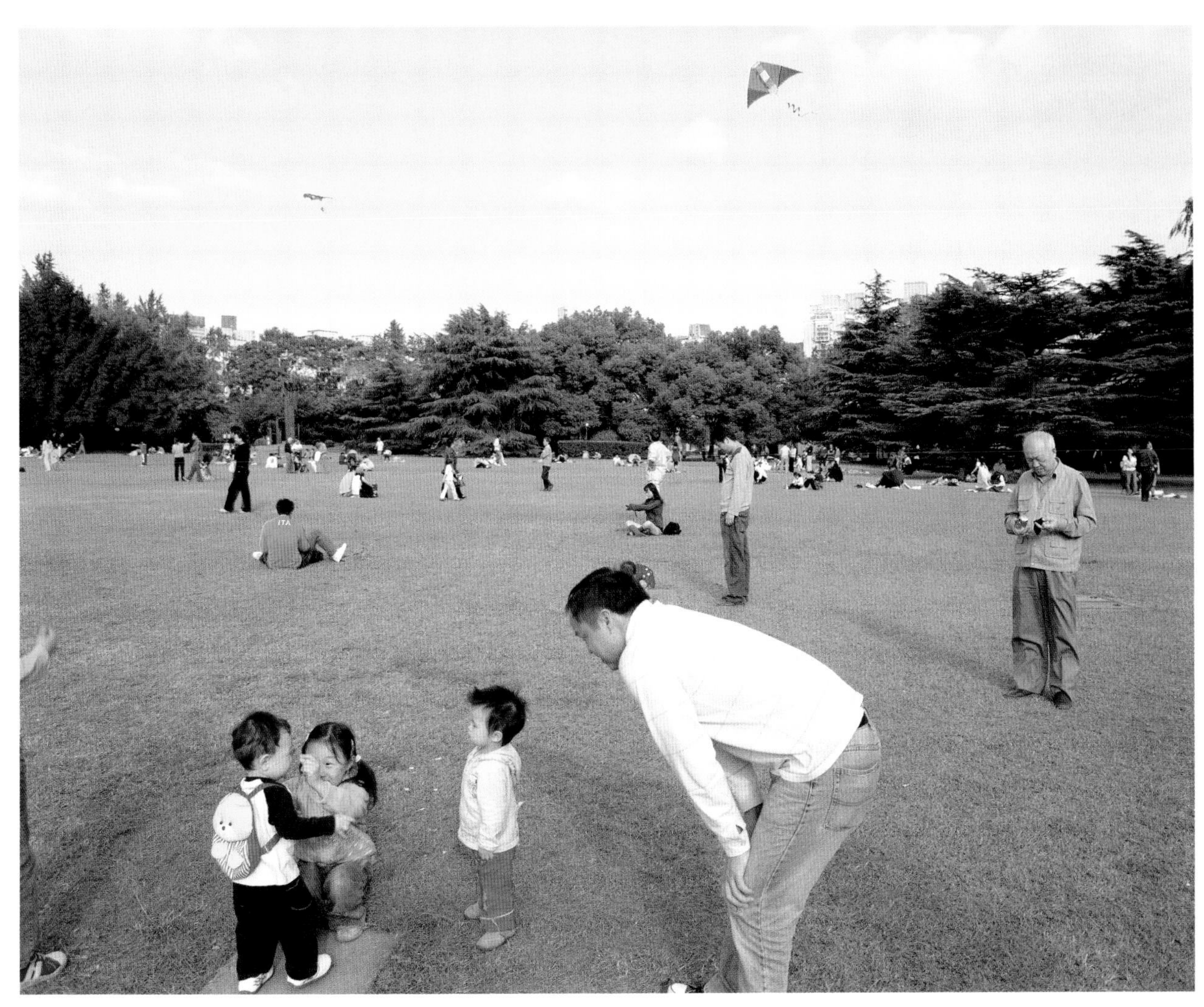

1 JULY 14, 3.30 IN THE AFTERNOON AT ZHONGSHAN PARK • 2007 • C-PRINT • 130 x 130 CM (x2)

2
3

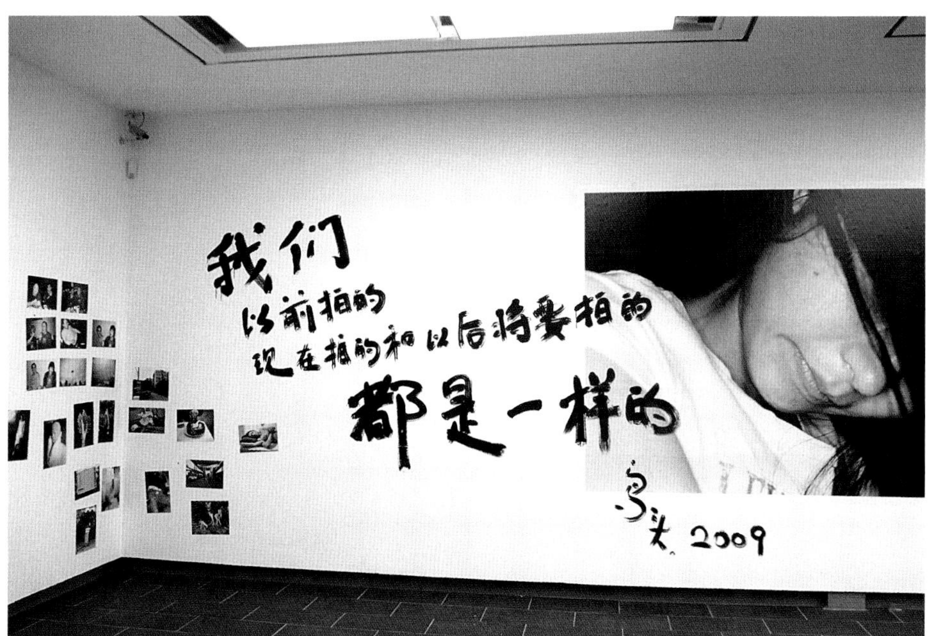

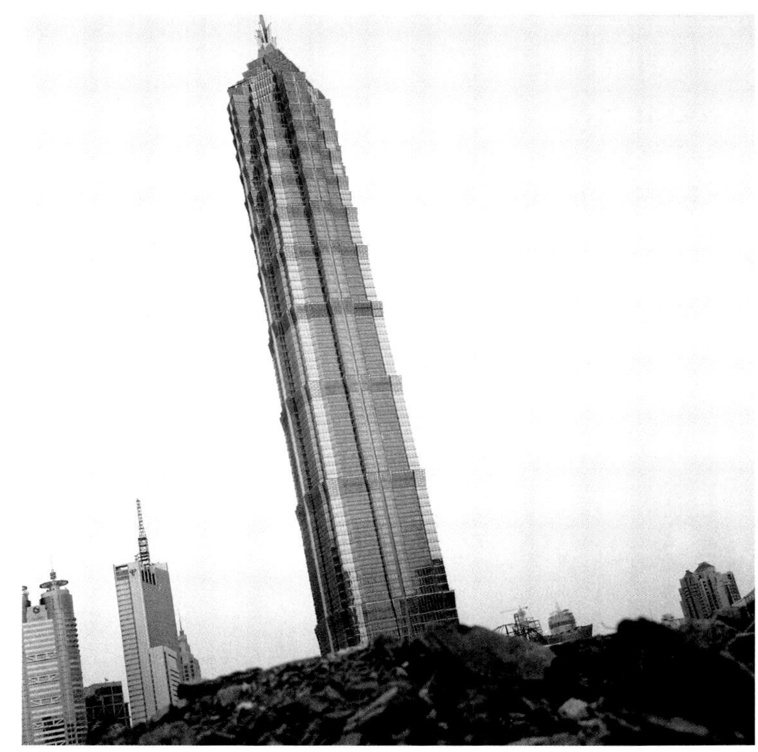

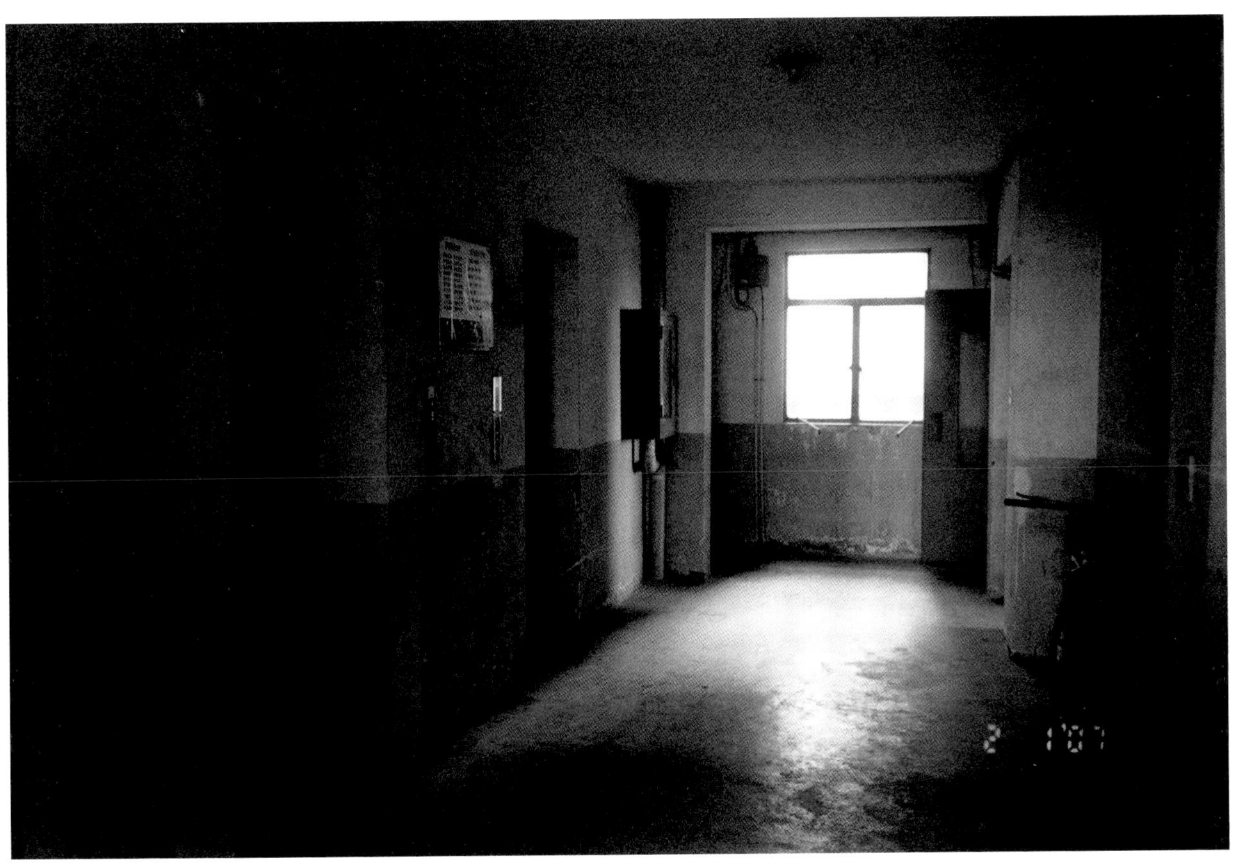

2 BIRDHEAD SOLO SHOW IN MANCHESTER, UK • 2009 • PHOTO • VARIOUS SIZES

3 BIRDHEAD 2005 • 2005 • C-PRINT • 60 x 60 CM

4 BIRDHEAD "XIN CUN" • 2006 • SELF-ADHESIVE PHOTO PRINT • 20.5 x 26 CM

5

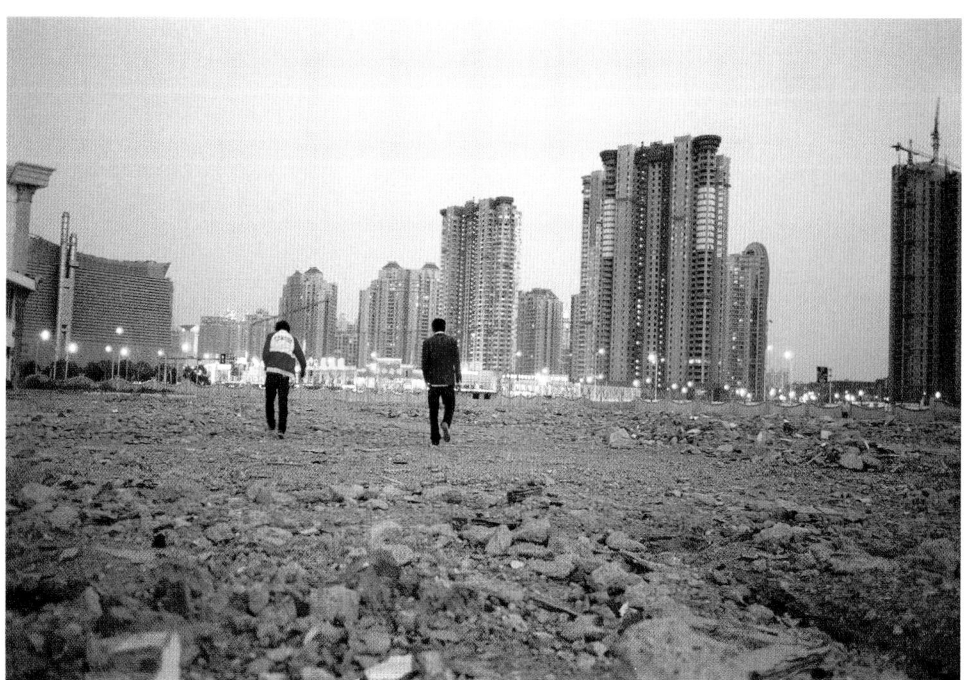

5 BIRDHEAD 2005 HALF YEAR (PRINT 262) • 2005 • C-PRINT • 40 x 60 CM

6 BIRDHEAD "XIN CUN" • 2006 • SELF-ADHESIVE PHOTO PRINT • 26 x 20.5 CM

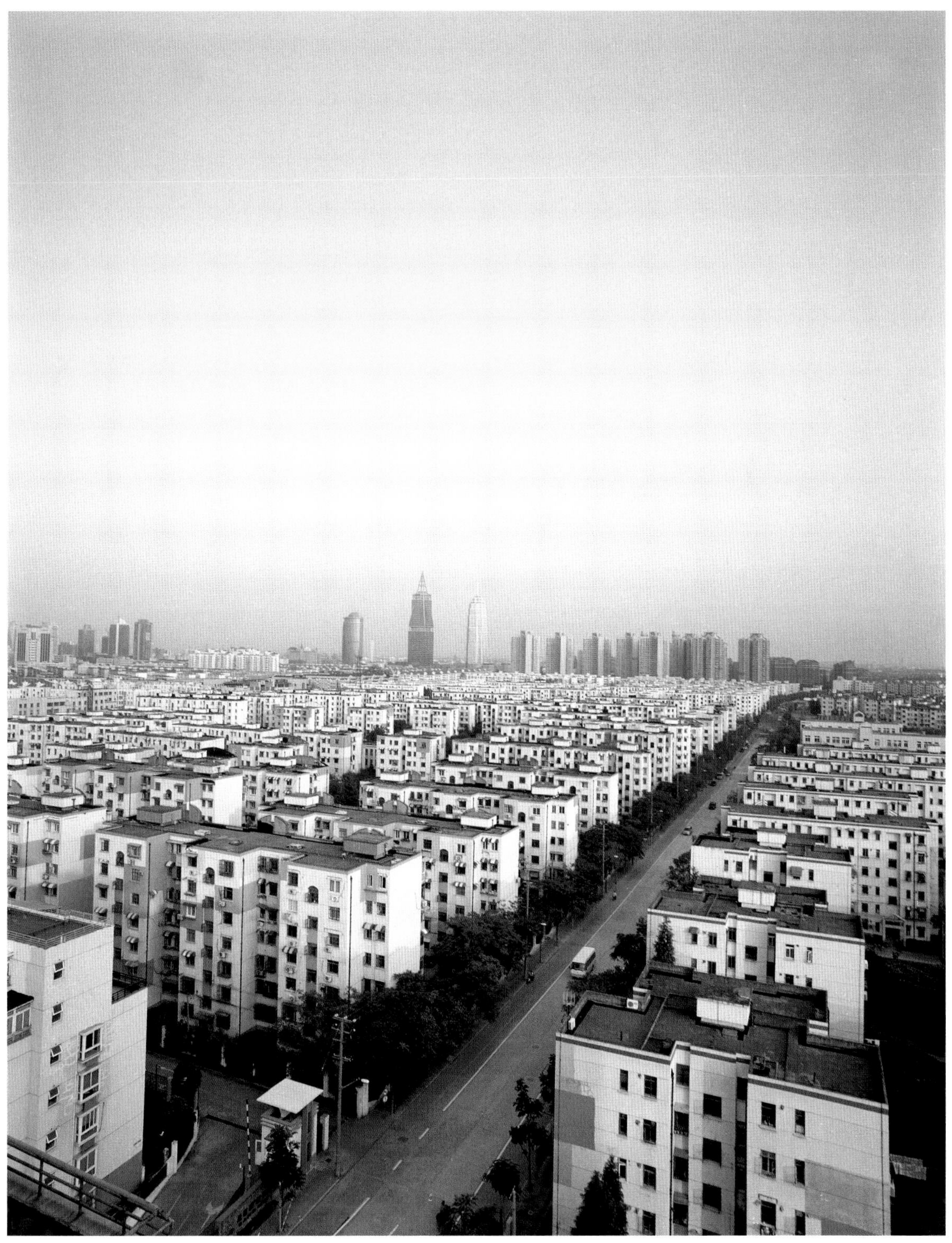

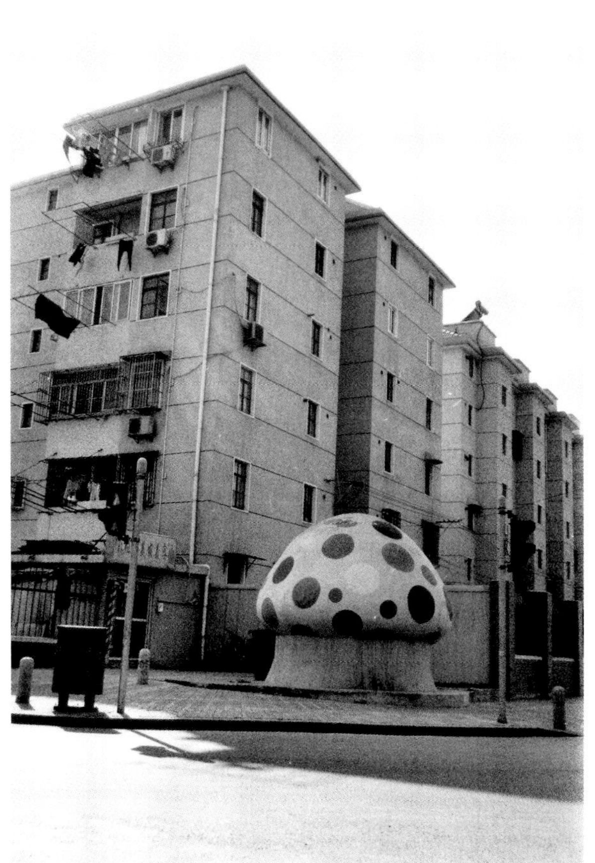

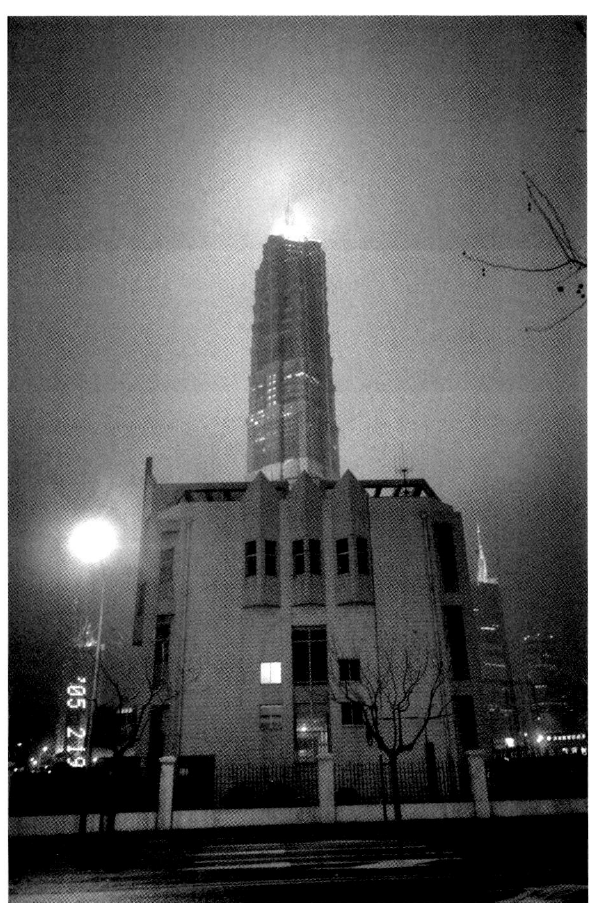

7 BIRDHEAD "XIN CUN" • 2006 • SELF-ADHESIVE PHOTO PRINT • 26 x 20.5 CM

8 BIRDHEAD 2005 HALF YEAR (PRINT 3030002) • 2005 • C-PRINT • 60 x 40 CM

QUESTIONNAIRE

5/11/08 • SONG TAO - SHANGHAI, JI WEI YU - SHANGHAI

SONG TAO'S RESPONSES (FIRST) • JI WEIYU'S RESPONSES (SECOND)

WHAT WAS YOUR FAVORITE CHILDHOOD TOY?

Toy guns.
Transformers.

WHAT DID YOUR PARENTS SAY TO YOU MOST OFTEN?

"Take care of yourself, don't sleep too late, and have meals on time."
"Don't cause trouble for others. Don't waste your money."

HOW DO YOU TRY TO STAY HEALTHY IN YOUR EVERYDAY LIFE?

Try my best to sleep early and have meals on time.
I don't try.

WHAT HAVE YOU BEEN WISHING FOR MOST RECENTLY?

To buy a car.
To get married and buy a car.

DO YOU BELIEVE IN TRUE LOVE?

Yes, I do.
No.

WHAT DOES YOUR IDEAL LIVING ENVIRONMENT LOOK LIKE?

Live at the end of Nanmatou Road, on the top floor of a high-rise building near the river. Every April or May, when the paulownia flowers bloom, I can smell and watch the small light-purple flowers on my balcony. The flowers can't resist gravity's attraction and they fall down eventually.
There is blue sky and a green field. I would prefer a place near the sea.

FROM WHICH TYPE OF MEDIA DO YOU DERIVE MOST OF YOUR INSPIRATION?

I rarely get any inspiration from media.
I get my inspiration from life and the Internet.

WHAT DO YOU LIKE/DISLIKE ABOUT BEING AN ARTIST?

I was born as an artist, so there is nothing I like or dislike.
It has nothing to do with "like" and "dislike." It's my job.

HOW DO YOU COMMUNICATE WITH THE AUDIENCE IN YOUR ART?

With my vision.
Through a love for life.

IF YOU HAD FIVE WORDS TO DESCRIBE YOUR GENERATION, WHAT WOULD THEY BE?

I can't think of any.
Luck, inferiority, arrogance, hypocrisy, and loneliness.

IF THE WHOLE WORLD WOULD LISTEN TO YOU FOR FIFTEEN SECONDS, WHAT WOULD YOU SAY?

"Take care of yourself, don't sleep too late, and have meals on time."
"Remember my name, and treasure what you have now!"

EXHIBITIONS

SELECTED SOLO EXHIBITIONS

2009
Birdhead - Song Tao + Ji Weiyu 2009 in Manchester,
Chinese Arts Centre,
Manchester, U.K.

2005
Welcome to Bird Head World: Photography by Bird Head 2004–2005,
ShanghART H-Space,
Shanghai, China

SELECTED GROUP EXHIBITIONS

2009
Warm Up,
Minsheng Center for Contemporary Art,
Shanghai, China

2008
New Photography in China: One of the Largest Surveys of Emerging Photography Talent from China,
Hong Kong Fringe Club,
Hong Kong, China

2007
ShanghART Autumn Exhibition,
ShanghART Gallery,
Shanghai, China

2007
Celebrating: Chinese Contemporary Photography Exhibition,
epSITE Shanghai,
Shanghai, China

2007
China Power Station: Part II,
Astrup Fearnley Museum of Modern Art,
Oslo, Norway

2007
Individual Position 2: Video, Photo, and Installation,
ShanghART H-Space,
Shanghai, China

2005
The 1st Lianzhou International Photo Festival: Double Vision,
Culture Square Lianzhou,
Lianzhou, China

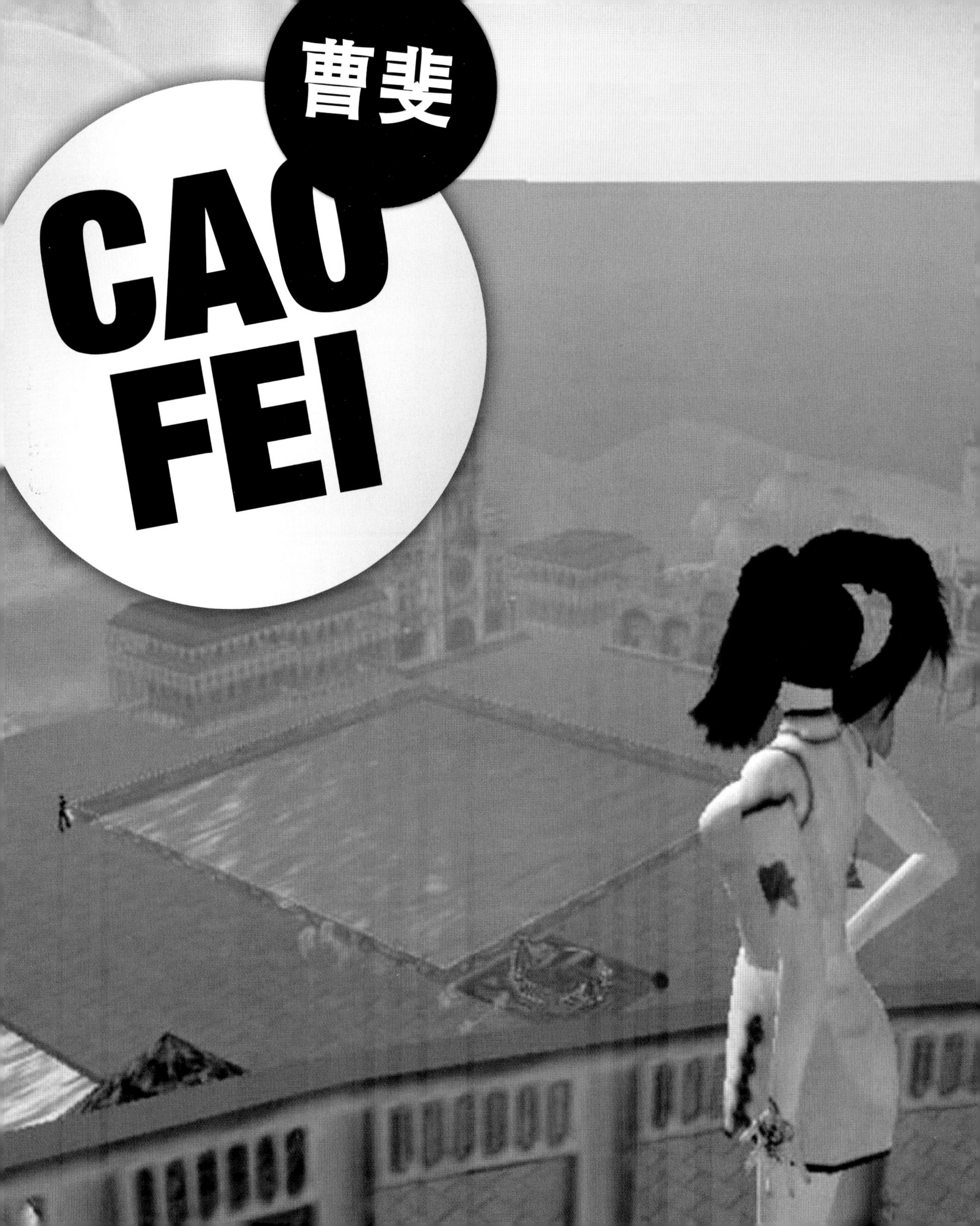
曹斐
CAO
FEI

NAME
CAO FEI
BORN IN
1978, GUANGZHOU
LIVES IN
BEIJING
STUDY
GUANGZHOU ACADEMY OF FINE ARTS, GUANGZHOU
MEDIA
INSTALLATION, INTERNET/ANIMATION, PERFORMANCE, PHOTOGRAPHY, VIDEO

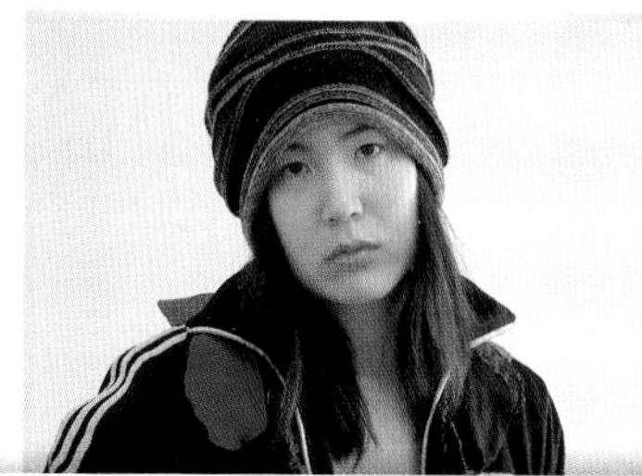

FANTASTIC REALITIES AND REALISTIC FANTASIES

There are many things that separate Cao Fei from her generational peers, but one clearly stands out: although she focuses on the fate of the individual, she fuses it with a deep concern for China's rapidly transforming social reality. Her oeuvre is expansive – ranging from photography, theater, performance, writing, and sound pieces, to short and feature-length films. It is in the blurring of the lines between reality and fantasy, in combining the obviously disparate, that she manages to both imbue her works with energy and with a cool freshness. She infuses them with a subtle, humorous yet piercing critique that is reflective of her character. "For me art is ... searching for connections in the gaps between things that are completely different."[1]

One of Cao Fei's earliest works that received wide international acclaim is her video and photography series *COSPlayers* (2004). Just like Cao Fei herself, many of the late-seventies and early-eighties generation have been deeply influenced by an exposure to Japanese manga and other anime in their childhood. Referencing the Japanese subculture of costume play, the artist addresses the alienation from traditional values as well as the sense of loss, disaffection, and melancholy felt by a large number of China's urban youth. It is in this gap between the realistic cityscapes and the fantastic havens these young people find in their heroic alter egos that Cao Fei discovers the fertile ground for a playful yet all the more acute critique of China's modernization process. "Cao Fei takes us on a wonderful adventure in the realm of the self-made myth of this new generation."[2]

While most of Cao Fei's work radiates with this cynical playfulness, one of her seldom-discussed photographic works, *Room 807* (2002), solely focuses on the abyss of anonymity and dislocation into which people can easily fall in the ever-changing environment of contemporary China. In the artist statement accompanying *Room 807* Cao Fei explains that she did this series of photographs in the summertime when she was traveling about different cities with another girl: afloat, lost, and feeling there was no way to return. The photographed scenes emulate murder and suicide scenes; the muted colors and the anonymity of the generic hotel room underline the sense of being adrift, displaced, detached, disposable, and utterly alienated from the real world from whence this tortured and abandoned figure came.

Five years after completing *Room 807*, Cao Fei picks up the theme of the traveling youth again. This time the atmosphere is not one of surrender but of defiance, and the issue discussed goes beyond an individual's inner world to the condition of a generation. The protagonists of *Nu River* (2006–7) are Cantonese and Yunnanese rappers who met on the Internet, where they searched for a companion to go backpacking in Yunnan in order to escape the pace of the city that seems to suffocate them. Cao Fei taps into China's active youth backpacking subculture, allowing her docudrama to be scripted by the stories written by other travelers on rocks along their path. The story circles around the feelings of alienation of China's youth through the rapid and often haphazard urbanization process and their fruitless search for paradise.

While the works discussed above revolve around the fantastic realities created by an escapist youth, other recent works by Cao Fei focus on another type of life, one in the realistic fantasy of Second Life, an Internet-based virtual world. *i.MIRROR – A Second Life Documentary Film by China Tracy* (2007) was completed for the China Pavilion at the 52nd Venice Biennale and shown inside a separate cloud-like tent placed in the pavilion's garden. In *i.MIRROR* Cao Fei documents her experiences in this fantasy world over the course of six months and explores the possibilities of living a totally different life as her avatar China Tracy. She watches the sunset on a lonely beach, she teleports to various places, has romantic experiences, and changes her appearance often. But although Cao Fei's avatar is free to do what she wills and be who she wants, a sense of loneliness and longing remains pervasive. Despite the vivid colors, the endless opportunities to do the unimaginable, this fantasy world remains a cold and detached place.

In *RMB City – A Second Life City Planning* (2007), Cao Fei continues her experiments in Second Life, this time focusing on the virtual world's rampant consumerism. RMB City is located in the middle of an expanse of water and, according to the artist, represents a rough hybrid of communism, socialism, and capitalism constructed out of a condensed incarnation of the various characteristics and architectural icons of contemporary Chinese cities. It is not only the virtual consumerism that Cao Fei comments on so tersely, but also the actual obsession with real-estate development in Chinese cities. These larger issues are underlined by a series of cynical stabs buried in RMB City's design, such as the Panda head that has replaced Mao's portrait on the Gate of Heavenly Peace, as well as the giant Mao sculpture floating off the shore, a clear allusion to New York's Statue of Liberty. To finance the costs of building this virtual city, the artist is selling its property in various locations that are set up to look like actual real-estate offices. The return of investment, after a period of two years, is a commemorative artwork by Cao Fei.

Cao Fei's art has become increasingly challenging, demanding, and socially engaged over the past ten years of her career. Her playful joggling of realistic fantasies and fantastic realities makes her work most pertinent to actual life experiences in contemporary China, something often lost in the staggering numbers of economic growth and the cant governmental promises of an utopian future where everyone's life will be better the next day. As such, "Cao Fei's work stands as a counter-representation of the very fiction of 'new' China."[3]

By Xenia Piëch

1 Interview with Cao Fei, in *ARTiT*, no. 15 (Spring/Summer 2007), p. 57.
2 Hou Hanru, "Cao Fei: A Cosplayer Recounts Alternative Histories," *ARTiT*, no. 15 (Spring/Summer 2007), p. 58.
3 Benjamin Thorel, "Cao Fei: The Adventure of the Self," *artpress*, no. 343 (March 2008), p. 43.

1

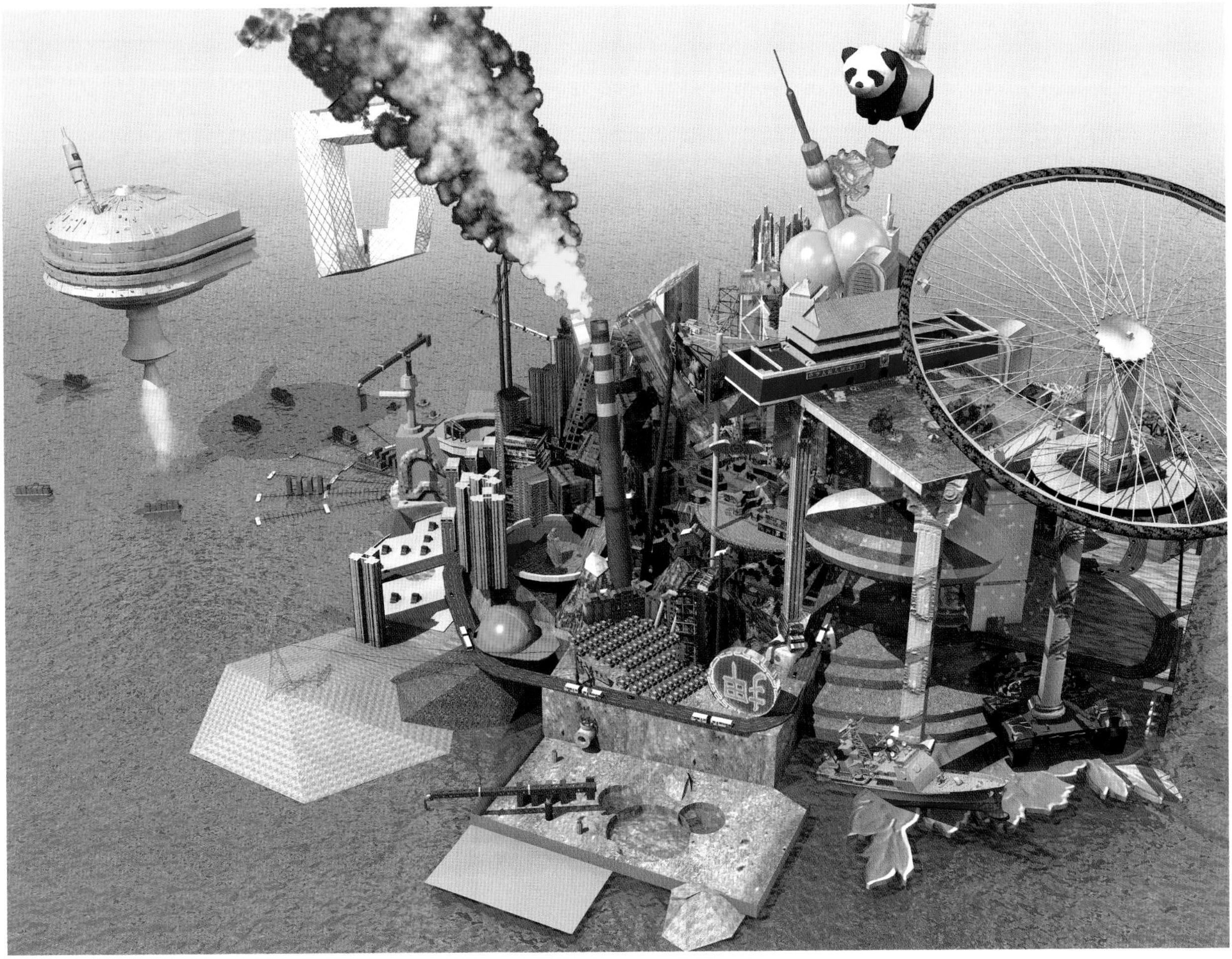

2

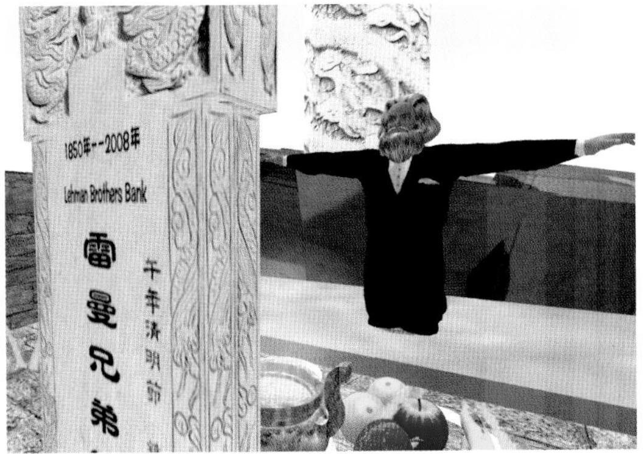

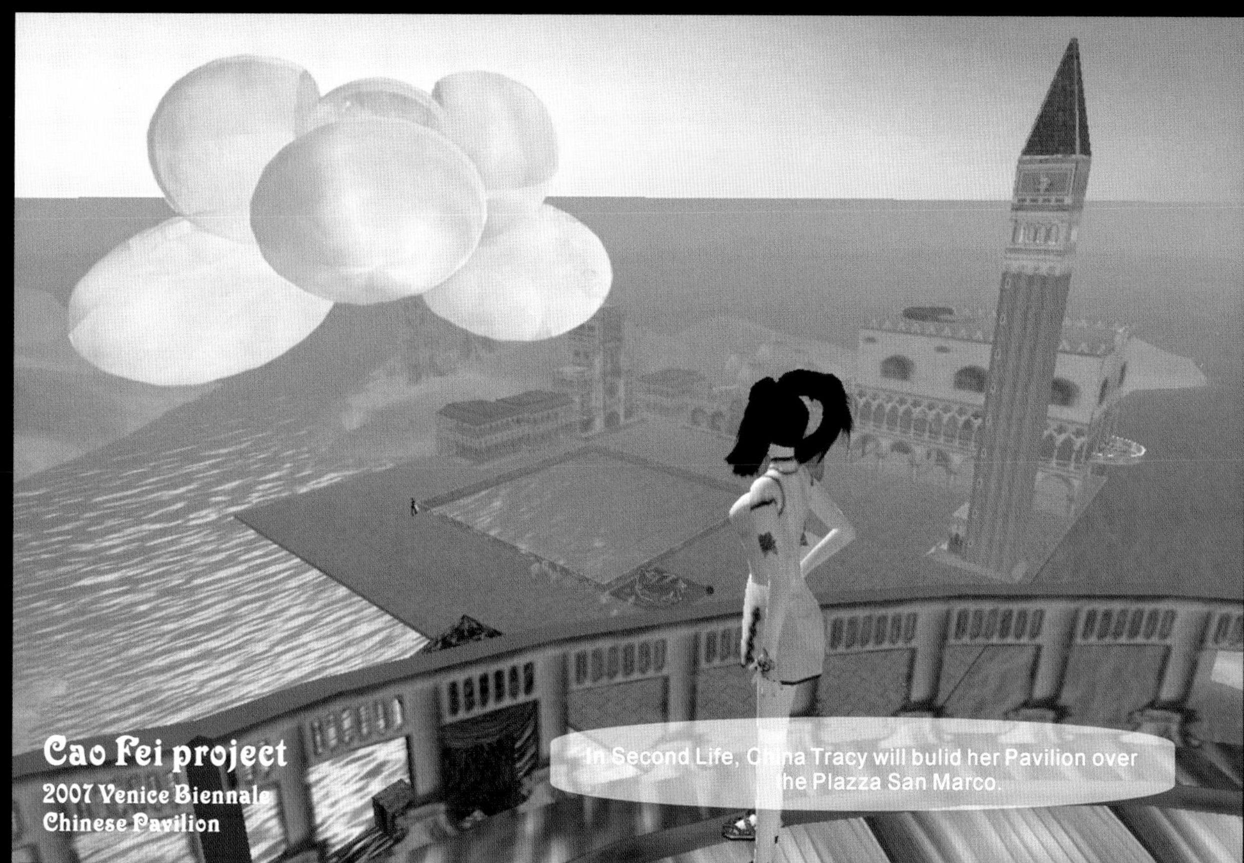

1 RMB CITY 4 • 2007 • C-PRINT • 120 x 160 CM

2 PEOPLE'S LIMBO IN RMB CITY • 2009 • VIDEO • 18'

3 I.MIRROR – A SECOND LIFE DOCUMENTARY FILM BY CHINA TRACY • 2007 • VIDEO • 28'

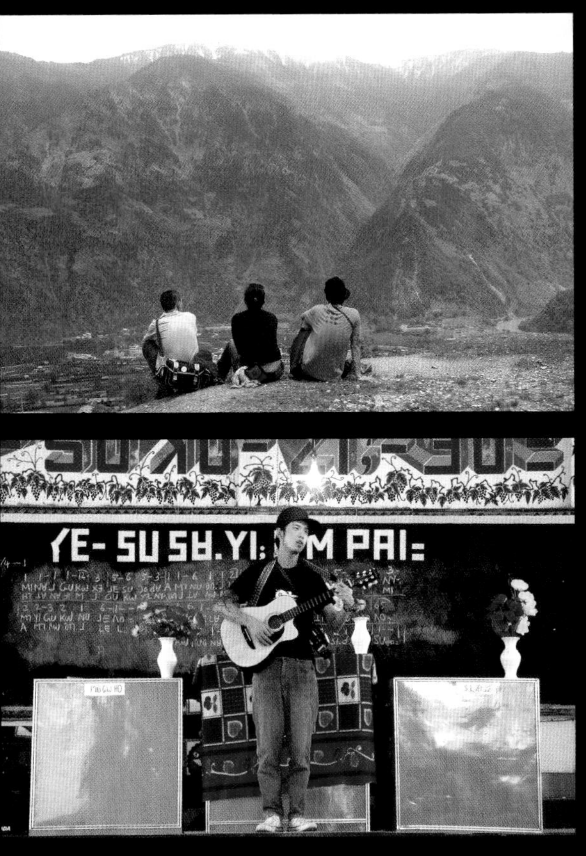

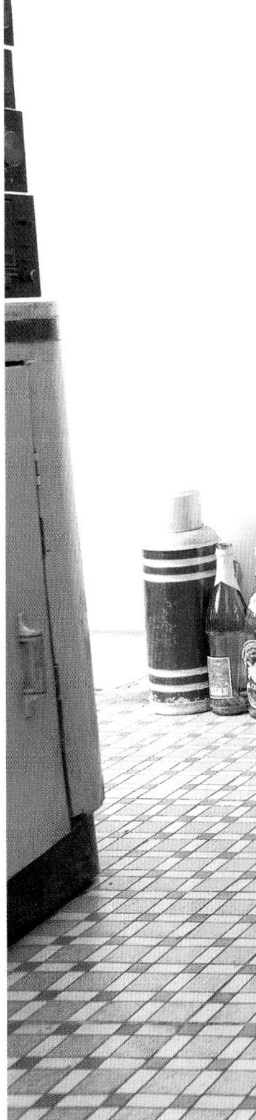

4 NU RIVER • 2006 • VIDEO • 53'

5 AH MING AT HOME (COSPLAYERS SERIES) • 2004 • C-PRINT • 74 x 100 CM

5

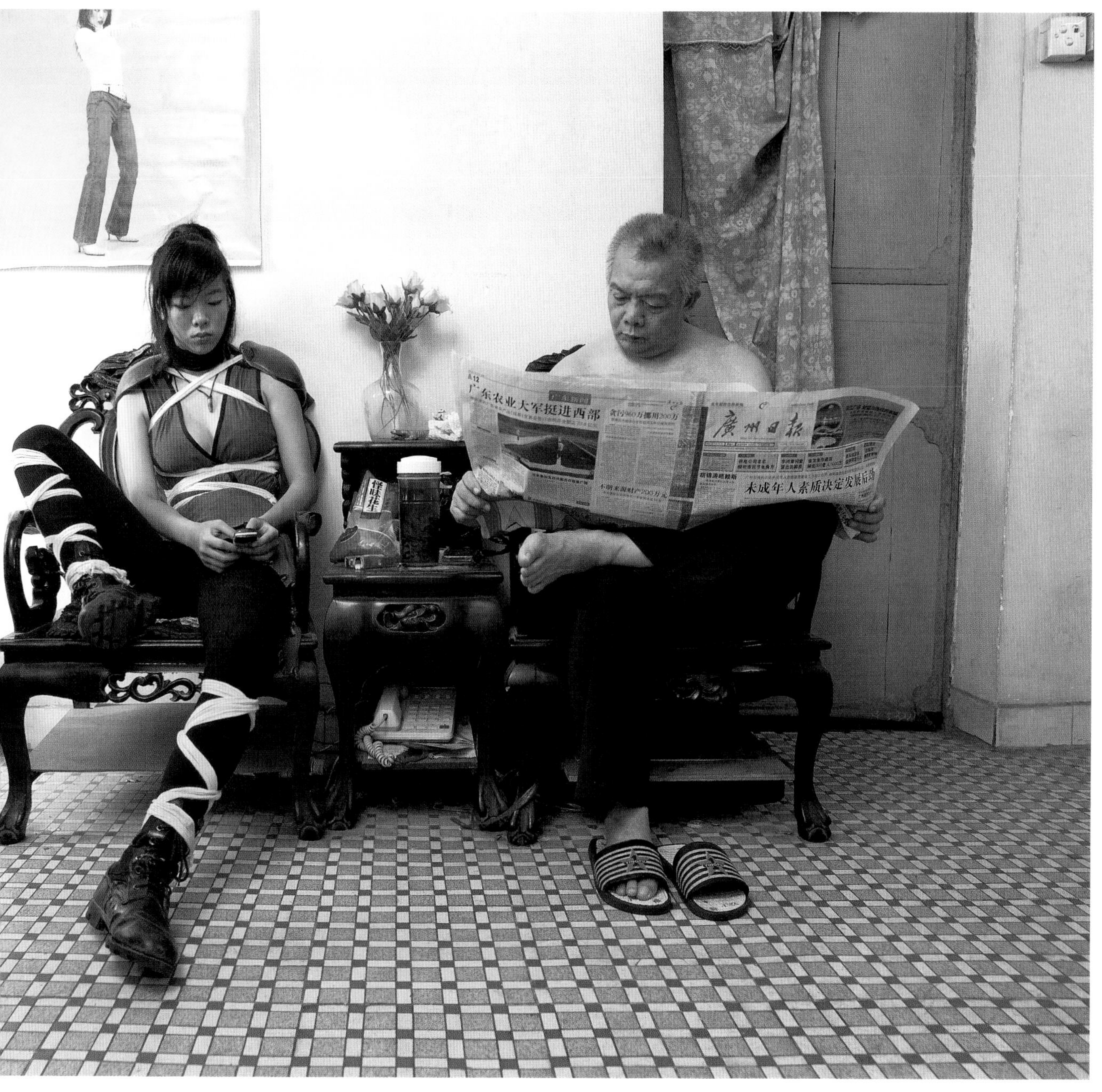
A12
广东农业大军挺进西部
贪污960万挪用200万
不明来源财产200万元
廣州日報
胡锦涛晤赖斯
未成年人素质决定发展后劲

6 7

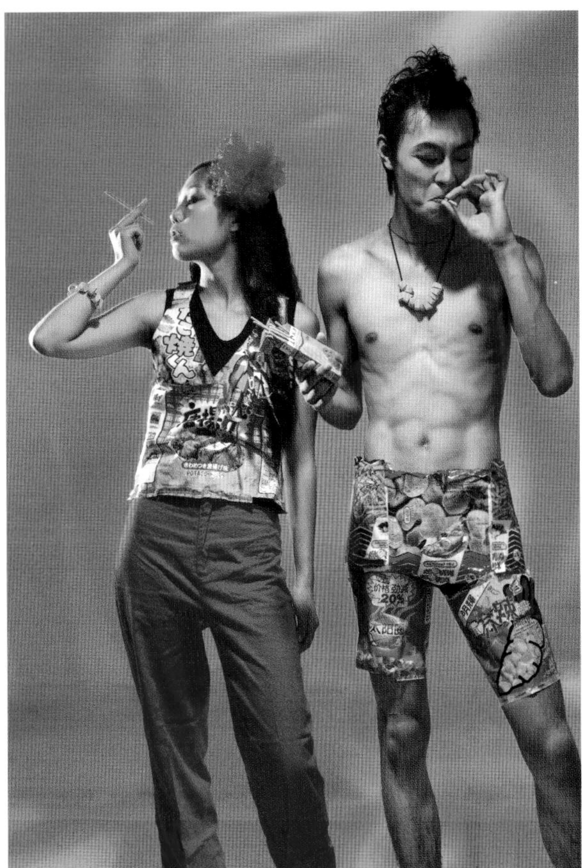

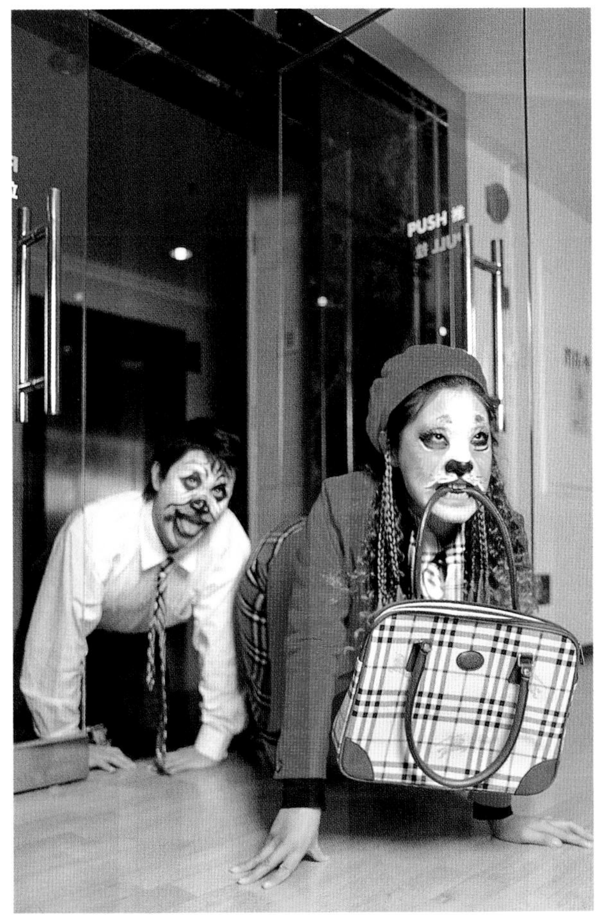

8

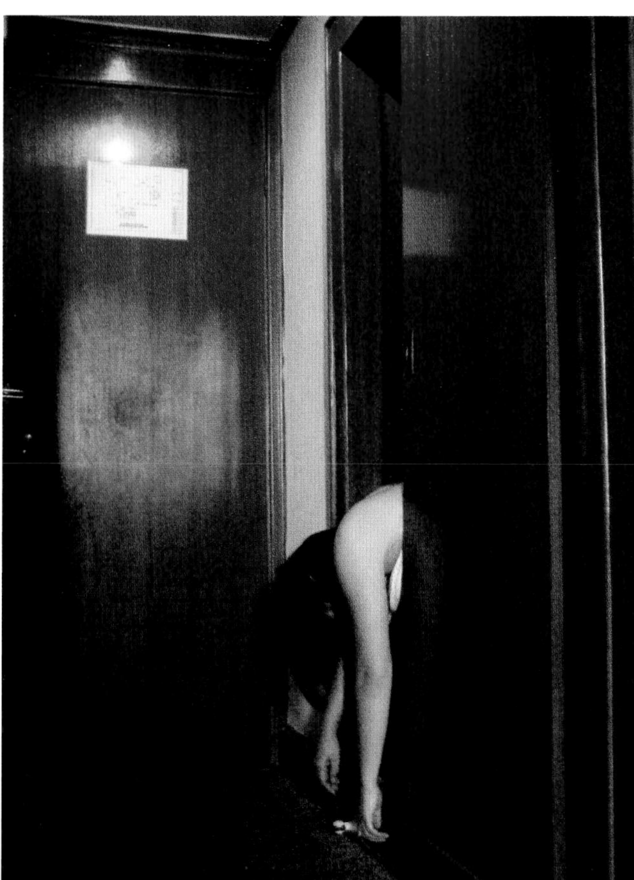

EXHIBITIONS

SELECTED SOLO EXHIBITIONS

2008
Cao Fei,
Kunsthalle Nuremberg,
Nuremberg, Germany

2007
Cao Fei: Whose Utopia,
Orange County Museum of Art,
Newport Beach, U.S.

2006
PRD Anti-Heroes,
Museum Het Domein,
Sittard, The Netherlands

2006
What are you doing here?,
Siemens Arts Program,
Fu Shan OSRAM Factory,
Guangzhou, China

SELECTED GROUP EXHIBITIONS

2009
The Generational: Younger than Jesus,
New Museum,
New York, U.S.

2007
52nd Venice Biennale,
Chinese Pavilion,
Venice, Italy

2007
10th Istanbul Biennial,
Istanbul, Turkey

2007
9th Lyon Biennial,
Lyon, France

2007
The Real Thing:
Contemporary Art from China,
Tate Liverpool,
Liverpool, U.K.

2006
15th Sydney Biennial,
Sydney, Australia

6 SNACK (FRESH SERIES) • 2002 • C-PRINT • 150 x 100 CM
7 DOG DAYS (RABID DOGS SERIES) • 2002 • C-PRINT • 90 x 60 CM
8 ROOM 807 • 2002 • C-PRINT • 72 x 54 CM

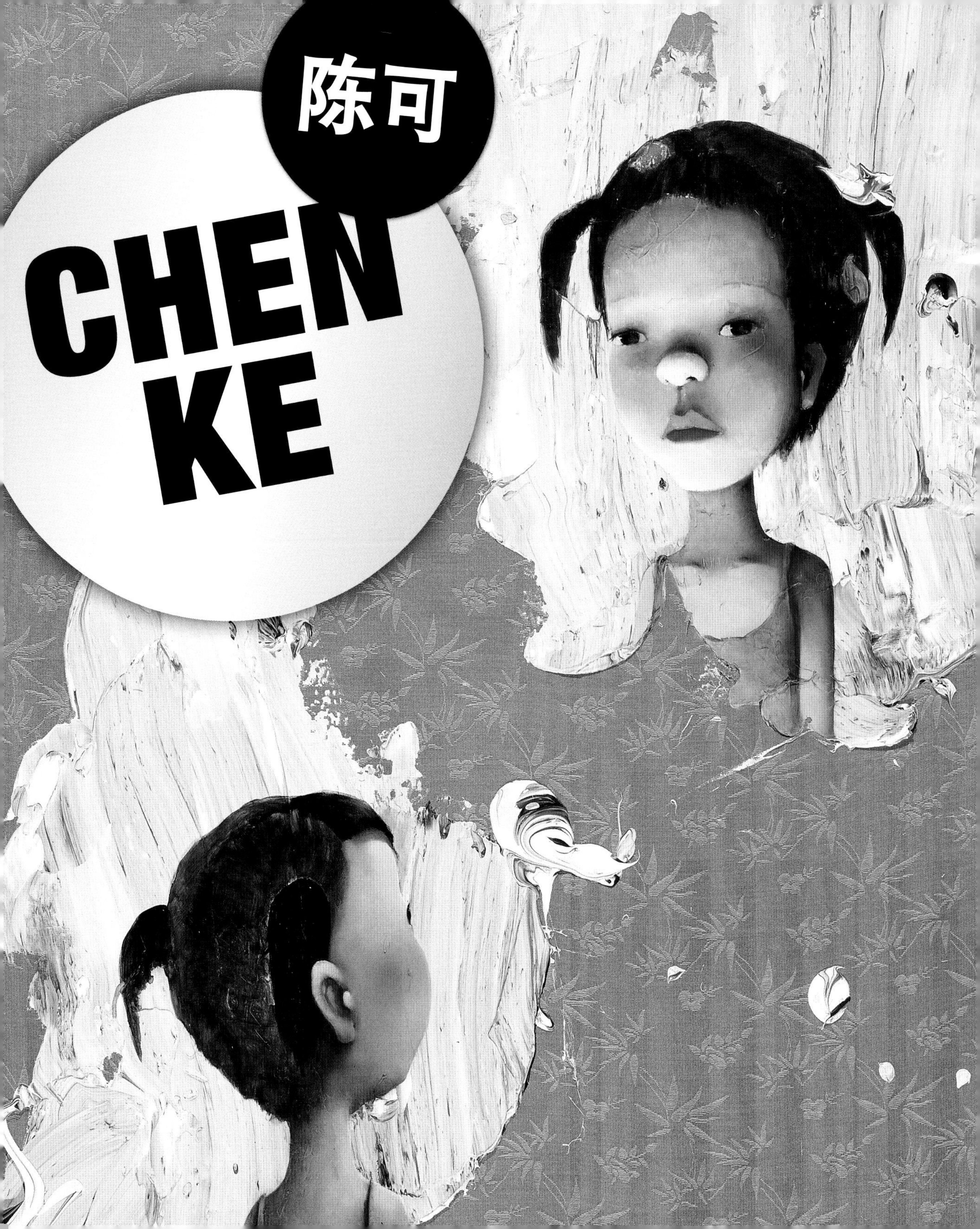
陈可
CHEN
KE

NAME
CHEN KE

BORN IN
1978, TONGJIANG

LIVES IN
BEIJING

STUDY
SICHUAN INSTITUTE OF FINE ARTS, CHONGQING

MEDIA
INSTALLATION, PAINTING, SCULPTURE

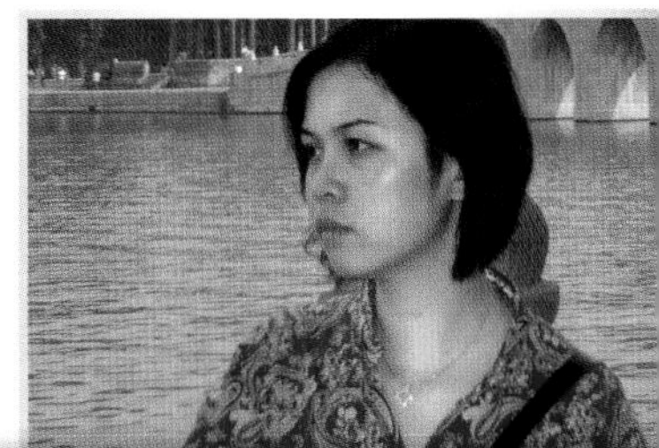

ONE GAME IS OVER, A NEW ONE BEGINS

"Game Over." In the Spring of 2008, the Beijing based artist Chen Ke embroidered this resolute statement in red pearls on the lower edge of her work by the same name. Two white-stockinged girl's legs project into the picture from above and stand on a glowing blue, volcano-like rise. Within glass balls swimming in the lava, gloomy yet romantic landscapes open up. This is the work of someone who has just quit the game.

Chen Ke has been painting her melancholy girl-women since 2004. In her early works she stationed them in the isolation of undefined space, only to later send them into extremely inhospitable fields in search of meaning. Demonstrative refusal to eat, useless weapons, shoulders hanging down, heavy eyelids – Chen Ke sounds out the psychic dynamics of her heroines and portrays them with a kind of trauma aesthetic. What once belonged to the genre of manga comics now segues into multidimensional art, especially in her most recent pieces. Flecks applied to the canvas float unanchored, becoming insecure bearers of the scenes placed within them. Layers of color over layers of color, breaking up like craquelure, or flowing like wash, allow surfaces just a few centimeters square to achieve their own life.

In the sculpture ensembles *With You, I Will Never Feel Lonely* (2007) and *Quartet* (2007), even pieces of furniture become image surfaces. Here modeling paste pours over the backrest of an upholstered chair, there over the body and keys of a toy piano. And every small surface seems populated with Chen Ke's girls. The prevailing mood of Chen Ke's works is concentrated in minimalistic gestures: the feelings of loneliness, exposure, and helplessness. In counterpoint to this dark attitude, she articulates memories of her childhood: "Even as a child I painted a lot. At the time, I felt free, but also sheltered. I could live completely in my own world." Her works keep these memories alive in the imaginative space of art. Some of the featured pieces of furniture come from her family's possessions. "But several of them I got at the flea market with my mother, because they resemble pieces that we owned before. The things tell stories from my past – the painting appends new stories."

In the works from 2008, Chen Ke experiments with expressing herself in new media. She has begun to leave whole pieces of the canvas unpainted, coated with a clear glaze. Then she embroiders wave formations and letters into her pictures with fine beads. Where before repeating patterns of doll-like girls' heads covered the surface we now encounter complex constellations of implied figures. "For me, these new works are like a diary. It's no longer just about readable picture stories, and it's also no longer about looking inward. For me, art is like an expedition, and I don't know where it's taking me."

During a visit to her studio, I find three picture books lying open before the unfinished painting *Is It Time to Do Something?* (2008). One presents classical Chinese landscapes, a second one American landscape photography, and the third is a monograph of C.D. Friedrich. It is astounding how similar the images of dead trees are in each. This end-time symbol has worked its way into *Is It Time to Do Something?*, only a few centimeters large and huddled beneath a rock formation with hulking masses of stone, like what one sees in Chinese scroll paintings. In front of this background the empty spaces of Chen Ke's new work attain concreteness just as the unformed space in classical landscape painting provided room for the viewer to rest and reflect. "With C.D. Friedrich's paintings, the similarity to Chinese landscape painting occurred to me at once. The atmosphere of these paintings also inspires me very much."

But what Chen Ke shows on the rest of the canvas has very little in common with either Western or Eastern models. Soft pink pours in, complementing the earthy green of the mountains; a snake approaches a small girl. And there again are the fin-like sweeps of beads, covering the whole surface. Chen Ke tells of the various symbolical correspondences she reads into her own painting: the opening, for example, of an exhibit or a play. She doesn't yet know how the picture will develop. One change she has deliberately implemented: putting the title of the picture within the picture – and in both English and Chinese. To her, intercultural dialogue is important and to foster any language barrier would only be a hindrance. And besides, contemporary Chinese art is no longer a purely Chinese affair.

Parallel to *Is It Time to Do Something?*, Chen Ke is working on the painting *Game Over* (2008). The title is again incorporated into the blue-black painting, and we are alarmed by both what we see and what we read. The voice of the artist takes on an aggressive undertone as she speaks of her intention behind this piece: "This picture represents a turning point. I would like to remove myself from the outside turbulence of the art world and other forms of isolation as much as possible. This game is not good for me." Here, art is becoming the mode of reflection on the external conditions of making art. In *Game Over*, Chen Ke is articulating a wish for the Chinese art world – with its very young history of success – that is often expressed among the artists of her generation: a return to self-determination. Thematically and technically, the works, which Chen Ke has completed in just the last few months, show that she has already started a new game.

By Ulrike Münter

1

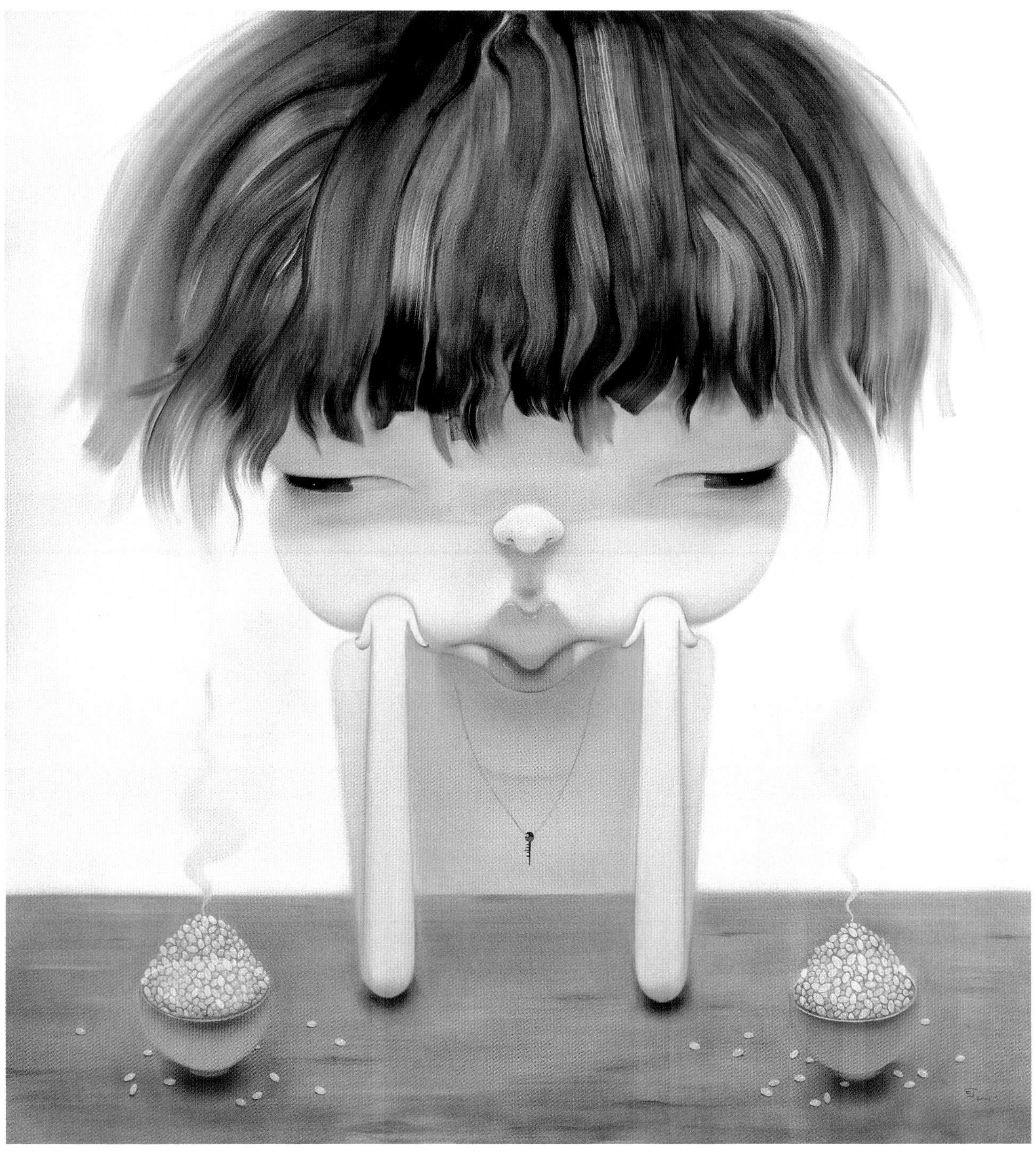

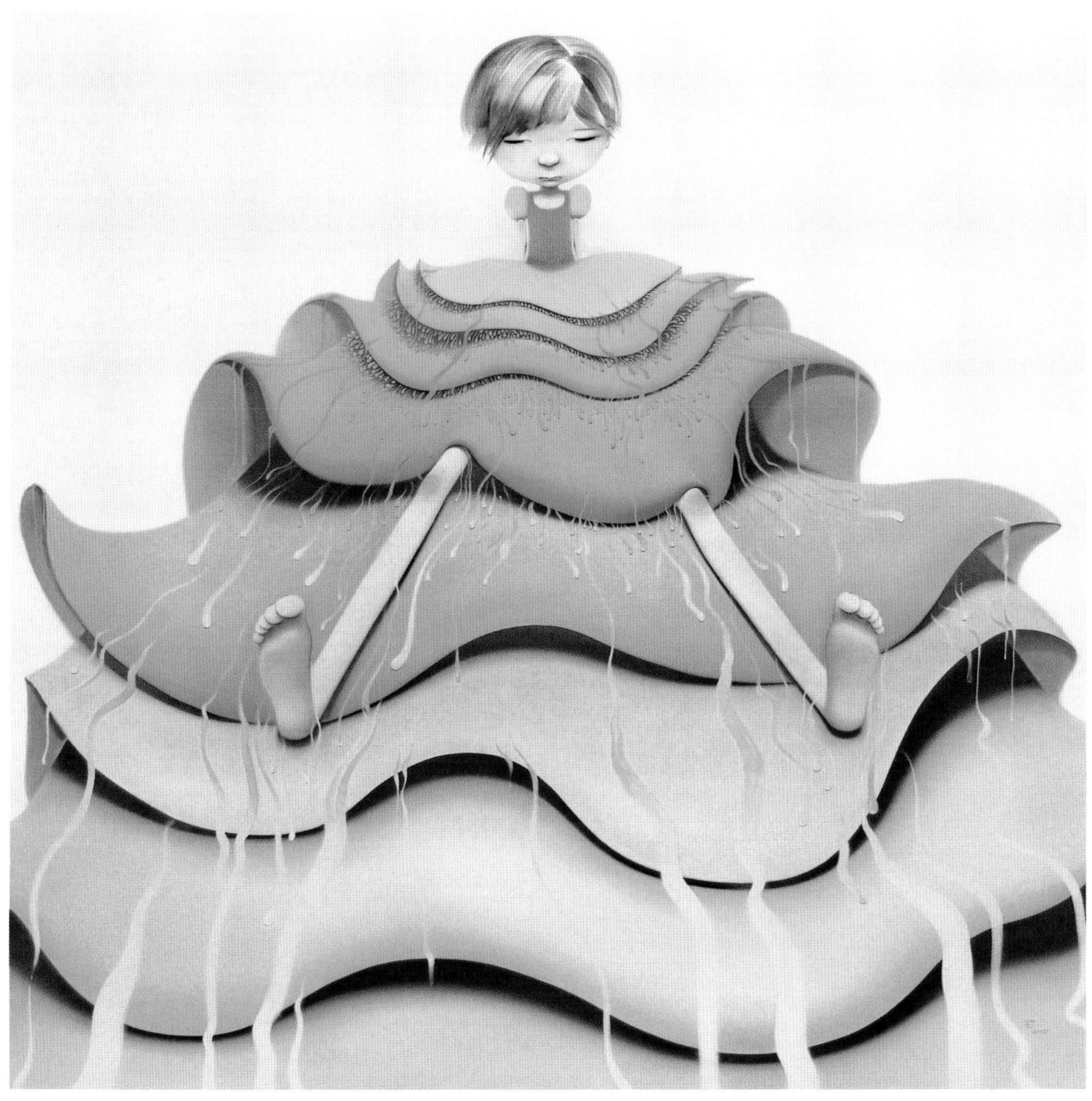

1 ANOREXIA • 2005 • OIL ON CANVAS • 150 x 140 CM

2 NINE-LAYER TOWER • 2005 • OIL ON CANVAS • 200 x 200 CM

3

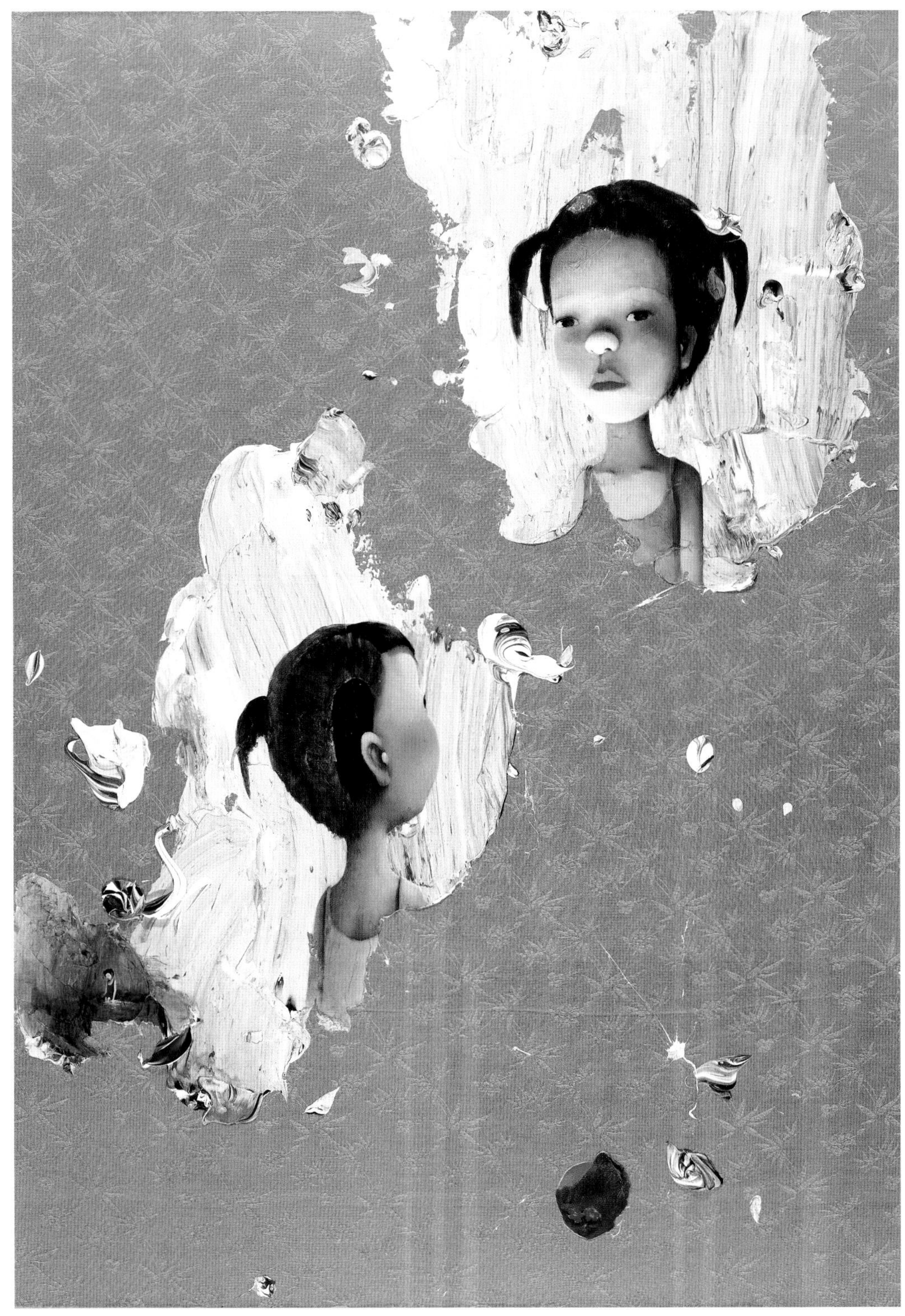

4

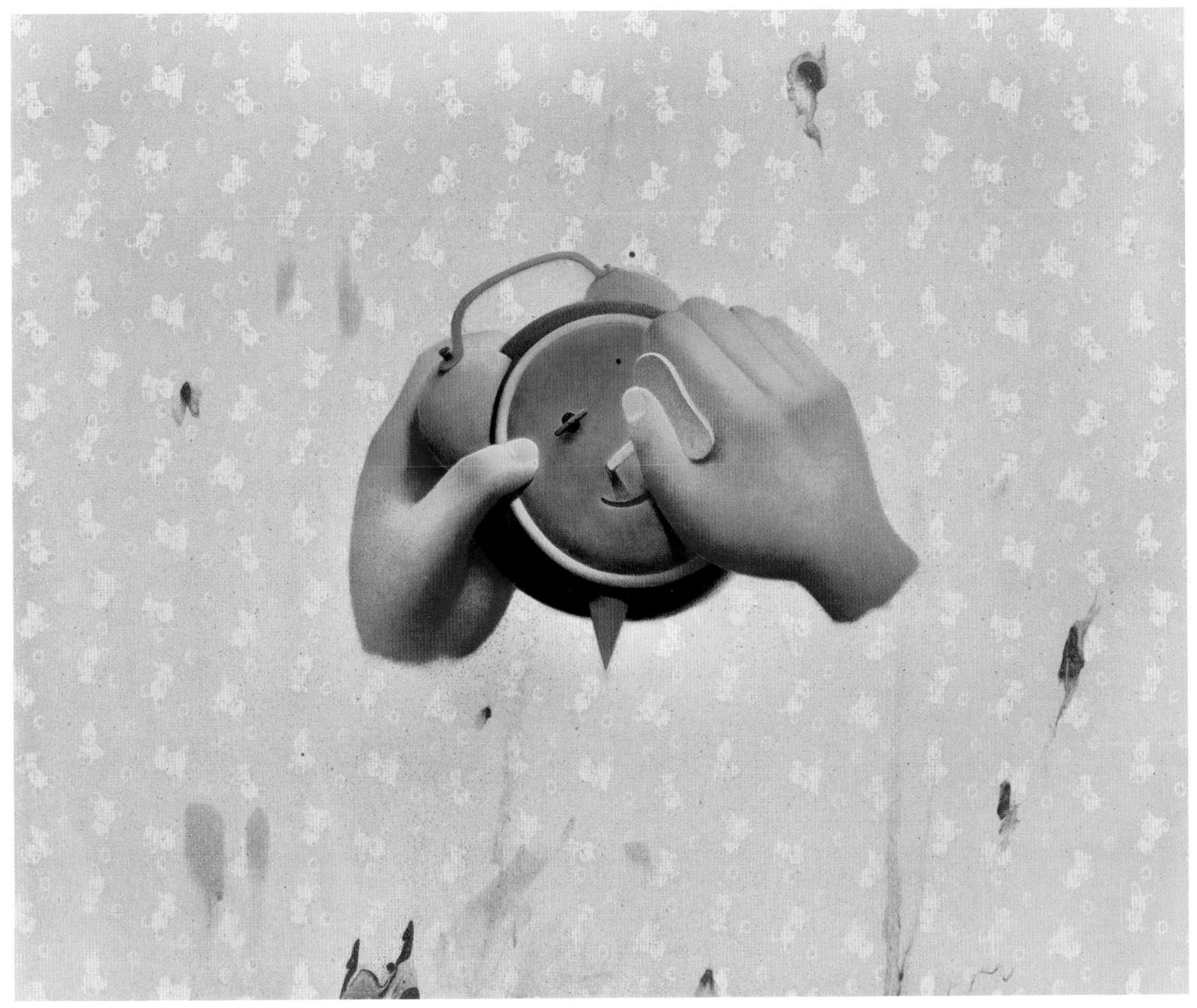

3 ANOTHER ME IN THE WORLD • 2007 •
MODELING PASTE AND OIL ON SILK • 170 x 120 CM

4 CLOCKWORK • 2009 • OIL COLOR AND
ACRYLIC MEDIUM ON PRINTED CALICO • 73 x 90 CM

5

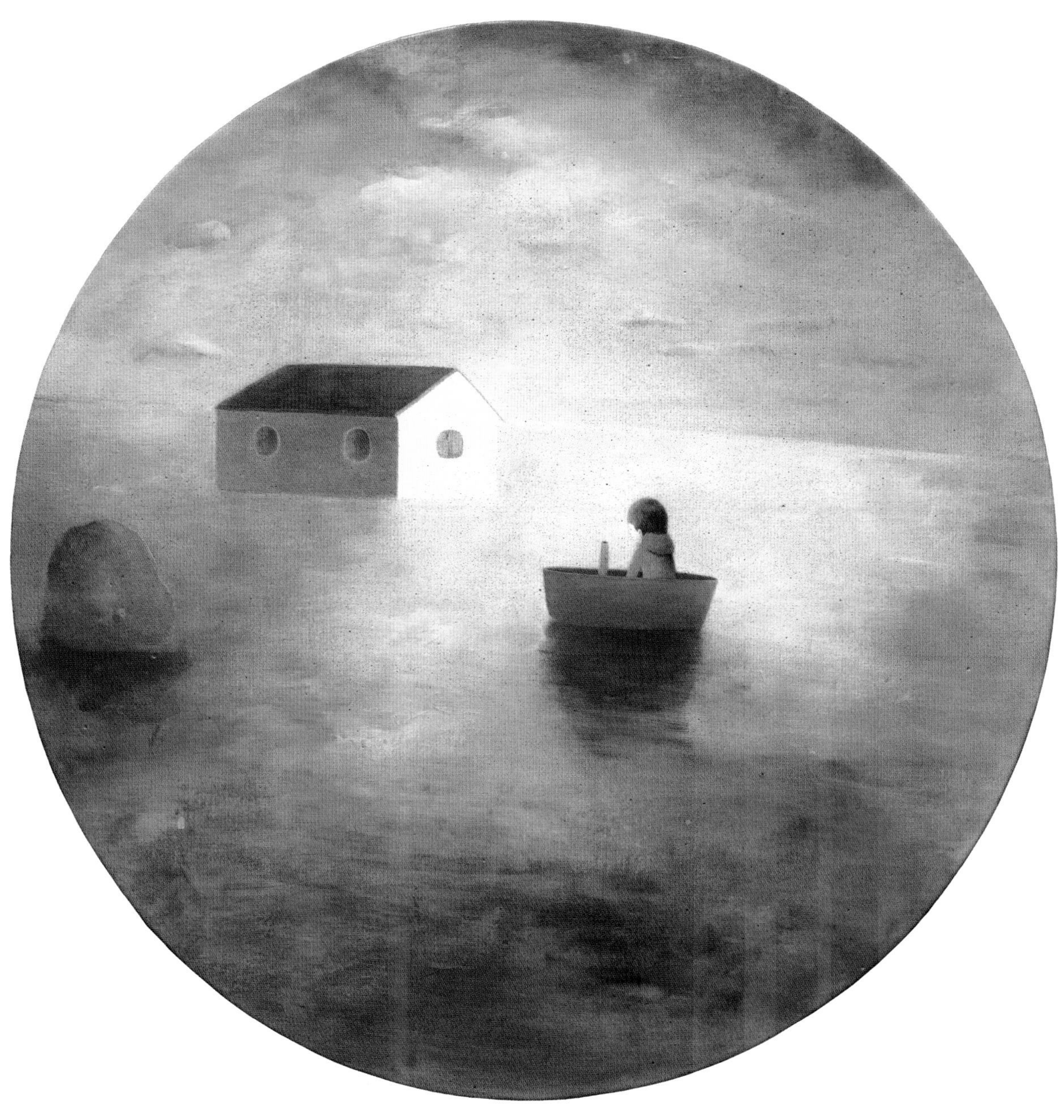

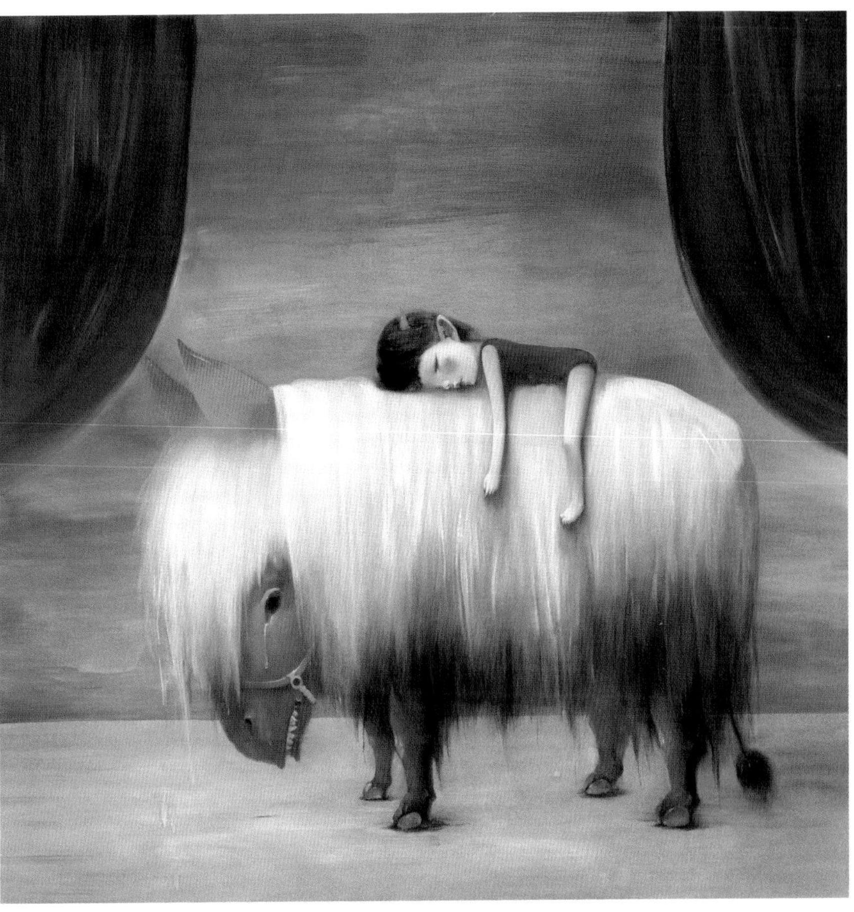

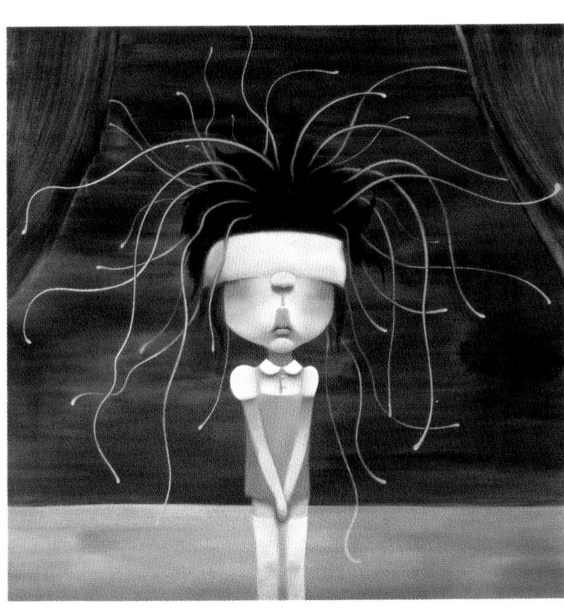

5 LITTLE BOAT • 2009 • ACRYLIC ON LINEN • 100 CM DIAMETER

6 MATADOR • 2006 • OIL ON CANVAS • 215 x 215 CM

7 SENSITIVE NERVE • 2006 • OIL ON CANVAS • 160 x 160 CM

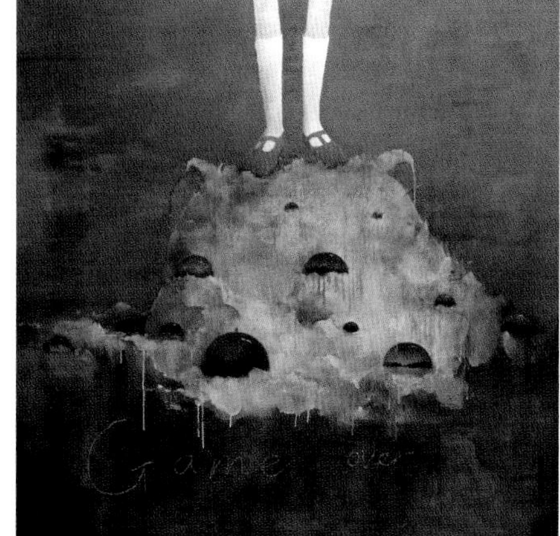

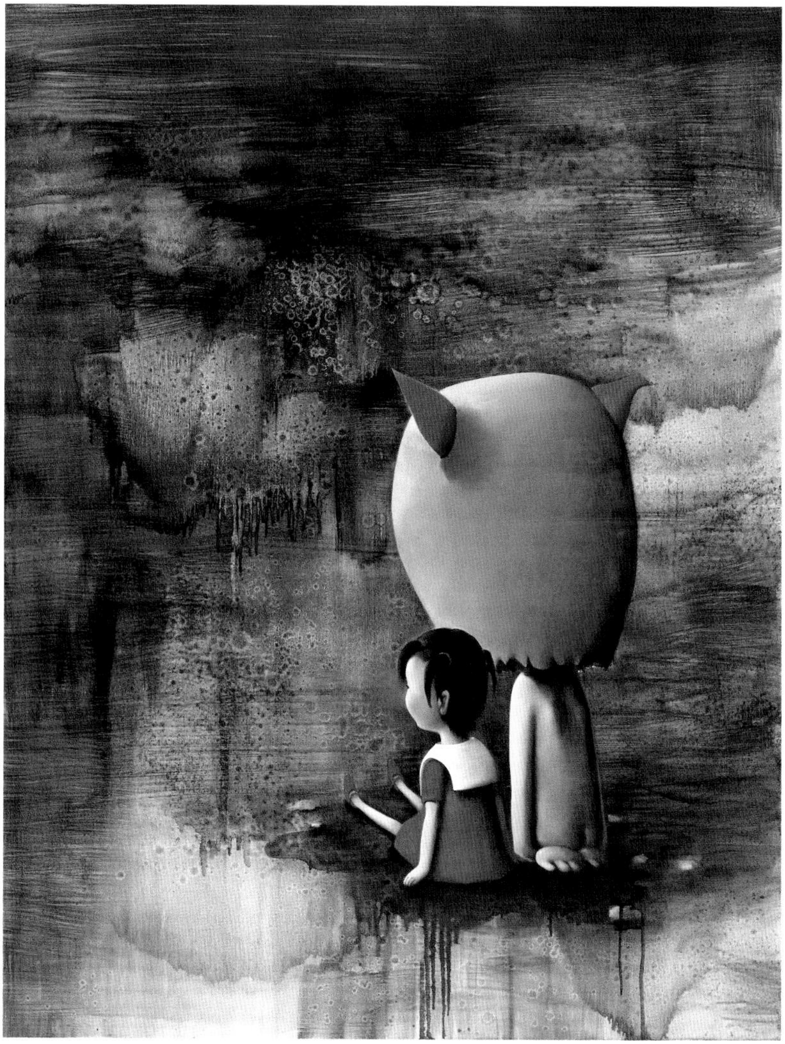

8 GAME OVER • 2008 • OIL AND BEADS ON CANVAS • 220 x 220 CM

9 TILL THE END OF THE WORLD NO. 4 • 2007 • OIL ON CANVAS • 130 x 100 CM

ONLINE CHAT WITH EDITORS

5/14/08 • LATE EVENING

[22:01:42] Thinking back: What was your favorite toy when you were a child?

[22:03:55] A doll. They were produced in China, but they looked like a western child. I remember about two or three dolls which I had, including a baby doll. I loved to tailor clothing for them.

[22:06:15] What did your parents say to you most often?

[22:07:30] When I was a kid, they often told me to wash my hands. Nowadays my mum asks me to eat more and regularly.

[22:07:45] This sounds familiar ...

[22:08:28] Moms worry about the same things all over the world.

[22:10:22] In your daily life, how do you try to stay healthy?

[22:12:34] One important thing is to eat not too much fast food; another thing is to do yoga.

[22:16:21] What have you been wishing for most recently?

[22:20:18] I really hope to be able to help the people who suffered a lot and lost their homes during the earthquake. It is very sad to realize that life can be so fragile.

[22:23:56] Do you believe in true love?

[22:28:05] That is so difficult to answer. I believe between parents and their child it can be 100%, between loving couples maybe 80%. But I think all humans have the ability to love.

[22:32:07] How does your ideal living environment look like?

[22:34:16] Having a home, which is close to a sea or a lake.

[22:38:38] Is there a certain place you have in mind?

[22:39:42] I would like to go back to the south of China when I get older. I like a place that is surrounded by nature and is sunny, like Yunnan. My hometown in Sichuan is a little too cloudy. But on the other hand, people in Sichuan are very kind.

[22:42:15] From which type of media do you derive most of your inspiration?

[22:43:26] From magazines, novels, and movies.

[22:45:47] And what do you like/dislike about being an artist?

[22:48:02] What I like: It is a job full of creation. Also you never feel bored, because you never know what the future brings. Also, I can arrange my life by myself. What I dislike about being an artist is that sometimes I feel a little lonely.

[22:50:30] How do you communicate with the audience in your art?

[22:53:47] By showing my works in exhibitions and also sometimes by good interviews.

[22:56:43] What do you think is the most effective way? Is it important for you that people understand your works?

[22:59:02] To let people come to watch the works in my studio. If I can't communicate with the audience only via my artwork, then the artwork is not good, as it doesn't speak on its own. For me it is not so important whether or not the audience gets the same message from the work as I do. If the audience gets something individual out of the work, then this makes it really valuable.

[23:02:49] If you had five words to describe your generation, what would they be?

[23:04:03] Sensitivity, visions, consumption, uncertainty, loneliness.

[23:08:18] "Uncertainty" seems very typical. Others mentioned this already. Why do you think many people of your generation feel uncertain and lonely?

[23:11:43] I often feel it, especially here in China. Maybe the speed of society is too fast. Many values were broken, yet they were just being built yesterday.

[23:13:01] If the whole world would listen to you for fifteen seconds, what would you say?

[23:15:40] "Be kind to people who love you, so that there will be nothing to regret tomorrow." Sometimes in the past I was very busy, I didn't have enough time for my parents. But on the day of the earthquake, I felt that for me it is the most important thing to stay with them.

EXHIBITIONS

SELECTED SOLO EXHIBITIONS

2009
Another me in the world,
Kunstverein Viernheim,
Viernheim, Germany

2007
With you, I will never be lonely,
Star Gallery,
Beijing, China

SELECTED GROUP EXHIBITIONS

2007/8
China: Facing Reality,
National Art Museum of China,
Beijing, China /
Museum Moderner Kunst Stiftung Ludwig,
Vienna, Austria

2007
Floating: New Generation of Art in China,
National Museum of Contemporary Art,
Seoul, South Korea

2007
Starting from the Southwest,
Guangdong Museum of Art,
Guangzhou, China

2007
Generation Süss-Sauer:
Chinas neue Künstler,
Mannheimer Kunstverein,
Mannheim, Germany

2006
Beyond Experience: New China!,
Arario Gallery,
Beijing, China

2006
The Originals: Neo-Aesthetics of Animamix,
MoCA,
Shanghai, China

2006
The Self-Made Generation:
A Retrospective of New Chinese Painting,
Zendai Museum of Modern Art,
Shanghai, China

2005
Archaeology of the Future:
2nd Triennial of Chinese Art,
Nanjing Museum,
Nanjing, China

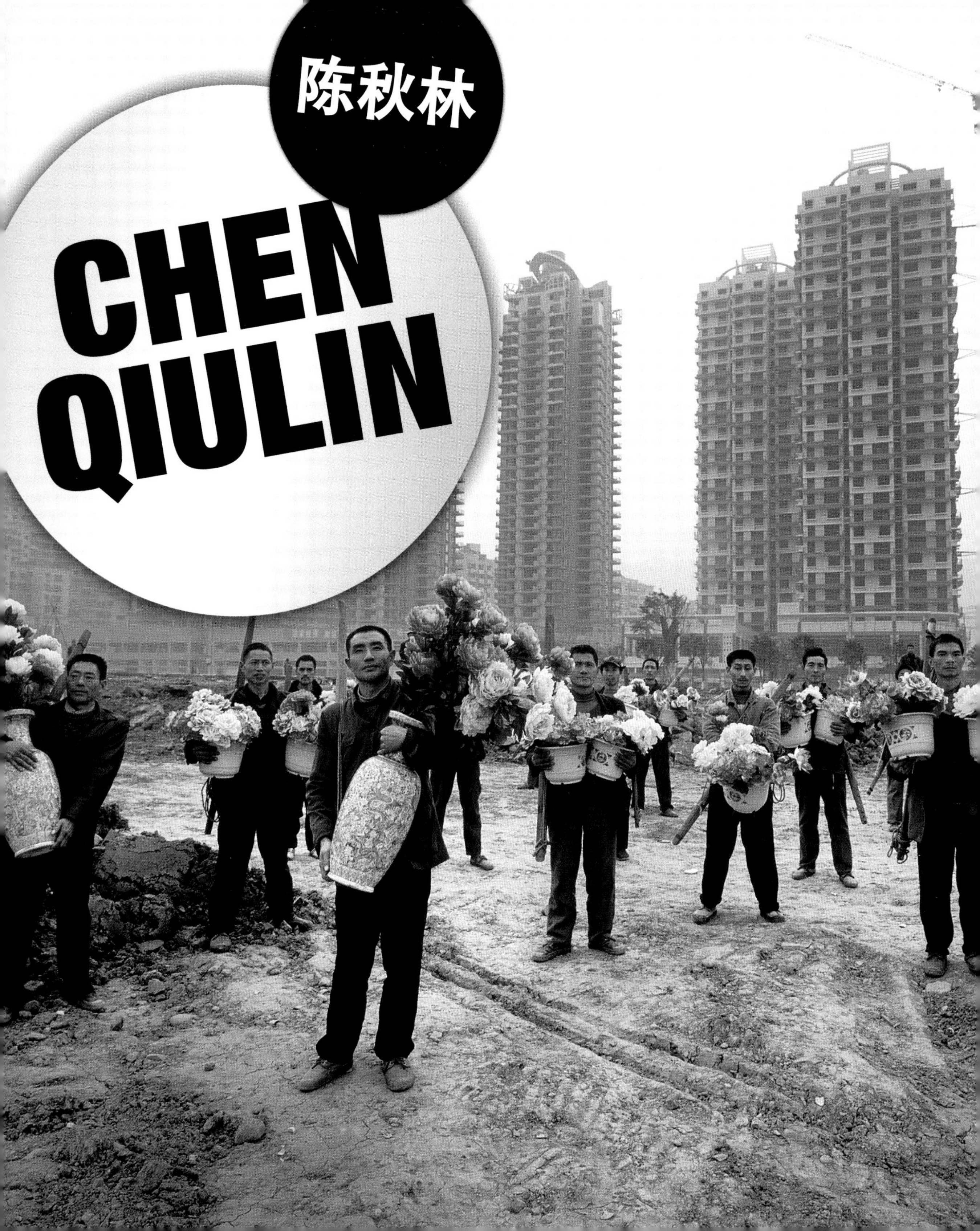

陈秋林

CHEN QIULIN

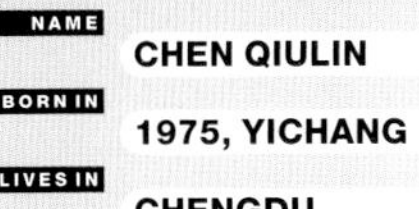

NAME
CHEN QIULIN
BORN IN
1975, YICHANG
LIVES IN
CHENGDU
STUDY
SICHUAN INSTITUTE OF FINE ARTS, CHONGQING
MEDIA
INSTALLATION, PERFORMANCE, PHOTOGRAPHY, VIDEO

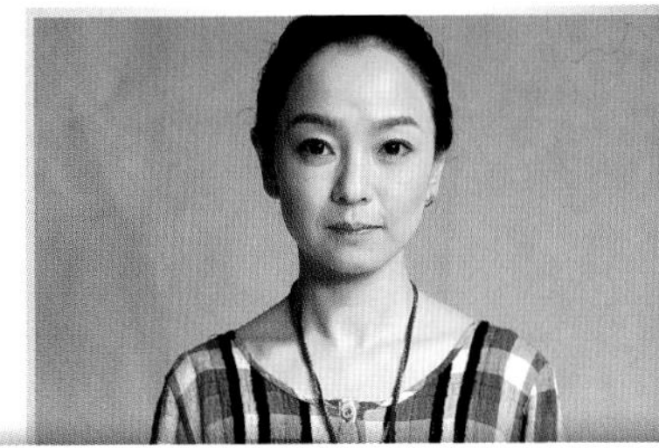

POETICS OF FAREWELL

Chen Qiulin's launching point as an artist coincided with the beginning of the disappearing process of her hometown. Shortly after she graduated from Sichuan Institute of Fine Arts in 2000, Wanxian, a small town on the shore of the Yangtze River, underwent systematic demolition and gradually became submerged by the rising waters of the Three Gorges Dam. Like 1.3 million others affected by the controversial project, Chen Qiulin was left alone to negotiate her memory of the past and adjust to a deformed "hometown" that she could no longer recognize. Born in 1975, Chen belongs to a new generation of Chinese artists who remember little about the political turmoil of the Cultural Revolution. For them, personal anguish and struggle, to a large extent, stem from the alienating temporal and spatial displacements brought by China's rapid urbanization in the last two decades. The resulting disorientation yields to a plethora of new artworks that address various problematic effects of the radical urban transformation. A key representative of this "urban generation," Chen Qiulin created a series of works bidding farewell to her lost hometown, a consistent theme of the artist's oeuvre since Wanxian was partially erased.

Using personal recollection and returning to her now-demolished home as a departure point, Chen Qiulin developed a combined language of documentary representation and poetic allegory. In 2002, she spent weeks filming the demolition process of Wanxian and a few soon-to-disappear towns nearby. In her fourteen-minute video *Farewell Poem* (2002), the documentary footage of the demolition process interchanges with segments of the Peking opera *Farewell My Concubine* staged on the ruin of a traditional opera theater. Dressed up as Concubine Yu herself, Chen Qiulin transforms the ill-fated opera character into an allegorical figure in memory of the lost cultural tradition of her hometown. Along a similar conceptual vein, Chen carved out hundreds of the most common Chinese family surnames on tofu blocks and displayed them in a local night market. Entitled *Tofu February 14th* (2004), this installation serves as an ephemeral homage to the human sacrifice made for the Three Gorges Dam project. A more extravagant gesture of commemoration underlines the installation *Migration* (2006). Chen shipped sixteen tons of original wood structure of several traditional shops and houses from Sichuan province to Beijing and restored them to the original form at the Long March Space.

Unmistakably, Chen Qiulin's arts of farewell are permeated with, to borrow theorist Svetlana Boym's term, "restorative nostalgia" – a sensibility based on a trans-historical reconstruction of the lost home, an attempt to return to the origins, to revive traditions and to call for the absolute truth embedded in origins.[1] On the one hand, the impulse of "restorative nostalgia" mourns the loss of an enchanted home with clear borders and values; on the other hand, it dwells on the impossibility of any return. Through the "restorative" lens, the history of a city is based on a linear unfolding of time, with urban demolition as a monumental rupture between the past and the future. Both urban development and urban nostalgia are based on the similar conception of unrepeatable and irreversible time. Hence, "restorative nostalgia" is not the antithesis, but rather the side effect of the teleology of urban progress. Here, we may pause to ask: can nostalgia move beyond a singular narrative of mourning and provide a more critical reflection on the dialectics of urban erasure and urban creation? Chen Qiulin's recent projects are pertinent to this question.

The highly-choreographed video *Color Line* (2006) centers on an ambiguous figure of a Chinese angel stranded in the temporal-spatial vacuum between demolition rubble and a post-industrial future. Wearing traditional opera makeup, the angel (performed by the artist) wears a costume made from the red, blue, and white striped tarp material commonly used for China's ubiquitous construction sites. Unlike Concubine Yu, a familiar opera character rooted in an idealized past, the angel appears to be inauthentic and even suspiciously alien to the Chinese eye. Neither an allegory for the irretrievable past nor an omen of the future, the ethereal angel resists being fixated in any temporal phase. Her aimless act of roaming between the sites of the past and the future does not suggest a forward movement to a better future, but a perpetual suspension from the linear temporal logic of urban development. Chen Qiulin's latest video, *Garden* (2007), continues to explore the dialectical potentials in the post-demolition setting of Wanxian. The fourteen-minute work presents dozens of peasant workers traversing the cityscape to deliver huge vases stuffed with gaudy plastic peonies. Through their repetitive walking and fruitless searching, the urban ruins, semi-demolished buildings, and new sterile constructions are overlapped into an expanded field of simultaneous reality. The futile task of delivery not only erases the differences of these spatial categories, but also ironically reveals the eerie resemblance between them. In a dialectic fashion of visualization, the artist renders the present as a circular movement between urban destruction, creation, and utopian imagination. It is this newly-acquired sense of circularity and interconnectedness that propels Chen Qiulin's works beyond a singular reflection of social reality or personal anguish, and thus gains critical potentials as a visual allegory for contemporary China.

By Miao Yu

1 Svetlana Boym, *The Future of Nostalgia* (New York, 2002).

1 TOFU FEBRUARY 14TH • 2004 • INSTALLATION

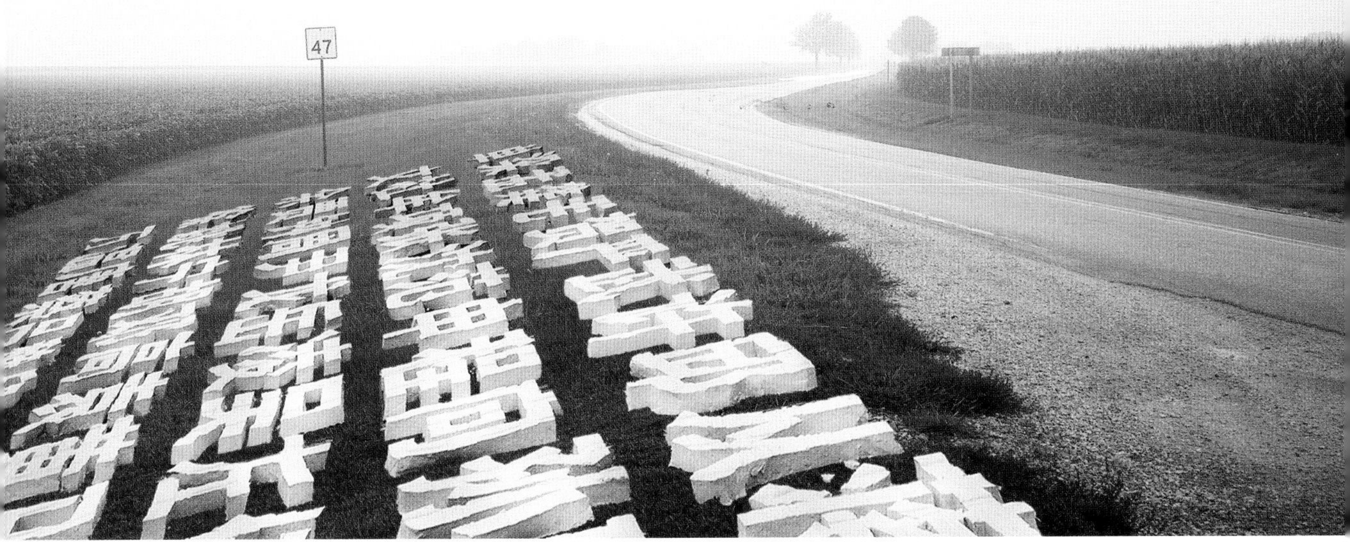

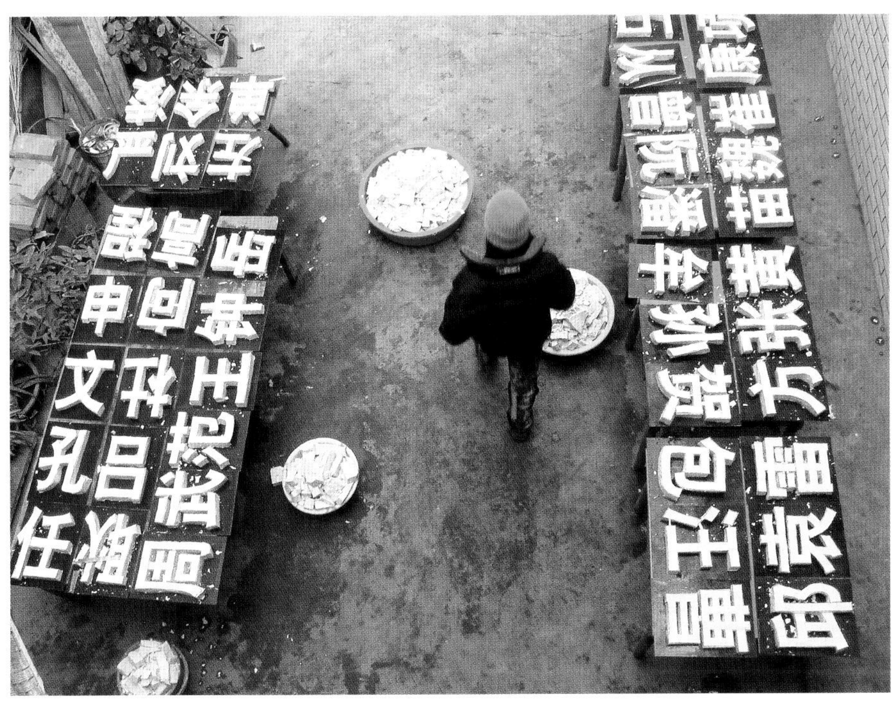

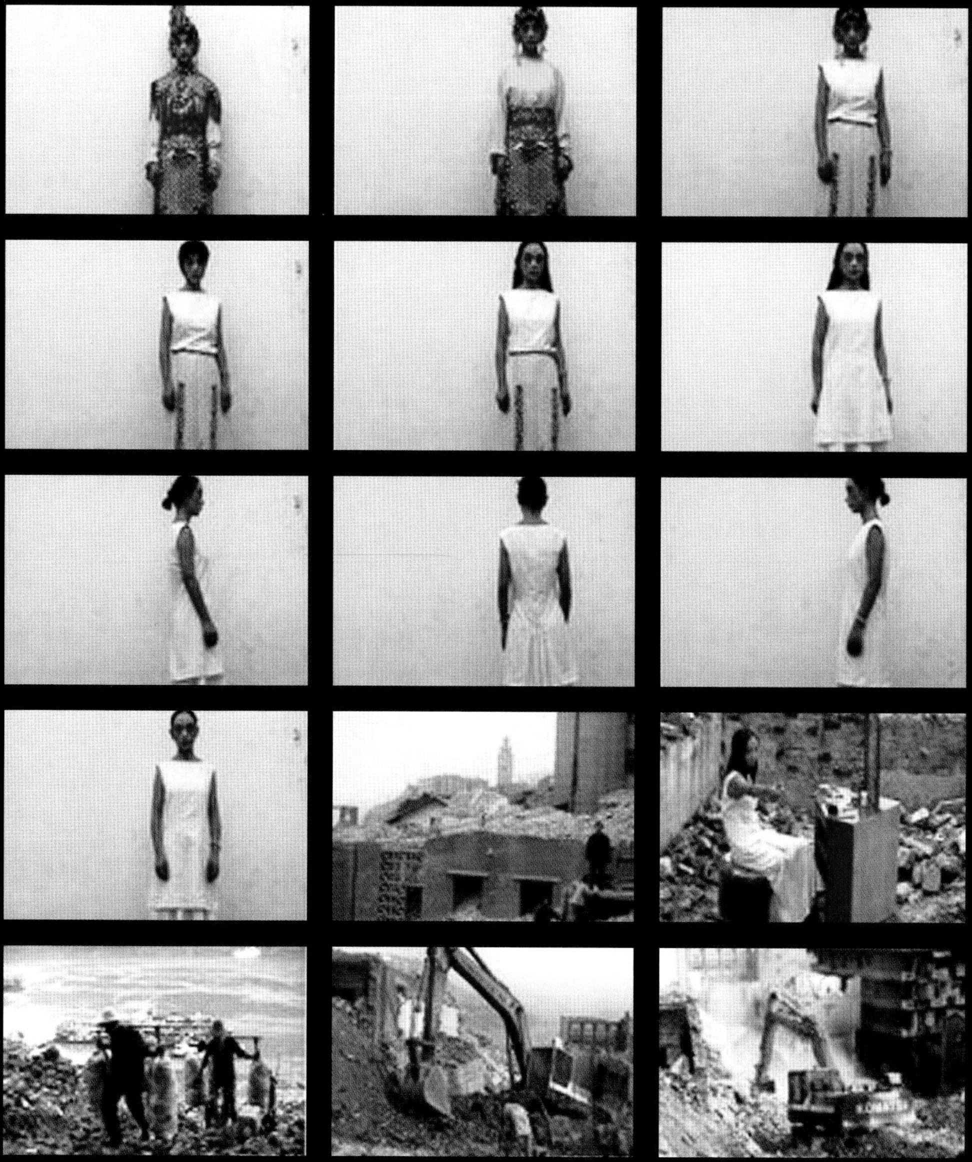

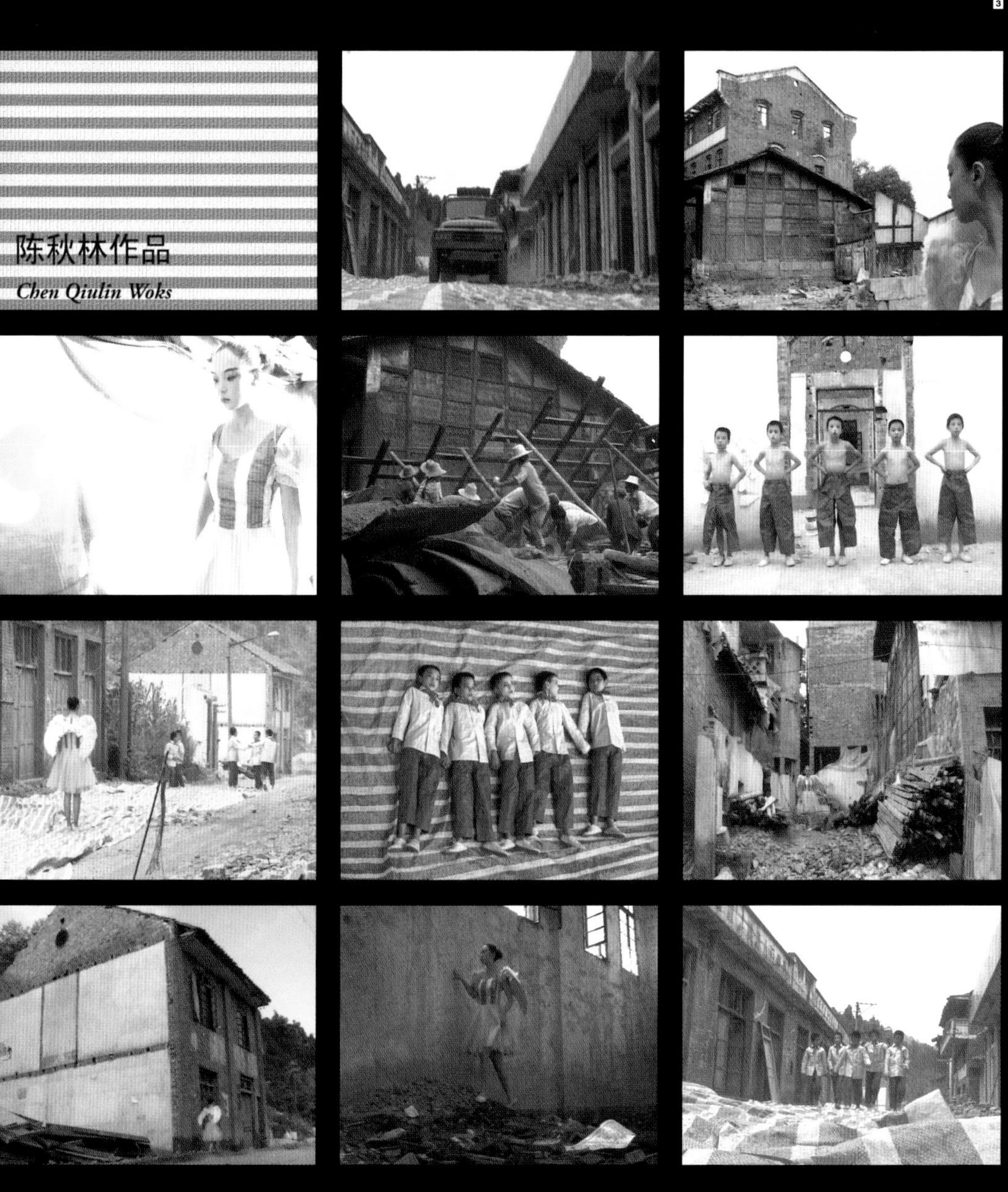

2 FAREWELL POEM • 2002 • VIDEO • 14'

3 COLOR LINE • 2006 • VIDEO • 8'08"

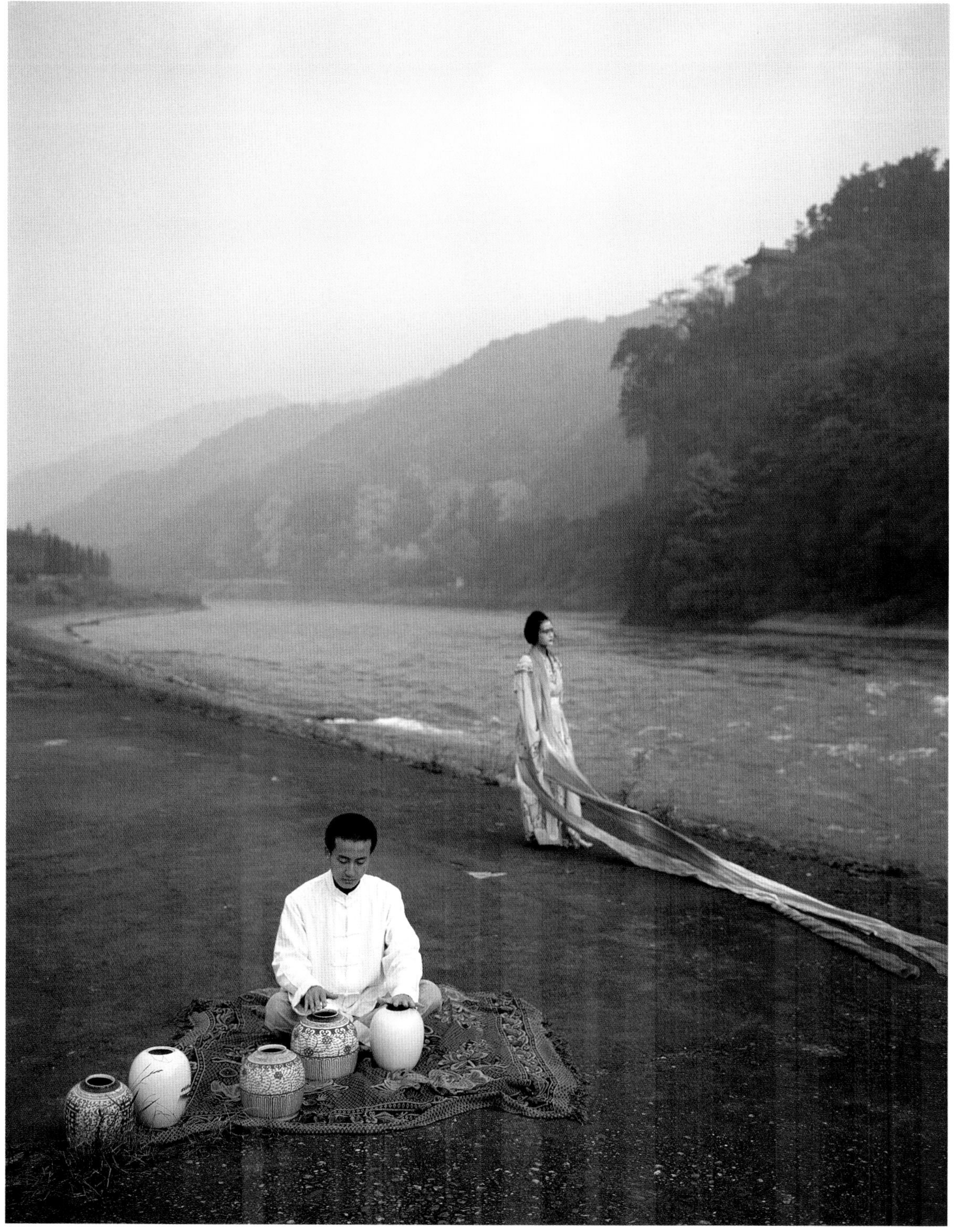

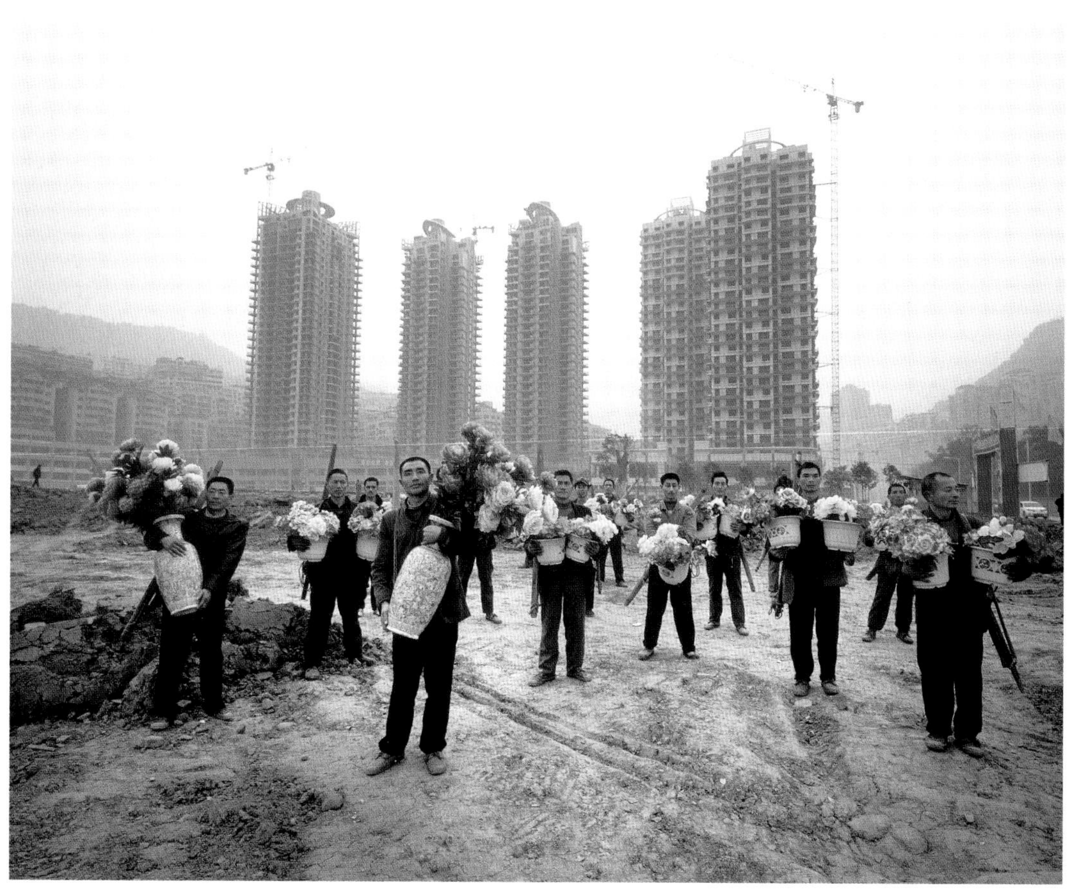

4 DAWNING BELL • 2009 • C-PRINT • 154 x 124 CM

5 GARDEN NO. 4 • 2007 • C-PRINT • 127 x 152 CM

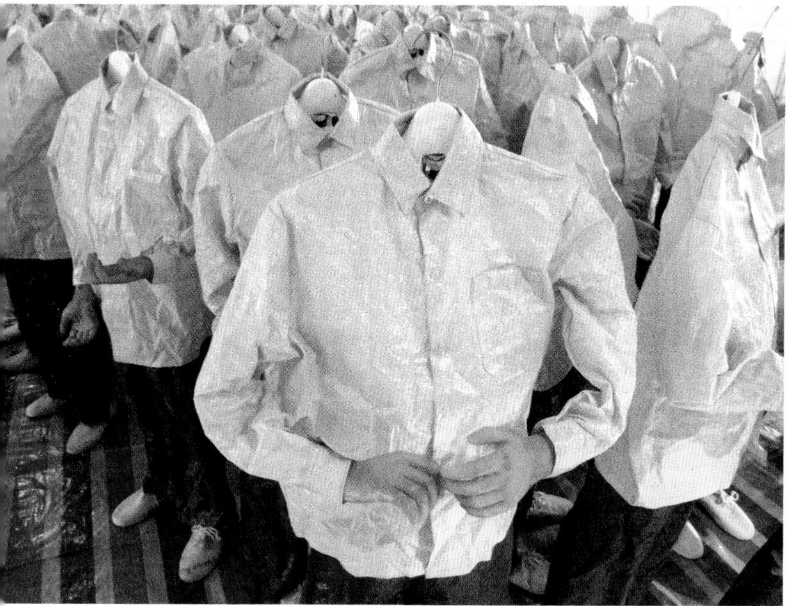

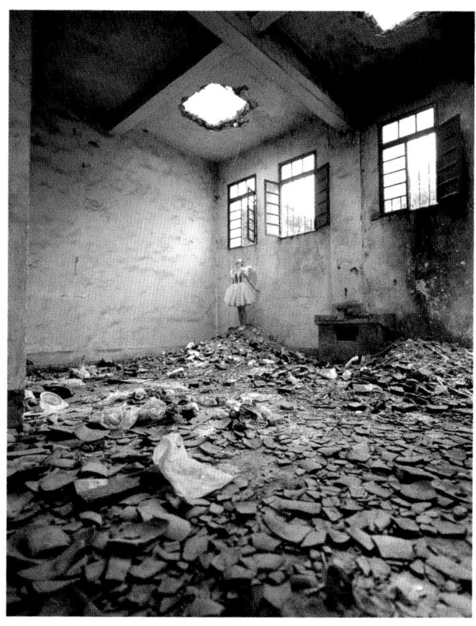

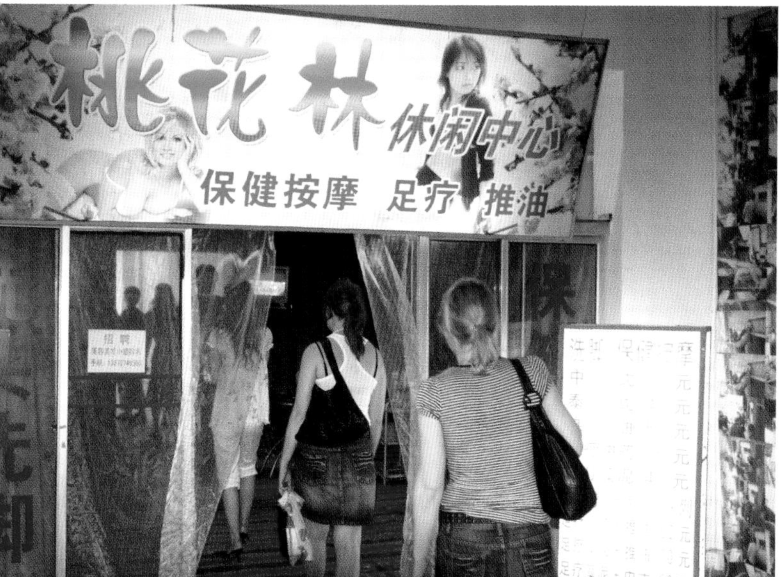

6 MIGRATION • 2006 • INSTALLATION

7 I AM AN ANGEL NO. 2 • 2006 • C-PRINT • 168 x 135 CM

PHONE INTERVIEW WITH EDITORS

5/15/08 • MORNING

EDITORS *Right now you are in Shanghai, right?*

CHEN Q. Yes, I am attending a conference.

EDITORS *Do you remember what your favorite toy was when you were a kid?*

CHEN Q. When I was a kid, there were hardly any toys. But I remember that my dad once made some handicrafts for me. It was a kind of toy made of dried leftovers of rice plants. I loved these toys very much.

EDITORS *What sentence did your parents say to you most often?*

CHEN Q. When I was a kid, they often told me to do or to avoid certain things. Now, most of the time they ask me to look after my health.

EDITORS *And how do you look after your health?*

CHEN Q. I belong to this group of people who do not really take care of their health. Sometimes I go to the gym, but I hardly find time to go. Also in regards to nutrition, I am not very careful. I eat a lot of snacks and sweets, but until now, luckily, I don't need to worry about gaining weight.

EDITORS *What have you been wishing for most recently?*

CHEN Q. It's in relation to the earthquake that happened on May 12th, close to my hometown in Sichuan. I hope the consequences of the quake will come to an end very soon.

EDITORS *Do you believe in true love?*

CHEN Q. Yes, I do. But it is important to experience real love over a long period of time. One shouldn't talk too much about it, but feel it.

EDITORS *What does your ideal living environment look like?*

CHEN Q. Right now, I am not sure how to answer this question. In the past, I had a quite naive idea of what my ideal environment should look like. I wished to be surrounded by forest and nature and hoped that all people would love each other. Right now, after all these happenings due to the earthquake, I am not sure anymore. Life is so fragile.

EDITORS *From which type of media do you derive most of your information?*

CHEN Q. From real life.

EDITORS *What do you like/dislike about being an artist?*

CHEN Q. First of all, I define myself not as an artist, but a person who does artistic work. I guess doing artistic work means that our social life and our communication can be much more direct and free than that of other people. For this reason I feel that we artists are very lucky. What I don't like is being indirect and dishonest.

EDITORS *How do you communicate with your audience in your art?*

CHEN Q. When I'm working on my artistic works, I always try to emphasize the atmosphere surrounding my works. It can influence the feeling of the audience very much. Another way is to exchange with the audience, e.g. in workshops when I discuss my artistic ideas and the development process of my works.

EDITORS *If you had five words to describe your generation, what would they be?*

CHEN Q. Illusion, hope, responsibility, loss, and beauty.

EDITORS *You are the first person to mention "beauty."*

CHEN Q. Many people search for an improvement either of the individual, the society, and/or the environment. I call this process "beauty." Most of my works are related to time and human illusions. Time is an important component of my artistic works, as the environment and the surrounding is changing over time. And time often includes the aspect of "losing something."

EDITORS *If the whole world would listen to you for fifteen seconds, what would you say?*

CHEN Q. I guess for me fifteen seconds would be too long, but of course everybody has a different personality and opinion on that. However, if this opportunity would come up, I would just say, "Hello, I am Chen Qiulin and I am an artist from China."

EXHIBITIONS

SELECTED SOLO EXHIBITIONS

2009
Chen Qiulin,
Hammer Museum,
Los Angeles, U.S.

2007
Chen Qiulin: Recent Work,
University Art Museum, University of Albany,
Albany, U.S.

2006
Migration,
Long March Art Space,
Beijing, China

2005
Big Factory,
1918 Art Space,
Shanghai, China

2004
Tofu February 14th,
Landing Art Centre,
Chengdu, China

SELECTED GROUP EXHIBITIONS

2009
The 6th Asia-Pacific Triennial of Contemporary Art,
Queensland Art Gallery / Gallery of Modern Art,
Brisbane, Australia

2007
Echoes: Chengdu New Visual Art Documentary Exhibition,
A Thousand Plateaus Art Space,
Chengdu, China

2007
China Power Station: Part II,
Astrup Fearnley Museum of Modern Art,
Oslo, Norway

2006
This Is Not For You: Diskurse der Skulptur,
T-B A21,
Vienna, Austria

2002
Harvest: Chinese Contemporary Art Exhibition,
Agricultural Exhibition Centre,
Beijing, China

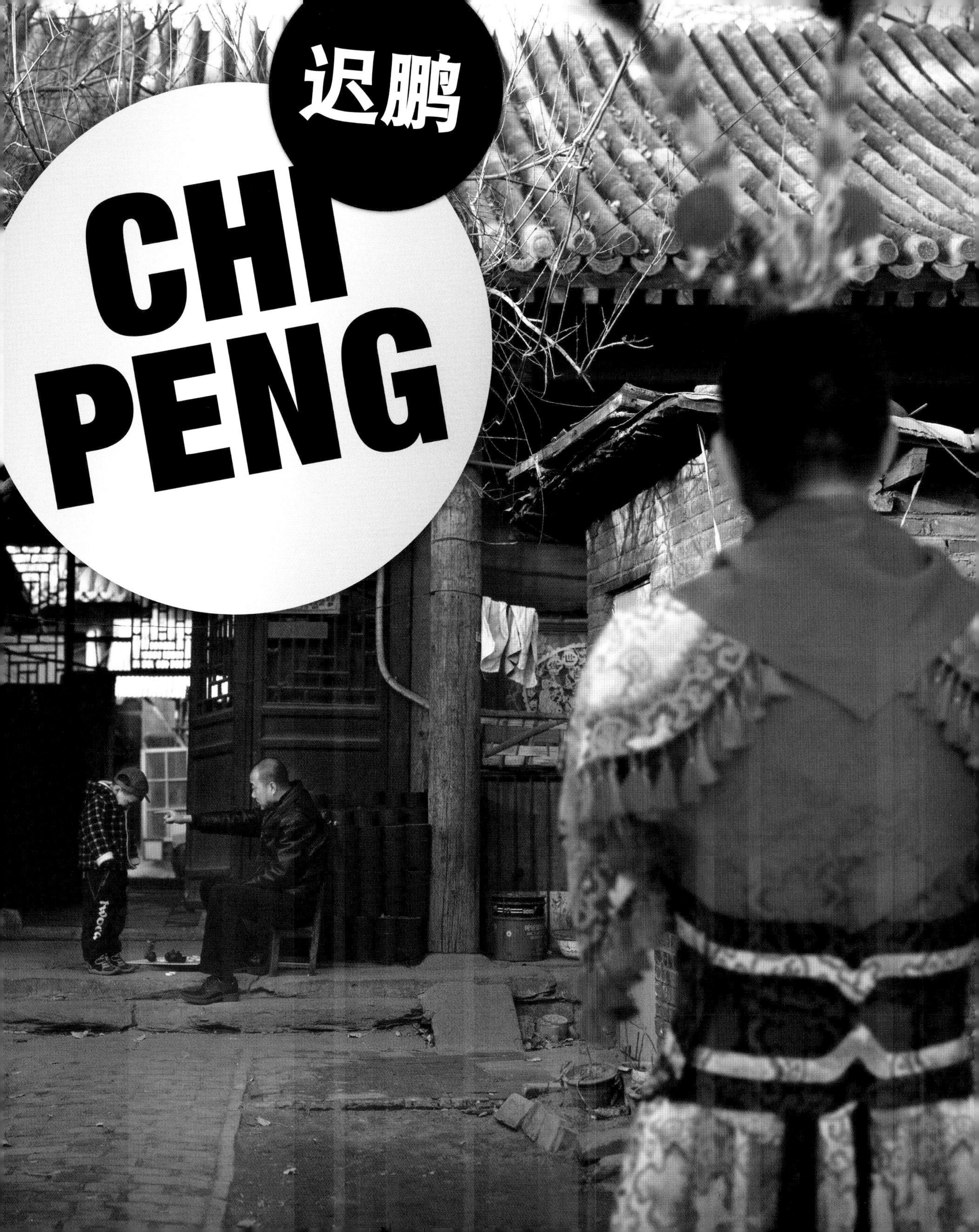

迟鹏

CHI PENG

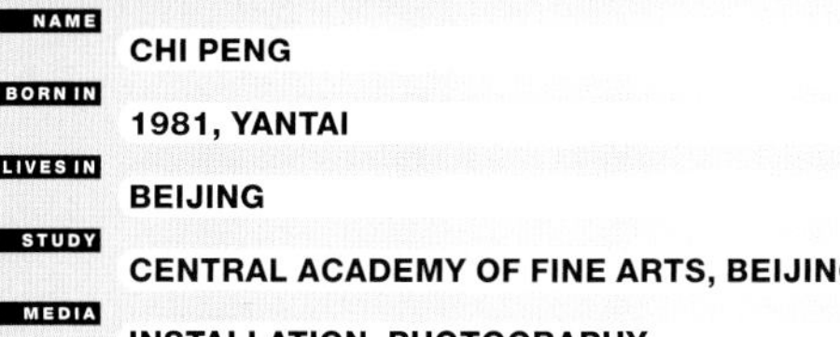

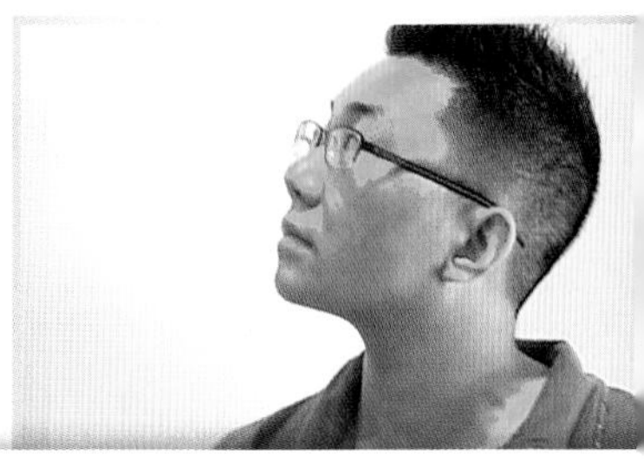

SPRINTING FORWARD, LOOKING BACKWARD

Chi Peng's digitally processed photographs seem restlessly moving in search of a goal. What he proposes visually hits the target dead-on; here the human is a lone warrior – even love relations become public acts mirroring the self. Up until 2005, the Beijing artist's fantastic-yet-real scenarios took place in the Chinese capitol, but after that they have dwelt increasingly in places outside of China. With the 2007 series *Journey to the West*, they have even moved into the realm of myth. The room installation *Soft* (2008) changes up the medium entirely, using 700 bed covers to build a bastion of temporary security.

Looking back, Chi Peng compares his studies – completed at the renowned Central Academy of Fine Arts in Beijing – with a pond full of croaking frogs, all practicing the high jump. It quickly became clear to him that his path would not lead to a specialty in painting or to the imitation of real objects or other artworks. In the combined play of concrete locations and flights of fancy, his pictures tell highly personal stories dealing with, for example, gender issues or homosexuality. His frieze-like works, often a meter long, avoid portraying a beginning or end. Emulating the effect of film stills, Chi Peng captures moments of intense psychic stress, physical exertion, or arousal. Thematically as well as technically, his pictures could not be more current. Chi Peng senses that digital photography and its opportunities for virtual manipulation (with the computer program Photoshop) grant his interests their most authentic articulation. His method attains both purpose and sensuality, as he meticulously constructs the scenes to be photographed, brings in friends and acquaintances as extras, composes the landscape, and even designs and tailors the costumes.

In the series *Sprinting Forward* (2004–5), paranoia pursues the artist's alter ego who multiplies himself and flees, mostly naked, through the Chinese capital. Anyone familiar with Beijing will recognize the locations. In *Apollo in Transit* (2005), it's the wall of the Forbidden City where a montage of figures find themselves curled up in oversized raindrops. In another image of the series, Chi Peng is stranded in front of the curved glass façade of the Hyatt Hotel, while glowing red airplanes fly past toward the horizon. The *Dream-Series* (2006) pursues the theme of an East-West axis, incorporating the Brandenburg Gate. We might ask ourselves which association appears more threatening: the traditional Chinese, in which the individual wiles away his life as a compliant but secure member of a group – or the kind of metropolitan loneliness Chi Peng articulates so well. The photo series *I Fuck Me* (2005) brings no relief, reducing homoerotic sex to a lonely and yet often public act of masturbation. Passionate togetherness becomes a virtual conflation of a doubled ego. Love in the time of egomaniacal self reference?

Chi Peng considers his series *Journey to the West* (2007), comprised of twelve photographs, to be his most important work to date. It reflects his usual elements of autobiography and critique, but expanded into a mythological and also inter-media dimension. Incorporating costuming, elaborated head ornamentation, and mask-like face painting one finds at the traditional Beijing Opera, Chi Peng transforms himself into the monkey-king Sun Wukong. There is no child in China who isn't enamored of this crafty fable character. But it's not the classic *Journey to the West* that interests the artist so much as the legend of the flying monkey king which is able transform into seventy-two different forms, and which has been adapted in countless Chinese and Japanese comics, TV series, and movies.

The titles of the *Journey* photos play on central themes of the classic story. The vertical-format work *Five Elements Mountain* shows Chi Peng, alias Sun Wukong, captured in a knotted spiral of skyscrapers. Pictures like *Red Boy* and *Three Fights against the White Bone Demon I* evoke more concrete allusions to humiliating childhood experiences. In *Mountain*, more than six meters long, the fantasy figure of the monkey king, exhausted, floats on a cloud through a craggy mountainscape wrapped in fog. Everyone familiar with traditional Chinese art will see in the details of the arrangement just how carefully Chi Peng has kept to the genre's formal guidelines of motif and perspective. This work actually references Wang Shen's masterpiece of the Sung Dynasty *The Light Snow in the Fishing Village*. But now the traditional work has become an opportunity for the artist's own personal reflection. When Chi Peng takes on the personality of the monkey king, he mirrors, kaleidoscopically, the relevant aspects of his own, self-determined life. "In the *Journey* series, it was my primary goal to find the images that would honestly and devotedly express my memories. That attitude is prerequisite for my art."

His newest work, the room installation *Soft*, uses 700 bed covers to create an oasis of stillness accessible to the visitor. Childhood memories and the current need for breathing space beyond the demands of daily life come together in this work. It once more makes it clear that the life of his generation in China, despite all its material advantages and freedoms, is a continual balancing act between nearly unlimited possibilities and the struggle for personal integrity.

By Ulrike Münter

1
2

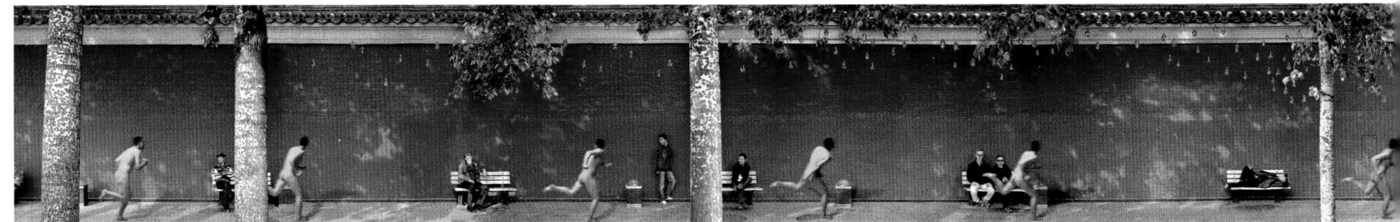

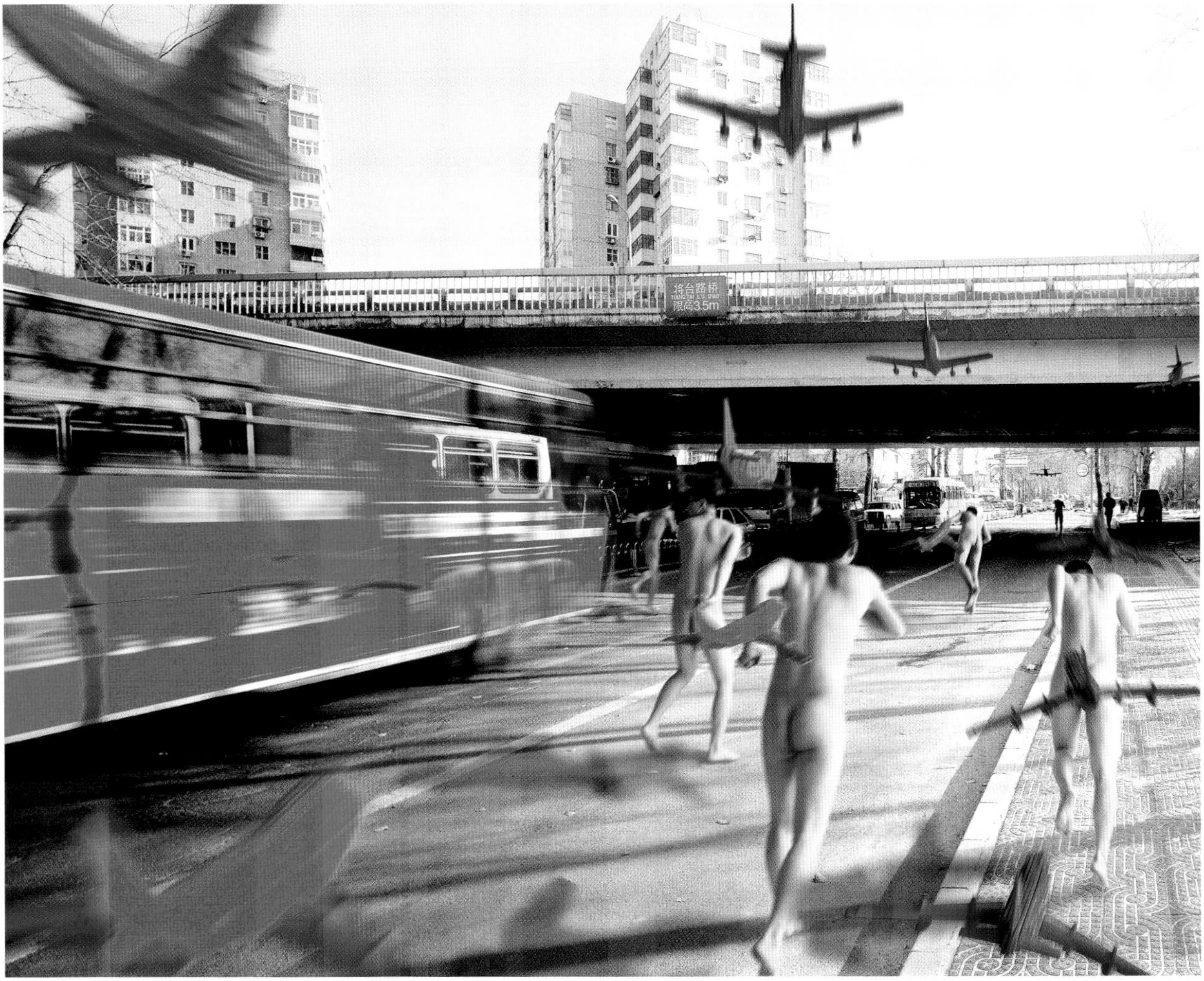

1 APOLLO IN TRANSIT • 2005 • C-PRINT • 33 x 400 CM

2 SPRINTING FORWARD – 2 • 2004 • C-PRINT • 120 x 152 CM

3 I FUCK ME – BATHROOM • 2005 • C-PRINT • 155 x 120 CM

3

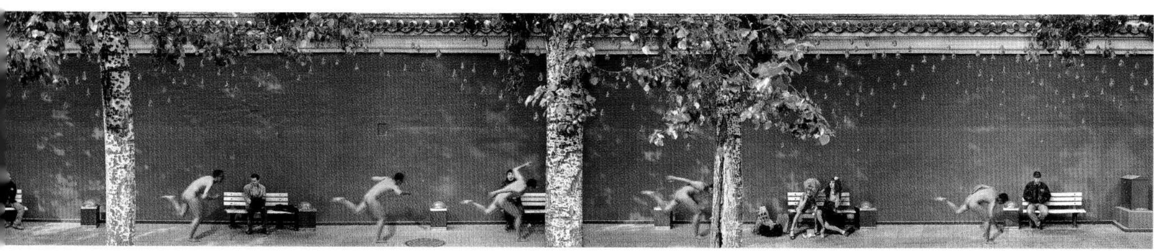

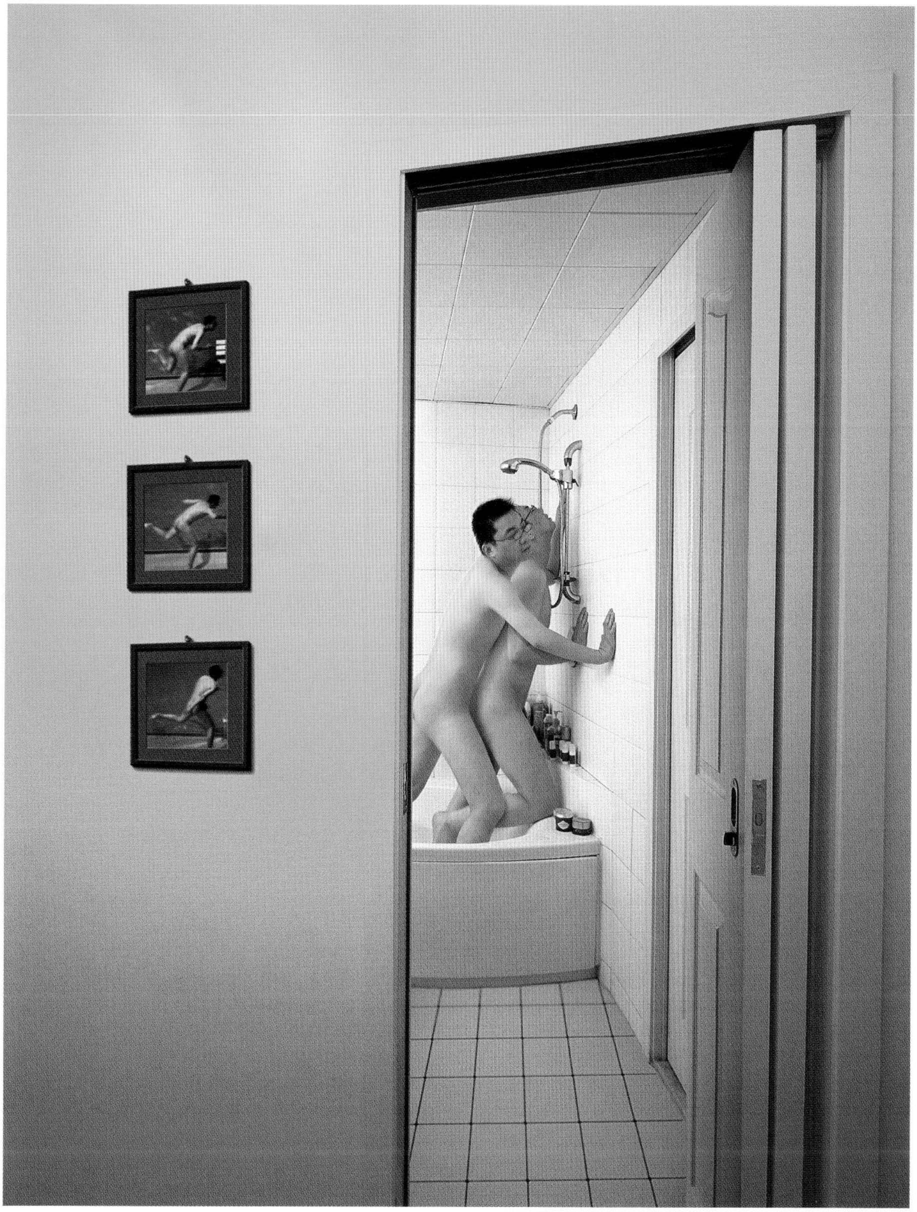

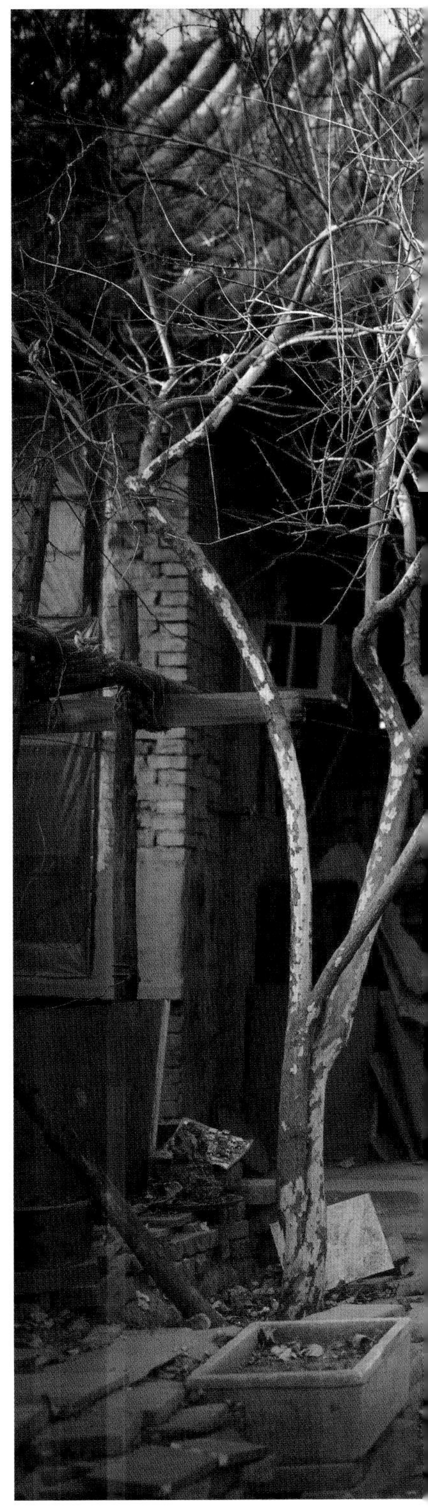

4 THREE FIGHTS AGAINST THE WHITE BONE DEMON 1 (JOURNEY TO THE WEST SERIES) • 2007 • C-PRINT • 175 x 222 CM

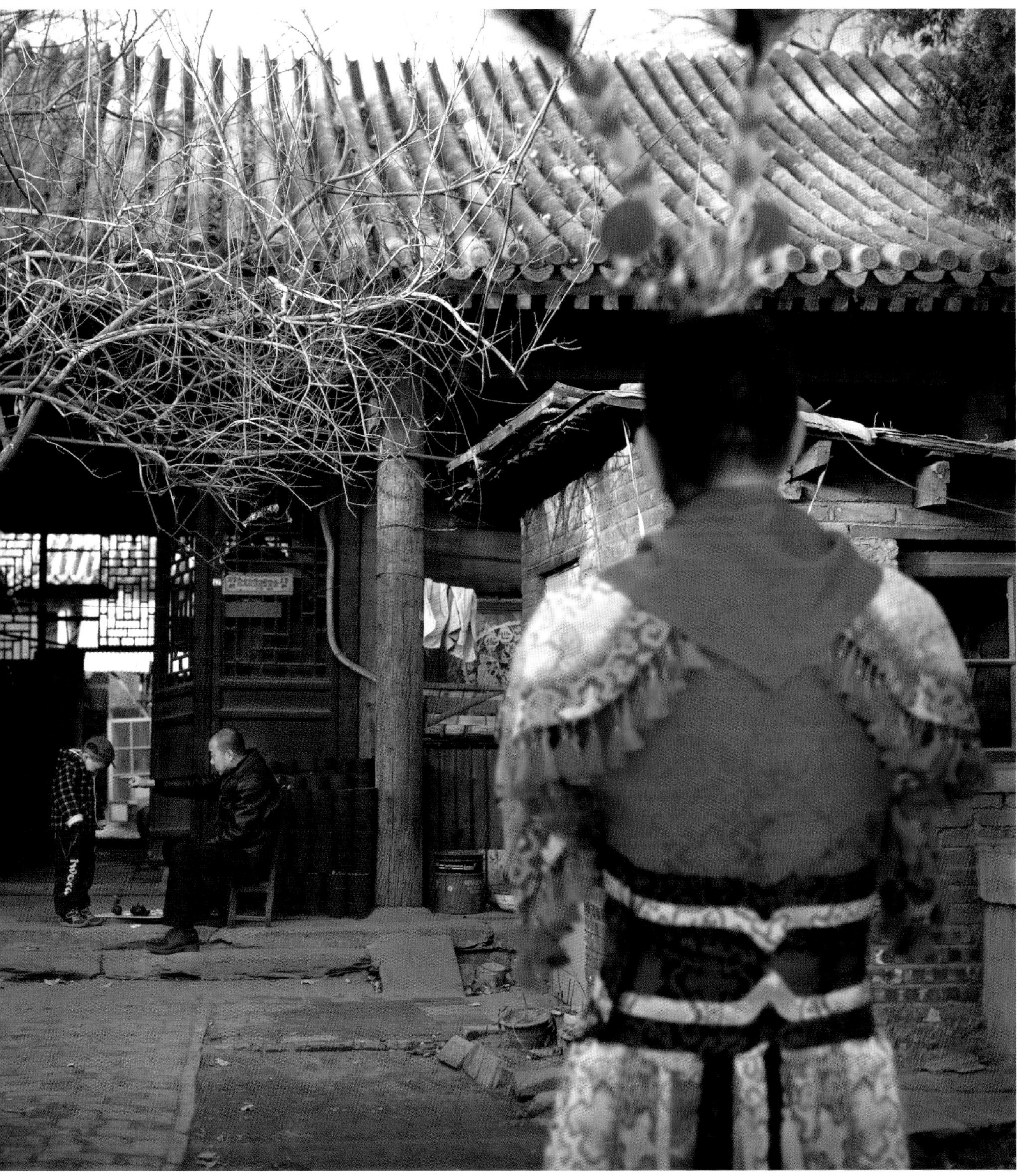

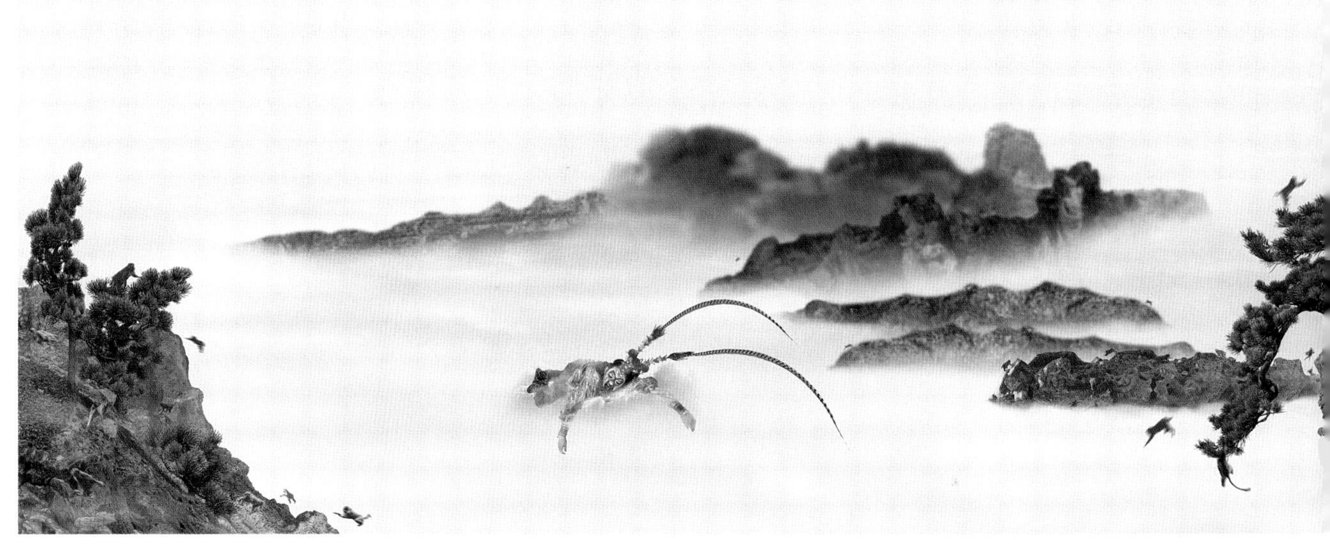

QUESTIONNAIRE

5/18/08 • BEIJING

WHAT WAS YOUR FAVORITE CHILDHOOD TOY?

When I was young my family couldn't afford to buy me any toys, so I loved any toys that I laid eyes on. Now, of course, I've grown up and can now afford to buy them myself. But I've lost interest.

WHAT DID YOUR PARENTS SAY TO YOU MOST OFTEN?

I've forgotten. You're better off asking them directly.

HOW DO YOU STAY HEALTHY IN YOUR EVERYDAY LIFE?

I would like to care for my health whenever I can. But, whenever I can, I often forget.

WHAT HAVE YOU BEEN WISHING FOR MOST RECENTLY?

Recently I've been so sad that I've even lost my wish.

DO YOU BELIEVE IN TRUE LOVE?

How could I dare not believe?

WHAT DOES YOUR IDEAL LIVING ENVIRONMENT LOOK LIKE?

It doesn't matter in which environment you live. It's more important that you assimilate to whichever environment you find yourself in, and that you maintain a balance in your heart.

FROM WHICH TYPE OF MEDIA DO YOU DERIVE MOST OF YOUR INSPIRATION?

Real artistic inspiration comes from your heart.

WHAT DO YOU LIKE/DISLIKE ABOUT BEING AN ARTIST?

I don't understand this question fully. Whether I "like" or "dislike" doesn't depend on whether I am an artist or not. Also, let's not forget that artists are human beings and have a lot in common with other people.

HOW DO YOU COMMUNICATE WITH THE AUDIENCE IN YOUR ART?

Art is a reflection of individual emotions. When one doesn't want to communicate, then there's no need to communicate. Likewise, when there's no need to communicate, then one just doesn't.

IF YOU HAD FIVE WORDS TO DESCRIBE YOUR GENERATION, WHAT WOULD THEY BE?

Selfish, narcissistic, and snobbish. These three words are enough.

IF THE WHOLE WORLD WOULD LISTEN TO YOU FOR FIFTEEN SECONDS, WHAT WOULD YOU SAY?

Nothing. Because in fifteen seconds you can't talk about anything substantial. Besides, even if you say something, you can't use it to make a difference. It would only be to satisfy myself, but it wouldn't have any other meaning or purpose.

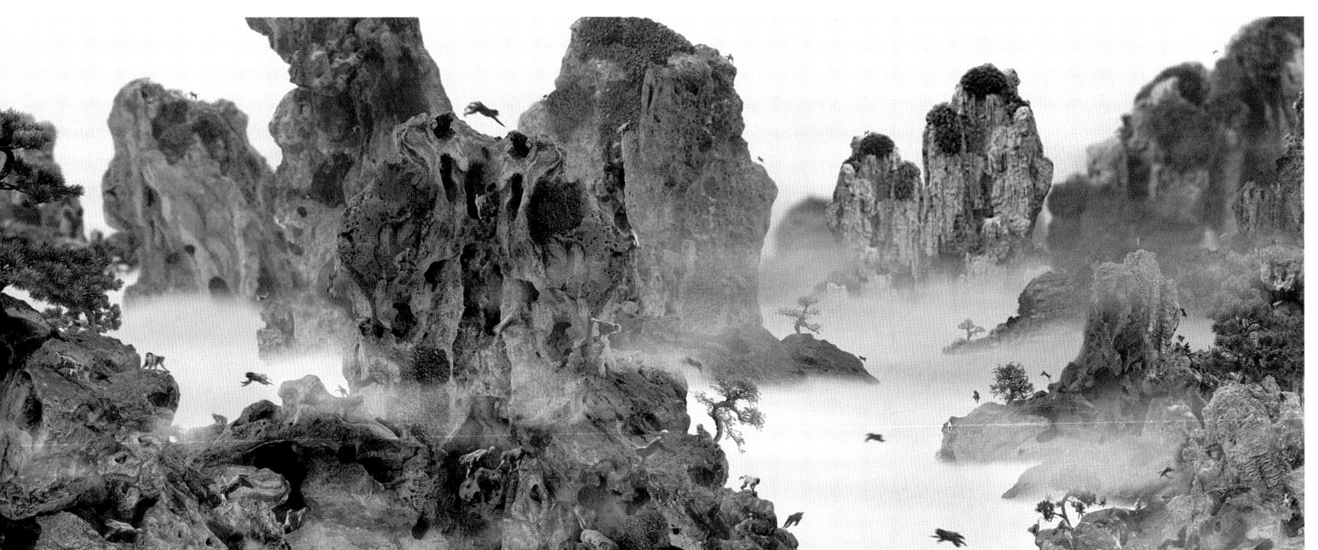

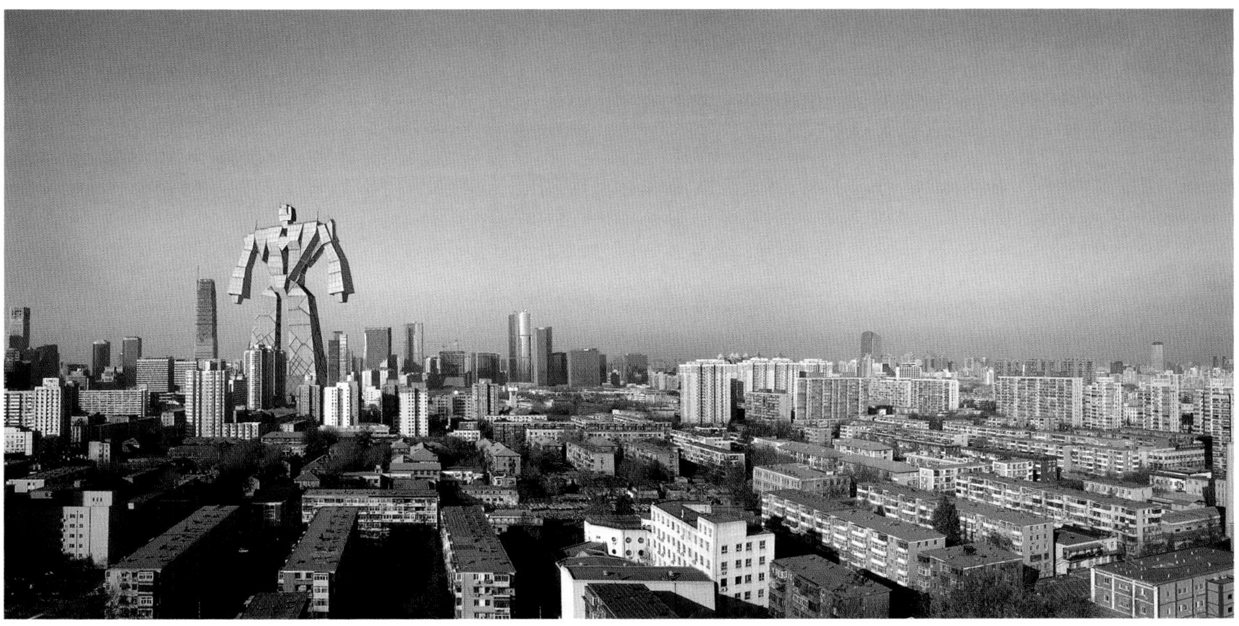

5 MOUNTAIN (JOURNEY TO THE WEST SERIES) • 2007 • C-PRINT • 120 x 629 CM

6 WHY SHOULD I LOVE YOU? • 2008 • C-PRINT • 120 x 249 CM

7

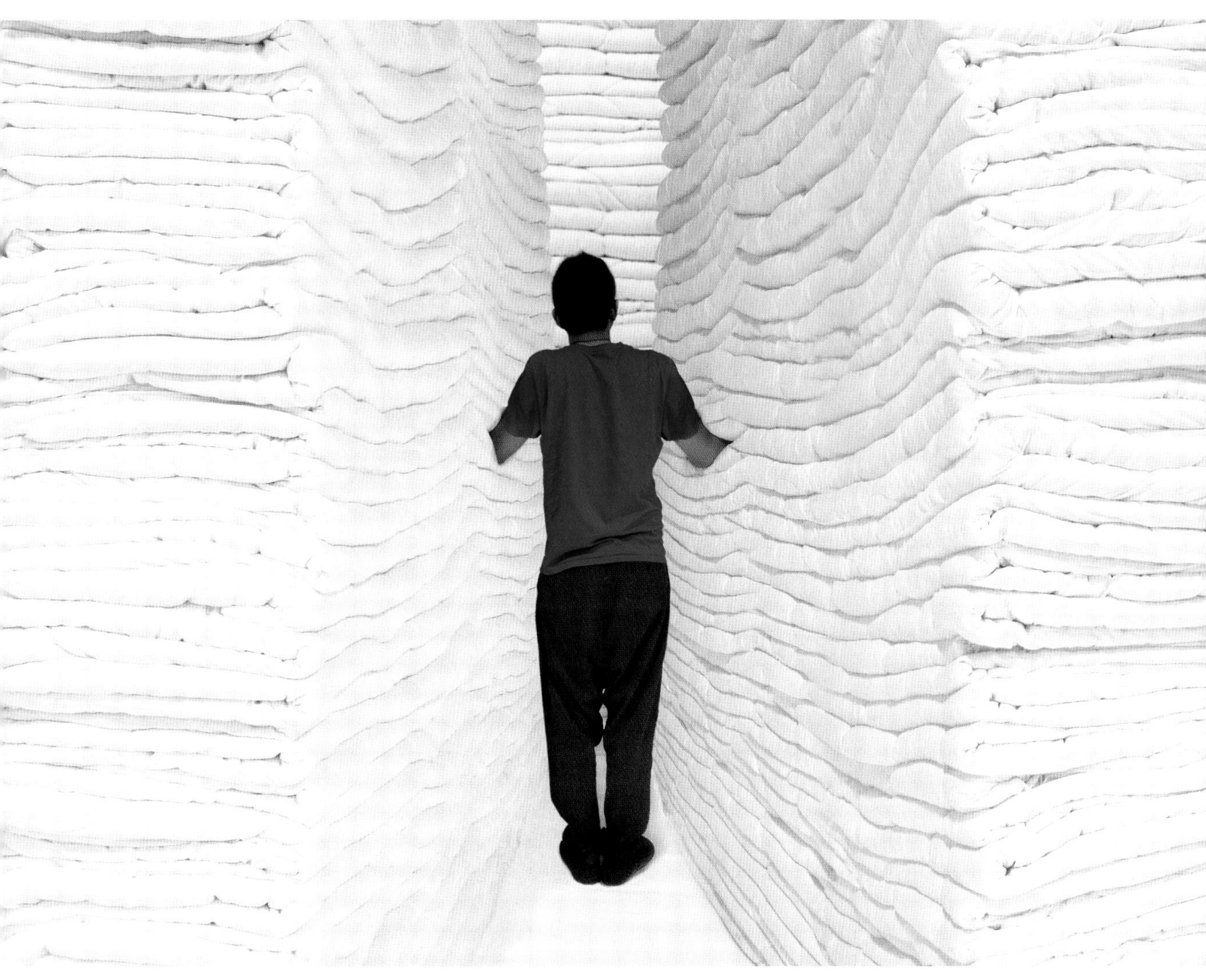

8
9

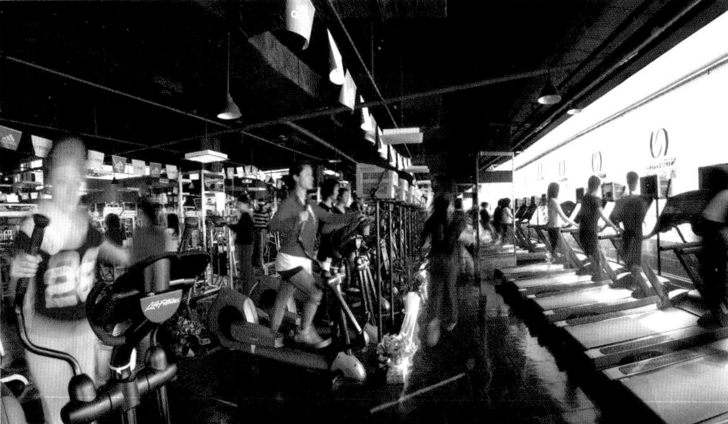

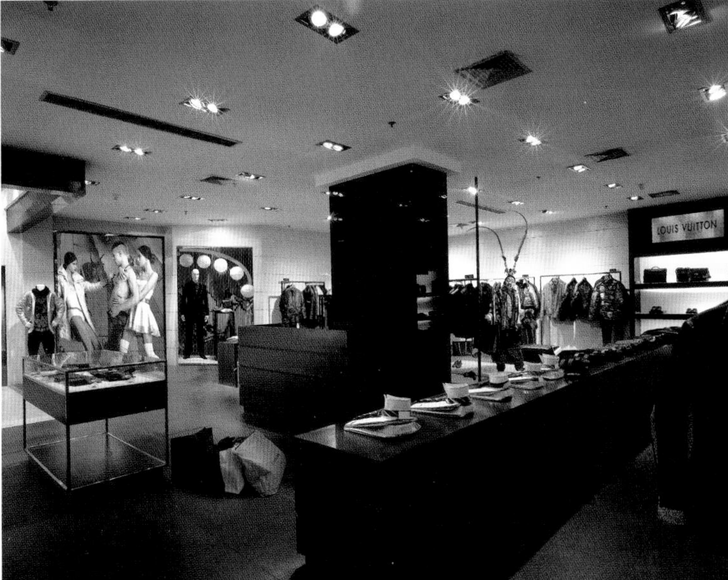

7 SOFT • 2008 • INSTALLATION: QUILT • 270 x 400 x 500 CM

8 WOMAN KINGDOM (JOURNEY TO THE WEST SERIES) • 2007 • C-PRINT • 172 x 300 CM

9 THE STEALING OF THE PEACHES (JOURNEY TO THE WEST SERIES) • 2007 • C-PRINT• 175 x 222 CM

EXHIBITIONS

SELECTED SOLO EXHIBITIONS

2009
Secluded Radius,
He Xiangning Art Museum,
Shenzhen, China

2007
Trading Pain,
Ludwig Museum,
Budapest, Hungary

2006
Physical Practice,
Zhu Qizhan Museum,
Shanghai, China

SELECTED GROUP EXHIBITIONS

2008
New World Order,
Groninger Museum,
Groningen, The Netherlands

2008
Prague Triennale 2008,
National Gallery,
Prague, Czech Republic

2008
Just Different!,
Cobra Museum,
Amsterdam, The Netherlands

2008
Body Language:
Contemporary Chinese Photography,
National Gallery of Victoria,
Melbourne, Australia

2007
Floating: New Generation of Art,
National Museum of Contemporary Art,
Seoul, South Korea

2006
China Now: Kunst in Zeiten des Umbruchs,
Sammlung Essl,
Klosterneuburg, Austria

2005
Karlsruhe Barcelona Cambridge Toronto,
Centre Georges-Pompidou,
Paris, France

龚剑

GONG JIAN

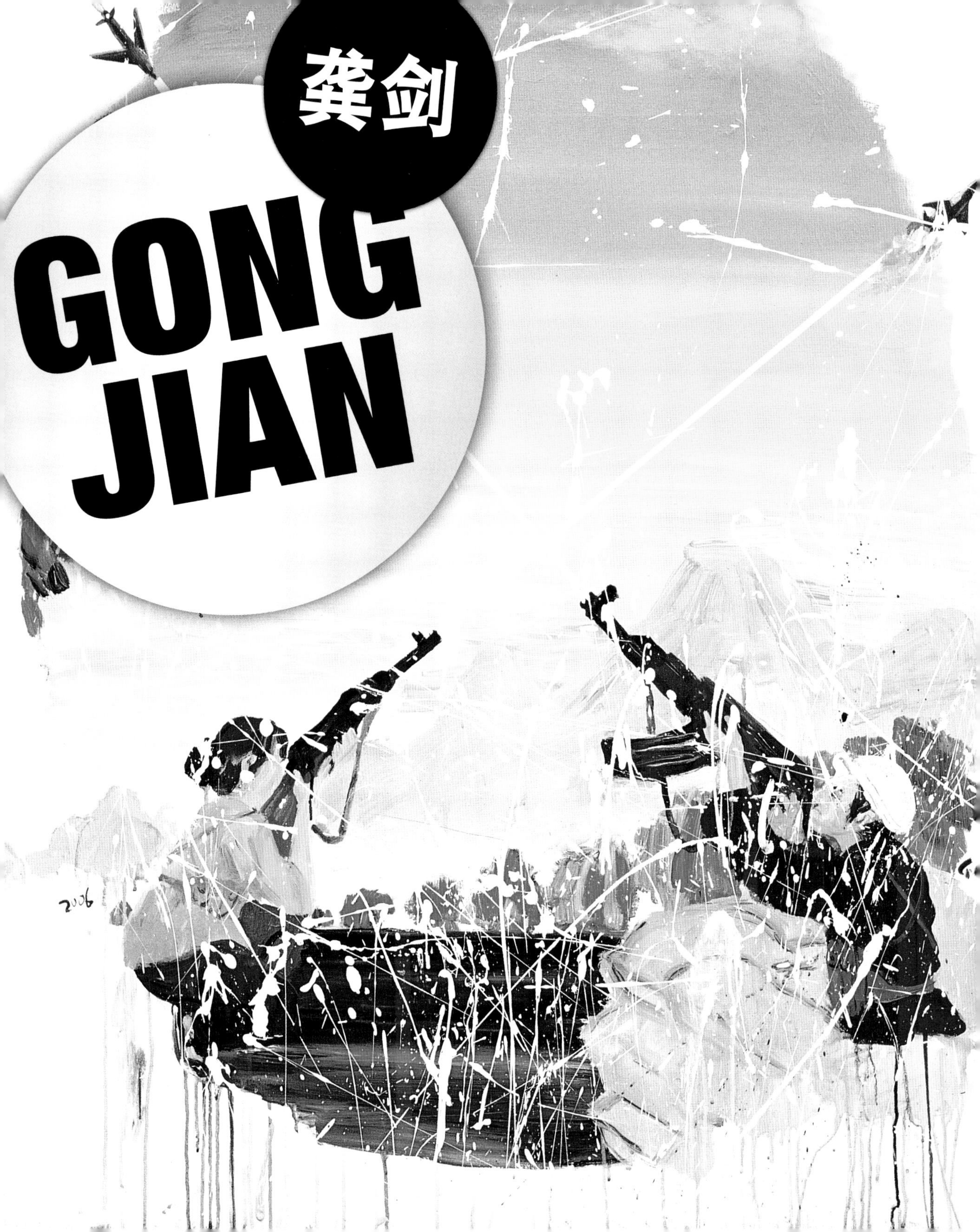

NAME
GONG JIAN

BORN IN
1978, HUBEI PROVINCE

LIVES IN
WUHAN

STUDY
HUBEI INSTITUTE OF FINE ARTS, WUHAN

MEDIA
PAINTING, PHOTOGRAPHY

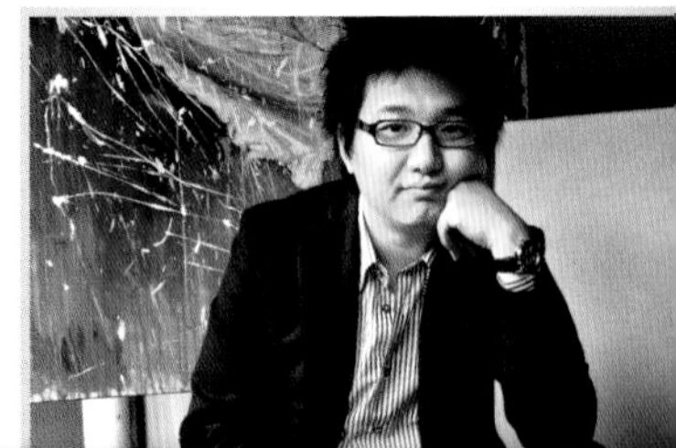

TEACH YOU TO SHOOT PLANES

Gong Jian has a gift for juggling honesty and tact, ferociousness and gentility, boredom and excitement. His works, particularly his paintings and drawings, are irreverent practical jokes juxtaposing time, space, history, society, and politics into the absurdity of his symbolic language. This type of irrationality – often reflected in his choice of subject matter, composition, and accompanying texts – creates a darkly humorous dramatic effect, a puzzling sense of ennui, and an uncontrollable destructive force. At the same time it brings forth an extremely *bad* set of aesthetic characteristics. This deliberate or inadvertent display of *bad taste* exposes the irreverent cynicism, subversiveness, independence, and sincerity of the artist; this courage to transgress taboos and public conventions is best described in the words of the photographer Terry Richardson: "Mediocrity is the last thing the world needs."

Gong Jian was born in Wuhan, Hubei Province, in 1978. After graduating from the Hubei Institute of Fine Arts he lived for many years in Wuhan, consciously keeping his distance from the country's artistic hubs. For this reason, it is rare to see the fashionable styles and methods of the contemporary Chinese art world in Gong Jian's work; in fact, his works are filled with an impetuous and unstable individualism. He immerses himself in his own visual games, unrestrained by conventional mores, playfully making sport of his subjects and themes, and cheerfully dispelling the po-faced seriousness of the art world. This attitude can be detected even in his earliest installations and photographs, such as a wall bearing graffiti which reads, "How can art overthrow?", an abandoned ticket kiosk in a park, and a detailed report about Wuhan's red-light district.

In a set of digital photographs from 2003 entitled *Mao Occupying South Baoan*, pubic hairs are computer processed and installed in an evening street in Shenzhen, giving the image a gloomy and mysterious atmosphere. The ambiguity of this image is elaborated further in the title; "mao", Chinese for "bodily hair" or "fur," is a tangible material and a private part of the body that is visible in the image, but also points to Chairman Mao Zedong, a symbol which has unique historical and psychological meaning for China. This linguistic double entendre combines with the image to create a rhetorical style in which the literal and implied meanings diverge significantly.

By 2004, the rhetoric of images and words had become a key feature in Gong Jian's concept of art. At the same time, his focus on – and allegorical treatment of – cultural memory, states of mind, and social intervention become even more apparent. His paintings are created with an unrestrained vigor, in which chaotic splashes of white pigment obstruct the narrative process of the image. This resistance to and the destruction of conventional painting is offset by opposing forces: the traditional and the modern, the fictional and the real, the frivolous and the solemn. Gong Jian frequently borrows elements from traditional Chinese painting such as Bada Shanren's birds, scenery from Zhao Mengfu's *The Autumn Colors on the Qiao and Hua Mountains*, and the bridges of Qi Baishi, as well as the cartoons of Feng Zikai. But are these cultural symbols simply the result of the artist's own memories? Although Gong Jian may regard them as commonplace things that he has seen since childhood and which may be found anywhere, his choices and the usurpation, provocation, concealment, and isolation of the images is entirely his own. He departs from their "legitimate" traditional meanings to make them reflect his individual passions.

However, while one can feel the pleasure the artist derives from painting his works, they are by no means simply the self-indulgent expression of his personal interests. A great deal of the pleasure comes from his transgressions against taboos, conventions, classic works, and systems, making him sometimes seem almost like the impetuous little child in *The Emperor's New Clothes*. It is obvious that Gong Jian is aware of the nature of this venture, thus enabling his works to gradually cross over from the individual to the public, from the entertaining to something deeper and more mature.

Sex, a common theme in Gong Jian's work, is addressed in the intimate relationship between the pandas Tuantuan and Yuanyuan (*Tuantuan and Yuanyuan – Blow Job*, 2006), in the demeanor of the bowing tiger, as well as in a number of scenes connected with revolutionary propaganda paintings, such as in the 2006 works *Teach You To Shoot Planes* (a euphemism for masturbation), *Fairy Cave*, and *Mother's Milk*. The irony underlining these words and images transforms bodily privacy into humorous banter on topics such as political rights and collective consciousness. It appears innocent while in fact playing a "dirty trick." In his last works, he has alluded to the recent sex-photo scandals in Hong Kong show business by depicting a rural scene containing boundless countryside and naïve spring flowers (*Glamour Shot*, 2008).

There is also another type of painting by Gong Jian that possesses a style all of its own. In works such as *Love Letter* (2005), *Love* (2006), and *The Diamond Sutra* (2008), the artist repeatedly writes a lover letter, a fictional story, or a religious text using either a paintbrush or his fingers. A monochrome palette is covered and smeared with layer after layer until the letters are no longer distinguishable. The repetitive brushstrokes create a sense of ceaseless agitation. At the same time, linguistic meaning is blurred to the point of total loss, leaving behind a simple, abstract beauty within the work. Such abstract intentions, continual questioning of concepts, definitions, emotions, and deeper truths during the painting process is Gong Jian's way of inquiring about the world until all concept of language has been destroyed, all reverence and beauty has been smashed, and the bottom line of the truth beneath heaves into view.

By Azure (Wei) Wu

1

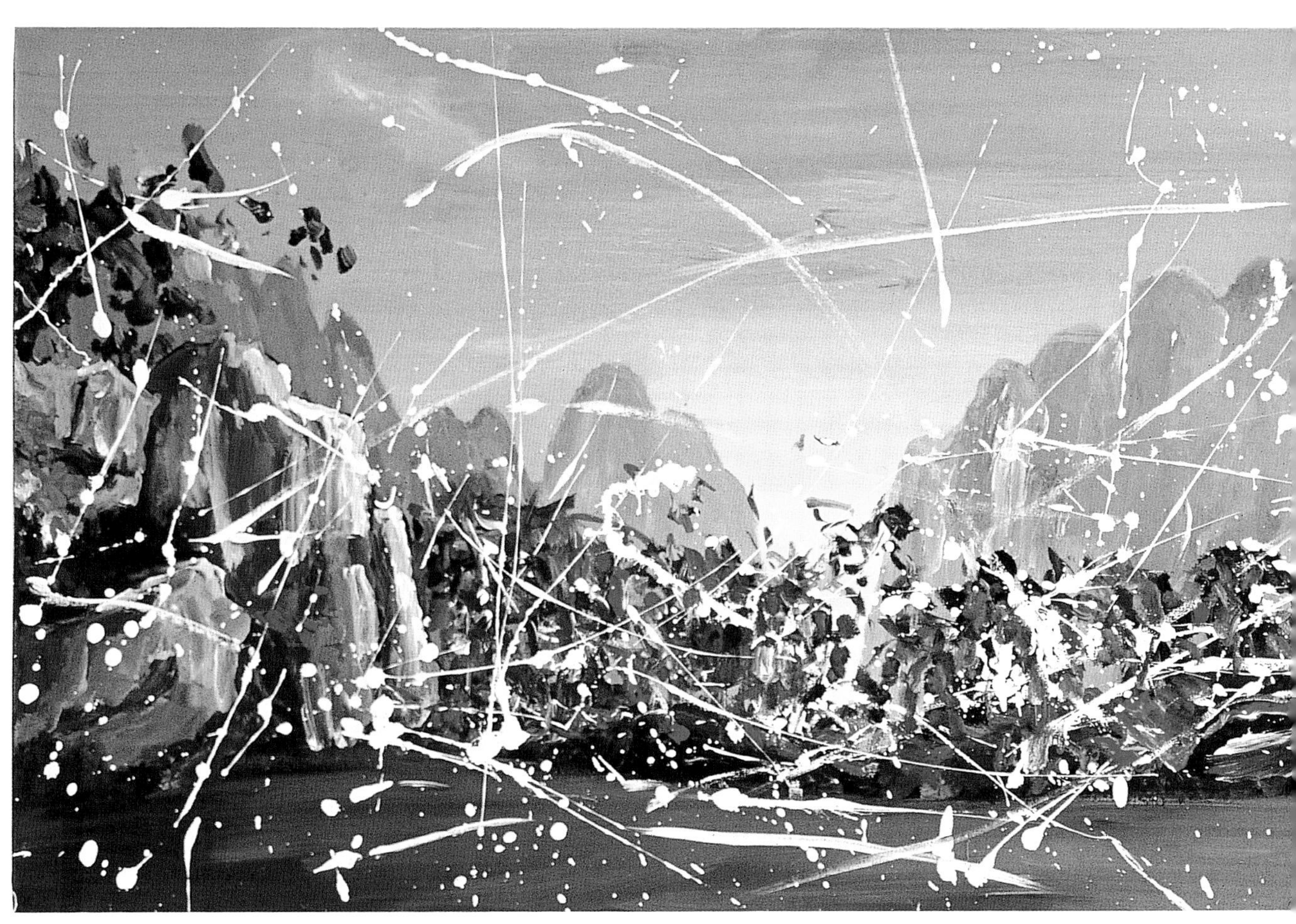

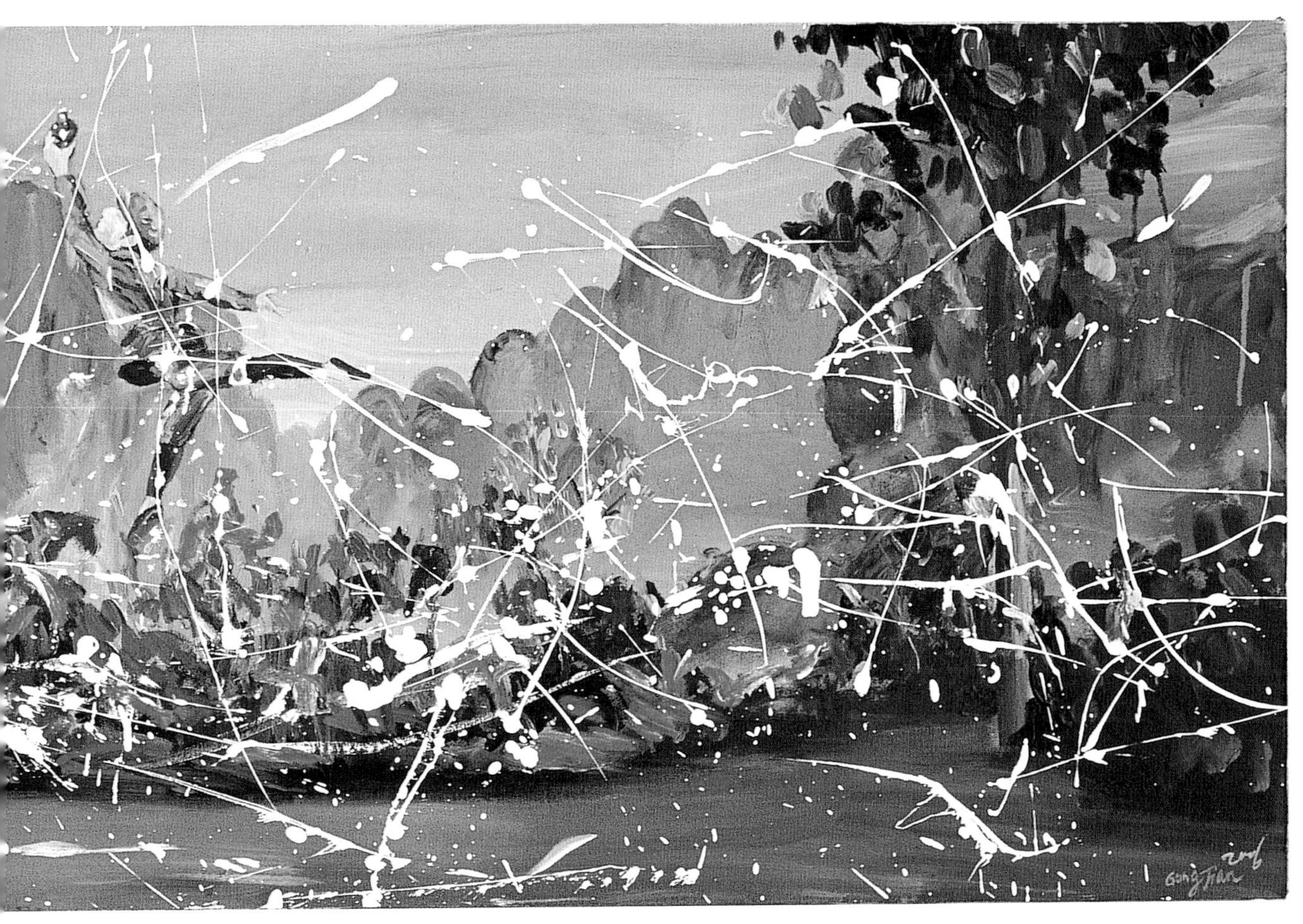

1 MOTHER'S MILK • 2006 • ACRYLIC ON CANVAS • 70 × 220 CM

2

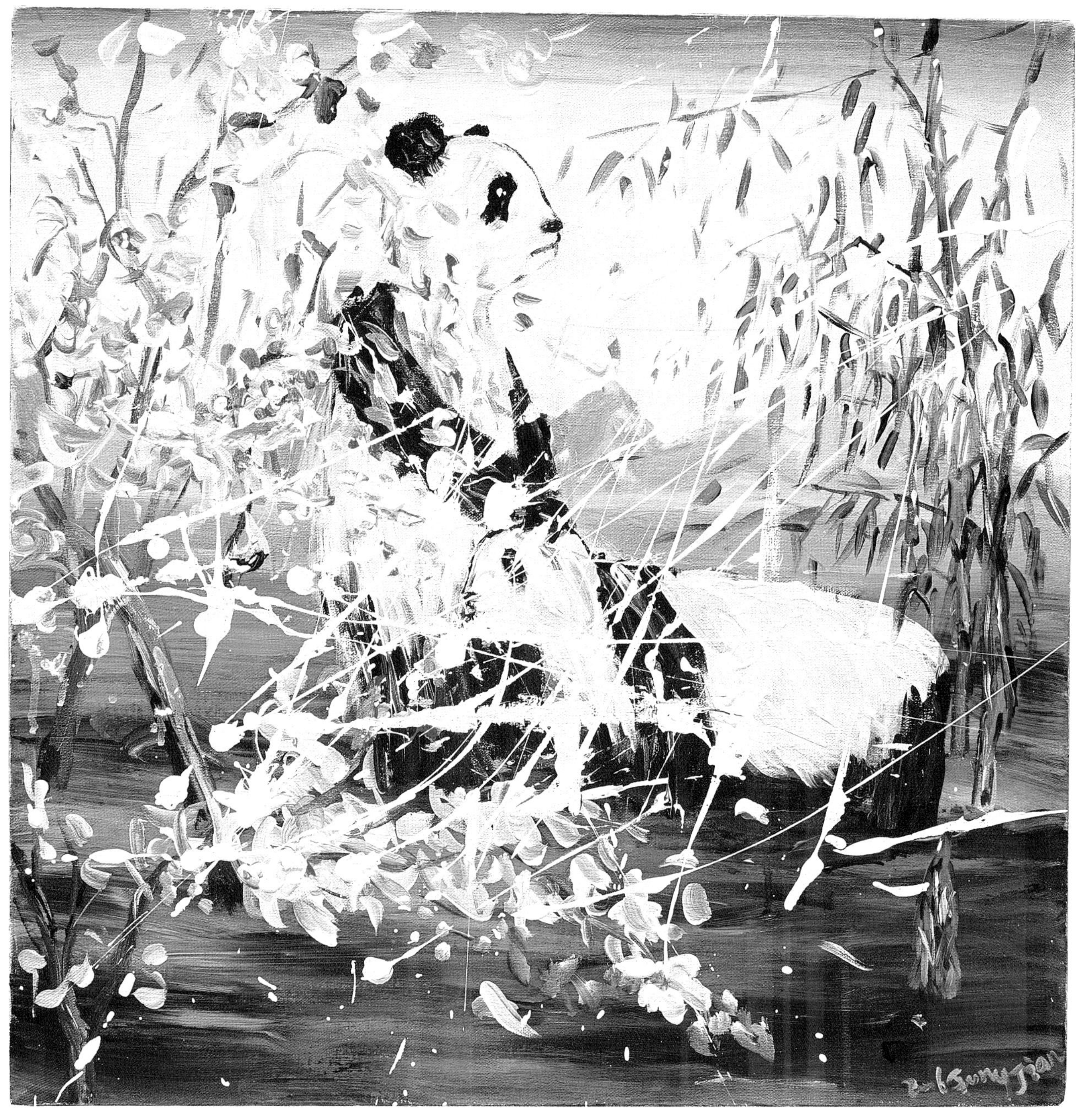

2 TUANTUAN AND YUANYUAN – BLOW JOB NO. 1 • 2006 • ACRYLIC ON CANVAS • 60 x 60 CM

3 TEACH YOU TO SHOOT PLANES NO. 2 • 2006 • ACRYLIC ON CANVAS • 150 x 120 CM

3

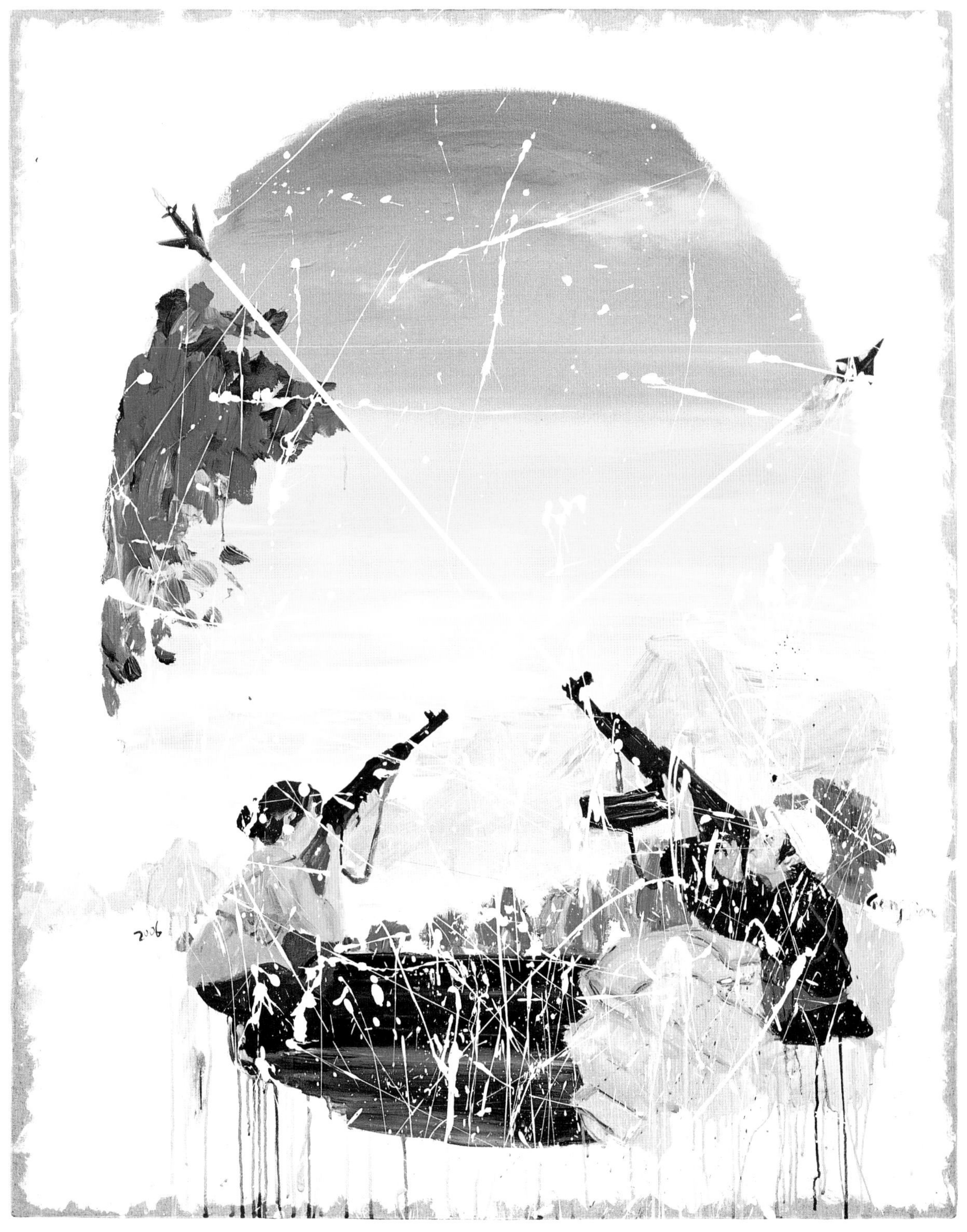

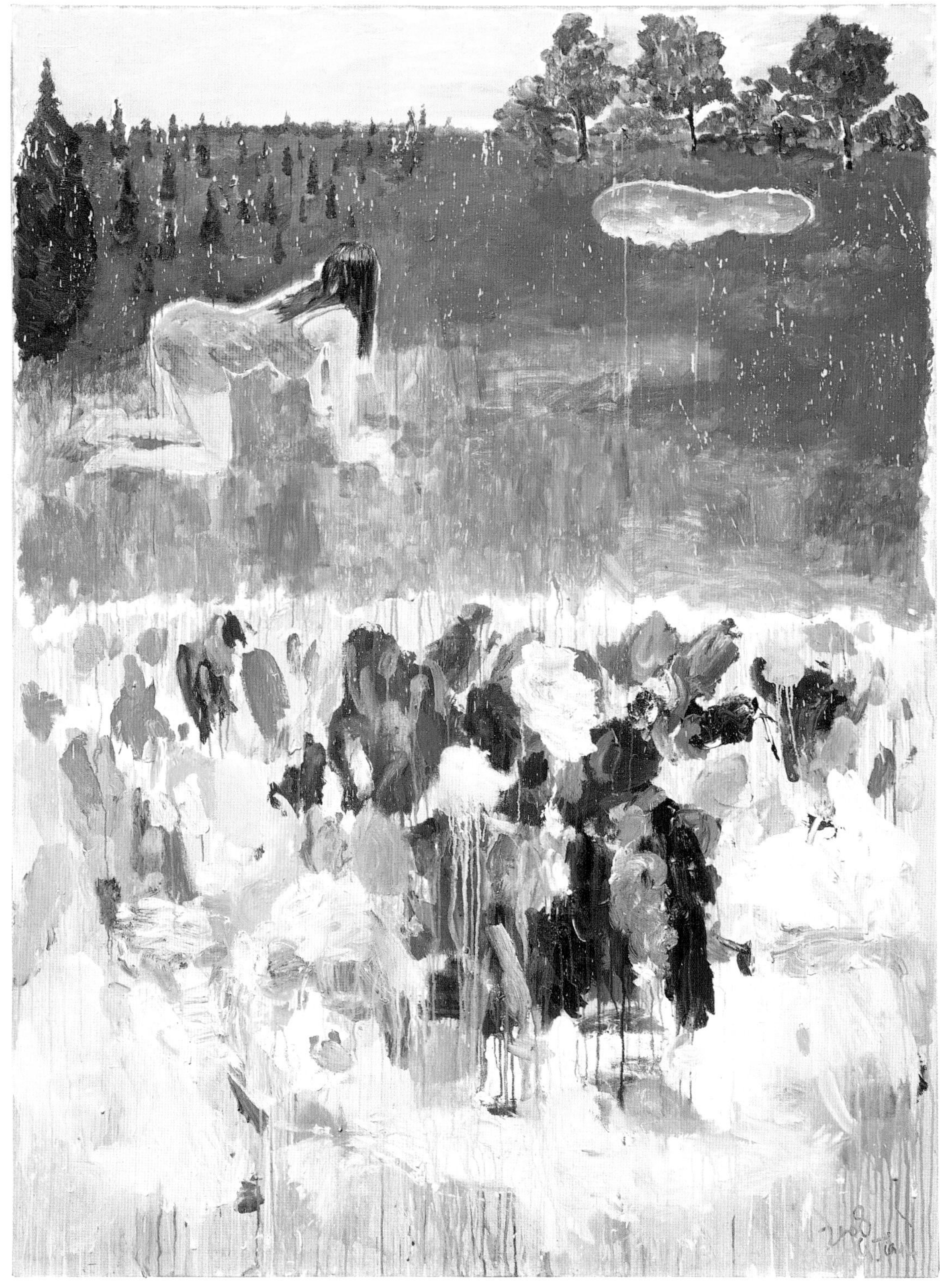

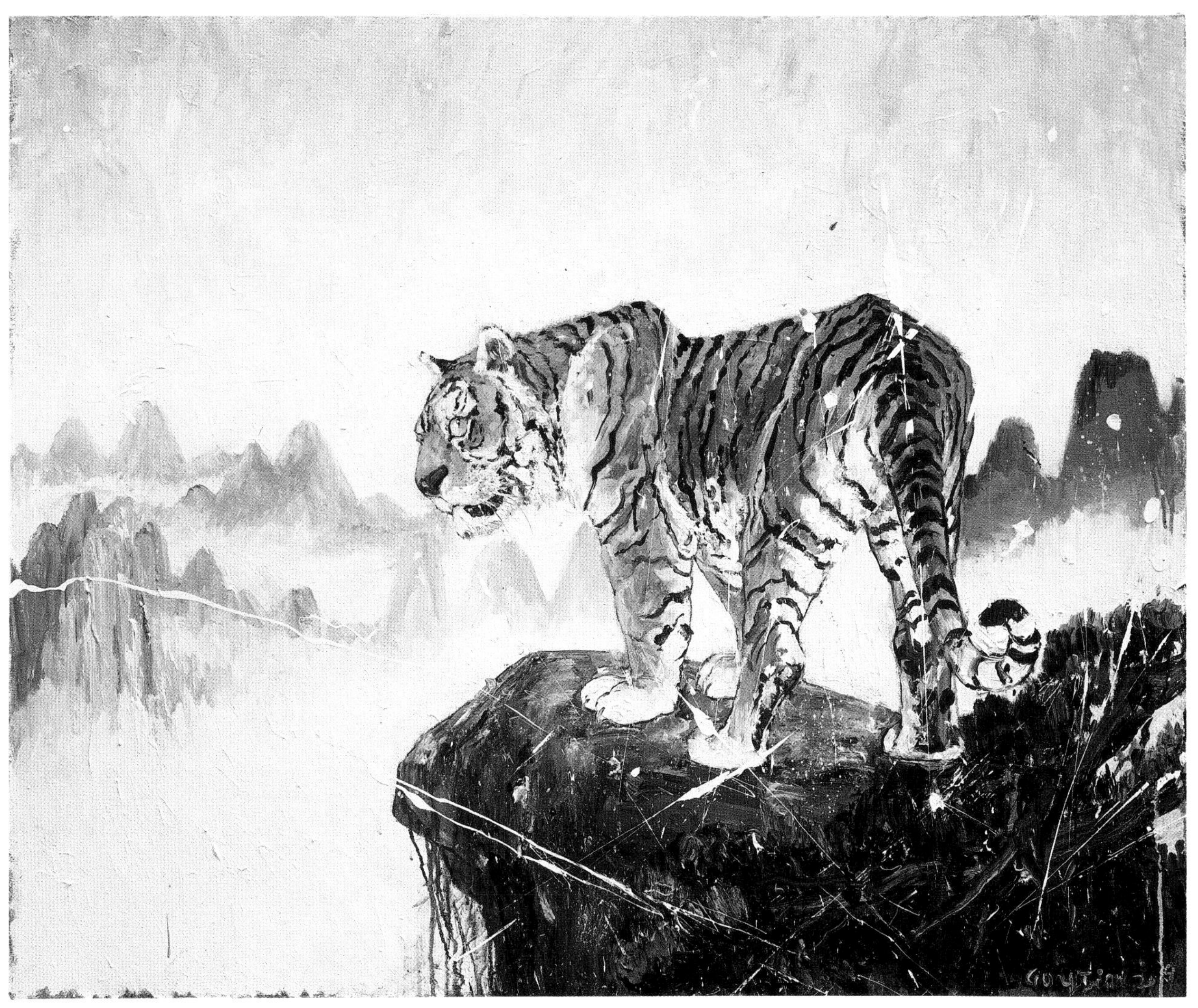

4 GLAMOUR SHOT • 2008 • ACRYLIC ON CANVAS • 220 x 165 CM

5 TIGER NO. 4 • 2009 • ACRYLIC ON CANVAS • 97 x 120 CM

6

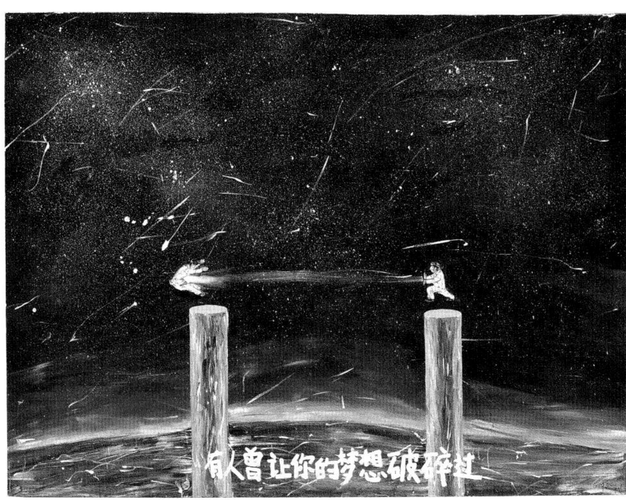

ONLINE CHAT WITH EDITORS

5/15/08 • LUNCHTIME

[12:09:23] What was your favorite toy when you were a child?

[12:13:01] My early memories are vague. My dad didn't really have enough money to buy me toys. What I remember is often being jealous of other kids having nice toys.

[12:16:16] What did your parents say to you most often?

[12:20:54] When I was a kid, I was quite naughty and very energetic. So, my parents would usually tell me to obey them. Now that I live on my own, they ask me whether I have eaten enough and remind me not to go to bed too late.

[12:22:46] How do you try and stay healthy?

[12:26:00] I hardly do anything to take care of my own health. But my plan for the future is to pay more attention to a lighter and fat-reduced diet, and I also want to try to get more sleep. But it's very hard to abandon my old habits.

[12:28:12] Do you usually work late at night?

[12:34:42] Yes. It's nice to work in the evenings as it gets quieter and I can concentrate much better. Afterwards I sometimes enjoy watching a movie or surfing on the Internet.

[12:38:03] What have you been wishing for recently?

[12:42:23] I hope to create some great new artworks very soon. And I would love to go on holiday. It would also be nice to find a girlfriend.

[12:09:23] Then the next question follows nicely. Do you believe in true love?

[12:09:23] I'm looking for true love and really hope to be able to find and enjoy this experience. But sometimes I am not sure whether I have somehow lost the ability to believe in the existence of this emotion.

[12:09:23] Describe your ideal living environment.

[12:09:23] I once watched an Al Pacino movie set in Miami. There was a white villa right by the sea, a huge pool, a little boat at the on-landing platform, and beautiful women everywhere. But this is only a fantasy, which I think is fun to dream of but not what I really want to set out to achieve.

[12:09:23] From which type of media do you look to for inspiration?

[12:09:23] I rarely watch television or read the newspapers, but spend most of the time on the Internet. Inspiration is manifold. In my case, the ideas mostly just pop up in my mind.

[12:09:23] What do you like about being an artist?

[12:09:23] It's great to have the opportunity to freely express all my thoughts and work in a very flexible way. I enjoy it a lot.

[12:09:23] But are there aspects you don't enjoy?

[12:48:19] Yes, the time pressure ahead of exhibitions, which can clash with my creative process. Apart from that I am a very happy and satisfied person.

[12:50:47] How do you communicate with your art?

[12:53:59] I can hardly bear communicating with my audience in my mind. I'm not sure if this is a disadvantage. I want to riddle my audience without providing a straight answer. I see my works as a magic entrance. Once you enter it's like wandering through a labyrinth.

[12:55:11] If you had five words to describe your generation, what would they be?

[12:59:03] That's hard. Each person has such a different personality, so it's a challenge to use only five words. But if I would try to describe myself, I would say optimistic and pessimistic, at the same time while also being lonely, selfish, empathic, and brave. I think I could list many more.

[13:00:59] One last question for you. If the whole world would listen to you for fifteen seconds, what would you say?

[13:05:42] I have too many things to say! But if I only had fifteen seconds, I would ask everyone to take care of each other. If they dislike someone, they still should try to respect the opposite view and try putting themselves in their place before making a decision.

6 SOMEBODY EVER SHATTERED YOUR DREAM • 2006 • ACRYLIC ON CANVAS • 165 x 220 CM

7 LOVE • 2006 • ACRYLIC ON CANVAS • 60 x 60 CM

8 LOVE LETTER NO. 1 • 2005 • ACRYLIC ON CANVAS • 110 x 110 CM

EXHIBITIONS

SELECTED SOLO EXHIBITIONS

2009
You should learn to wait,
Fine Arts Literature Art Center,
Wuhan, China

2008
Bored: Paintings of Gong Jian,
Fine Arts Literature Art Center,
Wuhan, China

SELECTED GROUP EXHIBITIONS

2009
Hubei and Hunan Chinese Contemporary Art 1985-2009,
Guangdong Museum of Art ,
Guangzhou, China

2008
Winter Group Show,
Boers-Li Gallery,
Beijing, China

2007
The 2nd Documentary Exhibition of Fine Arts,
Hubei Museum of Art,
Wuhan, China

2007
Visual Experiences,
China National Art Museum,
Beijing, China

2006
Twelve: Chinese Contemporary Art Awards,
Zendai Museum of Modern Art,
Shanghai, China

2006
DFOTO,
San Sebastian, Spain

2006
Limited & Freedom,
Fine Arts Literature Art Center,
Wuhan, China

2005
WHS+8,
Siemens Arts Program,
Construction Bank Building,
Wuhan, China

2002
Chinart: Contemporary Art from China,
Museum Küppersmühle, Duisburg, Germany /
Marco Museum, Rome, Italy /
Ludwig Museum, Budapest, Hungary

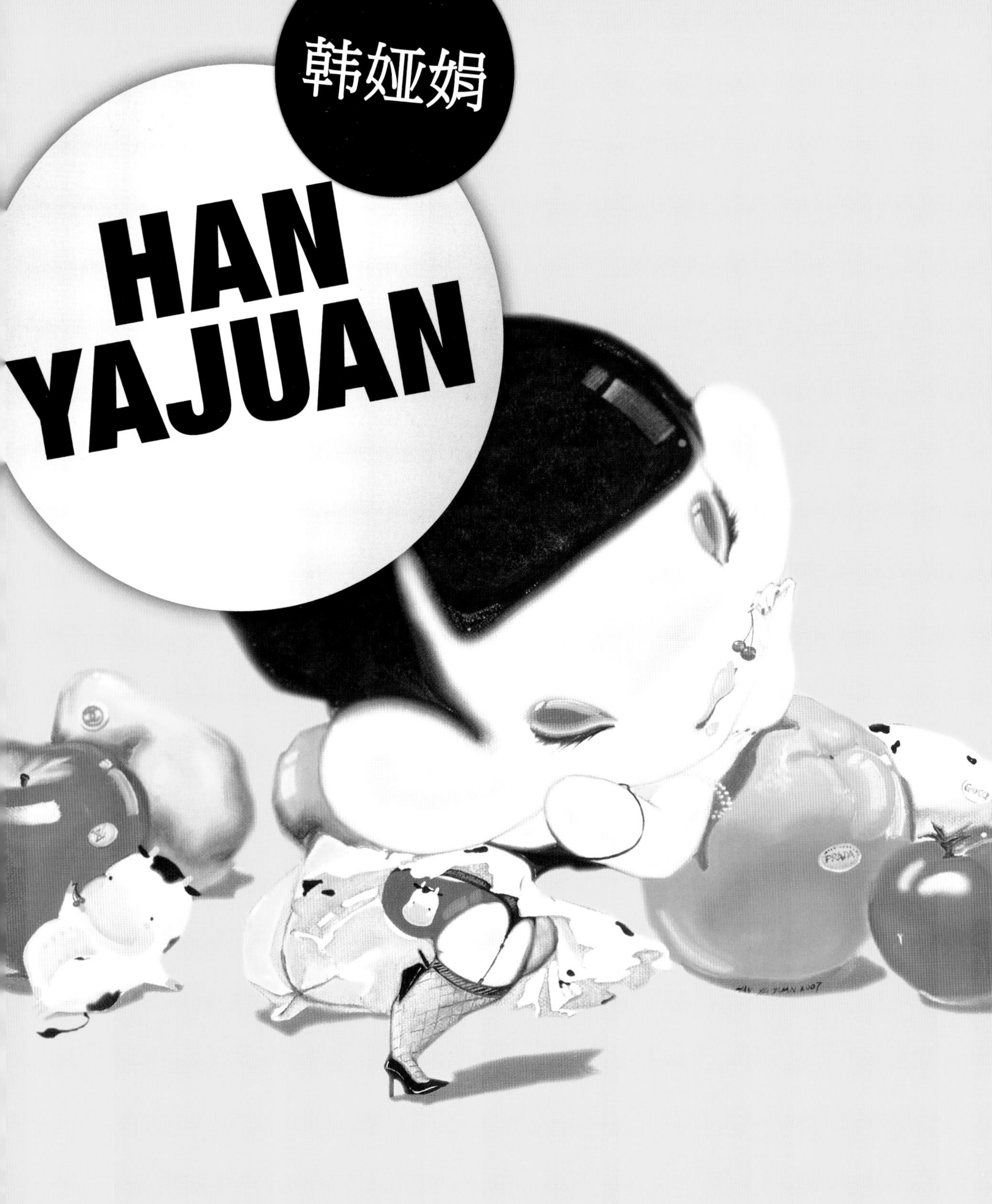
韩娅娟
HAN
YAJUAN
PRADA

NAME

HAN YAJUAN

BORN IN

1980, QINGDAO

LIVES IN

BEIJING

STUDY

CHINA ACADEMY OF ART, HANGZHOU

MEDIA

PAINTING

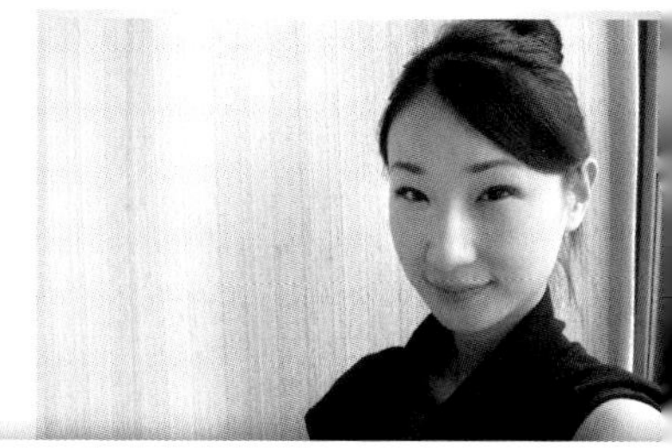

BLING BLING CHINA

Han Yajuan belongs to a new generation of Chinese artists who are among China's first single children, exposed only to times of rapid economic growth, a consumer-oriented society, and a life of material plenty. They didn't experience the monetary, social, and individual struggles that were the norm in the generation of their parents. Han Yajuan uses cartoonish playfulness in her paintings to express a fascination for high fashion and celebrity culture that is increasingly prevalent in China's rapidly growing urban centers. She portrays the fantasy life of young Chinese women reflecting the rising economy's promises of wealth, luxury, and new options of consumerism. "They are like my idols. They can be fashionable, but also brave. They can be really free and easy, fearlessly driving off in a VW Beetle, or being really successful. In short they can do lots of things I could not do."

Cartoon-style painting is an inherent part of the contemporary Chinese art scene. Its emergence is related to the visual stimuli of imported cartoon programs that this generation was exposed to in their youth. But using a cartoon style in their works does not only reflect childhood nostalgia. These are highly individualized worlds, showing feelings of love, desire or anxiety, dreams, and life experiences that may be deep or superficial, true or false. In addition, using a comic-inspired imaginary that already has an established international and intercultural visual diction enables Han Yajuan's generation to communicate their ideas and feelings to a global audience.

While many of the earlier Chinese artists have used brand emblems as a means of pointing out Western influence on traditional China, Han Yajuan applies them to celebrate the affluence and lifestyle luxury goods that these Western brands have brought to urban China. Female consumers in China's cities are spending much of their hard-earned cash on recreational activities, dining out, shopping, and pursuing urban leisure lifestyles. In *Travel Alone* (2007), for example, sparkling mineral-colored oils and flashy color shades are used to depict the rapid swirl of glamour. By painting her little heroine's having her heavily tinted eyes closed, the artist permits her actress to daydream in a parallel universe without being "disturbed" by reality.

Han Yajuan's earliest works, such as *My Chicks Kingdom* (2005), depicted Western girls and were dominated by beauty ideals. Her later works, however, showed an increasing use of international luxury brand logos. As the new values of China's consumer society seem to be confirmed and Western characters began to disappear from her paintings. The artist's little rouged girls engage in a variety of activities ranging from being hard at work to preparing for a date. *Pearl* (2006), for example, depicts a bunch of dressed-up girls along with their little cow friends posing and chilling in front of oversized pearl necklaces. Wearing cow-patterned petticoats, the little divas can be seen surrounded by various high-end fashion logos. Being accompanied by small cows prevents them from being lonely in the new settings of today's China, and also reflects the feeling of young women's pet-like existence. Though many changes happened to a women's role in society, the cows remind one of the traditional role which is still played by many girls.

In Han Yajuan's recent works, the mini-doll protagonists' minute bodies, along with their oversized heads, appear increasingly exaggerated. With this step into the world of fantasy, Han Yajuan subtly comments on this superficial appearance as a double-edged sword of desires and ideals. In these works, different aspects of a girl's life are illustrated while the background of the works changes from a previously unspecific monochrome space to particular insights into female privacy. Most of the scenarios display the "lucky-to-be" girls on their own, only having pet cows as "mini-me" companions. Looking at the conglomerate of divas such as in *Blue Fly* (2007), for example, one realizes that no interaction at all is taking place amongst the lonely-hearted and self-absorbed girls that have everything but love and security. But, as in *Sharing Life* (2007), Han Yajuan provides a closer look behind the scenes, as the bird's-eye perspective uncovers many little secrets of her divas' daily lives.

Apart from all the amusement, Han Yajuan is equally concerned to emphasize the negative effects of a culture made of famous brands and individual appearance. "When looking behind the scenes of glamour and luxurious lifestyles it becomes clear that living a life of plenty also implies loneliness and is definitely not a universal solution to all human problems and desires." By adopting this position, Han Yajuan's works manage to go beyond being purely a lovable product placement.

By Cordelia Noe

1

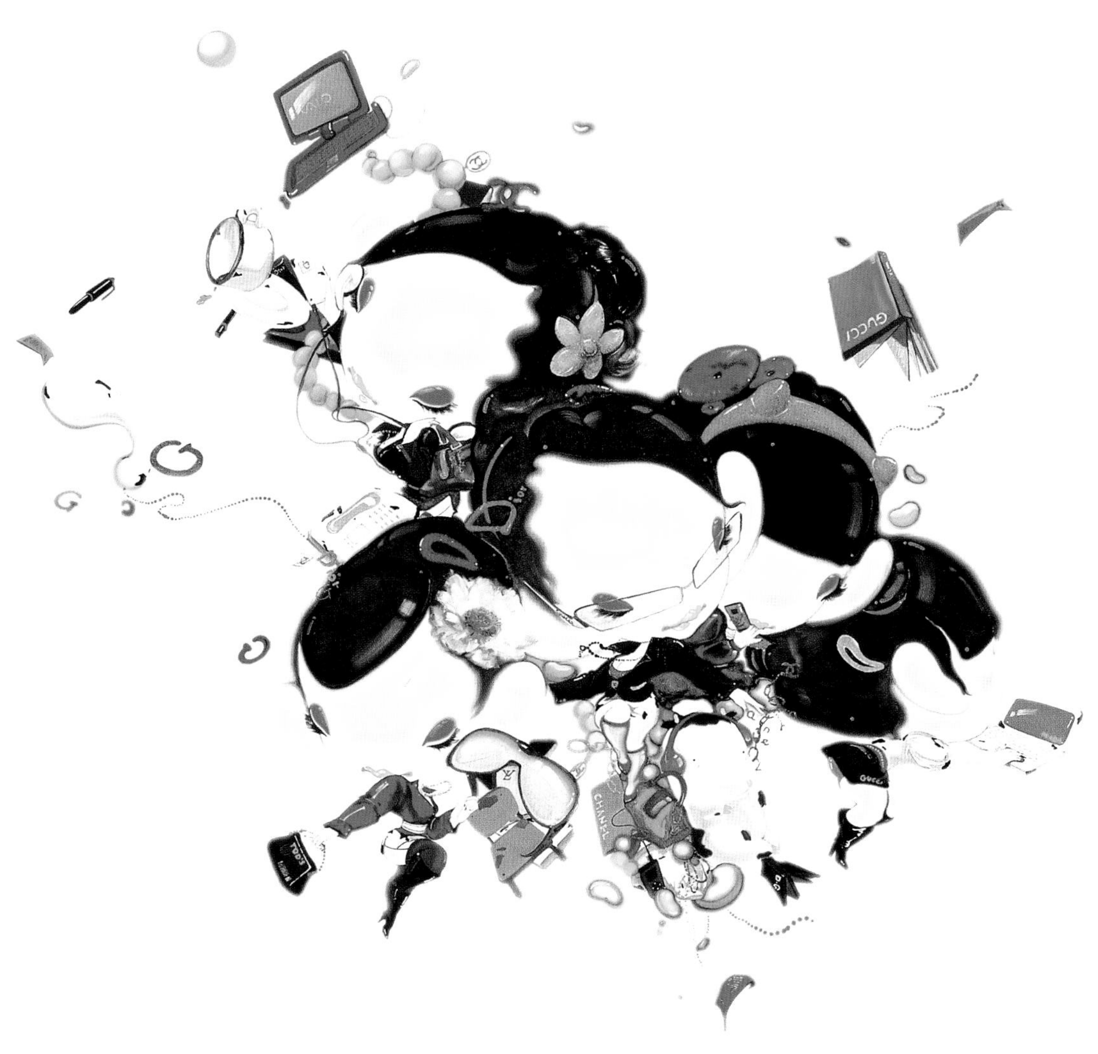

1 BLUE FLY • 2007 • OIL ON CANVAS • 150 x 150 CM

2 TRAVEL ALONE • 2007 • OIL ON CANVAS • 60 x 50 CM

3 OH DEAR, I AM BUSY • 2007 • OIL ON CANVAS • 100 x 100 CM

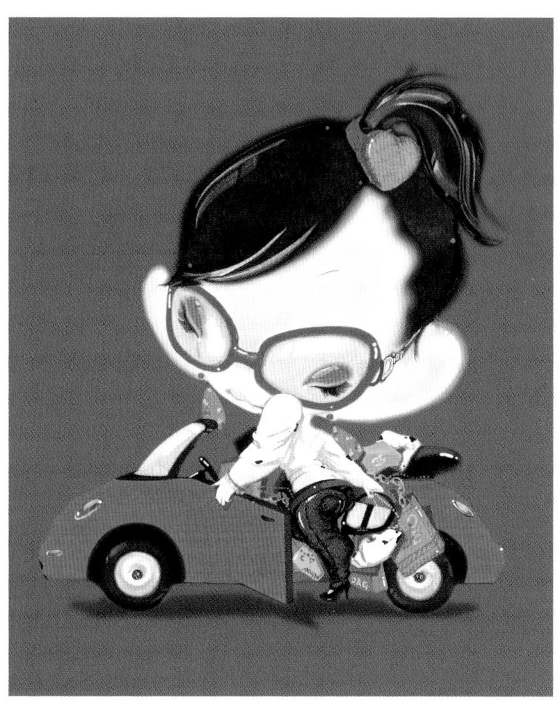

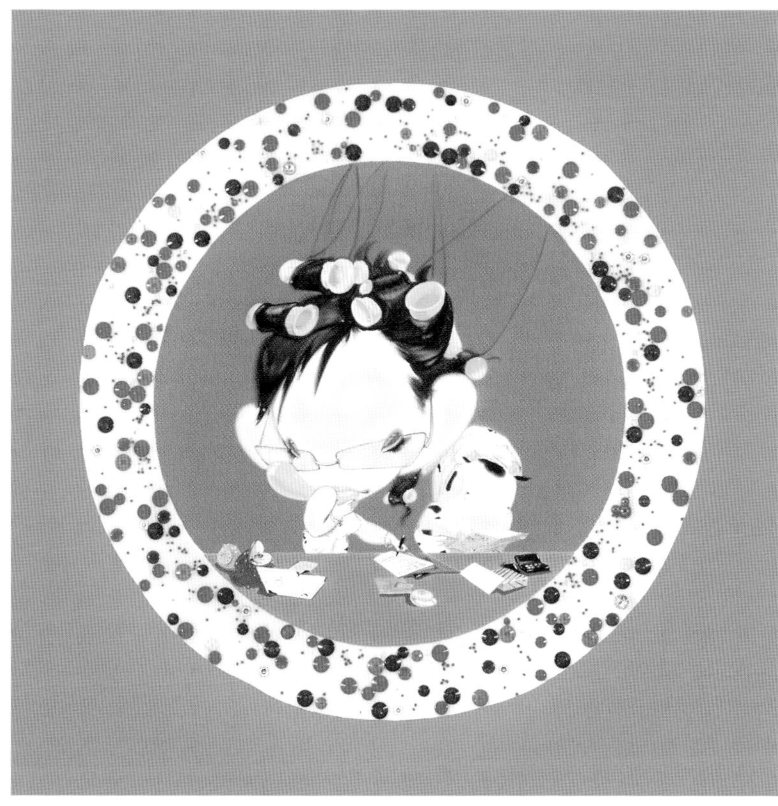

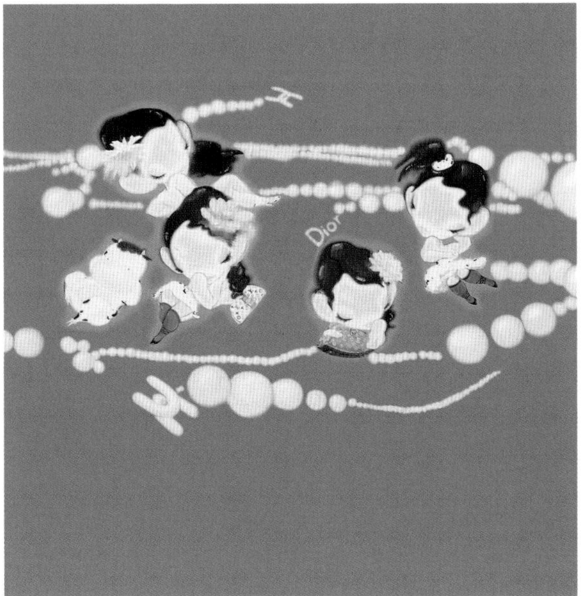

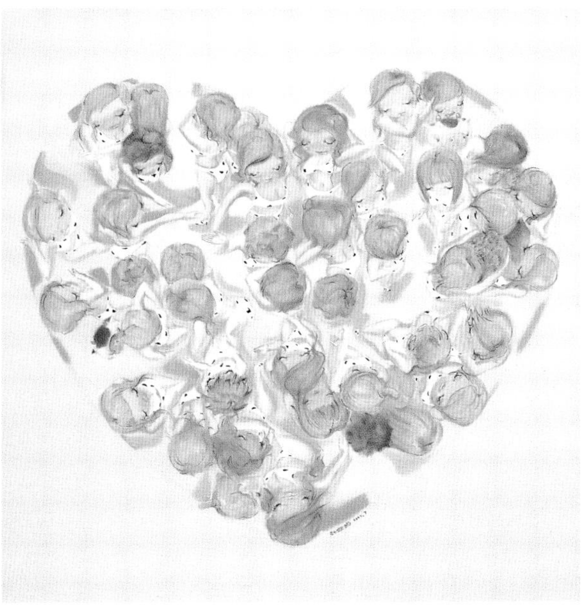

ONLINE CHAT WITH EDITORS

4/29/08 • LATE MORNING

[11:30:42] Looking back, what was your favorite childhood toy?

[11:32:15] Some dolls, which were made in China, similar to Barbies.

[11:34:03] What sentence did your parents say to you most often?

[11:36:20] After I left home to start studying at university, they often told me to eat regularly.

[11:37:16] How do you try to maintain good health in your everyday life?

[11:39:56] Well, mainly I try to eat healthy and on time.

[11:41:00] What is your recent wish?

[11:43:59] To go on a holiday. But I don't have any plans right now. If it is planned in too much detail, it loses its spontaneity and feels more like "accomplishing a mission."

[11:45:21] Do you believe in true love?

[11:48:04] Yes, I do. True love is full of responsibilities including mutual trust, encouragement, support, and tolerance.

[11:49:06] What does your ideal living environment look like?

[11:51:47] In my ideal environment, there should be a lot of sunshine and it should not be too far from the city. I hope it will be in China, but let s see.

[11:53:31] Which type of media provides you with most of your inspiration?

[11:55:43] If you are only asking about media, then I would choose the Internet. But generally speaking, most inspiration comes from my life.

[11:58:49] You have worked as an artist already for a couple of years. What do you like/dislike about being an artist?

[11:59:57] What I like about being an artist is having a more intense feeling about life and also getting the chance to express my feelings through my artworks. However, one point seems a little difficult for me: sometimes I am maybe too indulged in my work. This means I don't care enough about other people's ideas or thoughts, but create my own value system and develop it according to my own standards. I guess sometimes I should be more open and also get some feedback from outside.

[12:01:14] How can you communicate with the audience through your art?

[12:04:20] By the feelings I transfer to my audience via my works.

[12:06:50] In five words, how you would describe your generation?

[12:08:46] Individualism, materialism, courage, happiness, and simplicity.

[12:10:01] If the whole world would listen to you for fifteen seconds, what would you say?

[12:13:41] "Enjoy every moment of your life!"

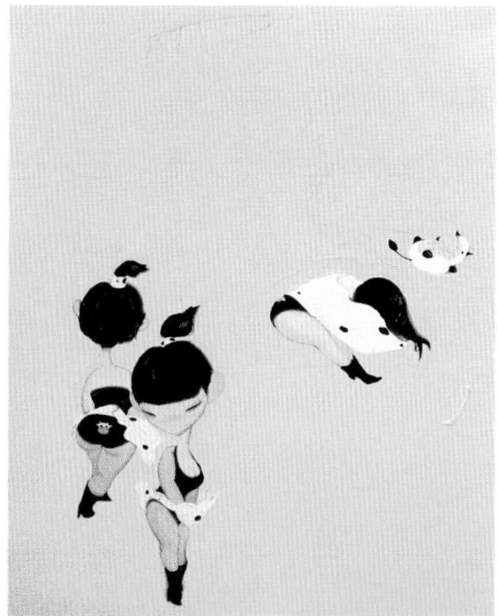

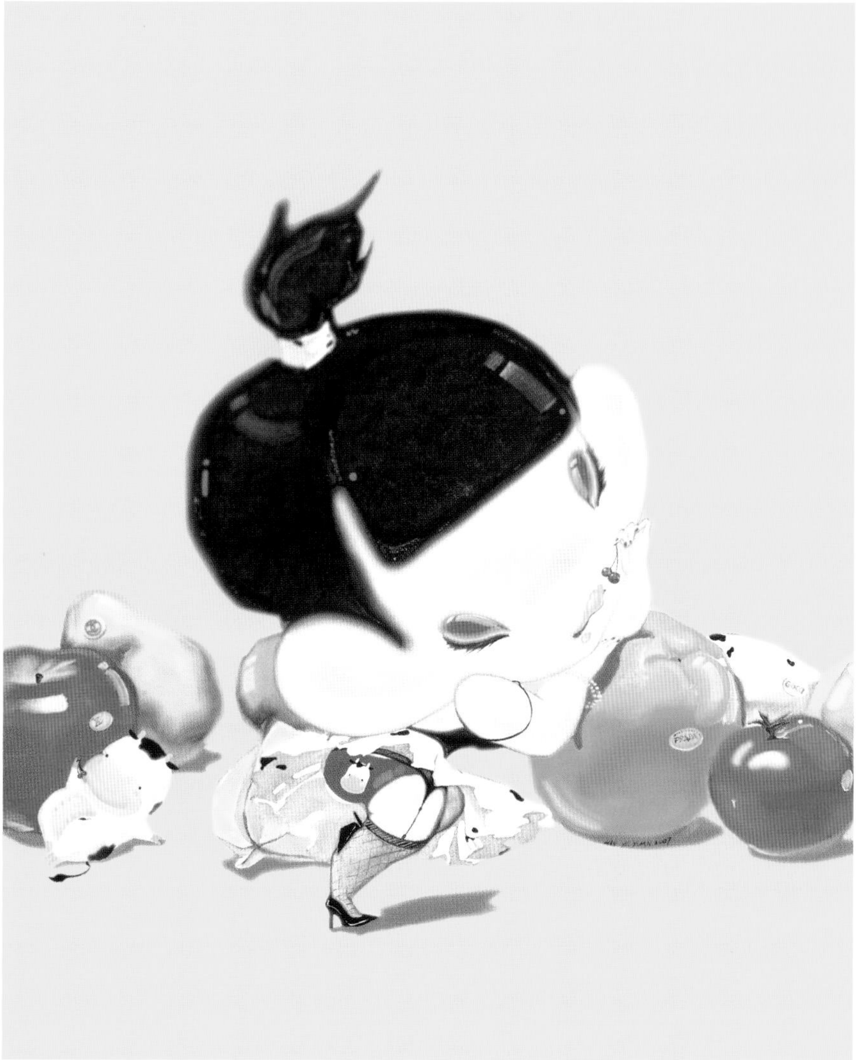

4 PEARL • 2006 • OIL ON CANVAS • 150 x 150 CM

5 MY CHICKS KINGDOM NO. 8 • 2005 • OIL ON CANVAS • 80 x 80 CM

6 I BELIEVE I CAN FLY NO. 18 • 2005 • OIL ON CANVAS • 60 x 50 CM

7 IMPORTED VITAMINS • 2007 • OIL ON CANVAS • 60 x 50 CM

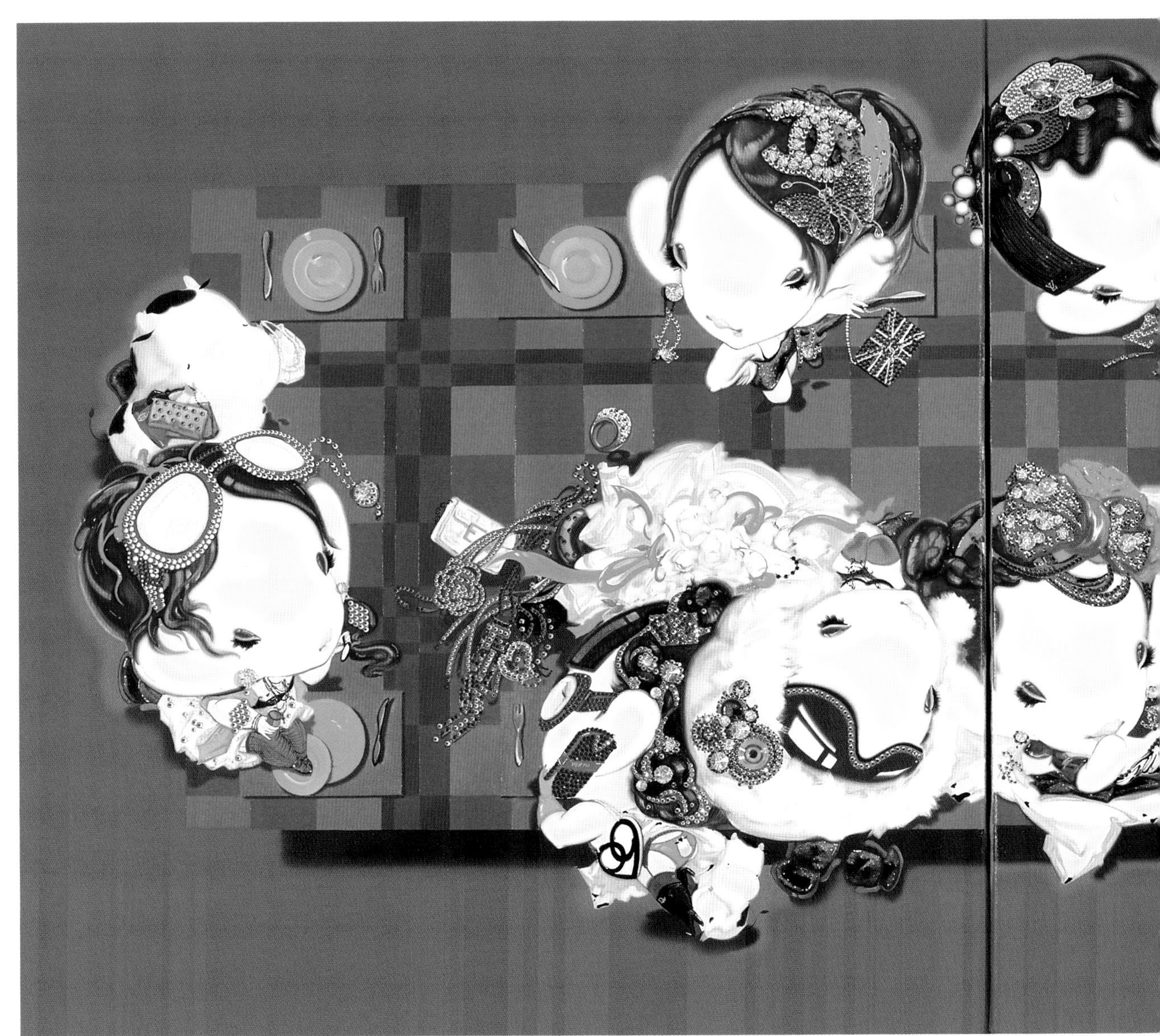

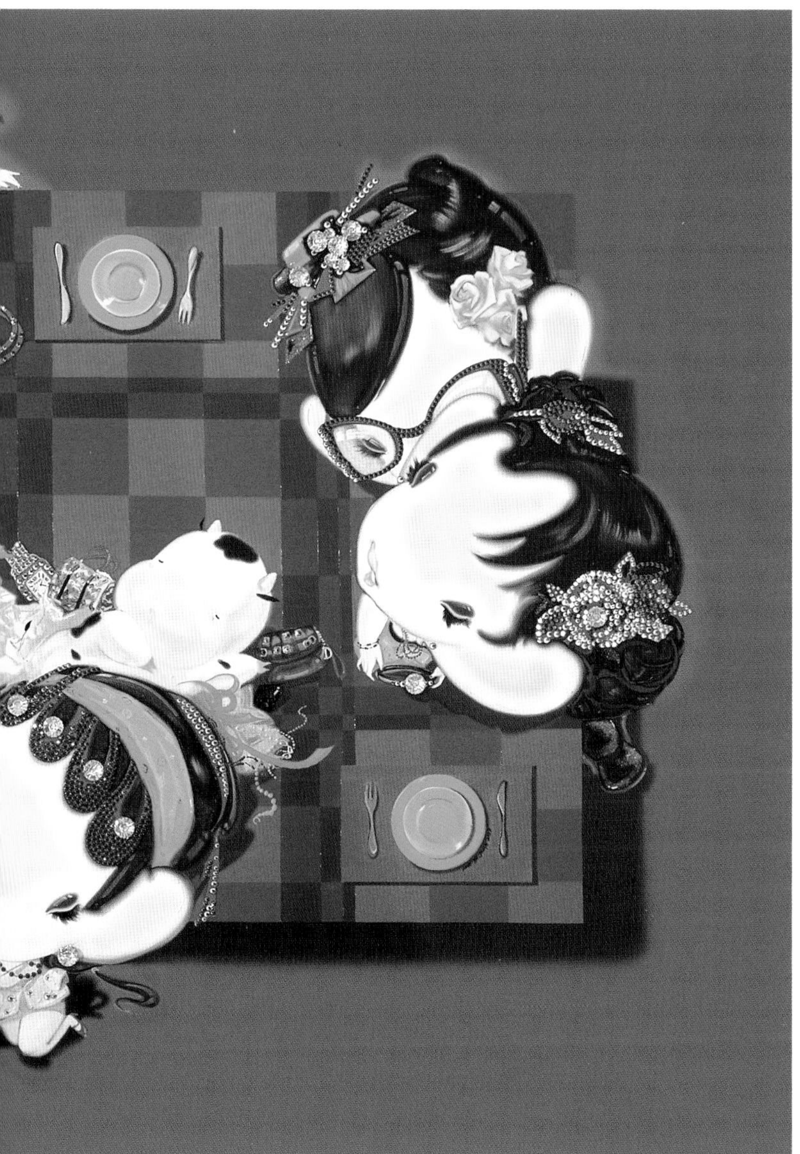

■ BLINGEE • 2009 • OIL ON CANVAS (DIPTYCH) • 150 x 300 CM

EXHIBITIONS

SELECTED SOLO EXHIBITIONS

2008
Herstory,
Marella Gallery,
Beijing, China

2008
Angels from Hell,
Olyvia Oriental,
London, U.K.

2007
Travel Alone,
Tokyo Gallery,
Tokyo, Japan

SELECTED GROUP EXHIBITIONS

2008
Free Zone: China,
BSI Art Collection,
Lugano, Switzerland

2007
La Cina e' vicina,
Palazzo delle Arti Napoli,
Naples, Italy

2007
Floating: New Generation of Art in China,
National Museum of Contemporary Art,
Seoul, South Korea

2007
Animange,
Maison des Arts de Créteil (MAC),
Paris, France

2006
Fiction@Love,
MoCA,
Shanghai, China

2005
Archaeology of the Future:
2nd Triennial of Chinese Art,
Nanjing Museum,
Nanjing, China

2005
After 70s:
The Generation Changed by Market,
Yuan Ming Culture & Art Center,
Shanghai / Beijing, China

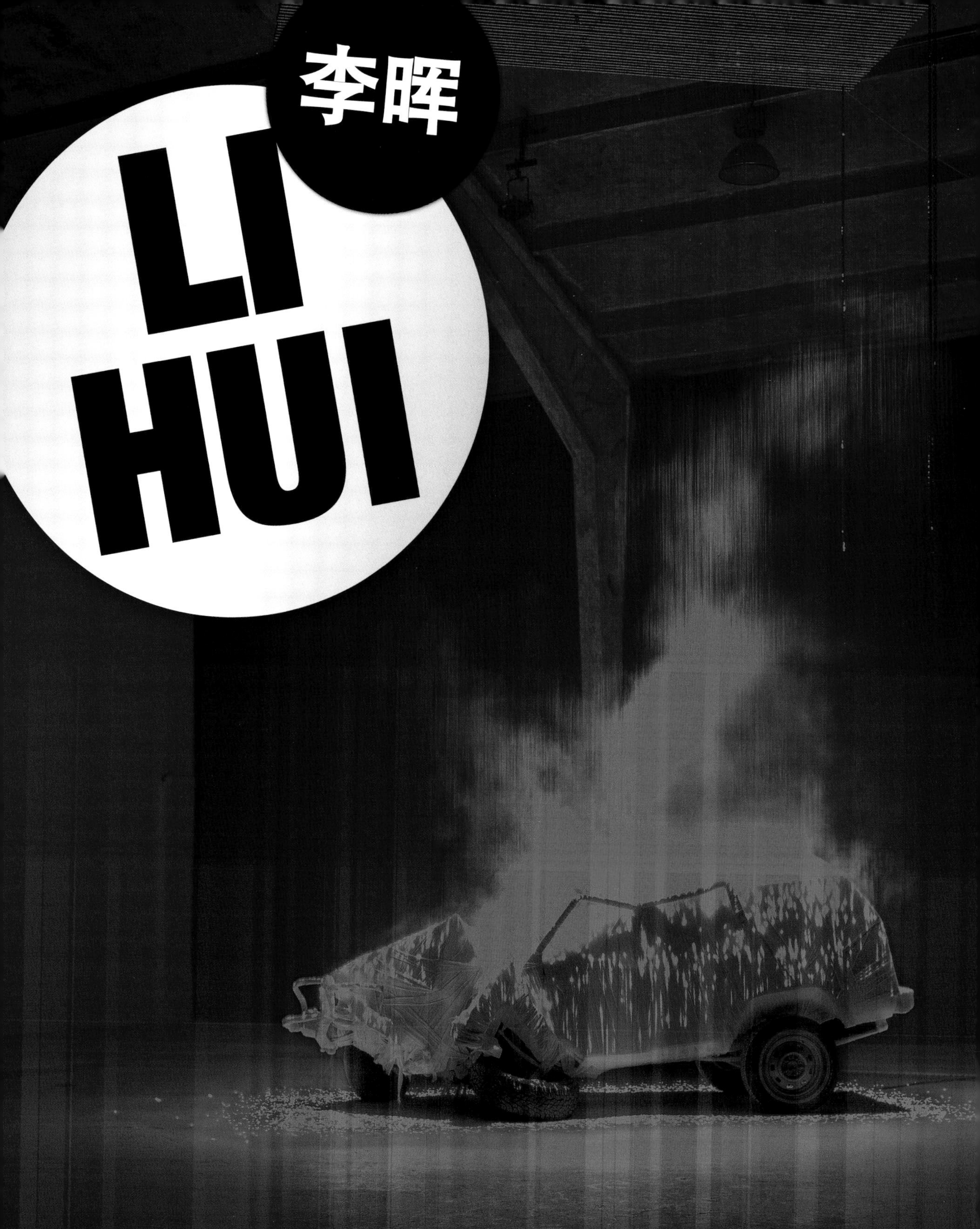
李晖
LI
HUI

NAME
LI HUI
BORN IN
1977, BEIJING
LIVES IN
BEIJING
STUDY
CENTRAL ACADEMY OF FINE ARTS, BEIJING
MEDIA
INSTALLATION, SCULPTURE

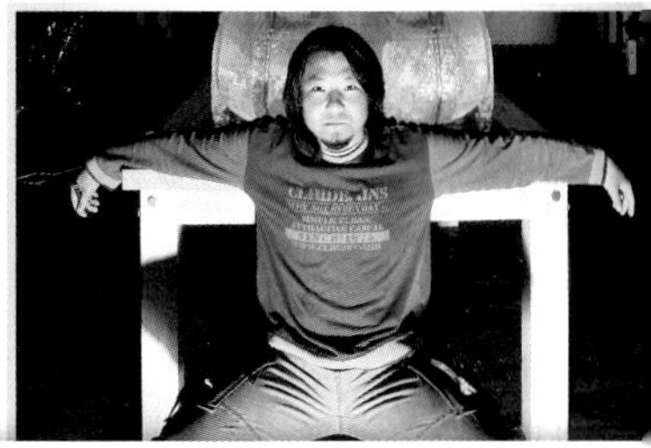

WHO IS AFRAID OF GREEN LIGHT?

There are works of art that captivate before they are understood – that bring something to light that's already intuitively intimate. The Beijing artist Li Hui avoids every categorization. Nothing about his works lets on that he comes from China. His sculptures and installations often take over the room – working with materials from stainless steel and wood to lasers and LED lights that stage dreamlike or dramatically charged environments. Ships, bursting open, are floating over our heads. Lustrous red light pours out over a bed. Under a Plexiglas cover rests a prehistoric skeleton. What is it that makes us recoil in fear before a cage made of green laser beams?

Renewing Jeep (2003), a vehicle made by welding together the front ends of two Jeeps, is based on his thesis work at the Beijing Central Academy of Fine Arts. "Looking back over my studies, I determined that we were instructed in Western artistic techniques, but in terms of content and even spirit, we learned from the Eastern tradition. I want to make this phenomenon, which is typical in today's China, visible in my work." *Renewing Jeep* objectifies the question of the "right way" – and at the same time nullifies the contradiction between "forward" and "backward." Li Hui is updating a traditional Eastern concept central to both Buddhism and Taoism: the movement itself becomes the goal.

In *Change* (2006), Li Hui shows just how much explosive power lies coiled in the tension between tradition and modernity – or to put it another way: in the encounter of Eastern and Western values. With merciless vehemence, a steel sheet rams into the hull of a simple wooden boat. Splinters fly through the air; the rudder no longer functions. In *Gu Zheng* (2006), the object destroyed is a traditional Chinese stringed instrument. The processes of detaching and fusing may be violently portrayed, but these works, like so much of Li Hui's output, also have the power to attract.

Surely the most impressive example of fear and agony shining out of a dreamlike production is the piece *Untitled (2007)*, in which a crashed car is bathed in red laser light and fog. "The car was actually wrecked in a real accident. In this installation, I want to make visible the experience of the people involved. Fog leaks out of the destroyed automobile and dissolves in the air – as do the souls of the victims." In *Reincarnation* (2007), too, Li Hui reveals what is invisible and even verbally inexpressible. Red laser light streams over a bed: Dreams / Nightmares? Joy of love / Fear of death? Convalescence / Exhaustion? What speech posits in pairs of opposites, art makes visible in a *single* image. But the gleaming, bewitching optics of both works may not have been thought up initially. "The idea of transforming something negative into something positive is deeply rooted in Chinese philosophy. Maybe I brought it over into these works unconsciously. I can't say for sure myself."

In the *Amber Series* (2006), Li Hui has piled up numerous layers of acrylic sheets on top of one another. White shapes resembling animal bones emerge from hollow spaces in the surfaces. The outside of the sculpture looks like a race car, glowingly illuminated with blue LED lights. Just as the real-life amber alluded to in the title preserves otherwise ephemeral relicts of plants or animals, so in *Amber* a symbol of speed and acceleration becomes the protective cover for an animal whose age and species is not readily discernable. With the *Amber* sculptures, Li Hui is fashioning a condensed expression of the Chinese understanding of history as continuum. The past – like a chamber holding more than 3,000 years – is preserved in every life form and even in things. And now in China's bustling metropolises another nuance of meaning pushes itself forward: is the human being himself – whether he is a willing participant in the accelerating processes of modernization or not – becoming a kind of fossil?

Li Hui articulates philosophical considerations with the help of the most modern techniques. An almost poetic aura surrounds the result. The light installations *Cage* (2006) and *The Door* (2007) deal with the existential experience of freedom and bondage. The artist uses green lasers to evoke a cage and red lasers for a gateway, leaving both accessible to the visitor. The immaterial question, as it were, then hangs in the air: which constraints and restrictions does the individual impose on himself voluntarily, which are accepted in the rush to obey, and which exist for real in themselves? The visitors' reactions show how potent this question can be: more often than not they shrink back in fear from these virtual boundaries to their freedom of movement.

By Ulrike Münter

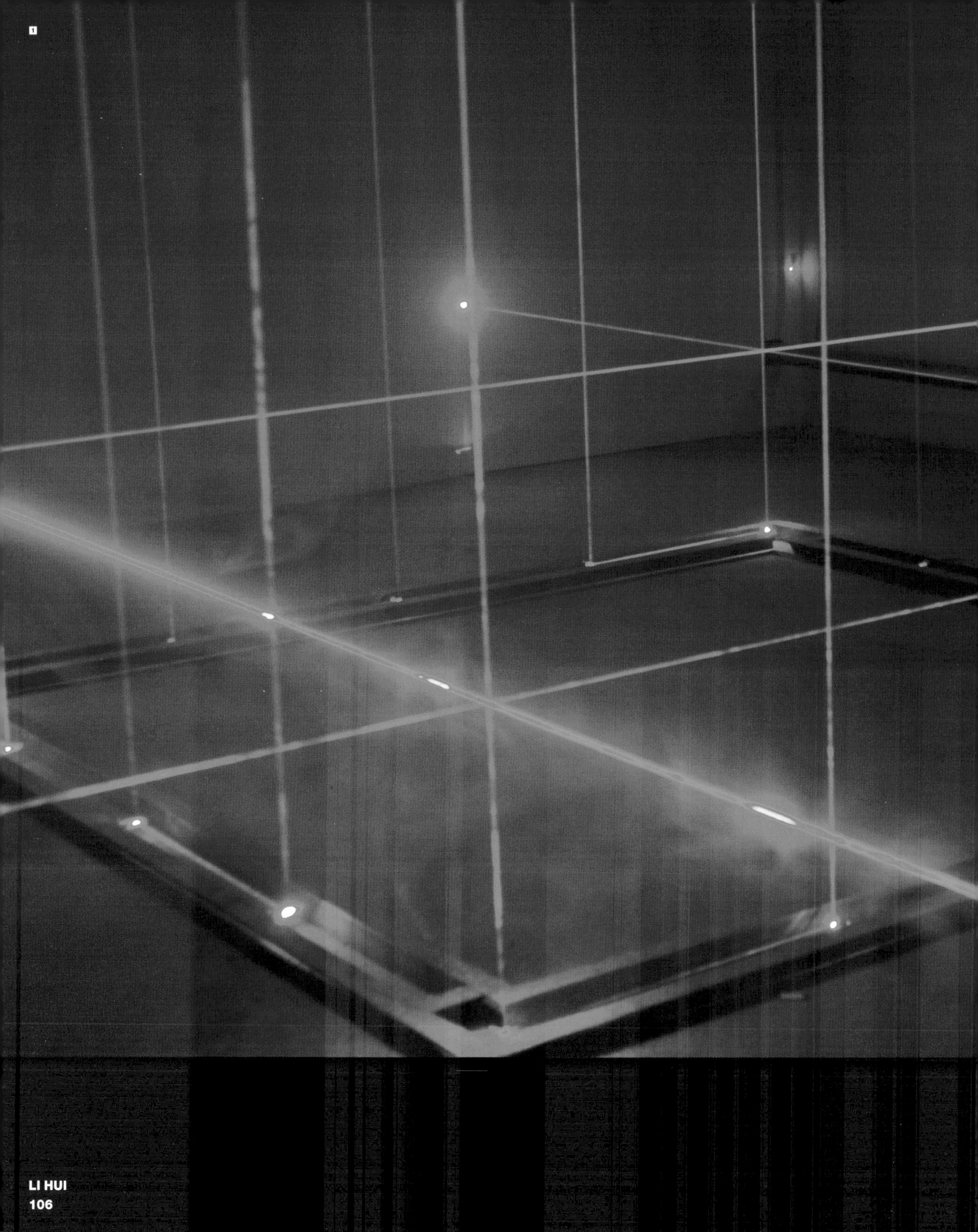

1

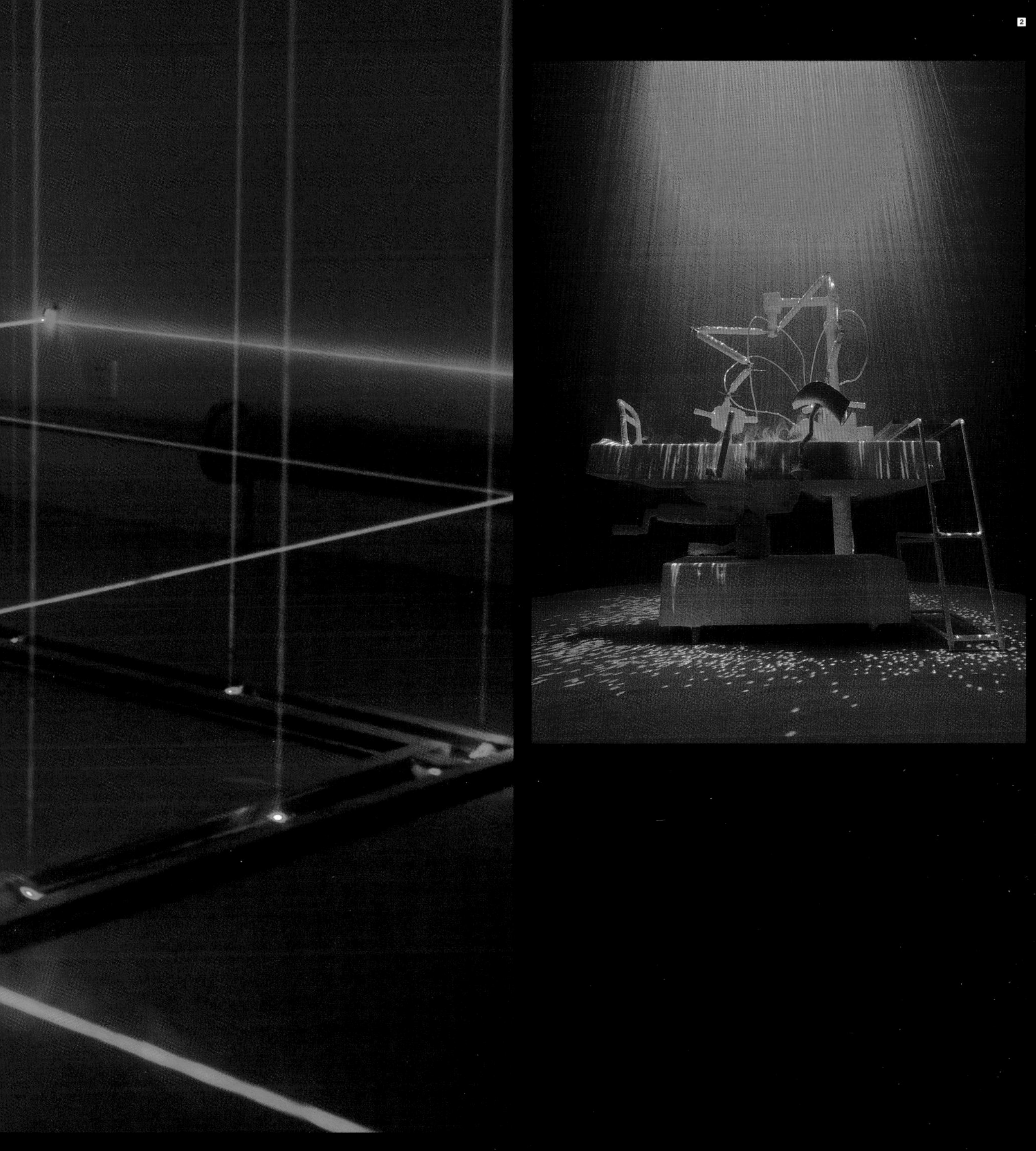

1 CAGE • 2006 • LASER, MIRROR, IRON • 300 × 200 × 200 CM

2 THE SOUL RELEASED BY REASON • 2009 • STAINLESS STEEL, LASER, FOG, GAUZE • 800 × 300 × 170 CM

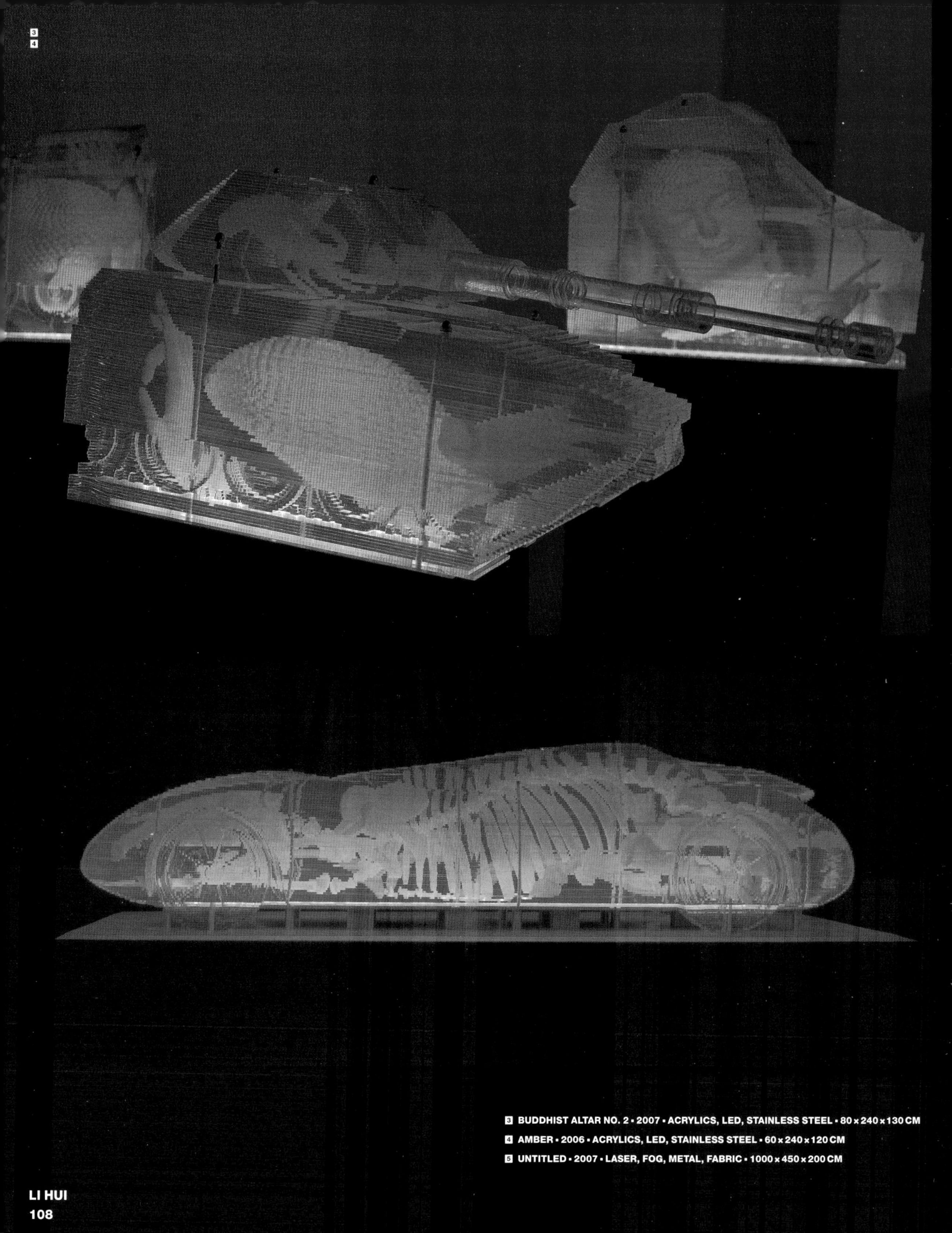

3 BUDDHIST ALTAR NO. 2 • 2007 • ACRYLICS, LED, STAINLESS STEEL • 80 x 240 x 130 CM

4 AMBER • 2006 • ACRYLICS, LED, STAINLESS STEEL • 60 x 240 x 120 CM

5 UNTITLED • 2007 • LASER, FOG, METAL, FABRIC • 1000 x 450 x 200 CM

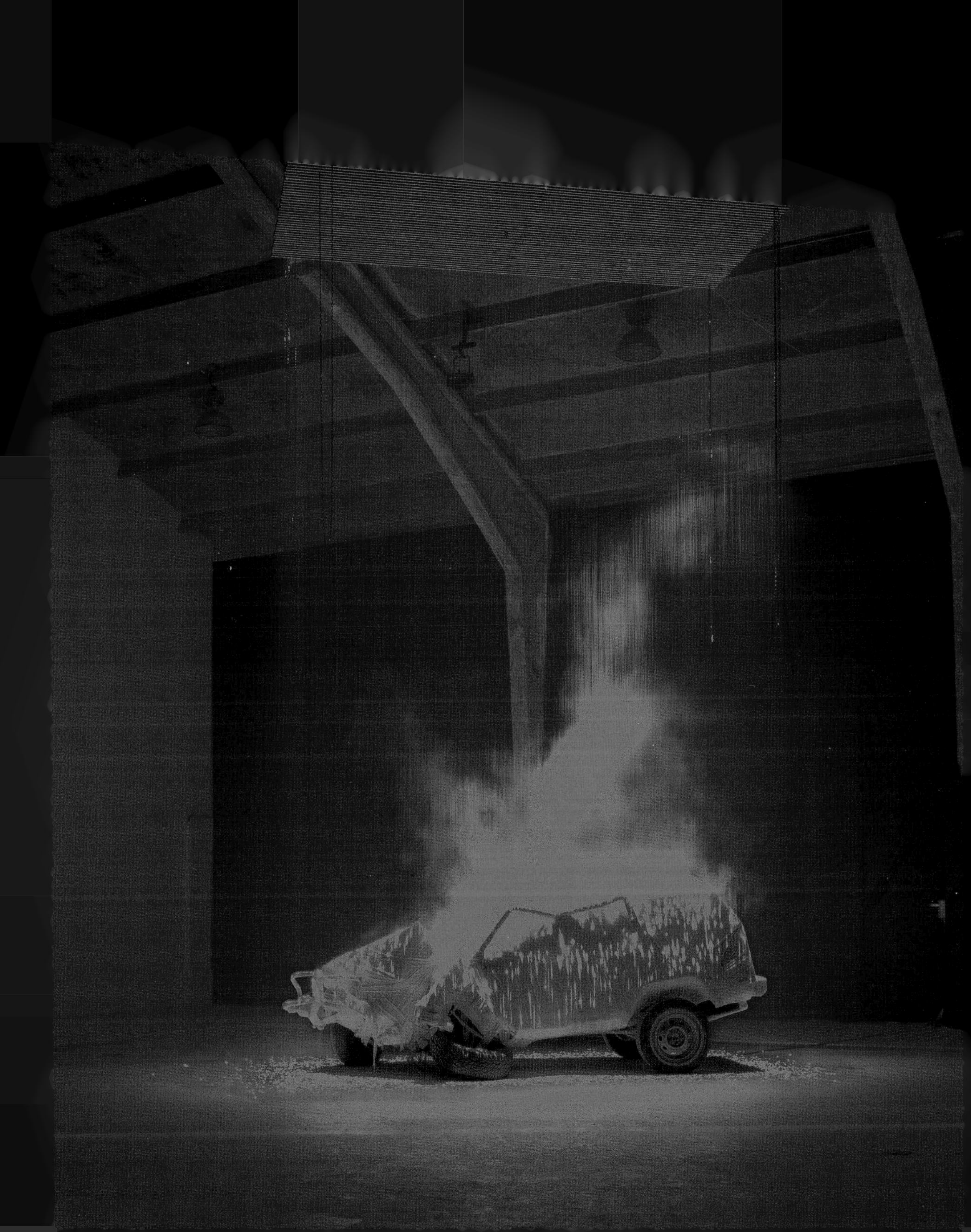

6
7

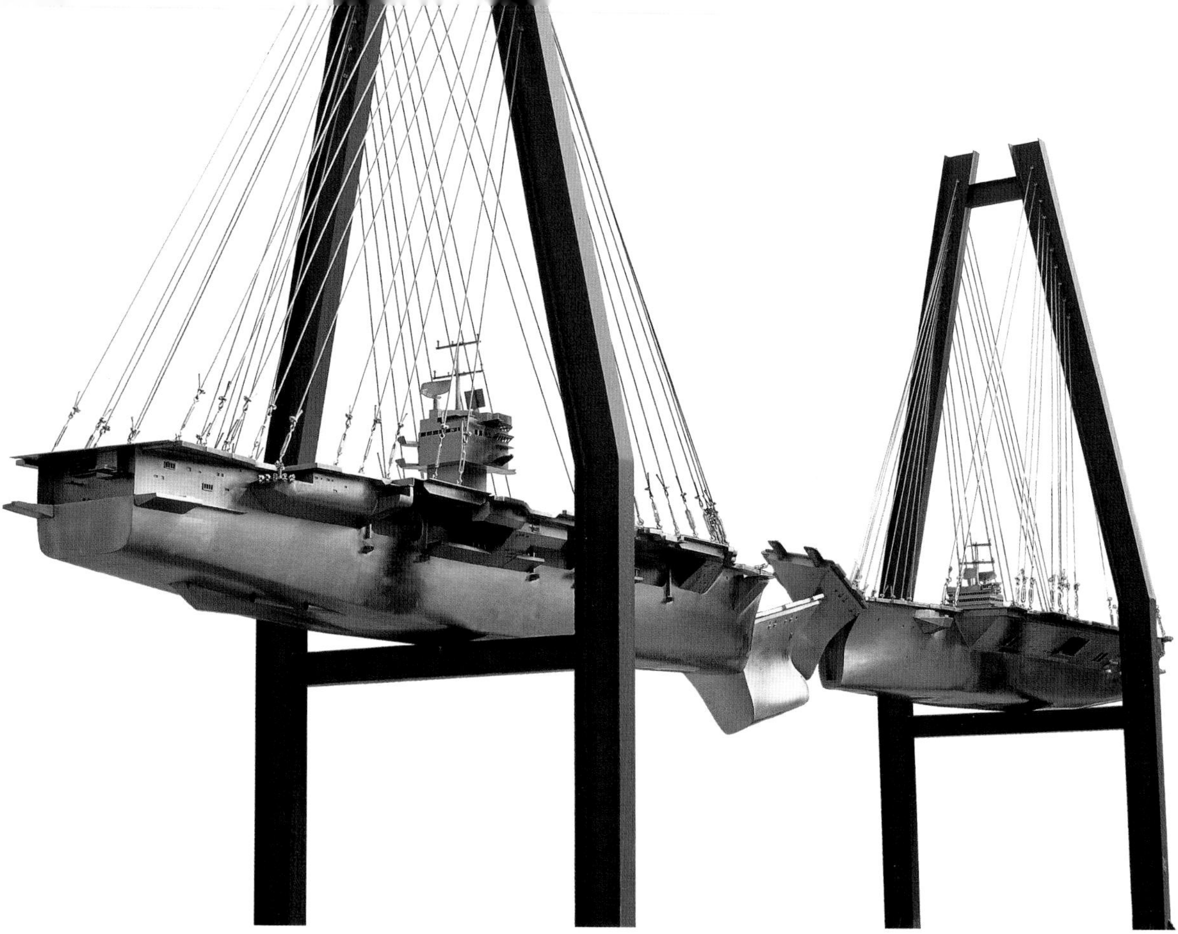

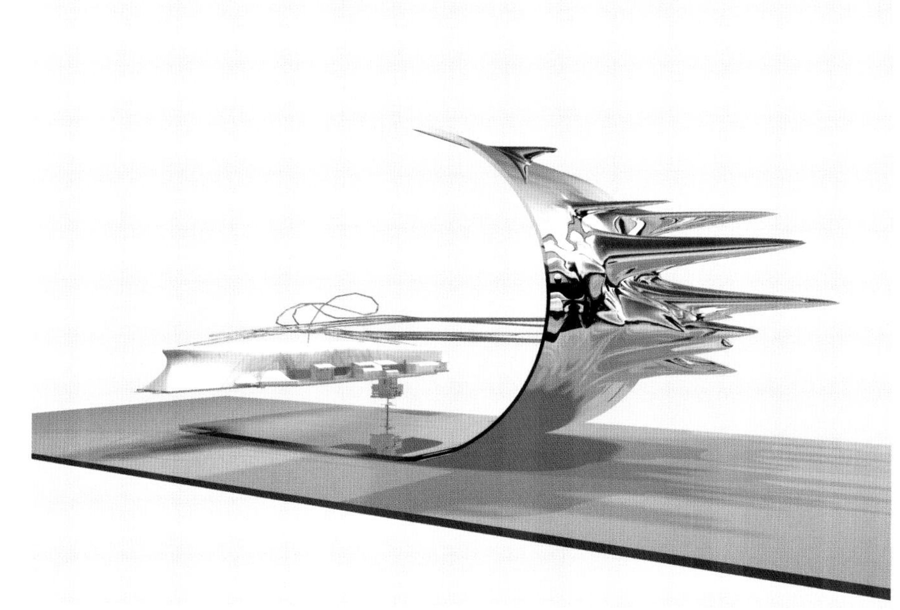

FACE-TO-FACE INTERVIEW WITH EDITORS

4/29/08 • LATE AFTERNOON • A CAFE CLOSE TO THE CENTRAL ACADEMY OF FINE ARTS, BEIJING

EDITORS *Let's talk about your childhood. Tell us first what was your favorite toy?* **LI HUI** When I was a kid I loved to play with modeling clay and shaping it into different things. **EDITORS** *Do you still remember what it was your parents said to you most often?* **LI HUI** When I lived with them they always told me, "You need to go to bed on time." **EDITORS** *Do they still tell you that today?* **LI HUI** No, not any more. After I moved out they ask me if I eat enough and regularly.

EDITORS *You just mentioned eating. Do you try to maintain a healthy lifestyle?* **LI HUI** I don't care too much about a healthy lifestyle. I usually work very intensively for a period of time. There is no time to think about anything else except work. After that period is finished, I can relax a bit and take better care of myself.

EDITORS *Name us a recent wish?* **LI HUI** I have to think about that. Can I give you an answer later? **EDITORS** *Of course. Then let's continue by asking if you believe in true love?* **LI HUI** Yes, I do! **EDITORS** *Your answer is very emphatic.* **LI HUI** Yes. But, I also think that not everyone can realize true love. **EDITORS** *What does your ideal living environment look like?* **LI HUI** I like it "natural," like the quadrangle courtyards you see in Beijing. In this "world" you can feel the harmony between nature and mankind.

EDITORS *Which type of media inspires you the most?* **LI HUI** I can't really differentiate where my inspiration comes from. Some comes from the media, particularly from the Internet, while less from television. I've banned myself from watching TV, because once I start watching I can't stop. However, inspiration also derives from simple things like chatting with friends.

EDITORS *What do you like about being an artist?* **LI HUI** I like the individualism, directness, and the honesty you can express with a piece of art. As an artist I can describe and express my ideas and then share them with others. **EDITORS** *Is there anything you dislike?* **LI HUI** I don't like the repetition of the artistic action. I think many artists are confronted with this challenge. Once they have a good idea they keep repeating it in different forms. If you do this too often it becomes embarrassing. A good artist has to face this challenge. The only way out is to continuously come up with new ideas and to reinvent.

EDITORS *Describe how you can communicate with the audience through your art?* **LI HUI** Just as poets communicate via their poems, artists communicate through their artworks. My own art allows me to address issues, which are often abstract to us, in a very direct way.

EDITORS *You were born in the mid-seventies. So, I want to ask you for five words that best describes your generation?* **LI HUI** This is difficult, but I guess individualism, subjectivity, reality, pluralism, and openness. **EDITORS** *If the whole world would listen to you for fifteen seconds what would you say?* **LI HUI** "What a wonderful time that it's my turn to speak." **EDITORS** *Finally, back to an earlier question. Give me one thing you've wished for recently?* **LI HUI** Well, I hope I can rest for a few days and find more time to play basketball with my friends.

6 BRIDGE • 2006 • STAINLESS STEEL • 360 x 800 x 160 CM

7 GU ZHENG • 2006 • STAINLESS STEEL • 200 x 300 x 150 CM

8

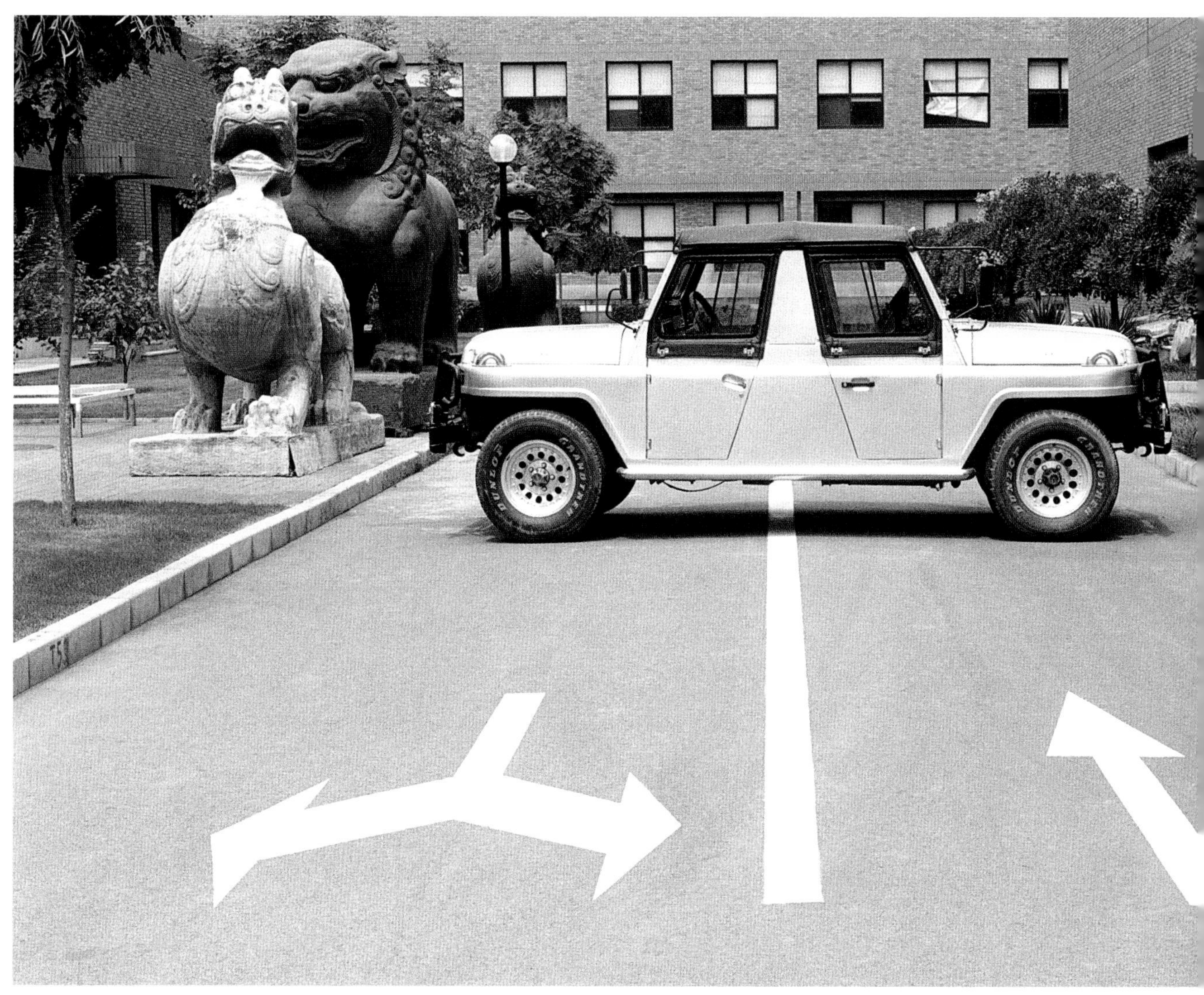

8 RENEWING JEEP • 2003 • CAR • 185 x 500 x 170 CM

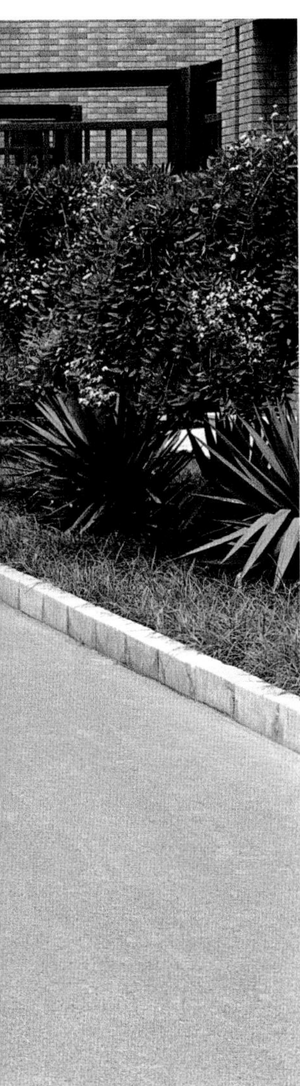

EXHIBITIONS

SELECTED SOLO EXHIBITIONS

2010
Transition,
Mannheimer Kunstverein,
Mannheim, Germany

2009
Between Dimensions,
Kuandu Museum of Fine Arts,
Taipei, Taiwan

2008
Samsara ,
Bund 18 Creative Center,
Shanghai, China

SELECTED GROUP EXHIBITIONS

2007/8
China: Facing Reality,
National Art Museum of China,
Beijing, China /
Museum Moderner Kunst Stiftung Ludwig,
Vienna, Austria

2007
The 6th Shenzhen Contemporary Sculpture Exhibition,
He Xiangning Art Museum,
Shenzhen, China

2007
Spin,
Tang Contemporary Art,
Beijing, China

2007
Floating: New Generation of Art in China,
National Museum of Contemporary Art,
Seoul, South Korea

2007
EXIT Festival,
Maison des Arts de Créteil (MAC),
Paris, France

2006
Busan Biennale,
Naru Park,
Busan, South Korea

2006
Shanghai Biennale,
Shanghai Art Museum,
Shanghai, China

2005
Chengdu Biennale,
Chengdu, China

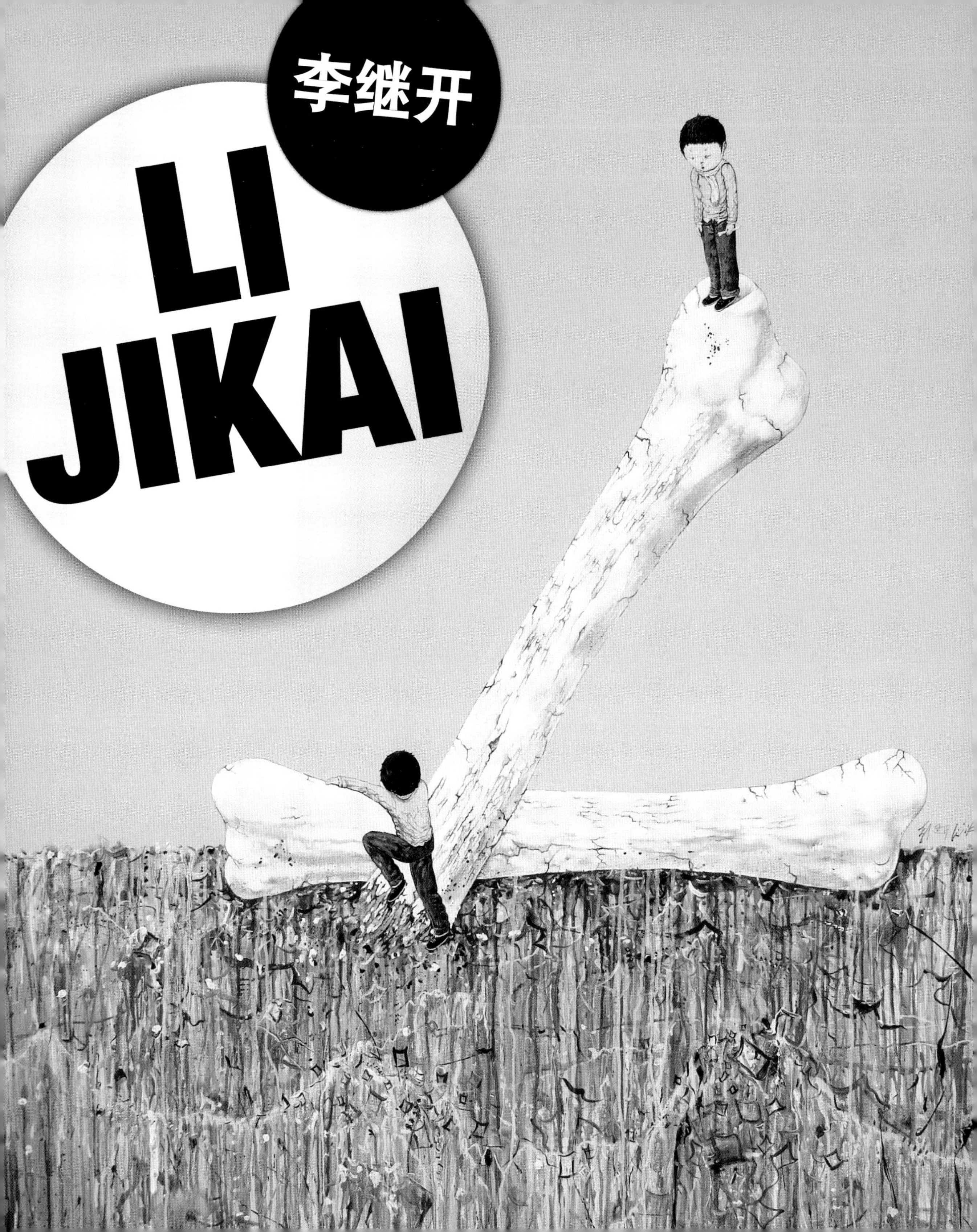
李继开
LI
JIKAI

NAME
LI JIKAI

BORN IN
1975, CHENGDU

LIVES IN
WUHAN

STUDY
SICHUAN INSTITUTE OF FINE ARTS, CHONGQING

MEDIA
PAINTING

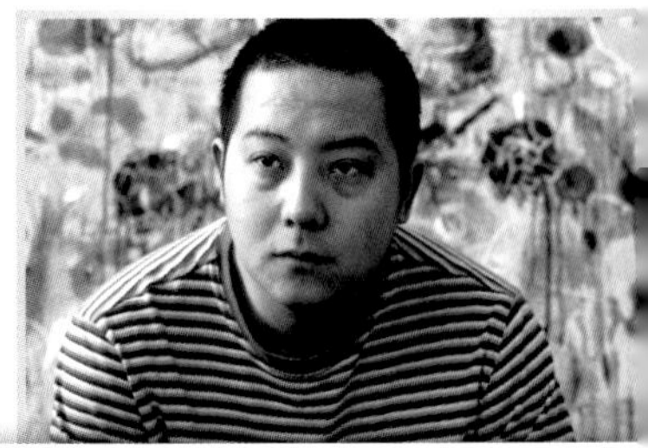

PAINTING THE DREAMS

Chinese artists born after the 1970s are today referred to as the "Me generation." One of the key exponents of this generation of artists is Li Jikai. His artistic expression has developed in a rapid and epoch-making fashion; it directly expresses new characteristics of self-psychology – confusion, loneliness, dejection, indecision, introversion, and ego. Li Jikai seems to remove himself entirely from the maelstrom of the world, taking the position of an observer of life. In his paintings he makes use of a surrealistic vocabulary to express personal reactions to the strangeness, absurdity, sorrow, suffering, and helplessness of the world. Unlike those involved with other artistic trends, Li Jikai has turned to an exploration of the subconscious activity of the personal psyche. As the metanarrative of contemporary political consciousness has gradually been eroded, the era of the collective unconscious has also drawn to an end. Replacing this is an excessive concern and protectionism of family ideology as well as the visual imagery and cultural information of the computer age. Li Jikai has begun a process of reflection on what the "self" truly means in such a cultural environment. As he sees things, "I" has been virtually transformed into a tame object like a helpless doll. But the self that he is concerned with is not mere narcissism, but rather an attempt to highlight a body of consciousness in relation to the self and the objective world.

Another key feature of Li Jikai's art is his reliance on dreamscapes. As dreams are emotional, unreal, surreal, and psychologically analytical, it is precisely these fantastic properties of dreamscapes that lead Li Jikai to reconstruct their illogical, abnormal images and absurd content. He subjectively binds "objects" (excrement, animals, airplanes, tables, garbage, building blocks, rowboats) and "people" together. This is a type of purely subconscious evocation and pursuit of dreams. In *Gigantic Dustheap* (2006), he portrays a lonely child amongst piles of garbage. The child's weak, skinny body creates a marked contrast, as the tiny figure seems to be drowning in the objects surrounding it. In *Bones of Giant* (2007), he portrays two people standing at either end of an enormous bone, metaphorically representing life and death. These two works both use a completely illogical narrative language, making them seem like daydreams. In *We Want to Go Afar* (2007) and *An End for a Start* (2006), Li Jikai very astutely situates the small person standing on the table and the child standing on a mushroom in reality, as if recounting his inner sorrow or a painful secret to the audience. Li Jikai's paintings contain neither a modernist exploration of absolute truth nor a postmodernist attitude of cynicism; instead they analyze the meaning of the existence of the self, and the indeterminate conflict between the inner psyche and the external world. It is this aesthetic tone that dominates the Post-70s "Me generation."

Li Jikai condenses "I" into an infant age and defines it as a memory of the most beatific moments in the process of life and maturation. In other words, he deliberately portrays "I" as a person who has never grown up, because the childhood psyche is always connected with a form of simple and pure memory. However, this fantasy of beauty is by no means the pursuit of absolute perfection; it is rather the psychological activity of leaving reality to delve into a certain type of personal unease. Works such as *Clear Day* (2005), *Take Off? Get Ready!* (2005), *Fragments* (2006), and *High Place* (2006) demonstrate the moral undertone of his paintings – worry, panic, and sorrow. It is from this that Li Jikai constructs his reflections on the past. He uses art to seek out the loss of the self, and it is in this seeking of the self that the true meaning of art lies.

It is worth noting that Li Jikai has strived to minimize the image of "I" in spatial terms, making the images more subjective. It is precisely this "minimization" of the selection and interception of people that "maximizes" the significance of space. He often places a solitary, lonely child in a vast, empty space, thereby creating a detached dreamscape. At the same time, the simple cartoonish images establish a humorous mood. He confines himself within a world of self, and yet immerses himself in a world where the self appears insignificant. In works such as *End of the World* (2006) and *Flying Firefly* (2006), he also highlights a turbulent atmosphere through the use of free-floating lines. These edgy, fairytale-like paintings are a surrealistic experience – a metaphor for the dreamscape of the self-psyche, an allegory of the deep extinction of the self.

Li Jikai's work fits into the overall trends of twenty-first-century contemporary Chinese art. By breaking out of mainstream consciousness, and due to the disappearance of a collective consciousness, artists are returning to the individual and looking back at personal experiences and values from a microcosmic perspective. In other words, they are describing their personal memories and circumstances using a personalized artistic vocabulary, while endowing their works with a vast palette of metaphorical meanings. Li Jikai's style of painting is both conventional and wild, with motion and stillness going hand in hand. The characters he creates have almost animalistic expressions on their faces. The round eyes, rabbit-like mouths, and disturbing expressions are characteristic of his works. The audience cannot help but be moved by pity, and grows to love each character.

By Huang Du

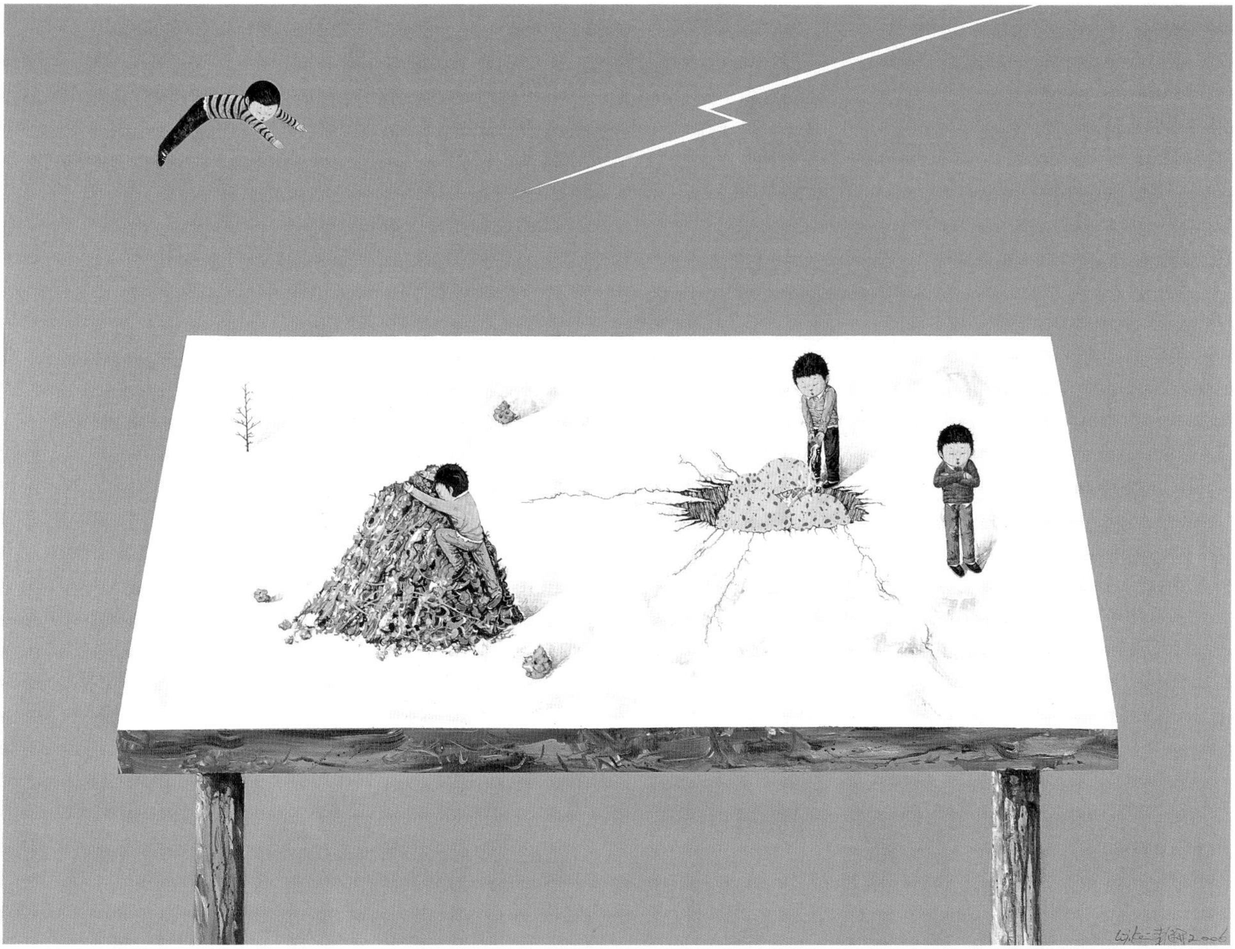

2

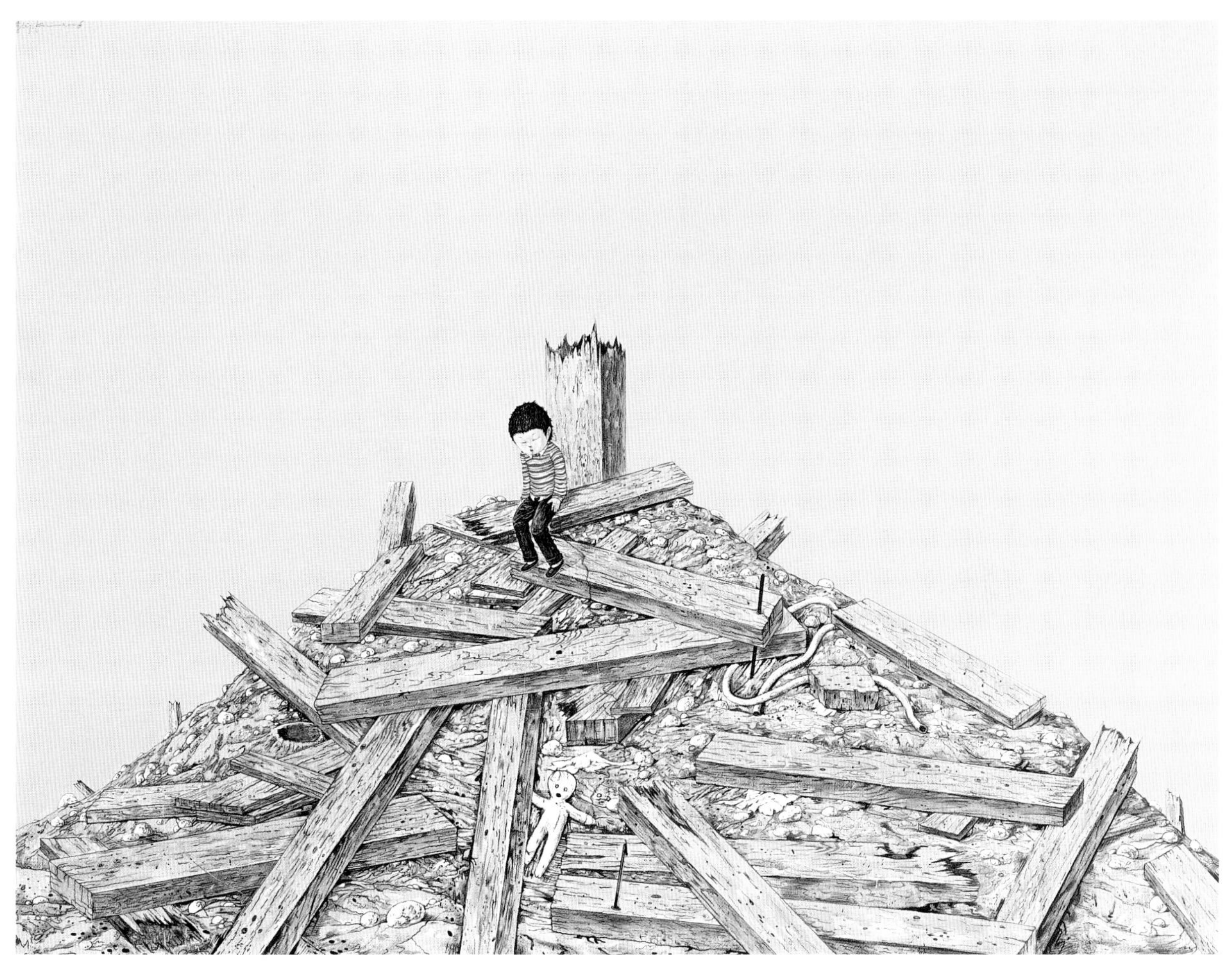

1 AN END FOR A START • 2006 • ACRYLIC ON CANVAS • 150 x 200 CM

2 GIGANTIC DUSTHEAP • 2006 • ACRYLIC ON CANVAS • 150 x 200 CM

3

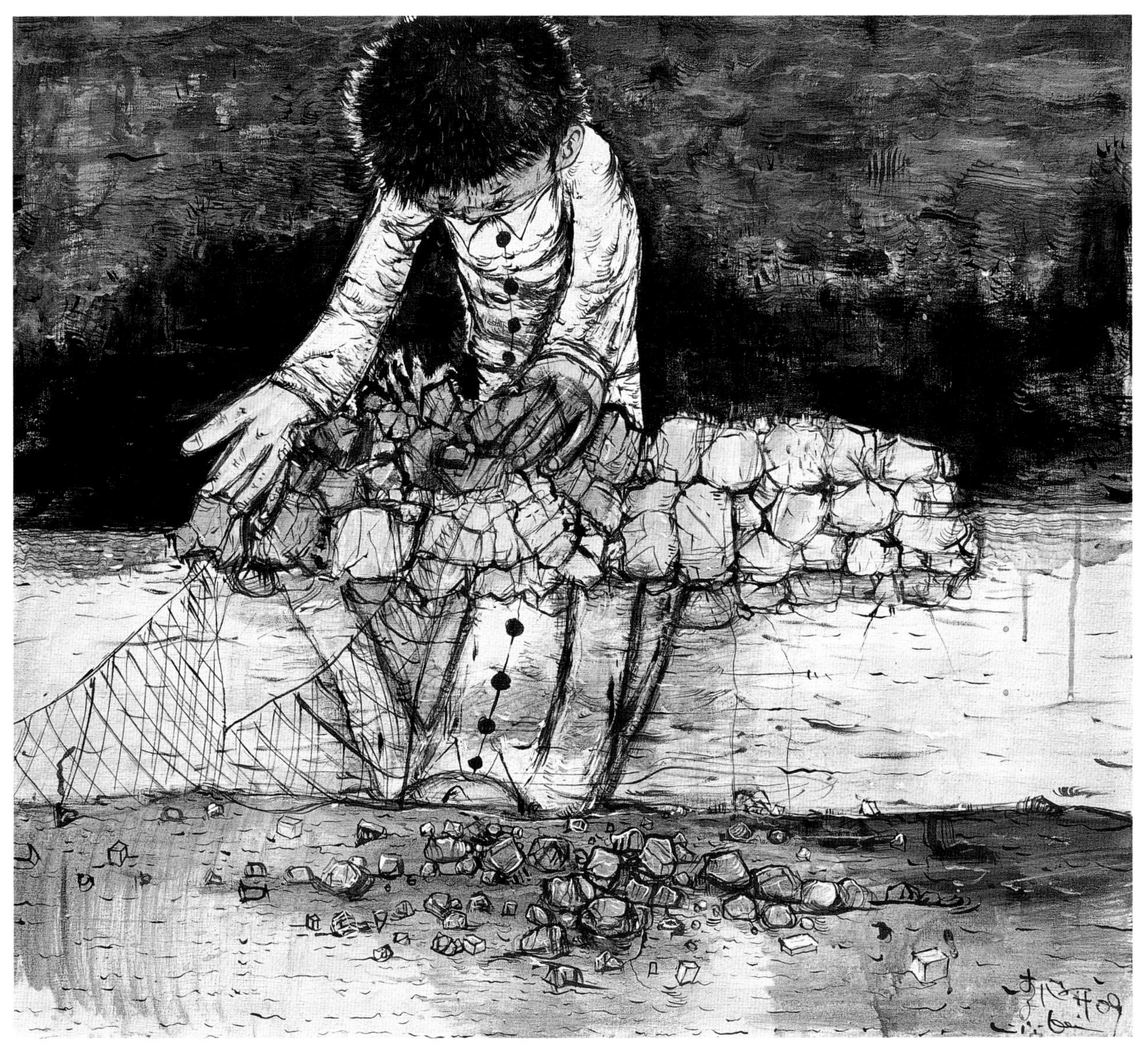

3 NET • 2009 • ACRYLIC ON CANVAS • 70 x 80 CM

4 SHARP KNIFE • 2004 • ACRYLIC ON CANVAS • 48 x 39 CM

4

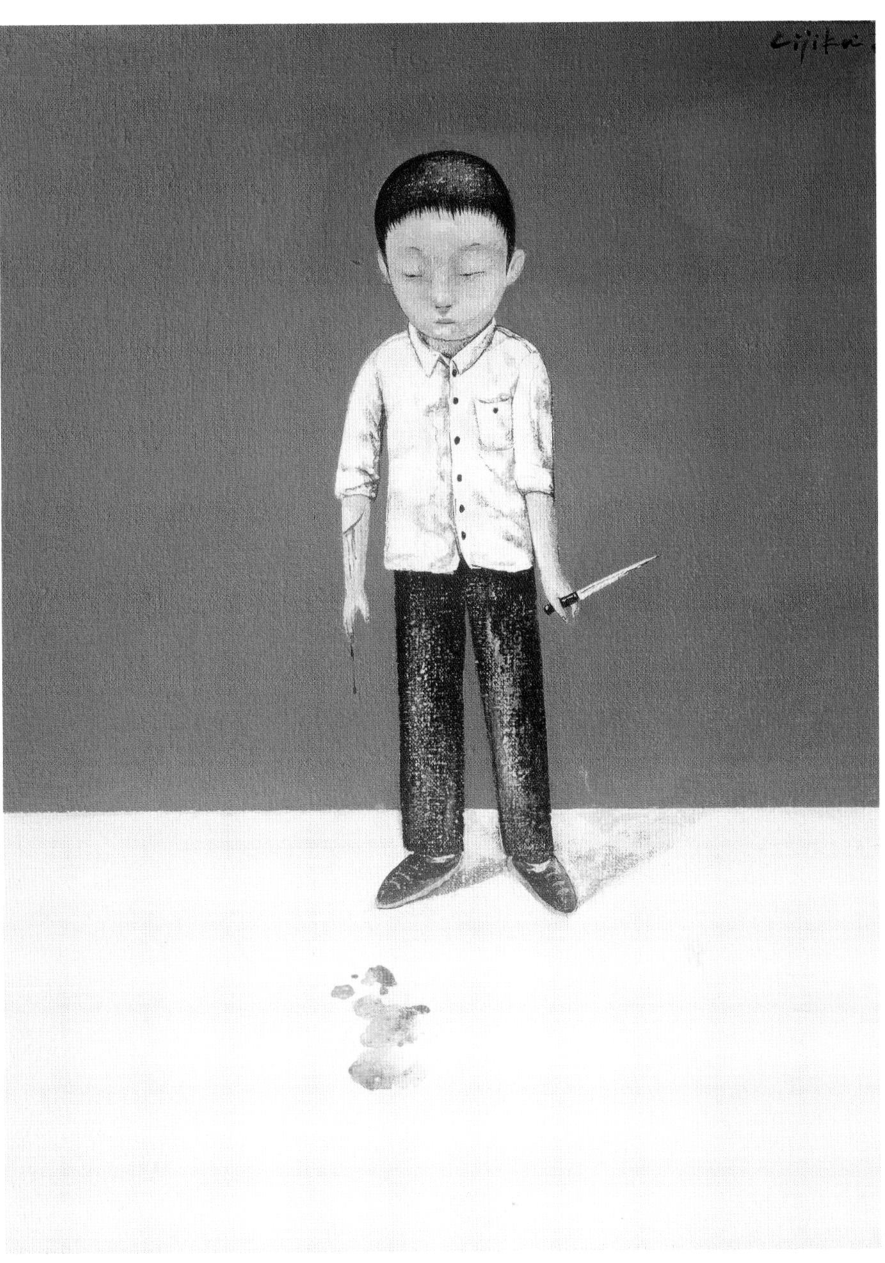

5

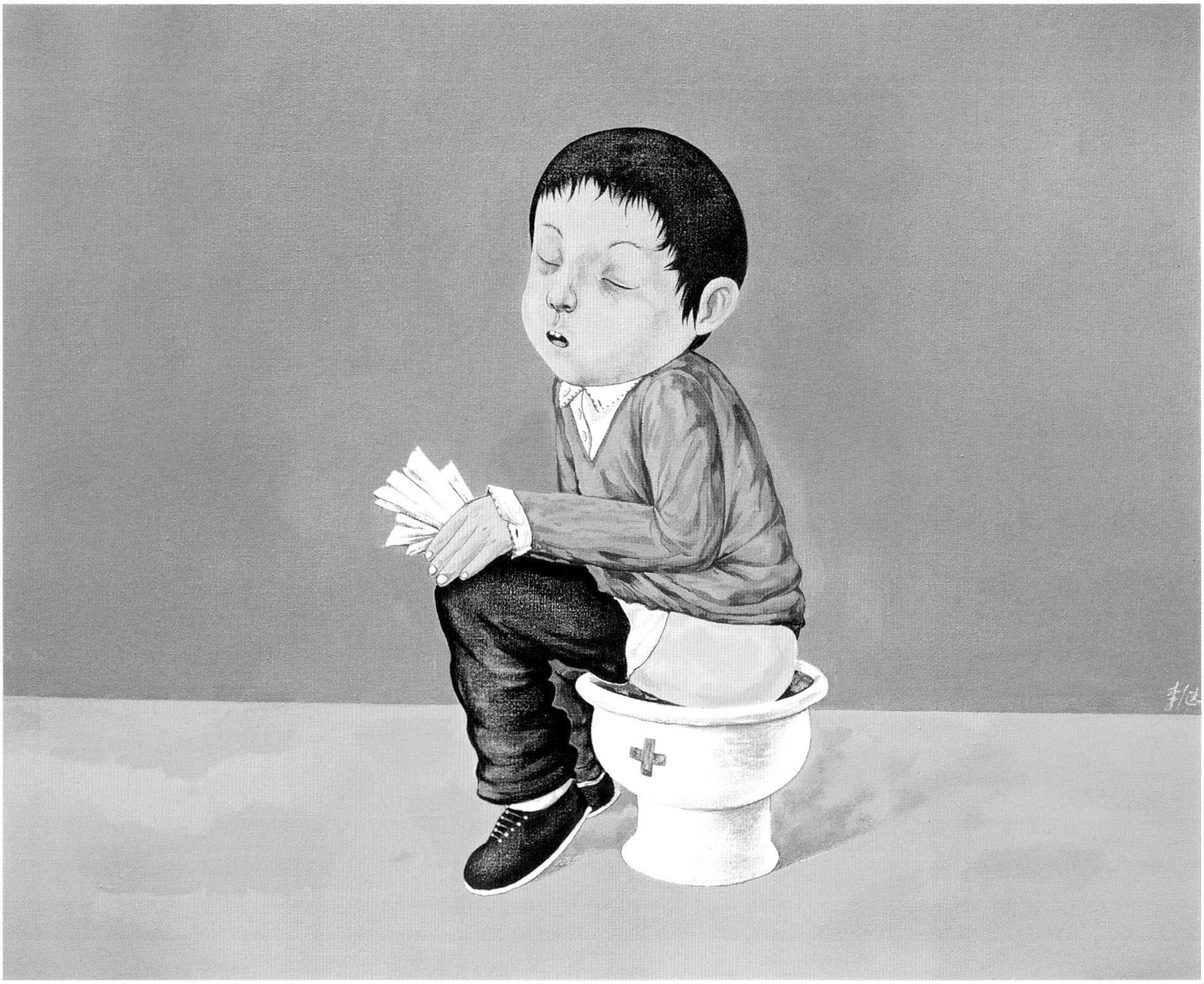

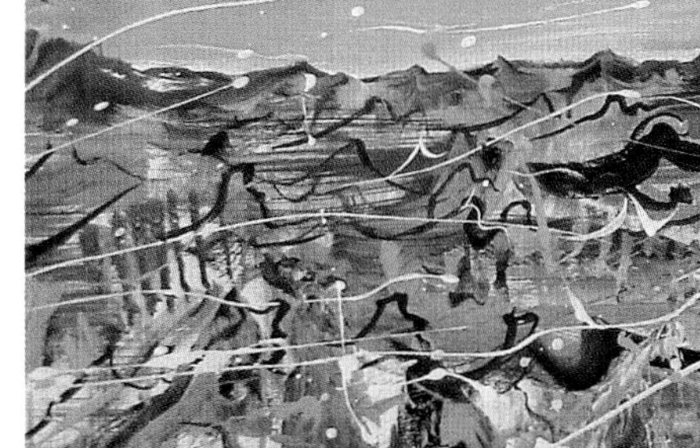

5 CLEAR DAY • 2005 • ACRYLIC ON CANVAS • 100 x 100 CM

6 BOY ON MUSHROOM • 2005 • ACRYLIC ON CANVAS • 200 x 150 CM

7 FLYING FIREFLY NO. 1 • 2006 • ACRYLIC ON CANVAS • 50 x 200 CM

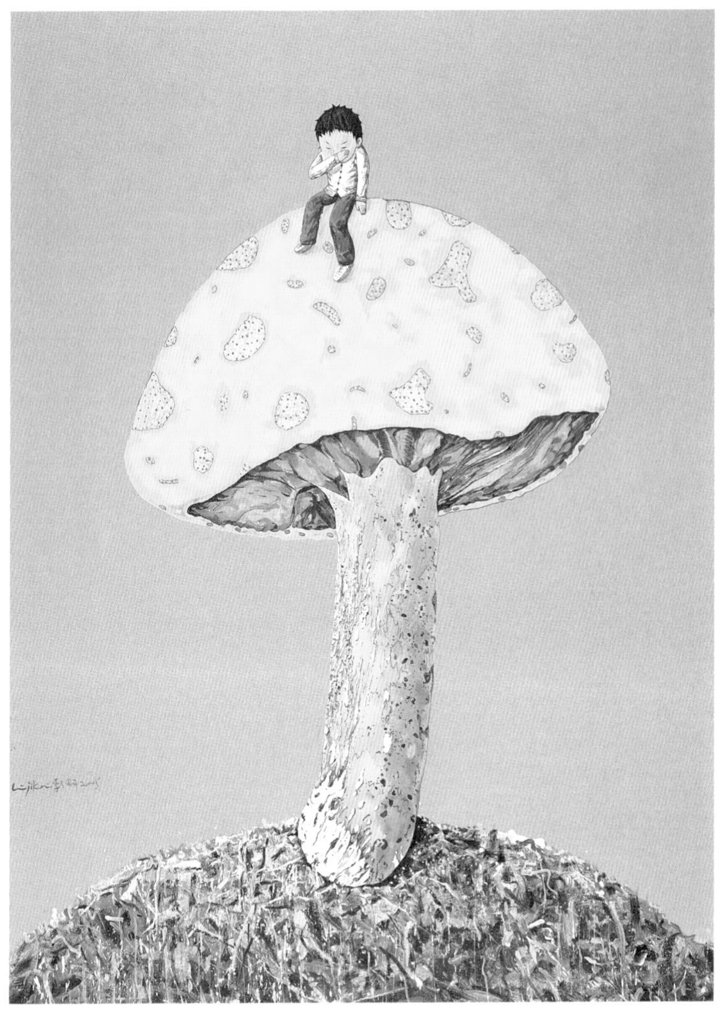

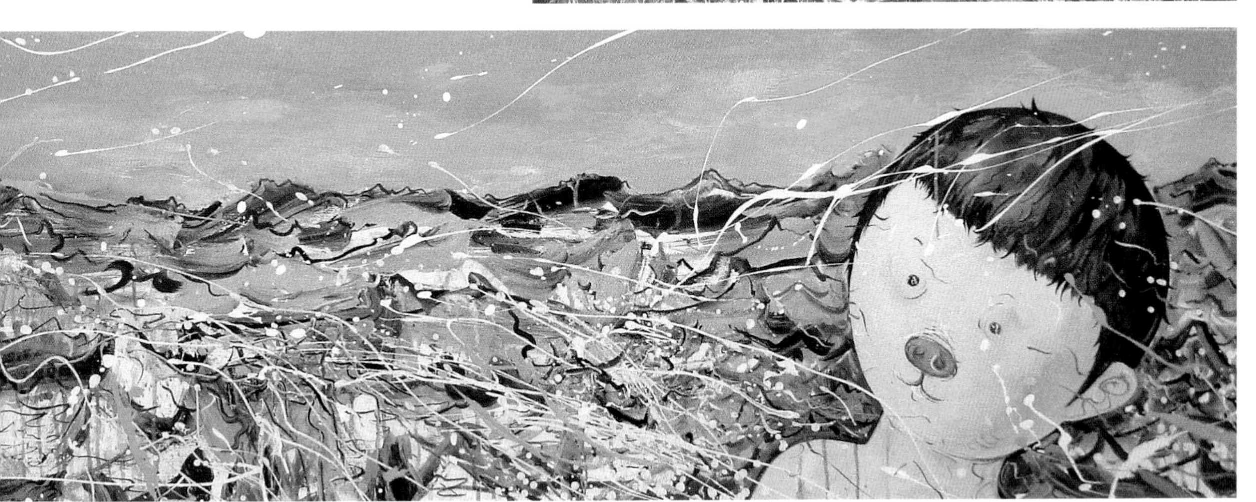

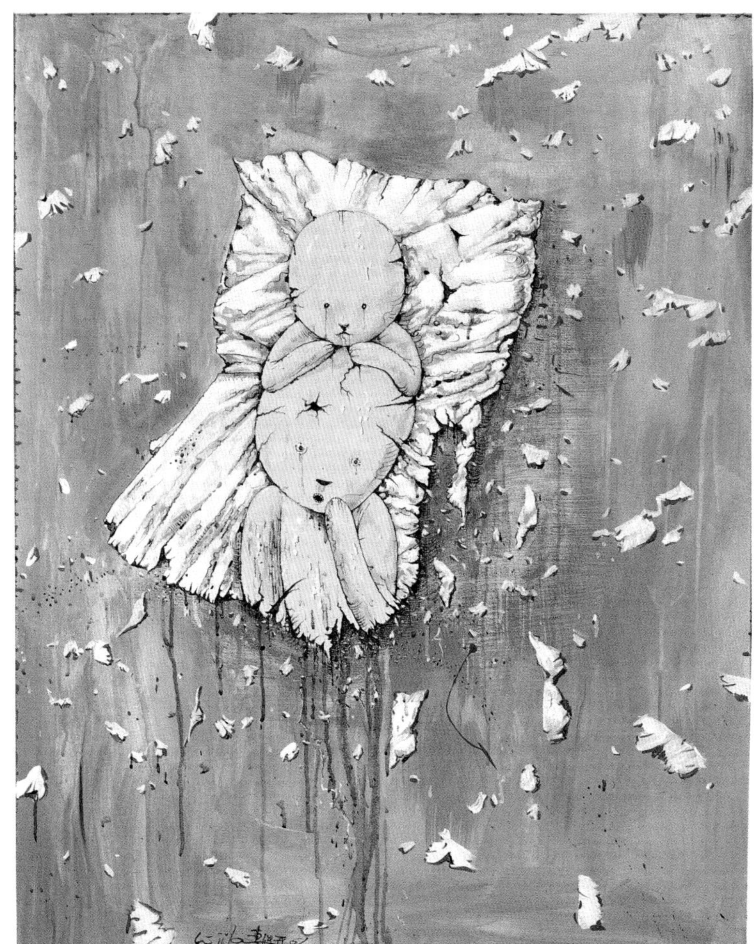

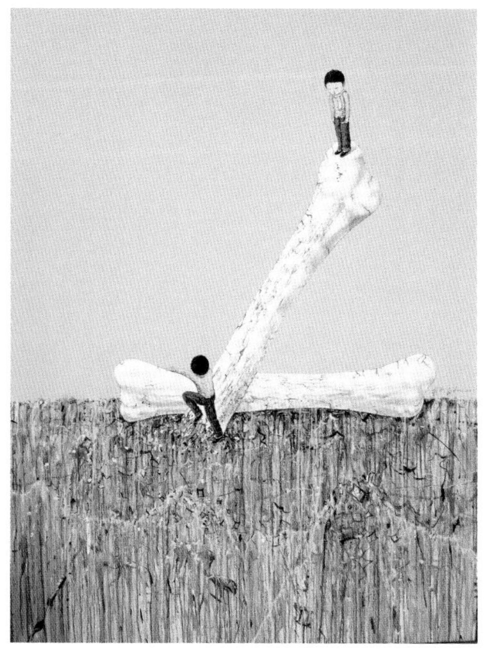

8 FRAGMENTS • 2006 • ACRYLIC ON CANVAS • 100 x 80 CM

9 BONES OF GIANT • 2007 • ACRYLIC ON CANVAS • 200 x 150 CM

QUESTIONNAIRE

BEGINNING OF MAY • WUHAN

WHAT WAS YOUR FAVORITE CHILDHOOD TOY?

An airplane and a peashooter.

WHAT DID YOUR PARENTS SAY TO YOU MOST OFTEN?

"What would you like to eat today?"

HOW DO YOU TRY TO STAY HEALTHY IN YOUR EVERYDAY LIFE?

I don't care much about my health. To me, healthy living means good eating, good sleeping, and appropriate exercise.

WHAT HAVE YOU BEEN WISHING FOR MOST RECENTLY?

To be able to relax in a quiet environment with nice scenery.

DO YOU BELIEVE IN TRUE LOVE?

Maybe.

WHAT DOES YOUR IDEAL LIVING ENVIRONMENT LOOK LIKE?

A place where there are hills and rivers ... and no mosquitoes.

FROM WHICH TYPE OF MEDIA DO YOU DERIVE MOST OF YOUR INSPIRATION?

I can get a lot of inspiration just from reading.

WHAT DO YOU LIKE/DISLIKE ABOUT BEING AN ARTIST?

I like that artists have relatively more freedom in their lives, and that they can do things they like to do.
I dislike that some people have no respect for artists.

HOW DO YOU COMMUNICATE WITH THE AUDIENCE IN YOUR ART?

Through my works, but it's a limited form of communication. My main purpose is to create works that fulfill my own needs.

IF YOU HAD FIVE WORDS TO DESCRIBE YOUR GENERATION, WHAT WOULD THEY BE?

Effort, egoism, confusion, naivety, and maturity.

IF THE WHOLE WORLD WOULD LISTEN TO YOU FOR FIFTEEN SECONDS, WHAT WOULD YOU SAY?

I've never thought about that. When it comes up, I think I will have something to say.

EXHIBITIONS

SELECTED SOLO EXHIBITIONS

2008
Li Jikai,
Arario Gallery,
Seoul, South Korea

2008
Unorderly Branches: Paintings of Li Jikai,
Fine Arts Literature Art Center,
Wuhan, China

2007/8
Clear: The Solo Exhibition of Li Jikai,
Today Art Museum,
Beijing, China /
Shanghai Art Museum,
Shanghai, China

SELECTED GROUP EXHIBITIONS

2009
Chinamania,
ARKEN Museum of Modern Art,
Copenhagen, Denmark

2007
From Rural Modernity to Urban Utopia,
National Art Museum of China,
Beijing, China

2007
China Now,
Cobra Museum,
Amsterdam, The Netherlands

2007
Varied Images:
China's Contemporary Paintings,
Shanghai Art Museum,
Shanghai, China

2007
The First Today's Documents:
Energy–Spirit, Body, Material,
Today Art Museum,
Beijing, China

2006
Beyond Dimension: Chinese New Painting,
Nanjing Square Contemporary Art Museum,
Nanjing, China

2006
The Self-Made Generation:
A Retrospective of New Chinese Painting,
Zendai Museum of Modern Art,
Shanghai, China

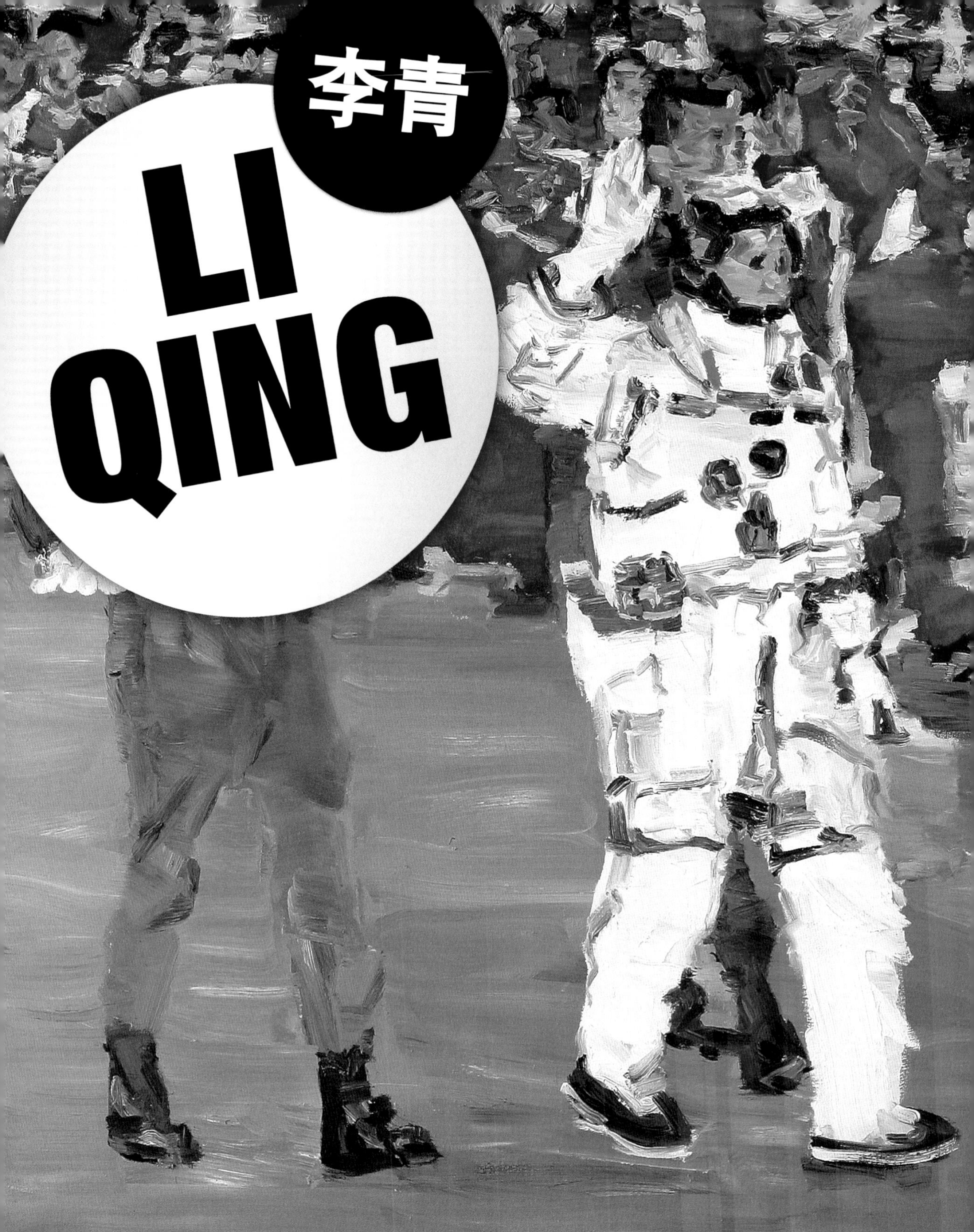
李青
LI
QING

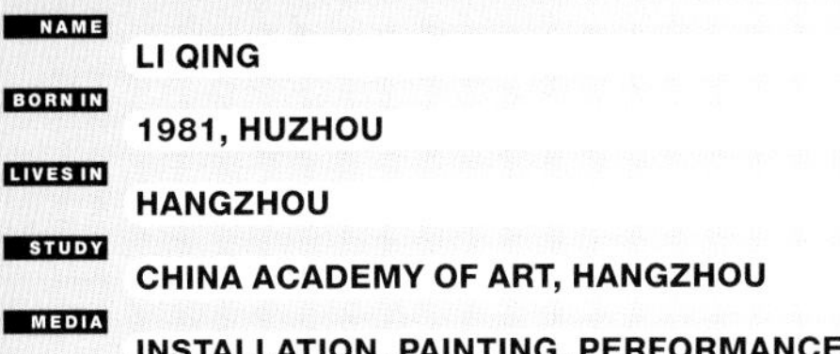

NAME LI QING
BORN IN 1981, HUZHOU
LIVES IN HANGZHOU
STUDY CHINA ACADEMY OF ART, HANGZHOU
MEDIA INSTALLATION, PAINTING, PERFORMANCE

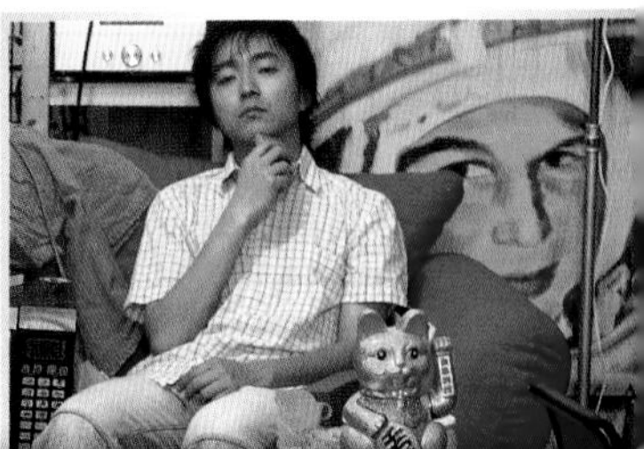

FISHING FOR THE WILLING

"Fishing for the willing" is both a common expression on Li Qing's blog as well as the phrase that best sums up his artistic spirit. In his works, Li throws out many hooks for the viewers, but is it also possible that the fisherman himself unwittingly becomes one of the willing that takes the bait? It is necessary to be aware that the birth of a work of art is an "event" in the history of art, which has both internal and external reasons. In the same way, the process of painting a painting is also an "event" – an event in a continuous context.

A look at Li Qing's works to date brings forth the following keywords: Magritte-like language games, multiple time perspectives, deconstruction, social image resources, form, etc. As with many other young artists, Li Qing's system of language is simple, powerful, and yet distinct. It is not so much that the language systems of "young artists" are imperfect, but rather that they are extremely difficult to generalize. What they reveal is not a system, but a fragment. Each work is like a cell, all of them sharing a common lineage; the thinking behind their rationale and consequences is undoubtedly interconnected, but the connection is not clear.

Commonly shared visual experiences often form the basis of Li Qing's work. This has its origins in the "deconstruction of the metanarrative." Li Qing's definition of this includes various forms of meaning and things that have already been over-utilized in historical culture, and of course also includes previously acknowledged rights, values, and methods of regulation. The series *Point out the Difference*, started in 2005, is probably the best-known series of his work. The inspiration comes from a computer game that tests the player's visual perception by finding the differences between two similar pictures. The differences are always focused on the gestures and expressions of the characters or on some surrounding details. In *Wedding* (2006), for example, Li Qing based his images on the documentary film of the wedding between Prince Charles and Lady Diana. The differences between the two images lie in the movements of the royal family members as well as in the child who accompanied the newlyweds. Many of these details provoke us to spontaneously associate the wedding with related things and secrets that have puzzled us until the present.

Li Qing doesn't intend to use the concept of "deconstruction of the metanarrative" in its philosophical sense, but rather uses the "deconstruction of records" in his own works to substantiate this concept. His approach stems from a process of doubting and inquiring about traditional linguistic resources. One could say that he is interested in the methodology of "deconstruction" itself. What he wants to deconstruct is vacuous expression. Li Qing's ultimate objective is to find a new methodology beyond deconstruction and to search for constructive meaning during the process of moving "behind the metanarrative."

So, in *People Swept Away by the Qiantang River Tide* (2007) a marked contrast is formed between the real scene and its visual appeal, as he defines such visual appeal within the scope of the "metanarrative." Many of the deconstructive methods found in Li Qing's works involve creating two images and allowing interplay between them. For this reason, his works often appear in pairs, such as *Point out the Difference* and *Collision* (2007). The creative thought process behind these works is consistent with that of *People Swept Away by the Qiantang River Tide;* a single entity is created from two pictures, one an impression and the other a real image, while a third picture is generated by the forcible fusion of the two.

"Even after the background and subject are removed, works retain their power and soul." This is what Li Qing expects of a perfect work of art, and it is also an important element in his artistic world – the essentially constructive nature of form. Consequently, he values the role of form in completing the process of interaction between a work and its audience. However, he says: "The work should tend towards conceptualization, while minimizing its conversion into experience."

In 2007, Li Qing began working on the series *Ping Pong*. In the first works of this series maps of China and America were painted on each side of a Ping Pong table. When the paint was still wet, he invited some friends to play Ping Pong using that table. The Ping Pong ball jumped on the wet paint, leaving blotches everywhere. In *Ping Pong 2* (2008), he chose a different approach. For this work, Li Qing first placed some wet paint smudges on the table and then put the Ping Pong balls on top of the still wet color. With the drying of the paints the balls became fixed. These soft things were inlayed in hard things, having both interaction and confrontation, just as the Ping Pong game. It is in the relationship between the two forces that Li Qing is interested. The *Ping Pong* series is a big step in the intensity of the artist's trans-media research. Now that he has made the first step to go beyond paintings, why not go all the way and shed the restriction of any media in general? This question has its roots in the doubts of the art circle about the production thoroughness of the post-eighties artist generation.

By Song Yi

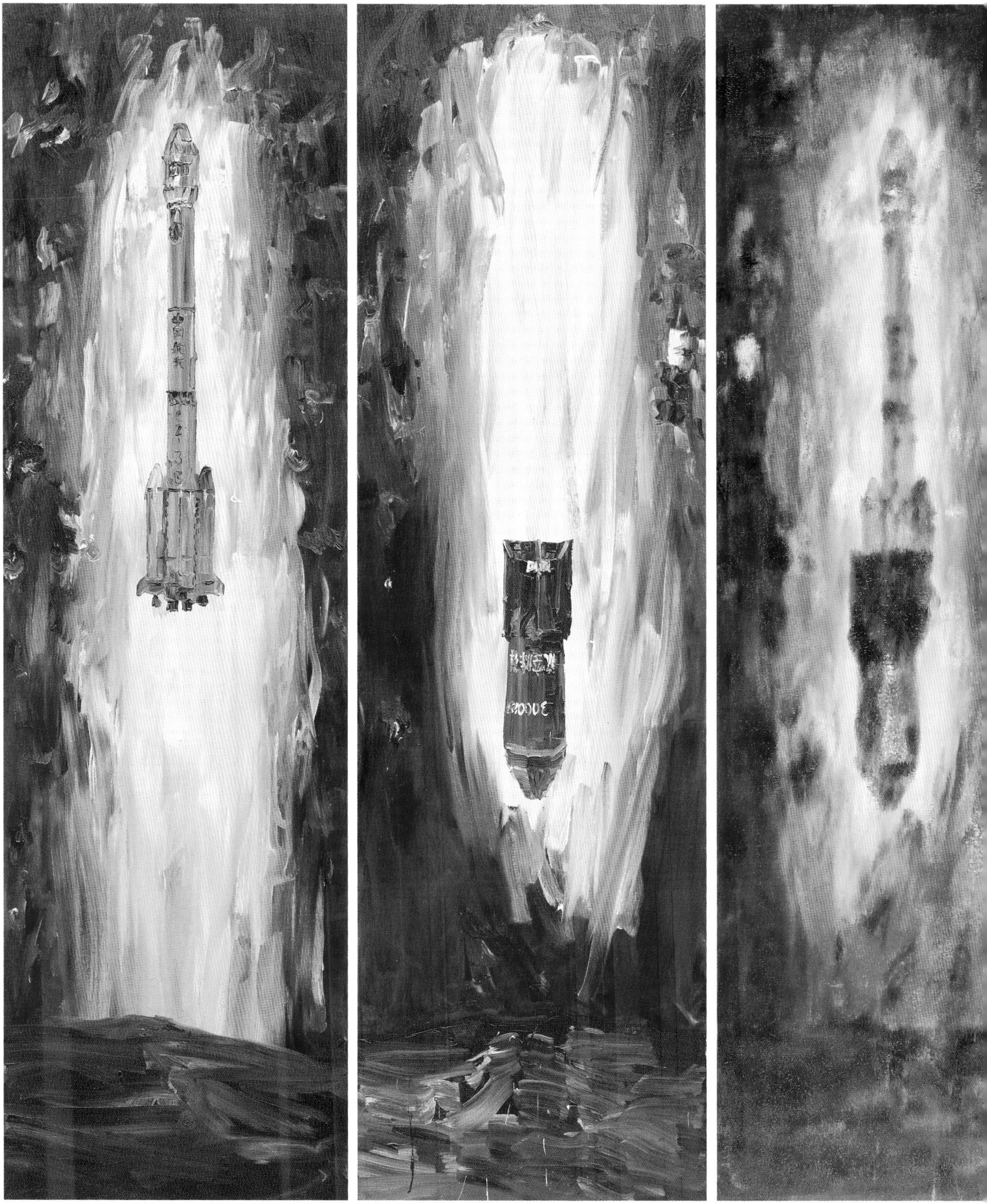

1
A B C D

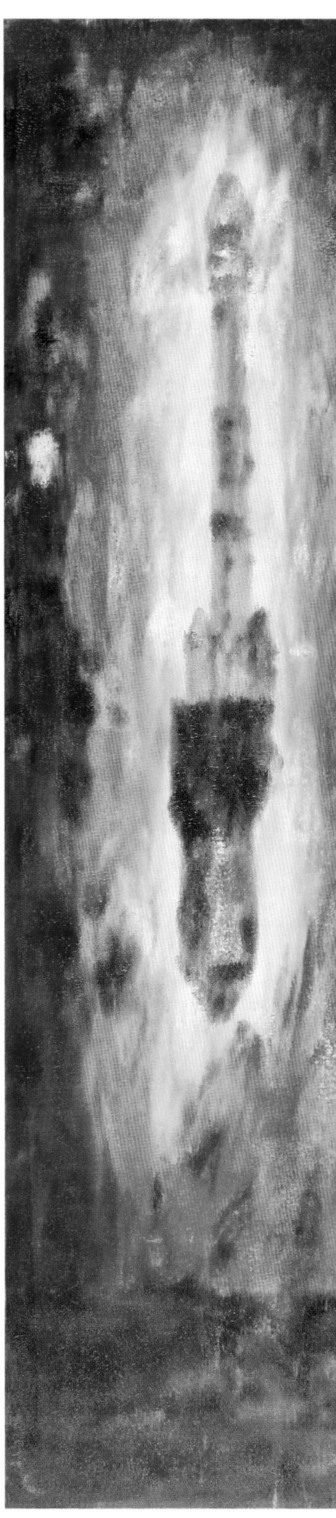

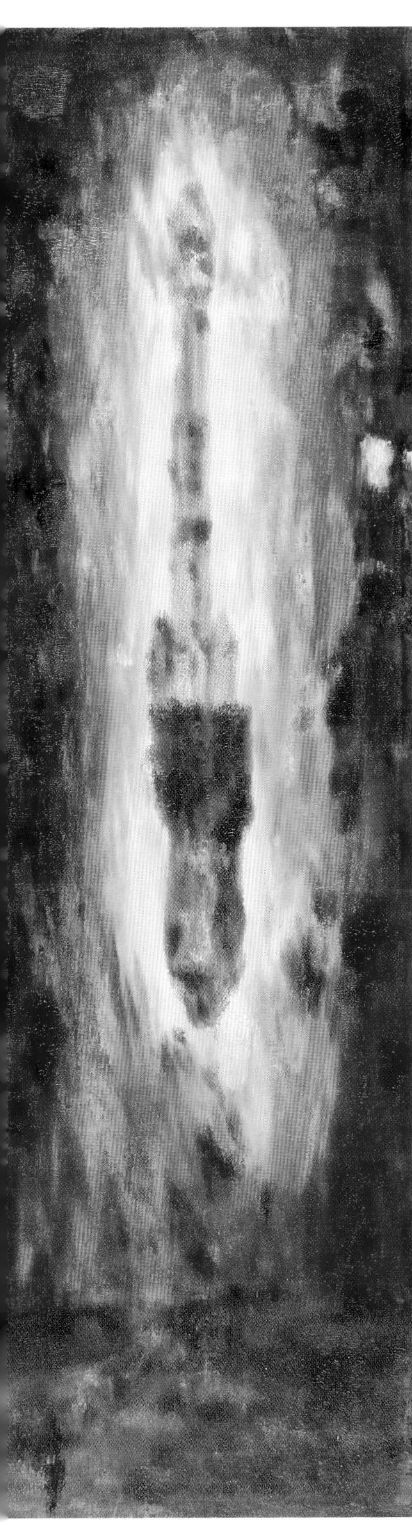

1 MUTUAL UNDOING AND UNITY: MIXED WEAPON • 2007 • OIL ON CANVAS • 300 x 90 CM (x4)

2
A B

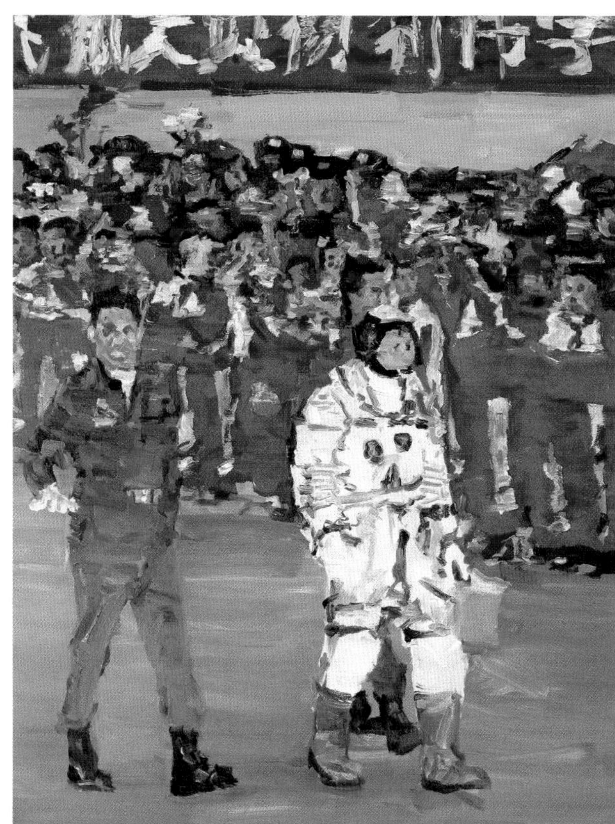

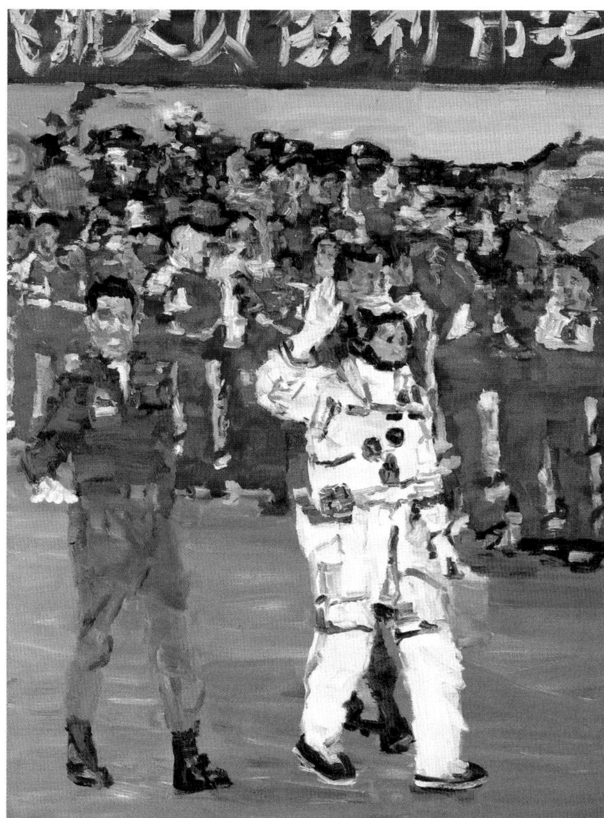

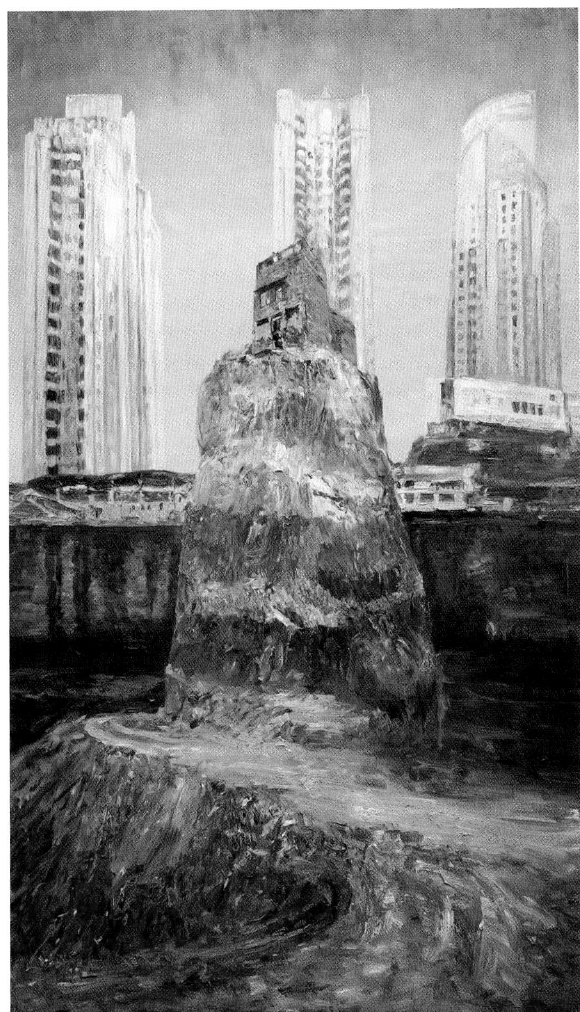

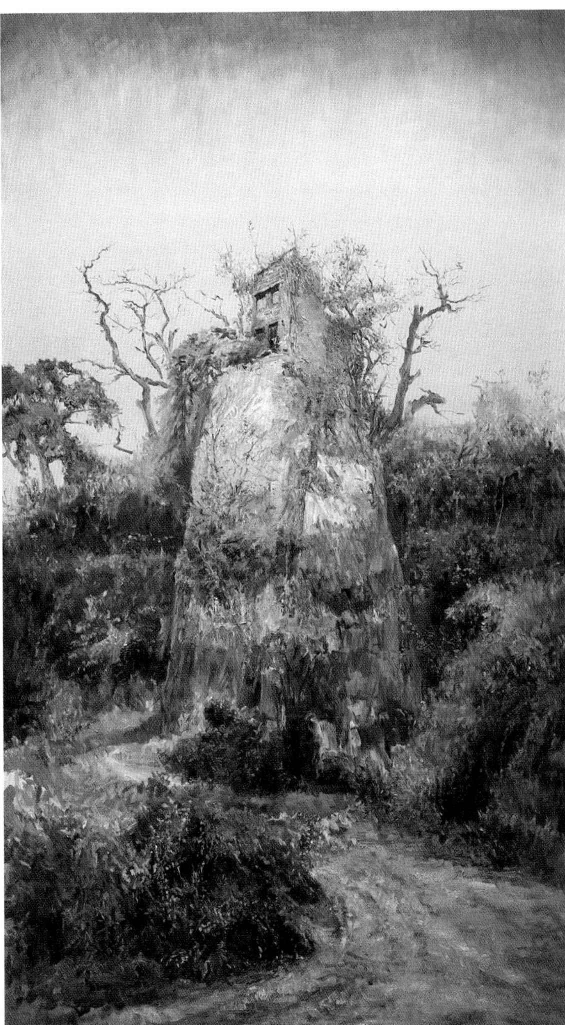

2 HERO'S RETURN (THERE ARE 8 DIFFERENCES IN THE TWO PAINTINGS) • 2005 • OIL ON CANVAS • 170 x 130 CM (x2)

3 A HUNDRED YEAR NAIL • 2008 • OIL ON CANVAS AND PHOTO • 365 x 210 CM (x2)

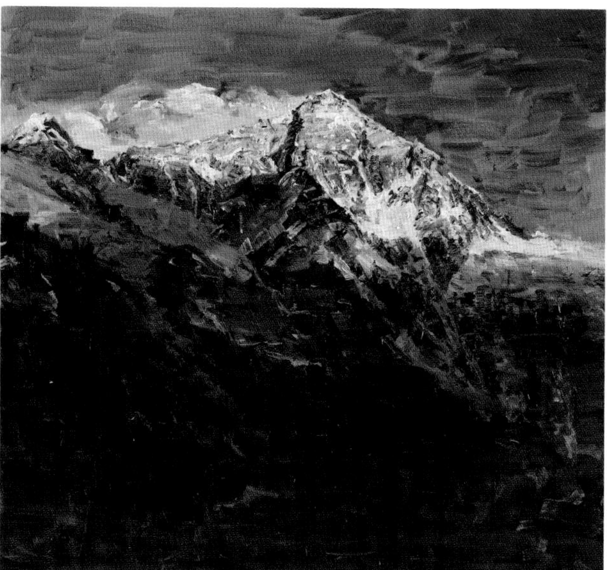

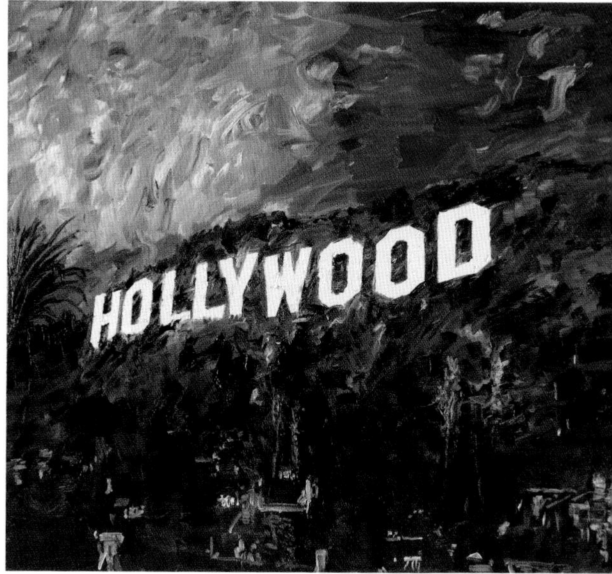

QUESTIONNAIRE

4/30/08 • HANGZHOU

WHAT WAS YOUR FAVORITE CHILDHOOD TOY?

Transformers.

WHAT DID YOUR PARENTS SAY TO YOU MOST OFTEN?

They hoped that I would be healthy. When I was a child, they said to me, "You should eat more." Now they often say, "You must have more rest."

HOW DO YOU TRY TO STAY HEALTHY IN YOUR EVERYDAY LIFE?

I don't care much about my health.

WHAT HAVE YOU BEEN WISHING FOR MOST RECENTLY?

To open a shop and sell interesting things.

DO YOU BELIEVE IN TRUE LOVE?

Yes, because I am just a human being. True love is a beautiful thing. Even hatred and harshness can not get in the way of true love.

WHAT DOES YOUR IDEAL LIVING ENVIRONMENT LOOK LIKE?

I will cite an advertisement, "You have a good sight of the hills and water, and you enjoy the prosperity whether you progress in your career or retire and friends come to visit you from far places." (This is an adaptation of a saying by the philosopher Confucius.)

FROM WHICH TYPE OF MEDIA DO YOU DERIVE MOST OF YOUR INSPIRATION?

My inspiration doesn't come from the media. The media is only an instrument, and we can decide whether to use it or not.

WHAT DO YOU LIKE/DISLIKE ABOUT BEING AN ARTIST?

I like the free and individual way an artist is able to work. It suits the people (including me) who hate boring regulations. The different contents of the work create a long-lasting feeling. I can be offensive in my works or I can break a taboo; in turn, this enables me to stay calm in living daily life as a simple person.
I don't like solving many technical problems. This feeling gets even stronger over time.

HOW DO YOU COMMUNICATE WITH THE AUDIENCE IN YOUR ART?

Those who are willing to understand can understand. The viewers have many things in their heart, but maybe they are unaware of it, so I make a "map of hidden treasures" for them. Whether they begin searching with the help of the map, and what they may find is up to them, and I can't influence that.

IF YOU HAD FIVE WORDS TO DESCRIBE YOUR GENERATION, WHAT WOULD THEY BE?

Conceit, sensibility, narcissism, bravery, and calmness.

IF THE WHOLE WORLD WOULD LISTEN TO YOU FOR FIFTEEN SECONDS, WHAT WOULD YOU SAY?

Fifteen seconds are too long. It's a waste of time for all the people.

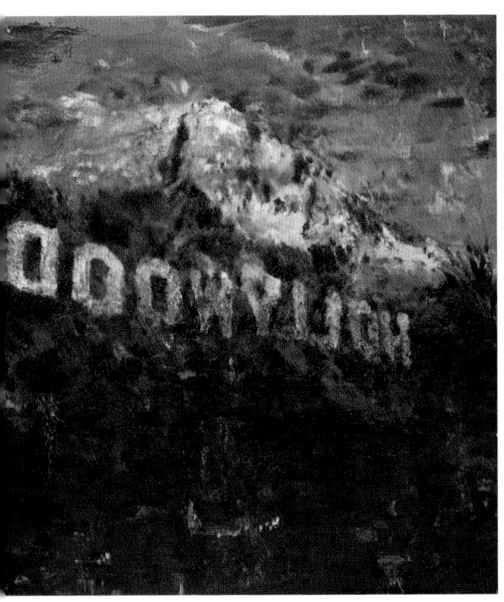
DOOWYLLOH

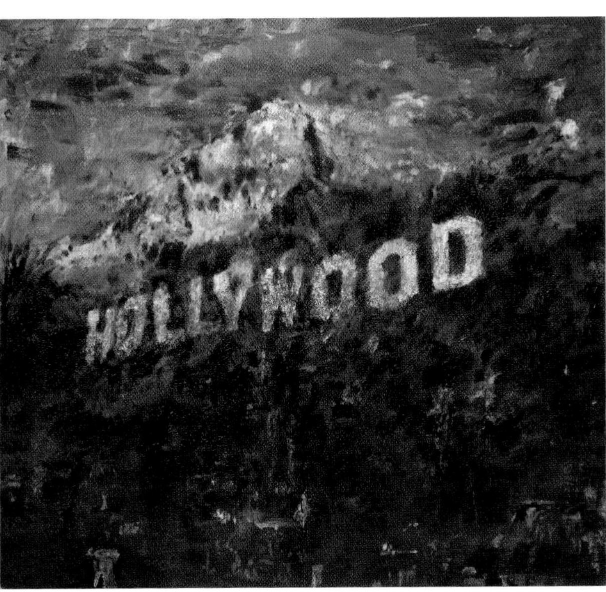
HOLLYWOOD

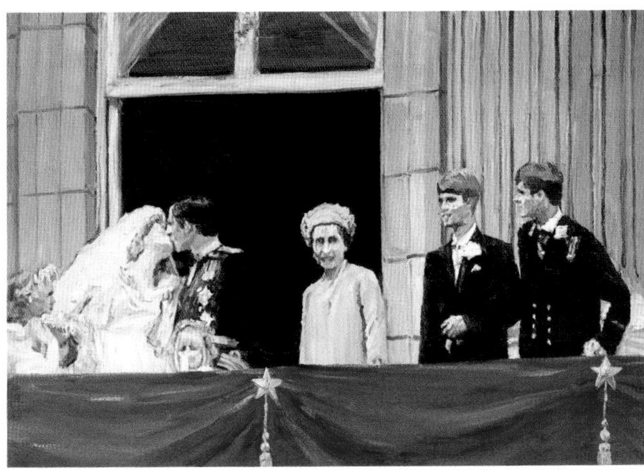

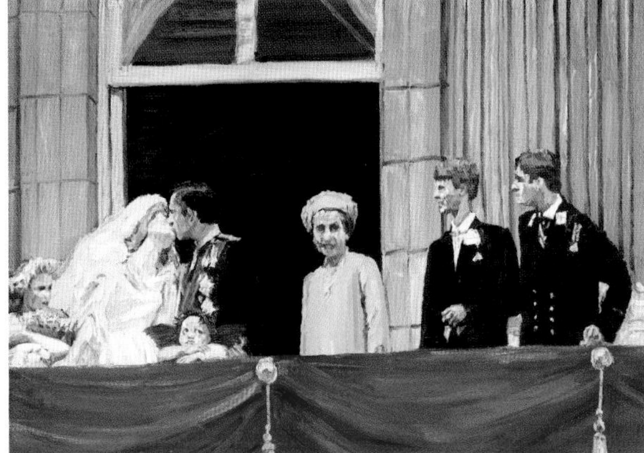

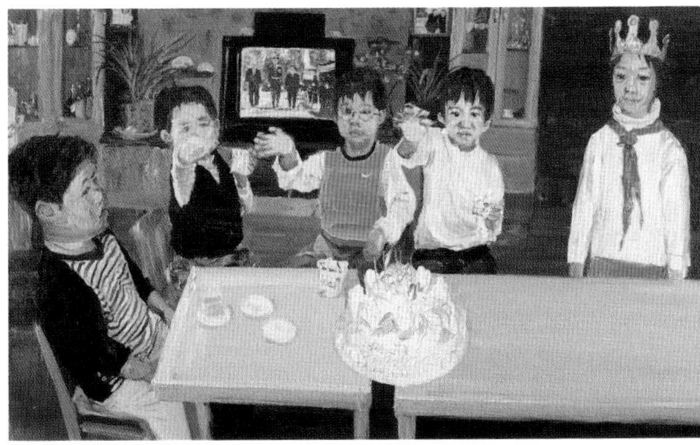

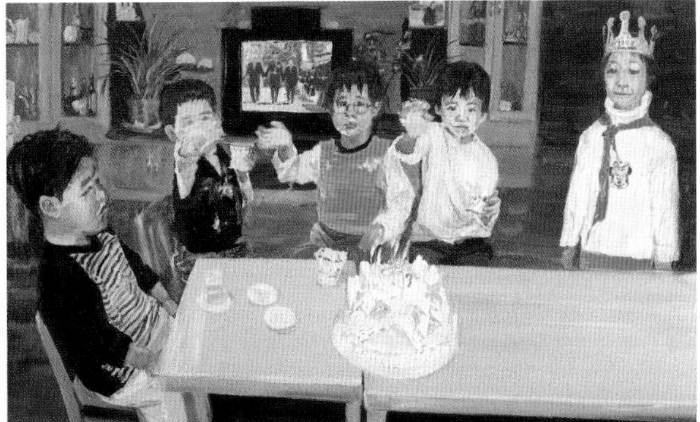

7
8

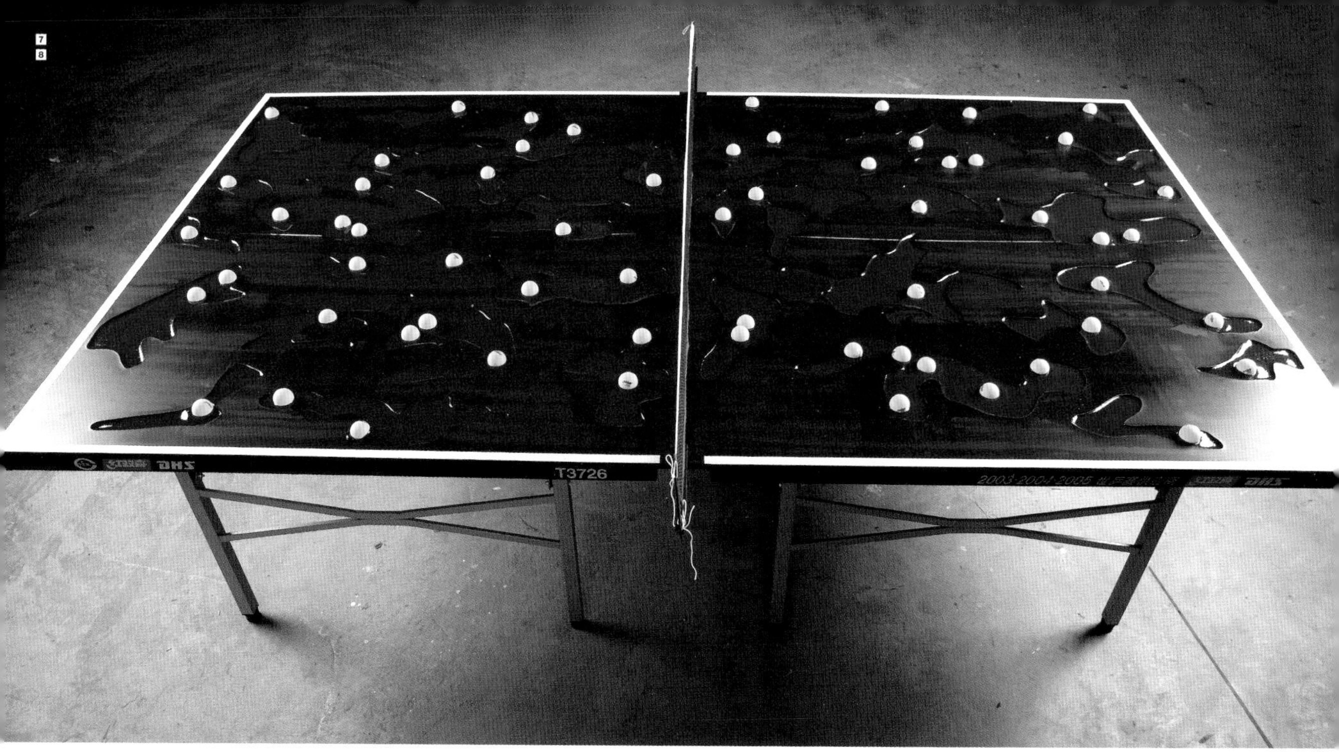

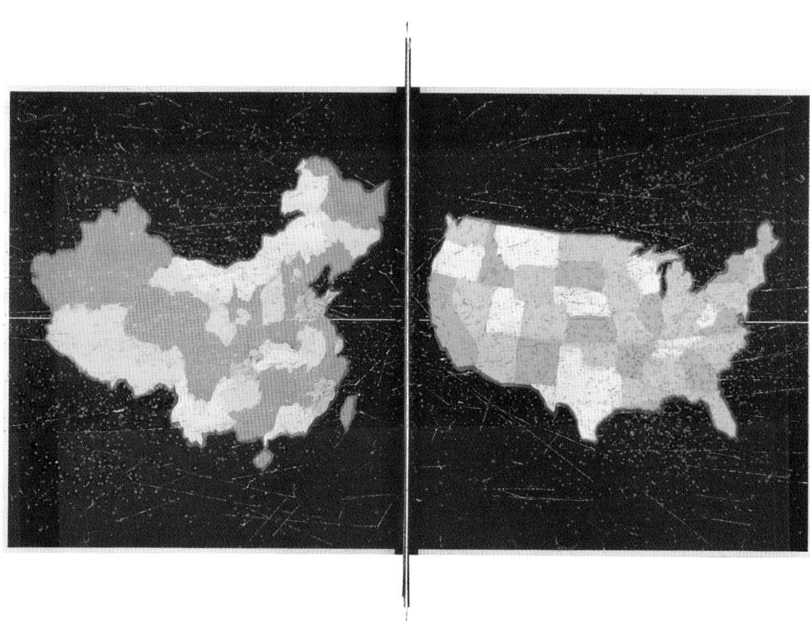

9

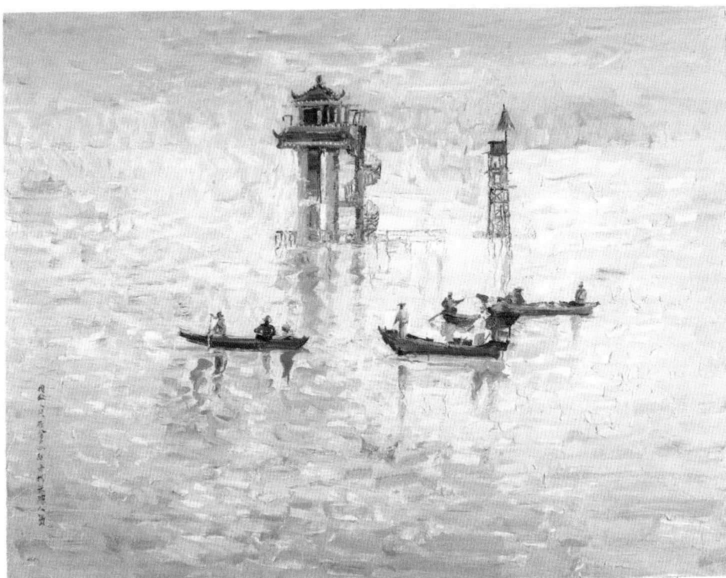

4 MUTUAL UNDOING AND UNITY: MOUNTAIN AND HILL • 2007 • OIL ON CANVAS • 200 x 220 CM (x4)
5 WEDDING (THERE ARE 6 DIFFERENCES IN THE TWO PAINTINGS) • 2006 • OIL ON CANVAS • 190 x 275 CM (x2)
6 COME TO EAT CAKE (THERE ARE 11 DIFFERENCES IN THE TWO PAINTINGS) • 2006 • OIL ON CANVAS • 150 x 250 CM (x2)
7 PING PONG • 2008 • OIL ON PING PONG TABLE, RACKETS, PING PONG BALL, VIDEO • 152 x 274 CM
8 PING PONG NO. 2 • 2008 • OIL ON PING PONG TABLE, PING PONG BALLS • 152 x 274 CM
9 PEOPLE SWEPT AWAY BY THE QIANTANG RIVER TIDE • 2007 • OIL ON CANVAS • 230 x 300 CM

EXHIBITIONS

SELECTED SOLO EXHIBITIONS

2008/9
Ghosting,
Iberia Center for Contemporary Art, Beijing
Duolun Museum Of Modern Art ,
Shanghai, China

2008
Collision in the Air,
DF2 Gallery,
Los Angeles, U.S.

2006
Finding Together,
F2 Gallery,
Beijing, China

SELECTED GROUP EXHIBITIONS

2009
Prague Biennale 4,
Karlin Hall,
Prague, Czech Republic

2008
55 Days in Valencia:
Chinese Contemporary Art,
Institut Valencià d'Art Modern,
Valencia, Spain

2008
The Revolution Continues:
New Chinese Art,
Saatchi Gallery,
London, U.K.

2007
Time Difference:
New Art from China and USA,
Initial Access,
Wolverhampton, U.K.

2007
The First Today's Documents:
Energy-Spirit, Body, Material,
Today Art Museum,
Beijing, China

2007
Beyond Image: Chinese New Painting,
Shanghai Art Museum,
Shanghai, China

2005
Young Chinese Contemporary Art,
Hangar-7,
Salzburg, Austria

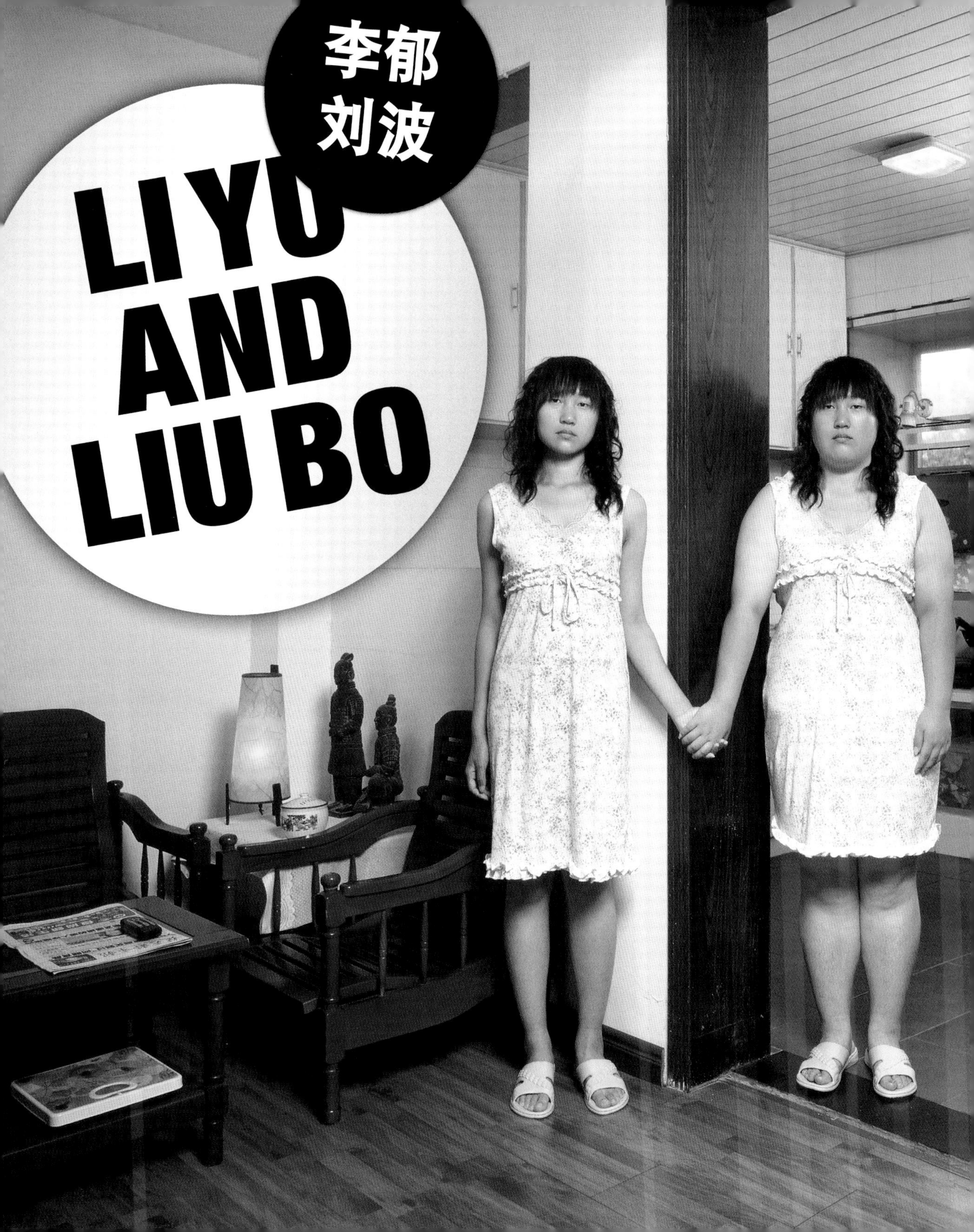
李郁
刘波
LIYU
AND
LIU BO

GROUP
LI YU AND LIU BO

NAME	LI YU	LIU BO
BORN IN	1973, WUHAN	1977, SHISHOU
LIVES IN	WUHAN	WUHAN
STUDY	CENTRAL CHINA NORMAL UNIV., WUHAN	HUBEI INSTITUTE OF FINE ARTS, WUHAN
MEDIA	PHOTOGRAPHY	

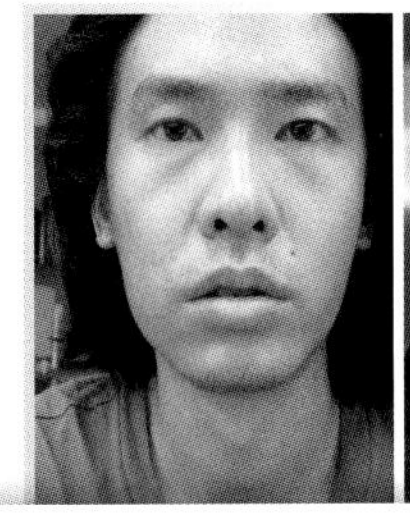
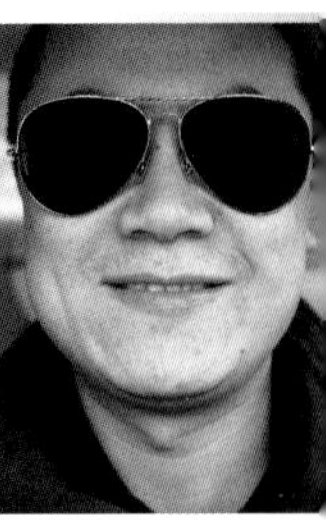

VICTIMIZATION AS AN OBJECT OF APPRECIATION

Since 2006, the Wuhan-based young photographer duo Li Yu and Liu Bo have worked closely on a series of news-based photographs entitled *13 Months in the Year of the Dog*. Their seamless collaboration continues into the making of *Victims* (2007), a second photography series revolving around the idea of victimization, trying to reconstruct victimizing situations and portray victimized subjects through the artists' own lens.

Liu Bo has been interested in the idea of harm and violence and the representation of violence in art since his time in art school. "I tend to think that human beings are vulnerable and easily hurt." It wasn't until he accidentally came across the book *New York Noir: Crime Pictures from the Daily News Archive* in 2005 that he was struck by the force of portraying violence and had the idea of re-enacting some of the scenes from the pictures in the book. The *New York Daily News* – established in 1919 – has documented the faces of last century's most violent criminals and their unfortunate victims and established the fashion of compressing each story into one arresting photograph. The content and equally the art of these journalistic photographs have exerted lasting influence on moviemakers and photographers.

Liu Bo soon realized that it would be extremely challenging to find all the necessary props and clothes to restage the crime scenes from the book. Li Yu then suggested they use the news stories from their own everyday life instead. The two hit it off and set to work right away. In 2006, the duo plunged into the archives of their local newspapers – in particular the *Chutian Metropolis Daily* and the *Chutian Golden Paper* – selecting twenty-six news events and retelling each of them in one photograph. Although most of the stories are related to victimization, no matter whether the victim is a dog or a group of migrant workers, the tone of their photographs is much less grim than news journalism. They, on the contrary, strike a light-hearted and surreal note that outweighs the depressing nature of the events they depict. Their images resemble sets and scenes from soap operas as the artists deliberately arranged the lighting to focus on the different elements in each composition. Unlike stage sets in a theater, though, each image is taken with a condensed depth of field so that there is no emphasis on any particular figure or detail. The scenes thus seem flat, much more ordinary and less dramatic than their stories would have suggested.

The gap between what is being photographed and the photographer is a popular subject of inquiry for contemporary artists. In Li Yu and Liu Bo's photographs the distance between the stories and the artists is even greater than that between news events and the journalists who are assigned to record them. This is a point that the two artists want to highlight in their work. Li Yu and Liu Bo are much more than onlookers or recorders of a past event. They were not present when the actual event took place and only read about the stories and their protagonists in the paper. Thus, they threw themselves into the bold and vivid reinvention of these events without the inhibition of not knowing every detail about what had actually happened. On the contrary, it has allowed them the liberty to devise what would go into the pictures to best benefit their storytelling.

In *She Follows You and Sleeps in Your Bed Naked. Who is This Lady?* (2006), a young lady, under the influence of drugs, follows a stranger home and lies down on his bed with her clothes off in the middle of the night. The man, who is supposedly the owner of the apartment, stands outside the bedroom door and looks at the naked woman soundly asleep in his bed. The sparse bedroom is oddly adorned; two illustrations of the pressure points on a human body are pasted on the wall, and a white plastic bag hangs around the lock of the door to suggest domesticity. In *Bedridden Man Dies in Grenade Explosion at Home* (2006), another common interior scene, a fifty-four-year old man is about to set off a grenade to kill himself after having being bedridden for more than a year. The ordinariness of the home setting offsets the desperation that charged the old man to make such a drastic decision. The tacky karaoke room in the image of *Karaoke Girl Forced to Take Drugs – Police Starts Investigation* (2007) is both over-decorated with elaborate wall fixtures and furniture, yet also seems bare without any of the messiness and commotion habitually found in an environment. The news story that gave form to this photograph was about a client of a karaoke bar forcing a bar girl to take drugs. The background gives focus to the estranged relationship lurking underneath the two protagonists alone in the room, hinting at the imminent hit of tragedy.

Despite the hopelessness, excitement, or disturbing nature of these photographs it is frustratingly impossible to make out the expressions of the characters, which is an intentional device of the artists. These people, be they victims or perpetrators, show no emotion at all and seem mechanical and extremely removed from the actual happenings. Yet they are physically present, as if they have been delivered into a dreamscape. Li Yu and Liu Bo's works consistently lay bare the constructed quality and artifice of the scenes in their photographs. Some of them even appear like scenes straight out of computer games. The heightened illusiveness of their photographs is on par with the absurdity of the actual events, defying our comprehension and experience. At the same time they reduce the gravity of these everyday tragedies. Indeed, we tend to only be able to endure the misfortunes of others by pretending that it is just hearsay or simply looking the other away. The less genuine they appear, the more tolerable they are.

By Carol Yinghua Lu

1

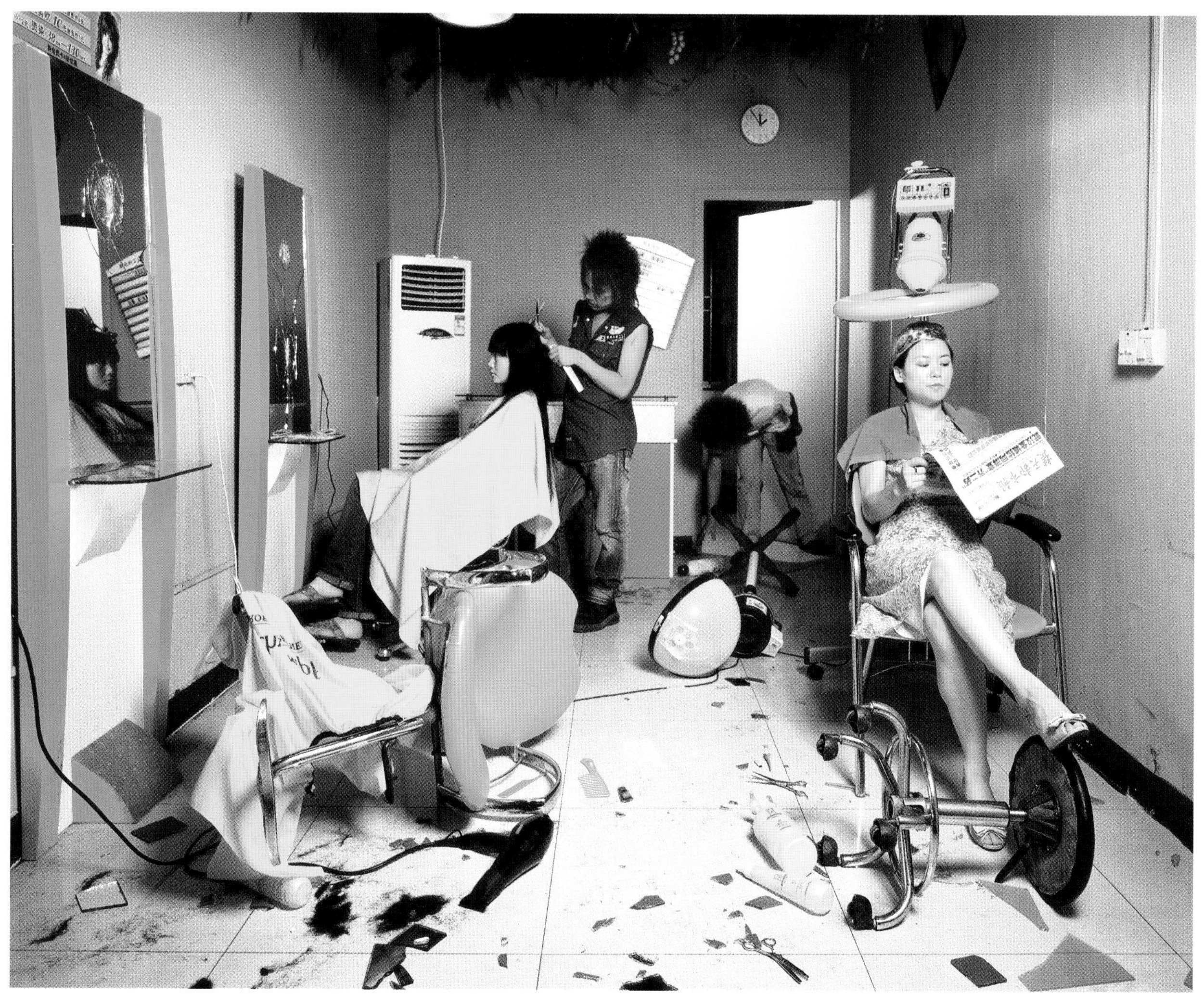

Chutian Golden Paper 2006-04-30
Hair Salon Wonder –
Hairdressing while Smashing

At 2:00 p.m. yesterday, a group of people rushed into the hair salon at 87 Renhe Road, Hanzheng Street. They began smashing the store while telling the salon owner not to do business there anymore. Two female customers, unhurried by the commotion, demanded that the stylists finish their respective haircuts.

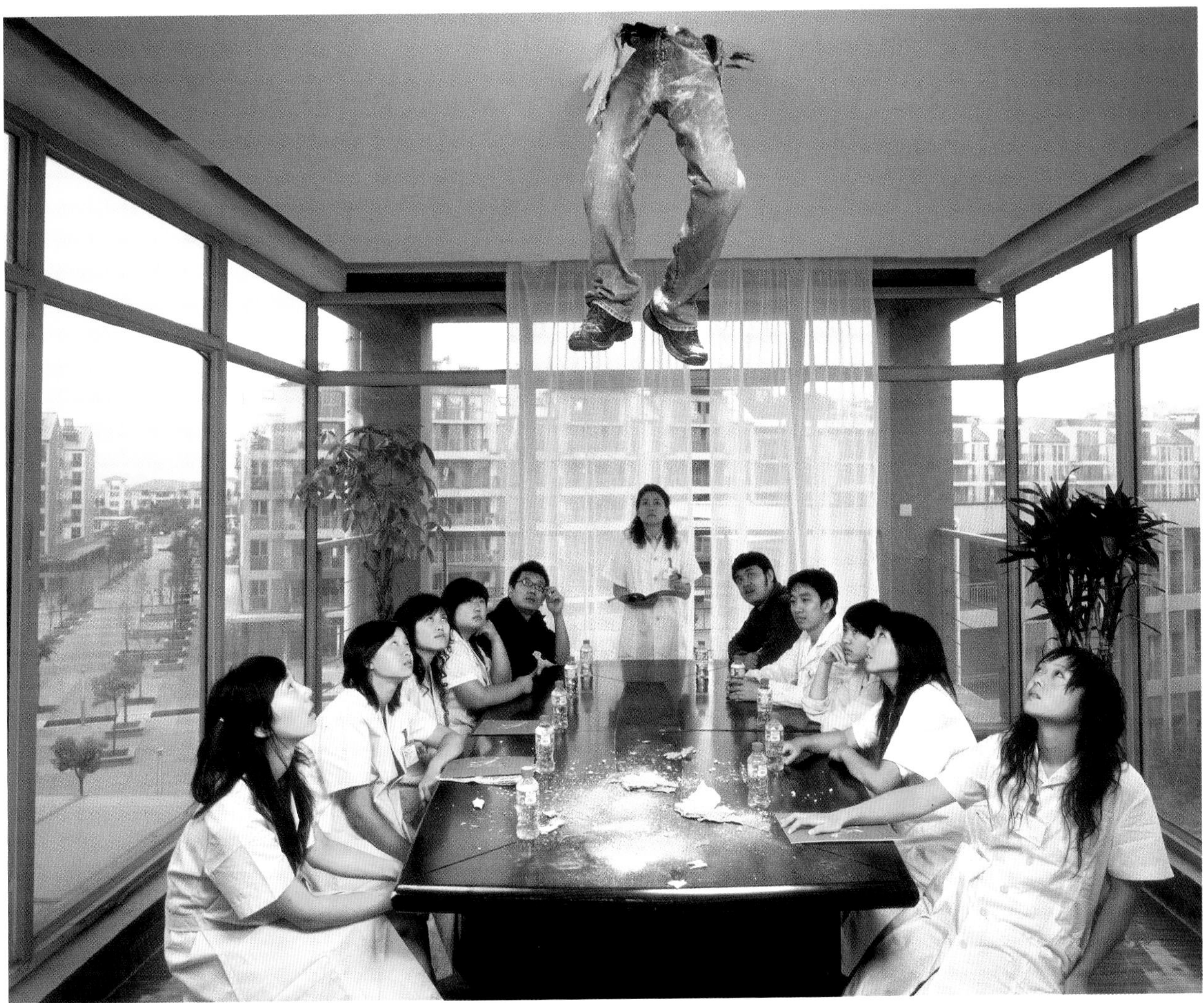

Chutian Golden Paper 2007-08-13
During a Pursuit Someone Jumped Down Through the Roof and Scared Others

According to Miss Yan, on August 10th a conference took place at her beauty salon's meeting room, which was attended by fifty people. Around 6:00 p.m., there suddenly was a big bang from the ceiling ...

1 HAIR SALON WONDER – HAIRDRESSING WHILE SMASHING • 2006 • C-PRINT AND LIGHTBOX • 122 × 152 CM

2 DURING A PURSUIT SOMEONE JUMPED DOWN THROUGH THE ROOF AND SCARED OTHERS • 2007 • C-PRINT AND LIGHTBOX • 122 × 152 CM

ONLINE CHAT WITH EDITORS

5/13/08 • AFTERNOON

LI YU'S RESPONSES

LIU BO'S RESPONSES

[14:01:13] What were your favorite childhood toys?

[14:03:10] I loved to play with wooden building bricks.

[14:03:36] My favorite toy was a self-made bow and arrow. I grew up in the countryside and spent a lot of time outdoors hunting small birds and even mice.

[14:05:23] What did your parents say to you most often?

[14:08:24] My parents always tell me to take good care of myself.

[14:09:57] Me, too. When I was a kid, my parents always told me to take care of myself and not to get involved in anything dangerous. These days, they tell me to get enough rest and to look after my health.

[14:12:54] It seems that the keyword here is "health." How to you keep fit and healthy?

[14:15:21] I recently stopped smoking and walk everyday to work.

[14:16:01] I get up early every morning and try to walk a lot outside.

[14:17:23] Do you also pay attention to good nutrition?

[14:20:47] Well, it's important to drink enough water every day ...

[14:21:41] ... and you need to drink less wine.

[14:22:58] Okay. What have you been wishing for since we last spoke?

[14:24:14] I have a daughter who is fifteen months old, and I really hope that she will grow up well and will always be in the best of health.

[14:24:56] Right now I'm taking driving lessons and I'm trying to drive carefully and without any accidents.

[14:27:00] Do you believe in true love?

[14:31:13] Yes, strongly. But it's very hard to understand the real meaning of love. You always need to listen to your heart and to your feelings. Nobody can explain it to you.

[14:32:01] I completely agree with you.

[14:34:20] Let's talk about your idea of your perfect living environment. What does it look like?

[14:36:10] For me, it's a life without financial and health problems and, more practically, I would love to live near a lake.

[14:37:41] Even in a turbulent world, I want peace in my heart.

[14:39:14]

[14:41:47] What media inspires you?

[14:42:26] Mainly TV and newspapers.

I guess in my work there are only limited sources for inspiration. Of course I watch TV and read the newspapers, but my ideas for new artworks are mainly influenced by real life and real situations.

[14:44:38] What do you like/dislike about being an artist?

[14:45:11] Usually I like all things that make me excited and capture my attention. But, as I get older, I'm also learning to deal with situations that don't excite me too much and which may even appear "boring" at first sight.

[14:47:00] There are many different kinds of artists. I would not consider us to be "typical" artists, as the life of the typical artist has hardly anything in common with real people's lives.

[14:50:17] How do you communicate with the audience with your art?

[14:52:12] There's no way! The viewers get only out of the works what they want to get out of them, and they will only see what they want to see.

[14:54:18] I agree. What we can "see" in our works can't always be transferred to the people looking form the outside. Not everybody will understand what an artist set out to express. What people associate with when they look at our works can't be influenced by us, but only by themselves. We only can control our own thoughts, but not those of others.

[14:55:10] Give me five words that you think accurately describe your generation ...

[14:58:13] Diligence, sensibility, melancholy, curiosity, and calmness.

[14:58:27] Agreement, excitement, anxiety, liveliness, and foolishness.

[14:59:42] If you had the world's attention for fifteen whole seconds, what would you say?

[15:01:40] I wouldn't say anything. Everybody should use that time to have a little rest.

[15:03:11] First, everyone should switch his mobile to the vibration mode ... and, after that, the fifteen seconds will be over.

3 BEDRIDDEN MAN DIES IN GRENADE EXPLOSION AT HOME • 2006 • C-PRINT AND LIGHTBOX • 122 x 152 CM

4 SHE FOLLOWS YOU AND SLEEPS IN YOUR BED NAKED. WHO IS THIS LADY? • 2006 • C-PRINT AND LIGHTBOX • 122 x 152 CM

Chutian Metropolis Daily 2006-10-21
Bedridden Man Dies in Grenade Explosion at Home

Mr. Xiao, a fifty-four-year-old patient living in No. 3 Community, Qingshan, Wuhan Petroleum Group Co. set off a grenade at home and committed suicide last night. It is said that he had been kept in bed for one year by muscular atrophy and other diseases. When the grenade blew up, his son and a friend were in another bedroom while his wife was in the living room.

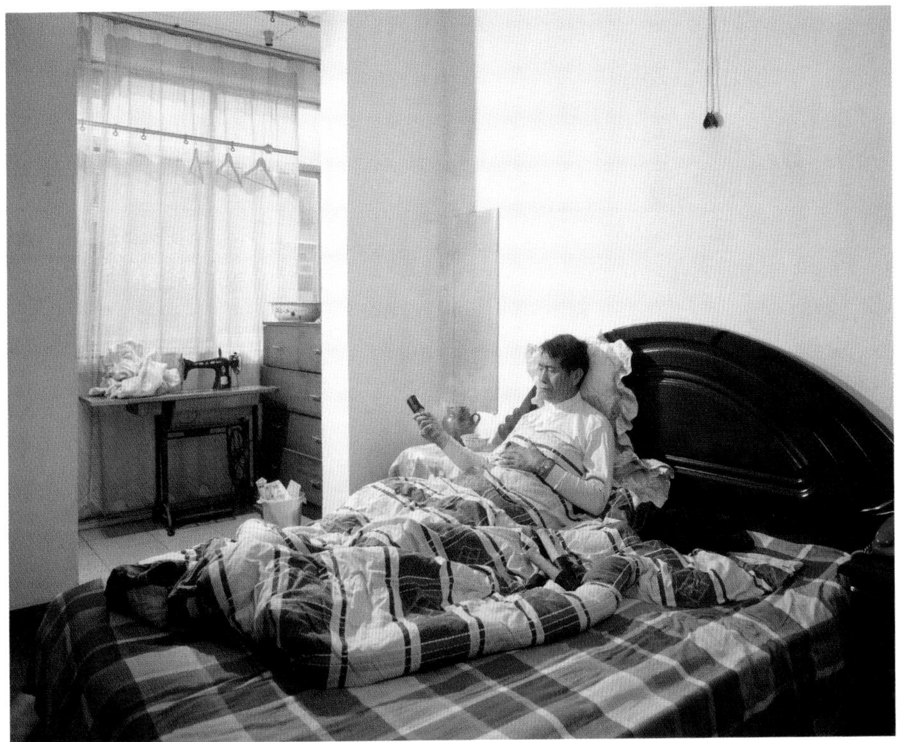

Chutian Metropolis Daily 2006-03-21
She Follows You and Sleeps in Your Bed Naked. Who is this Lady?

At 11:00 a.m., Mr. Yang, living in 2-1 Xiaozhi Chun, Xinhua Road, Hankou, went back home with his relative. An unknown lady wearing an overcoat followed them into the apartment, unclothed, and went to sleep in Mr. Yang's bed. Frightened, Mr. Yang immediately called the police. After examining the girl, doctors concluded that she was addicted to drugs.

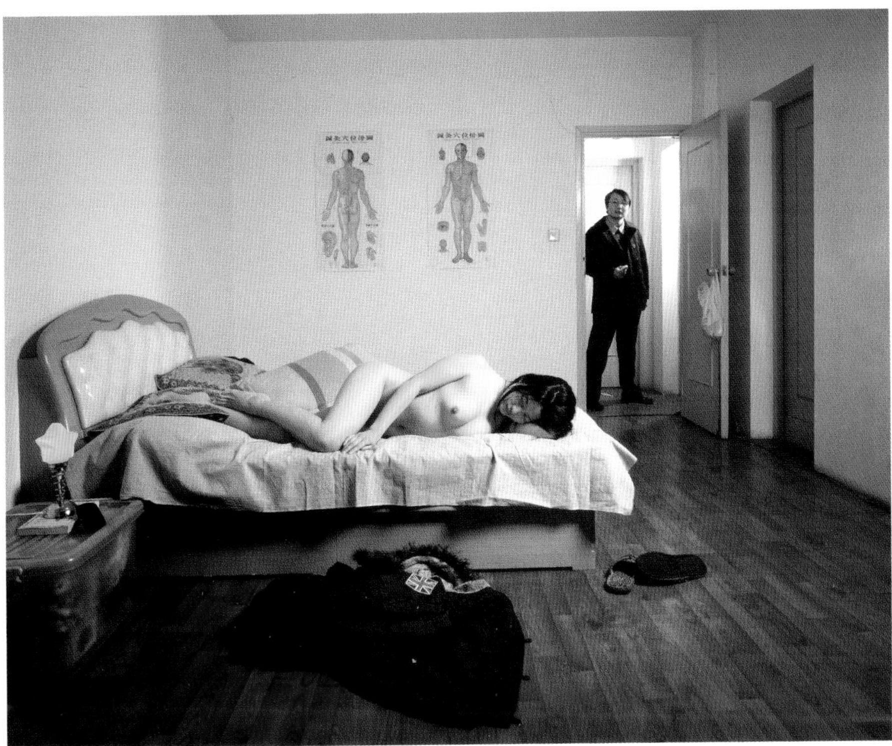

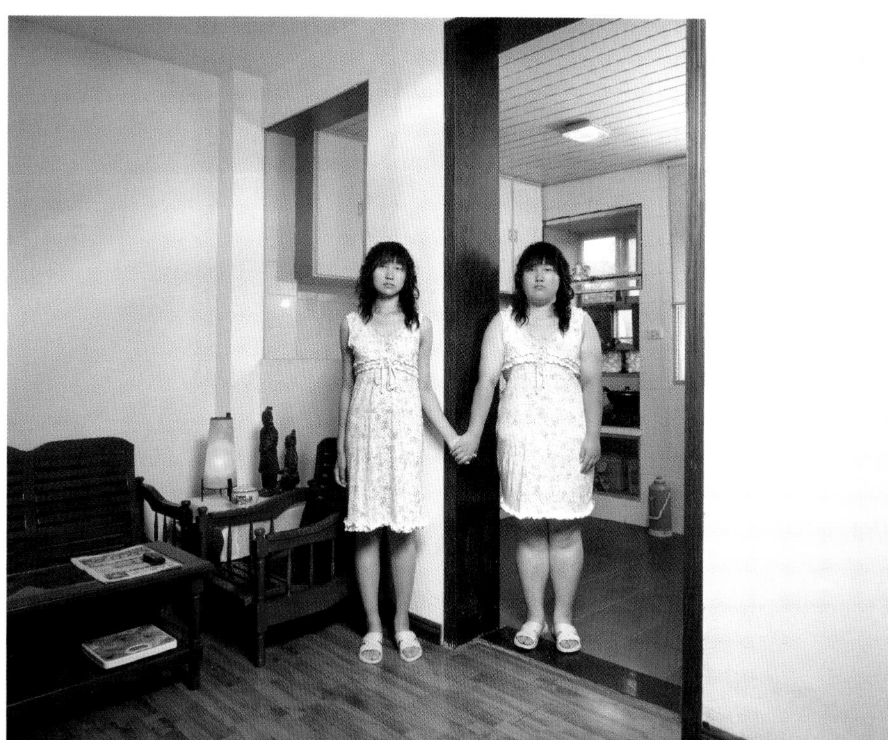

Chutian Metropolis Daily 2006-8-15
Same Face, Different Weight

At first glance, it's hard to tell the twin sisters apart; but as you look more closely you will see that one is plump while the other is slim. This startling change dates from March when the younger sister was sent to Beijing for two months of advanced study. During her stay in Beijing she took Paiyousu diet pills and lost fourteen kilograms (31 lbs.).

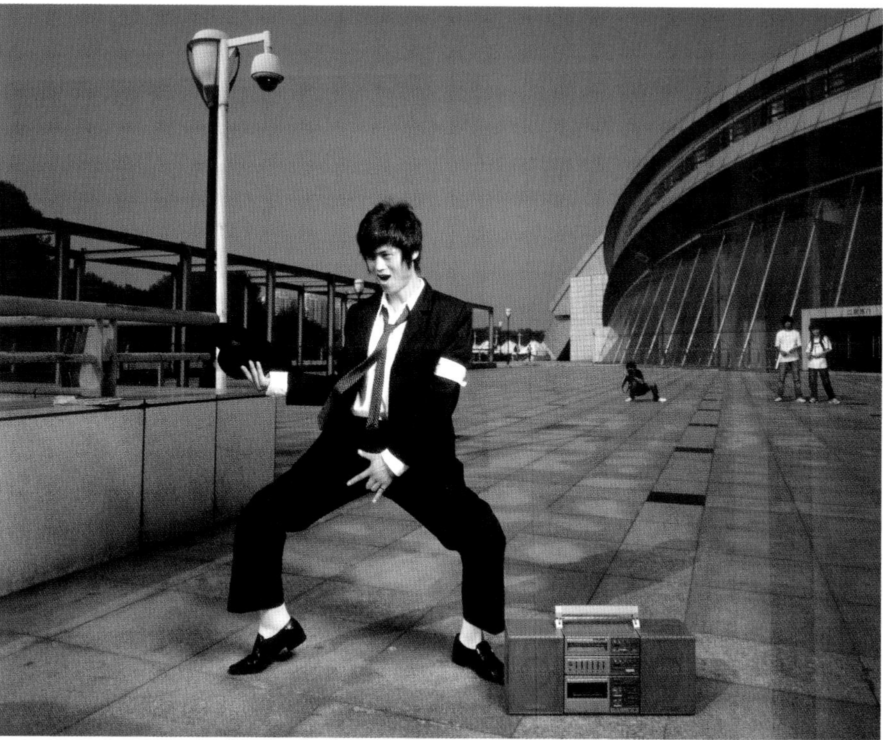

Chutian Metropolis Daily 2008-6-22
Dancing in the street for decompression

Yesterday noon, a young man was waving body fanatically in Jiefang Road, Simenkou ,Wuchang, disregarding other people present. He proclaimed himself Mr. Li, an insurance salesman. To relieve the tremendous pressure from his poor work performance, he often imitated his idol, Michael Jackson, the American pop music superstar, dancing in the street.

7

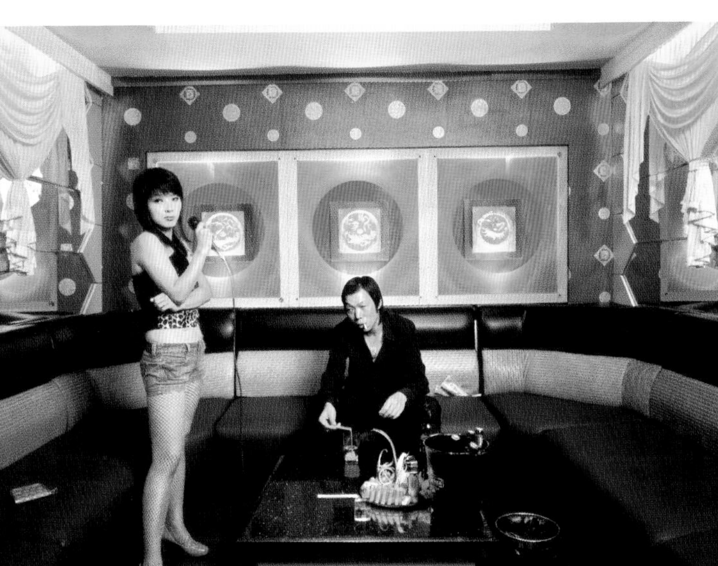

Chutian Golden Paper 2007-05-02
Karaoke Bar Girl Forced to Take Drugs – Police Starts Investigation

Last night at 11:50 p.m., a karaoke bar waitress was forced by a male guest to take around 10 ml of drugs in form of a pink liquid. After the girl had refused his advances the guest poured it into a glass and forced her into finishing the drink.

5 SAME FACE, DIFFERENT WEIGHT • 2006 • C-PRINT AND LIGHTBOX • 122 x 152 CM

6 DANCING IN THE STREET FOR DECOMPRESSION • 2008 • C-PRINT AND LIGHTBOX • 122 x 152 CM

7 KARAOKE GIRL FORCED TO TAKE DRUGS – POLICE STARTS INVESTIGATION • 2007 • C-PRINT AND LIGHTBOX • 122 x 152 CM

EXHIBITIONS

SELECTED SOLO EXHIBITIONS

2009
13 Months in the Year of the Dog,
Porsgrunn Kunst Forening,
Porsgrunn, Norway

2008
13 Months in the Year of the Dog,
Hubei Institute of Fine Arts Gallery,
Wuhan, China

SELECTED GROUP EXHIBITIONS

2009
Getxophoto,
Getxo, Spain

2007
2nd Documentary Exhibition of Fine Arts Forms of Concepts,
Fine Arts Literature Center,
Wuhan, China

2007
Refresh: Emerging Chinese Artists,
Zendai Museum of Modern Art,
Shanghai, China /
Arario Gallery,
Beijing, China

2007
Strange Encounters: Chinese Videos,
Kunsthalle Wien,
Vienna, Austria

2007
Umweg über China,
Hebbel Am Ufer,
Berlin, Germany

2006
Regenesis,
Museum of Contemporary Art,
Haikou, China

2005
What are they doing here?,
Siemens Arts Program,
SLC,
Wuhan, China

2005
920 Kilograms,
Duolun Museum of Modern Art,
Shanghai, China

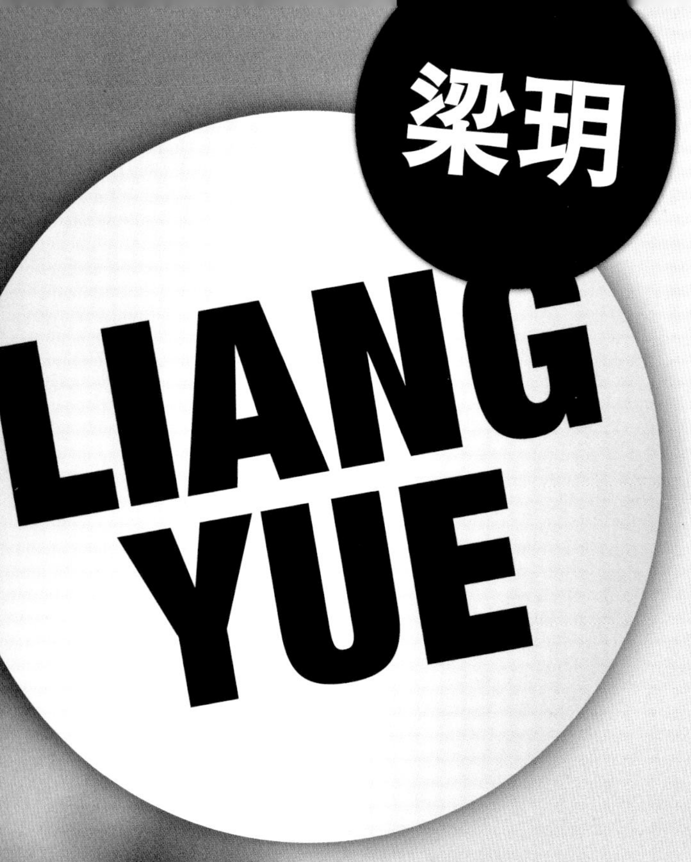
梁玥
LIANG
YUE

NAME

LIANG YUE

BORN IN

1979, SHANGHAI

LIVES IN

SHANGHAI

STUDY

SHANGHAI FINE ARTS COLLEGE, SHANGHAI

MEDIA

PHOTOGRAPHY, VIDEO

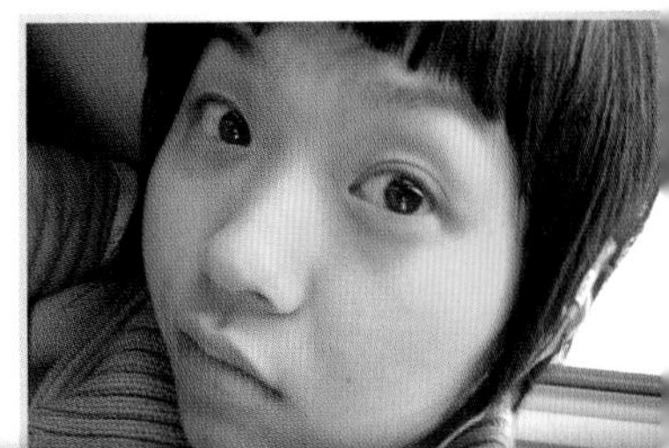

NIGHT MOVES

For Liang Yue, like so many Chinese photographers born after the mid-1970s, an important stepping off point is the textures of contemporary urban China. The city is a presence in much of her work, both as antagonist and accomplice. Yet the environmental features in both her video and photography pieces can most often be read as markers on an interior and often highly personal journey.

Pictures from the nighttime series *Early Fall Rain* (2005) focus on buildings in her hometown of Shanghai. The image *Early Fall Rain #3* is shot from Liang Yue's apartment window and catches the top floor and roof of a neighbor's apartment in the flare of the camera flash, which it illuminates brilliant white against the dark clouds. The slightly off-focus, snapshot feel of the work gives the scene a shimmering otherworldliness that is reflected in many of her pictures. In the series *Snow White Window* (2005), she exchanges late-night atmospherics for a heavy snowfall, while *In The Night, In The Mist* (undated) is an eerie series of color and black-and-white images of commuter traffic and streetlights in heavy rain and fog. Each of these series was executed at night, a time of day when the clamor of the city has died down and when, according to Liang Yue, "there are fewer people and fewer distractions and common places and objects are transformed." Yet, as much as these works are based in peace and quiet, they are simultaneously filled with the traces of humanity. The drawn curtains and distant lights on the highway suggest a multitude of lives and stories unfolding.

This idea finds an echo in video pieces such as the three-channel *Will The Weather Be Fine Tomorrow* (2002). Here the artist conjoins the sequence of a girl washing her hair in a bathroom on one channel with street scenes and sequences of passing traffic in the others. Liang Yue invites identification with the monotony of intimate, everyday routines, and in so doing pierces the impersonality and anonymity of the city. Further such video works enforce this view. *The Morn* (2003) presents a variety of urban locations that include a figure holding a flashlight whose beam is turned towards the viewer and periodically switched on and off. The video also forms the basis for the photography series *Morse Code* (2003/04). In one of these images the figure is shown standing in the distance on a pedestrian footbridge. People pass by and traffic can be seen rushing beneath. The scene is a blur of movement and activity except for the tiny beam of the flashlight that gives an intimate point of contact across space and time and suggests sympathy for individual consciousness within an indifferent environment.

These two works are notable for providing a rare intersection between her photography and video works. At the same time they are a convenient marker from which the character of her video and photography appears to undergo a change in emphasis. Similar themes continue to inform both sides of her output, yet subsequent videos generally take on a more informal character. *Traveling Day* (2005) and *Lady Lady* (2007), among others of this period, have the feel of diary pieces. The first documents a day out with friends to a small town in Zhejiang province, not far from Shanghai. The characters can be seen scuffing around a lake and aimlessly wandering the streets, engaged in the casual back and forth of everyday conversation. Similarly, *Lady Lady* documents a shopping trip to Hong Kong. The action takes place in coaches, a cheap hotel, and around Hong Kong's shopping district of Tsim Sha Tsui, where the artist films a friend visiting restaurants and buying huge amounts of cosmetics.

The intimacy and ordinariness of such pieces provides a common link to her earlier work and perhaps has precedence in *Happiest Winter* (2001), which documents a day drifting around Shanghai. Yet, where previous videos generally tend to be more reflective and conceptually finite, later pieces show a more fluid approach. Moreover, *Lady Lady* is striking for its light, giggly tone and is almost certainly a reflection of the artist's changing personal circumstances ahead of having her first baby.

By contrast, Liang's photography of the same time grows more tightly composed and thoughtful as she explores the medium at more depth. The triptych *On The Way*, from the *April Snow* (2006) series, develops the color manipulation techniques used in earlier series such as *Don't Worry* (2004), in which photos of tree branches at night are presented in negative and saturated in violent orange. In *On The Way* we see a heavily laden truck laboring along a snowy mountain road. Each panel shows the identical image transformed: as a black-and-white shot, reverse negative, and washed in dark, threatening red. Later series such as *Above The Sky* (2006) continue this process of refinement, although this time in form rather than technique. Here we are presented with black-and-white images of swirling clouds whose dissolving shapes approach total abstraction. The works contain a different emotional weight compared to the recent development of her video and seek to explore more formal ideas of perception and ambiguity.

More significantly, these pieces can also be seen as fulfilling a kind of functional balance for the artist. The present dialogue between Liang's video and photography works suggests that her output in one medium provides both psychological space and conceptual support for the other. Yet however tenuous the connection sometimes appears to be, the direction of both forms are united by a highly personal search for identity and purpose. The certainty of impermanence is what lends so much of her work its pathos.

By John Millichap

1

1 EARLY FALL RAIN #3 • 2005 • C-PRINT • 90 x 110 CM

2 IN THE NIGHT, IN THE MIST • UNDATED • PHOTOGRAPHY • 45 x 68 CM

3 MORSE CODE • 2003 • C-PRINT • 80 x 120 CM

2
3

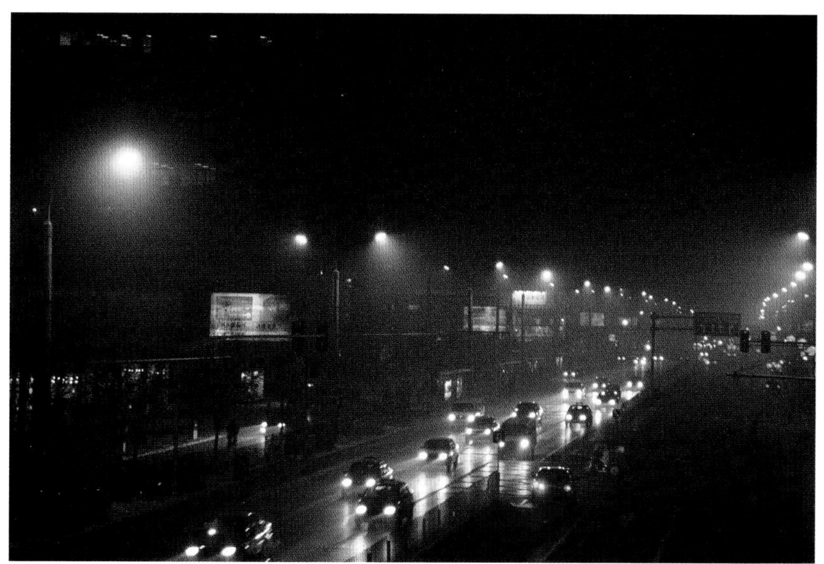

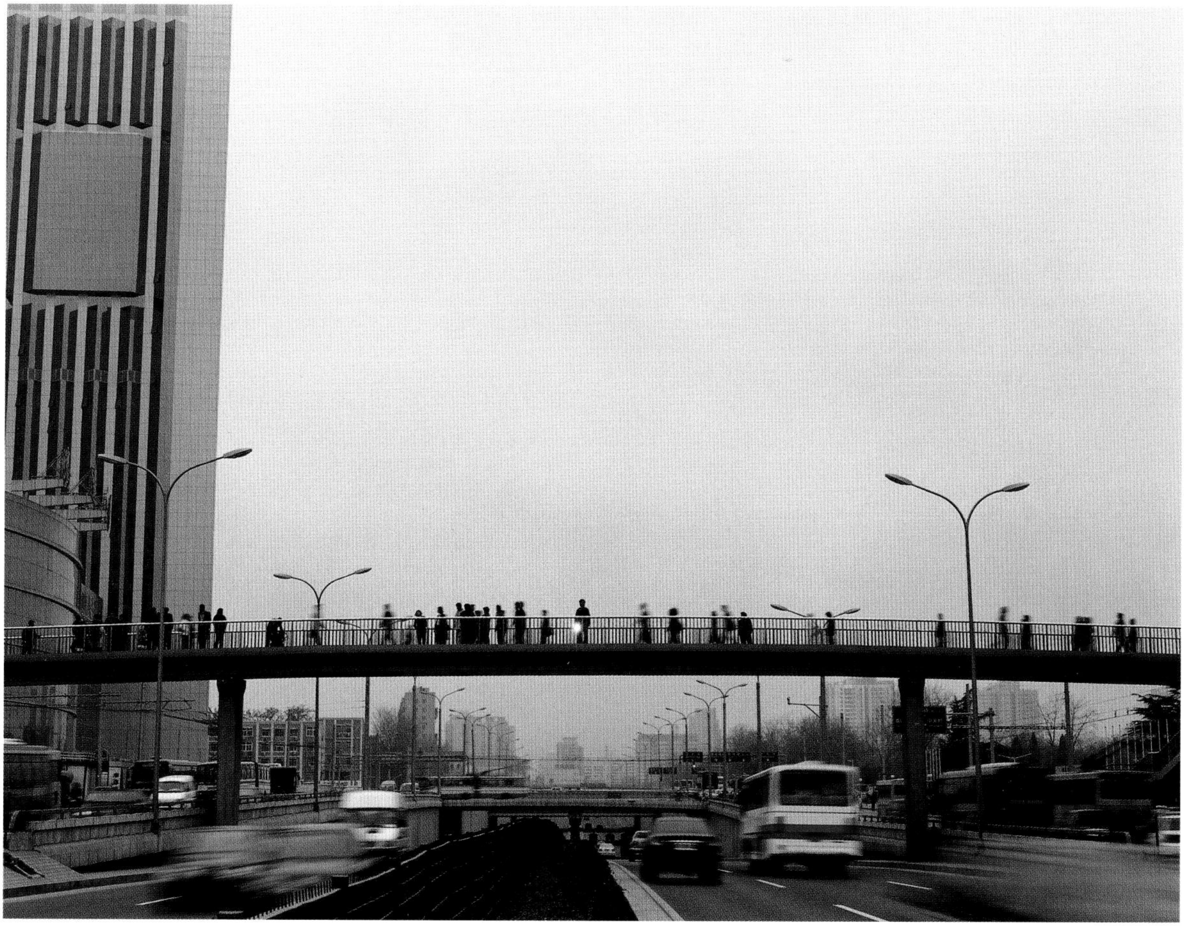

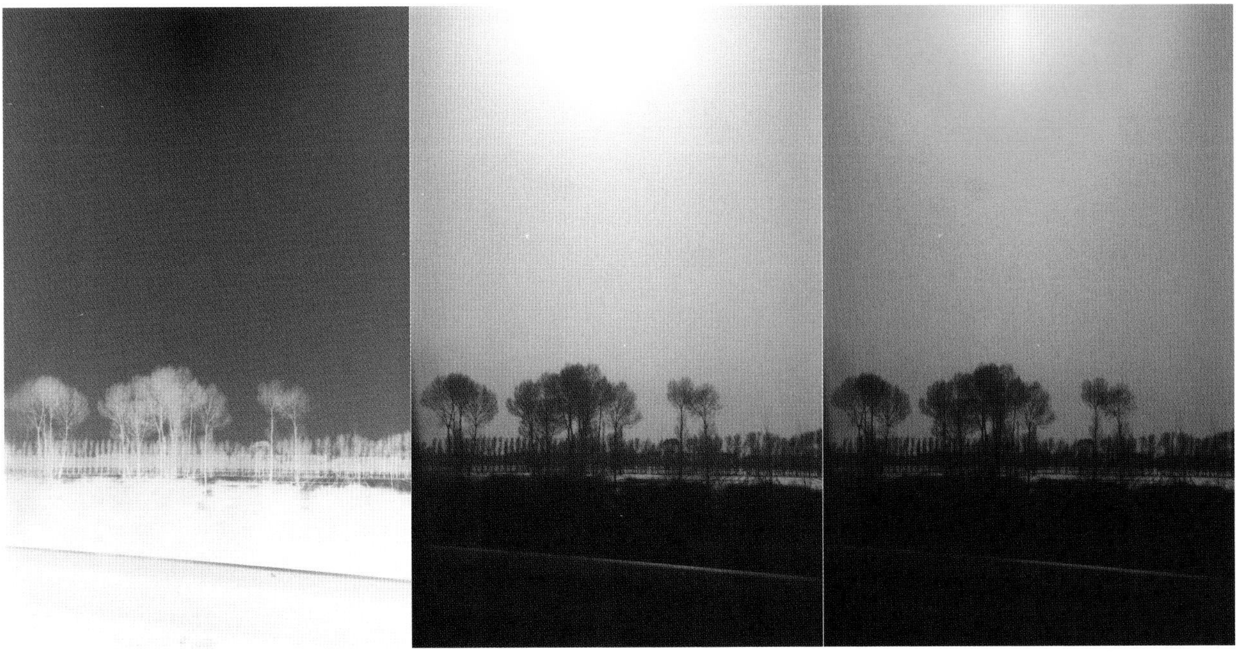

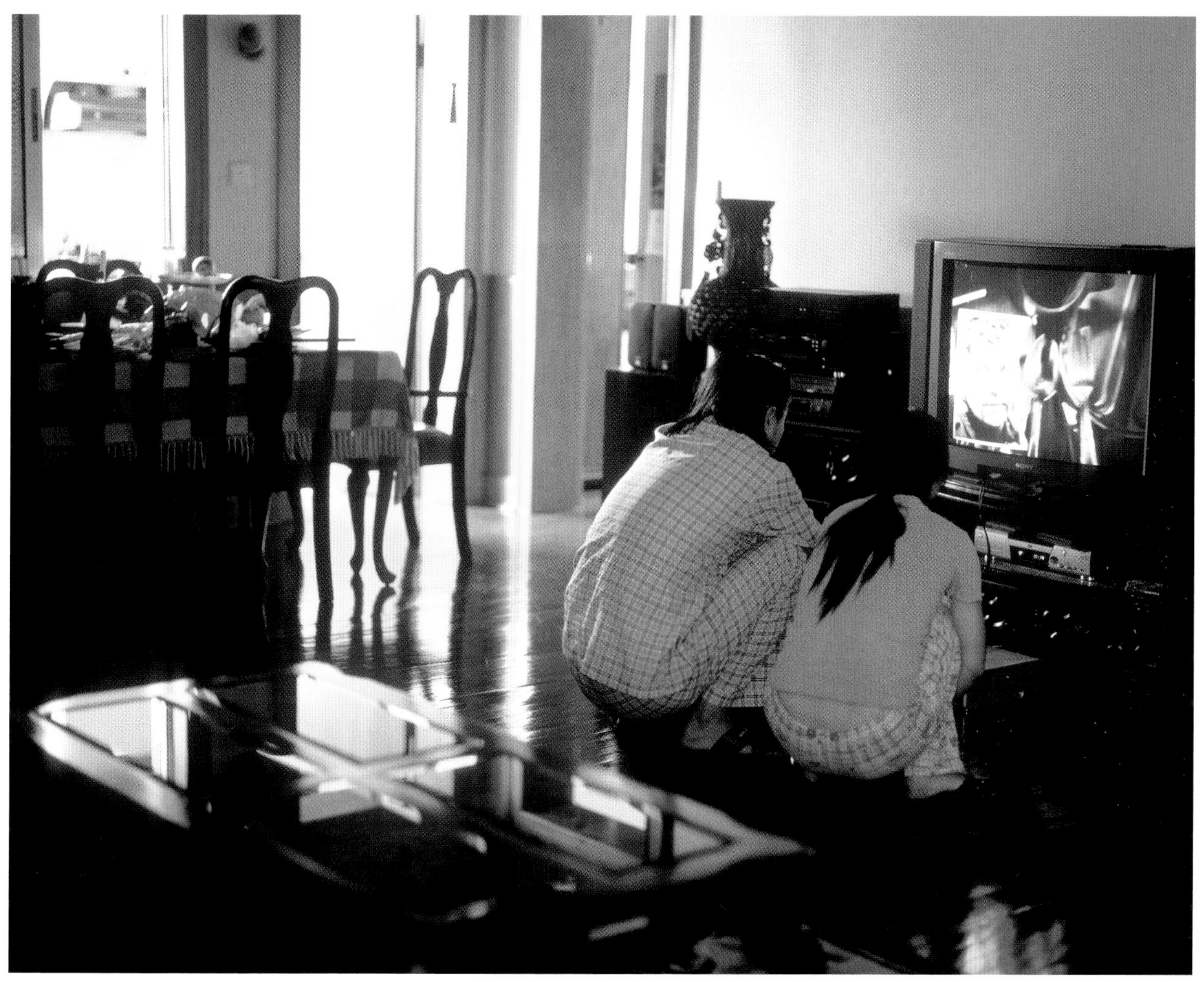

4 I LOVE SUNSHINE (APRIL SNOW SERIES) • 2006 • C-PRINT (TRIPTYCH) • 150 x 100 CM (x3)

5 ABOVE THE SKY (DETAIL) • 2006 • C-PRINT (TRIPTYCH) • 145 x 114.5 CM (x3)

6 IN SUMMER • 2004 • C-PRINT • 108 x 130 CM

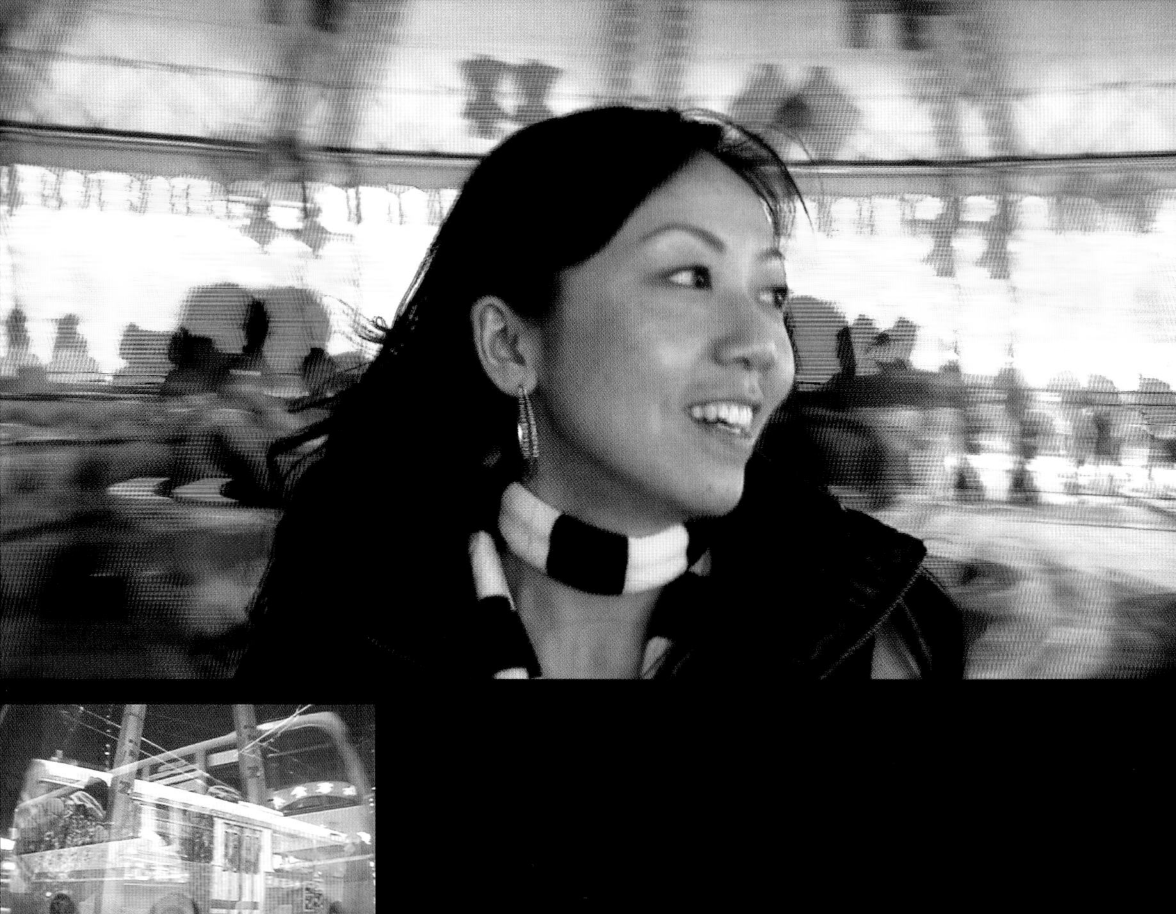

QUESTIONNAIRE

5/3/08 • SHANGHAI

WHAT WAS YOUR FAVORITE CHILDHOOD TOY?

An accordion.

WHAT DID YOUR PARENTS SAY TO YOU MOST OFTEN?

My mother said: "Lunch is ready. Let's eat."
My father would ask me: "Do you need some pocket money?"

HOW DO YOU TRY TO STAY HEALTHY IN YOUR EVERYDAY LIFE?

I don't care much about healthy living. I spend some time sleeping, daydreaming, or listening to music to rest and regulate my health. But basically I'm always very busy.

WHAT HAVE YOU BEEN WISHING FOR MOST RECENTLY?

To win 50 million RMB in the lottery.

DO YOU BELIEVE IN TRUE LOVE?

Yes. But I'm not sure how it will look like.

WHAT DOES YOUR IDEAL LIVING ENVIRONMENT LOOK LIKE?

I would like to have more spare time to do things I like.

FROM WHICH TYPE OF MEDIA DO YOU DERIVE MOST OF YOUR INSPIRATION?

It depends on the situation.

WHAT DO YOU LIKE/DISLIKE ABOUT BEING AN ARTIST?

I like the freedom I have as an artist. I don't need to go work in an office and I don't have to get involved in business activities.
I don't like when my works can't be sold, then I won't have any money. If I have no money, I can't do my work.

HOW DO YOU COMMUNICATE WITH THE AUDIENCE IN YOUR ART?

Through telepathy. I hope I have that ability.

IF YOU HAD FIVE WORDS TO DESCRIBE YOUR GENERATION, WHAT WOULD THEY BE?

I don't know which generation I belong to. I suggest the following words: uncertainty, boredom, waiting, and loss.

IF THE WHOLE WORLD WOULD LISTEN TO YOU FOR FIFTEEN SECONDS, WHAT WOULD YOU SAY?

I don't want to say anything.

EXHIBITIONS

SELECTED SOLO EXHIBITIONS

2008
The World of Other's,
MoCA,
Shanghai, China

2007
An Exhibition,
Wellside Gallery,
Shanghai, China

2005
Stop Dazing:
Liang Yue Photos & Videos in 2003–2005,
BizArt Art Center,
Shanghai, China

2003
Several Dusks,
ShanghART Gallery,
Shanghai, China

SELECTED GROUP EXHIBITIONS

2007
China Power Station: Part II, Astrup Fearnley Museum of Modern Art,
Oslo, Norway

2007
Artissima Cinema, Shanghype!:
Portrait of the City from Dawn to Dusk,
Mirafiori Motor Village,
Turin, Italy

2006
China Power Station: Part I,
Battersea Power Station,
London, U.K.

2006
Never Go Out Without My DV Cam:
Video Art from China,
ICO Foundation,
Madrid, Spain

2006
Twilight,
Albert & Victoria Museum,
London, U.K.

2006
Restless: Photography and New Media,
MoCA,
Shanghai, China

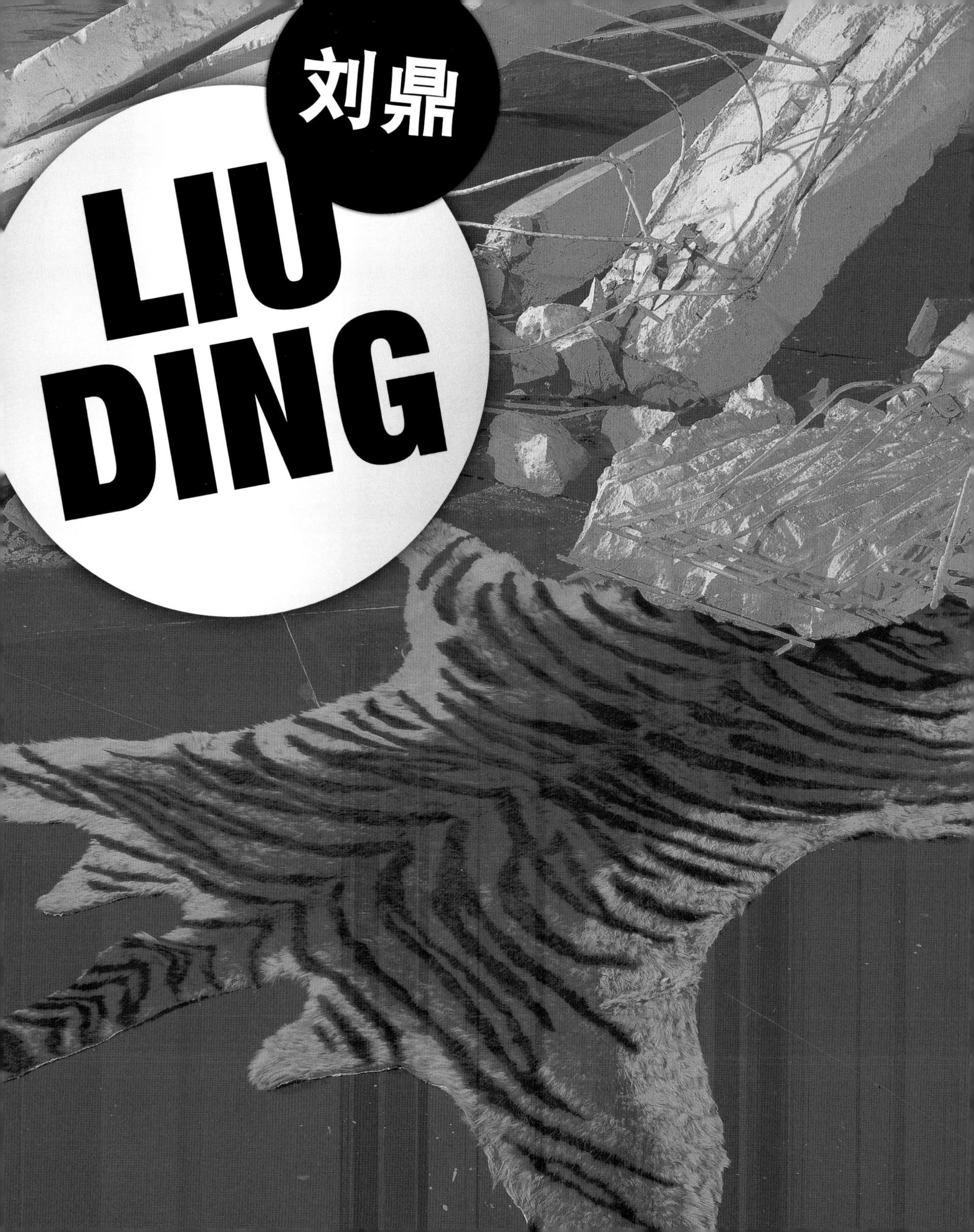
刘鼎
LIU
DING

NAME

LIU DING

BORN IN

1976, CHANGZHOU

LIVES IN

BEIJING

MEDIA

INSTALLATION, PAINTING, PERFORMANCE, PHOTOGRAPHY, SCULPTURE

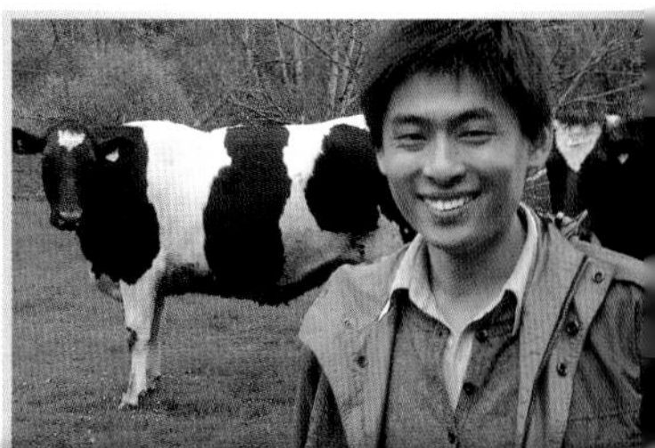

TRACING THE SURFACE

The setting is a cavernous exhibition space at *Beyond: The 2005 Guangzhou Triennial.* Arranged upon a pyramid shaped series of platforms are twelve painting easels and approximately twelve "master" painters hired by the artist Liu Ding to "perform" their everyday job – painting near identical oil paintings of Western-style landscapes. Hailing from Dafencun Art Village, the epicenter of oil painting production in southern China, the workers are positioned according to manual task: those at the bottom paint out the background – blue skies tinged with pink clouds; others studiously sketch in trees, waterfalls; and those at the top add finishing touches – white egrets in flight or finely rendered pine branches. Simultaneously embodying performance and installation, Liu's *Products* (2005) situates the hidden processes of "artistic creation" squarely within the framework of the large-scale international exhibition, at once questioning the site of the museum as a space for exhibition and manufacture while offering a critique of China's complicit role in the assembly-line mass production of art objects. Openly challenging the relationships between artists/producers and viewers/consumers and assumptions of high vs. low art, *Products* firmly established Liu Ding's status as an artist capable of multi-layered, piercing cultural critique.

Liu Ding was born in the southern city of Changzhou in 1976. Liu's father studied Chinese medicine, a factor that perhaps led Liu to incorporate aspects of medicine, drugs, and remedies into his early photographs and installations. Liu Ding's independent nature soon led him to abandon formal education and move to Shanghai, where he started up his own curatorial/art/design outfit Pink Studio in 2001. Freed from the regimen of an art school curriculum, Liu's artistic practice is overwhelmingly diverse, encompassing installation, painting, photography, and theater set design and production. His professional skills are equally varied, including work as a magazine editor, television producer, film director and, more recently, curator. The range of his practices are not easily contained under one rubric and, like many of his generation, he defies categorization, favoring instead the designation of "contemporary artist" over any media-specific label or nomenclature. Owing in part to his background in theater and set design, and as a product of "new China," Liu has a developed affinity for the surface texture and external appearance of things. Under his direction, these objects, materials, and daily items are readily configured to highlight the absurdities and exaggerated features characteristic of his generation. His heightened interest in all things visual – evident through his penchant for mirrors, polished surfaces, precious materials, and dramatic use of color – tackle the surface in order to get at something much deeper and darker residing beneath. It is through these elements that Liu's prevailing concerns with desire and disillusionment, reality and fiction, rational and irrational, find unique form and expression.

Liu's *Samples from the Transition* (2004–5) is an ongoing series in which the artist draws upon themes of desire and consumption through examining certain complexities in contemporary Chinese society on a microcosmic level. For the third installment of this series, *Treasure* (2005), the artist dug a hole in the ground, filled it with various gems and crystals, and used special lighting to give the effect of a found or lost treasure. The work presents a fantasy of wealth and fortune that is just beyond reach, expressing underlying material desires that permeate China's runaway capitalist economy.

Continuing on the theme of longing, Liu participated in *The Amber Room,* a 2006 exhibition in San Francisco which invited artists to respond to the mysterious disappearance of the eighteenth-century Amber Room – a baroque inspired structure made out of precious amber originally sited in St. Petersburg. *Forevermore* (2006) is an interactive installation covering the gallery's windows with colored acrylic panels inset with peepholes that invite viewers to peer onto the street below. With peepholes spelling out the word *Forevermore* – a double entendre that suggests an endless process of material accumulation and a future projection of the eternal – the work links viewers through the simple act of looking. Though standing shoulder to shoulder in the gallery space, when viewers look through the peepholes they are transported to individual realms of distorted reality, forever out of touch and disconnected from one another. The artwork intends to evoke the experience of continually searching alongside a growing feeling of loss and disappearance.

The heady themes Liu addresses in his work also have a way of manifesting themselves in intimate, more ephemeral ways. Perhaps this is most accurately summed up in his performance *Tracing the Wind and Shadows* carried out at the Miami Basel art fair in 2006. Liu uses a large paintbrush to trace the fleeting shadows projected against a white scrim background of people as they walk by. Yet Liu's actions with the brush cannot keep up with the moving crowds, and the visual result is a dizzying array of incomplete gestures and outlines, as if to signify the frenetic pace of today's contemporary art world and his own tenuous place within it.

By Pauline J. Yao

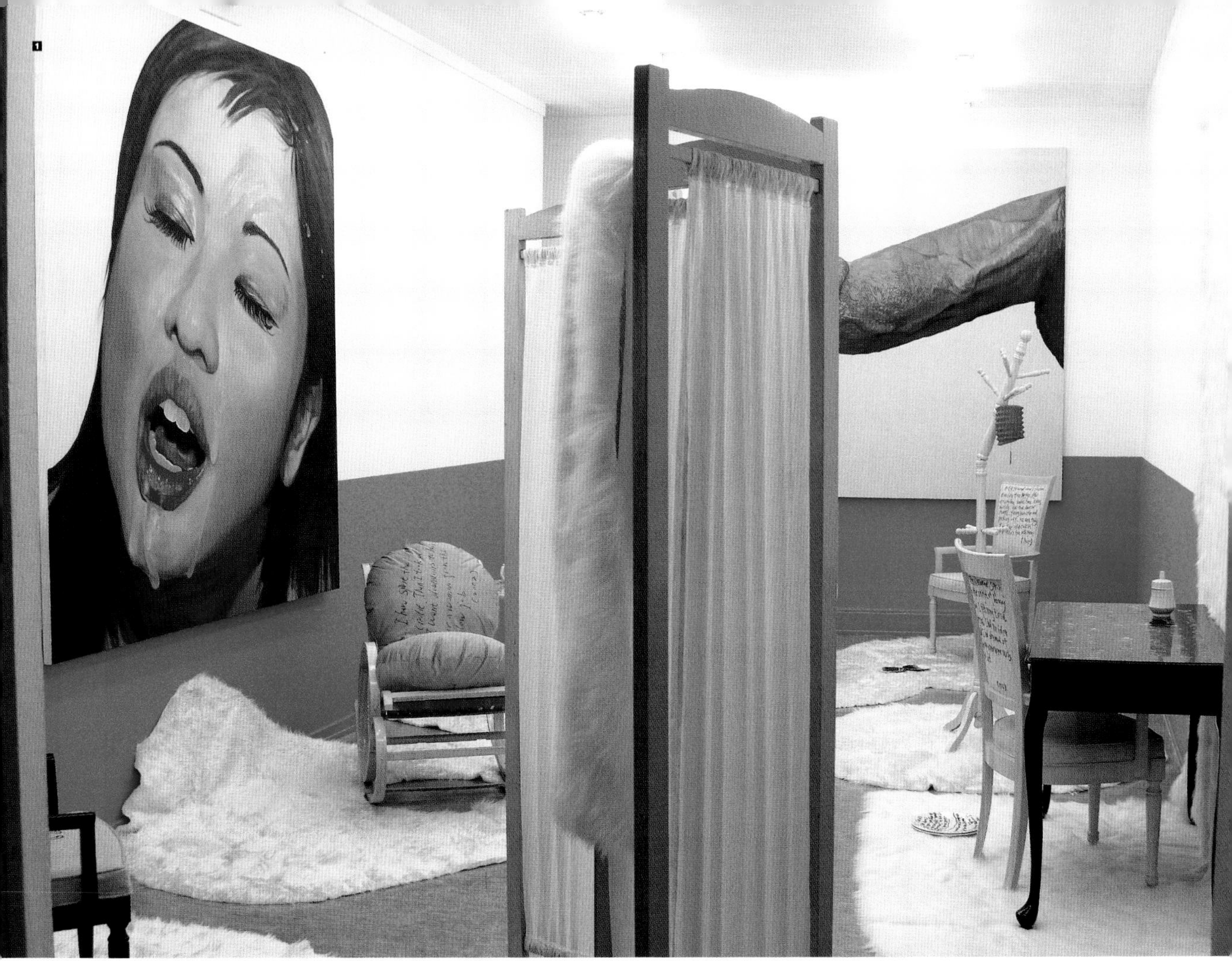

1 TRACES OF SPERM • 2008 • INSTALLATION: BLACK DESK, YELLOW CHAIR, GREEN CHAIRS (2), BLACK CHAIR, WHITE PORCELAIN PLATES (2), GREEN FLOWER STAND, PURPLE TEA TABLE, PINK ROCKING CHAIR & CUSHION, TRIPLE-COLOR PORCELAIN PLATES (2), SCREEN, COAT HANGER, WINE CUP, MILK CUP, CARPET, PAPER LANTERN, OIL PAINTINGS (2) • VARIABLE

2 PRODUCTS • 2005 • PERFORMANCE AND INSTALLATION IN TWO PARTS: 40 PAINTINGS, TRADITIONAL LIVING ROOM FURNITURE

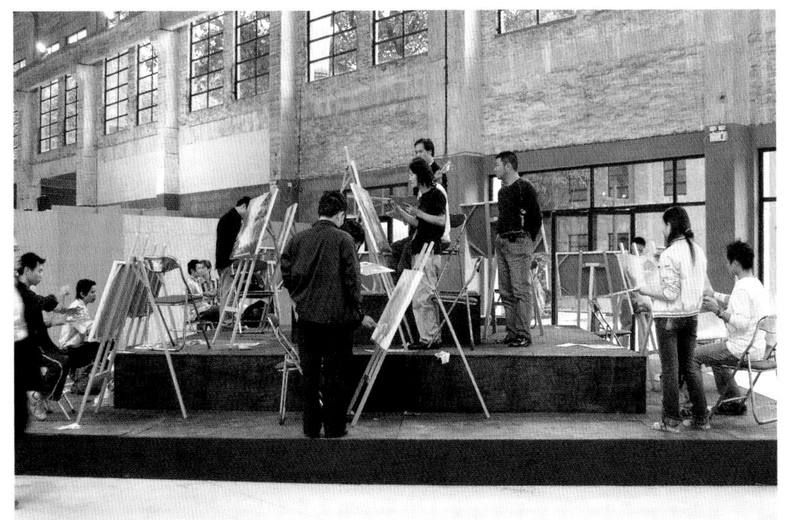

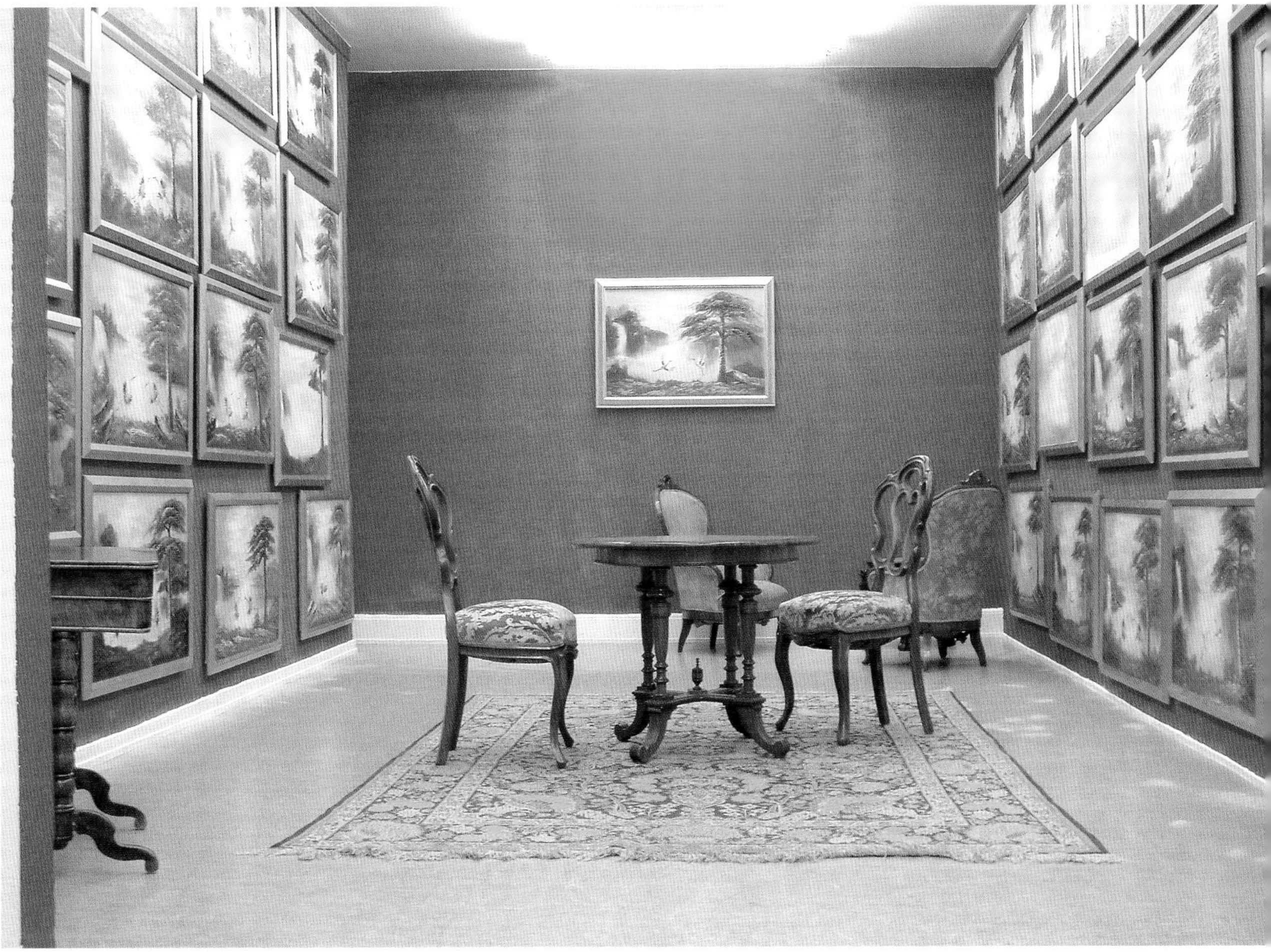

3
4

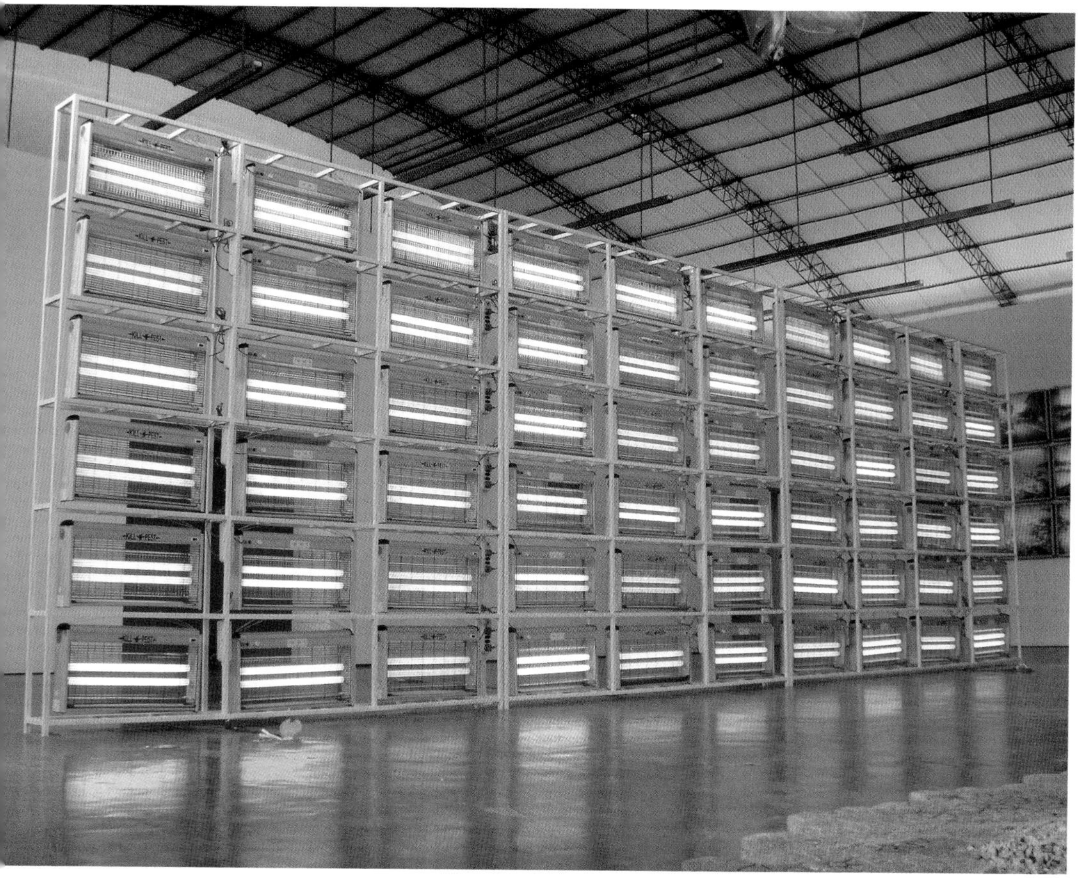

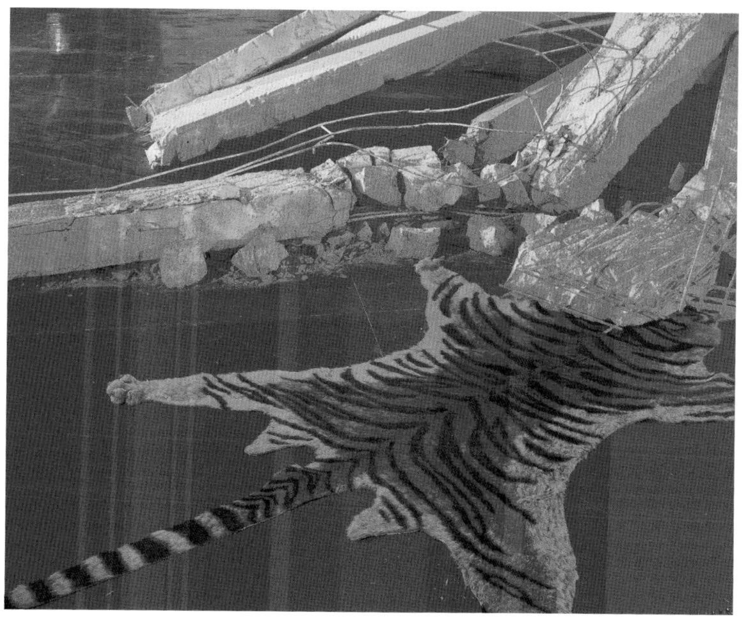

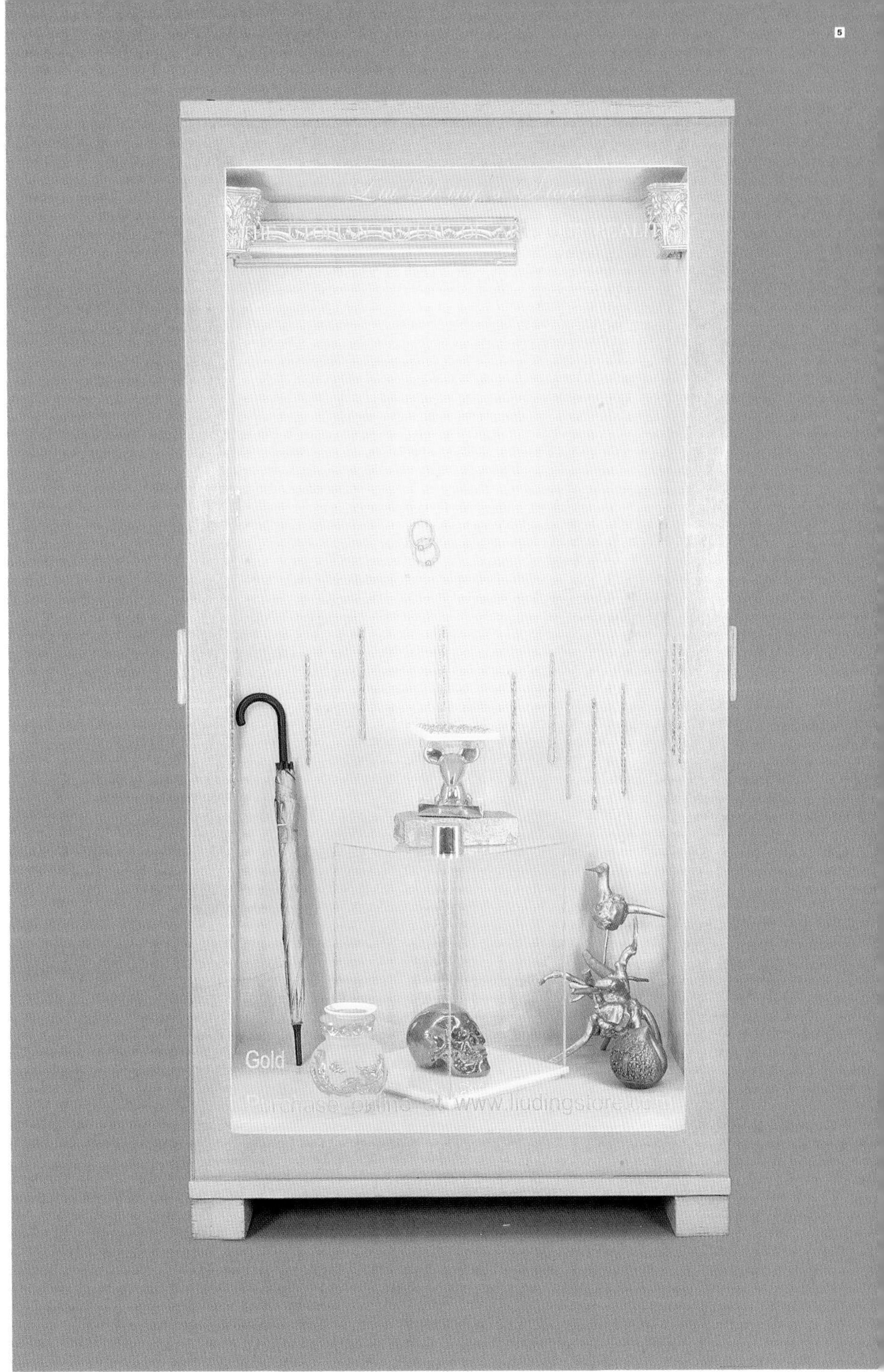

3 IT'S A WAR • 2006 • INSTALLATION: 60 INSECT KILLERS, 30 MOSQUITO BATS, IRON SHELF • 260 x 830 x 40 CM

4 TIGER • 2007 • INSTALLATION: CONCRETE, ARTIFICIAL TIGER SKIN, ACRYLIC MIRROR, BLUE LIGHT • VARIABLE

5 LIU DING'S STORE - THE UTOPIAN FUTURE OF ART. OUR REALITY: GOLD • 2009 • 200 x 100 x 70 CM

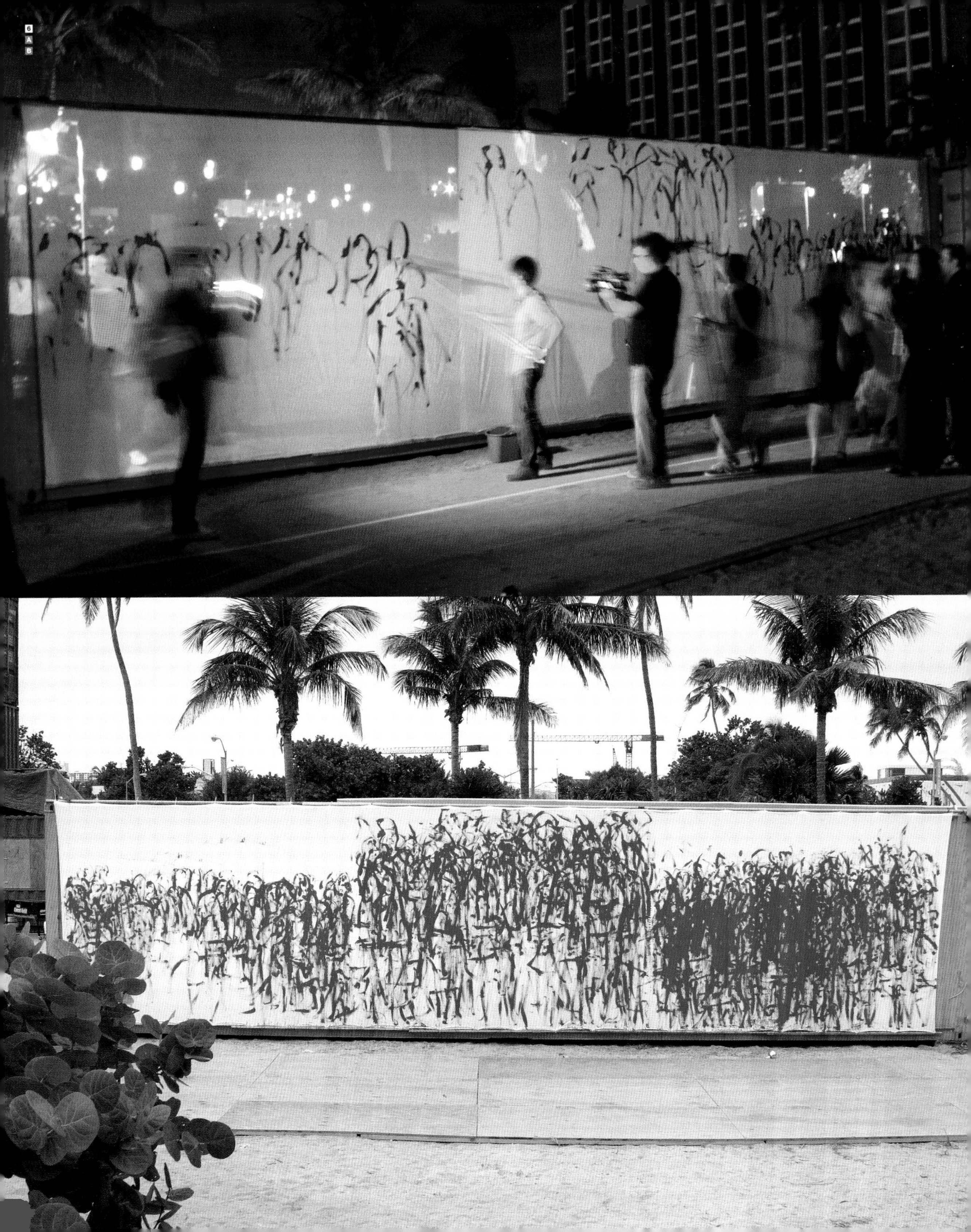
6
A
B

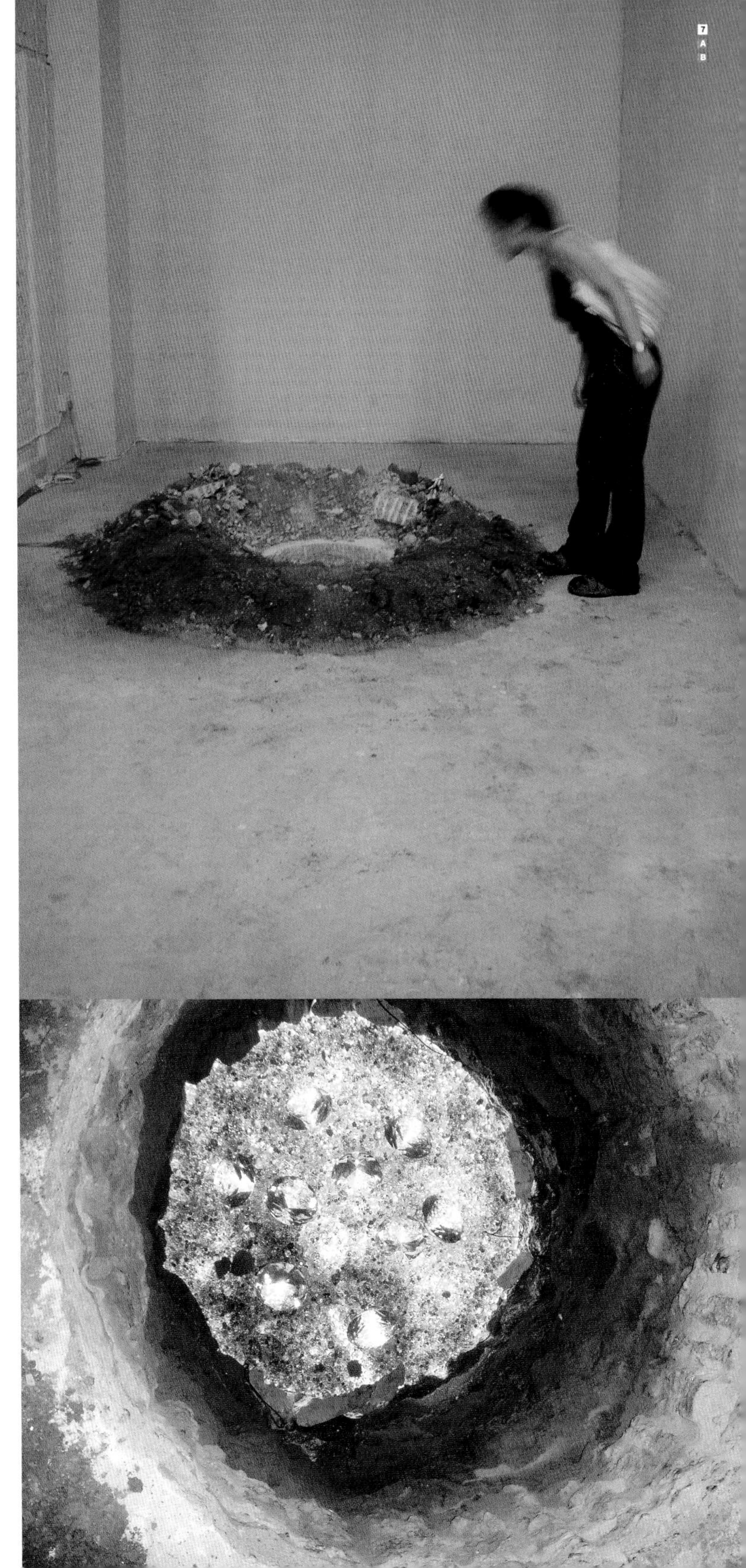

6 TRACING THE WIND AND SHADOWS • 2006 • PERFORMANCE: CANVAS, BLUE PAINT, THREE VIDEO CAMERAS, THREE PROJECTORS • 300 x 1200 CM

7 TREASURE • 2005 • INSTALLATION

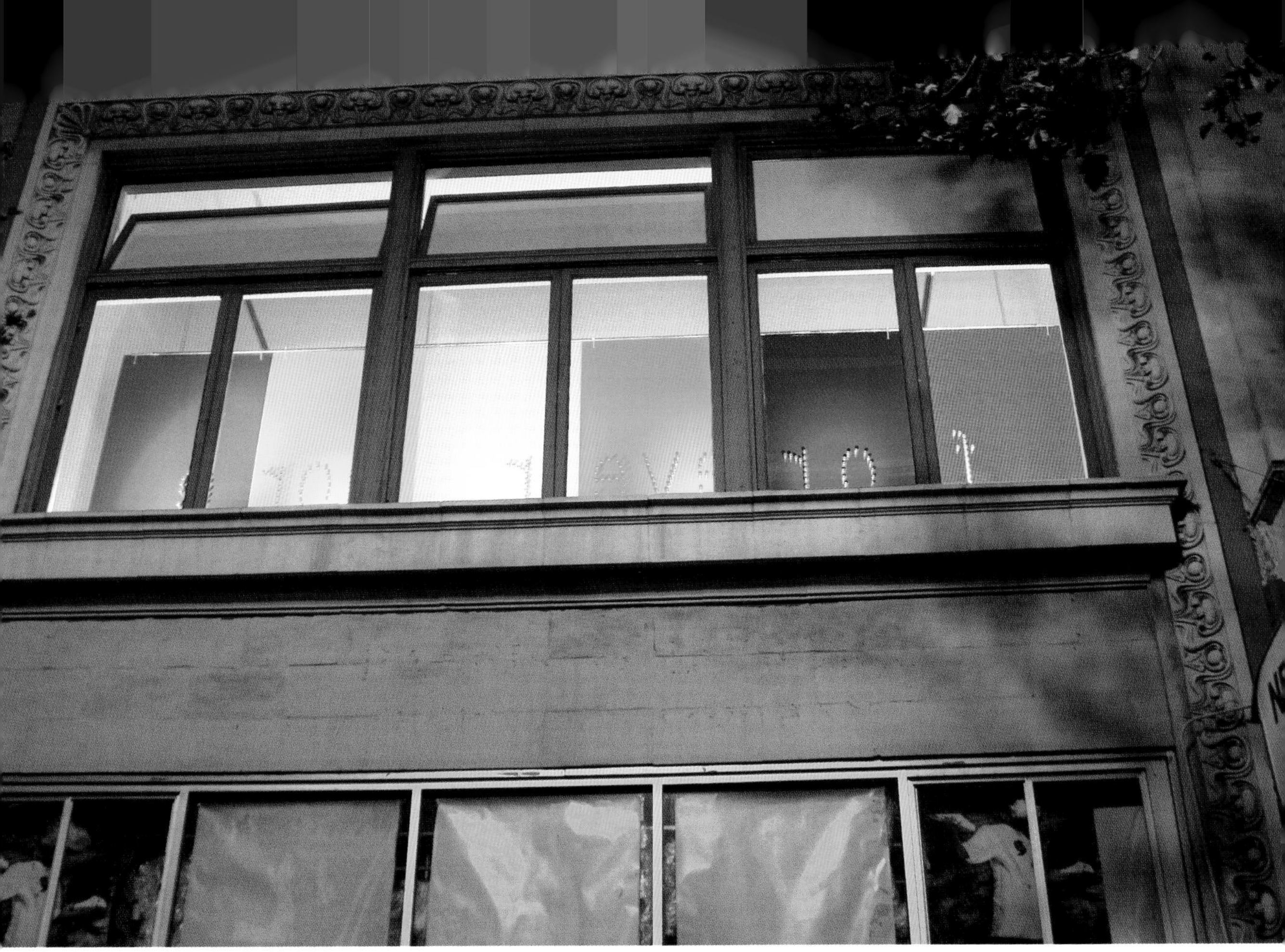

8 FOREVERMORE • 2006 • INSTALLATION

QUESTIONNAIRE

5/7/08 • BEIJING

WHAT WAS YOUR FAVORITE CHILDHOOD TOY?

I've forgotten.

WHAT DID YOUR PARENTS SAY TO YOU MOST OFTEN?

I can't remember.

HOW DO YOU TRY TO STAY HEALTHY IN YOUR EVERYDAY LIFE?

Take more rest.

WHAT HAVE YOU BEEN WISHING FOR MOST RECENTLY?

That my baby will be born healthy.

DO YOU BELIEVE IN TRUE LOVE?

Yes.

WHAT DOES YOUR IDEAL LIVING ENVIRONMENT LOOK LIKE?

An environment where I don't know anyone around me, a completely strange world.

FROM WHICH TYPE OF MEDIA DO YOU DERIVE MOST OF YOUR INSPIRATION?

From books.

WHAT DO YOU LIKE/DISLIKE ABOUT BEING AN ARTIST?

I like being an artist, but not so much creating artworks.

HOW DO YOU COMMUNICATE WITH THE AUDIENCE IN YOUR ART?

I create a suitable environment and atmosphere to communicate with my audience.

IF YOU HAD FIVE WORDS TO DESCRIBE YOUR GENERATION, WHAT WOULD THEY BE?

We have no sense of identity.

IF THE WHOLE WORLD WOULD LISTEN TO YOU FOR FIFTEEN SECONDS, WHAT WOULD YOU SAY?

I would keep silent for fifteen seconds.

EXHIBITIONS

SELECTED SOLO EXHIBITIONS

2009
I wrote down some of my thoughts,
Galerie Urs Meile,
Lucerne, Switzerland

2008
Traces of Sperm,
L.A. Gallery,
Frankfurt, Germany

2007
Tiger,
Universal Studio,
Beijing, China

SELECTED GROUP EXHIBITIONS

2009
53rd Venice Biennale,
Chinese Pavilion,
Venice, Italy

2008
New World Order,
Groninger Museum,
Groningen, The Netherlands

2007
China Power Station: Part II,
Astrup Fearnley Museum of Modern Art,
Oslo, Norway

2007
Forms of Concepts,
Center for Documentary Exhibition of
Fine Arts,
Wuhan, China

2006
AllLookSame?,
Fondazione Sandretto Re Rebaudengo,
Turin, Italy

2006
Dual Realities: The 4th Seoul International Media Art Biennale,
Seoul Museum of Art,
Seoul, South Korea

2006
China Power Station: Part I,
Battersea Power Station,
London, U.K.

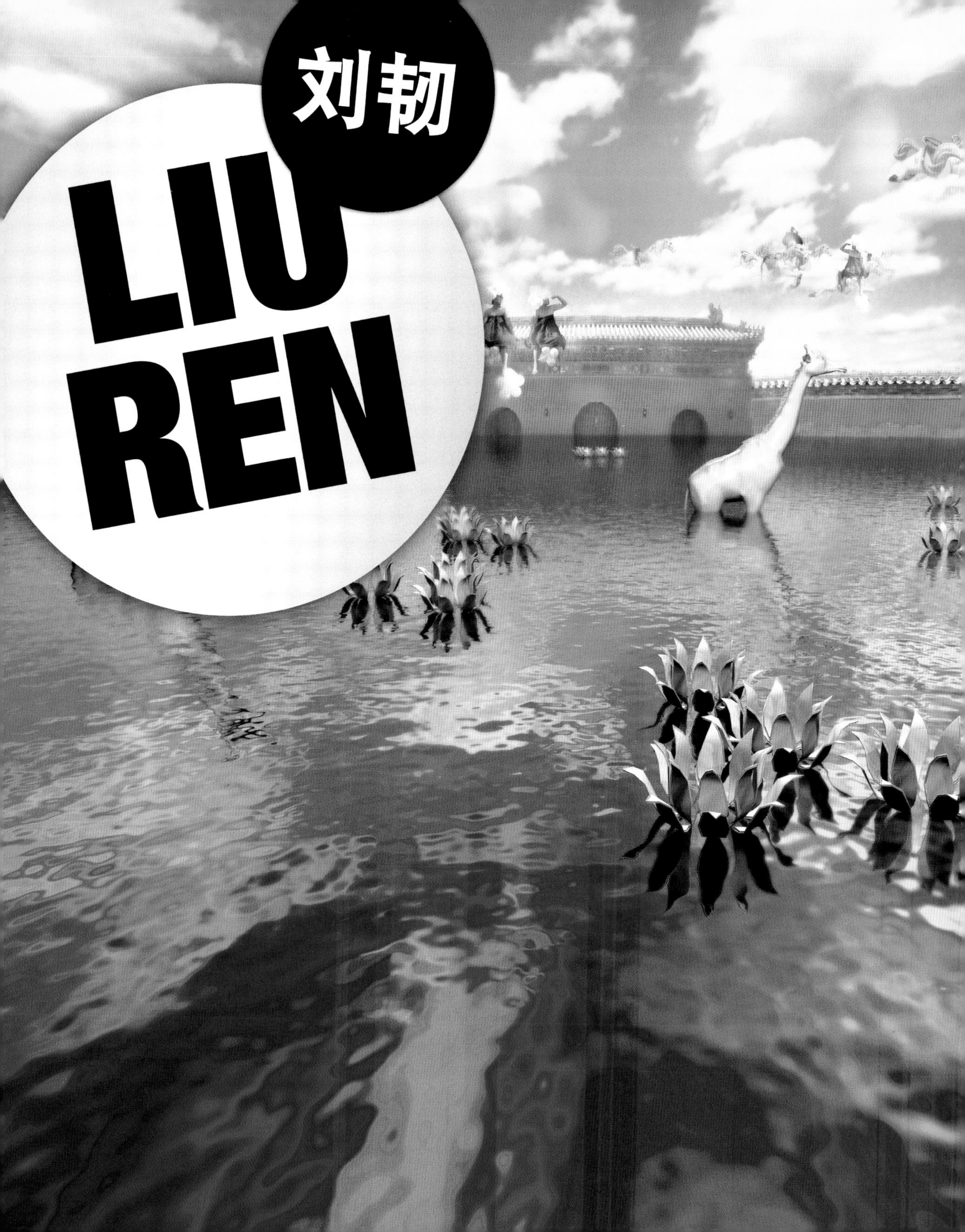
刘韧
LIU
REN

NAME
LIU REN

BORN IN
1980, QINHUANGDAO

LIVES IN
BEIJING

STUDY
CENTRAL ACADEMY OF FINE ARTS, BEIJING

MEDIA
PHOTOGRAPHY

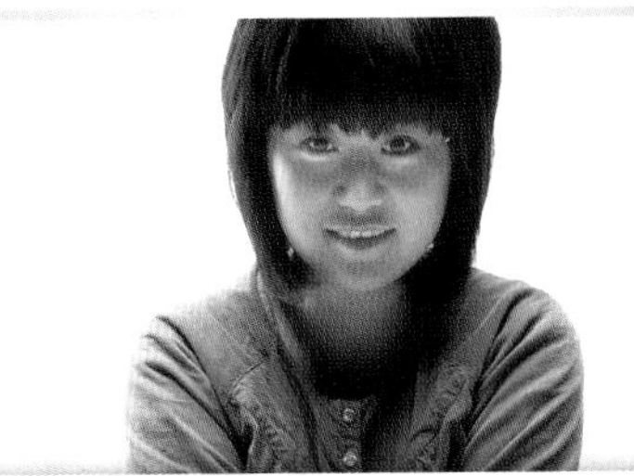

RECORDING MY INNER WORLD

The primary concern of Liu Ren's works is not so much with society, politics, and history on a grand scale, but rather it revolves around her own emotional life. The abstracted and surreal virtual spaces of her images forcefully conjure up dreamscapes. At the same time, however, Liu Ren's works are not at all unrelated to her socio-cultural background. It is very important to her to generate a feeling of time and history, often conflated into one abstracted space. Her nods to classical Chinese painting are reflected in the recurring round image format imitating traditional fan painting. Similarly, ancient architecture features in her works repeatedly. But, she stresses, she only uses these tools when it is relevant to express the main subject of her work: her inner world.

Liu Ren remembers her youth as carefree, dreamy, and leisurely. She still vividly remembers the after-school hours spent daydreaming while the gentle breeze would rush white clouds along the bright-blue sky of her seaside hometown. Liu Ren first completed a BA in industrial design and then worked in a design company for several years. But she felt this work was too stifling for her dreamy character and thus started to contemplate life as an artist. The then newly opened department for photography at the prestigious Central Academy of Fine Arts in Beijing took her on as an MA student in 2004. Liu Ren specialized in digital photography and it is through this media that the artist describes and records her experiences of everyday life, her feelings, dreams, and impressions. "Life is the creator of art, while I am the one recording her."

The first series of works by Liu Ren, completed during the initial year of her MA studies, is entitled *Memory* (2005). The images resonate with loss and melancholy and, according to the artist, record her feelings of lament and distress about her waning youth. This distress is not located in her physical but rather in her emotional aging – the loss of a child's carefree attitude and capacity to dream. The shipwreck in *Memory No. 2* intimates a passage taken, a person having arrived at the other shore and moved on. It is only Liu Ren's memory – giant eyeballs strewn all over the sandy bank – that has remained in this now desolate place.

Liu Ren's series *Someday Somewhere*, also completed in 2005, consists of twelve images. While some of the images are somber, even apocalyptic, others reflect a happy playfulness as well as the artist's penchant towards daydreaming. "The inspiration for most of my works has come from my randomly following my own thoughts all day." *Someday Somewhere No. 2* shows Liu Ren lounging on a couch in her electronically well-equipped apartment. The viewer gets the feeling of catching her in the creative act. It is a sunny winter afternoon; the dozing figure has just turned off the TV and is contemplating her life as a goldfish. Both the symbolism of the goldfish and the round format of the picture – imitating traditional fans as well as entry ways into the inner chambers that by tradition are associated with the female and thus reclusive members of the family – push the viewer, who is linked into the picture by the second glass of tea on the coffee table, into the position of a voyeur.

With time, the works of Liu Ren seem to move out of the deeply private into more general yet still personalized spheres of imagination. *Clouds Floating in Front of My Eyes* (2007) is as much a sentimental ode to the ungraspable passage of time and events as a personal lament about things in her life she could not hold on to – in this case her experiences and thoughts on love. "There are only a few lucky people that can capture love for their whole lifetime. But mostly love is sorrowful. Although it has been sad for me, it still is the most beautiful thing I know." It is this optimism and romanticism that radiates from *Clouds Floating*, yet the pictorial vocabulary clearly documents the dual nature of love such as in the mythological Chang E, living in the moon, forever separated from her husband Hou Yi and the two white horses, united in their purity and love, grazing on the banks of the other shore.

Animals and water are recurring elements in Liu Ren's artworks. They do not merely serve symbolic functions, but are a direct link to the artist herself. It is in the seaside town of her youth that Liu Ren's sensibilities matured, and it is in animals that she feels she can find and reflect the true essence of people's character. Her works are thus often multilayered and there are also those instances where an artwork turns out to be much more critical than Liu Ren originally intended. *Sleepwalker – Great Hall of the People* (2007) is such a case. This is a subversively funny image yet the artist admits that she only saw the work in that light after a viewer asked her about the political implications. "Actually," she said, "it was just a recording of a crazy dream I had."

By Xenia Piëch

1

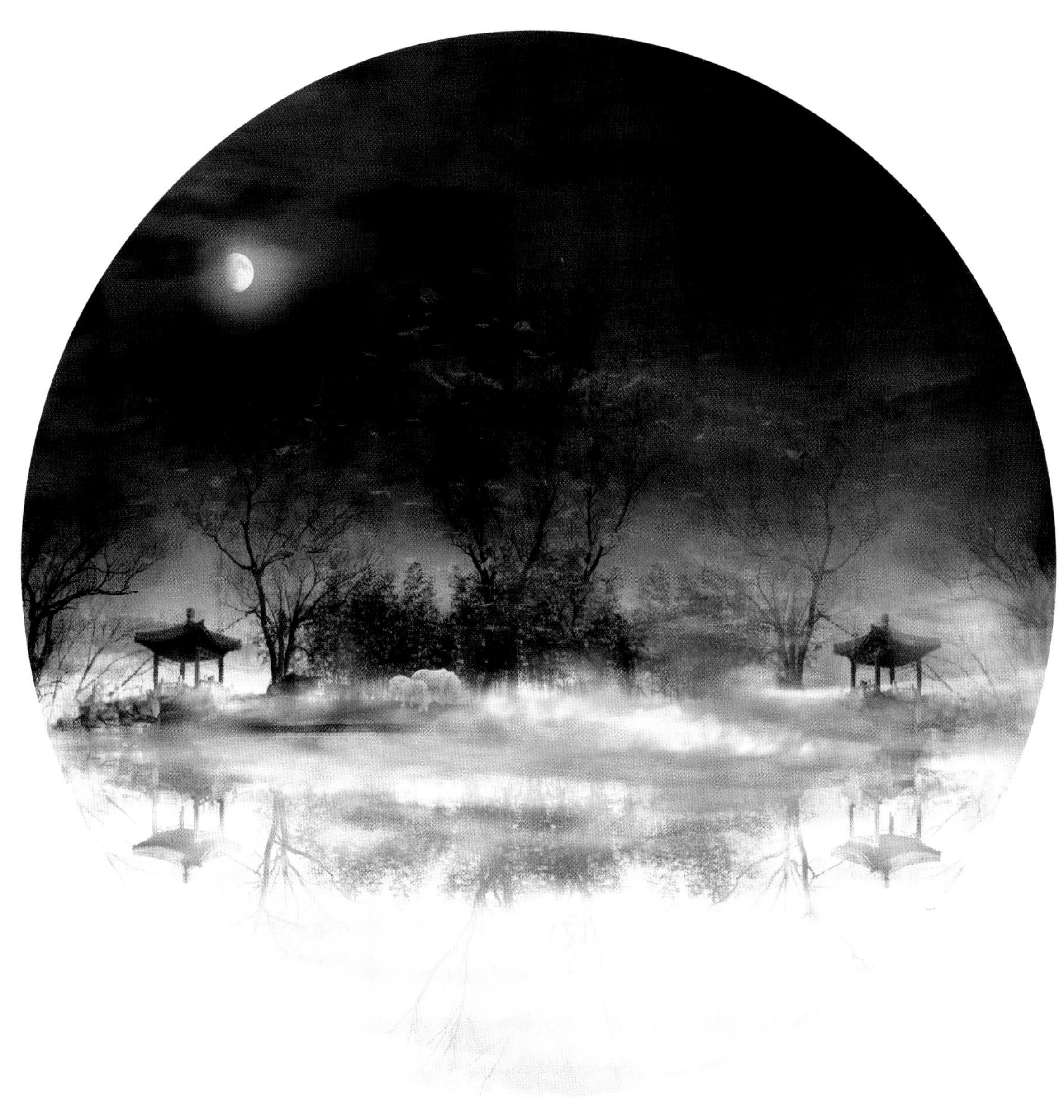

1 CLOUDS FLOATING IN FRONT OF MY EYES • 2007 • C-PRINT • 120 x 120 CM

2 SOMEDAY SOMEWHERE NO. 11 • 2005 • C-PRINT • 100 x 100 CM

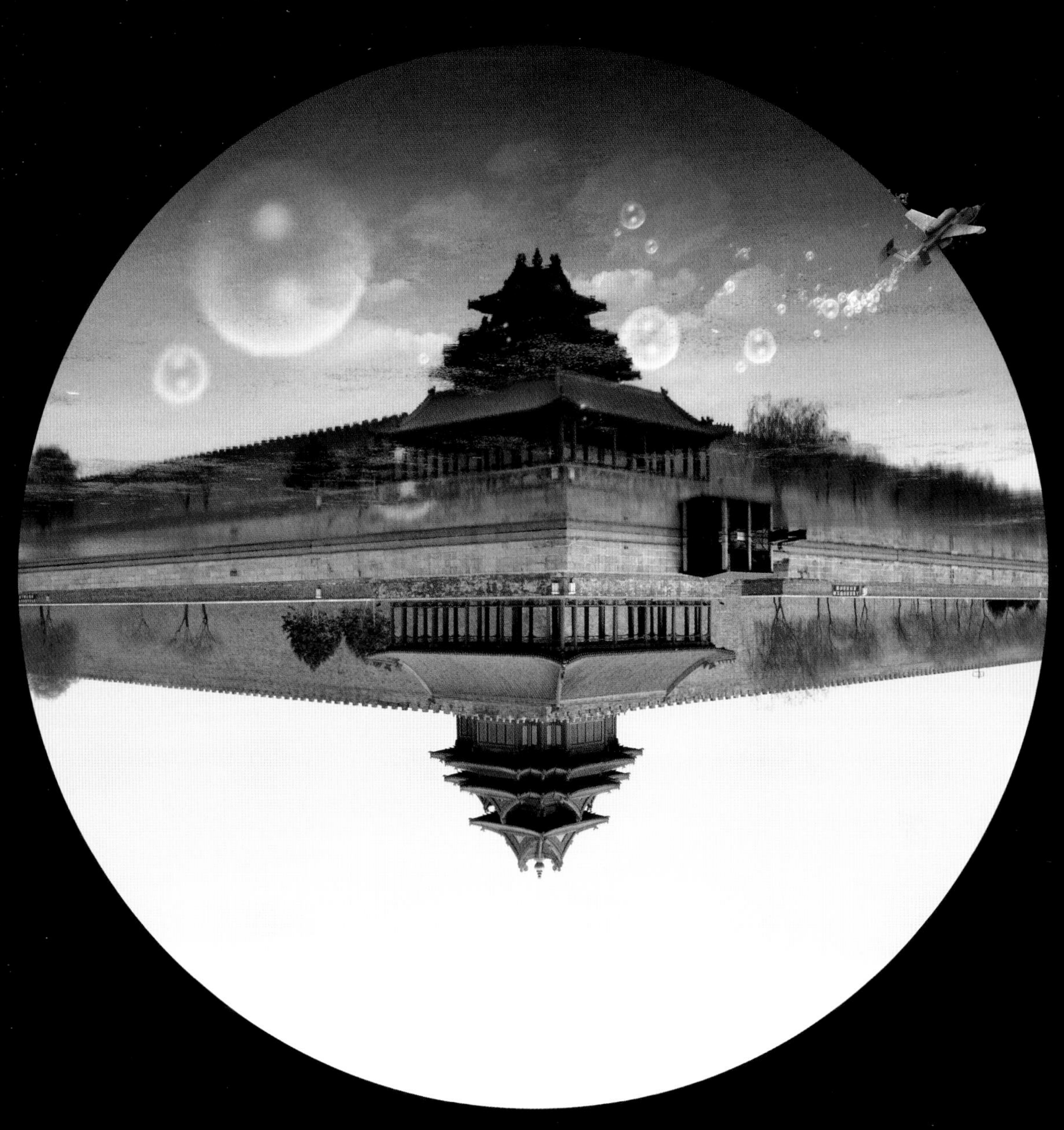
2

3

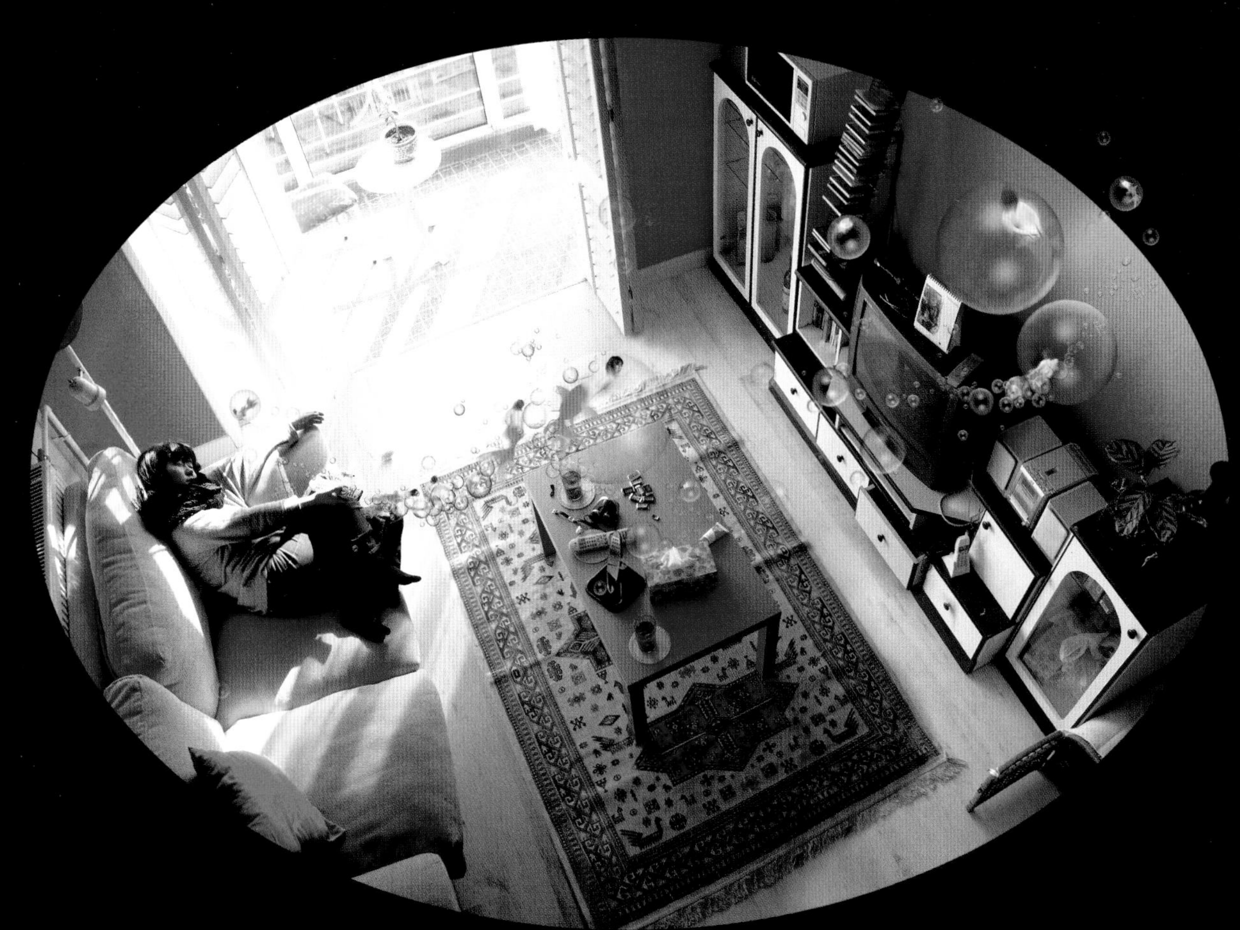

3 SOMEDAY SOMEWHERE NO. 2 • 2005 • C-PRINT • 70 x 100 CM

4 MEMORY NO. 2 • 2005 • C-PRINT • 100 x 75 CM

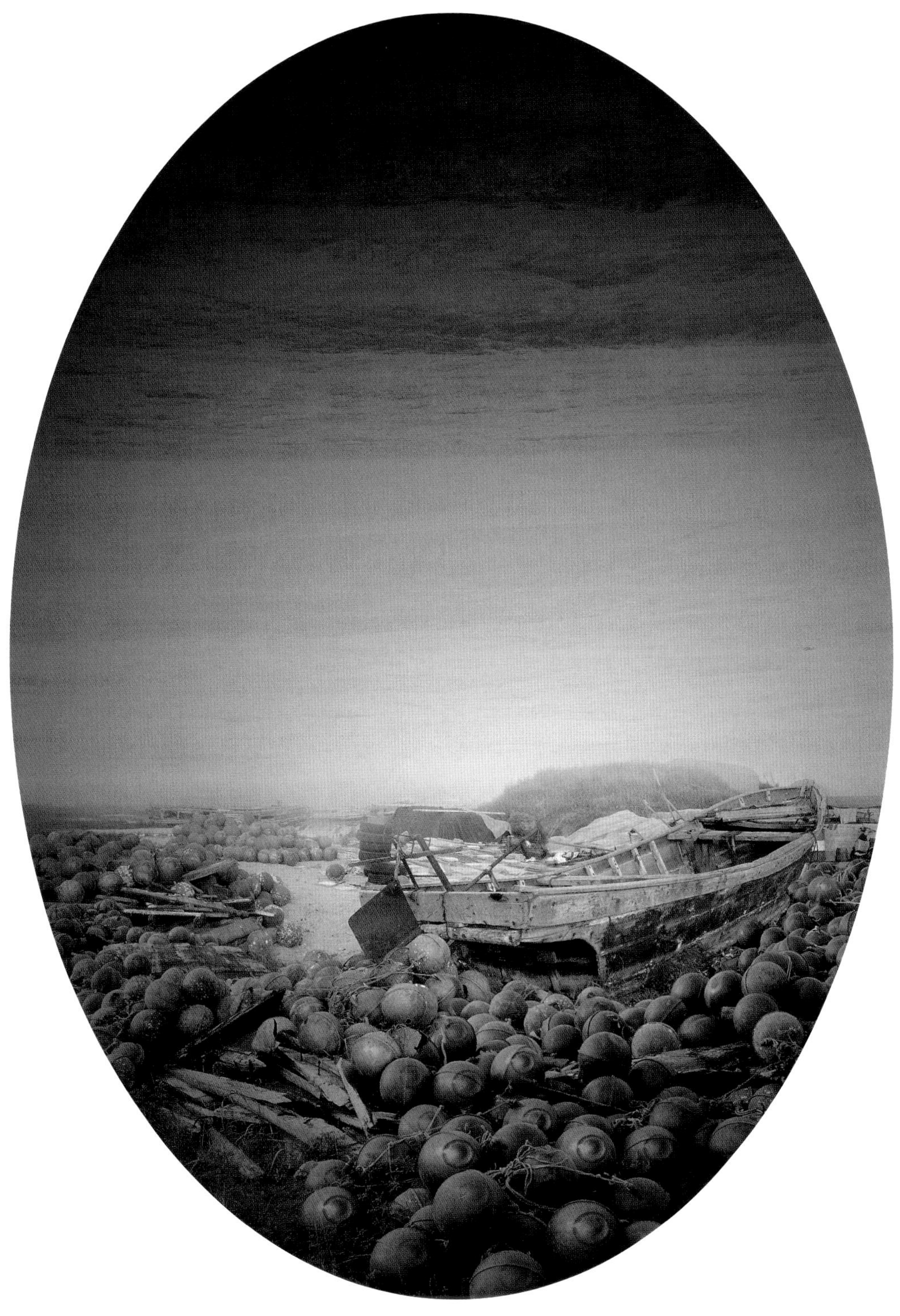

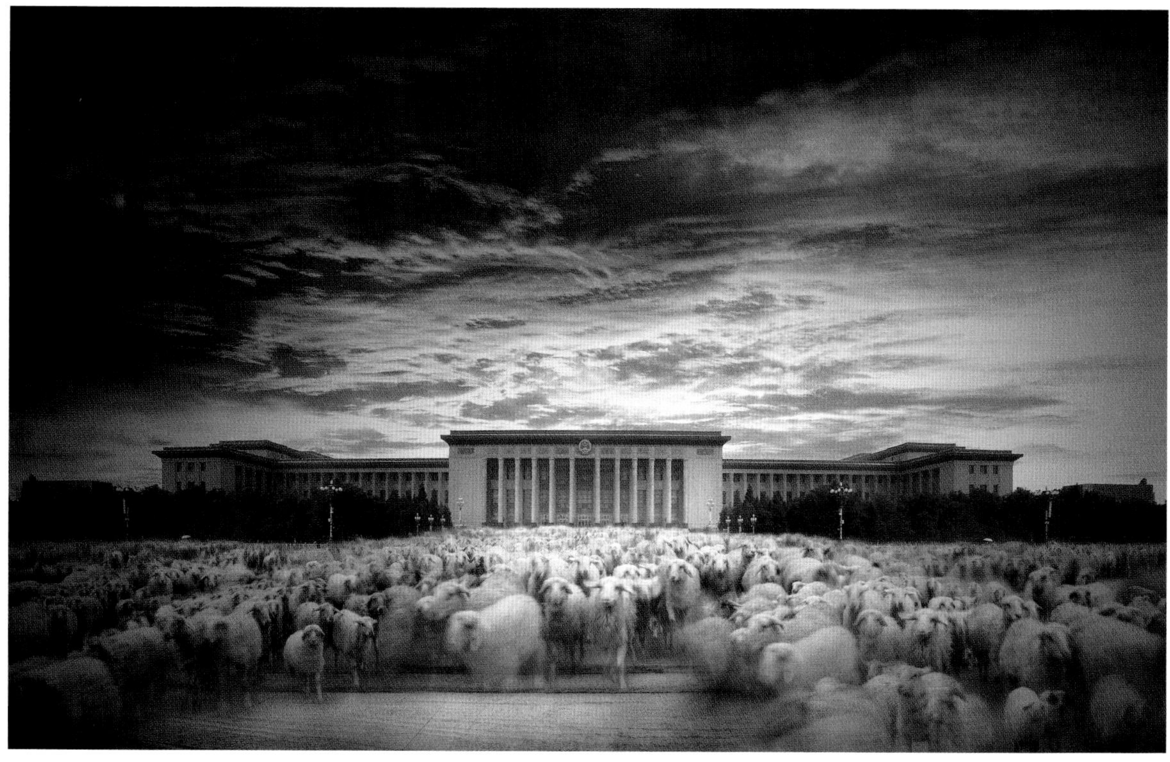

ONLINE CHAT WITH EDITORS

4/24/08 • AFTERNOON

[14:18:17] How's your day been so far?

[14:21:49] I haven't done anything special. Actually, I have thought of different ideas and concepts for a while and a lot of my inspiration comes from these spontaneous thoughts.

[14:23:10] What was your favorite childhood toy?

[14:28:34] A Donald Duck puppet. It was a gift from my parents. My dad spent nearly his month's salary. When I was a child, it was very hard to buy something special. But I always could find something around me to play with; I could be preoccupied with a tiny marble for a whole day.

[14:30:45] Which sentence did your parents say to you most often?

[14:36:17] That depends very much on the situation. For example, right now, they're always encouraging me to fall in love very soon. And while I was studying for my Masters, they told me not to get too tired. They influence me in many parts of my life.

[14:38:00] Did you always listen to them?

[14:40:13] I think I'm generally a "good child," and that I've made my parents very proud.

[14:41:41] How do you keep up a healthy lifestyle?

[14:44:07] Currently, my everyday routine is pretty irregular, and even if I tried to go to the gym I wouldn't be able to continue. But I try not to eat out too often.

[14:46:36] Can you tell us something about what you've been wishing for most recently?

[14:49:13] I have so many wishes, but if I can only name one ... let me think. I guess to meet my "Mr. Right" and to get married.

[14:51:00] What's your ideal living environment?

[14:53:19] I would like to live in a big house. The ideal location would be having the advantages of a city while enjoying the silence of the countryside. I would also love to have a few good friends around me, as well as my parents and my future children. In my spare time I would draw and read poems.

[14:57:50] What do you like or even dislike about being an artist?

[14:59:17] I especially appreciate the "powerful" characteristics that come with being an artist. You have to be determined.

[15:01:40] How do you communicate with the audience through your art?

[15:02:47] My art often shows at exhibitions and published in catalogues and magazines.

[15:05:10] Five words to would describe your generation?

[15:08:22] Idealism, romance, responsibility. And, two more, selfhood and materialism.

[15:11:05] And finally: If the whole world would listen to you for fifteen seconds, what would you say?

[15:14:55] "All of you should listen to me and my thoughts forever."

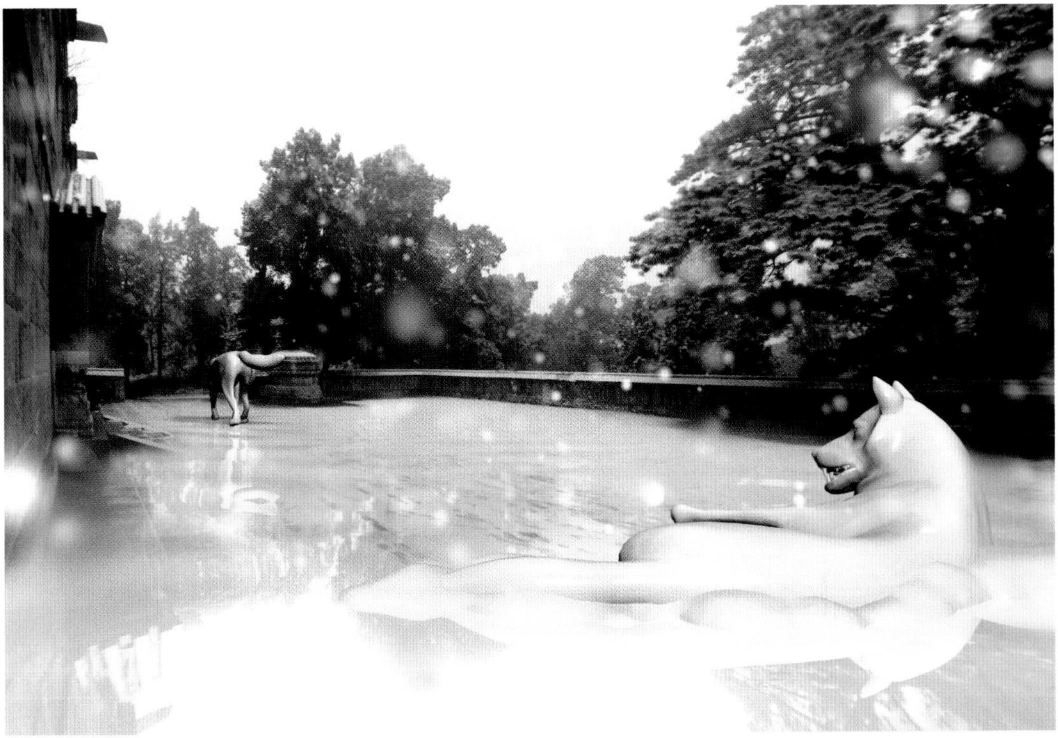

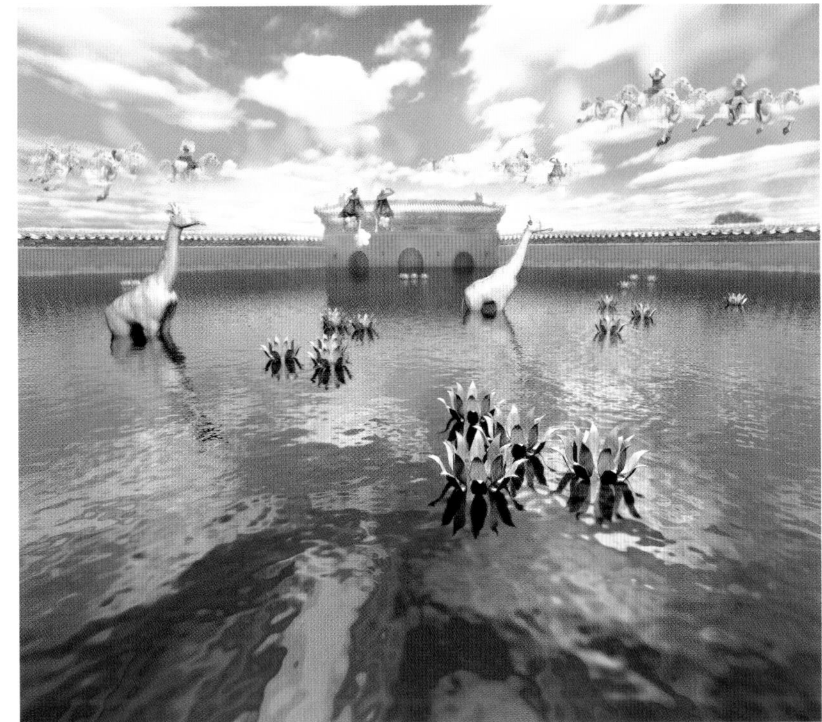

5 SLEEPWALKER – GREAT HALL OF THE PEOPLE • 2007 • C-PRINT • 90 x 145 CM

6 DREAM SEEKING NO. 1 • 2009 • C-PRINT • 120 x 179 CM

7 PARADISE NO. 1 • 2006 • C-PRINT • 90 x 100 CM

8

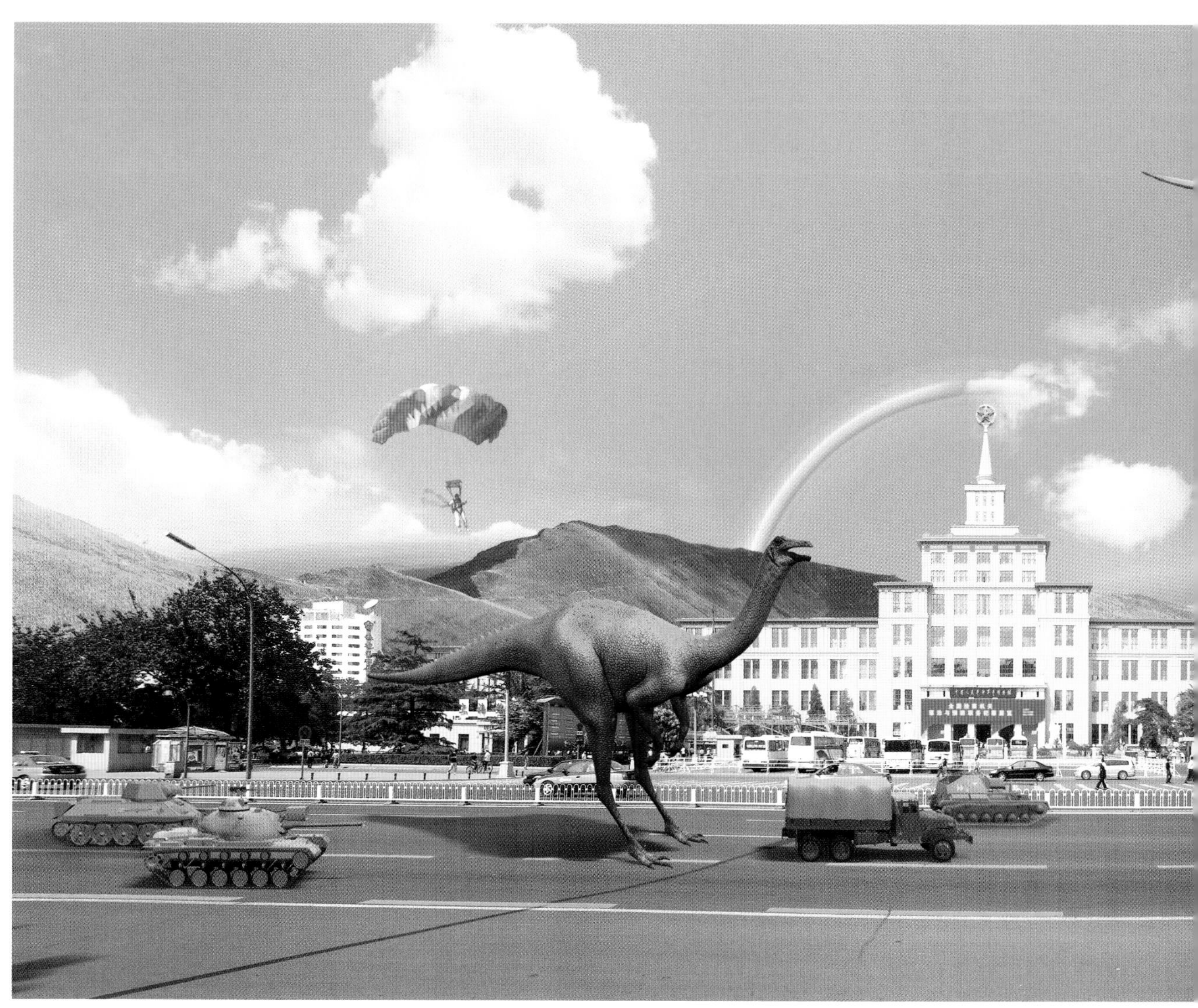

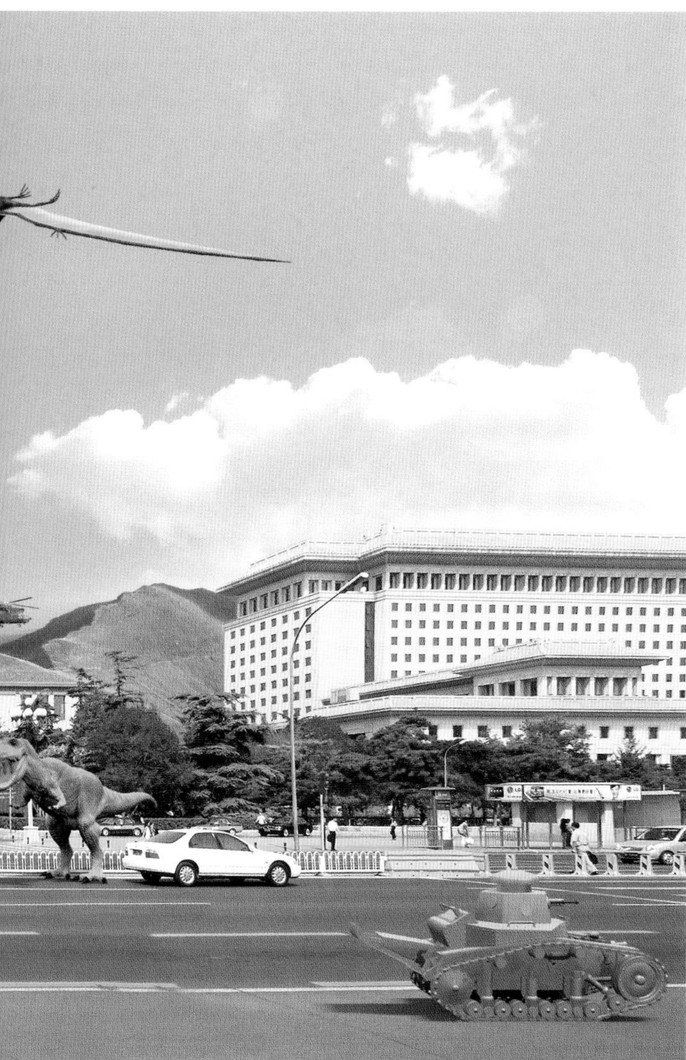

8 SLEEPWALKER – THE MILITARY MUSEUM • 2007 • C-PRINT • 90 × 185 CM

EXHIBITIONS

SELECTED SOLO EXHIBITIONS

2008
Between the Real and the Surreal,
VIPS International Art Galleries,
Rotterdam, The Netherlands

2006
Someday Somewhere,
Paris-Beijing Photo Gallery,
Meridian International Center

SELECTED GROUP EXHIBITIONS

2009
Metropolis Now,
Meridian International Center,
Washington, U.S.

2008
Fotofest 2008,
Houston, U.S.

2007
Between Reality and Illusion,
Marty Walker Gallery,
Dallas, U.S.

2006
Les Rencontres d' Arles,
Arles, France

2006
Changing China,
London Gallery West & University of Westminster,
London, U.K.

2006
Ultra-Sense,
Seoul International Photography Festival,
Seoul, South Korea

2006
Pingyao International Photography Festival,
Pingyao, China

2005
The Second Reality:
Photographs from China,
Piazza of the Berlaymont Building,
Brussels, Belgium

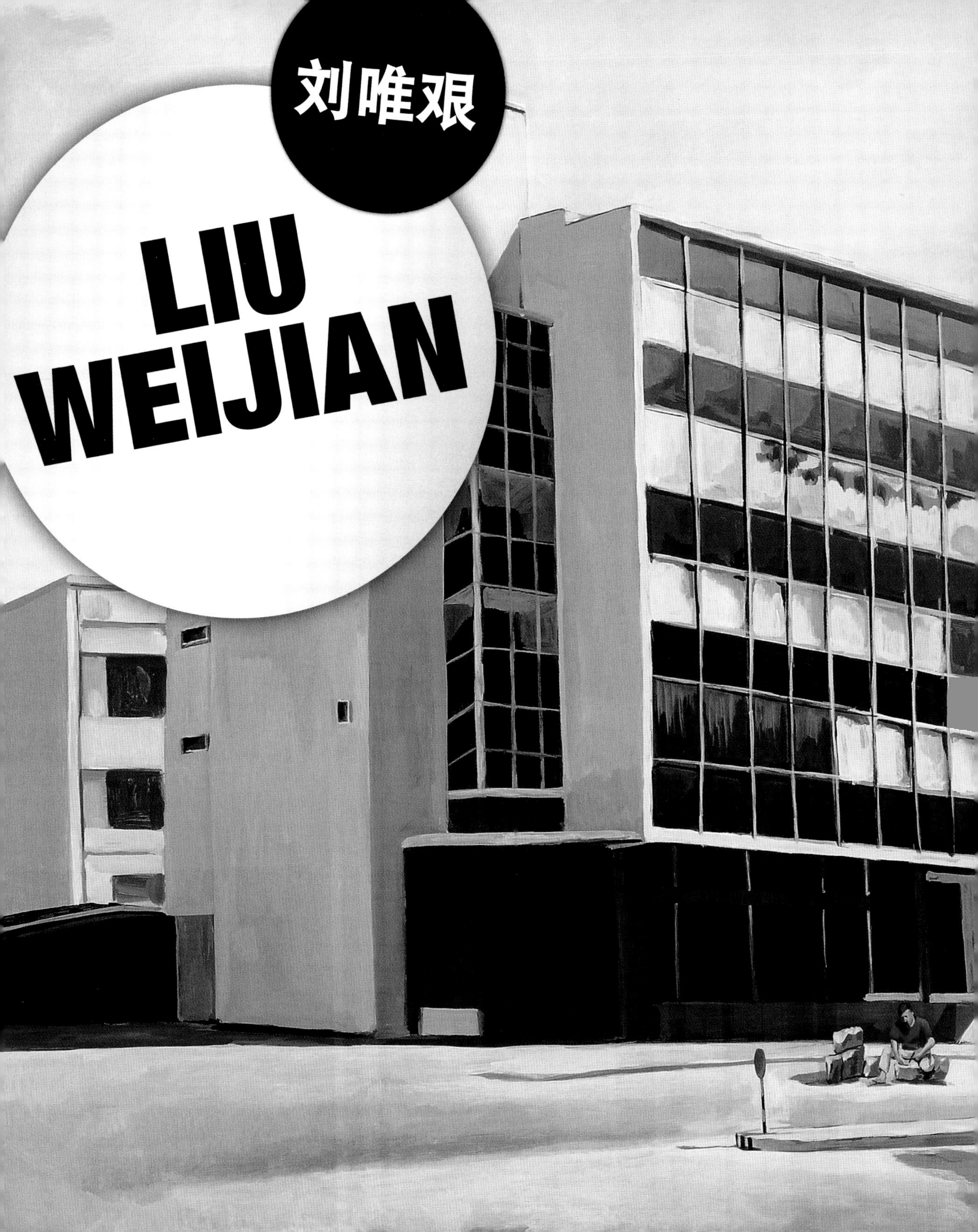
刘唯艰
LIU
WEIJIAN

NAME
LIU WEIJIAN

BORN IN
1981, HUNAN PROVINCE

LIVES IN
SHANGHAI

STUDY
SHANGHAI NORMAL UNIVERSITY, SHANGHAI

MEDIA
PAINTING, PHOTOGRAPHY

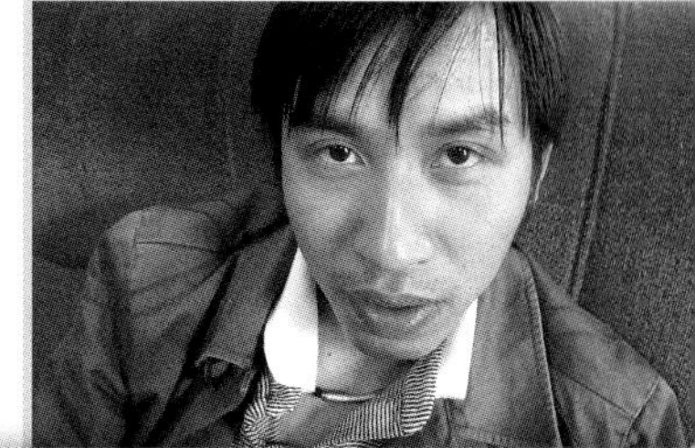

MIND MAPPING

Appearances can be deceiving in the paintings of Liu Weijian. Very often they convey the impression of twisted realities or fragments of dreams half remembered, eccentric encounters and expansive horizons. Yet despite such ambiguities his work navigates a reasoned if crooked path between the rational and metaphysical.

In early works such as *Wanted Hero* (2004), the viewer looks down across a vast, apparently deserted landscape of high-rise apartments and factory buildings that recedes in the distance to near-geometric abstraction. The relentless gray tones give the scene a grim, Orwellian monotony that is enforced by the presence of a loudspeaker on a tall pillar in the center of the picture whose proclamations can be read in scratchy red characters. Almost unnoticed beneath a balcony, two tiny figures can be seen conferring, as if conspirators in a hostile environment.

This nameless urban setting is a persistent feature of Liu's work and has possible antecedence in the mushrooming tower blocks of Shanghai, where Liu has lived since attending the Fine Art College of Shanghai Normal University from 2001 to 2005. Yet the architectural lines are not only a handy way of bracing his compositions, but also act as Liu's accomplices in the events they frame.

In later pieces he tightens the scene within courtyards, rooms, and car parks. In *Without Story* (2007), the picture is dominated by a multistory office block in front of which is a dwarfed, lone figure, apparently carving a block of stone. Meanwhile, in *Partial Problems* (2007) a technician in a white boiler suit peers intently into an open metallic hatch. Banks of similar hatches line the walls of a long, windowless gallery that streams away from the viewer towards a distant doorway. In each case the ambiguity of the busily engaged figures keeps the viewer at a distance. It is a feeling that is heightened by the incongruity of the subjects and their surroundings, and suggests a kind of psychoanalytic landscape.

In *Waiting* (2007), the sensation of unknowable activity is magnified by Liu's focus on two, white-coated figures who attend to a scientific-looking apparatus. Here, context is subordinated to a preoccupation with intense, anonymous activity. The feeling of spatial and temporal separateness is enforced by Liu's use of an archive black-and-white photograph as a model for the painting. It fixes the activity within a remote place and time that is distinct both from the artist's real-life experience of it, and magnified for the viewer by the artist's transformation of the event in paint.

All of Liu Weijian's paintings, with the exception of two, are based on magazine photos to which different, dislocated elements are frequently added. Sometimes these are present as discreet settings that are not immediately obvious, but very often they are much more apparent and directly contribute to the awkward strangeness of his pictures and the conceptual discussion taking place. His own photography provides an additional conceptual guide, however he has not shown any of this work except for a small number of exhibitions.

In *Waiting*, the straight, painterly translation of an already reported event strips the image to its conceptual essentials and narrows our interpretation to labor without obvious purpose. Such dryness finds an echo in the more recent series entitled *Properties* (2007), in which the artist isolates such objects as electrical appliances, switch boxes and fire hydrants and can be most simply read as "function."

The idea of "work" or "function" as a defining characteristic of being therefore has genuine resonance for Liu. The artist's name, "Liu Weijian," can be translated as "Only with hard work," and was given to him by his uncle. Meanwhile, his father kept the family's farm in Hunan Province in order to support Liu's uncles in their university studies. Today, one is an architect and the other is a microbiologist. For his son, Liu Weijian's father envisioned a future as a scientist. But as an artist Liu appears to believe it is his function to examine the ground on which this idea stands, and more specifically its relationship to the wider human condition at the beginning of the twenty-first century. As Liu explains, his paintings typically combine parallel forms of consciousness; worlds of the known and the unknown; "of hard facts and science and emotion or magic," he says. "A photograph is a real record of time and space, but by transferring it to paint it is emotionally transformed."

The complementary themes in Liu's work rise and fall, sometimes intersecting and sometimes finding resolution; yet the general path of his work is continually unfolding and with each new configuration reveals fresh lines of divergence. Within the context of contemporary Chinese painting, Liu Weijian's position is slippery. The fact that many of the photographs from which he works feature Chinese faces is conceptually incidental. Instead, the artist focuses on elemental themes that transcend specific cultural categories and connect to the contradictory nuances of the human condition within an increasingly alienating environment.

By John Millichap

1
2

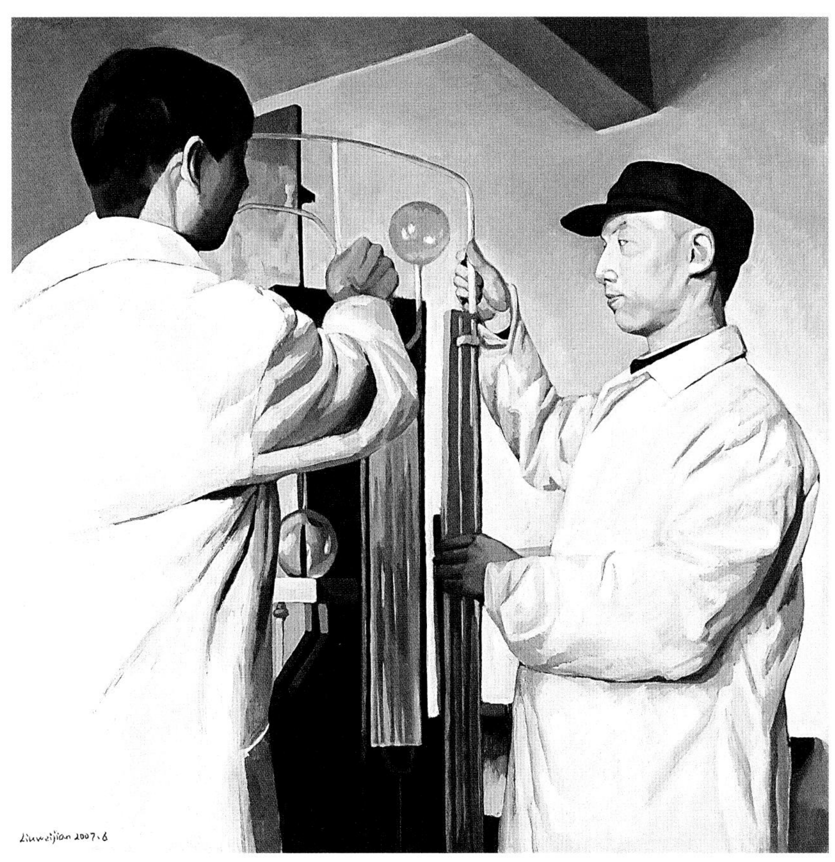

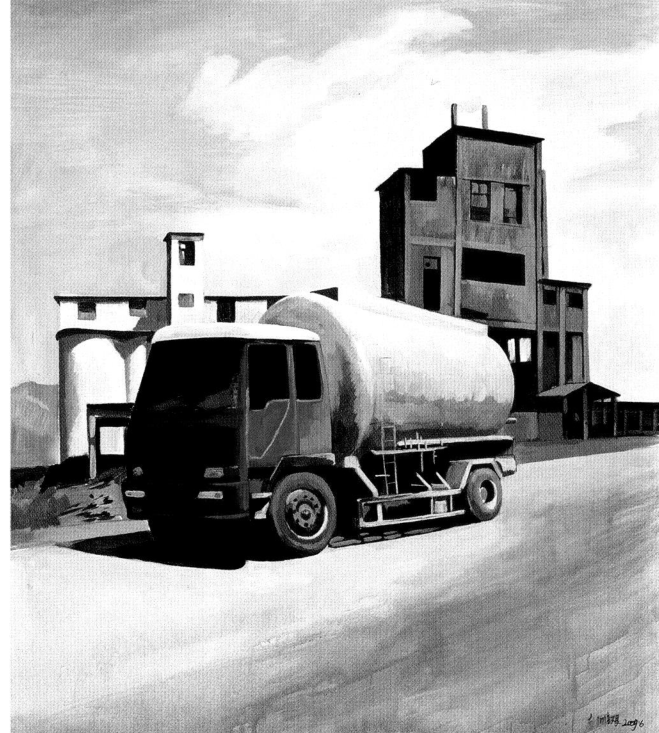

3

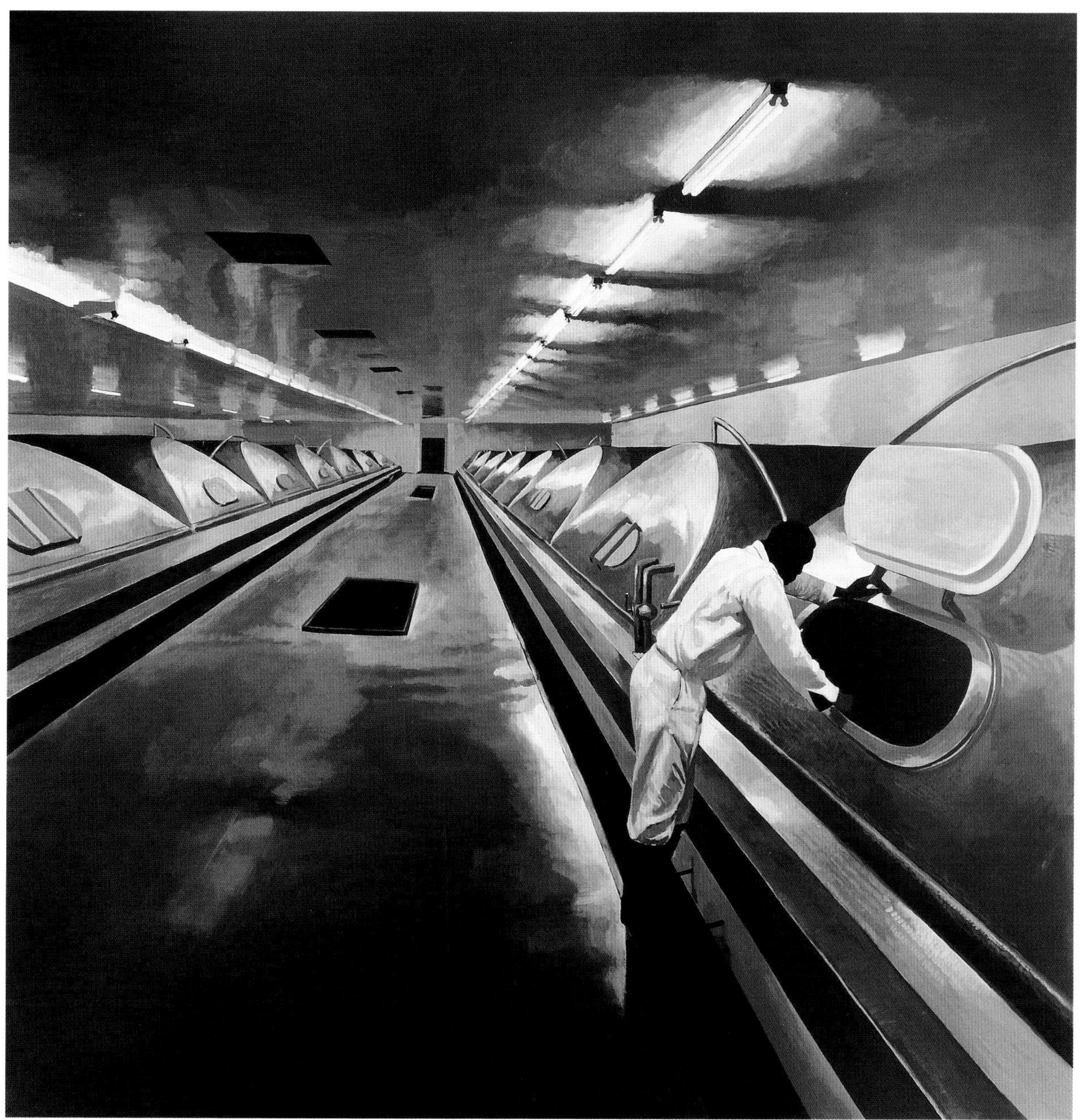

1 WAITING • 2007 • ACRYLIC ON CANVAS • 100 x 100 CM

2 DANGEROUS ONGOING • 2009 • ACRYLIC ON CANVAS • 170 x 150 CM

3 PARTIAL PROBLEMS • 2007 • ACRYLIC ON CANVAS • 150 x 150 CM

4

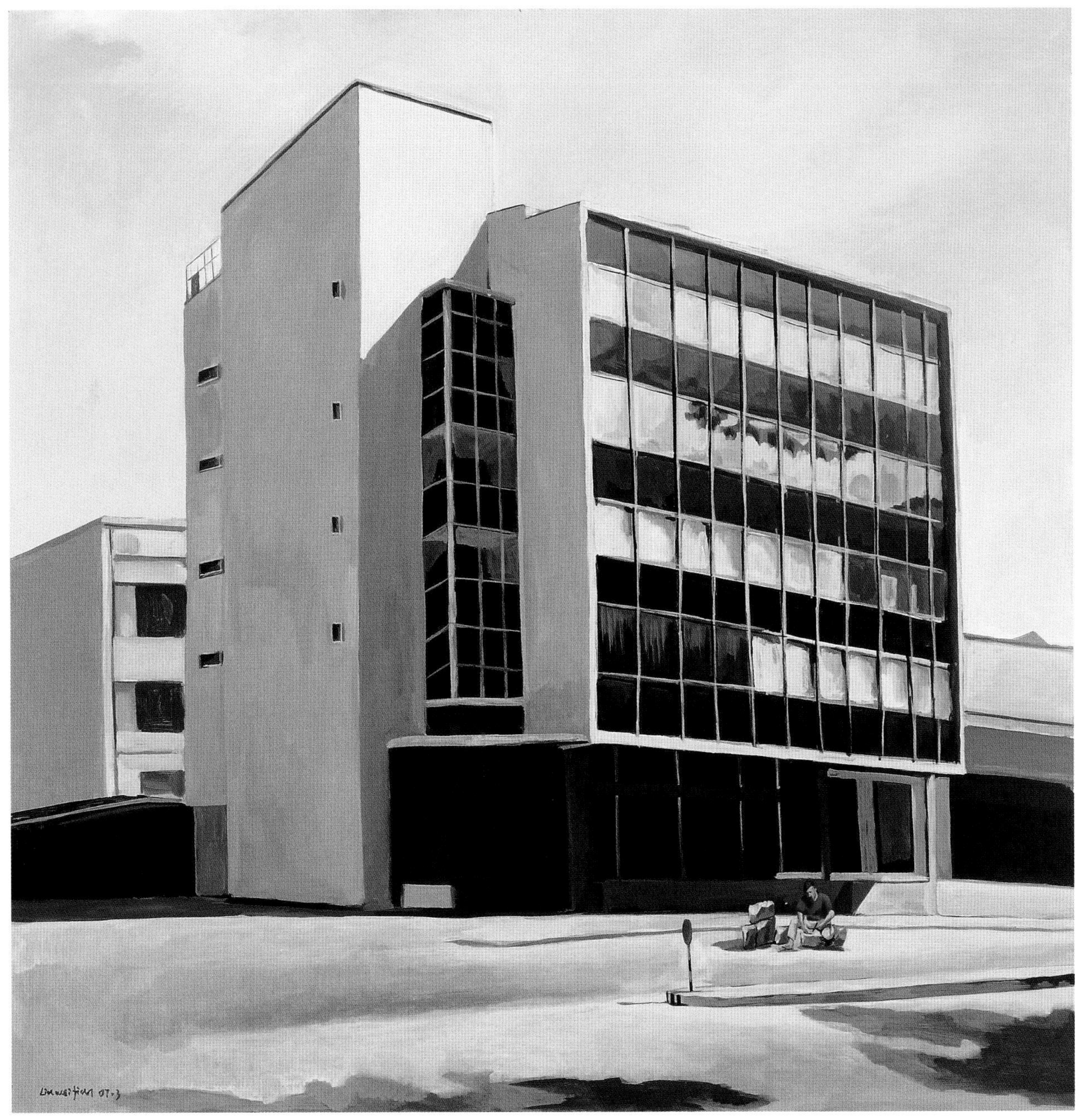

4 WITHOUT STORY • 2007 • ACRYLIC ON CANVAS • 100 x 100 CM

5 KEEPING A CERTAIN MEANING • 2007 • ACRYLIC ON CANVAS • 120 x 160 CM

6 GUARDING ROOM • 2007 • ACRYLIC ON CANVAS • 120 x 160 CM

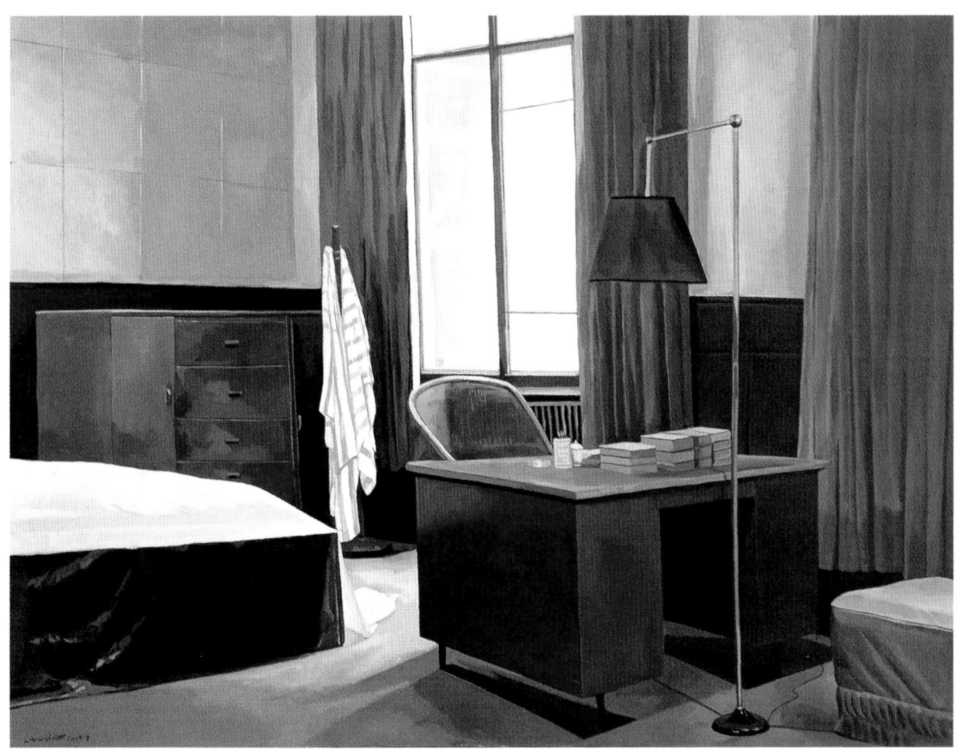

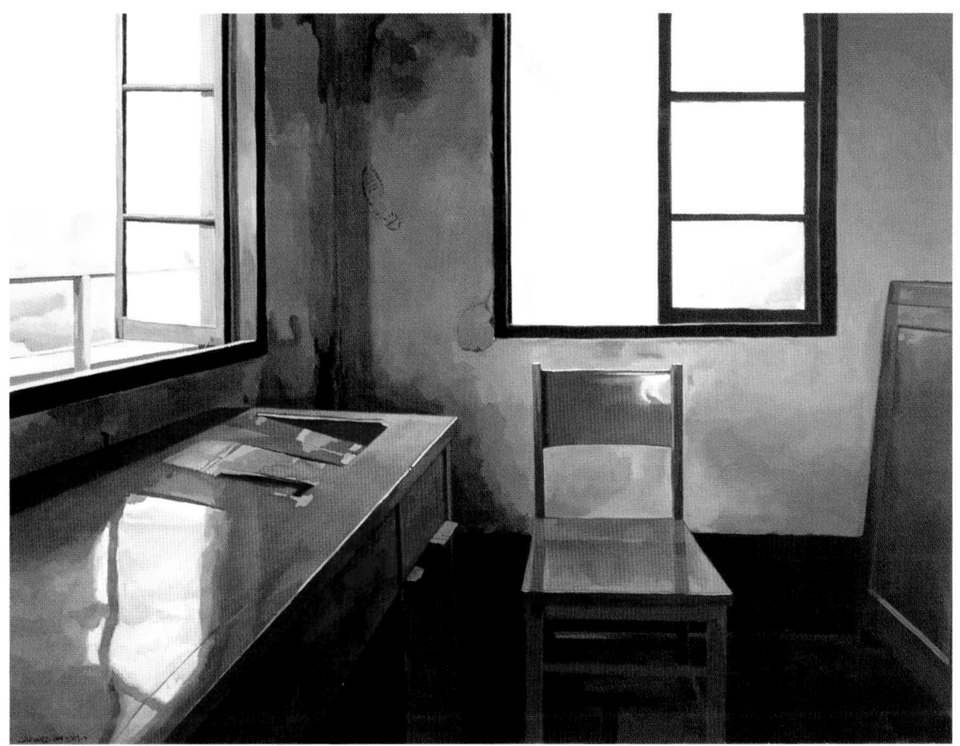

7

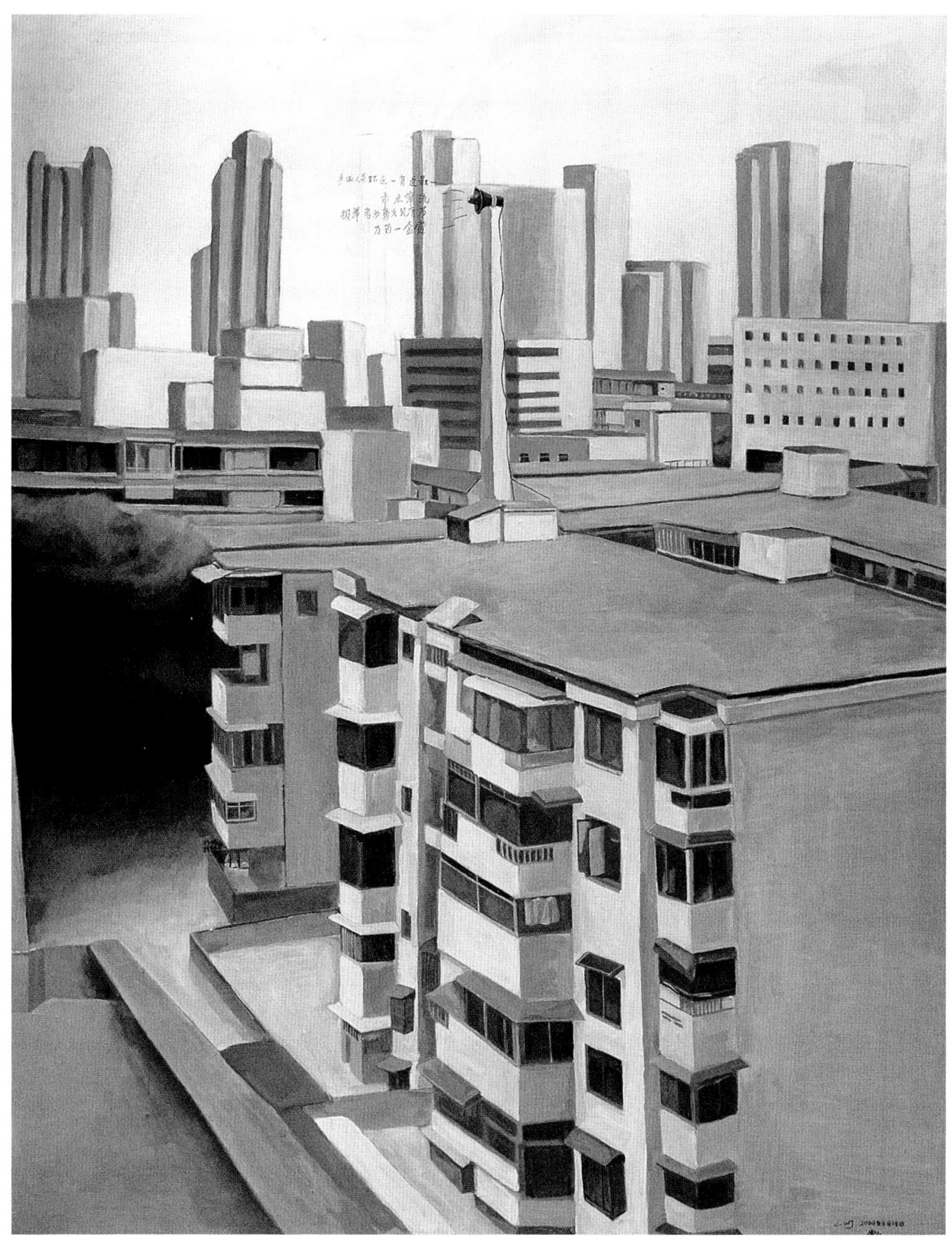

7 WANTED HERO • 2004 • ACRYLIC ON CANVAS • 190 x 150 CM

8 NATURAL SELECTION IS THE ONLY SOURCE OF ORDER • 2005 • C-PRINT • 80 x 120 CM

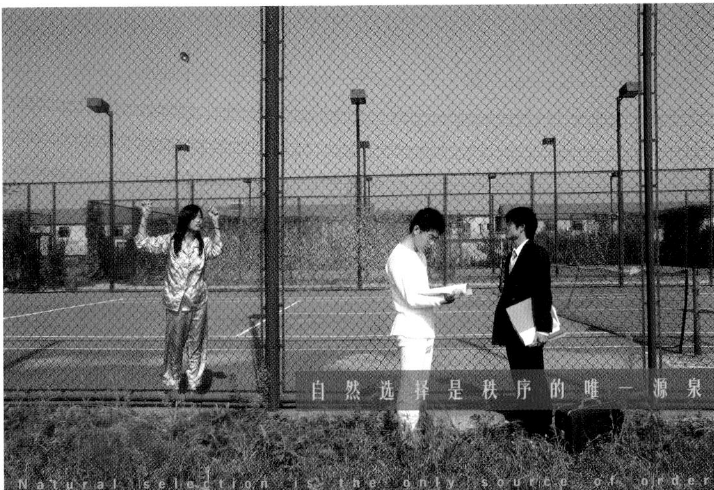

QUESTIONNAIRE

5/2/08 • SHANGHAI

WHAT WAS YOUR FAVORITE CHILDHOOD TOY?

Small cars which I made.

WHAT DID YOUR PARENTS SAY TO YOU MOST OFTEN?

"Have you eaten your meal?"

HOW DO YOU TRY TO STAY HEALTHY IN YOUR EVERYDAY LIFE?

I never think about that.

WHAT HAVE YOU BEEN WISHING FOR MOST RECENTLY?

To have exhibitions in some foreign countries.

DO YOU BELIEVE IN TRUE LOVE?

Yes, I do. It can be like the life of a monk.

WHAT DOES YOUR IDEAL LIVING ENVIRONMENT LOOK LIKE?

Having freedom and no worries.

FROM WHICH TYPE OF MEDIA DO YOU DERIVE MOST OF YOUR INSPIRATION?

All of them are a source of inspiration. But they are not the main source.

WHAT DO YOU LIKE/DISLIKE ABOUT BEING AN ARTIST?

I like it because I find it no trouble. There's nothing I dislike.

HOW DO YOU COMMUNICATE WITH THE AUDIENCE IN YOUR ART?

Through my exhibitions.

IF YOU HAD FIVE WORDS TO DESCRIBE YOUR GENERATION, WHAT WOULD THEY BE?

I don't know which generation I belong to.

IF THE WHOLE WORLD WOULD LISTEN TO YOU FOR FIFTEEN SECONDS, WHAT WOULD YOU SAY?

I have nothing to tell the people of the world.

EXHIBITIONS

SELECTED SOLO EXHIBITIONS

2009
Liu Weijian,
ShanghART,
Shanghai, China

2007
The Call of the Crows,
BizArt Art Center,
Shanghai, China

2006
Specimen and Secret,
Creative Garden,
Shanghai, China

SELECTED GROUP EXHIBITIONS

2007
Amateur World,
Platform China,
Beijing, China

2007
The First Today's Documents: Energy-Spirit, Body, Material,
Today Art Museum,
Beijing, China

2007
China Power Station: Part II,
Astrup Fearnley Museum of Modern Art,
Oslo, Norway

2006
Gifts 2: A Case of Contemporary Art,
Fanren Villa,
Hangzhou, China

2006
Satellite 2006,
Contemporary Art Pavilion,
Shanghai, China

2006
2nd Shanghai Duolun Exhibition of Young Artists,
Duolun Museum of Modern Art,
Shanghai, China

2006
China's Cutting Edge: New Video Art From Shanghai and Beijing,
Anthology Film Archives,
New York, U.S.

马延红

MA YANHONG

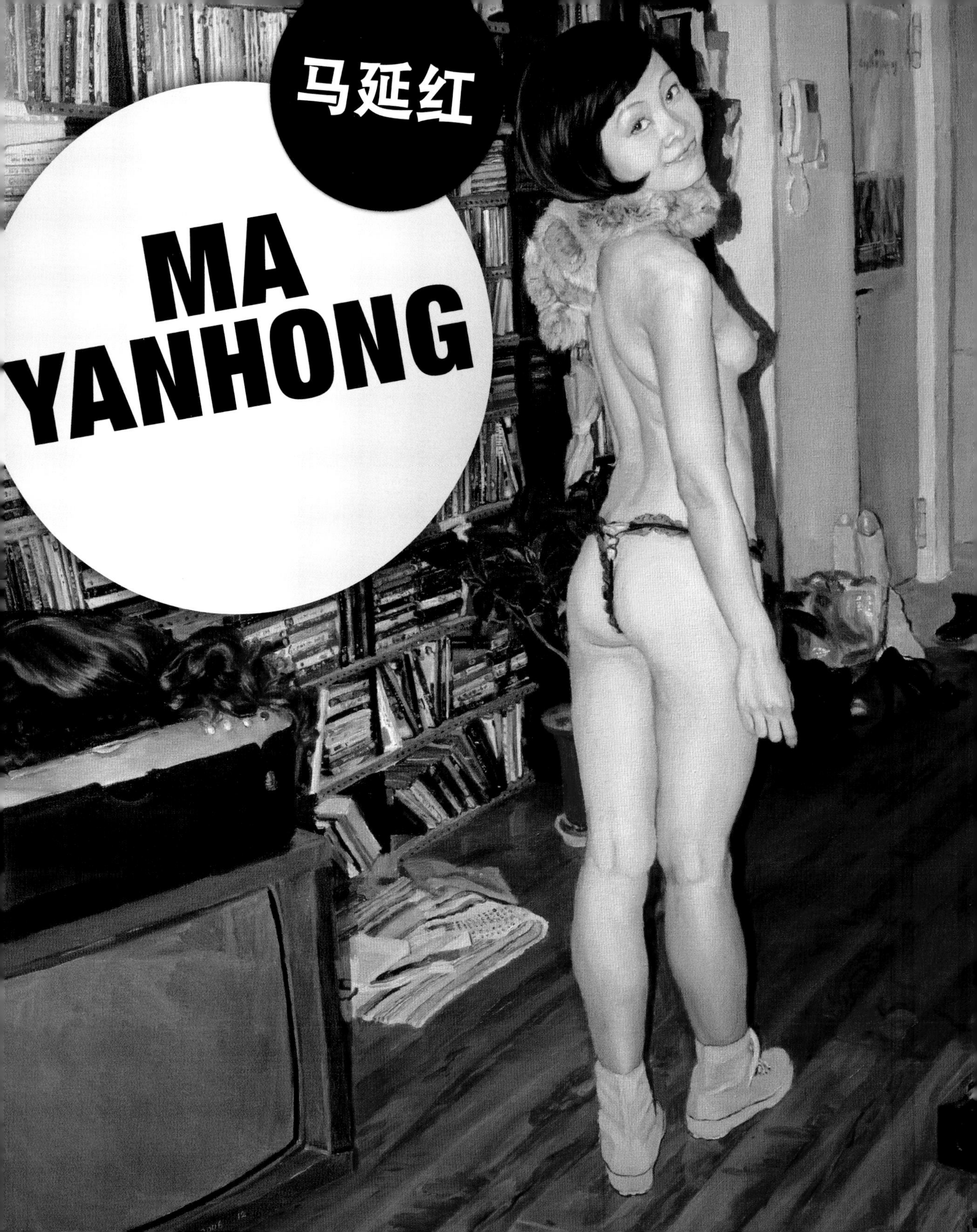

NAME

MA YANHONG

BORN IN

1977, SHANXI PROVINCE

LIVES IN

BEIJING

STUDY

CENTRAL ACADEMY OF FINE ARTS, BEIJING

MEDIA

INSTALLATION, PAINTING

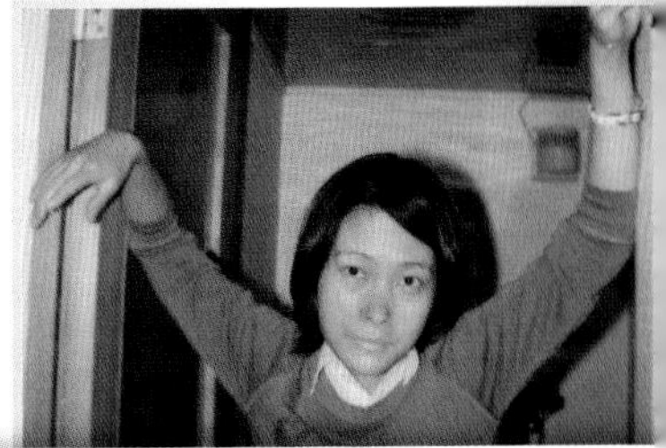

THE COLORS OF SKIN

In traditional Chinese art, detailing the depiction of the human body was simply deemed uninteresting. In its "aesthetic of floating" (François Jullien), the physical appearance of an individual – with its quality of arresting the moment – lost its meaning. On the contrary, Ma Yanhong's art takes its place in a new tradition of Chinese female artists who look beyond the borders of their own culture, seeking an authentic mode of expression for their generation to discuss femininity and physicalness in the medium of painting.

Sparsely clothed, leaning against a white wall next to each other, Ma Yanhong takes photos of three of her fellow students during a lunch break in one of the studio rooms of Beijing's Central Academy of Fine Arts. The pictures painted from the photos portray the young women as purposeful, but in no way relaxed. Embarrassed, one of them crosses her arms over her breasts; another totters on the outer edges of her heavy boots. Defiantly, the woman with the ponytail looks directly into the camera, staring the potential viewer in the face. The scene feels ostentatious – there is nothing self-explanatory about it. Here something is being proclaimed – and demanded. A perceptible agreement exists between the photographer/painter and her models. Ma Yanhong presented these images – entitled *Where There is No One* (2002) – in the exhibition rooms of the Academy as part of her thesis work. "Everyone was nervous, the women in the pictures and the students, who recognized them at once. But what's the difference between these pictures and the nudes which we constantly paint in class?", the artist asks.

The themes of her work during the last years prove that for Ma Yanhong this is not about simple provocation. The series *Idols* (2004), for example, features famous women from various origins and professions – such as the artists Frida Kahlo, Georgia O'Keeffe, Camille Claudel, and Cindy Sherman, the writers Simone de Beauvoir, Marguerite Duras, and Virginia Woolf, as well as a few actresses and female singers. To the right of the portraits, the artist placed a representative work of each subject or some other indication of their accomplishments. It's not the female body that commands attention here but the wealth of each woman's ideas. In the room installation *Talkative Women* (2007), Ma Yanhong staged a virtual women's discussion group. On the walls of the room she hung photos and extracts of conversation representing the women participating. A table with an ashtray full of stamped-out cigarettes is placed in the center of the room. "Each woman tells how she imagines her future. What's important for me is the feminine solidarity," Ma explains.

The realistic painting style used by Ma Yanhong often gets conflated with that of her well-known teachers Liu Xiaodong and Yu Hong. A few of her early works do indeed show a similar expressive, wide brush stroke, and an almost abrasive, alienating, and distanced use of dramatic color. "Certainly my teachers shaped me, but I'm developing ever further away from this painting technique. I am concerned with the beauty of the people I paint, their erotic charisma. And it's not just any random model, but I have a personal connection to the women. We set up the scenes together." And it is precisely this that grounds the intensity of her paintings. If Liu Xiaodong's works pursue studies of a scene or fixate on moments of societal breakdown, Ma Yanhong mirrors her own search – and that of her immediate environment – for a life commensurate with their ideals. Today's women of urban China seize upon the same right to femininity that their parents' generation, embroiled in the androgenic policies of the Cultural Revolution, considered morally reprehensible.

In Ma Yanhong's works from 2007 the artist herself starts playing the role of the recurring actress, showing her posing with blonde or white curly wigs, kneeling naked in a chair, wearing seductive lingerie and red bunny ears, or posing lasciviously with a feather boa on a white sheepskin rug. Shortly after China opened up in the 1970's, it was permissible to show pleasure in the classical beauty of Western art and even hang paintings of partially or fully undressed women in a museum. But up until a few years ago, any exhibition of excitement and lust in the work of a Chinese artist was classified as a forbidden provocation and moral danger. An attitude that is understandable against the backdrop of the female image formed by Mao Zedong: the pragmatic, proletariat one-style-for-all uniform hid every feminine charm. Women were also expected to work until physically exhausted – the security of "family" was considered "bourgeois." "My mother was worried about me because even as a child I liked to stand in front of the mirror. My desire to be pretty made my parents anxious. Now of course they are glad that I can live off the sale of my pictures. Still, I can't talk to them about my art."

How does a cool wooden floor feel when one lolls about it naked on a hot summer day? And when anything is possible, how can one decide what's right? The three-part series *Lonely Summer* (2007) reflects the sensual indulgence of undisturbed private time, but also the melancholy that such an intense form of self-reference brings. *Before Rendezvous* (2007), on the other hand, is marked with the pure joy of awaiting one's approaching lover. Currently, Ma Yanhong is working on two male nudes. In all of her works, the artist feels her way in close proximity to her subject, conferring a balancing brush flow that varies from painting to painting, and by that turning her subject's skin into a declaration of love to the beauty of the human body.

By Ulrike Münter

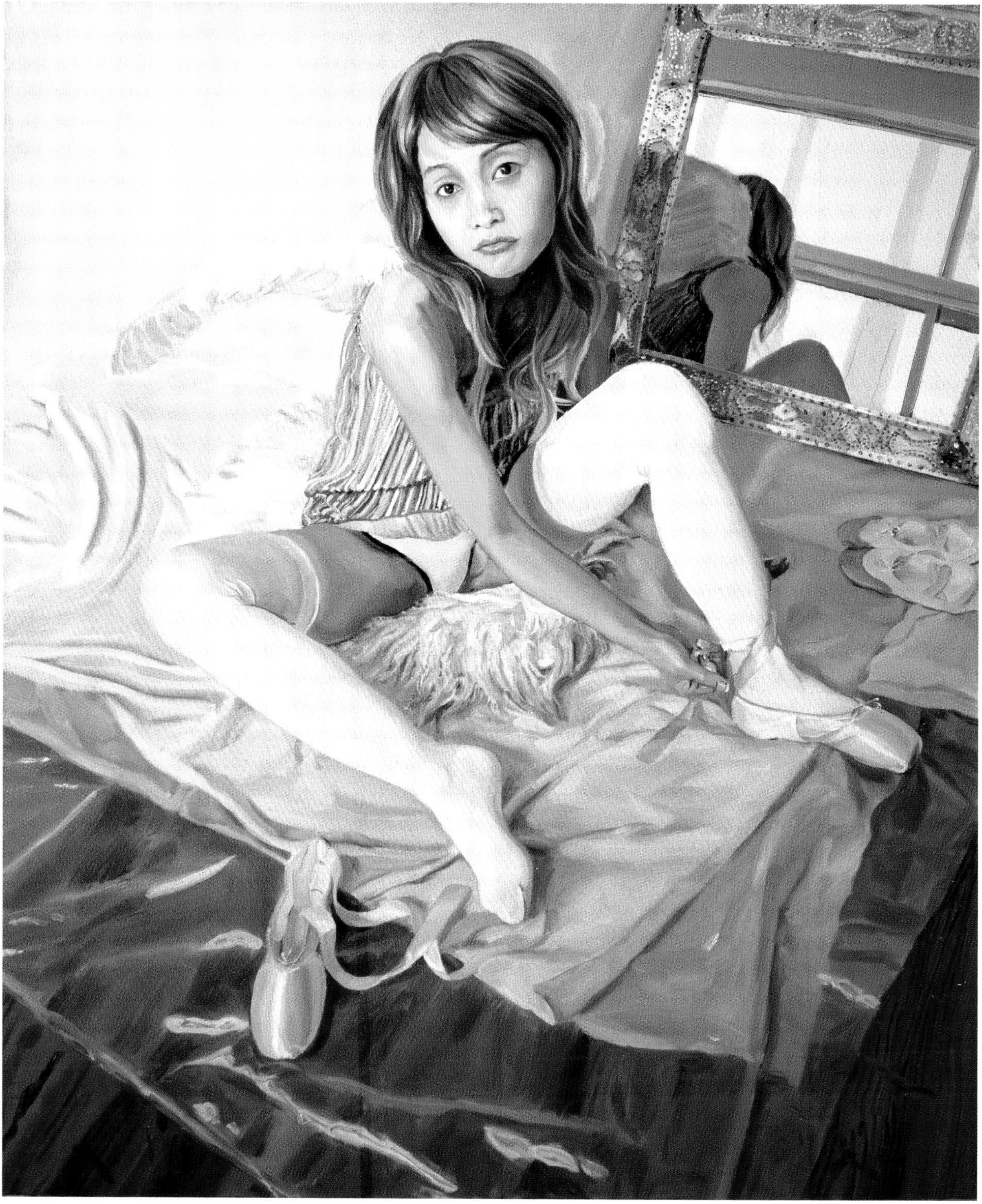

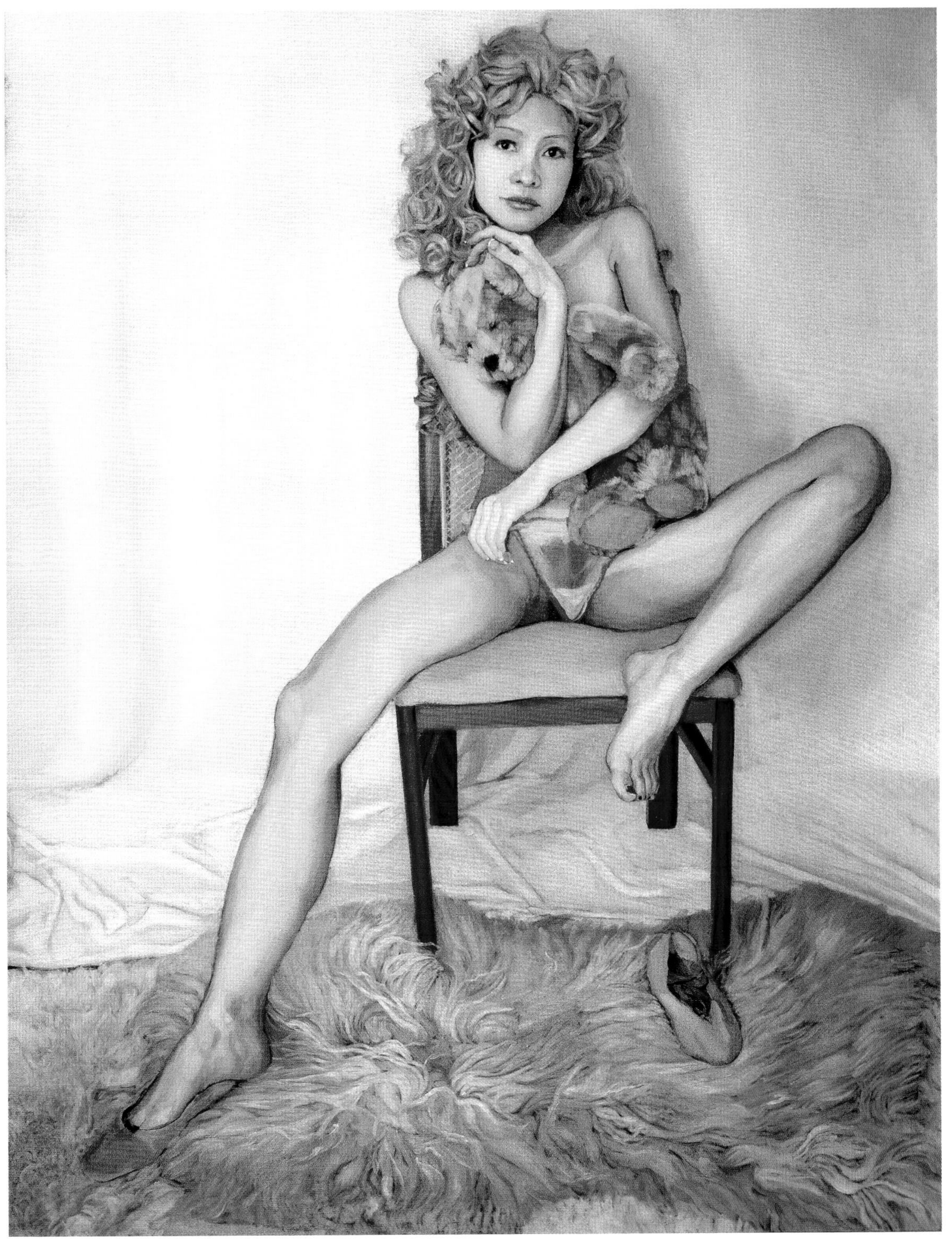

3

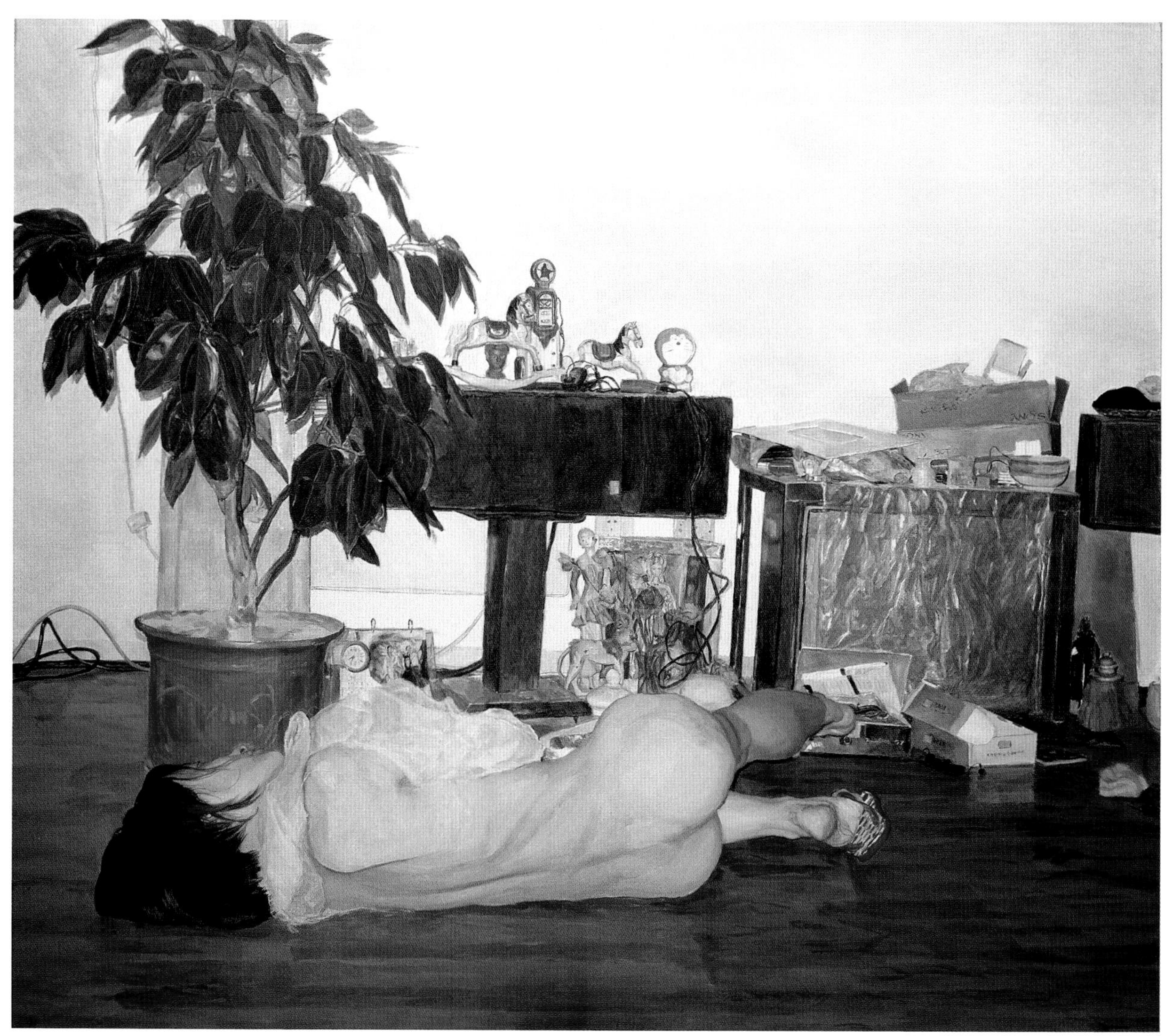

1 SEATED ANGEL WITH BALLET SHOES • 2006 • OIL ON CANVAS • 160 x 135 CM

2 MO MO WITH BEAR IN ARMS • 2007 • OIL ON CANVAS • 150 x 118 CM

3 LONELY SUMMER • 2007 • OIL ON CANVAS • 140 x 165 CM

4 BEFORE RENDEZVOUS • 2007 • OIL ON CANVAS • 210 x 144 CM

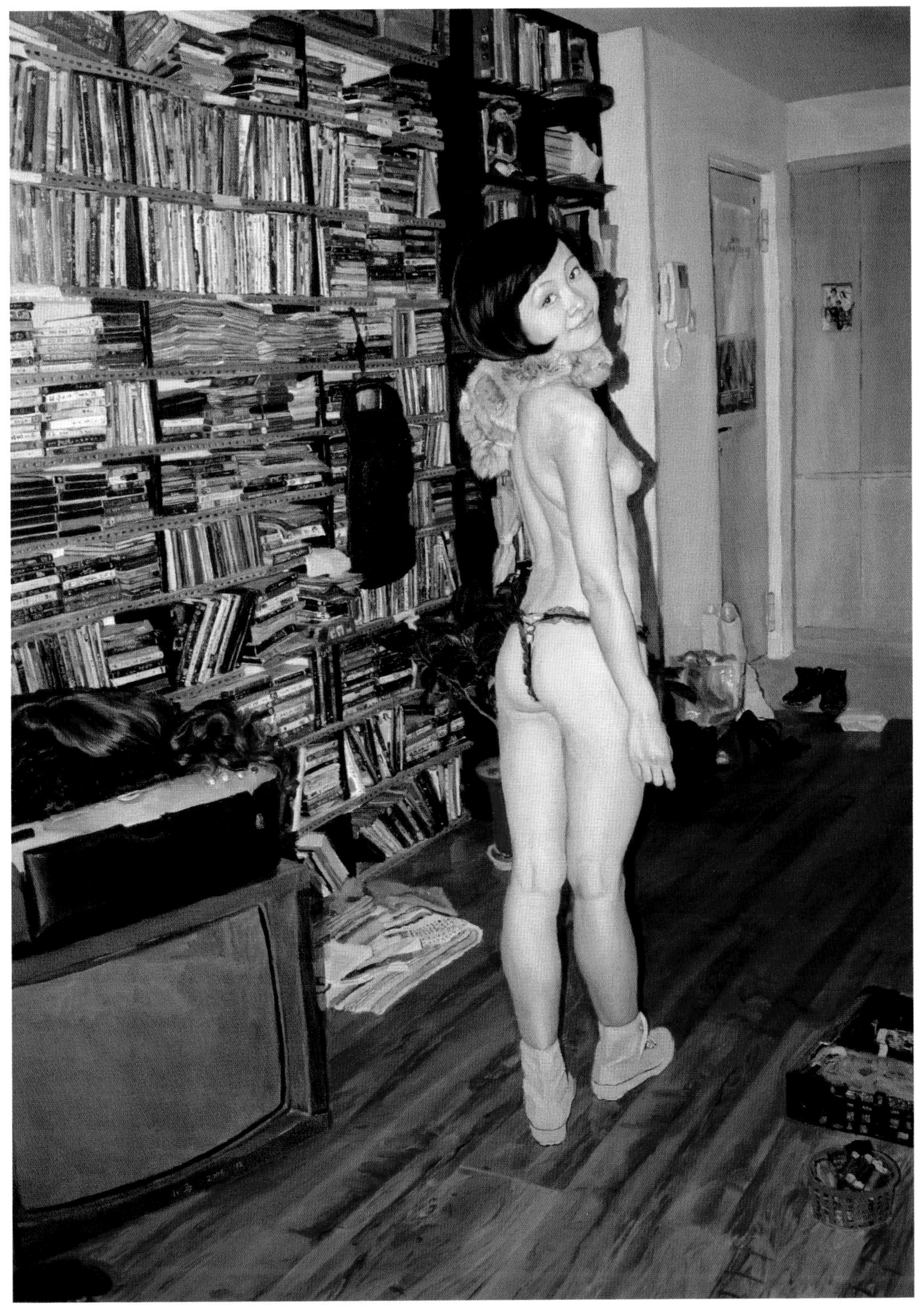

5

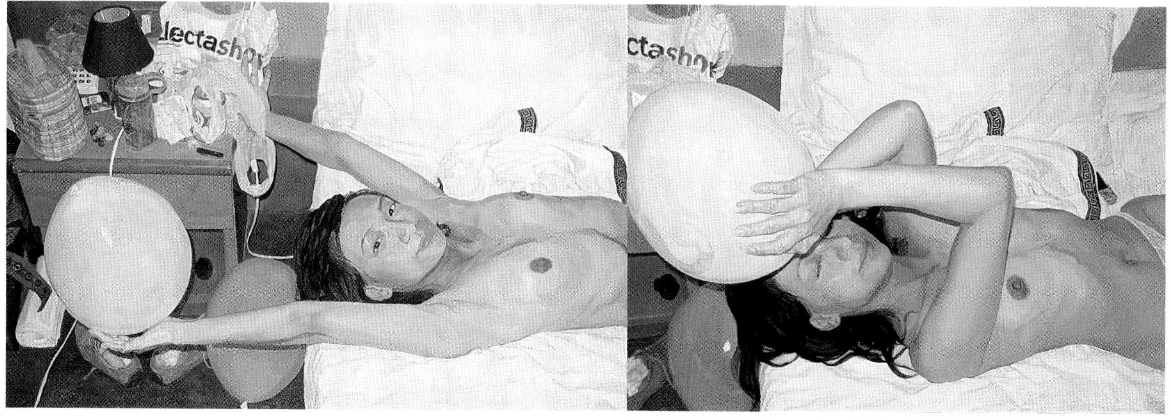

5 WHITE BALLON • 2009 • OIL ON CANVAS • 60 x 180 CM

6 WHERE THERE IS NO ONE • 2002 • OIL ON CANVAS • 165 x 140 CM

PHONE INTERVIEW WITH EDITORS

4/29/08 • MORNING

EDITORS *Thinking back to your childhood, can you still remember what was your favorite childhood toy?*

MA Y. When I was a kid, there was not a big variety of toys to choose from. My favorite toy was plastic tableware.

EDITORS *And what was the sentence your parents said to you most often?*

MA Y. My parents also live in Beijing, however I don't live with them anymore. They care a lot about me and quite often ask me where I am and what I am doing at the moment.

EDITORS *I suppose your life as an artist is very busy. Do you try to stay healthy in your everyday life?*

MA Y. I like to do yoga. I don't have enough time to join classes at the gym, but I have a yoga DVD and try to find some time to work out at home.

EDITORS *Could you reveal what you recently wished for?*

MA Y. I guess that my life would be less busy, and that I could have more time again for leisure.

EDITORS *Do you believe in true love?*

MA Y. Yes, I do. But I think in real life it is a little difficult to fulfill true love, although it exists. To me true love means a sincere and healthy relationship, which includes tolerance and reciprocity.

EDITORS *Life in Beijing is quite busy. If you could choose, what would your ideal living environment look like?*

MA Y. The environment in Beijing is not very ideal. I've been in many other countries and felt that many of them were more like a big garden. In my ideal environment the air should be clean—not as bad as in Beijing—and there should be fewer people and traffic jams then there are here. The environment where I am living right now can't really provide me with these conditions. But also, changing my living environment and living in a more silent place with fewer people is just a dream. Many friends live nearby my place and there are many artistic activities and exhibitions around this area. All of these things are also necessary for my life. In these terms, my current place is very convenient. It's a paradox.

EDITORS *Which type of media provides you with most of your inspiration?*

MA Y. My inspiration comes from newspapers and DVDs of mostly foreign literary films and movies displaying life in foreign cities.

EDITORS *You have worked as an artist for a couple of years already. What do you like/dislike about being an artist?*

MA Y. I like the environment in the art world where humans have more freedom, where you can experience more tolerant and open-minded people. I don't like the absolutism, which asks for a general criteria or ideas among the people. When I paint some new works, I want to paint whatever I want.

EDITORS *How can you communicate with the audience through your art?*

MA Y. I guess mostly through my exhibitions. During an exhibition I can see people's reactions, which is very interesting for me.

EDITORS *You were born in 1977. If you could use five words, how would you describe your generation?*

MA Y. Realism, relative rationality, materialism, freedom, individuality.

EDITORS *If the whole world would listen to you for fifteen seconds, what would you say?*

MA Y. "In the whole world there should be not so much chaos, people should all live in an ideal environment without so many wars and conflicts—especially religious conflicts." Also, I would wish that people would be more tolerant of each other.

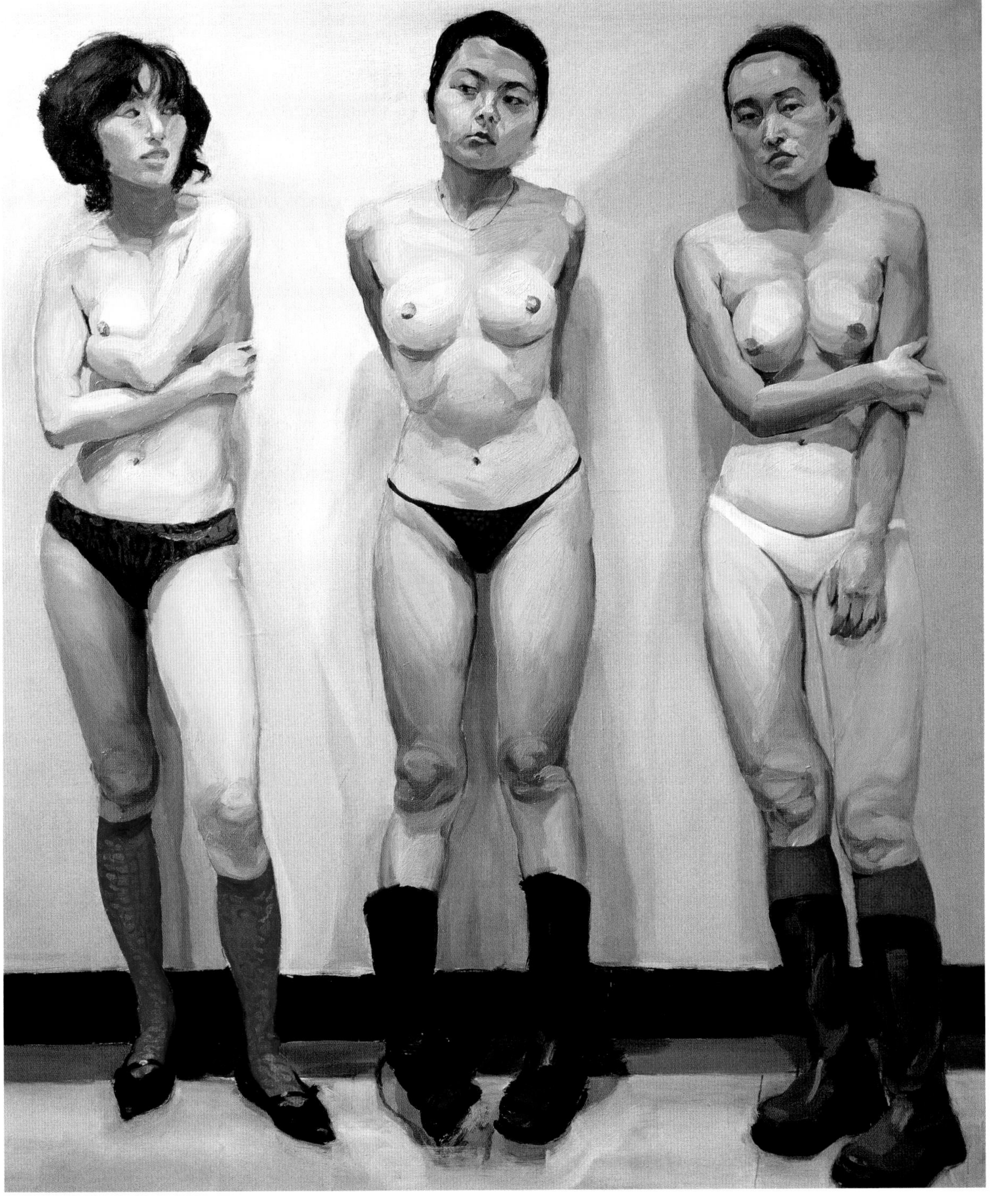

7
8

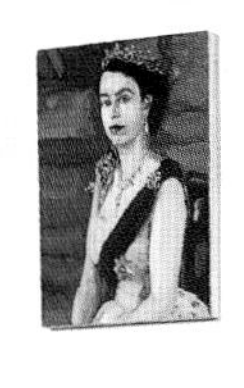
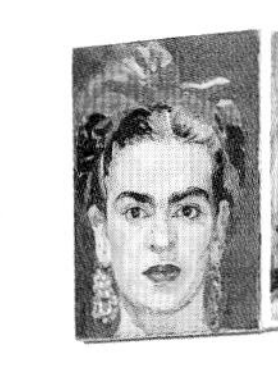
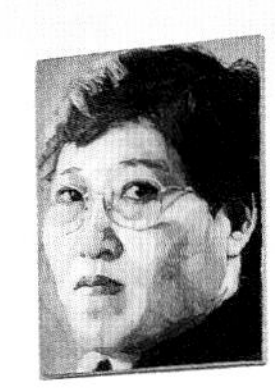
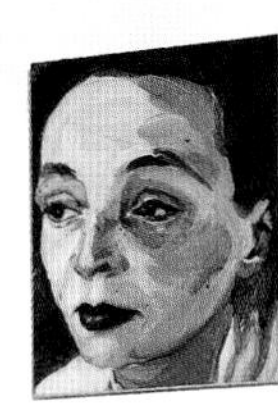
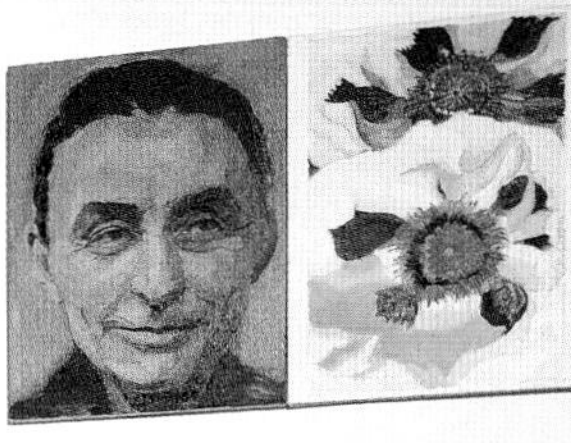
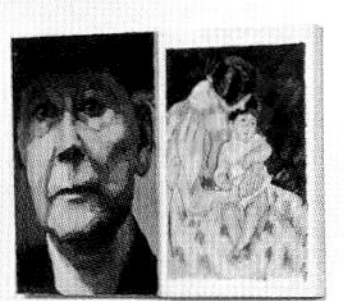
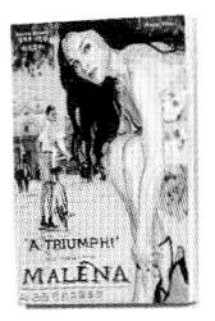

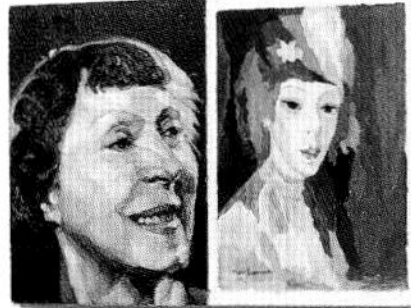
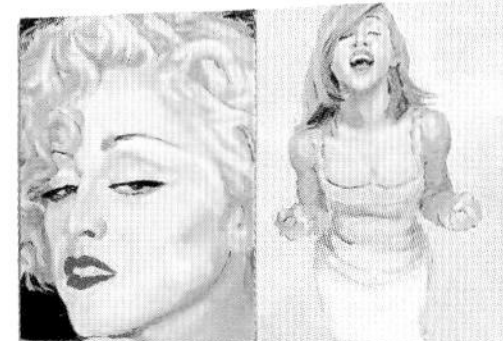
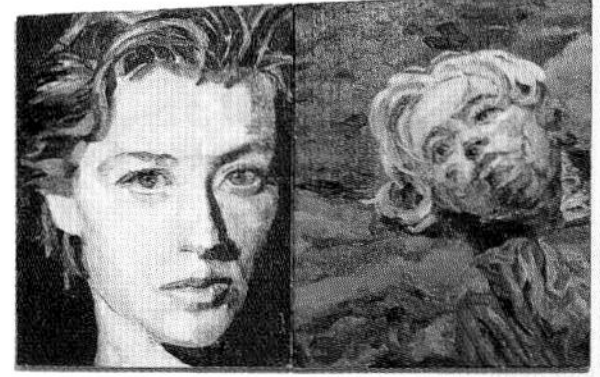
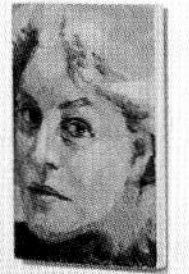
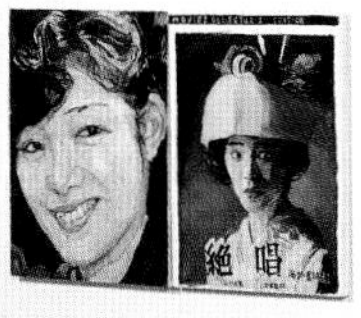

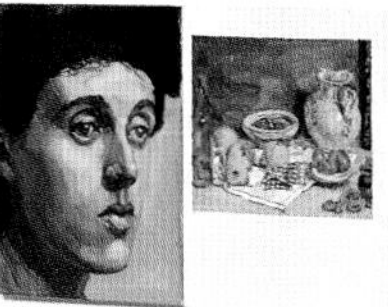
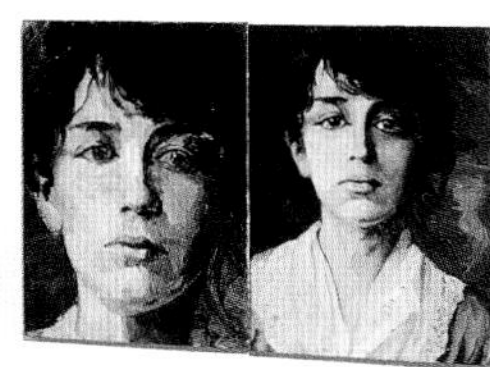
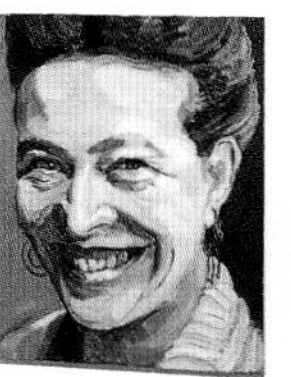
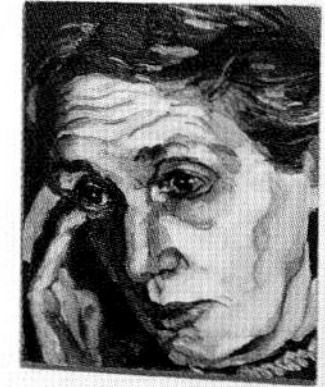
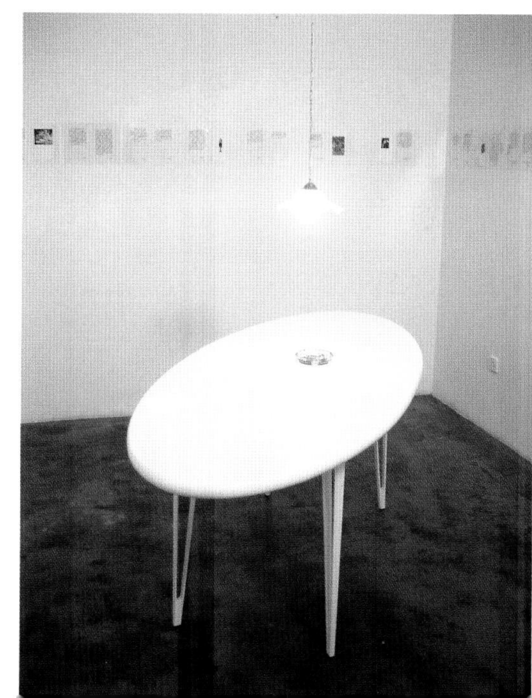

9

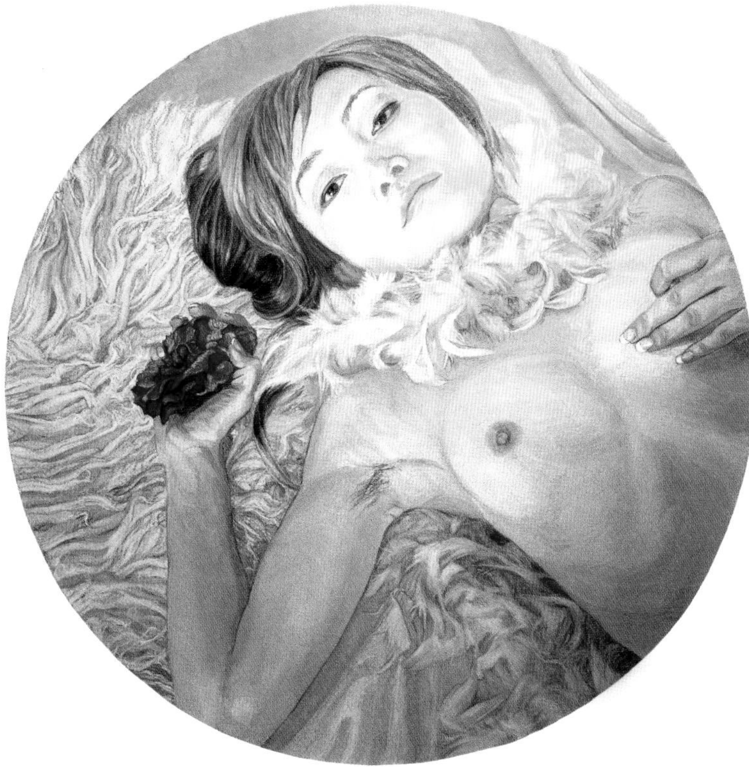

EXHIBITIONS

SELECTED SOLO EXHIBITIONS

2008
Recent Works by Ma Yanhong,
Goedhuis Contemporary,
New York, U.S.

2007
Xiao Ma's Forest,
C5 Art Gallery,
Beijing, China

SELECTED GROUP EXHIBITIONS

2007/8
Made in China: The Estella Collection,
Israel Museum,
Jerusalem, Israel /
Louisiana Museum of Modern Art,
Humlebæk, Denmark

2006
N12 – No.4,
C5 Art Gallery,
Beijing, China

2005
The Next Generation: A Return to Painting,
Goedhuis Contemporary,
New York, U.S.

2005
N12 – No.3,
Gallery of Central Academy of Fine Arts,
Beijing, China

2005
Young Chinese Contemporary Art,
Hangar-7,
Salzburg, Austria

2005
Contemporary Visions,
Macao Museum of Art,
Macao, China

2004
New Wave,
China Art Seasons Gallery,
Beijing, China

2003
The 3rd Exhibition of Chinese Oil Paintings,
National Art Museum of China,
Beijing, China

7 IDOLS • 2004 • OIL ON CANVAS • 53 x 41 CM (EACH)

8 TALKATIVE WOMEN • 2007 • INSTALLATION: 32 PIECES • VARIOUS SIZES

9 MO MO WITH FLOWER IN HANDS • 2007 • OIL ON CANVAS • 80 x 80 CM

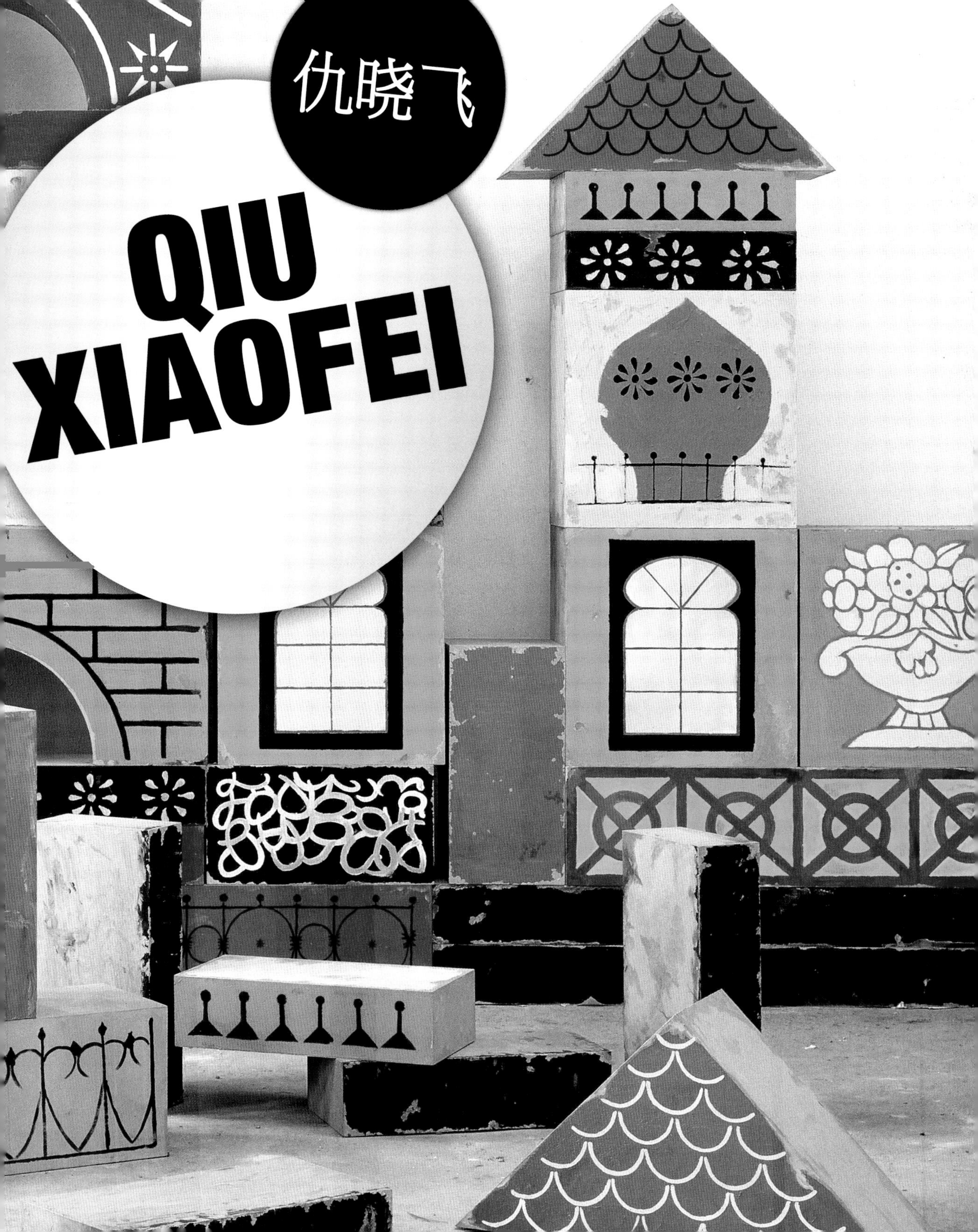
仇晓飞
QIU
XIAOFEI

NAME
QIU XIAOFEI

BORN IN
1977, HARBIN

LIVES IN
BEIJING

STUDY
CENTRAL ACADEMY OF FINE ARTS, BEIJING

MEDIA
INSTALLATION, PAINTING, SCULPTURE

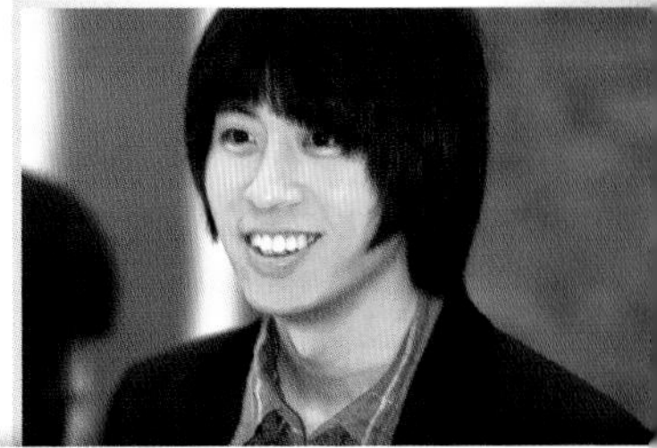

TOKENS FROM CHILDHOOD

Our brains work in mysterious ways. Sometimes we forget the most important things in life, other times we fixate upon the seemingly most trivial or insignificant. Memories can be likened to faulty cameras in our minds, they occasionally produce vivid glimpses into reality and at other times fail to capture anything at all. Artist Qiu Xiaofei manages to bring his own memories into sharp focus, illuminating his personal past while mediating the intangible forces of collective memory. In Qiu's paintings of toys, photos, and ephemera of his youth, we are confronted less with ideas of uniqueness or individuality than with sameness; the lingering feeling that the objects gleaned from his own personal history are identical to those shared by nearly everyone of his generation. In fact it is this awareness of equivalence that lends Qiu's practice a social dimension, albeit clouded by an interest in individual perception and memory and the tendency to approach remembrances as points of individual departure within a larger constellation of reality and imagination.

Growing up in the northern province of Heilongjiang, Qiu Xiaofei experienced a fairly standard and somewhat unremarkable upbringing. Yet the long hours spent at home waiting for his father to return from work seemed to have left indelible traces in Qiu's mind, provoking the artist to revisit these moments later in life through evocative and intimate paintings. At age twelve Qiu moved to Beijing and began to study art, eventually entering the oil painting department at the Central Academy of Fine Arts (CAFA). The oil painting courses Qiu was enrolled in rarely strayed from the well-honed path of realism, and yet the atmosphere of art school was enough to cultivate a newfound sense of individuality and freedom. Early exposure to 1990s experimental art forms like installation art and new media art also opened Qiu's eyes to new possibilities and may have effected his incorporation of these styles into his painting.

Following graduation in 2002, Qiu Xiaofei moved in with a fellow student and began to paint while earning a living through teaching remedial art classes. For the first time, he was faced with an option to paint whatever he desired. Inspiration came when he happened upon an old family photo album which triggered memories of his childhood in Heilongjiang. Revisiting the small streets, neighbors, and friends from his childhood, Qiu created a series of diminutively sized paintings that, owing to his lack of a proper studio were on one-to-one scale with the original photos themselves. Works like *Summer Palace* (2004) allude to a single event – a tourist outing perhaps – while the more detailed *Photo Album* (2005) is a comprehensive record of twenty-two paintings covering a stretch of time. The intimacy of *Photo Album* gives the viewer the feeling of peering into another person's life story. But it is a disjunctive narrative, conveniently bracketed off from the tumultuous events that precede or follow. Juxtaposing an anonymous and ambiguous "past" with the specific conditions of the present, the pale hues and dim scenes of Qiu's paintings are significant not only for what they leave out but for their conflicting relationship to the vast and unprecedented cultural changes occurring around him.

When it comes to the grand cultural narratives and socio-political critiques – so favored by artists a generation before him – Qiu is curiously silent, preferring instead to retreat into notions of the past through matters of perception and materiality. Tokens and objects from his childhood – a Ferris wheel, found photographs, a toy car, or toy piano – surface in Qiu's work as bizarre signifiers of a lost past, markers of a subjective history that exists only in memories. There is a certain snapshot quality to these paintings that suggests a deeper connection to photography, in particular its circumspect relationship to "objective" reality and subjectivity. Seeking to break beyond the picture plane, so to speak, Qiu took to painting three-dimensional objects themselves, using oil paint on wood to recreate, in painstaking detail, the worn appearance of childhood toys. *Bus* (2004), with its ruddy, slightly grimy surface, recalls the boxy shape of Soviet-style buses, some of which are still in circulation today in China but in decreasing numbers. Another piece, *Baby Piano* (2004), hints at the artist's ongoing interest in music. These objects are characteristic of Qiu's innovative approach to the medium of painting, extending it beyond the two-dimensional surface to deal with shifting notions of reality and artifice. Charged with representing reality in physical form, Qiu's objects are anything but, instead they exist as deeply constructed icons fashioned out of his own subjective memory shrouded with the curious effects of time.

House of Recollected Fragments, Qiu's multi-layered solo exhibition in 2008 revolves around these concerns, extending his ideas from painting to incorporate a variety of three-dimensional installation works: oversized children's building blocks recall the distorted perspectives we inhabit as youngsters (*Ruins*, 2007); a series of sculpted and painted doors suggest inaccessible entry into imagined worlds; sets of fabricated propane tanks emitting the sound of leaking gas summon an image of death and violence from Qiu's childhood (*Cakravada Mountain 2*, 2006–7); and photographs of the artist alongside a slowly burning mosquito coil form a tranquil meditation on the loneliness and solitude Qiu experienced as a product of the one-child policy (*Night by Night*, 2007). Seen collectively, these components exhibit Qiu's poignant reserves for exploring, ruminating upon, and eventually representing the disjointed space between memory and lived experience.

By Pauline J. Yao

1

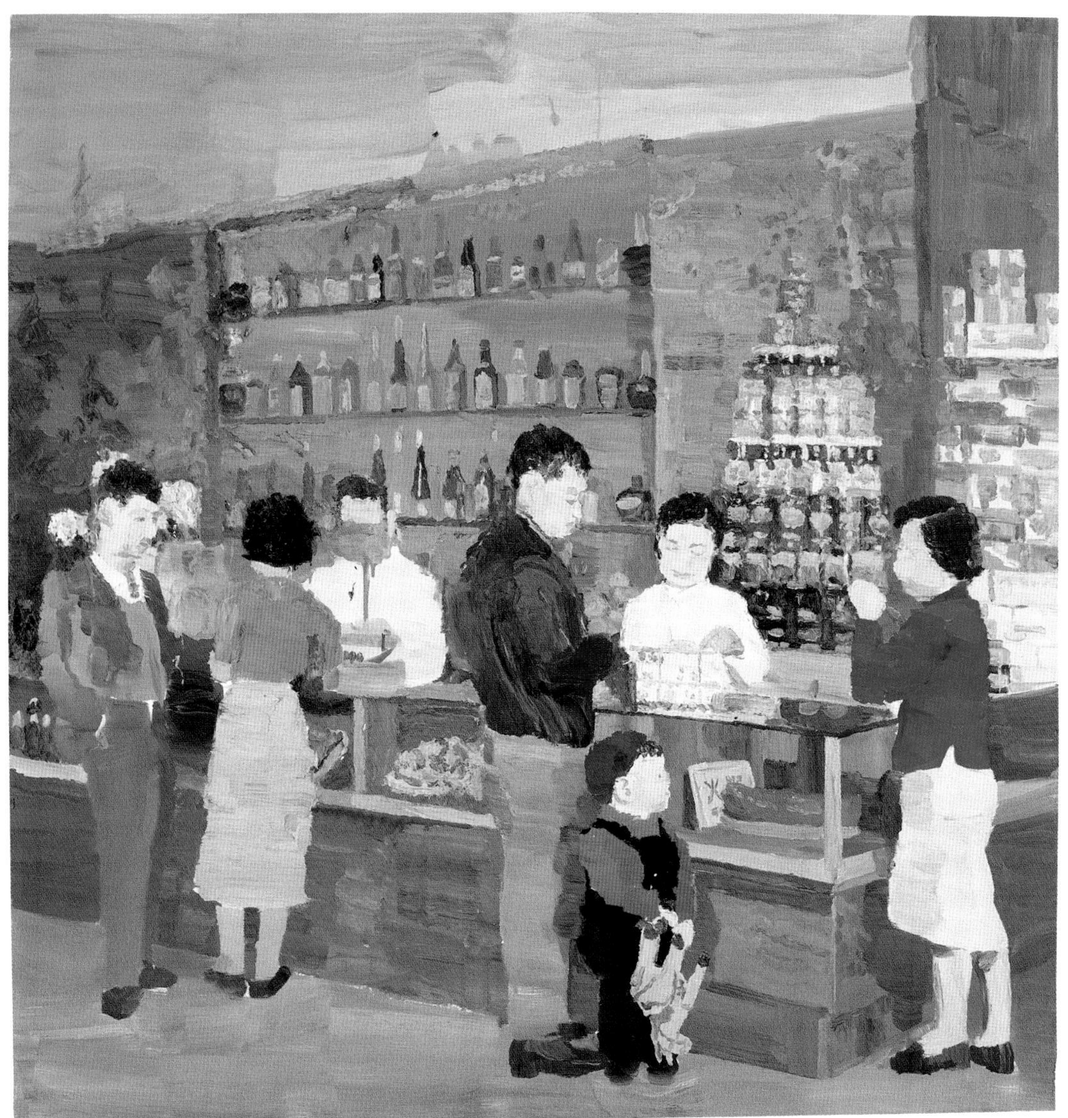

1 SHOPPING MALL • 2005 • OIL ON CANVAS • 205 x 210 CM

2 RENEW CORDIAL RELATIONS • 2009 • OIL ON CANVAS • 200 x 200 CM

3 PHOTO ALBUM • 2005 • OIL ON CANVAS (22 PIECES) • VARIOUS SIZES

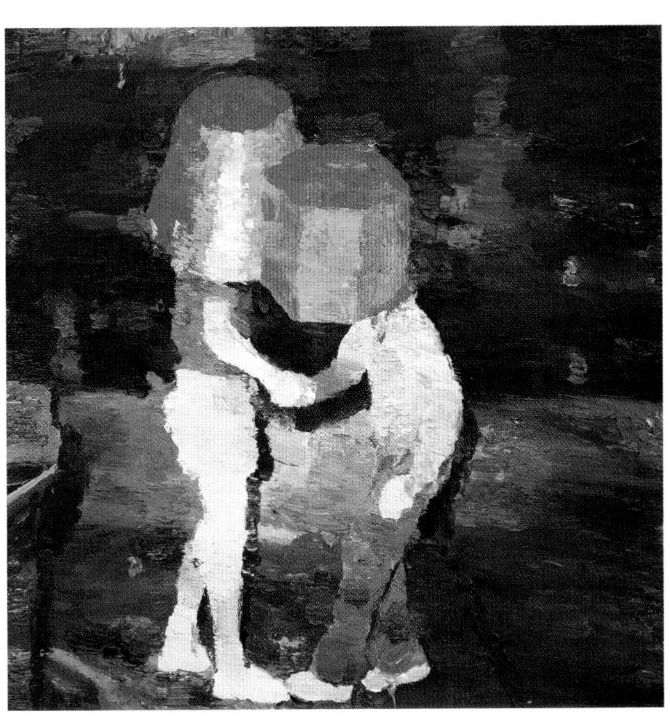

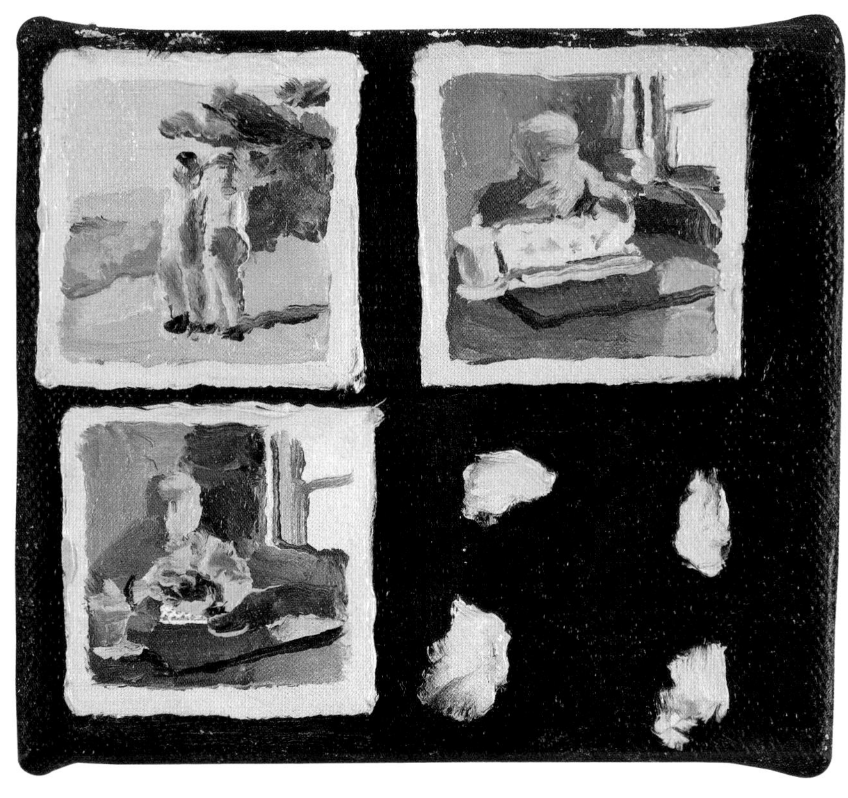

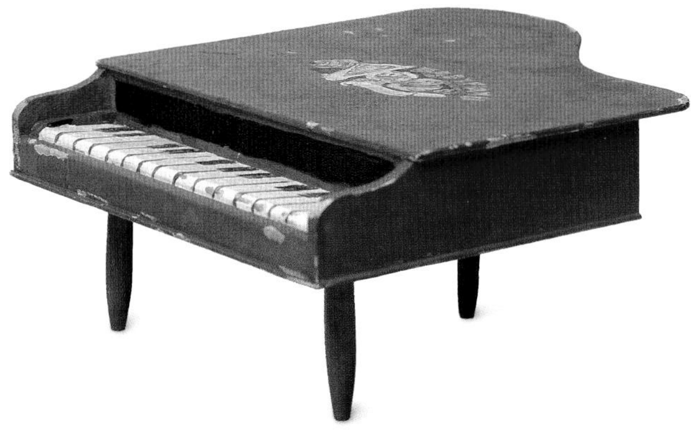

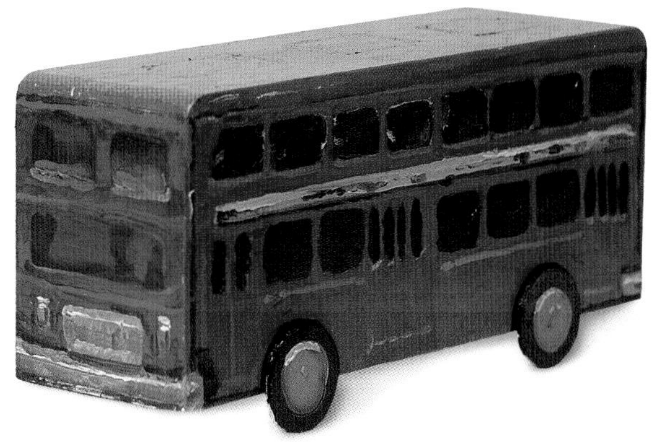

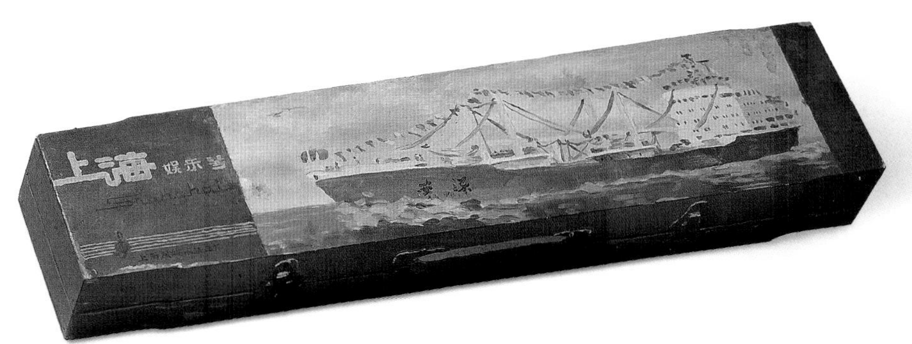
上海
娱乐琴

7

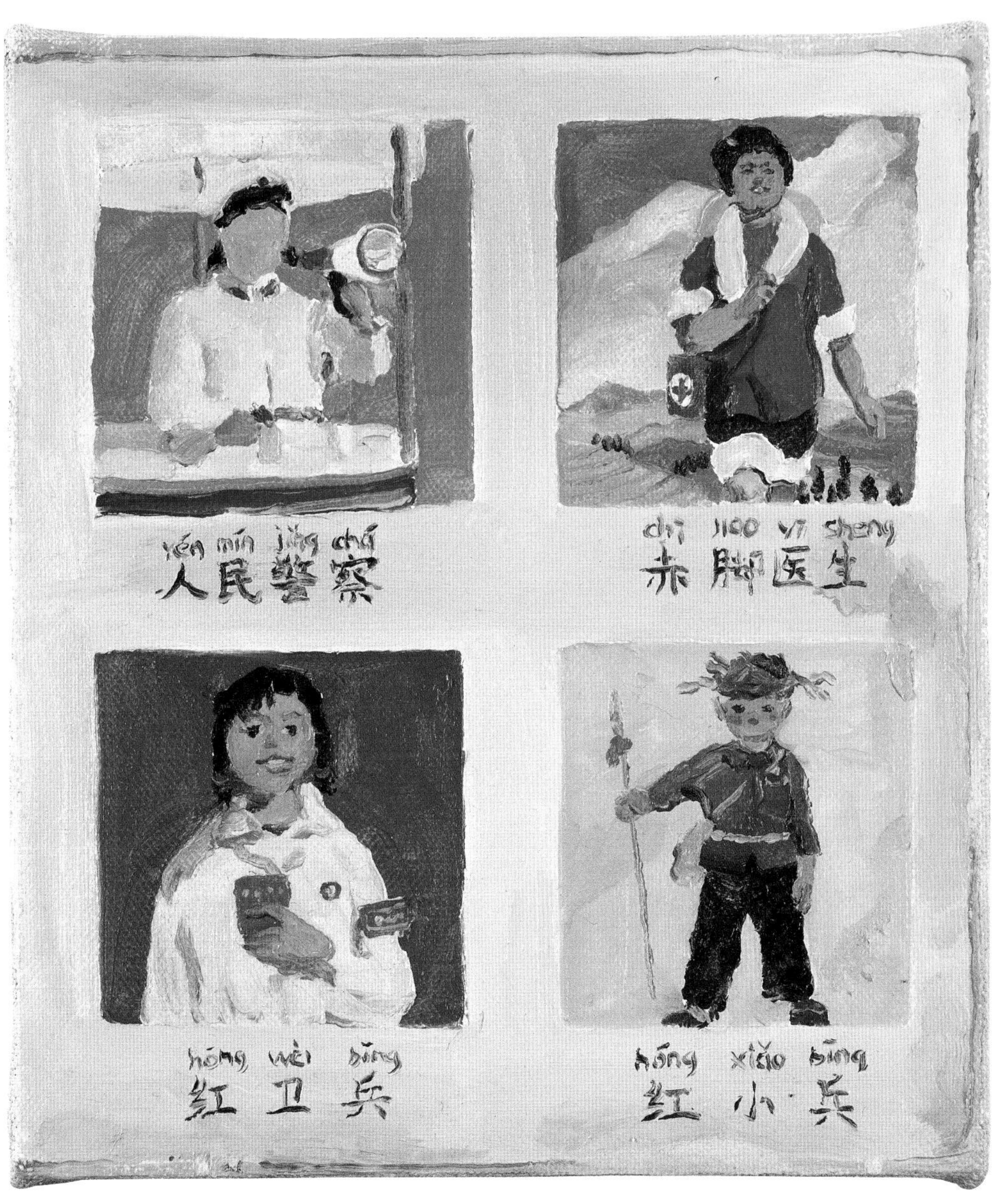

4 BABY PIANO • 2004 • MODEL, OIL PAINTING • 14 x 29 x 32 CM

5 BUS • 2004 • MODEL, OIL PAINTING • 12 x 25 x 7.5 CM

6 ZITHER • 2004 • MODEL, OIL PAINTING • 7 x 62 x 14 CM

7 VOCABULARY CHART • 2003 • OIL ON CANVAS • 26 x 23 CM

8

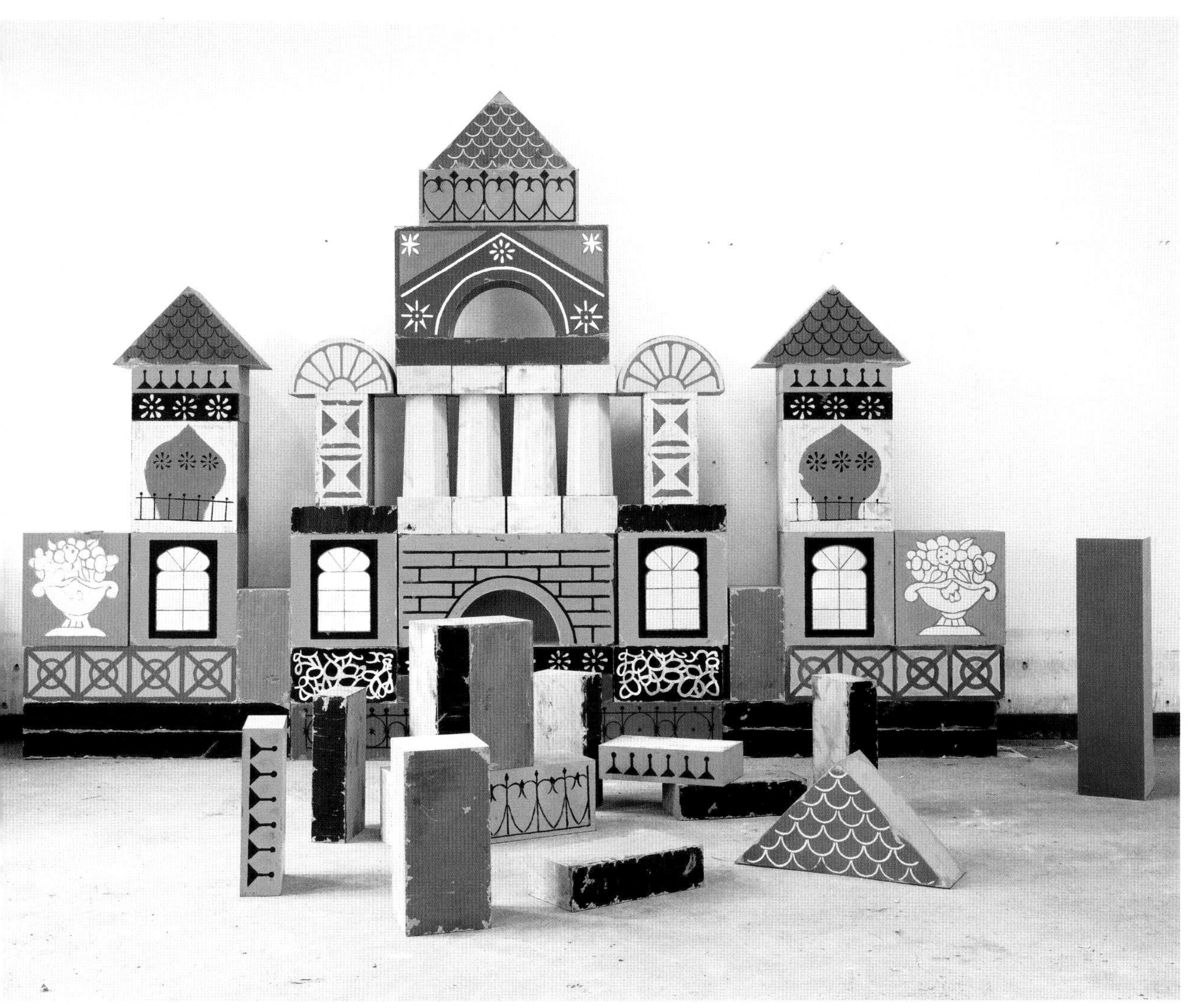

8 RUINS • 2007 • INSTALLATION: OIL ON WOOD AND PROPYLENE • VARIABLE

9 NIGHT BY NIGHT • 2007 • INSTALLATION: ACRYLIC ON FIBERGLASS, STEEL / 2 PHOTOGRAPHS • 63 x 136 x 136 CM / 85 x 120 CM (x2)

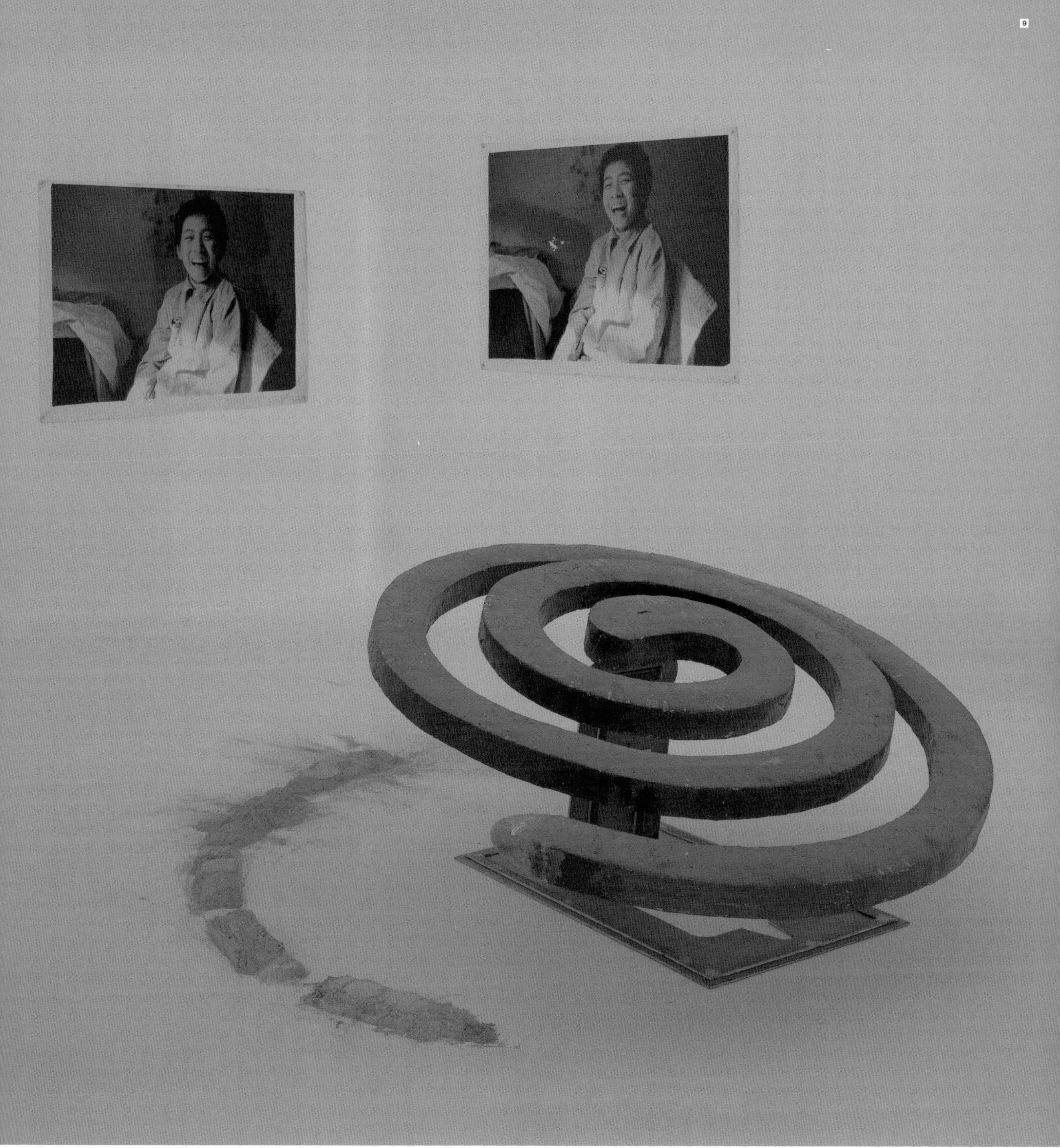

9

10

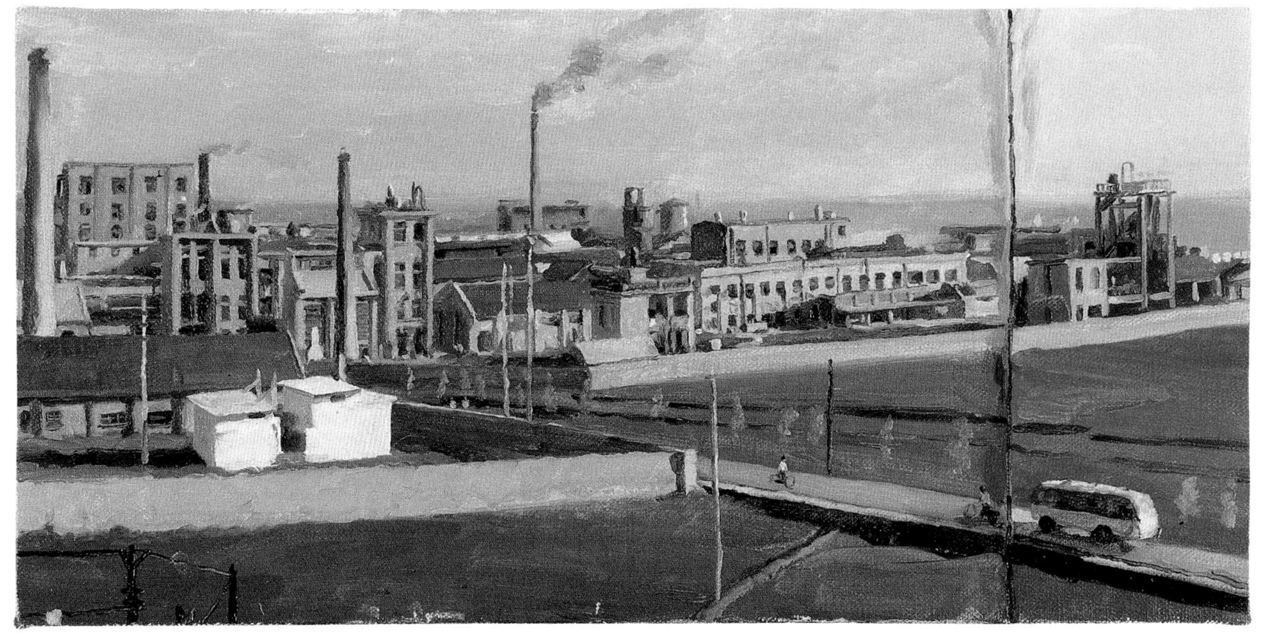

10 FACTORY IMAGE FROM A MAGAZINE • 2004 • OIL ON CANVAS • 20 x 45 CM

QUESTIONNAIRE

5/16/08 • IN A HOTEL, SPAIN

WHAT WAS YOUR FAVORITE CHILDHOOD TOY?

Maybe Transformers.

WHAT DID YOUR PARENTS SAY TO YOU MOST OFTEN?

They called me by my nickname a lot, even if they had nothing to tell me.

HOW DO YOU TRY TO STAY HEALTHY IN YOUR EVERYDAY LIFE?

I have never tried to take conscious care of my health. I never exercise and never play sports. I will always drive instead of walk. I go to bed and get up whenever I want.

WHAT HAVE YOU BEEN WISHING FOR MOST RECENTLY?

To finish this questionnaire.

DO YOU BELIEVE IN TRUE LOVE?

Of course, I do.

WHAT DOES YOUR IDEAL LIVING ENVIRONMENT LOOK LIKE?

I prefer to live life as it is. I don't have any particular dreams about that.

FROM WHICH TYPE OF MEDIA DO YOU DERIVE MOST OF YOUR INSPIRATION?

From whatever I have available to me.

WHAT DO YOU LIKE/DISLIKE ABOUT BEING AN ARTIST?

What does "artist" really mean? I am curious. You know, an "artist" is just an artist.

HOW DO YOU COMMUNICATE WITH THE AUDIENCE IN YOUR ART?

The audience can get whatever they want from my works.

IF YOU HAD FIVE WORDS TO DESCRIBE YOUR GENERATION, WHAT WOULD THEY BE?

Male, female, classmates, friends, relatives.

IF THE WHOLE WORLD WOULD LISTEN TO YOU FOR FIFTEEN SECONDS, WHAT WOULD YOU SAY?

I would not say anything. I am not a dictator.

EXHIBITIONS

SELECTED SOLO EXHIBITIONS

2009
Invisible journeys,
Doosan Art Center,
Seoul, South Korea

2008
House of Recollected Fragments,
Boers-Li Gallery,
Beijing, China

2006
Heilongjiang Box,
Art Museum of the Central Academy of Fine Arts,
Beijing, China

SELECTED GROUP EXHIBITIONS

2008
New World Order,
Groninger Museum,
Groningen, The Netherlands

2007
The Real Thing: Contemporary Art from China,
Tate Liverpool,
Liverpool, U.K.

2007
Thermocline of Art: New Asian Waves,
Center for Art and Media (ZKM),
Karlsruhe, Germany

2006
Chaos City,
Universal Studios,
Beijing, China

2006
N12 – No. 4,
C5 Art Gallery,
Beijing, China

2005
Mahjong: Contemporary Art from the Sigg Collection,
Kunstmuseum Bern,
Bern, Switzerland

2005
Retrospective Exhibition of Chinese Oil Painting,
National Art Museum of China,
Beijing, China

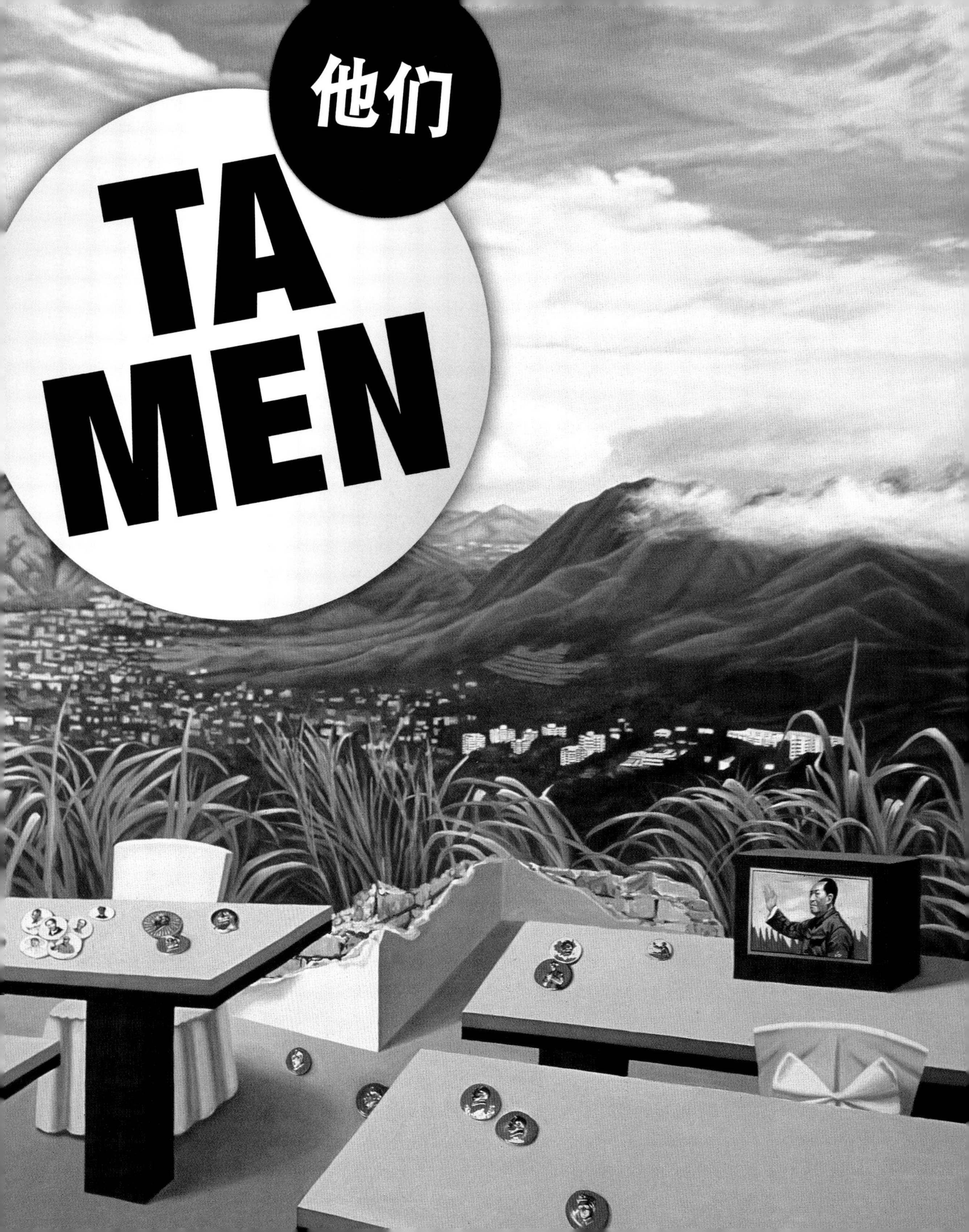
他们
TA
MEN

GROUP
TA MEN (THEY)

NAME	**LAI SHENGYU**	**YANG XIAOGANG**
BORN IN	**1978, HUNAN PROVINCE**	**1979, HUNAN PROVINCE**
LIVES IN	**BEIJING**	**BEIJING**
STUDY	**CENTRAL ACADEMY OF FINE ARTS, BEIJING**	
MEDIA	**PAINTING, PHOTOGRAPHY**	

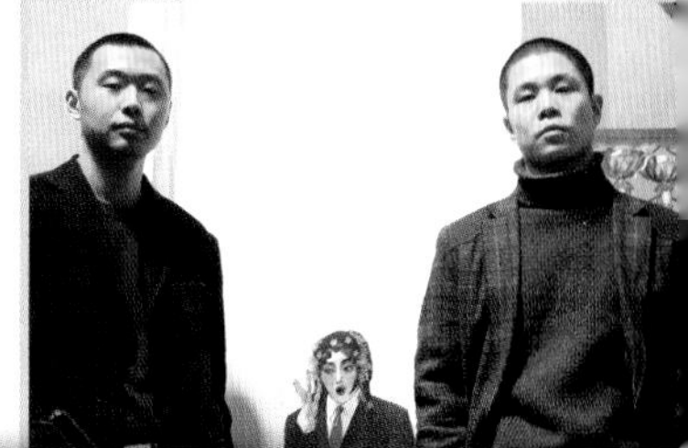

WE ARE THE OTHERS

Since 2005 the artist duo Ta Men have been staging hysterically exaggerated big-city scenes in a strangely furnished room featuring a huge window front. Whether set in Beijing, Shanghai, or Hong Kong – whether executed as works in oil on canvas or through the means of digital photography – Ta Men's analysis of the state of China's new affluence does not evoke confidence. The topics of their works reach from the lonely city dweller's melancholy, shopping mania, prostitution, and torture, to the desire for a harmonious cooperation between humanity and nature.

Originally Lai Shengyu and Yang Xiaogang had joined with Chen Li to form Ta Men, but since 2006 they have been working as a duo. "We are called 'they' in the sense of 'the others,' because it is not our own personal stories which stand at the center of our work. Our pictures hold up a mirror to contemporary China. This mirror should not just show the outer layer of reality. We are much more concerned with the psychological effects of China's rapid modernization on the people who live here." Before they paint a picture, Lai and Yang start by discussing the theme and the setting of the scene. Next they decide who will paint which parts of the picture. Each one always has the right to change or add to the work of the other. As the artists put it: "For us, it's a new form of collectivism. But it has nothing to do with the forced obedience that was demanded of individuals in the Cultural Revolution. For our generation, that's the past. We aim for a voluntarily chosen symbiosis of individualism and collective spirit."

Depending on the theme, Ta Men execute their works either through the medium of painting, or they enact scenes, photograph their posing friends, and then process the pictures on the computer. What is important to them are the varying degrees of virtuality. While various glimpses of China's past and future are more prominent in the painted pictures, the "insanity of the everyday" dominates Ta Men's photographic works. Yet both paintings and photographs share a similar basic arrangement: two rows of tables and a cabinet with a switched-on TV standing in a room effusing an aseptic new-construction aesthetic. On the left, a huge window front offers an open view of a landscape that differs from picture to picture. In some images the wall separating inside from outside is crumbled. This type of "stage curtain" was inspired by Ta Men's enthusiasm for René Magritte (*The Listening Room*, 1952) and Edward Hopper (*Sunlight in a Cafeteria*, 1958). Both painters worked, as Ta Men now do, with the dynamic between inside and outside space. At the same time, Magritte's symbolism and Hopper's portrayal of lonely cities find their echo in Ta Men's art.

One thing that immediately stands out is the detachment of the people populating Ta Men's scenes. The artists fit them into the scenery in an unpretentiously realistic style. Almost autistic and resembling decorative figures, they take their allotted places. The artists make it unmistakably clear that these are role-players and not real people. One recurring motif is a usually male figure who has his back turned to the viewer. "The 'back figure' both reflects our position as observer and makes us the director of the scene. In second instance, the figure represents the viewer." Through this trope Ta Men's art becomes both a projection screen and a reflective surface.

"In our work, we want to discuss social problems. As we understand it, art must stay a step ahead of real life. To make the consequences of today's way of life visible we often reach for very drastic means of expression." In *Freedom Leading Demos* (2005), for example, a blood-red sky stretches over the heads of a mass of bloodstained people. The TV, significantly, only gives off a distorted flicker. The message is unmistakable. While Ta Men here clearly engage the political level, the focus of most of their pictures is more critical of social conditions. The scenario in *Eating Snakes* (2005) is simply disgusting: in the middle of a surrealistic scene two women are depicted devouring snakes. Bank notes are flying about, snakes are taking over the furniture, and cockroaches crawl up the wall. Unidentifiable female heads and a rubber doll are suggestive of other lusts. A more crass testimony to moral decay is hardly imaginable.

Equally blatantly, Ta Men visualize what is probably the most significant characteristic of the Chinese metropolis: the simultaneousness of the contemporary and the past. Beijing Opera masks are put in a toy bank, a fire pot stands next to a McDonald's menu, and a traditional landscape painting decorates the wall, while the Olympic stadium is visible outside. Western status symbols and folklore-laden kitsch become the two sides of a coin that makes up today's China.

Ta Men's pictures can be decoded like a classical still life, but most of the symbols they use are taken from a catalog of the everyday. The scenes – occupying quasi-public rooms enriched with reference symbols like the television, status symbols, known personalities, and other artworks – make the separation between private sphere and society permeable. What happens outside affects the individual, and the individual is completely participatory in societal developments. In the pictures where the artists' signature "stage curtain" is partially broken, this interdependency becomes all the clearer. One of the most recent works of Ta Men, *Jiang Shan (Mountains and Rivers* (2008), shows a vision: beyond the almost completely vanished walls are houses harmoniously fitting into a hilly, green landscape that extends into the distance. A dream shortly before the completion of the CCTV towers in Beijing.

By Ulrike Münter

1

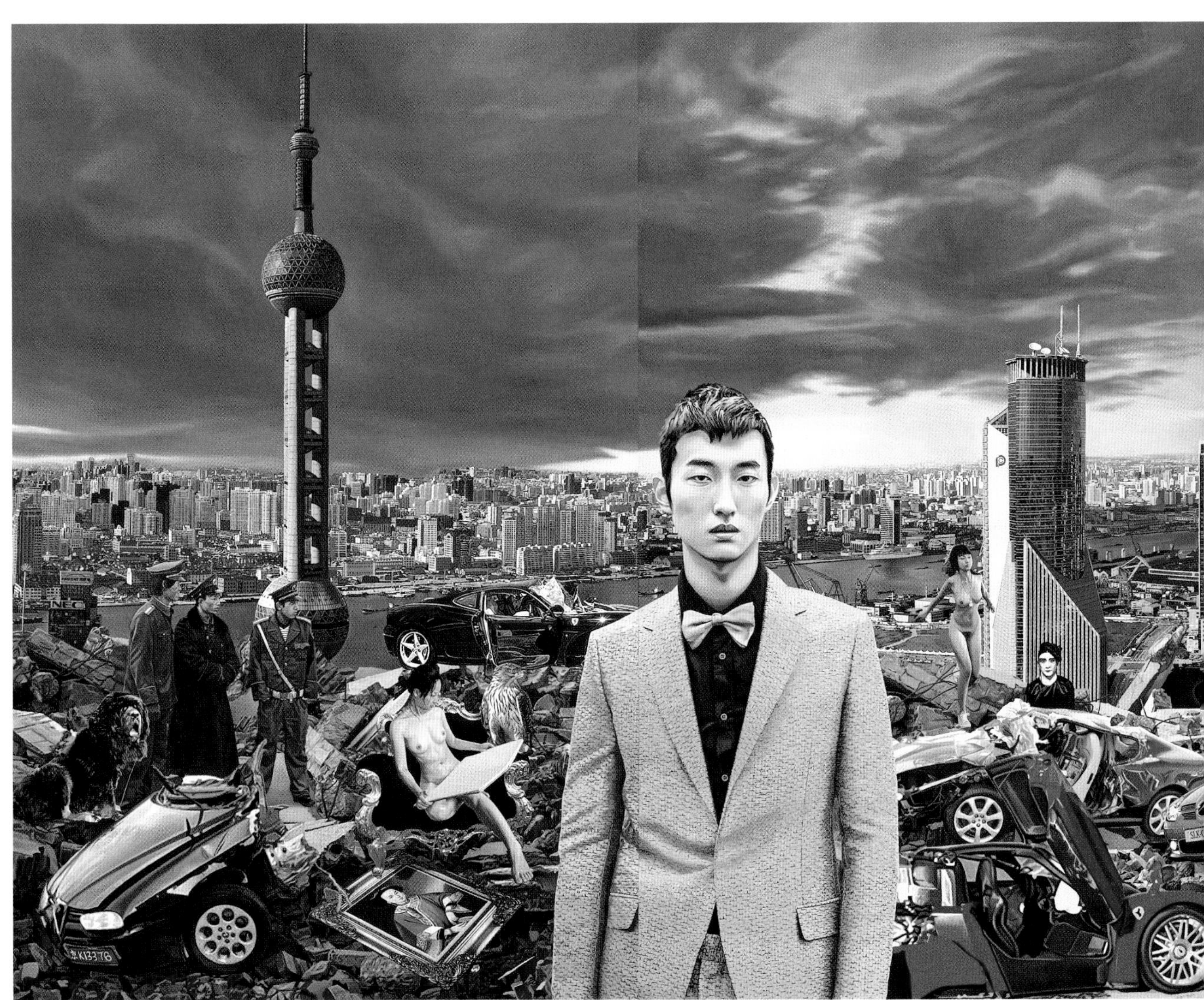

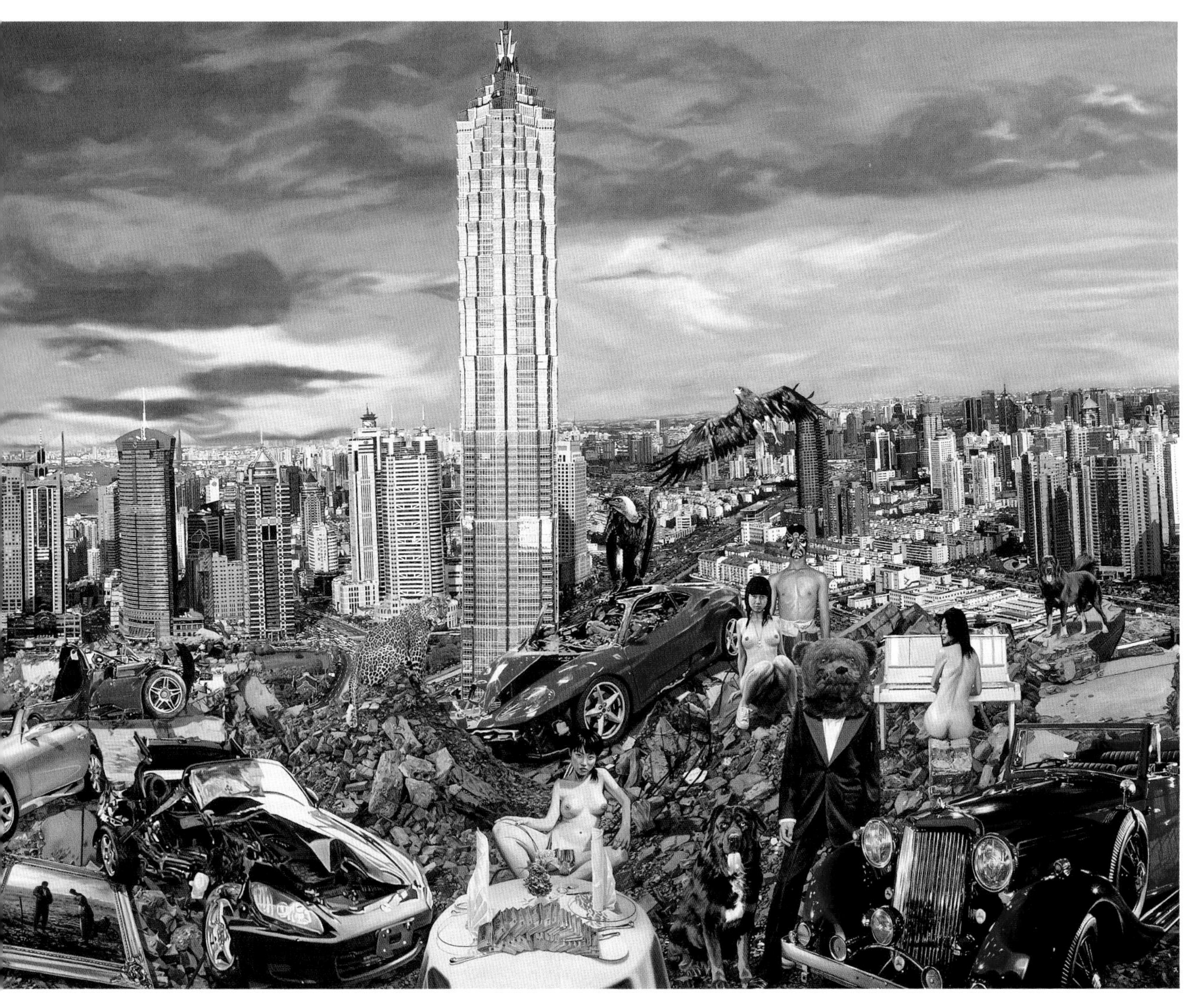

1 LOST HEAVEN NO. 2 • 2008-2009 • OIL ON CANVAS • 380 x 1000 CM

2

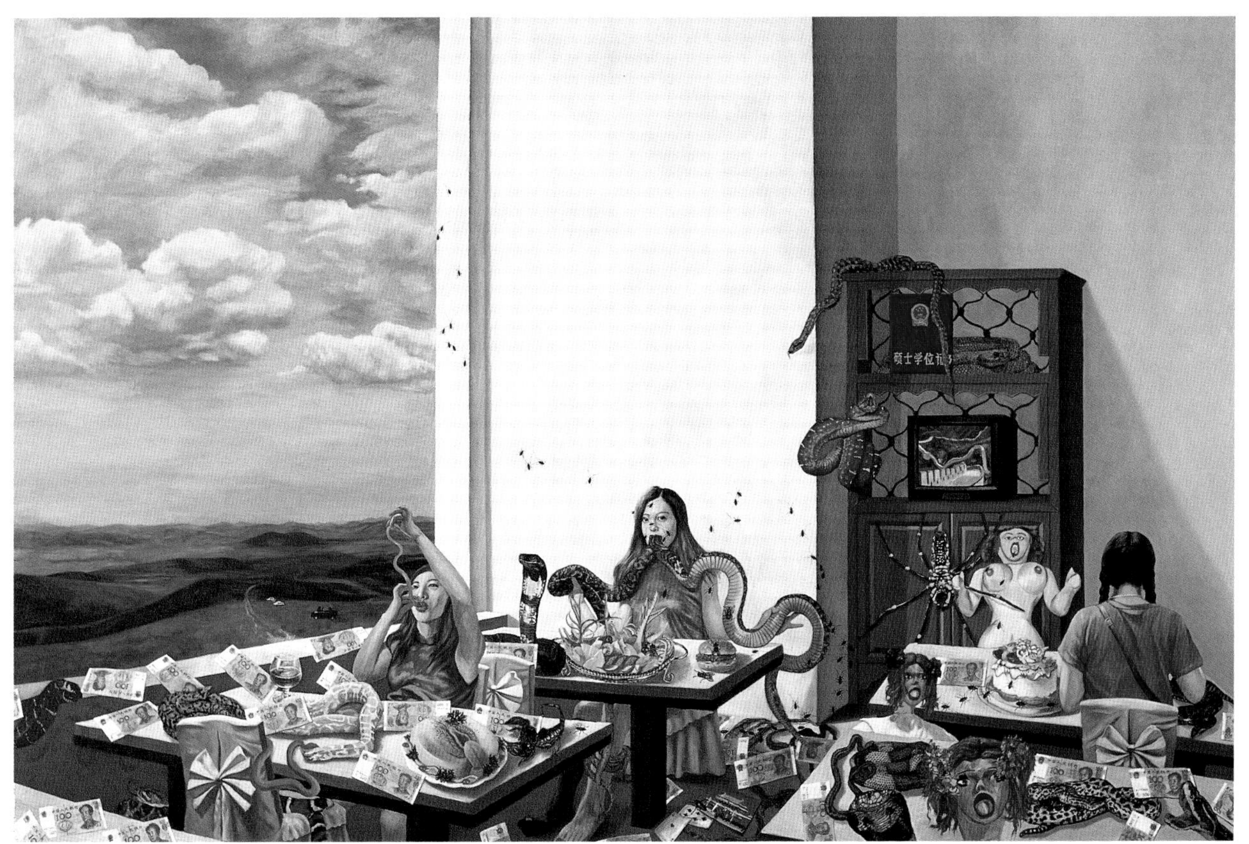

2 EATING SNAKES • 2005 • OIL ON CANVAS • 180 x 280 CM

3 SHANGHAI LUNCH • 2007 • C-PRINT • 160 x 210 CM

4 GUNFIGHT NO. 2 • 2007 • C-PRINT • 160 x 210 CM

3
4

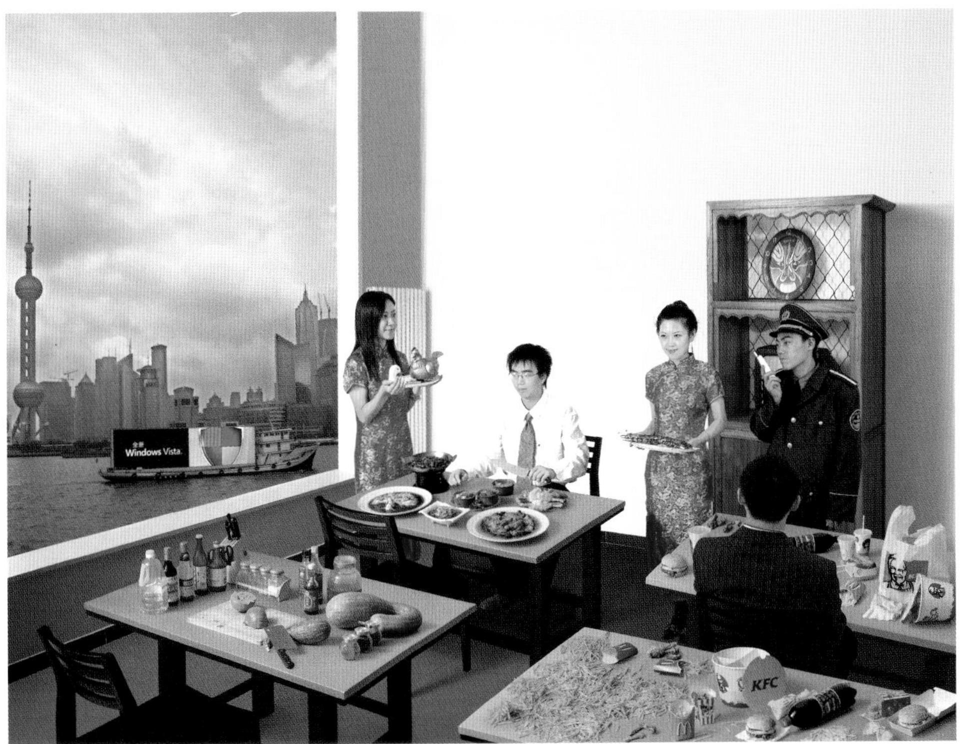

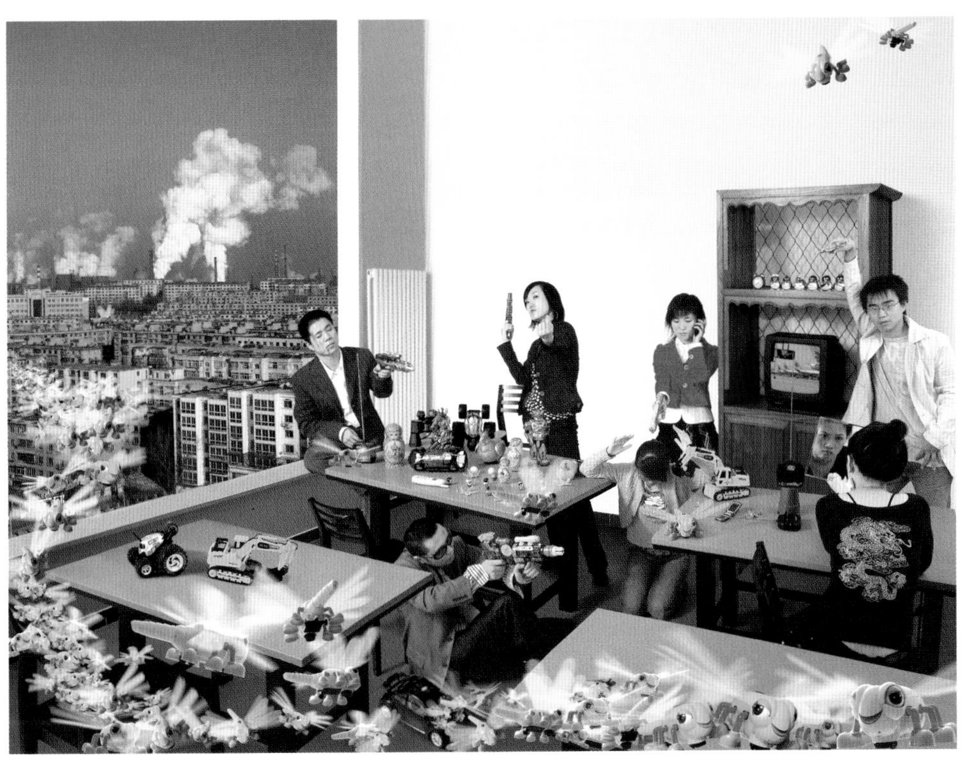

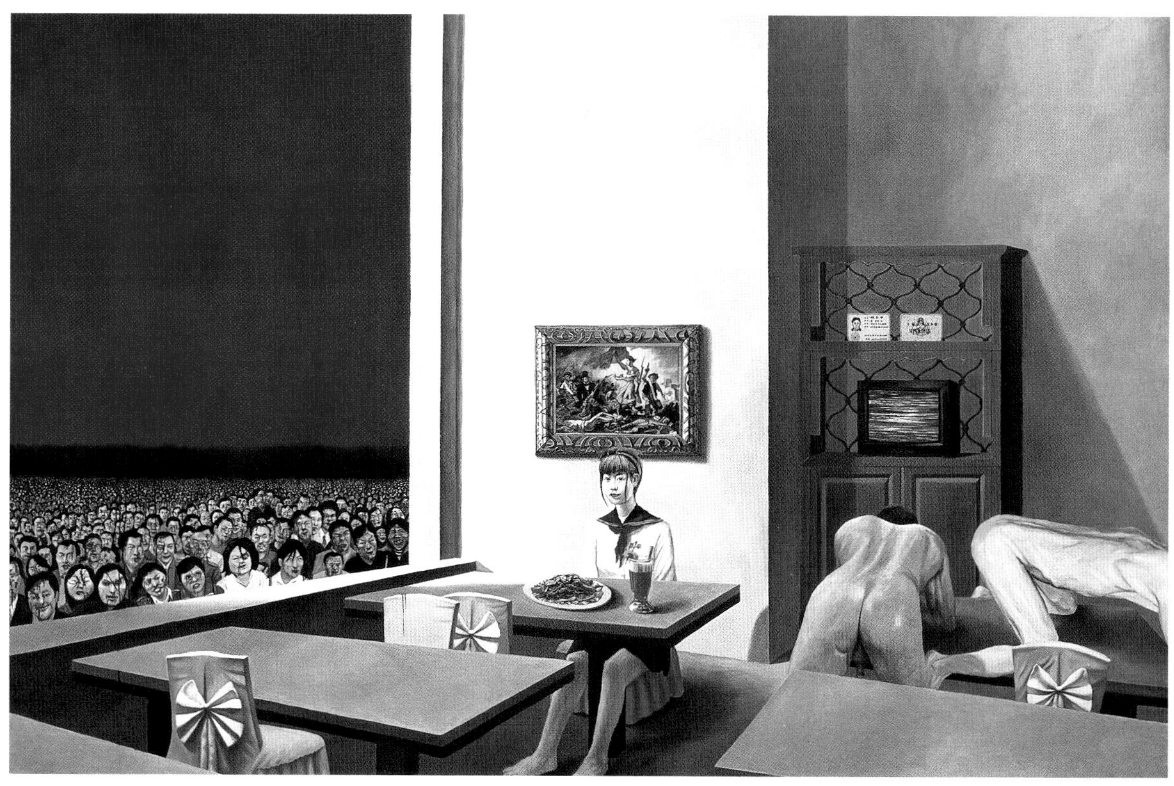

PHONE INTERVIEW WITH EDITORS

5/13/08 • AFTERNOON

EDITORS *What were your favorite childhood toys?*

TA MEN Marbles, metal rings, and toy pistols.

EDITORS *What sentence did your parents say to you most often?*

TA MEN "You have to be a good person!"

EDITORS *How do you try to stay healthy in your everyday life?*

TA MEN There are a lot of things in our everyday lives that keep us healthy. For example, the physical activity of painting, traveling around, and searching for new objects. And also photographing.

EDITORS *What is your recent wish?*

TA MEN To invent new ideas.

EDITORS *Do you believe in true love?*

TA MEN Definitely! For us this means being faithful to the person you love. This can be your wife, your lover, your kids, or anyone else.

EDITORS *What does your ideal living environment look like?*

TA MEN You have freedom to do the things you want to do. And also, there must be fair competition.

EDITORS *What do you like and dislike about being an artist?*

TA MEN We dislike "dishonest" works that lack content, imagination, and concept. And we like exactly the opposite.

EDITORS *How can you communicate with the audience through your art?*

TA MEN We are communicating with the audience via the content of our paintings. The prerequisite is a connection between the content and our society. Whatever we paint, we see it from of the perspective of others. For us, it's important that the viewer understands our concept but we are also afraid that not everyone can access our art.

EDITORS *Five words that describe your generation?*

TA MEN Self-centeredness, freedom, rebellion, initiative, and realism.

EDITORS *If the whole world would listen to you for fifteen seconds, what would you say?*

TA MEN This is a very strange question! Well, probably we would answer by saying something like, "Thank you very much for listening. Please pay more attention to the existence of the human beings."

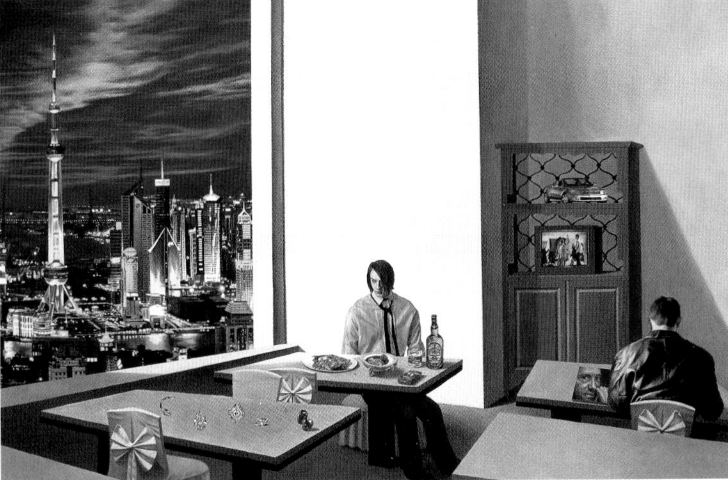

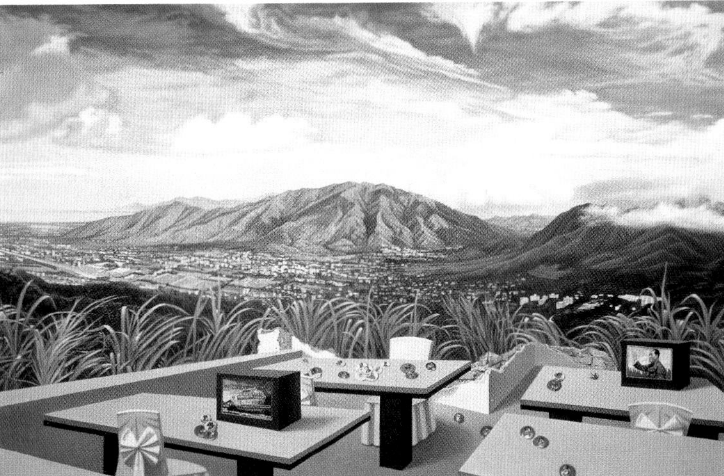

EXHIBITIONS

SELECTED SOLO EXHIBITIONS

2009
The lost Heaven,
Hunan Provincial Museum,
Changsha, China

2006
Ta Men,
PYO Gallery,
Seoul, South Korea

2004
Therefore It Is and Surely It's Them,
798 Art Space,
Beijing, China

SELECTED GROUP EXHIBITIONS

2009
Chengdu Biennale,
Chengdu, China

2007/8
China: Facing Reality,
National Art Museum of China,
Beijing, China /
Museum Moderner Kunst Stiftung Ludwig,
Vienna, Austria

2007
Thermocline of Art: New Asian Waves,
Center for Art and Media (ZKM),
Karlsruhe, Germany

2007
Floating: New Generation of Art in China,
National Museum of Contemporary Art,
Seoul, South Korea

2006
China Now: Kunst in Zeiten des Umbruchs,
Sammlung Essl,
Klosterneuburg, Austria

2006
Beyond Experience: New China!,
Arario Gallery,
Beijing, China

2005
*Grounding Reality:
New Chinese Contemporary Art*,
Seoul Art Center,
Seoul, South Korea

5 FREEDOM LEADING DEMOS • 2005 • OIL ON CANVAS • 180 x 280 CM

6 SHANGHAI NO. 1 • 2006 • OIL ON CANVAS • 180 x 280 CM

7 JIANG SHAN (MOUNTAINS AND RIVERS) • 2008 • OIL ON CANVAS • 180 x 280 CM

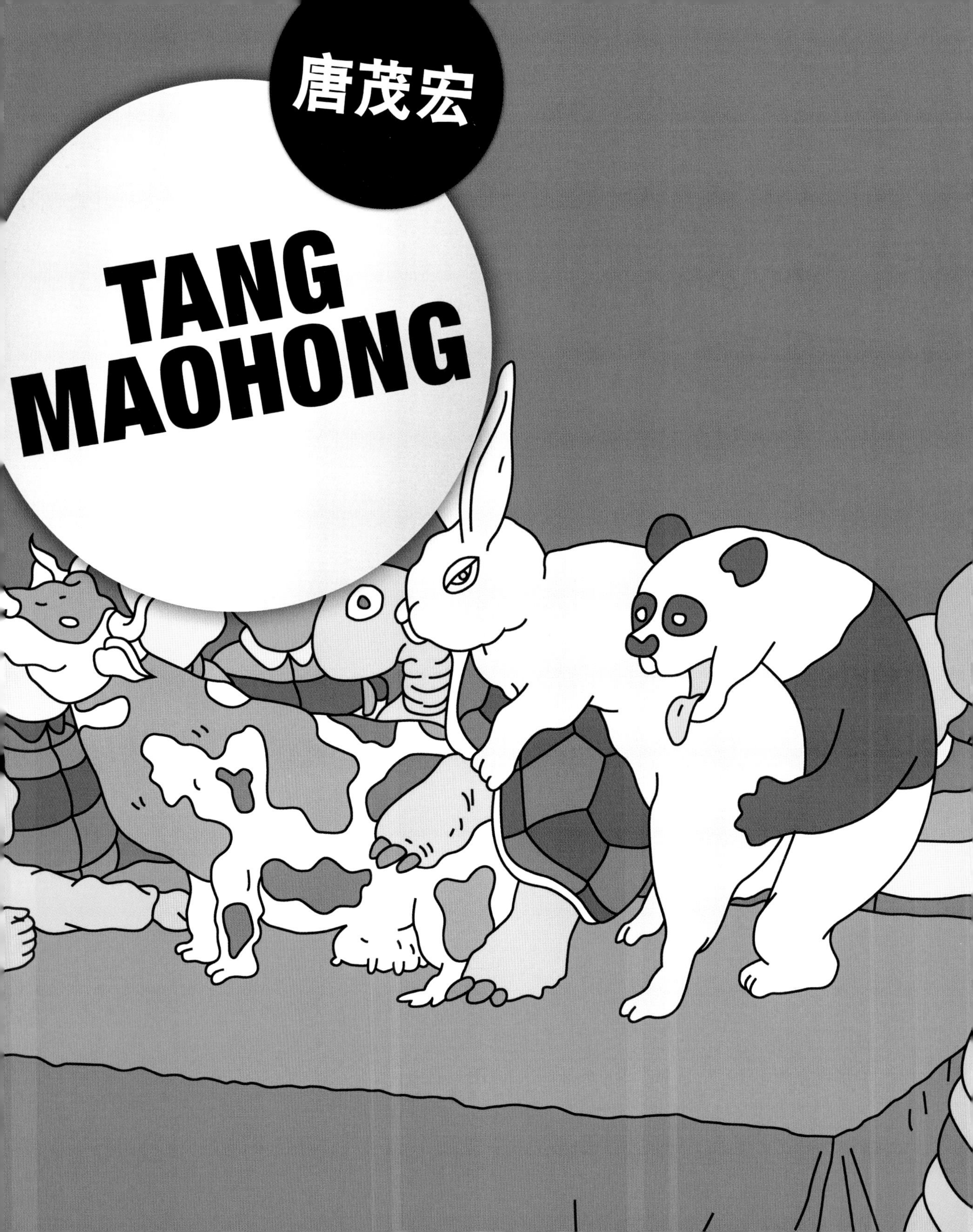
唐茂宏
TANG MAOHONG

NAME
TANG MAOHONG
BORN IN
1975, LINGCHUAN
LIVES IN
SHANGHAI
STUDY
CHINA ACADEMY OF ART, HANGZHOU
MEDIA
ANIMATION, PERFORMANCE

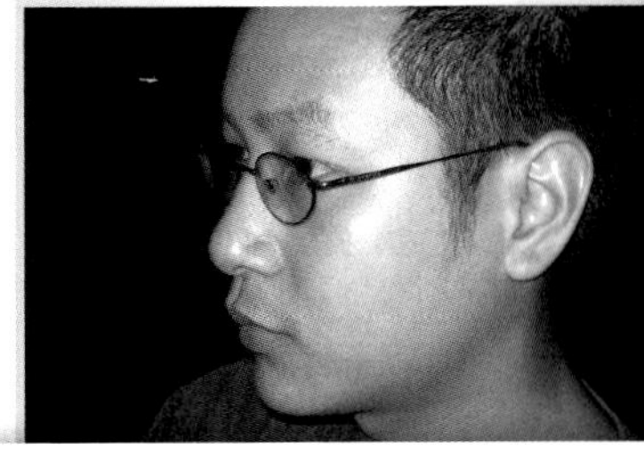

A MAGICAL WORLD

Tang Maohong calls himself an experimental animation artist. He was born in 1975 in a small city in Guangxi Province, and after graduating from the Chinese Academy of Art, Hangzhou, in 2000 he went to Shanghai to live and work. Tang's films are full of different scenes and illustrate his playful acquaintance with the most diverse images. All of them are elements of our life and imagination: politics, childhood, the Internet, pornography, history, the Chinese zodiac, violence, the body, fantasy, illusion, she, he, it ... The images in each different scene perhaps allow the viewer to experience the power of the imagination of artists and the magical power of artistic expression.

At the beginning of his artistic career, Tang Maohong worked on two performance art projects. In *Photosynthesis* (2000), the artist drew the outlines of corresponding shadows on his body, following the rays of the sun at twelve different times of the day. For *Walk* (2000), he walked barefoot, took the bus, the train, and the metro to go from the Hangzhou Zoo to the Shanghai Museum.

In 2005, Tang Maohong started creating experimental animations. *Orchid Finger* (2005) – Tang Maohong's first experimental animation – is a three-screened animation installation in which he uses images to express "crazy thoughts." The artist sees the surface appearance of images as the medium that can express his ideas in a broader and fuller way. In *Orchid Finger-3*, circular picture frames are lined up in the middle of the screen. The content of the scene constantly changes; there is nothing linking the images, as every image in the series can be chosen at random and can stand alone as an independent image. The animation itself is full of strange, magical scenes: girls with long tails, huge snails, rabbits mating with everyone, masked people with rabbit's ears, dazzling mushrooms, etc. The extraordinary level of imagination in Tang Maohong's works surprises the audience and pushes them to look for a deeper meaning to his work.

Being interested in an extensive scope of areas, many of the images Tang Maohong uses as inspiration for his works are downloaded from the Internet. The materials for *Sunday* (2006) are almost all taken from ready-made Web images. This work, however, is not an investigation into the reproducibility of images. It abandons the question-and-answer function of art by focusing on random choice and alteration of images. On could say that Tang Maohong chooses a lazy or passive method to think about art. *Sunday* is different to *Orchid Finger* in that it lines up five round picture frames in the middle of the screen. The increased number makes the images more powerful and enforces the sense of space. But this work keeps in line with the former as it uses the same fragmented image style. It seems that viewers are hardly asked to respond to the dynamic images that are constantly flowing across the screen; all of them funny and fantastic, they show a mixture of obsession and oppressiveness. Music has an important effect on the overall atmosphere in both *Orchid Finger* and *Sunday*, and the artist friends recruited by Tang Maohong delivered soundtracks that fit well with the fragmented and lost feeling of the films.

Tang Maohong's strange daydreams are beautifully reconstructed in these two hand-drawn animation works. In tune with the strong rhythm of the drums, a sequence of absurd images and unordered plots flow like clouds across the screen. Gorgeous mushrooms, elegant flowers and plants, towering pagodas, faceless crowds, crazy animals are all displayed, and all find their place in the round frames on the screen. These images express a strange, fantastic world, but also create a realistic metaphor. It is Tang Maohong's translation of the strange, subjectively rich and abundant daily life of the world. This is the artist's characteristic language, which builds realism, fantasy, and experience into a strange and magical surreal image.

By Huang Du

1

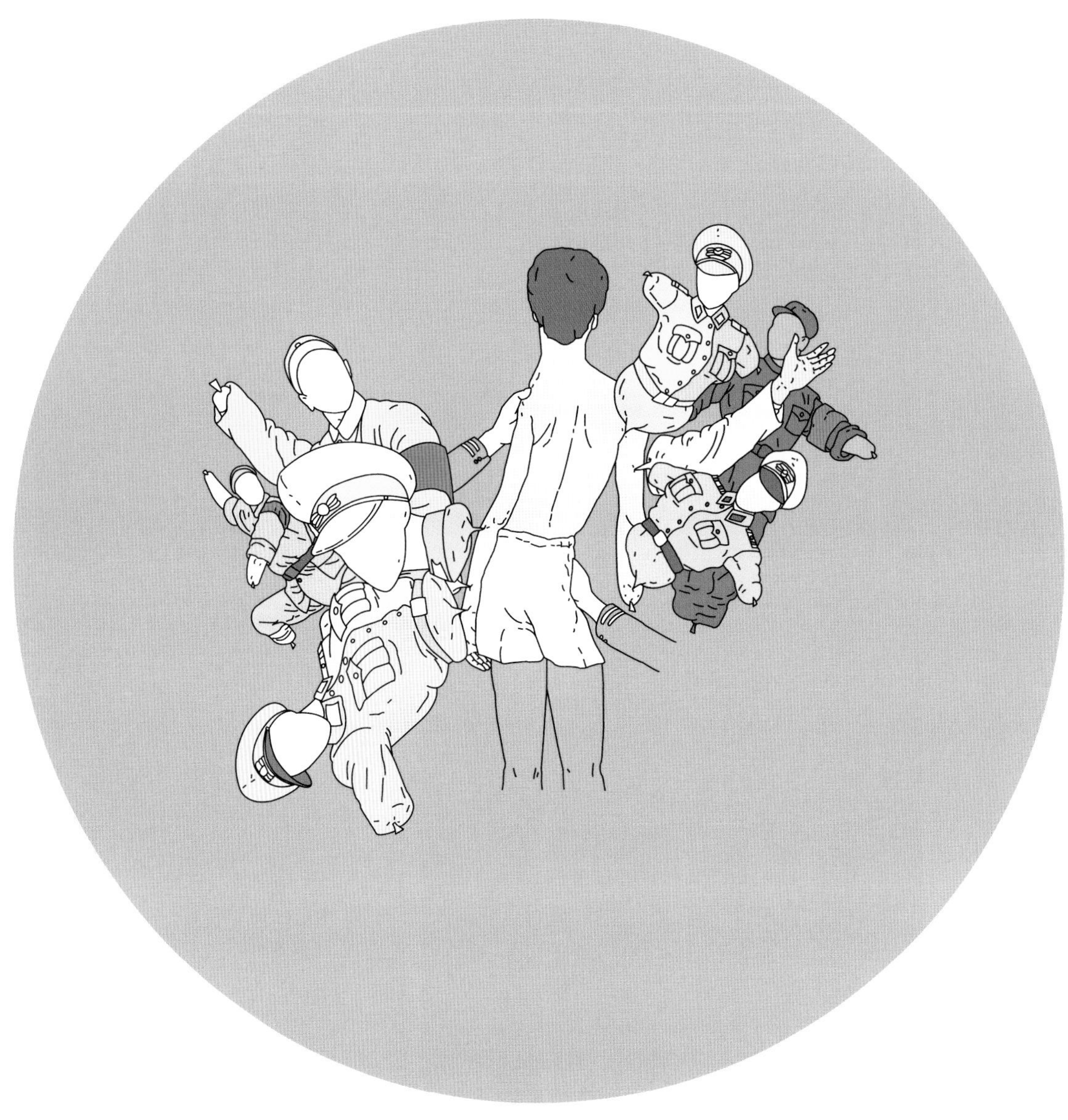

1 ORCHID FINGER-9 • 2005 • SILKSCREEN PRINT • 45 x 45 CM

2 ORCHID FINGER-12 • 2005 • SILKSCREEN PRINT • 45 x 45 CM

3 ORCHID FINGER-4 • 2005 • SILKSCREEN PRINT • 45 x 45 CM

2
3

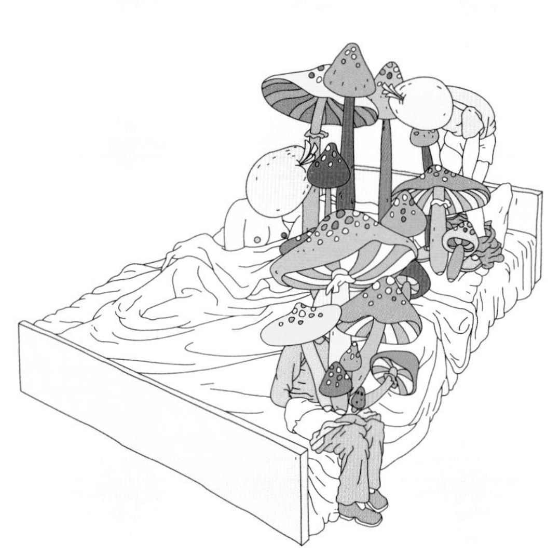

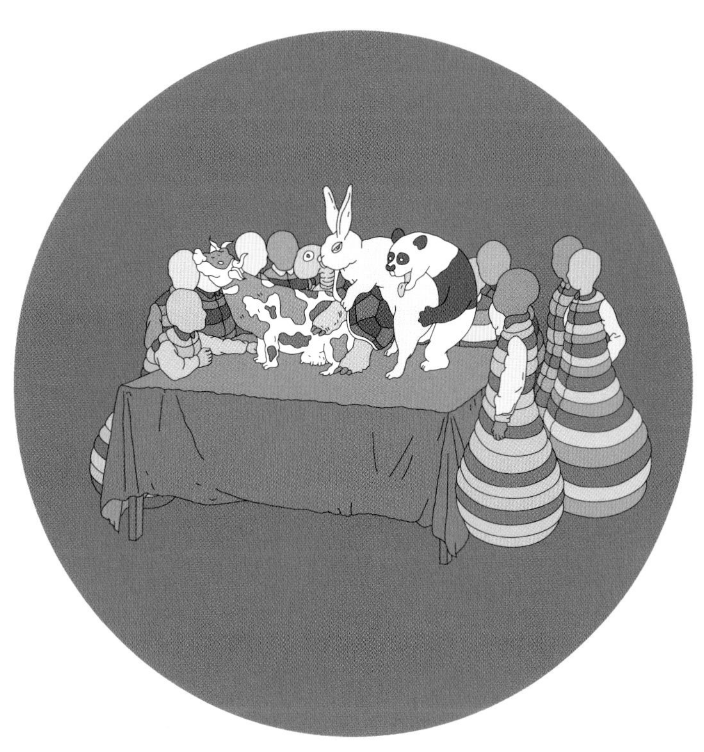

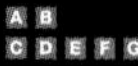

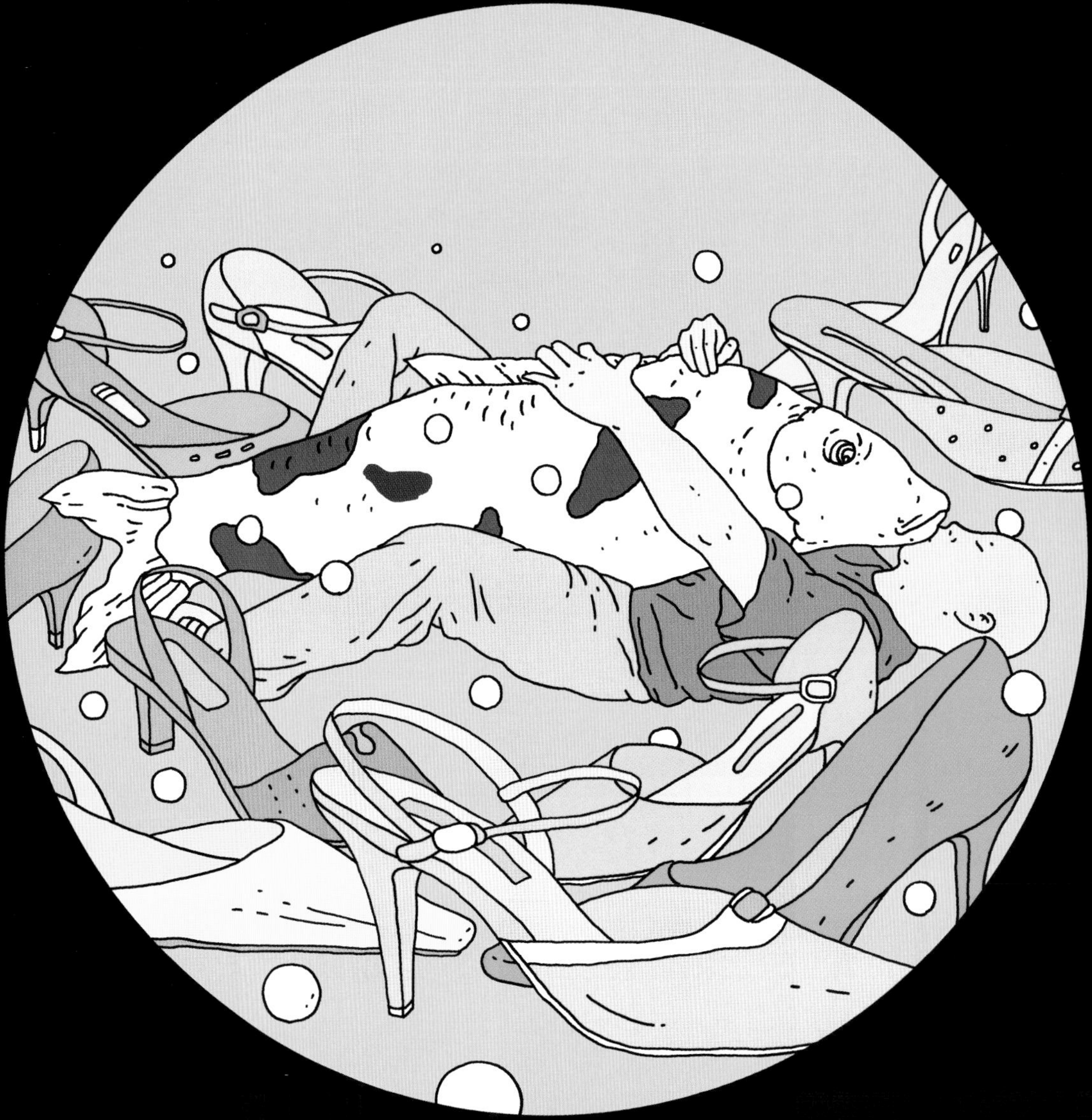

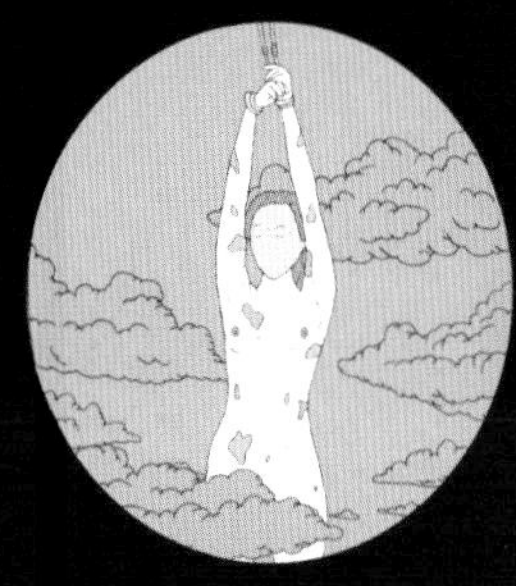

4 SUNDAY • 2006 • VIDEO, MULTI-CHANNEL • 6'

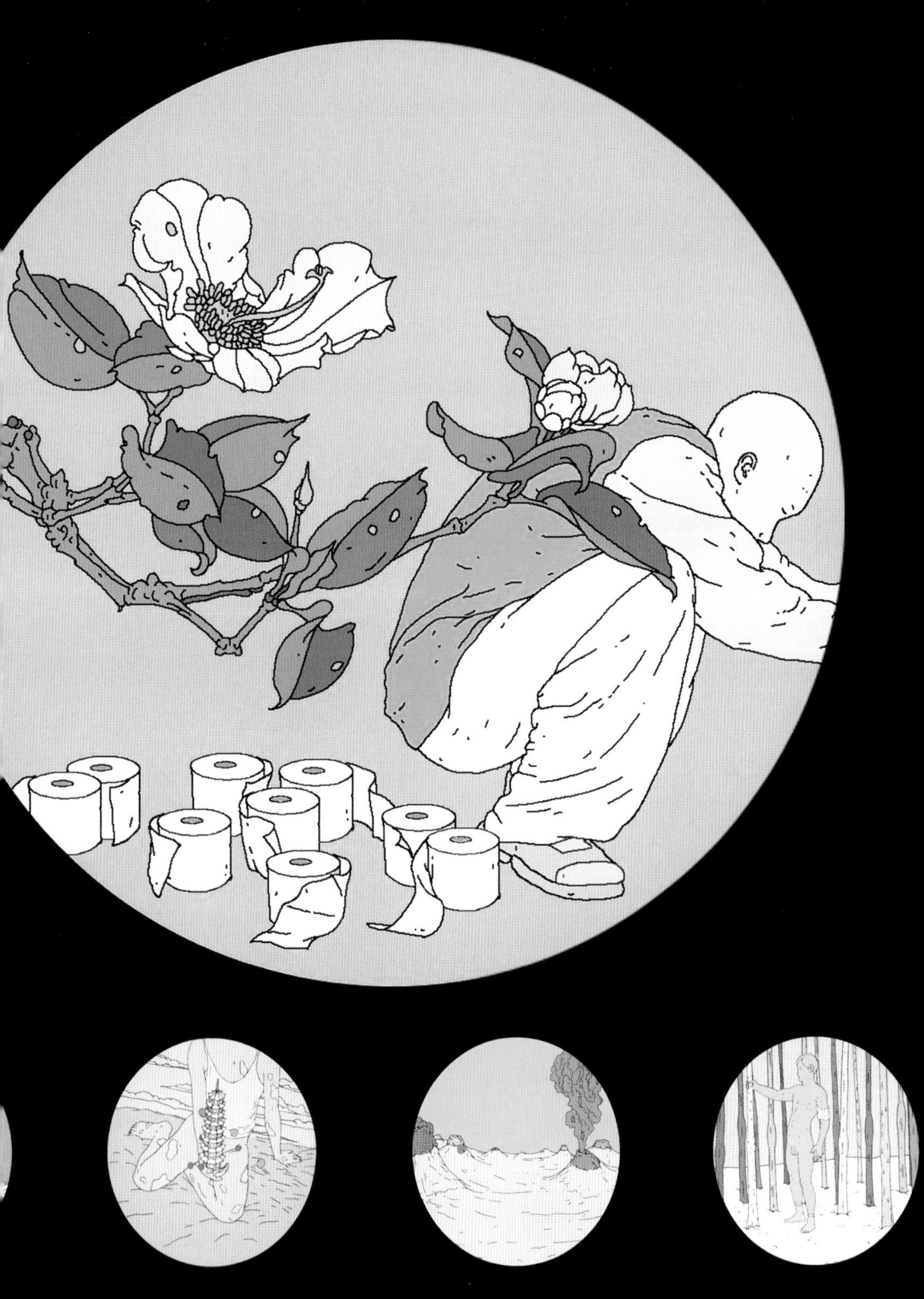

QUESTIONNAIRE

5/2/08 • SHANGHAI

WHAT WAS YOUR FAVORITE CHILDHOOD TOY?

A sword.

WHAT DID YOUR PARENTS SAY TO YOU MOST OFTEN?

"Take care of your health."

HOW DO YOU TRY TO STAY HEALTHY IN YOUR EVERYDAY LIFE?

I eat regularly.

WHAT HAVE YOU BEEN WISHING FOR MOST RECENTLY?

To be able to drink green tea at night without suffering from insomnia.

DO YOU BELIEVE IN TRUE LOVE?

Yes.

WHAT DOES YOUR IDEAL LIVING ENVIRONMENT LOOK LIKE?

Tolerant and natural.

FROM WHICH TYPE OF MEDIA DO YOU DERIVE MOST OF YOUR INSPIRATION?

From the Internet.

WHAT DO YOU LIKE/DISLIKE ABOUT BEING AN ARTIST?

I like the freedom of the job, but I dislike that the job is too free compared to other jobs.

HOW DO YOU COMMUNICATE WITH THE AUDIENCE IN YOUR ART?

With as much honesty as I can.

IF YOU HAD FIVE WORDS TO DESCRIBE YOUR GENERATION, WHAT WOULD THEY BE?

Naivety, ambition, disorder, violence, and incredulousness.

IF THE WHOLE WORLD WOULD LISTEN TO YOU FOR FIFTEEN SECONDS, WHAT WOULD YOU SAY?

If it's possible, I'd like to sell this chance by auction.

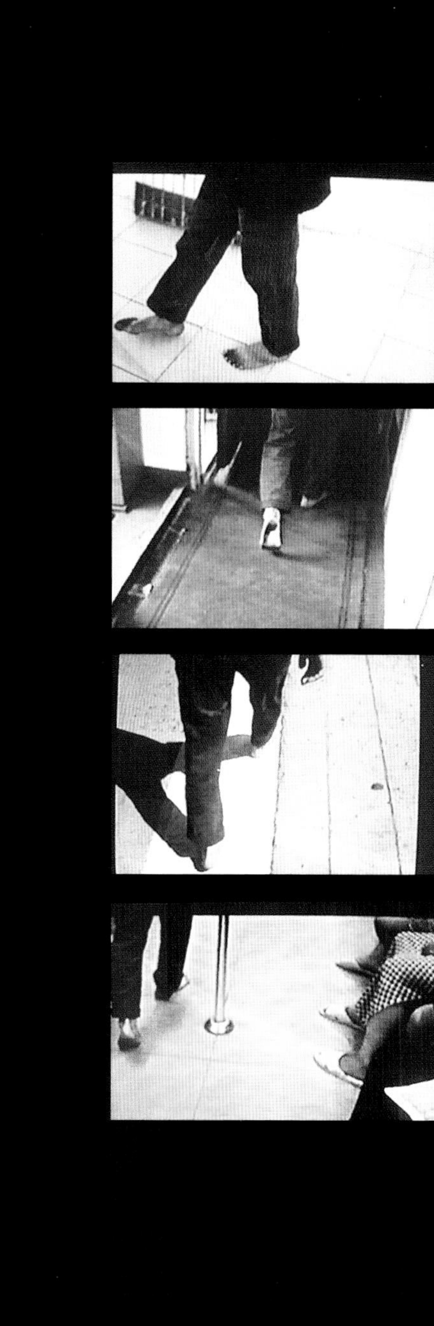

5
A
B
C
D

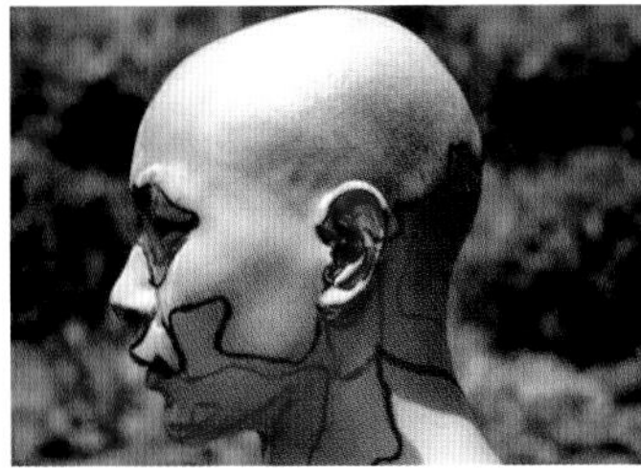

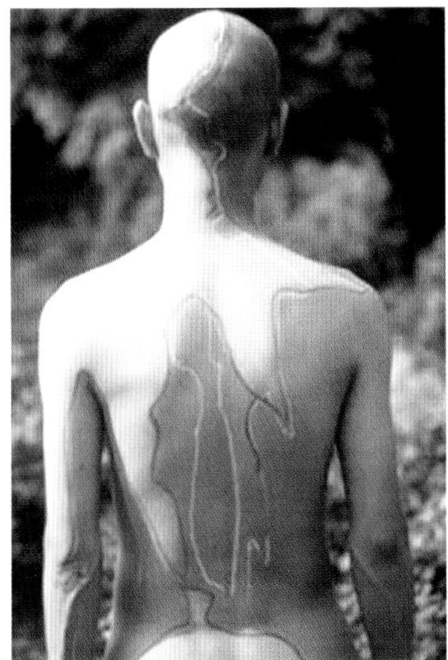

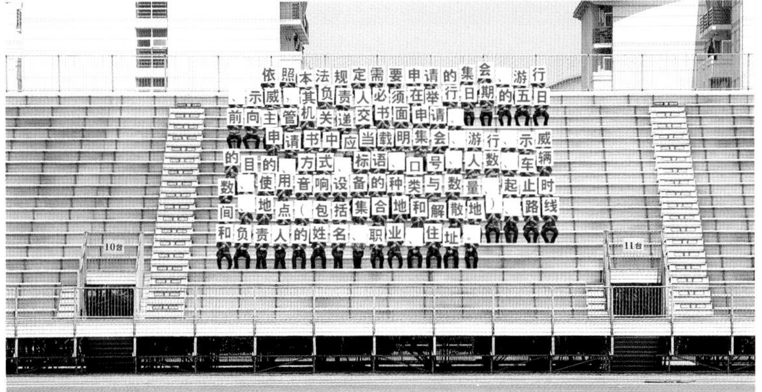

5 WALK • 2000 • PERFORMANCE

6 PHOTOSYNTHESIS • 2000 • PERFORMANCE

7 SILENT FILM: LAW OF THE PEOPLE'S REPUBLIC OF CHINA ON ASSEMBLIES, PROCESSIONS AND DEMONSTRATIONS • 2009 • VIDEO • 8'

EXHIBITIONS

SELECTED SOLO EXHIBITIONS

2006
Orchid Finger: Video & Silkscreen Prints,
ShanghART H-Space,
Shanghai, China

2006
Sunday,
Creative Center 2577 Longhua Road,
Shanghai, China

SELECTED GROUP EXHIBITIONS

2008
7th Shanghai Biennale - Translocalmotion,
Shanghai Art Museum,
Shanghai, China

2008
Building Code Violations II,
Long March Space,
Beijing, China

2007/8
China: Facing Reality,
National Art Museum of China,
Beijing, China /
Museum Moderner Kunst Stiftung Ludwig,
Vienna, Austria

2007
Shenzhen & Hong Kong Bi-City Biennale of Urbanism,
Shenzhen, China

2007
Rejected Collection,
Ke Center for Contemporary Arts,
Shanghai, China

2007
Thermocline of Art: New Asian Waves,
Center for Art and Media (ZKM),
Karlsruhe, Germany

2007
New Nature,
Govett-Brewster Art Gallery,
New Plymouth, New Zealand

2005
Asian Traffic,
Zendai Museum of Modern Art,
Shanghai, China

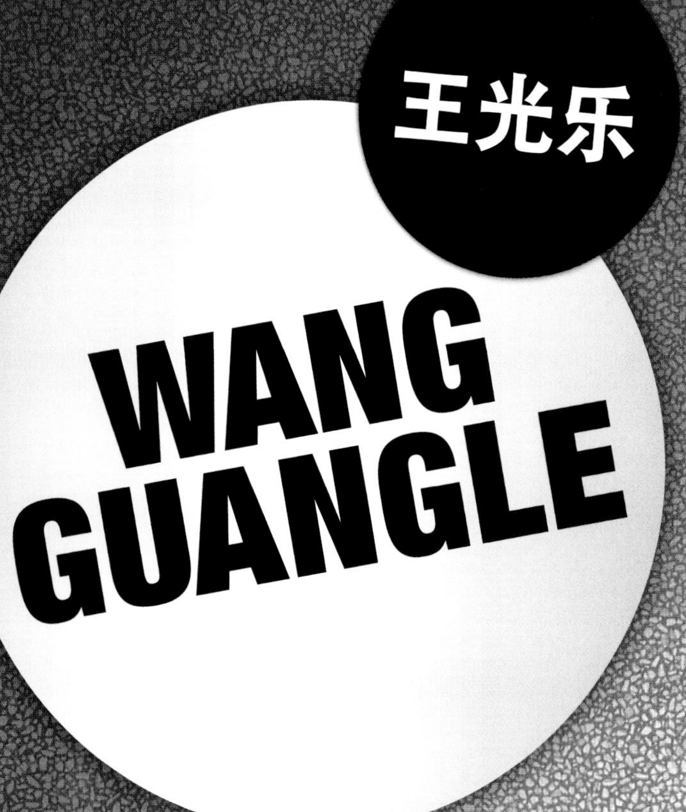
王光乐
WANG
GUANGLE

NAME
WANG GUANGLE

BORN IN
1976, SONGXI

LIVES IN
BEIJING

STUDY
CENTRAL ACADEMY OF FINE ARTS, BEIJING

MEDIA
INSTALLATION, PAINTING, SCULPTURE

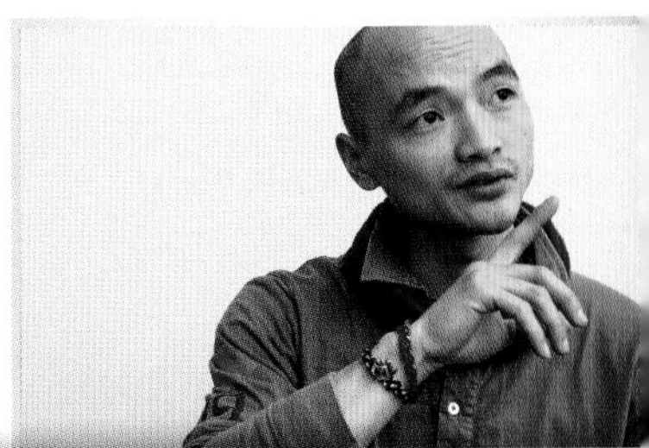

VISIBLE TIME

Wang Guangle's thesis piece at Beijing's Central Academy of Fine Arts – *3 to 5 p.m.* (2000) – earned him first prize in the annual academy contest. It also powerfully established the theme of his later work. In this three-part series (oil on canvas), the artist shows an empty room, darkened by a curtain. A single, narrow chink between the wall and the fabric lets in a beam of light. We see how the light's angle of incidence changes, captured in the painting at irregular time intervals. Here as well as in subsequent works, Wang Guangle visualizes time at once in its duration and fickleness. In the delirium of big-city progress – where the present means nothing but a stepladder to the future – the Beijing based artist makes a plea for the irretrievable significance of the here and now.

The *Terrazzo* series connects thematically to *3 to 5 p.m.* The first picture (*Untitled*, 2003) shows a beam of light falling on marbleized flooring named after the Italian city of Terrazzo. This affordable mixture of concrete and other materials was much loved in the artist's own home province, but in recent years it has increasingly given way to other materials considered more modern. "My memories of my home are bound up inseparably with this material. When I paint it, I feel freed from specific forms – I can virtually look inward." In the paintings that make up the rest of the series, the light beam is nowhere to be seen. A diffuse timelessness permeates the veined surface. "I was unhappy with my first works. I had indeed marked a specific time point in the image, but what I wanted was to convey the experience of time itself. And that should in turn be reproducible for the viewer. Therefore I left the light beam out." And it is precisely this tangible sense of time that characterizes Wang Guangle's painting process. With the finest brushstrokes he recreates the seams in the concrete around the inlaid pieces and splinters of stone. The pictures that emerge possess a delicate ornamental aesthetic in gray and green tones, sometimes even in soft rose. In the minimal contours the viewer can readily imagine his fixed gaze as well as the sharp concentration in Wang Guangle's handling of the brush. Millimeter by millimeter the canvas fills itself, becoming the archivist of the artist's lifetime. Often taking numerous months of work, he transforms a stone structure into a "picture structure." "When I paint, I frequently have the feeling that I am writing calligraphy – which I enjoy immensely."

For Wang Guangle, painting becomes ritual, such as when, in 2004, he spent three months painting a Terrazzo image on the wall of a house doomed for demolition (*The Wall*, 2004). It is the act, not the product, which is the intent of his work. "For me, the most important thing is not the 'what' of painting, but the 'how'." A comparison to Buddhist sand mandalas would be appropriate – blown away by the wind as soon as they are finished – and Wang Guangle himself affirms the connection to Buddhist thinking. "I believe that something exists beyond the world of appearances." The intensity of contemplating a picture, analogue to the demanding process of painting, posits a spiritual counter-trend to the daily haste that throws away every moment and is totally preoccupied with distant goals, either self- or externally defined.

The existential element in Wang Guangle's work reveals itself again in his *Coffin Paint* series, begun in 2004. An old tradition in his home province of Fujian inspires the series; when someone feels that his life nears its end, he orders a casket, paints it in red lacquer, and keeps it on the second floor of his home. Every year that he still finds himself alive, he paints it again. There could hardly be a clearer application of the ancient saying "Memento Mori" – "Remember that you too shall die." On the basis of this ritual, Wang Guangle adds a layer of paint – twice daily, morning and evening – that more or less covers the canvas. The tone scale varies from monochrome to two or more colors. Since each application begins a little further removed from the edge, and is allowed to drip along the outer edge of the frame, the works attain a nearly plastic dimension. The association with a coffin is intended as the center of the canvas builds up the thickest layer of paint, classifying his *Coffin Paint* works close to sculptures.

In a variation on this technique, Wang Guangle applies every layer of paint the same distance from all four sides of the canvas's outer edge. In the center of his piece *041230* (2004) he has achieved a kind of suction affect. "Viewers have already told me that this work makes them think of a time tunnel." In another variation from 2007 (*070506* and *070508*), the paint surfaces are applied in the form of a circle, reminiscent of a tree's annual rings. The aesthetic affect of the coffin paintings, depending on the choice of colors, can range from a buoyantly cheerful, dramatic, or even gloomy aura, all the way to a contemplative gesture that invites the eye to wander. Wang Guangle's monochrome white or black compositions are particularly intense. They become reflective surfaces, mirroring the attention almost unavoidably back upon the viewer.

Wang Guangle's works are simultaneously timeless and current. They refresh a traditional Chinese phenomenon that is best articulated in Chinese landscape painting. While it is the nature of Western painting to deliver moments in time, Chinese landscape painting often features the same person several times within the same picture. The viewer is thus invited to simply follow the figure's wandering. Such traditional and other similar stylistic motifs achieve what Wang Guangle' paintings achieve abstractly and conceptually: making the passing of time visible.

By Ulrike Münter

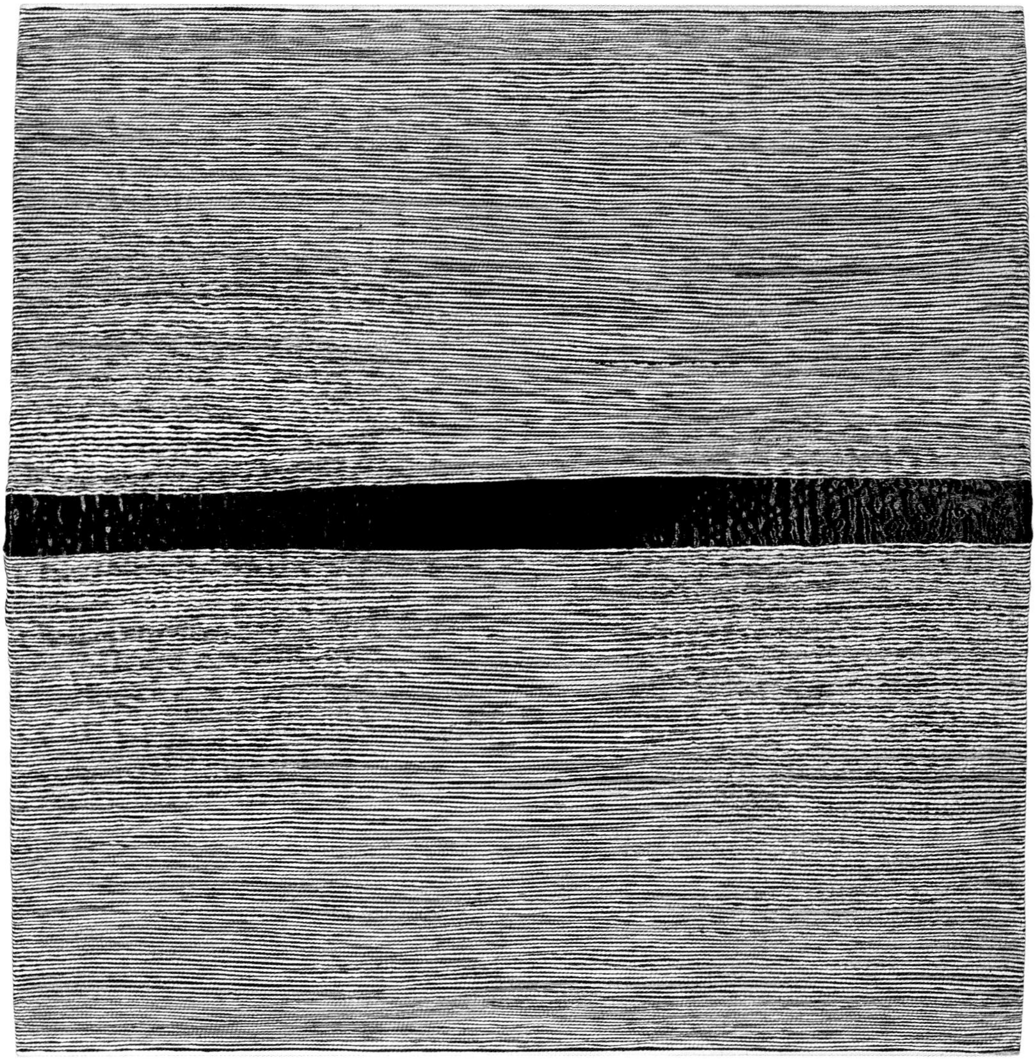

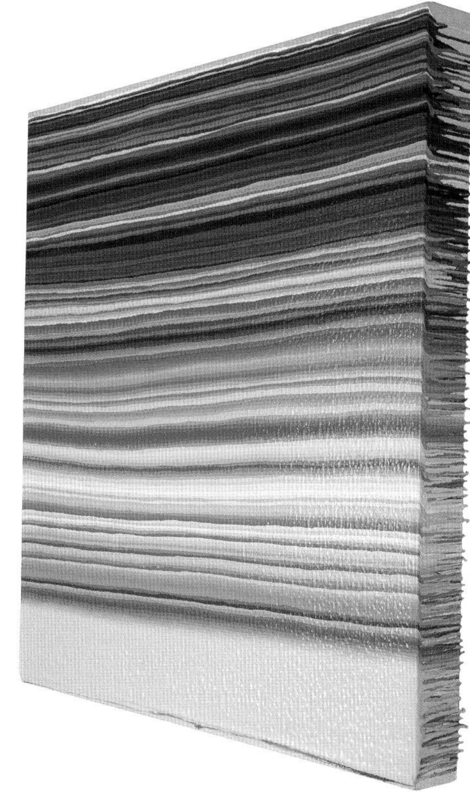

1 061213 • 2006 • ACRYLIC ON CANVAS • 116 x 114 CM

2 070613 • 2007 • ACRYLIC ON CANVAS • 116 x 114 CM

3 4
5

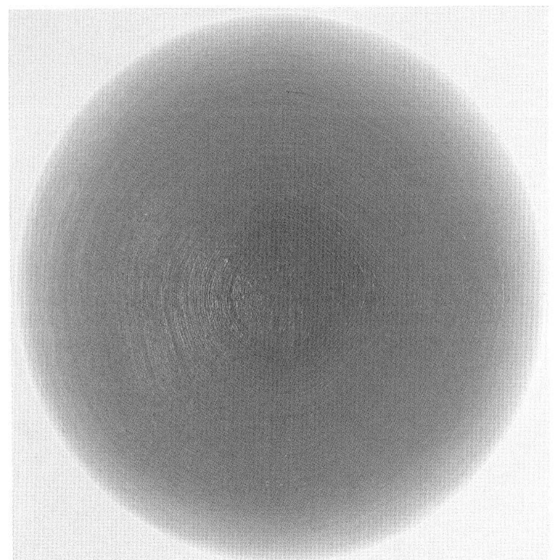

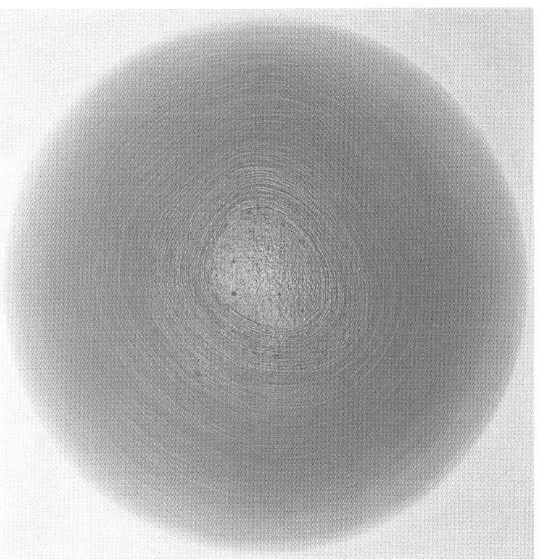

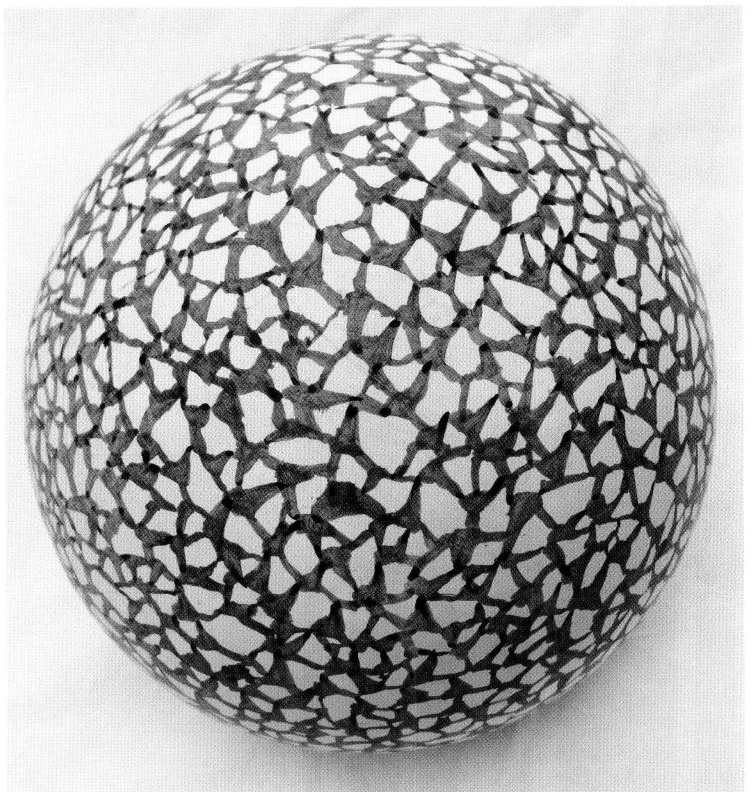

6

3 070506 • 2007 • ACRYLIC ON CANVAS • 112 x 112 CM

4 070508 • 2007 • ACRYLIC ON CANVAS • 112 x 112 CM

5 MEMORY BALL • 2004 • ACRYLIC ON GYPSUM • 20 CM DIAMETER

6 090119 • 2009 • ACRYLIC ON CANVAS • 230 x 180 CM

7

WANG GUANGLE

WANG GUANGLE

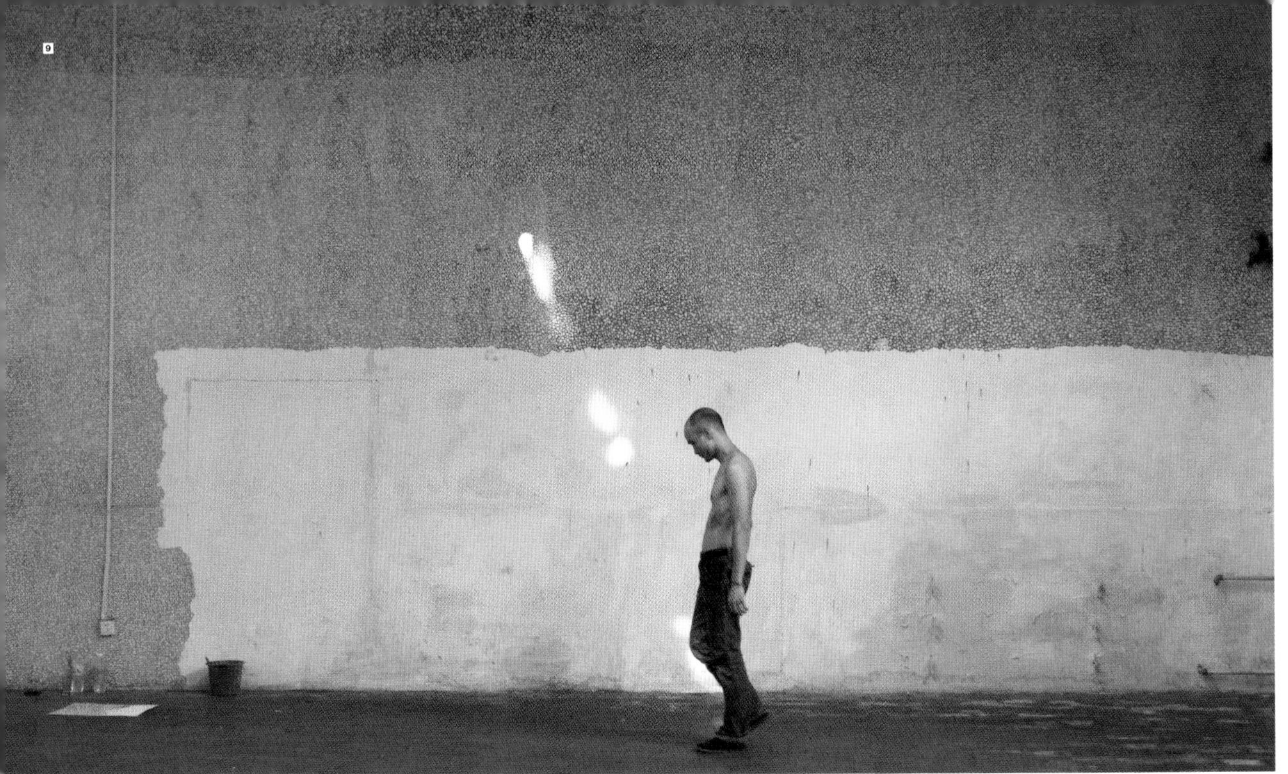

FACE-TO-FACE INTERVIEW WITH EDITORS

5/12/08 • EARLY EVENING • OFFICE OF THE MINISTRY OF ART, BEIJING

EDITORS *Thinking back to your childhood, what was your favorite childhood toy?* **WANG GUANGLE** I loved making my own toys. **EDITORS** *For example?* **WANG GUANGLE** I modeled little toy guns out of wire.

EDITORS *What did your parents say to you most often?* **WANG GUANGLE** My parents actually said different things. My mom said, "If you think something is good, then it will be good." My dad said, "Don't go to bed too late!" **EDITORS** *Still today?* **WANG GUANGLE** Yes. Actually, both of them still tell me these things today.

EDITORS *How do you try to maintain your health in your everyday life?* **WANG GUANGLE** I try to do some sports; for example, I play badminton and also sometimes soccer.

EDITORS *What is your most recent wish?* **WANG GUANGLE** I guess it is related to health. I would like to smoke less in the future.

EDITORS *Do you believe in true love?* **WANG GUANGLE** Of course I do! I also think that this true love can be not only between lovers but also between parents and their kids, etc. **EDITORS** *What does your ideal living environment look like?* **WANG GUANGLE** Having at least 60 percent greenery around my living place, and also a very clean environment is important to me. Unfortunately, my current living place does not fulfill that requirement, but my hometown in Fujian Province does.

EDITORS *Which type of media provides you most of your inspiration?* **WANG GUANGLE** Hardly any of my inspiration comes from the media.

EDITORS *Where does it come from?* **WANG GUANGLE** It comes from the real life. For example, from people I meet, things that I encounter, and so on.

EDITORS *What do you like and what do you dislike about working as an artist?* **WANG GUANGLE** I like that as an artist you are not fixed to one role only, as maybe a doctor is, who would be primarily seen by society as a doctor first and not as a person. Also you have a lot of freedom and are able to meet many new people. The freedom one has can be used to bring good things and ideas to society. However, I dislike that some artists misuse this freedom, feel superior, and become very arrogant.

EDITORS *How can you communicate with the audience through your art?* **WANG GUANGLE** I believe that there are many ways to communicate with the audience. Nowadays, a lot of paintings are figurative. This makes the viewer determine what the content of this painting is. My paintings don't show any action and the viewers do not have to think about it. They have to think about why the artist did the work in a certain way.

EDITORS *What is the reaction of the viewers when they suddenly do not have to think about the content any more?* **WANG GUANGLE** There are different reactions to my paintings. Nowadays, life has become very fast, so many people pass by the paintings without having any thoughts. But I got feedback that many of the viewers think about the paintings later. So my paintings seem to take a while to process.

EDITORS *If you would describe your generation with five words only, what would they be?* **WANG GUANGLE** This is very difficult to answer, as the people within this generation are so different.

EDITORS *If the whole world could listen to you for fifteen seconds, what would you say?* **WANG GUANGLE** Fifteen seconds are so short! I would say, "This feeling is good (that everyone is listening)" ... and then I guess the time would already be over.

10

EXHIBITIONS

SELECTED SOLO EXHIBITIONS

2009
Wang Guangle,
Beijing Commune,
Beijing, China

2007
Coffin Paint,
Aye Gallery,
Beijing, China

SELECTED GROUP EXHIBITIONS

2009
Prague Biennale 4,
Karlin Hall,
Prague, Czech Republic

2007
Refresh: Emerging Chinese Artists,
Zendai Museum of Modern Art,
Shanghai, China /
Arario Gallery,
Beijing, China

2007
New Interface 3,
Liu Haisu Art Museum,
Shanghai, China

2006
Unclear and Clearness,
Heyri Foundation,
Seoul, South Korea

2005
N12 – No.3,
Art Museum of Central Academy of Fine Arts,
Beijing, China

2004
Ideal of New Generation: Chinese New Generation Artists Award Exhibition,
He Xiangning Art Museum,
Shenzhen, China

2003
The 3rd Exhibition of Chinese Oil Paintings,
National Art Museum of China,
Beijing, China

2003
Prayer Beads and Brush Strokes,
BTAP,
Beijing, China

7 TERRAZZO 2005.6/8 • 2005 • OIL ON CANVAS • 180 x 150 CM

8 TERRAZZO 2003.5 • 2003 • OIL ON CANVAS • 180 x 143 CM

9 THE WALL • 2004 • ACRYLIC ON WALL • 600 x 900 CM

10 3 TO 5 P.M. • 2000 • OIL ON CANVAS • 170 x 70 CM

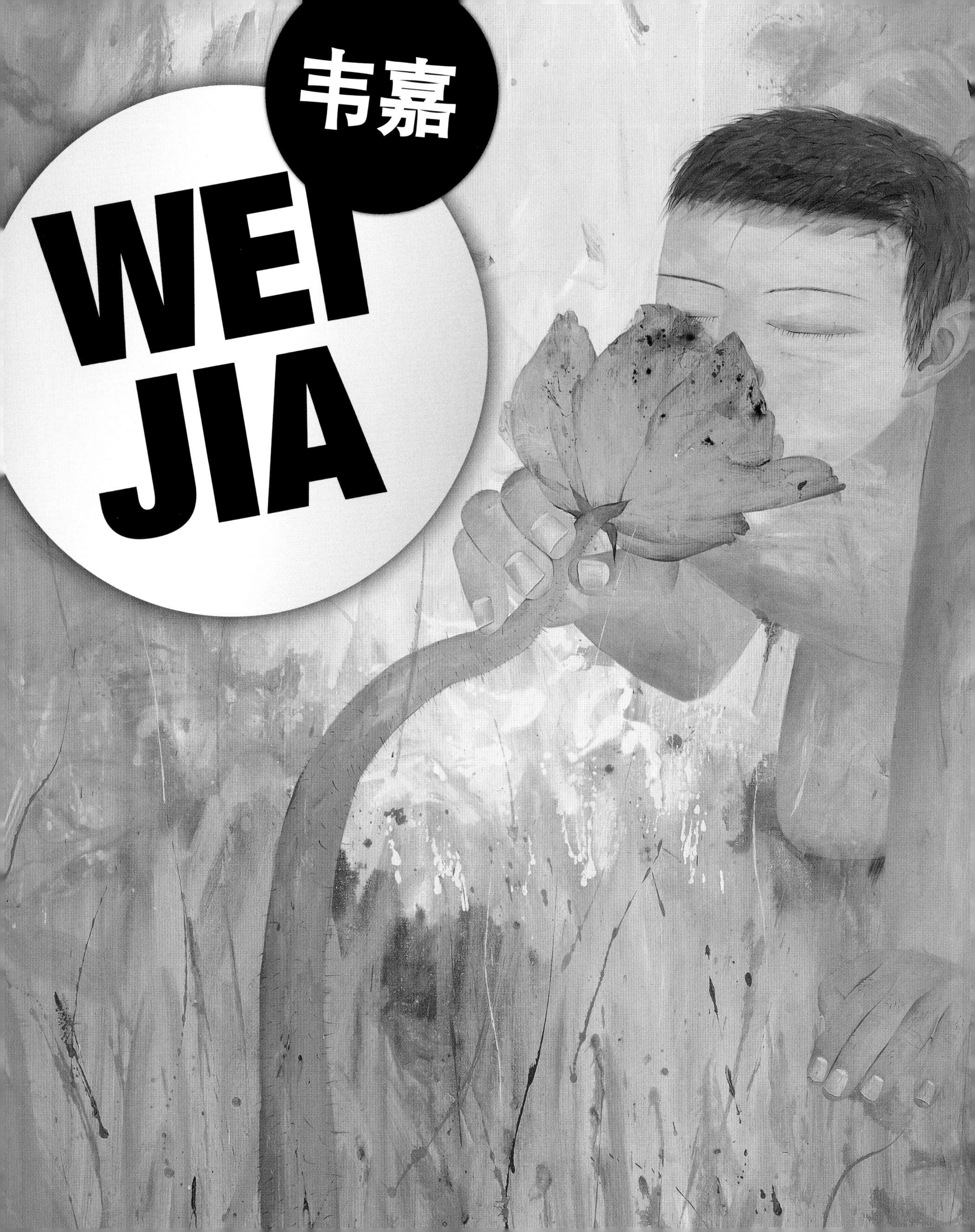
韦嘉
WEI
JIA

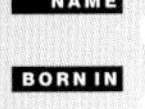

NAME
WEI JIA

BORN IN
1975, CHENGDU

LIVES IN
CHONGQING

STUDY
CENTRAL ACADEMY OF FINE ARTS, BEIJING

MEDIA
LITHOGRAPHY, PAINTING

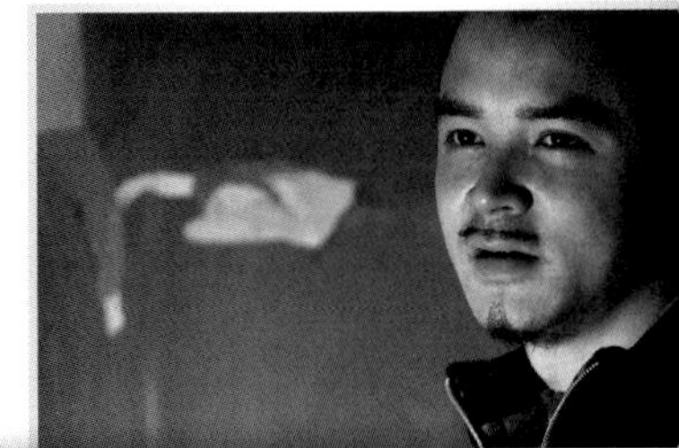

PSYCHOLOGY OF PAIN

Wei Jia is regarded as one of the representatives of the new generation of contemporary Chinese painters. The figures in his paintings display a unique sense of form; their expressions appear solemn or serious to the extent that they seem consumed by feelings of morbidity, desolation, exhaustion, and lethargy. As an artist Wei Jia values intuition and regards art as a part of life. He thus reinterprets his personal life experiences by viewing memories of a child growing into adulthood through the prism of psychological analysis.

Starting with multi-colored lithographs in his college time, after 2004 he gradually turned to acrylic painting. The accurately drawn figures in Wei Jia's paintings all appear extremely flat, thus giving off a sense of isolation from real life. There is no spatial relationship between one figure and another, or between figures and their background. There is simply a structural relationship and it is that which can be identified as Wei Jia's unique artistic vocabulary. In his works, the figures are expressionless, and there is no narrative connection between the figures. The characters are not simply isolated from one another but also stand apart and seem detached from their environment and background.

If You Could Fly, Where Could You Go? (2006) is indicative of this characteristic isolation. Here Wei Jia simplifies the images of the figures in the painting while simultaneously endowing them with a sense of life, thereby describing a very human sense of solitude and loneliness. The relationships between the figures, as well as between the figures and their environment, are like an endless dream world, where life seems like a never-ending journey of loneliness. The artist places particular emphasis on the personal experience of facing an ever colder and more isolated world in which one may find that only one's internal experiences are real.

This sense of solitude is particularly depicted in works such as Wei Jia's recent series *David* (2007–8). In these paintings he expresses personal life circumstances, enveloping them in a melancholy lyricism. The figures exude a feeling of worry, loneliness, and bitterness that is the key to unveiling their true meaning and enable the viewer to feel the pain of life himself.

In terms of form, the heart of Wei Jia's works does not lie in the painstaking pursuit of a strict artistic process but rather in the subjective emancipation of his own inspiration and intuition, which he expresses both through emotional and manual freedom. The freedom of Wei Jia's paintings is reflected in their numerous traces of childlike imagery. This naïveté is not intended to produce a naïve form, as he is striving to paint more naturally and intuitively. The intention, in fact, is to expose the unconscious world within this naïve state. Wei Jia's empty, dreamlike vistas only serve to reinforce the sense of loneliness and create an almost somniloquent atmosphere. His works seem to regard life as a game, just as to a child everything in the adult world is a game. The depiction of children in his works – whether they be children holding different kinds of weapons or blood dripping from a gash on a child's head – is filled with violent symbols and allegories based on memories of childhood and adolescence. These spiritual symbols hint at things we find difficult to express in words.

Wei Jia's paintings are always a quiet attempt to release a variety of disturbing emotions from his inner world. Because his form implicates an individual reality, his works embody a spiritual experience that comes from his own memories.

By Huang Du

1

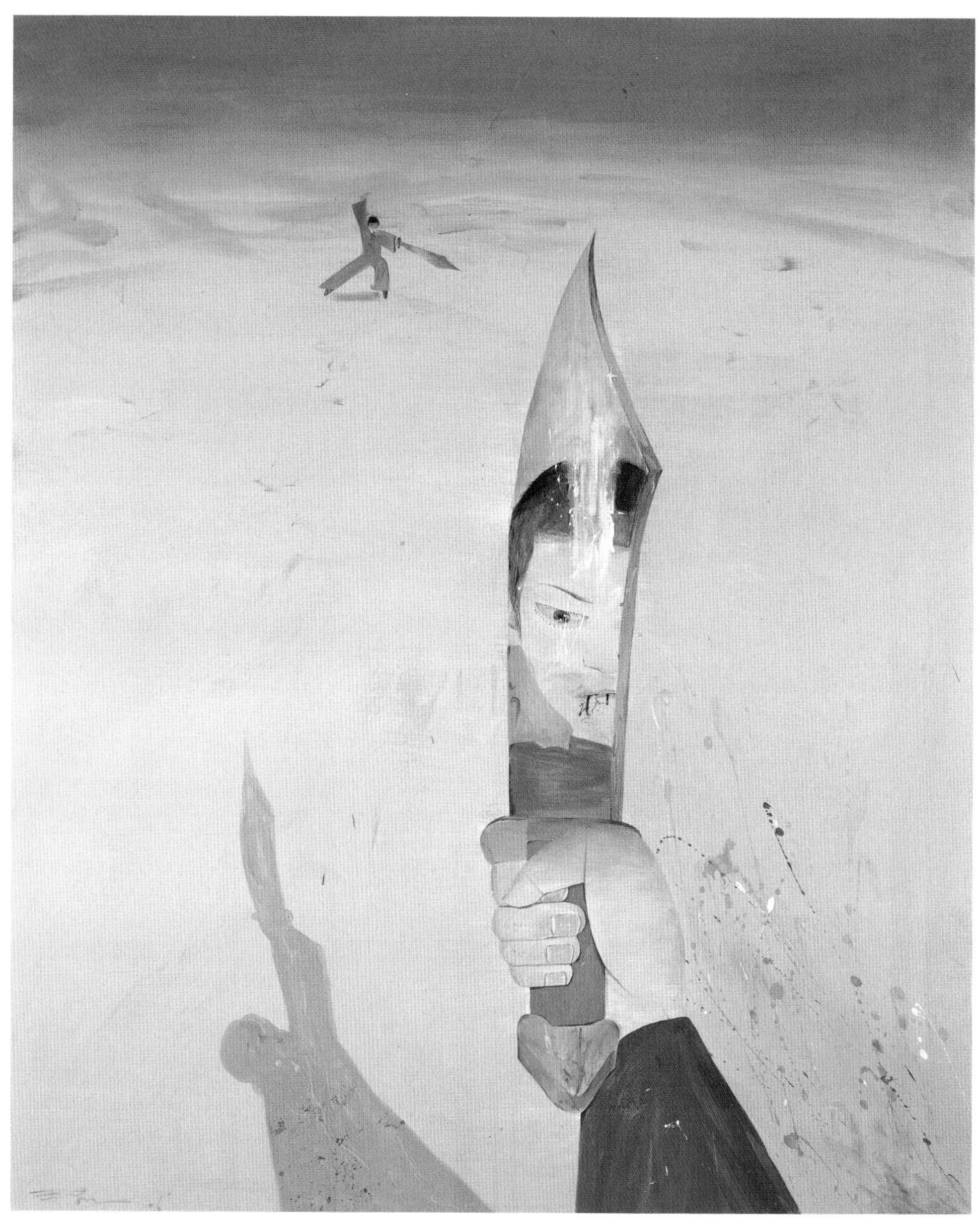

1 THE HEAT OF BATTLE • 2006 • ACRYLIC ON CANVAS • 120 x 100 CM

2 IF YOU COULD FLY, WHERE COULD YOU GO? • 2006 • ACRYLIC ON CANVAS • 250 x 170 CM

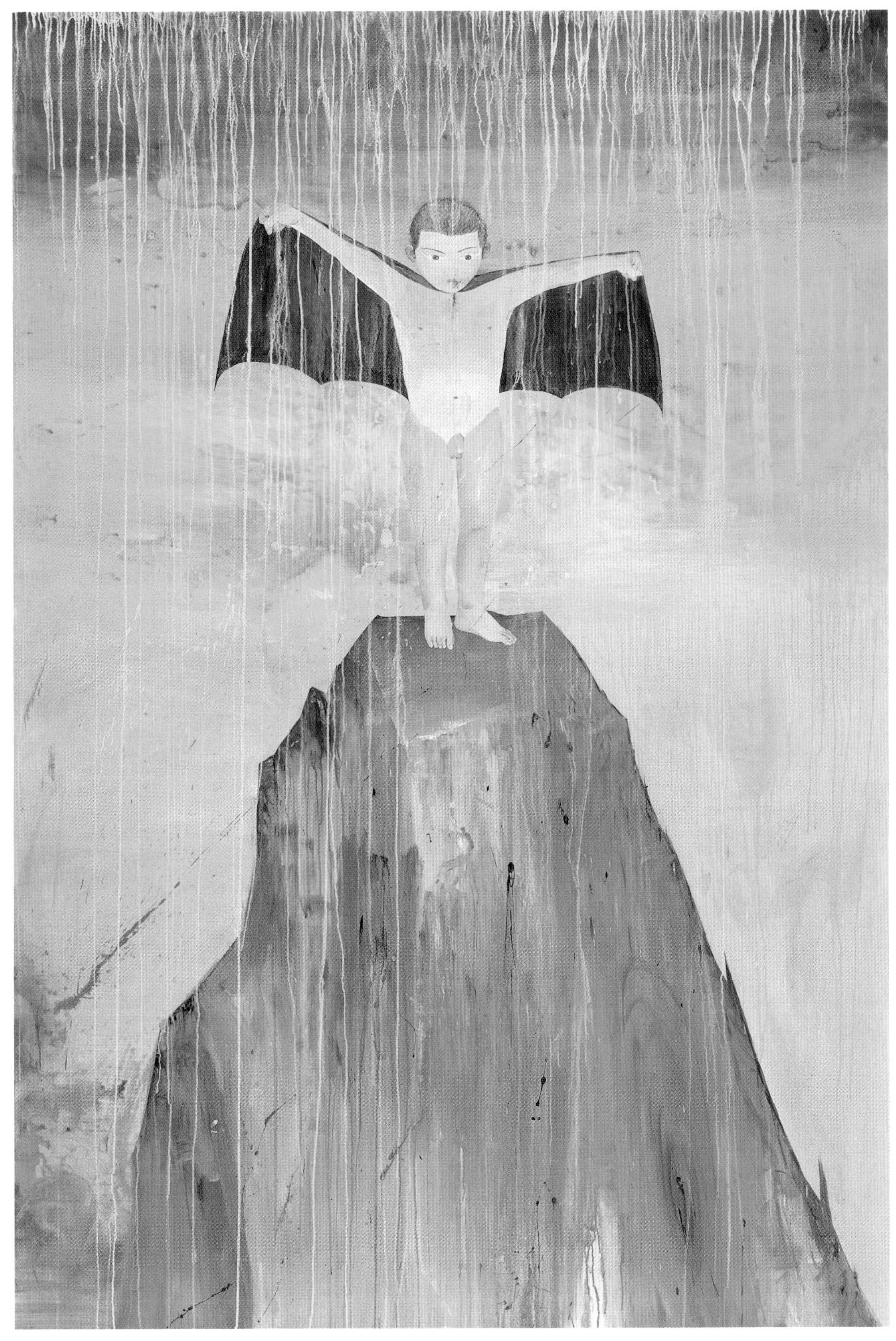

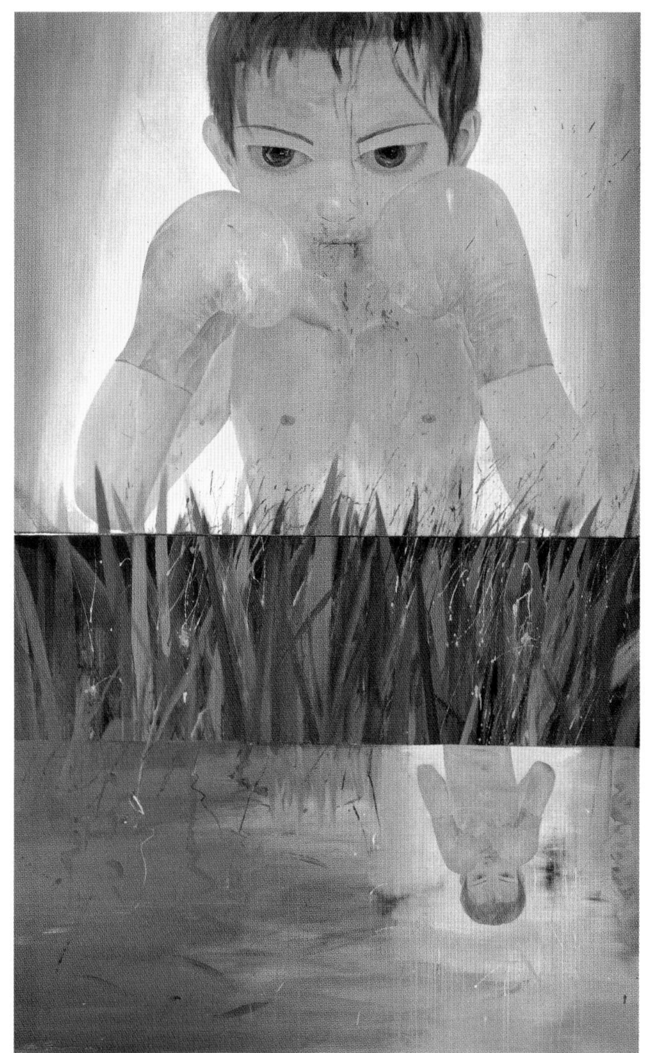

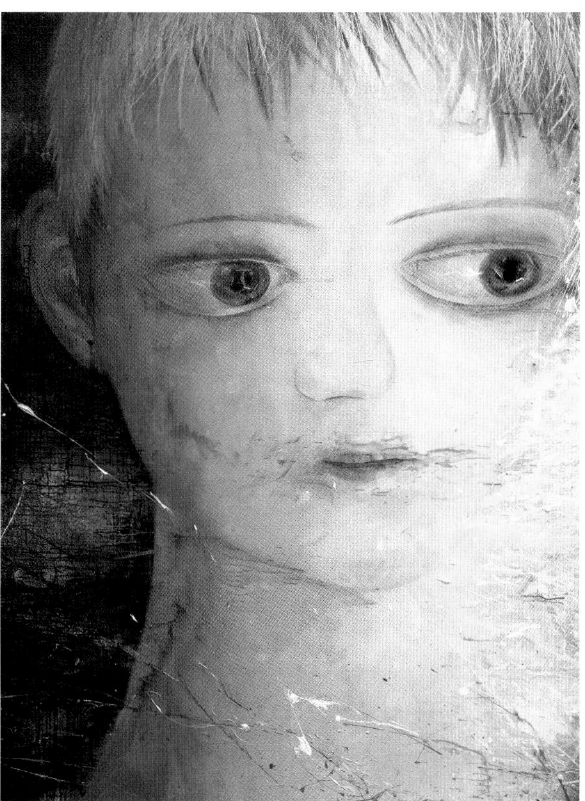

3 I'M STILL YOUNG, IT IS OKAY TO FAIL • 2007 • ACRYLIC ON CANVAS (DIPTYCH) • 240 x 150 CM

4 DAVID NO. 3 • 2007 • ACRYLIC ON CANVAS • 300 x 150 CM

5 FLOWER AND TREE BOY NO. 1 • 2006 • ACRYLIC ON CANVAS • 200 x 150 CM

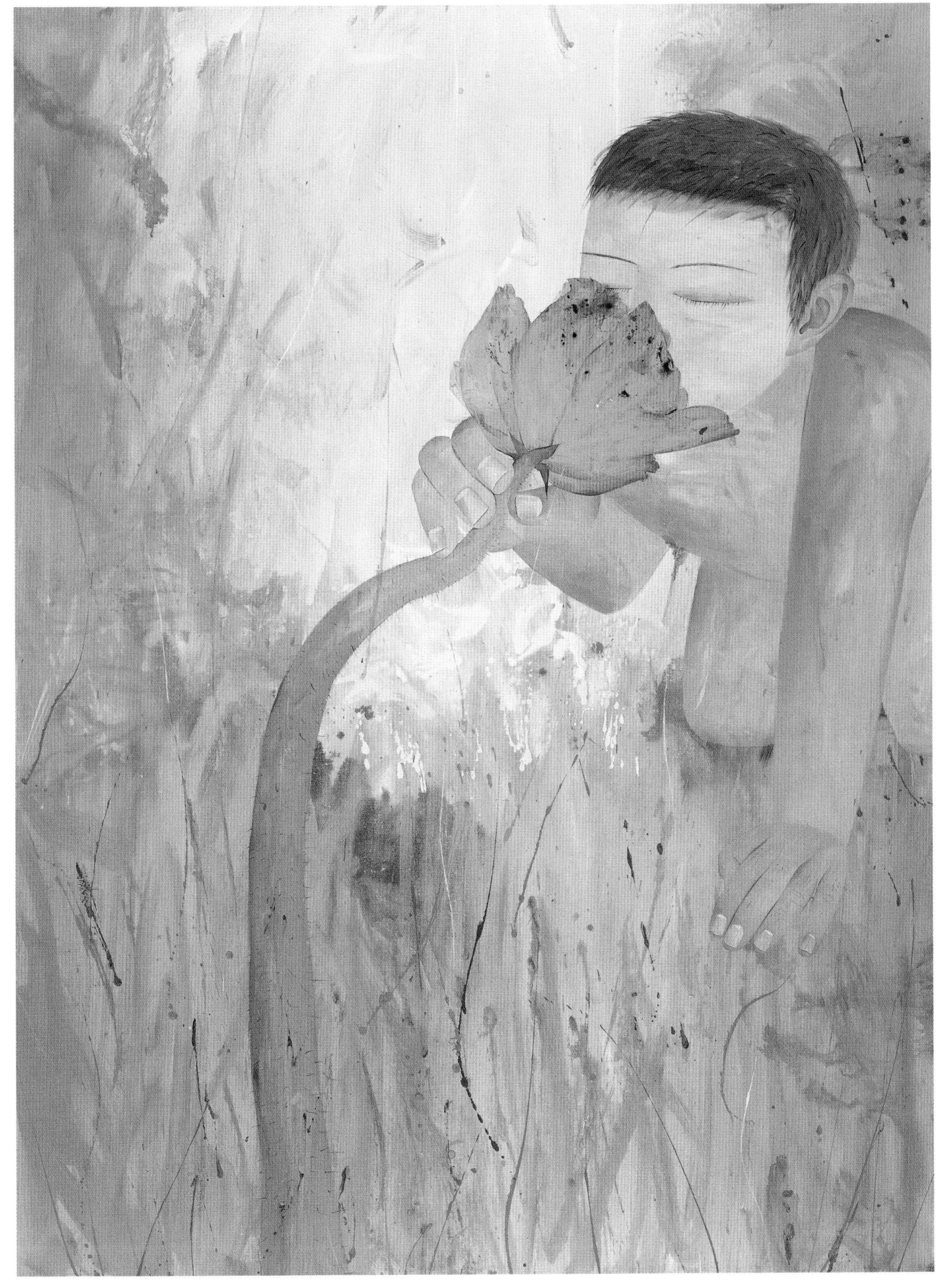

PHONE INTERVIEW WITH EDITORS

5/13/08 • MORNING

EDITORS *When you were a little boy, what was your favorite toy?*

WEI JIA It was a little car and I played with it a lot.

EDITORS *And do you still remember what sentence your parents said to you most often?*

WEI JIA What they told me when I was a kid I have forgotten, as it was such a long time ago. But nowadays they tell me not to burn myself out, and to take good care of my health.

EDITORS *Related to that is my next question: how do you try to stay healthy in your everyday life?*

WEI JIA You know, after one turns thirty it gets more important to take care of health issues. When you are young, you don't eat and sleep regularly, and it's no problem as you recover very quickly. But to do these things now, which were so easy a couple of years ago, is now more harmful. So I try paying attention to that.

EDITORS *What have you been wishing for most recently?*

WEI JIA Right now I am preparing a solo exhibition in Taiwan and I hope that it will be successful, as I am very excited about it. That's my most recent wish, I guess.

EDITORS *Would you say that you believe in true love?*

WEI JIA Yes, I definitely believe in true love. Love for me means that all other surrounding things in life are not important, and love is the only thing you care for.

EDITORS *Now you are living in Chongqing. Would you say that you have found your ideal living environment, or if not what would it look like?*

WEI JIA I prefer a relaxed and quiet environment, where I have the freedom to choose a suitable job and lifestyle. In Chongqing this idea can be more or less fulfilled. Just sometimes it is not as quiet as I wish it would be.

EDITORS *From which type of media do you derive most of your inspiration?*

WEI JIA Most of the time, before I start to paint, I have a very clear image how the work will look like and my works are mainly created out of my own ideas. But of course it also happens that different media have an impact on my works.

EDITORS *Since quite some years you are working as an artist. What do you like/dislike about it?*

WEI JIA As an artist I like the honesty of my job. What I don't like are the constrictions and hypocrisy you are sometimes confronted with.

EDITORS *What would you say, how do you communicate with the audience in your art?*

WEI JIA I mainly communicate directly via my works. Other ways of communication are not so important for me. I guess an artist should not primarily transfer his own ideas to the world, but should try to encourage his audience to develop their own ideas about the works and find parallels matching their own life.

EDITORS *You are also part of the Post-'75 generation. If you had five words to describe your generation, what would they be?*

WEI JIA Dream, freedom, fate, and confusion. Let me explain why I mention fate. We search for something that can help us to escape from our fate and have control of our own lives. But often when something unexpected happens, we realize that we have to accept our fate.

EDITORS *And what do you mean by confusion?*

WEI JIA The generation of our parents got educated about idealism and they were taught to be dutiful. But my generation experienced a kind of social shock due to missing and not matching values, and sometimes we don't know what our common dream is.

EDITORS *If the whole world would listen to you for fifteen seconds, what would you say?*

WEI JIA If I only had fifteen seconds, I wouldn't even start to speak at all. I guess fifteen seconds are meaningless. It is too short, as the audience wouldn't really understand my meaning or remember my words.

6
7
8

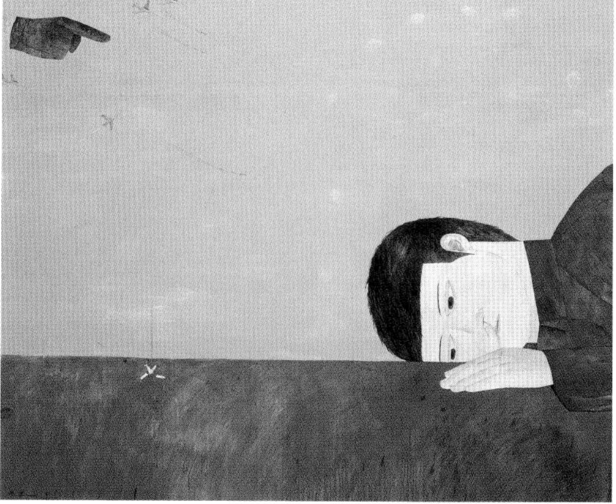

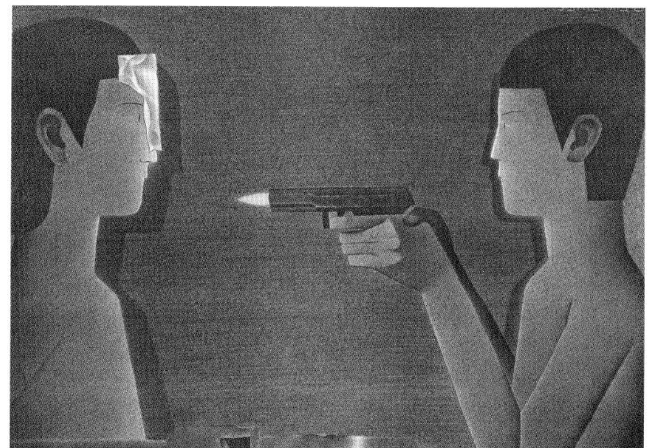

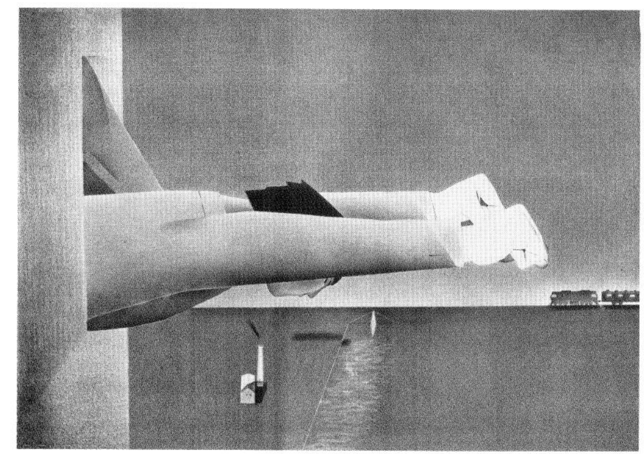

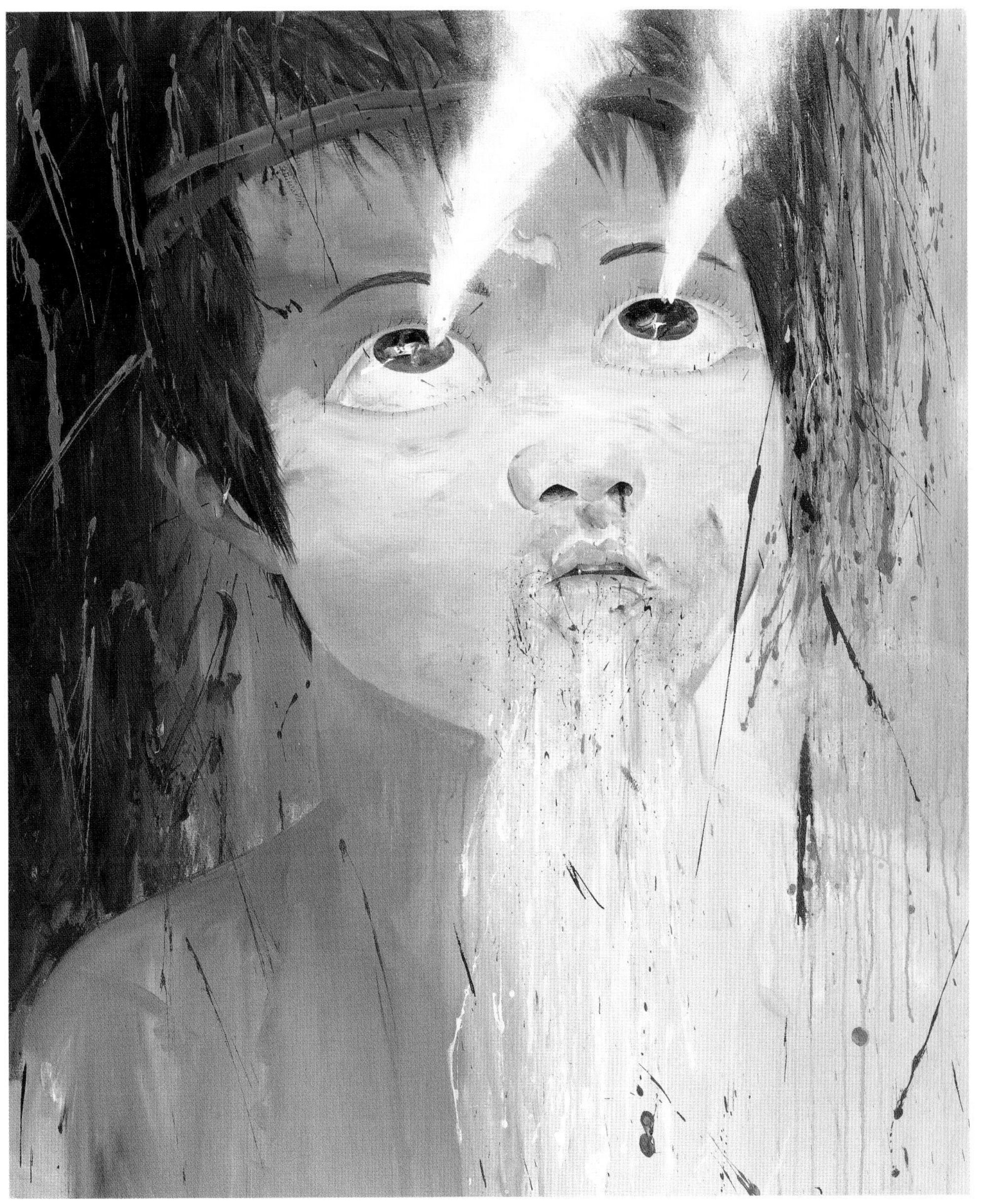

6 COLLAPSING ON THE ROAD TO ADVANCEMENT • 2005 • ACRYLIC ON CANVAS • 160 x 200 CM

7 DON'T MOVE • 2003 • LITHOGRAPHY • 53 x 70 CM

8 SUPERMAN • 2002 • LITHOGRAPHY • 50 x 73 CM

9 PAINFUL PLEASURES NO. 3 • 2006 • ACRYLIC ON CANVAS • 120 x 100 CM

10 DOOR • 2008 • ACRYLIC ON CANVAS • 180 x 250 CM

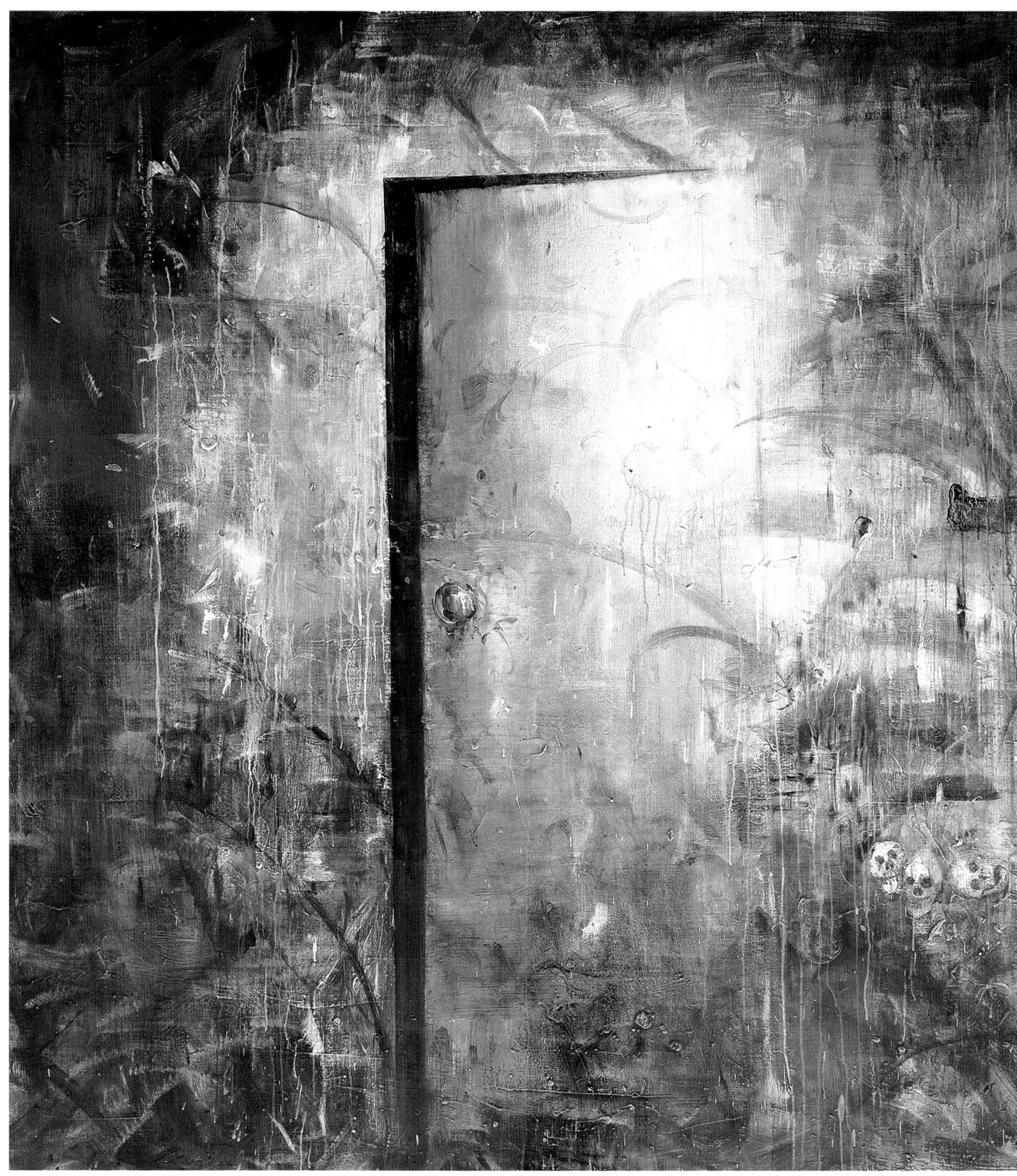

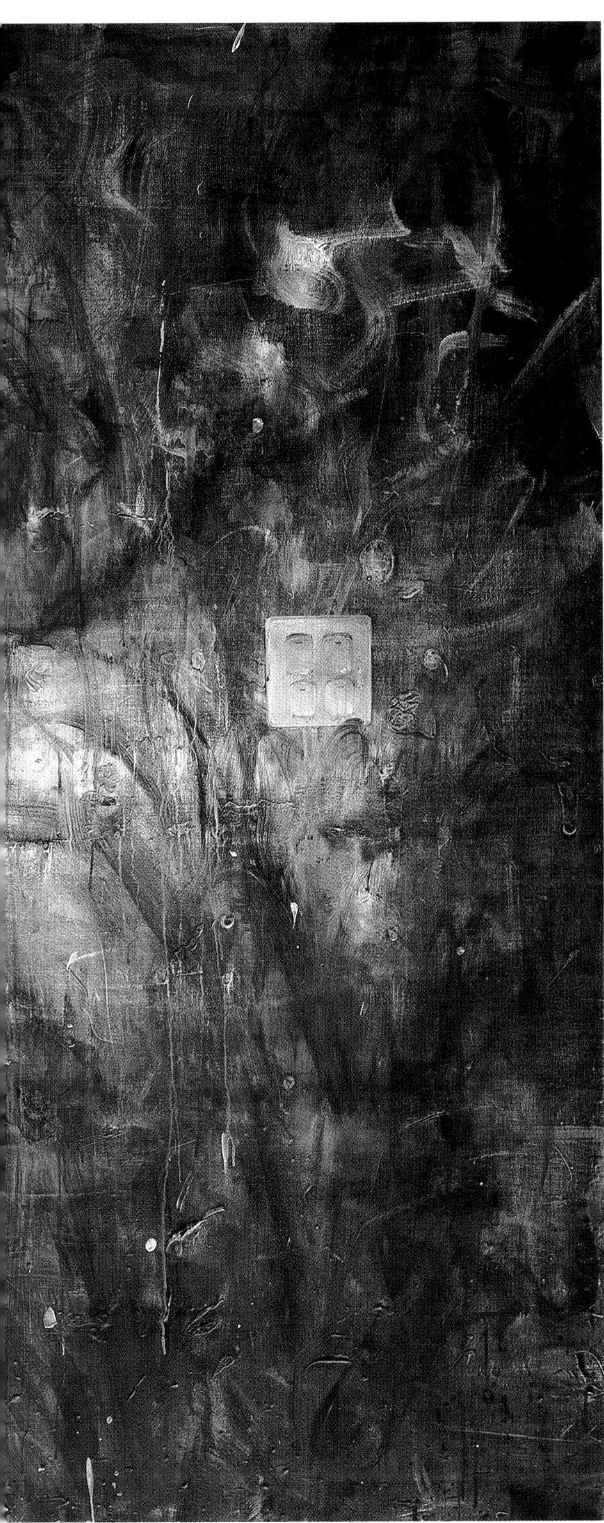

EXHIBITIONS

SELECTED SOLO EXHIBITIONS

2008
Wei Jia's Works from 2004-2008,
Star Gallery,
Beijing, China

2007
If You Could Fly, Where Could You Go?,
Aura Gallery,
Shanghai, China

SELECTED GROUP EXHIBITIONS

2009
Chinamania,
ARKEN Museum of Modern Art,
Copenhagen, Denmark

2007
The First Today's Documents:
Energy–Spirit, Body, Material,
Today Art Museum,
Beijing, China

2007
Sport in Art by adidas,
Shanghai Contemporary Art Museum,
Shanghai, China

2007
Starting from the Southwest,
Guangdong Art Museum,
Guangzhou, China

2006
Playful Images,
Shenzhen Art Museum,
Shenzhen, China

2005
Next Station, Cartoon?,
He Xiangning Art Museum,
Shenzhen, China

2005
The Self-Made Generation:
A Retrospective of New Chinese Painting,
Zendai Museum of Modern Art,
Shanghai, China

2004
Ideal of A New Generation:
The Chinese New Generation,
He Xiangning Art Museum,
Shenzhen, China

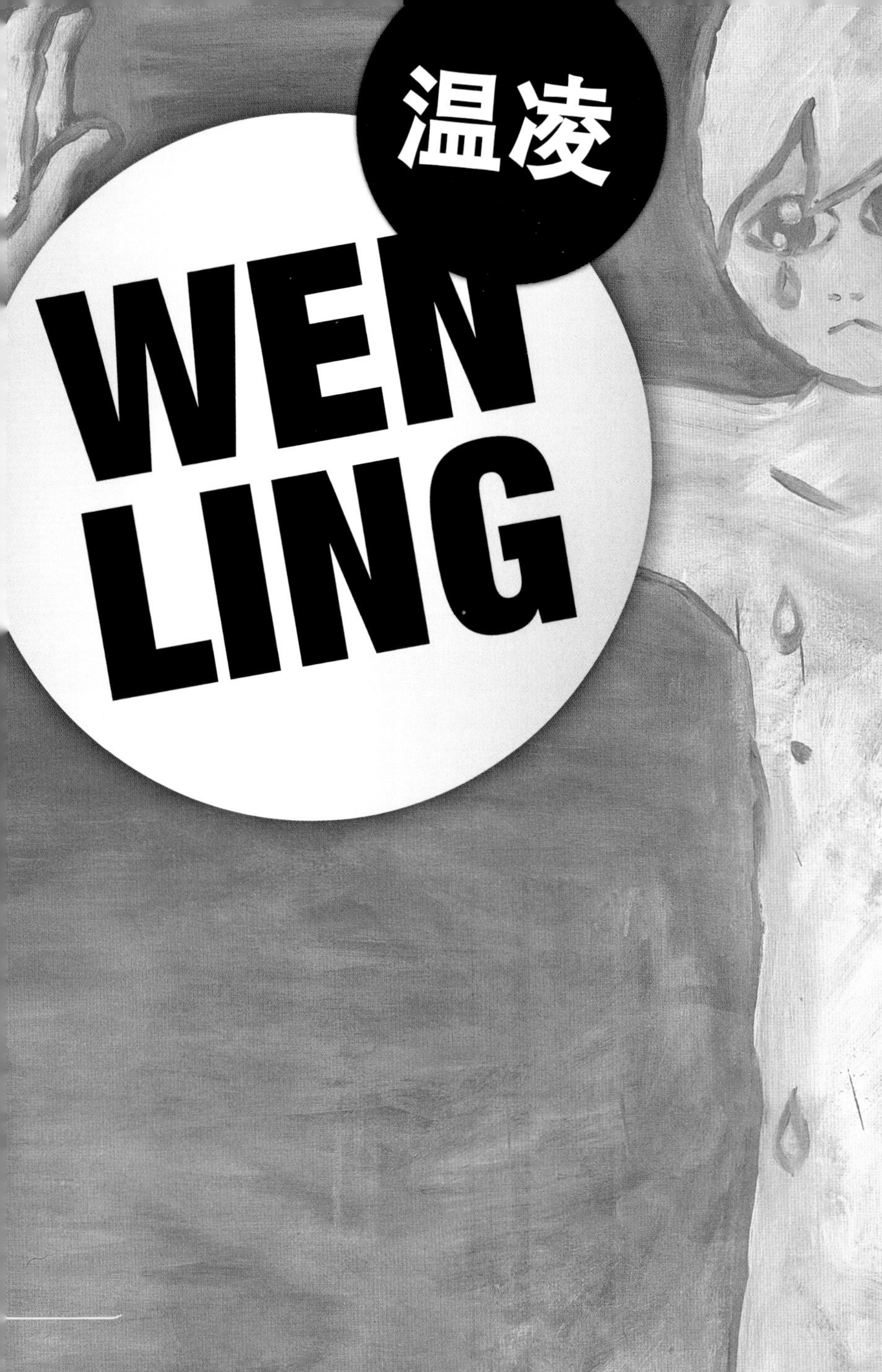
温凌
WEN
LING

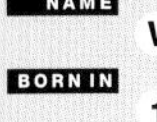

NAME
WEN LING

BORN IN
1976, HARBIN

LIVES IN
BEIJING

STUDY
CENTRAL ACADEMY OF FINE ARTS, BEIJING

MEDIA
ANIMATION, PAINTING, PHOTOGRAPHY

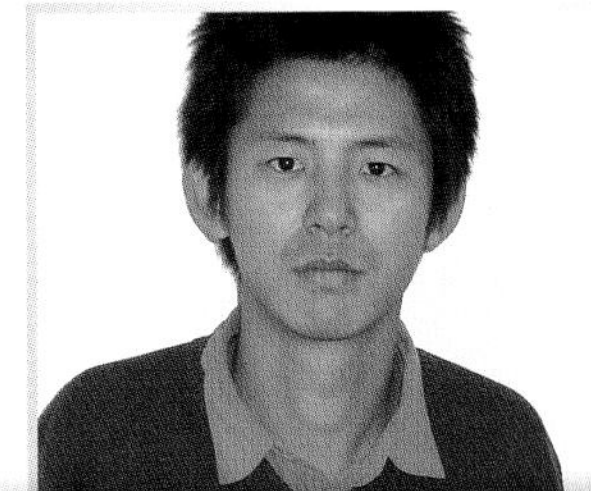

MINI ME

Wen Ling's work, like that of a number of his contemporaries, makes use of the most diverse media. In the beginning of his artistic career he made a name for himself as a photographer of everyday Chinese scenes. His international fame was jump-started later by creating China's first ever photo blog. While photography is the medium that has launched his career as an artist, Wen Ling equally works with comics-like video animation and oil painting.

Barely touching on his personal life, Wen Ling's photographic work mostly observes life in the big city from various angles. Following the basic principles of his photo blog – to make daily urban life accessible to the broader public, especially outside of China – he captures snap-shots of society, public events, or close friends and family. *2005.10.1* (2005), for example, is made up of snap-shots from the Beijing Midi music festival, thus documenting the boundless enthusiasm of the concertgoers and giving us a glimpse into China's youth culture. In turn, *2006.2.6* (2006) depicts the changing of the guard on Beijing's Tiananmen Square. Although the approach seems to suggest intimacy, Wen Ling's photographs maintain objective distance, hardly allowing a deeper look into the artist's intimate world of thought.

When it comes to his animation and painting, however, Wen Ling presents a completely different line of argument and intent. Their most recognizable characteristic is a very child-like visual language which, coupled with biographical themes, constitutes his artistic strategy. In the history of art, artworks have repeatedly adopted child-like designs, using this unbiased view, as it were, to break through to the original understanding of a thing, reflecting upon it anew. For Wen Ling, too, such a partial return to childhood becomes an act of release, opening the way to unrestrained imagination and free association. This approach helps him to recall past emotions, and then express them with a completely different intensity and vulnerability. The central theme of his work is sexuality and the body, and it is his goal "to portray confusion and fantasy around sexuality."

Nowadays, the morals of communist China, which forbade every form of sexualized physical contact, are clearly beginning to crumble and new sexual role models are starting to establish themselves. Growing up with the fundamentally conservative attitude of his parents' house, Wen Ling hardly had any chance of discussing such topics. Even outside of the family environment, as among friends, very little opportunity presented itself for open discussion of taboo topics like love and sexuality.

Wen Ling's work *Two Girls and Six Boys* (2006) depicts a band of little boys having tears in their eyes and clinging to the very feminine figures. They embody both motherly and sexually compelling qualities and protectively cover the boys' heads with their hands. The artist's inner restlessness is clearly expressed in the motifs themselves but also in the impulsive and two-dimensional application of background colors, switching from strong blue shades to expansive, even pastel nuances. Together with the brown-outlined, loosely sketched figures, this elusive background brings into focus the materialization of inner images and visions. This kind of composition provides the characters access to plenty of space – often they stretch beyond the image, seemingly reaching out of the canvas.

Don't Look At Me! (2005) works with the same compositional strategy. In the center, a child – smothered by family and societal expectations – desperately extends his arms in an effort to remove himself from parental authority and to preserve the last bit of free space left to him. In Chinese culture and society, not least because of the "one child policy," children are exposed to the focused attention of parents and extended family. This is the source of abundant tension and latent conflict that provides the theme of this work. The child ends up torn as it longs for contact, but when it reaches out only finds itself faced with social and family expectations. In his 2002–3 animation *54boy*, Wen Ling proposes an escape from this oppressive authority. After being humiliated by his teacher and a stranger in public, the main character transforms himself into *54boy*. As a kind of caped superhero he takes off through the air into an ideal world. There, far away from school and family, he and his beloved pass the hours together indulging in his idea of a perfect day.

Wen Ling employs a variety of media and never settles on a single technique in his work. The artist himself feels that it is necessary for him to fuse these different modes in order to adequately express his various feelings and experiences. Only the combination of his starkly biographical painting and animation on the one hand, and his socio-analytical photography on the other, allows Wen Ling to conceptualize his complex images and present them to the viewer.

By Cordelia Noe

1

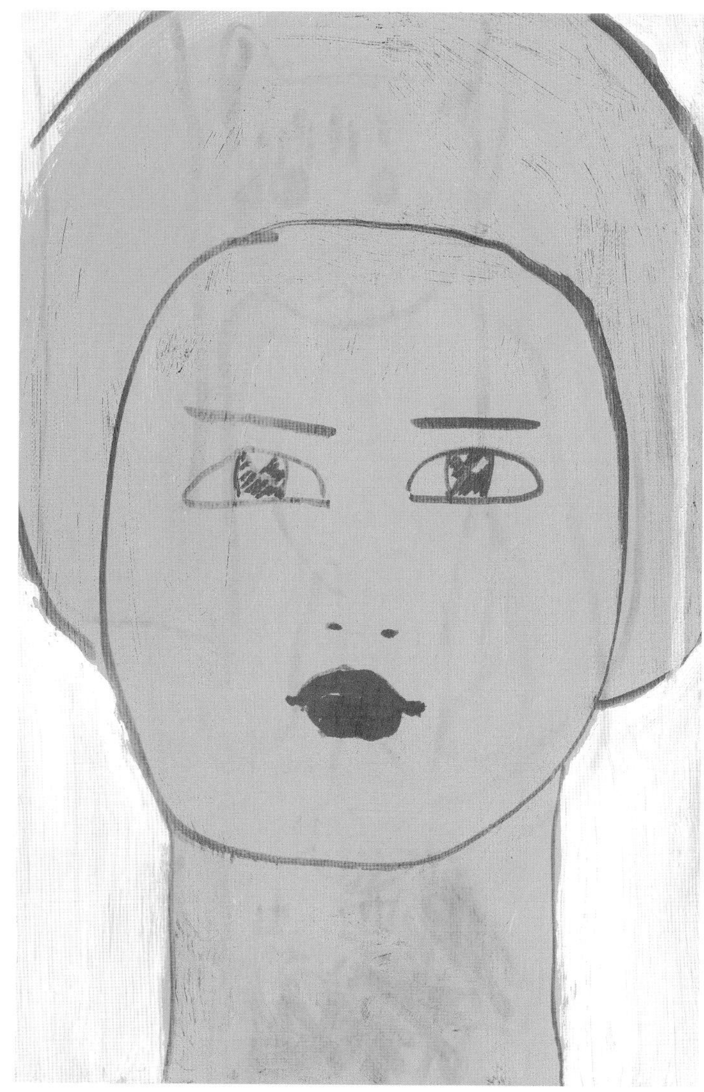

1 LVXIAO 2008 NO. 36 • 2008 • ACRYLIC AND MARKER ON CANVAS • 35 x 23 CM

2 LVXIAO 2008 NO. 46 • 2008 • ACRYLIC AND MARKER ON CANVAS • 38 x 25 CM

2

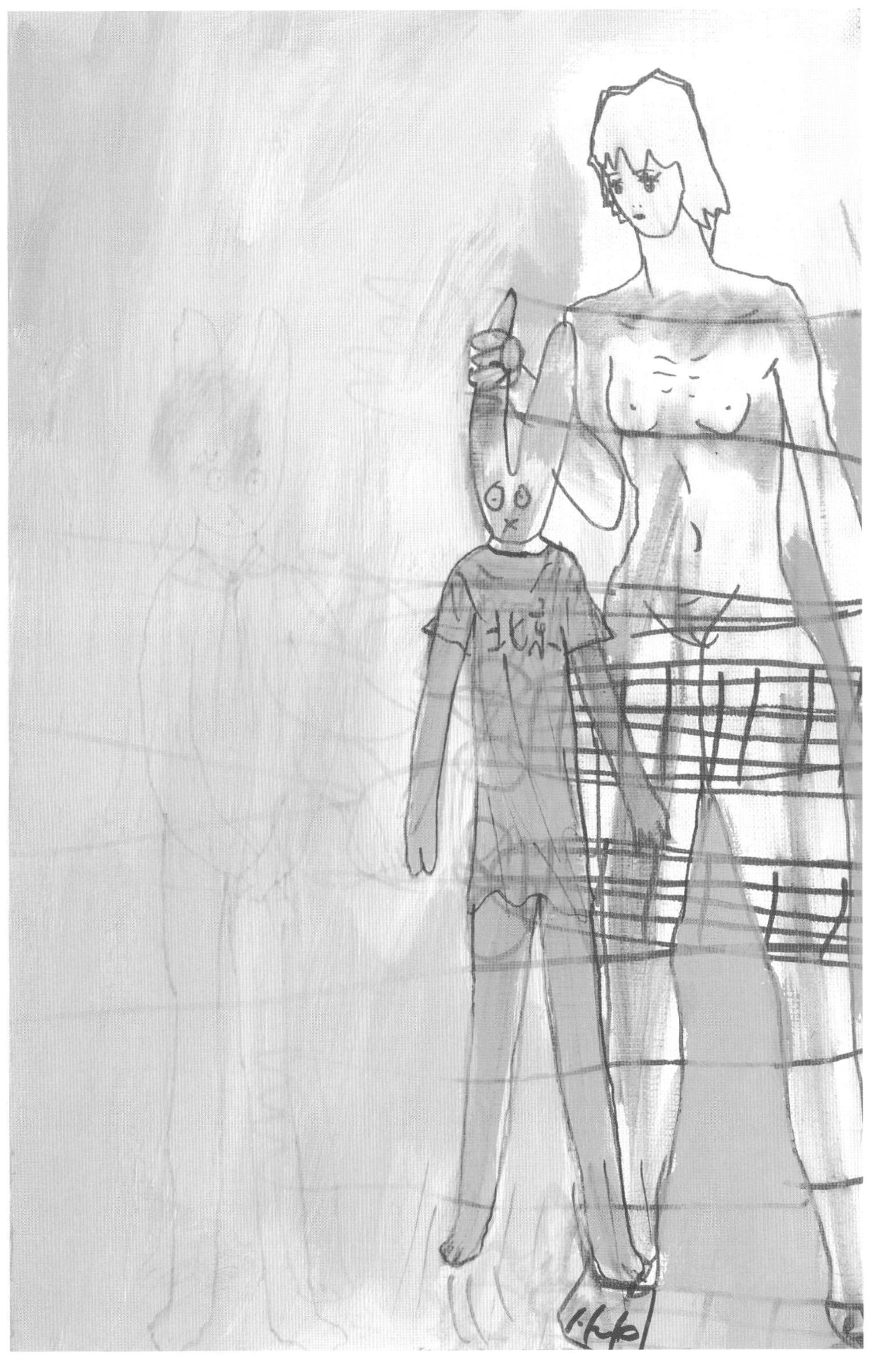

3

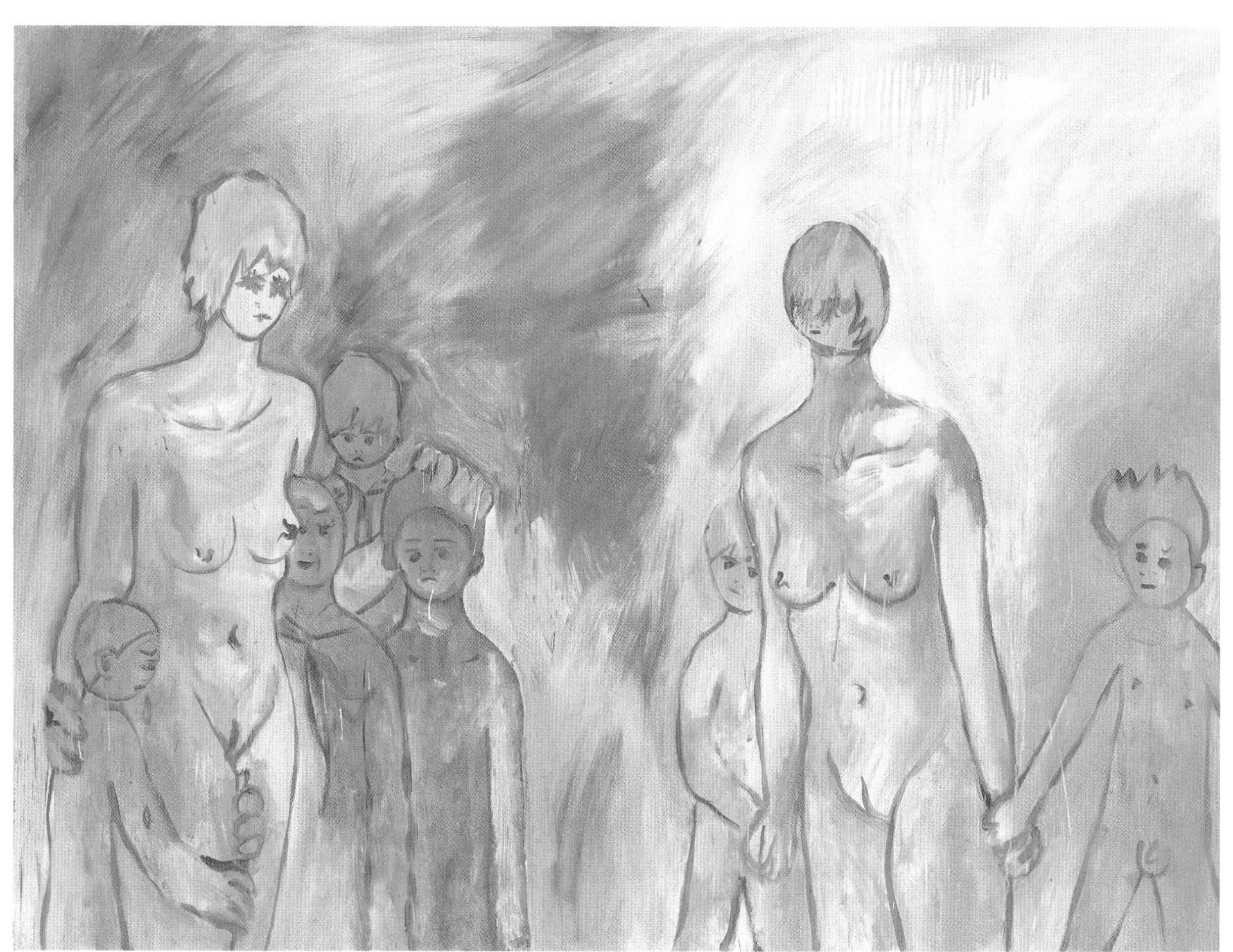

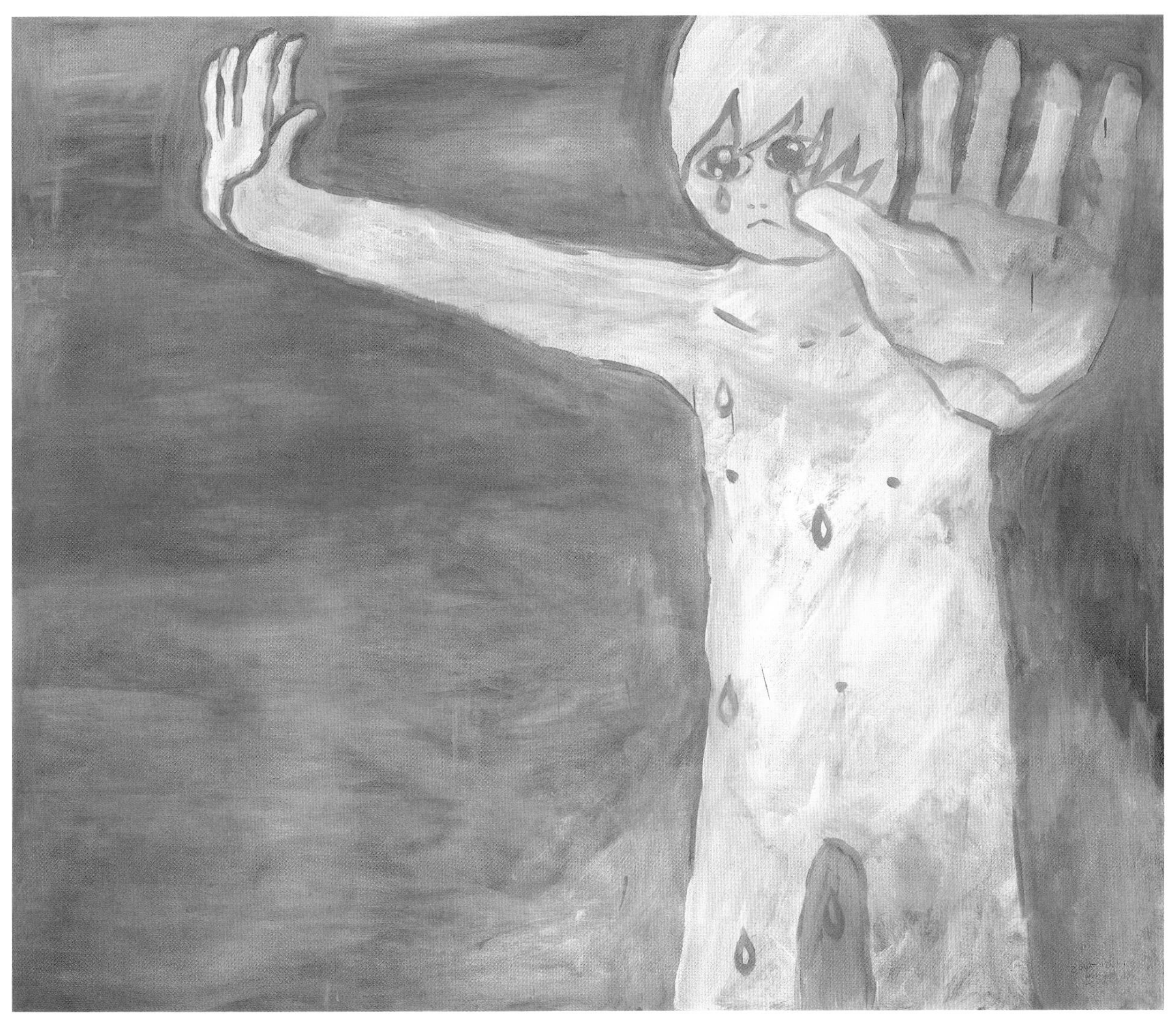

3 TWO GIRLS AND SIX BOYS • 2006 • OIL ON CANVAS • 140 x 180 CM

4 DON'T LOOK AT ME • 2005 • OIL ON CANVAS • 150 x 180 CM

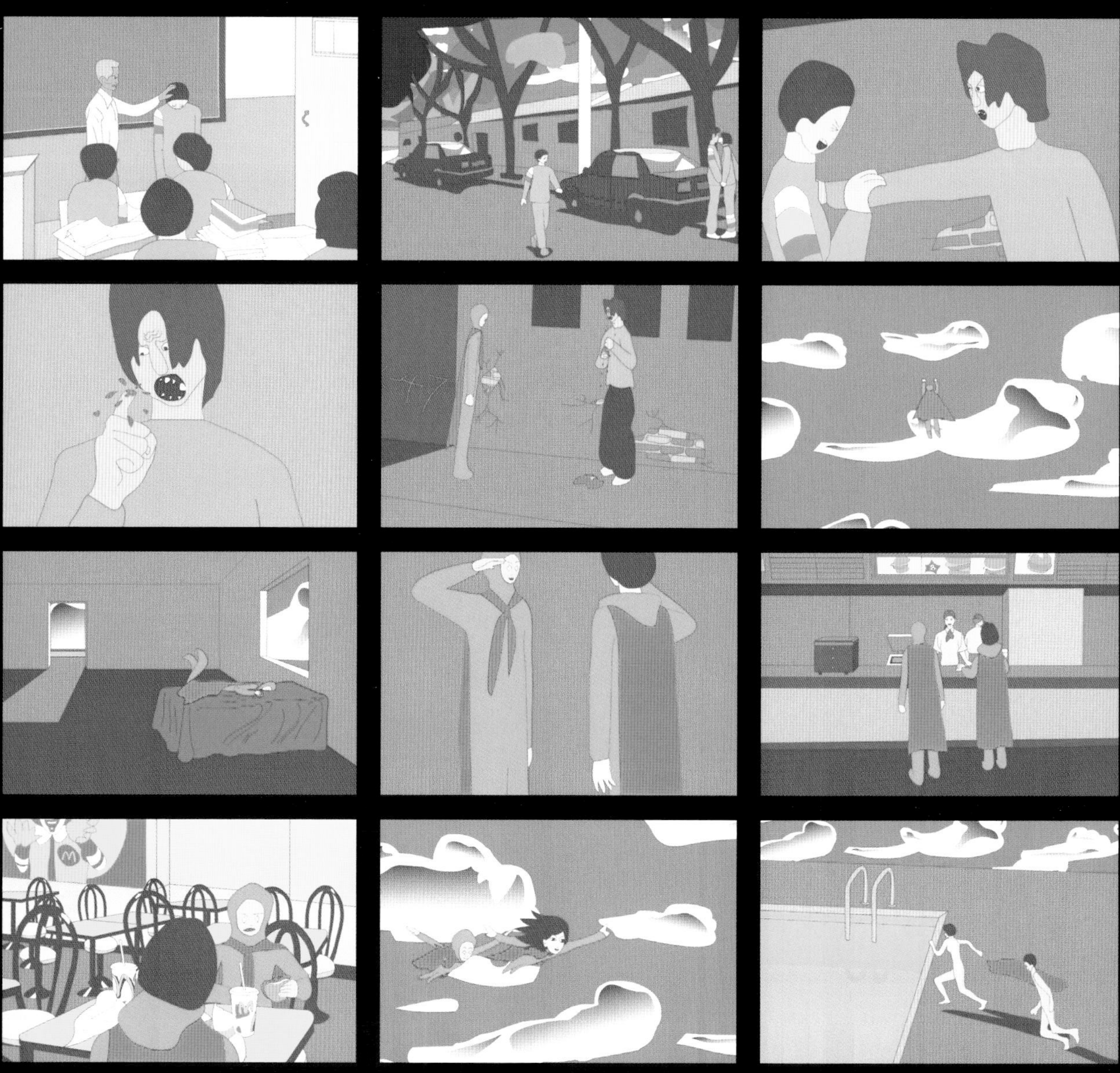

5 54BOY • 2002–3 • ANIMATION • 2'20"

6 2005.10.1 • 2005 • PHOTOGRAPHY • BLOG

7 2006.2.6 • 2006 • PHOTOGRAPHY • BLOG

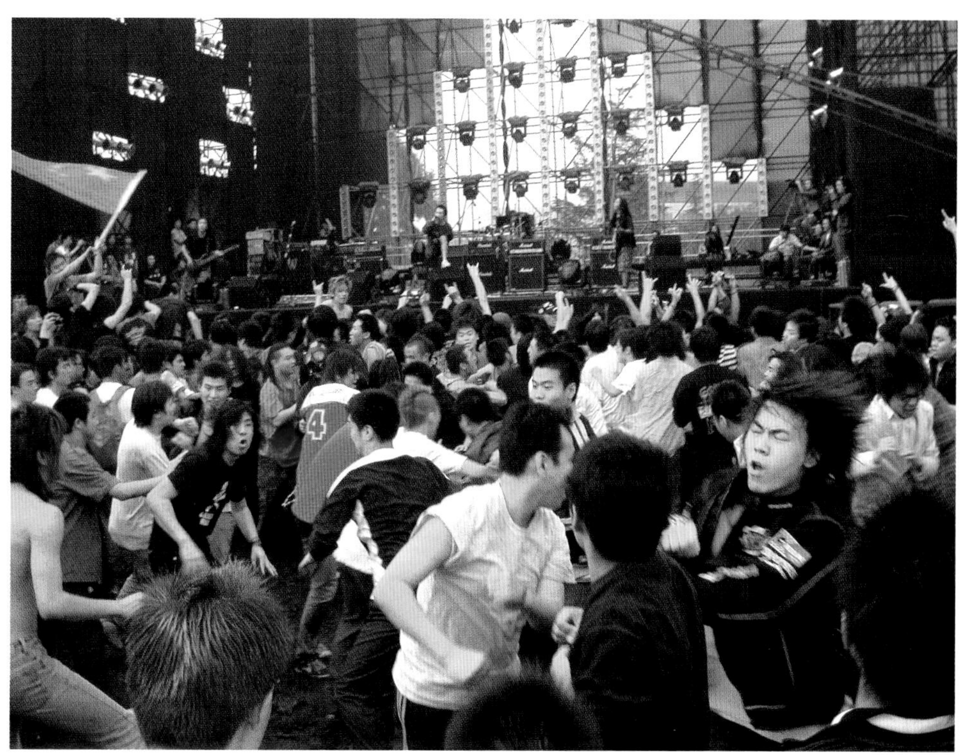

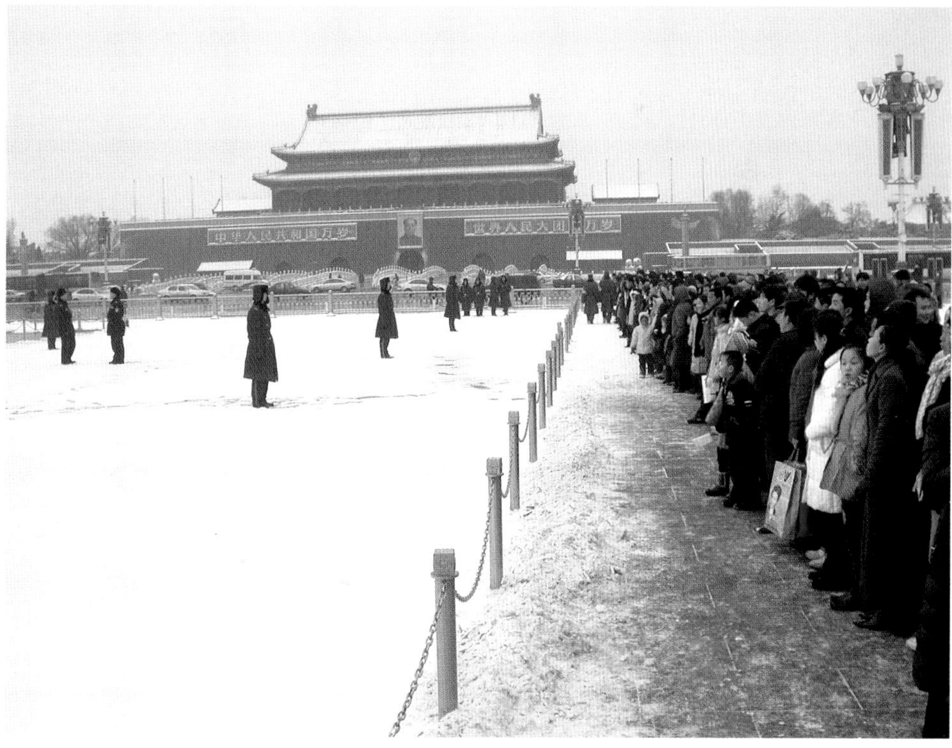
中华人民共和国万岁
世界人民大团结万岁

8 9
10

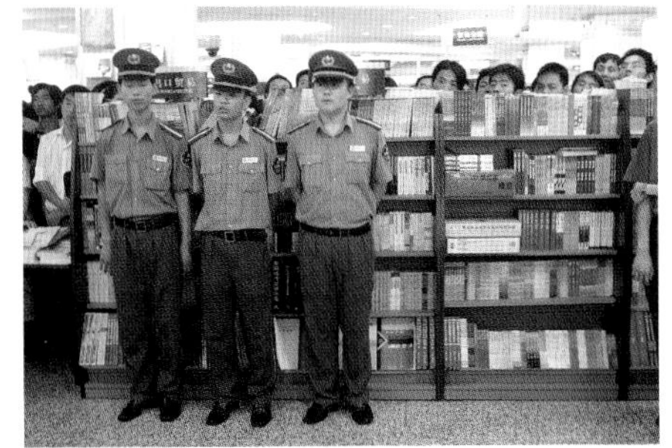

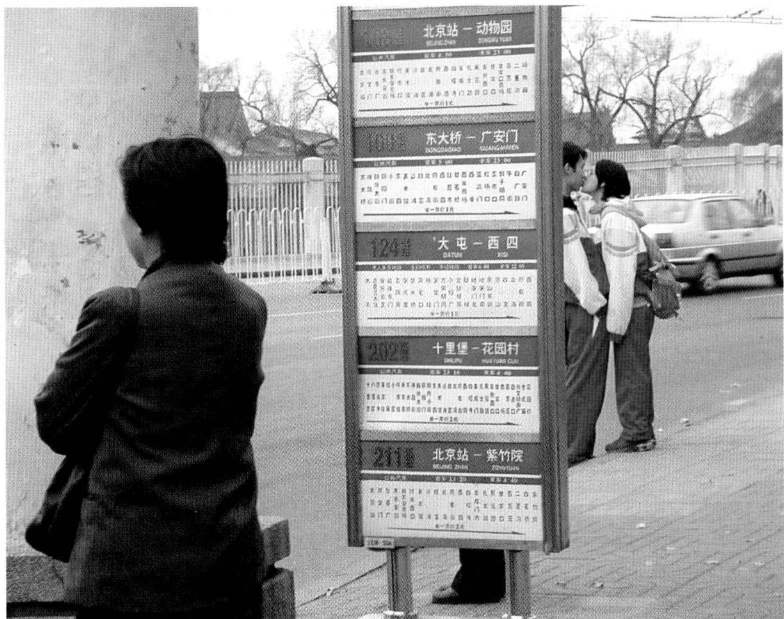

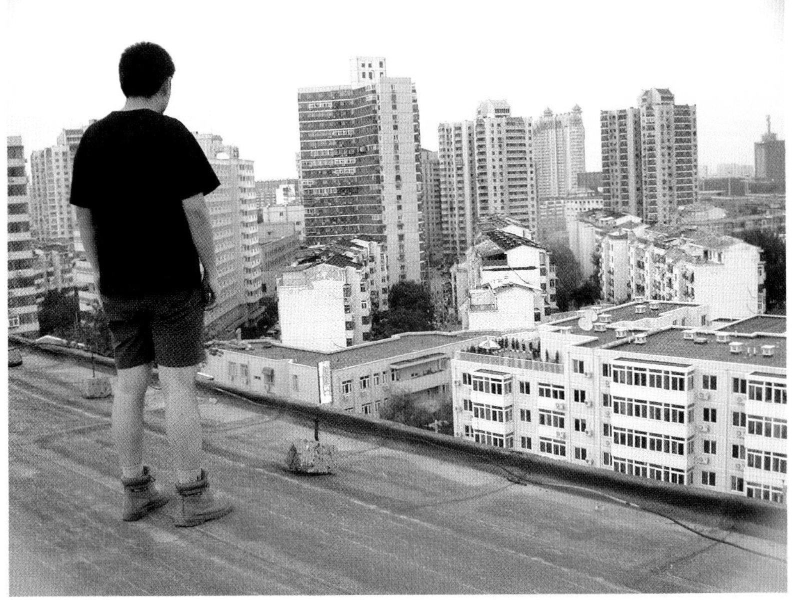

ONLINE CHAT WITH EDITORS

4/29/08 & 4/28/08 • MORNING (BEIJING) & EVENING (EAST COAST U.S.)

[09:15:11] Okay, let's kick off with our opening question ... your favorite childhood toy?

[09:17:45] I think what I liked best were guns. Toy guns.

[09:18:01] Water guns?

[09:18:59] No, without water. "Normal" toy guns.

[09:20:44] What sentence did your parents repeat most often when speaking to you?

[09:22:17] They would remind me not to be sleepy all day!

[09:24:04] Which type of media gives you most inspiration?

[09:24:56] Definitely the Internet!

[09:26:34] And what in particular? Blogs?

[09:28:00] For example imomus.livejournal.com or jeansnow.net

[09:28:57] Do you take care of your health; and if so, how?

[09:31:13] I eat more vegetables and less meat. I also try to get more relaxation and not to work too much. In the summer, I sunbathe and swim from time to time.

[09:32:27] Name us a recent wish of yours?

[09:32:58] A car.

[09:34:31] Do you believe in true love?

[09:36:13] Hard to say.

[09:36:39] Why?

[09:37:56] To answer I would need to disclose the secret of the universe.

[09:39:22] What does your ideal living environment look like?

[09:42:40] To live in an unpolluted environment, in a house where I could feel safe and maybe also have a nice view.

[09:44:51] What do you enjoy about being an artist?

[09:48:32] I like being able to turn my passion into my profession. That's a great feeling.

[09:49:17] And is there anything you dislike?

[09:50:08] Not really.

[09:52:01] How do you communicate with your audience?

[09:55:23] Through the Internet and especially through my photography blog. Millions of people have already visited my site. Some of them leave messages. About thirty thousand "netizens" surf my blog each day.

[09:57:22] What five words describe your generation?

[09:59:20] Internet, reform, and opening. Also, not having to worry about food and clothing, rebellion, and little respect for their elders.

[10:00:44] Last question. If the whole world could listen to you for fifteen seconds, what would you say?

[10:02:30] I would read them paragraphs out of the *Diamond Sutra*.

8 **2003.8.23 • 2003 • PHOTOGRAPHY • BLOG**

9 **2003.4.1 • 2003 • PHOTOGRAPHY • BLOG**

10 **2003.7.9 • 2003 • PHOTOGRAPHY • BLOG**

EXHIBITIONS

SELECTED SOLO EXHIBITIONS

2009
Wen Ling
Beijing Art Now Gallery,
Beijing, China

2006
Here: "Photoblogger"
Ziboy's Self Expression,
Dimensions Art Center,
Beijing, China

SELECTED GROUP EXHIBITIONS

2008
Looking for me,
Minsheng Center for Contemporary Art,
Shanghai, China

2008
FotoGrafia: Rome's International Festival,
Rome, Italy

2007
Inspiration Indecently Exposed,
MIM Studio,
Sittard, The Netherlands

2007
Infantization,
Shanghai Art Museum,
Shanghai, China

2007
Mini Me,
Prima Kunst, Stadtgalerie Kiel,
Kiel, Germany

2006
N12 – No.4,
C5 Art Gallery,
Beijing, China

2005
Naughty Kids,
3818 Gallery,
Beijing, China

2005
Les Nuits Magiques,
Bordeaux, France

吴俊勇

WU JUNYONG

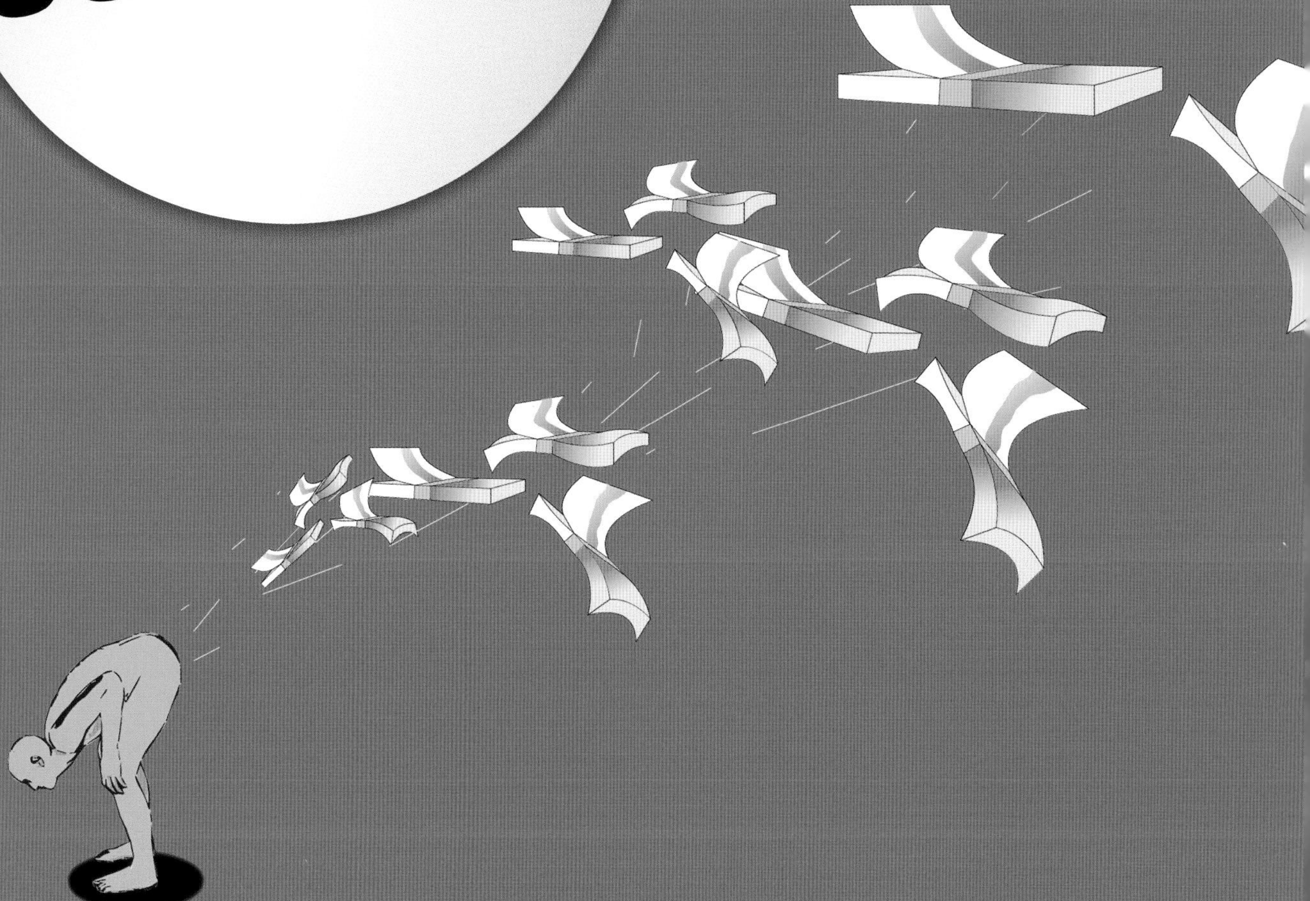

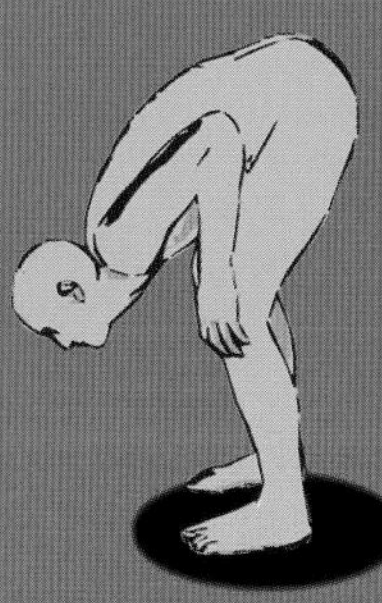

NAME
WU JUNYONG

BORN IN
1978, FUJIAN PROVINCE

LIVES IN
HANGZHOU

STUDY
CHINA ACADEMY OF ART, HANGZHOU

MEDIA
ANIMATION, PAINTING

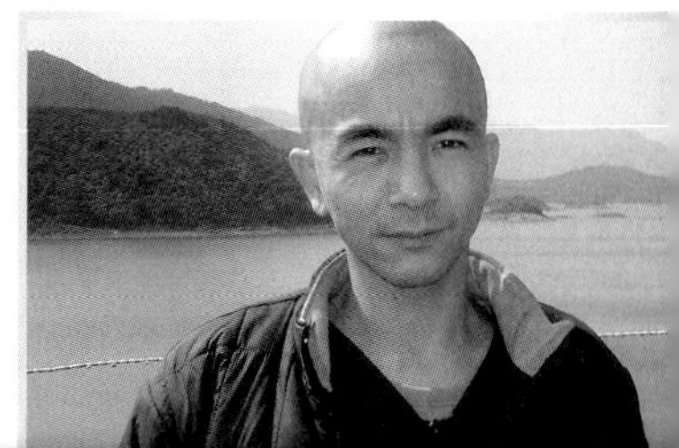

FROM OBSERVATION TO ANIMATION

Wu Junyong can be considered as one of the most famous Flash Art practitioners in China. His work is inclined towards self-entertainment and sees New Media art as a tool to liberate artistic concepts. It is this idea that he uses in his creation as it allows the boundaries of art to be extended into new domains. For Wu Junyong, New Media provides the ability to quickly put into practice a person's many different ideas. His artistic principles are very individualistic as he almost never predicts the outcome of his work and tends to work in a very random way, sometimes thinking about what he wants to do as he is doing it, and sometimes simply doing it while thinking about it.

To date, *Wait Us Rich* realized in 2005 is Wu Junyong's most important work. The work has its roots in the Internet culture. Surfing on the web he encountered the song "The Day That I'm Rolling With Money" by Zhou Xixi. The song moved and affected him because it echoed his own taste and thus inspired him to create this work. *Wait Us Rich* – made in Flash MV – uses a large red background and Zhou Xixi's powerful rock song to attack the viewer's visual and aural senses. A naked man with a flashing dollar sign on his head is sitting in the middle of the screen. With the rise and fall of the music, social issues such as the New Rich, extravagance, inflation, and the pursuit of blatant materialism are parodied as absurd phenomena. The naked man lifts his bum up in the air and sprays out an endless stream of paper money. At the same time a row of headless men in western suits parade across the screen with briefcases located where their heads should be. A little bald man in black clothing drives a black Rolls Royce whose wheels are replaced by feet, thus seemingly walking across the screen and pulling a limousine behind. With this work Wu Junyong addresses many much-discussed social topics and shows an innate understanding of human nature. *Wait Us Rich* is on the one hand critical of society, and on the other full of entertainment; it is satirical and at the same time funny. It builds a perceptual world that is based upon the vulgar and shallow world of humanity, being both a mirror held up to reality and the vulgar world of one person's imagination.

An important part of contemporary Chinese culture is the love of idols and entertainment. In this cultural context, Wu Junyong's work tries to create a world based on bizarre morals enveloped in the crazy atmosphere of a game that is built on the tedium and joy of collective absurdity. Undeniably, contemporary American and Japanese cartoons have had a large effect on Chinese aesthetics. Wu Junyong believes that the affects of today's culture are felt in every aspect of life, and his work is filled with these influences. The images in his works are largely based on traditional illustrated books for the lower classes as well as folk art. *Parade* (2006), for example, was influenced by folk histories, and the *Opera* series – *Opera I*, *Opera II*, and *Opera III* – realized between 2006 and 2007, is based on old communal stage performances. In this animation work Wu Junyong satirically expresses his observations on politics by making politicians perform on a stage.

Wu Junyong likes things that are funny and full of knowledge. His aesthetic principals are based in normal culture, but his work often reflects a less than ordinary meaning.

By Huang Du

1

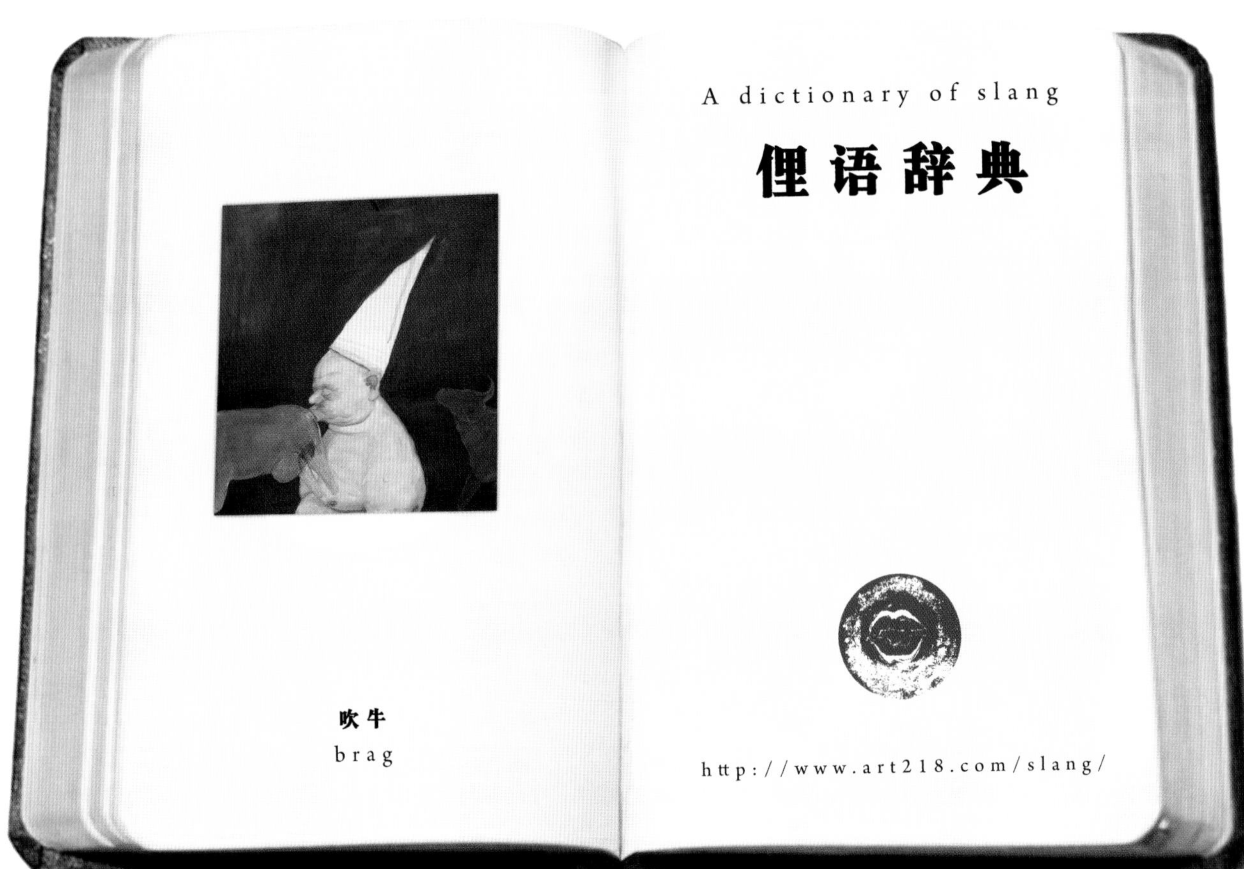

1 A DICTIONARY OF SLANG • 2008 • BOOK, PAINTING, INTERNET

2 CIRCLE OF SPIDER • 2008 • ANIMATION • EIGHT SCREEN

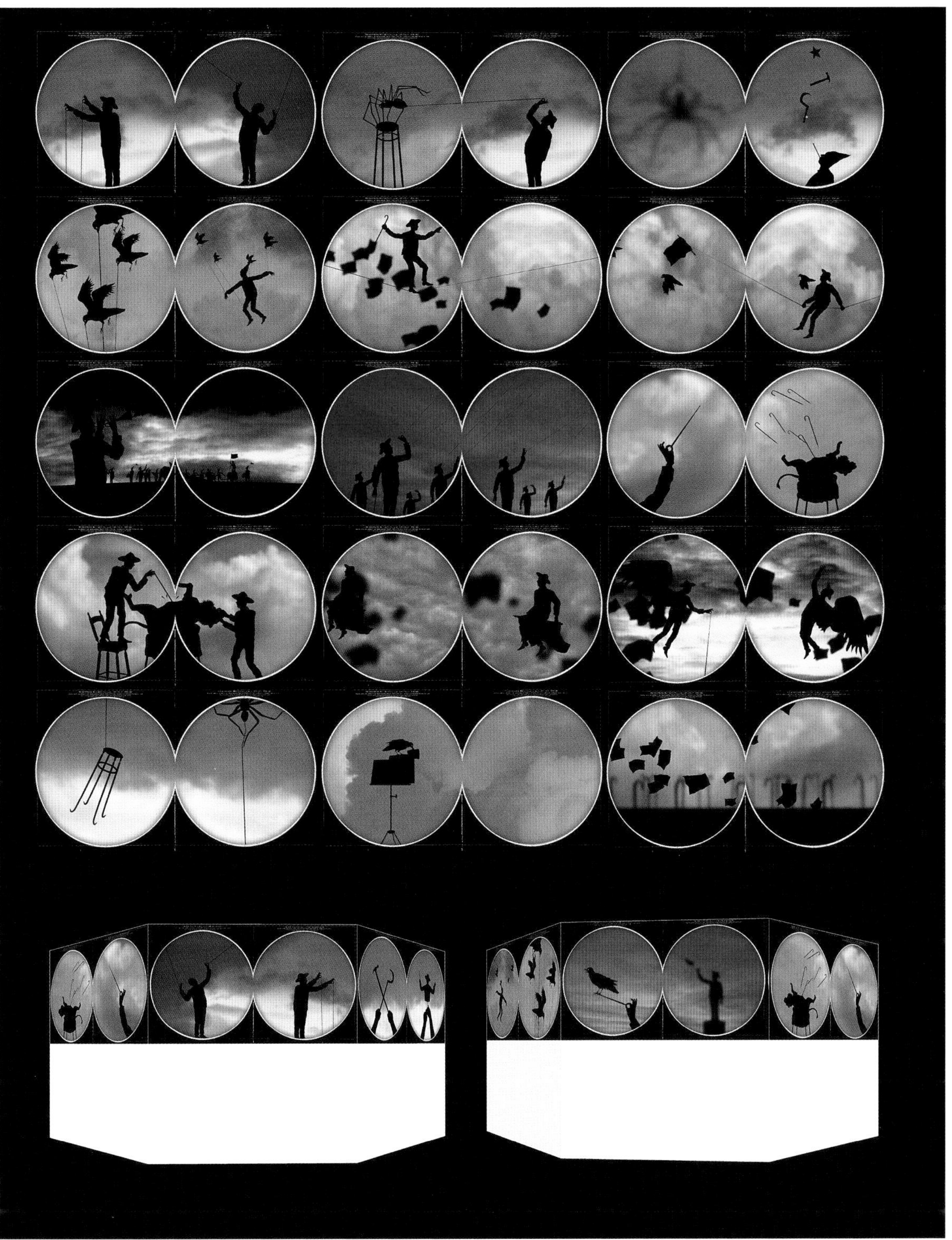

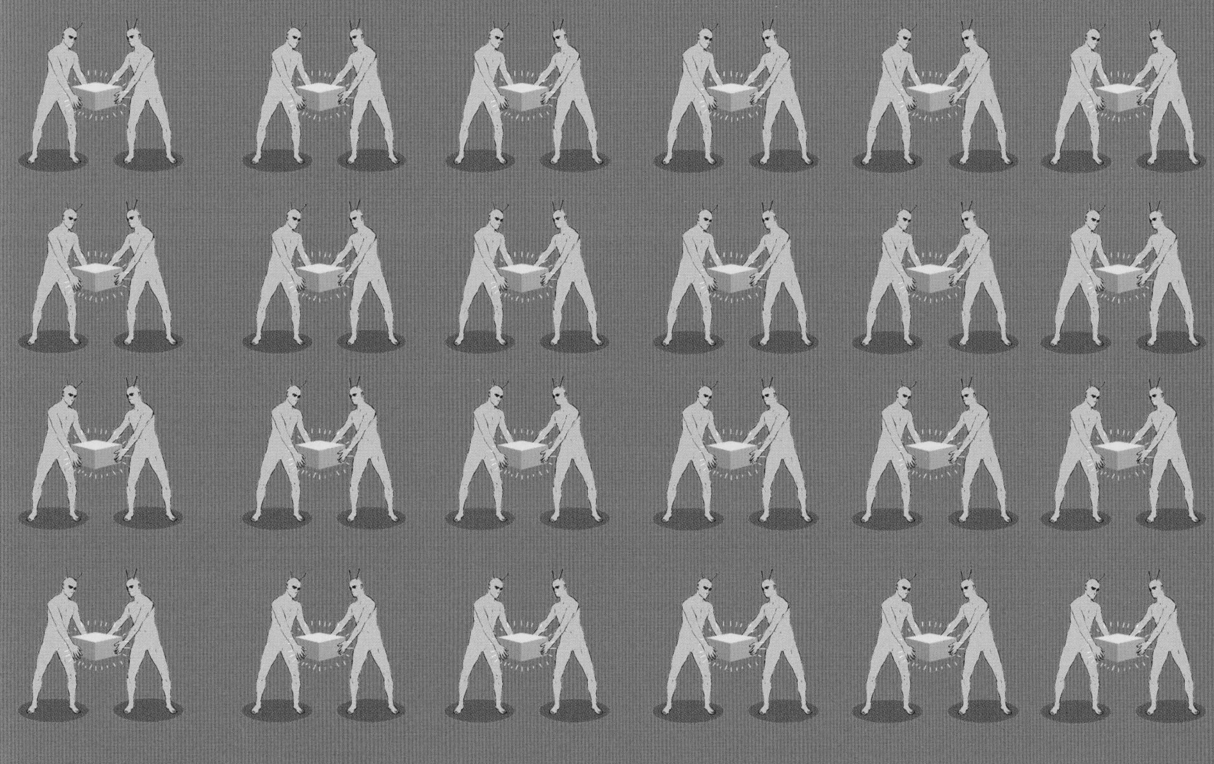

等咱有钱了

wait us rich

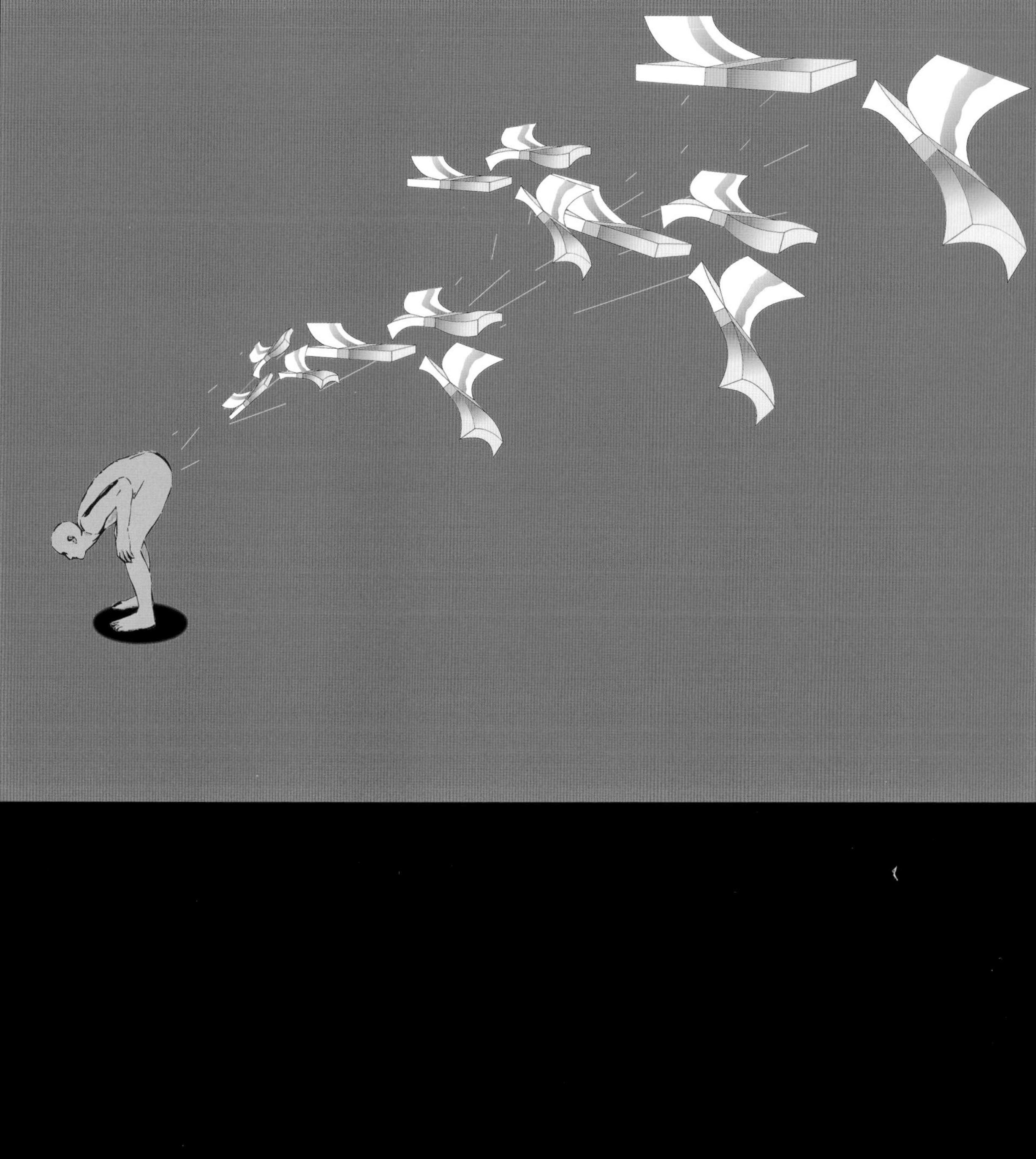

WAIT US RICH, 2005, ANIMATION, 1'50"

4

5 6

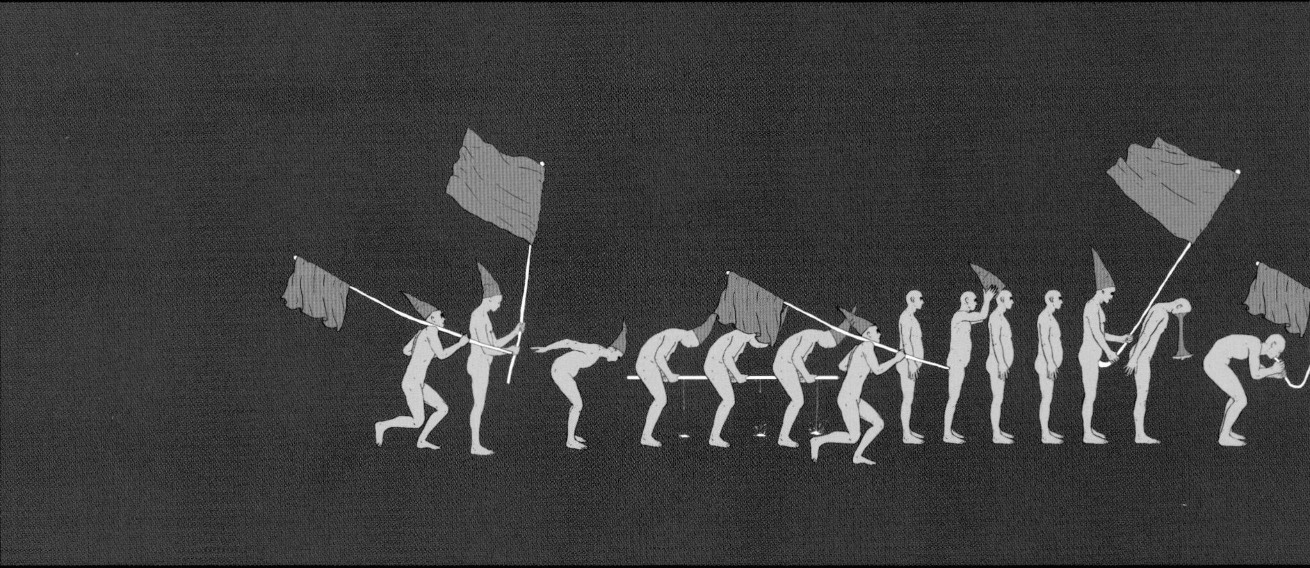

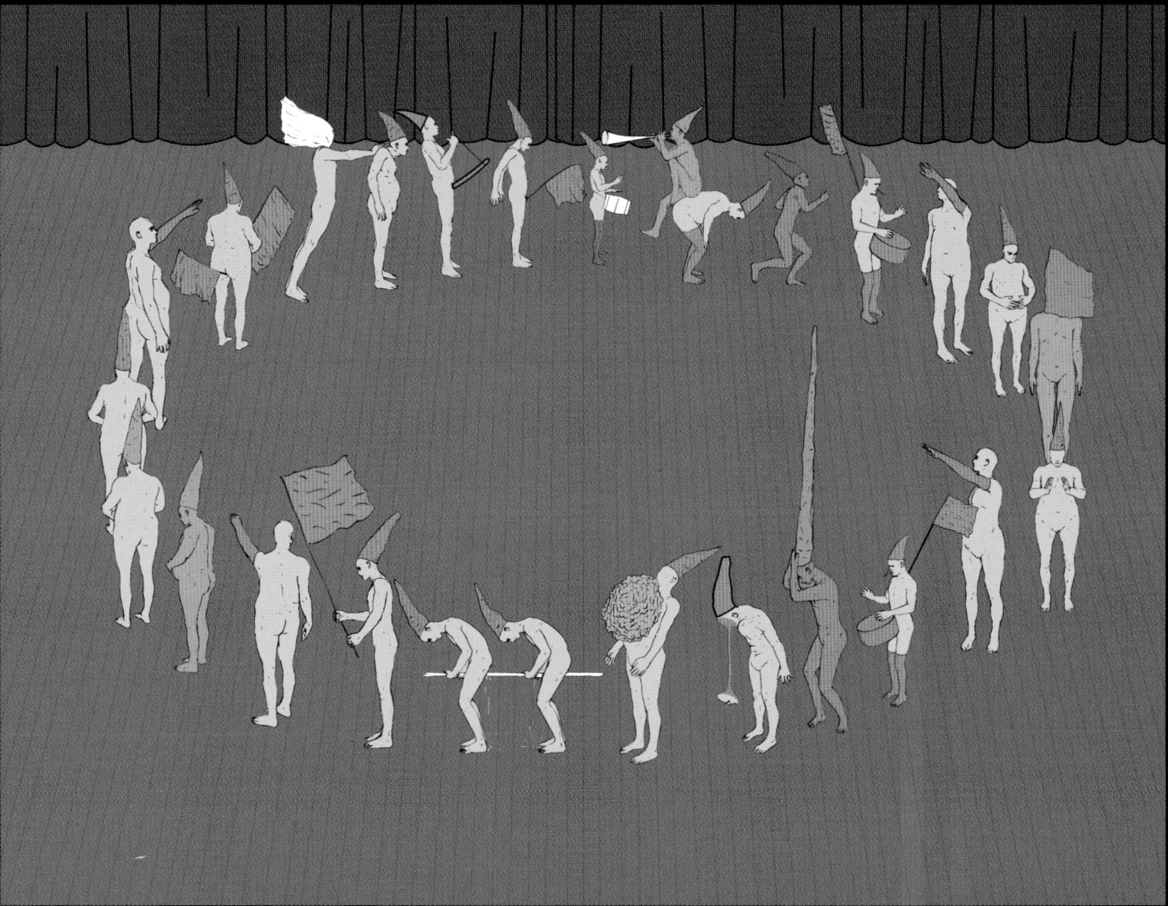

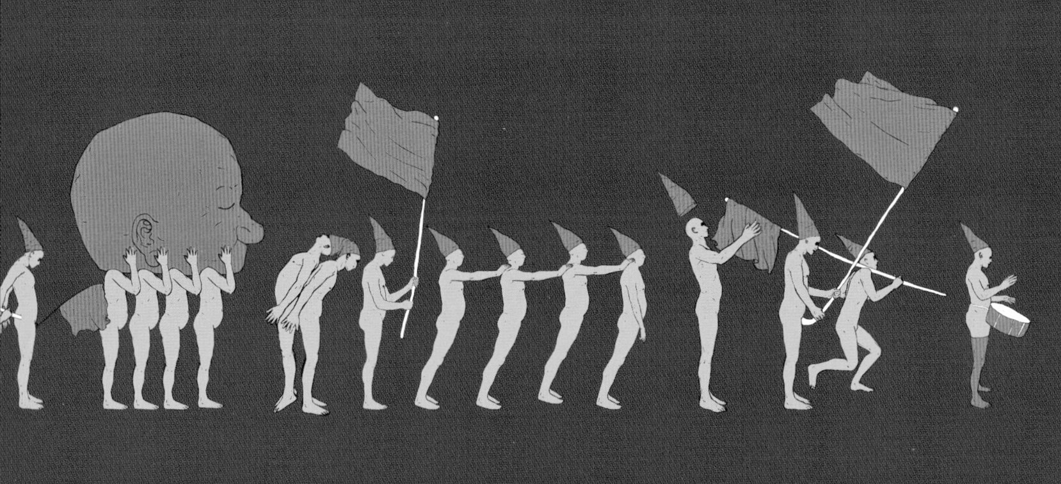

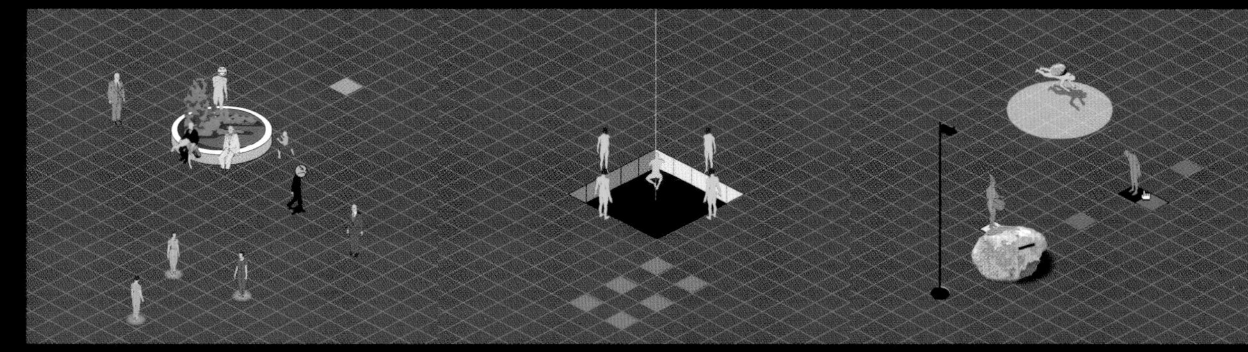

4 PARADE • 2006 • ANIMATION • 4'35"

5 OPERA III • 2007 • ANIMATION • 4'30"

6 SQUARE • 2006 • INTERACTIVE VIDEO, 3 PROJECTORS

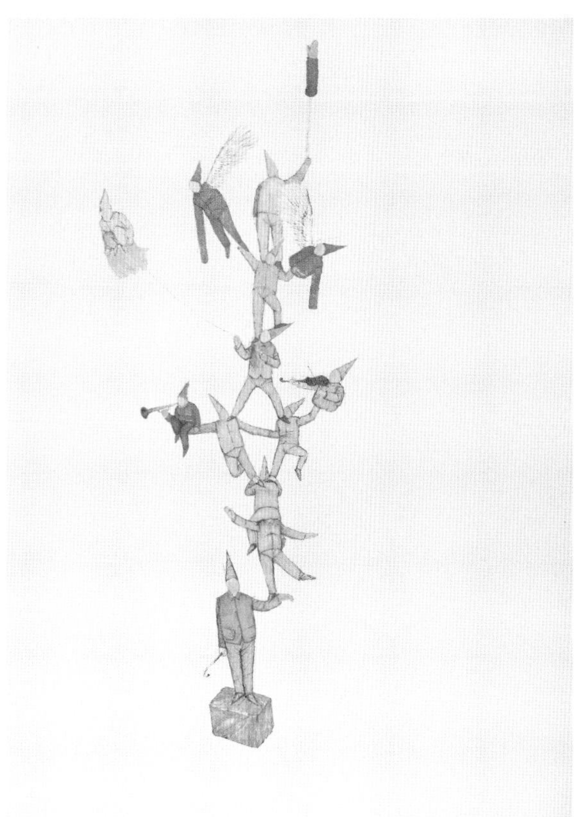

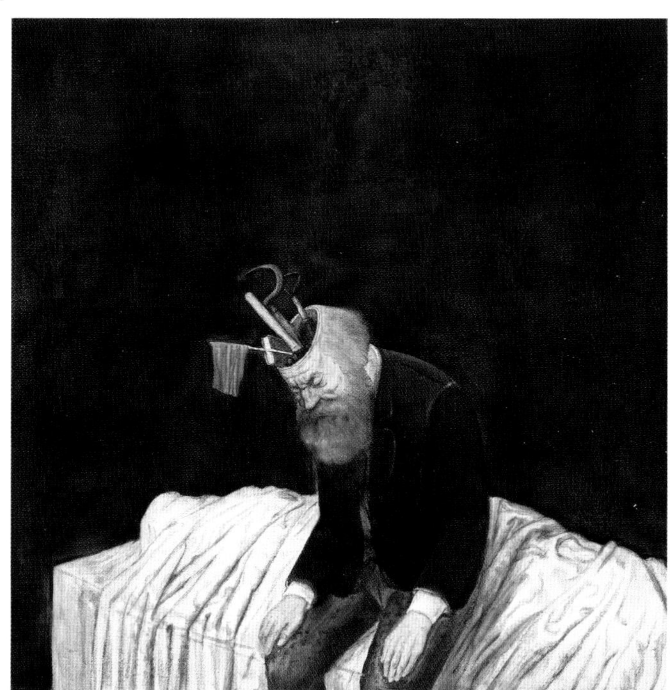

ONLINE CHAT WITH EDITORS

5/20/08 • AFTERNOON

[16:30:28] What was your favorite toy as a child?

[16:35:11] When I was a kid, my family didn't have money to buy me toys. But I often played with animals like chickens, kittens, or small insects. I also remember that one of my good friends had a little bookshelf filled with many children books. I loved it.

[16:36:43] What did your parents say to you most often?

[16:38:55] When I was little, they told me to become a successful man in the future, and nowadays they especially care about my health.

[16:39:36] How do you try to stay healthy in your everyday life?

[16:42:01] I hardly take care of my health, except when I am feeling sick. Also I don't do any sports nor do I care about my nutrition.

[16:44:14] What have you been wishing for most recently?

[16:48:50] Unfortunately, no one could predict the earthquake that happened last week in Sichuan (5/12/08). I wish someone could have.

[16:49:22] Do you believe in true love?

[16:50:56] Normally, I don't really believe in it. Sometimes I do, but then this is only temporarily, until the love is over.

[16:51:40] What does your ideal living environment look like?

[16:55:09] It should be close to a lake or the sea, with mild temperatures in spring when the flowers should bloom. For me, the ideal environment is based on the harmony between industrialization on one side and nature on the other side.

[16:56:49] From which type of media do you derive most of your inspiration?

[16:58:10] Mainly from the Internet. I very often use search engines like Google.

[16:59:58] What do you like and dislike about being an artist?

[17:00:57] I love the freedom; this is why I decline commissioned artworks.

[17:02:29] How do you communicate with the audience in your art?

[17:05:18] Certain visual effects can arouse individual memories in one's heart. This is what I am reaching for.

[17:07:21] Could you name an example?

[17:08:43] For example, I painted a person "blowing up a bull."

[17:09:07] What does "blowing up a bull" mean?

[17:12:18] This is a Chinese saying, which refers to people who are snobbish and continuously sing their own praises. But in the end they fail with that behavior.

[17:14:12] If you had five words to describe your generation, what would they be?

[17:16:27] Change of location, dreams, memories of the past, sticking to one's principles.

[17:17:01] What do you mean by "change of location"?

[17:18:38] Nowadays, many people move away from the places where they were born?

[17:19:40] If the whole world would listen to you for fifteen seconds what would you say?

[17:20:11] 1-2-3-4-5-6-7-8-9-10-11-12-13-14-15 :)

7 CIRCUS • 2008 • DRAWING • 115.5 x 67 CM

8 KARL MARX'S WORRIES • 2008 • OIL ON CANVAS • 40 x 40 CM

EXHIBITIONS

SELECTED SOLO EXHIBITIONS

2008
Club Primavera,
Hanart TZ Gallery,
Hong Kong, China

2007
Opera,
Chinese Contemporary Gallery,
New York, U.S.

2005
Fantasy,
China Academy of Art,
Hangzhou, China

SELECTED GROUP EXHIBITIONS

2008
The Third Guangzhou Triennial,
Guangdong Museum of Art,
Guangzhou, China

2008
Kunstvlaai 7,
Westergasfabriek,
Amsterdam, The Netherlands

2008
Intrude: Art & Life,
Zendai Museum of Modern Art,
Shanghai, China

2008
55 Days in Valencia: Chinese Contemporary Art,
Institut Valencià d'Art Modern,
Valencia, Spain

2007
The Toronto Reel Asian International Film Festival,
Toronto, Canada

2007
The First Today's Documents: Energy–Spirit, Body, Material,
Today Art Museum,
Beijing, China

2006
China Gate,
Art Center Arko,
Seoul, South Korea

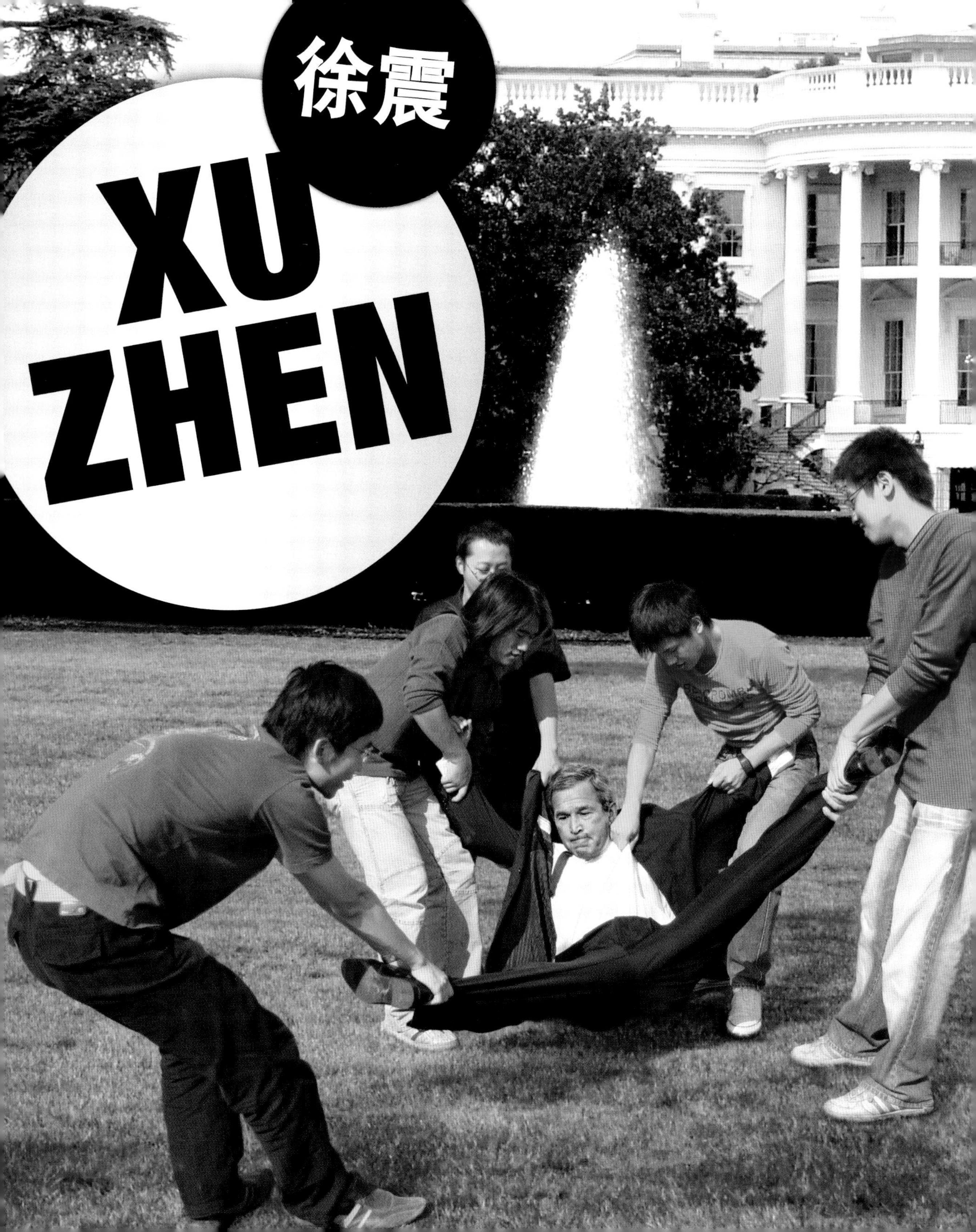
徐震
XU
ZHEN

NAME
XU ZHEN
BORN IN
1977, SHANGHAI
LIVES IN
SHANGHAI
STUDY
SHANGHAI ARTS & CRAFTS INSTITUTE, SHANGHAI
MEDIA
INSTALLATION, PERFORMANCE, PHOTOGRAPHY, VIDEO

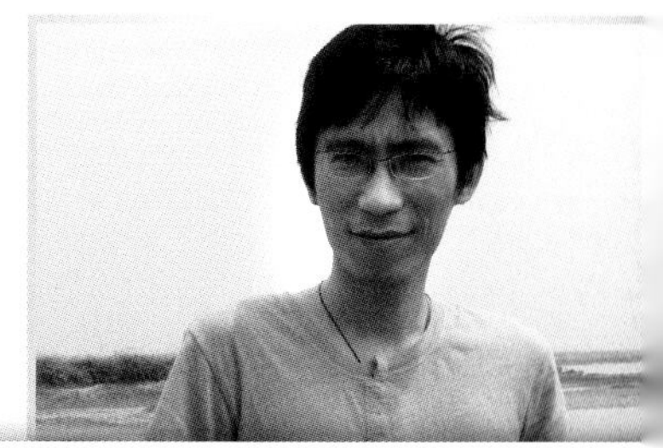

SHANGHAI'S MERRY PRANKSTER

Xu Zhen is among the earliest of a generation of Chinese artists who grew up unburdened by history, at once amused by and critical of their situation. Trained not at the elite art academies of Beijing or Hangzhou, but at a local Shanghai institute, he emerged in the late 1990s alongside Shanghai co-conspirators Yang Fudong and Yang Zhenzhong in a series of unofficial exhibitions – often of his own design and organization – such as *310 Jinyuan Road* (1998), *Supermarket* (1999), and *Useful Life* (2000). In 1999, his video *Rainbow* (1998) was included in the Harald Szeemann-curated 49th Venice Biennale, making him at twenty-two the youngest Chinese artist ever included in that major exhibition – a record that holds today.

It is in these works – raw pieces that begin with the controversial *I Am Not Asking for Anything* (1998), in which the artist wields a cat by its tail, repeatedly whipping it against wall and floor until its bloodied, limp carcass comes apart – that we see the genesis of Xu Zhen's sarcastic humanism. *Rainbow* shows the artist's back becoming increasingly red against a soundtrack of flagellation; the whip responsible for his suffering, however, is never shown. In *Shouting* (1998, 2005), he captures the only momentary pause and panic of Shanghainese passers-by on major urban thoroughfares as they hear pre-recorded screams of agony. Within seconds, these pedestrians have returned to their ordinary routines, ignorant to the death knell that has provided just an instant of bemusement. Much of Xu Zhen's work accomplishes its aesthetic work in that brief second where the viewer realizes that he or she is being assaulted with a "shout" of ambiguous meaning.

In the early part of the present decade, Xu Zhen's works grew in scope to encompass larger site-specific and performative projects, often dealing with abnormality and perversion. For *Twins*, a satellite show to the 2002 Shanghai Biennale organized in a warehouse on Jinshajiang Road by the curatorial collective BizArt which he founded in 1998 with the Italian Davide Quadrio, he hired one hundred local students and dressed them in the uniforms of insane-asylum inmates, instructing them to follow viewers around the exhibition. Much to the viewers' discomfort, these performers clung to their every move. In *Actually, I Am Also Dim* (2000), he created an installation of post-it notes imprinted with explicit pictures downloaded from the Internet and tacked up around a given space. The culturally constructed notions of clean and dirty were not far from Xu Zhen's mind, leading him to create works such as *Careful, Don't Get Dirty* (2002), in which a model vehicle moves around a Berlin gallery space spouting saliva collected from Chinese participants. Realized two years later in Lyon, *Comfortable* (2004) turns a "filthy" Chinese minibus into an oversized washing machine, its passenger area now filled with soapy water and clothes.

In 2003 and 2004, Xu Zhen's work took a turn for the social and political, perhaps best marked by his piece *Dang Dang Dang Dang* (2003) for that year's Shanghai Biennale. In this work he convinced the management of the state-run Shanghai Art Museum to speed up the clock that tops the museum building, which was formerly the colonial-era Jockey Club of the British. For the two months of the biennale, the clock turned such that a minute seemed to pass with each second – an apt metaphor for the urban condition of Shanghai in that year of unprecedented construction. Likewise, *Less Than 100,000,000 mm²* (2003) placed a tiny island in the shape of Taiwan below the surface of a lake in Shenzhen. At night, the island would poke through to the water's surface, visible in the glow of the gaudy neon lights surrounding the lake. *In the Blink of an Eye* (2005) positioned migrant laborers on elaborate support structures hidden beneath their clothes, such that these typically unseen underpinnings of the Chinese economy appeared constantly suspended as if about to fall to the ground. For *Tank* (2005), he simply placed a battered foam replica of an army tank, its gun flaccid, in the courtyard outside the Nanjing Museum – Nanjing of course being the site of the worst atrocities during Japan's occupation of China in the 1930s and 40s.

Xu Zhen's recent work has grown more light-hearted, if predicated on the notion of elaborate fictional scenarios. In one 2007 work (*Fitness*), he rigged exercise machines with remote control technology so that the viewer can get a virtual "workout" by pressing buttons that in turn move weights up and down. His best-known piece to date is perhaps *8848-1.86* (2005), an installation and video documenting the process by which he and his friends "climbed Mt. Everest" and removed a piece of the peak equivalent to the artist's height. *OK My Club* (2005) entails a purported global band of gangsters who collect donations from friends over the Internet to fund excursions devoted to "beating up" senior international politicians. A monumental untitled 2007 riff on Damien Hirst's early dissected-animal sculptures likewise presented a "brontosaurus" segmented in two, revealing behind vacuum-sealed glass a set of organ systems that actually consisted of cow parts.

Throughout his constantly evolving practice, Xu Zhen has shown himself to be an artist of remarkable wit and sensitivity, his works functioning as both snide rejoinders and enduring responses to a distinct set of historical, political, and urban conditions.

By Phil Tinari

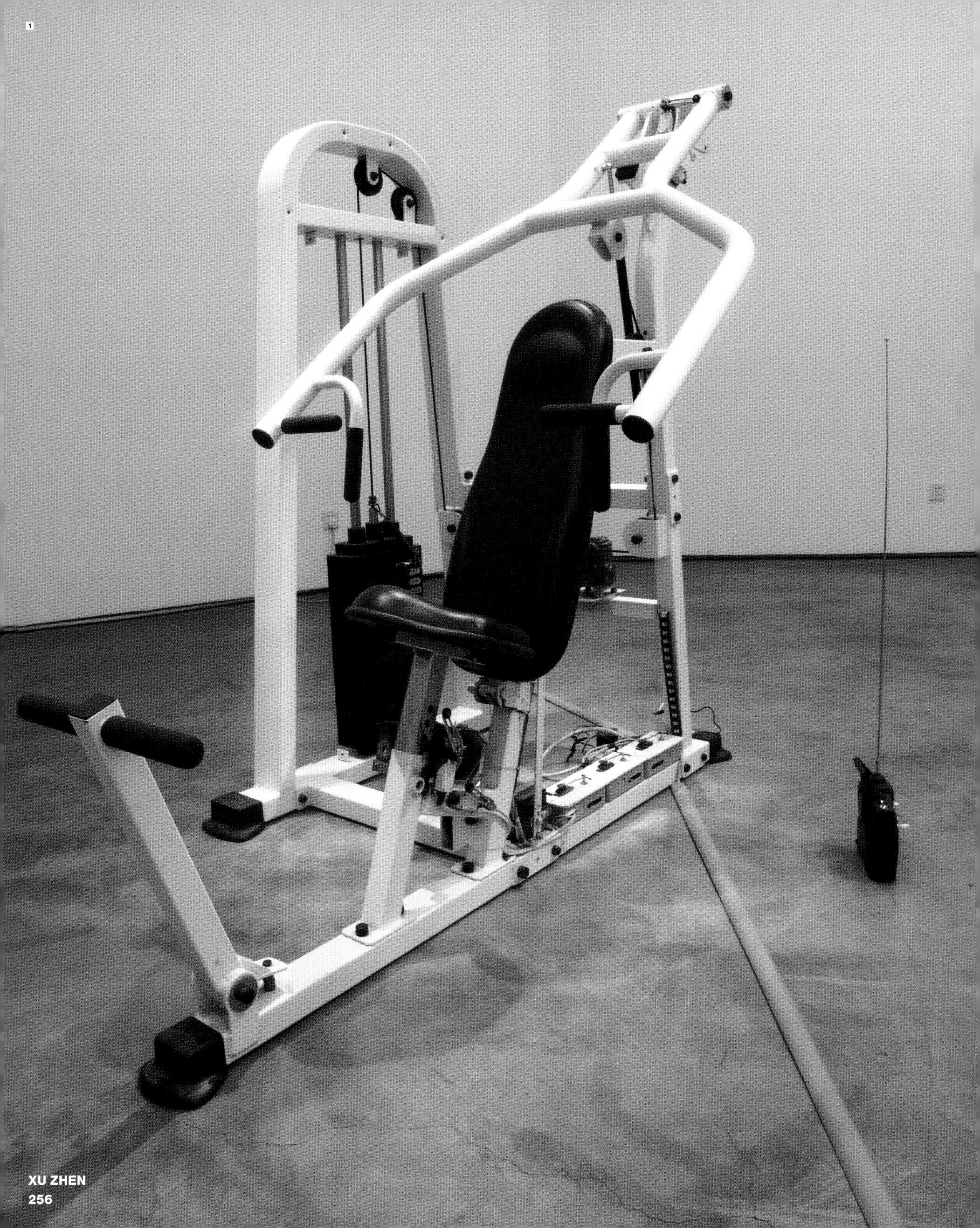
1

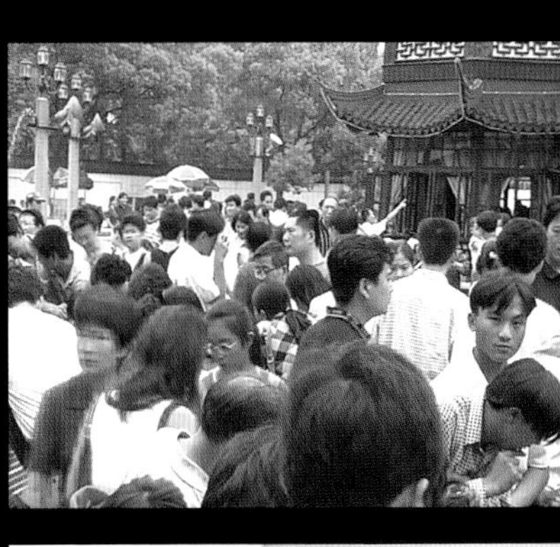

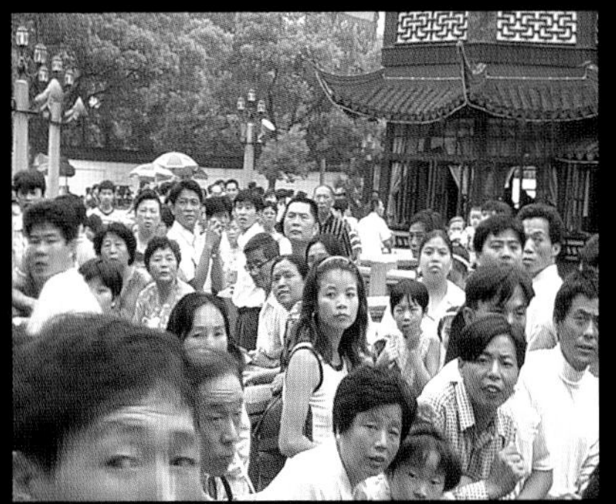

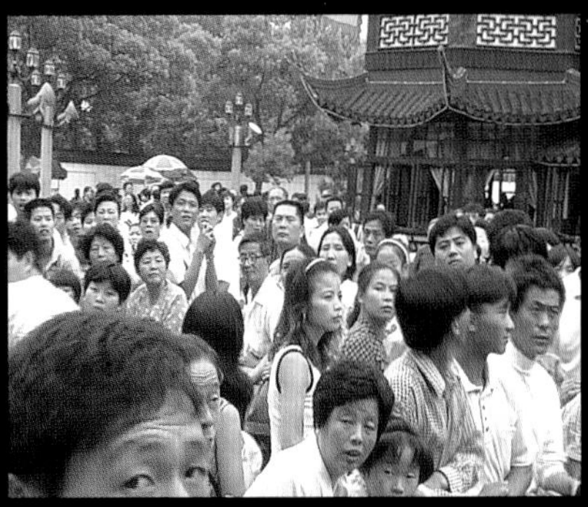

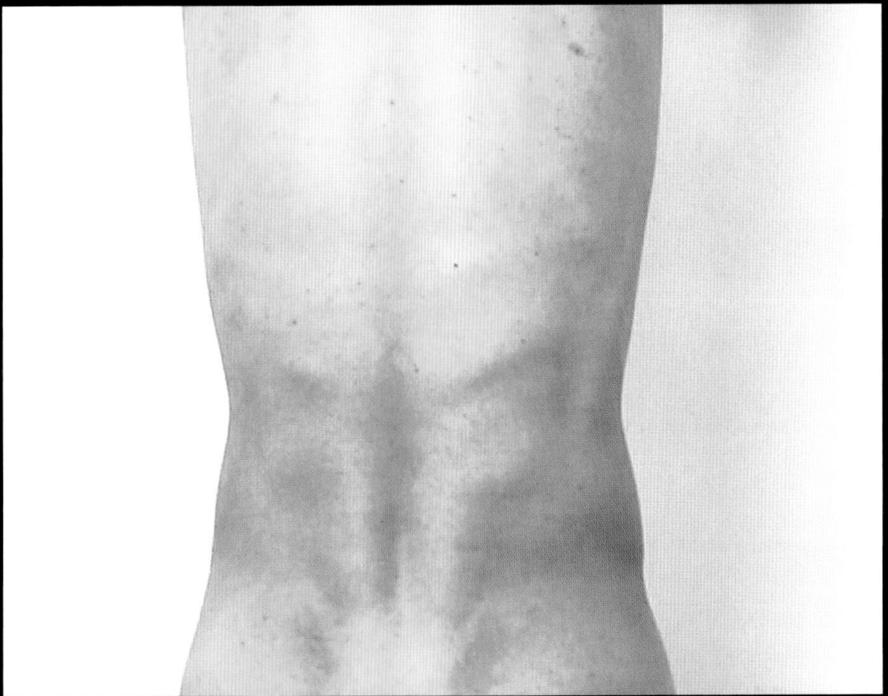

1 FITNESS • 2007 • INSTALLATION: FITNESS EQUIPMENT, MOTOR, REMOTE CONTROL

2 SHOUTING • 1998 • VIDEO • 4'

3 RAINBOW • 1998 • VIDEO • 3'50"

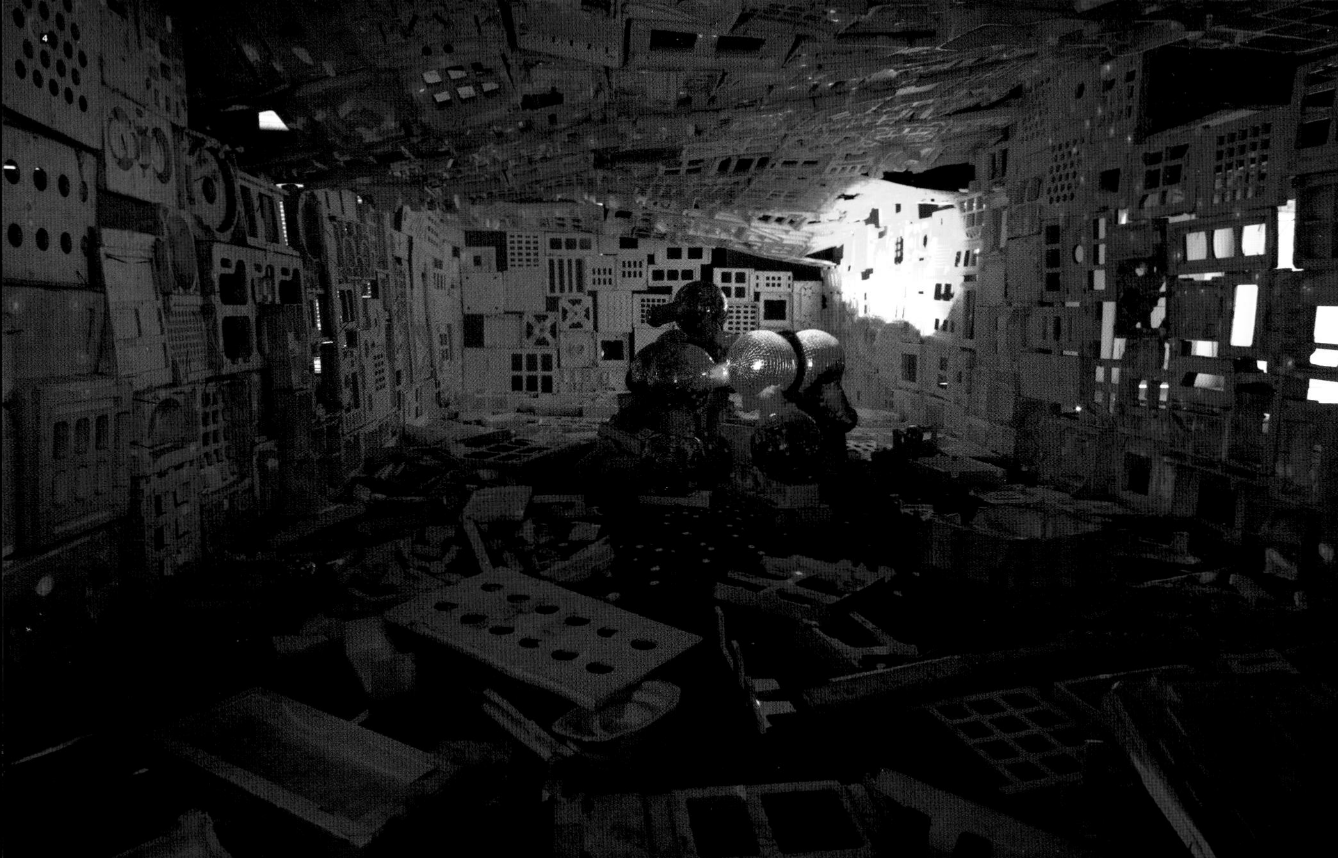

QUESTIONNAIRE

5/2/08 • MY HOMETOWN

WHAT WAS YOUR FAVORITE CHILDHOOD TOY?

Nothing.

WHAT DID YOUR PARENTS SAY TO YOU MOST OFTEN?

Put your toothbrush in the right place.

HOW DO YOU TRY TO STAY HEALTHY IN YOUR EVERYDAY LIFE?

I am not able to take care of my health.

WHAT HAVE YOU BEEN WISHING FOR MOST RECENTLY?

To have more time to sleep.

DO YOU BELIEVE IN TRUE LOVE?

Yes.

WHAT DOES YOUR IDEAL LIVING ENVIRONMENT LOOK LIKE?

The same as it is now.

FROM WHICH TYPE OF MEDIA DO YOU DERIVE MOST OF YOUR INSPIRATION?

All kinds of media.

WHAT DO YOU LIKE/DISLIKE ABOUT BEING AN ARTIST?

I don't like to answer this kind of question very often

HOW DO YOU COMMUNICATE WITH THE AUDIENCE IN YOUR ART?

In the most direct way possible.

IF YOU HAD FIVE WORDS TO DESCRIBE YOUR GENERATION, WHAT WOULD THEY BE?

Lively, vivid, taking the initiative, warm-hearted, selfish.

IF THE WHOLE WORLD WOULD LISTEN TO YOU FOR FIFTEEN SECONDS, WHAT WOULD YOU SAY?

I would just count the seconds.

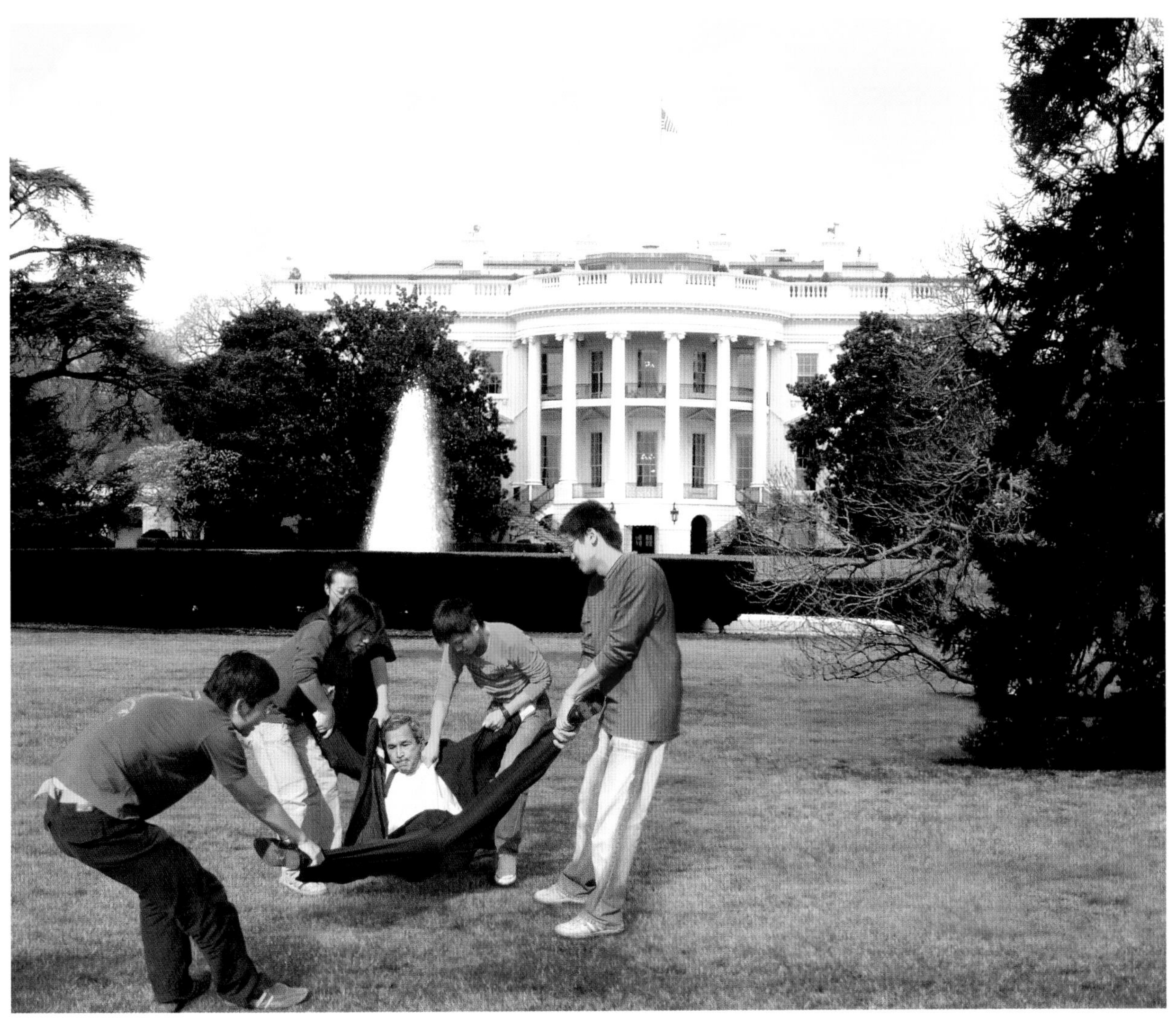

4 LOVE IN FACT RESULTS FROM AN EXCESS OF DOPAMINE IN THE BRAIN • 2009 • INSTALLATION FOAM BOARD, DISCO LIGHTS, FOOTBALL, BASKETBALL, VOLLEYBALL

5 OK MY CLUB • 2005 • C-PRINT • 120 x 160 CM

6

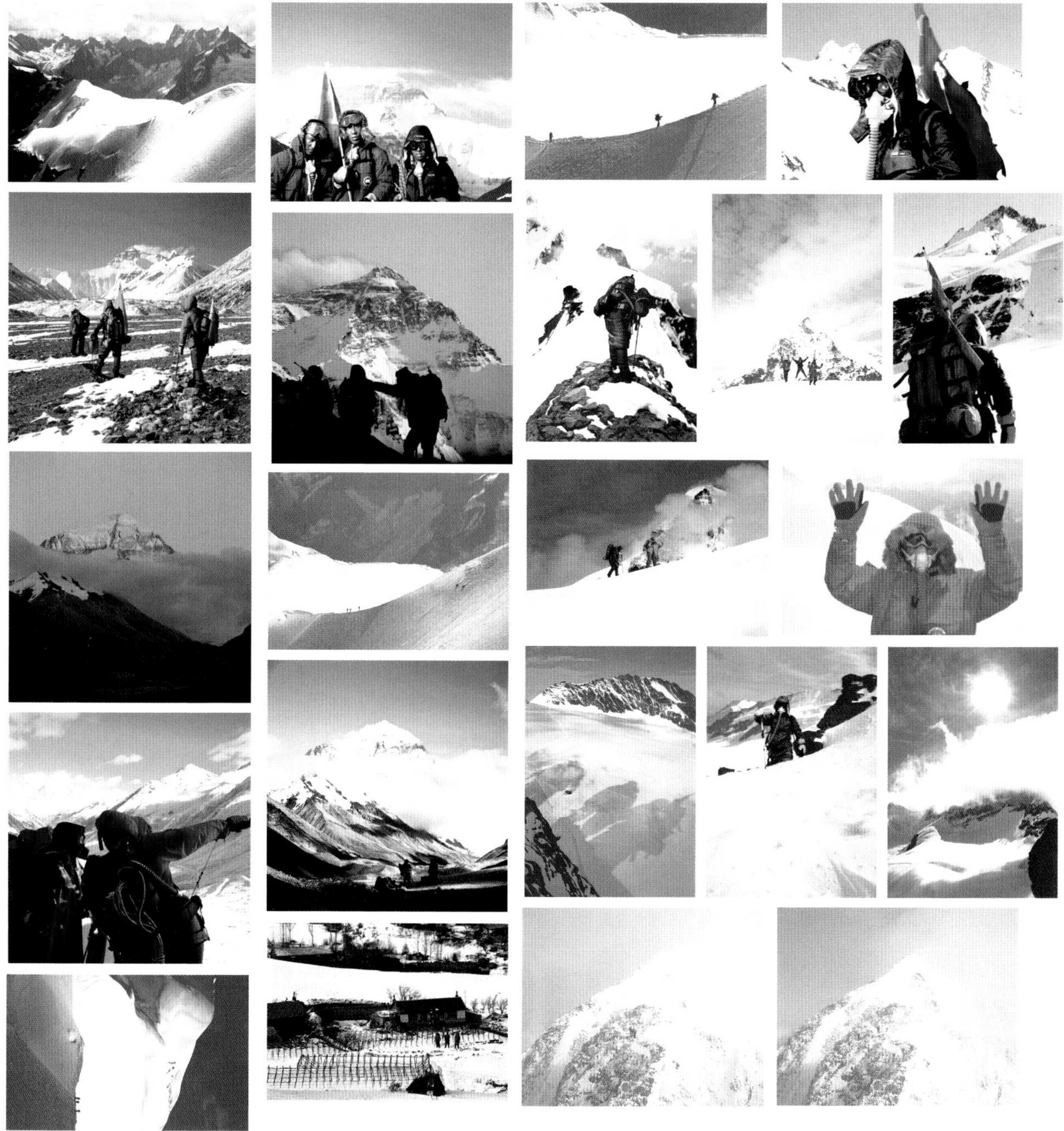

6 8848-1.86 • 2005 • C-PRINT (22 PIECES) • VARIOUS SIZES

7 DANG DANG DANG DANG • 2003 • INSTALLATION

8 COMFORTABLE • 2004 • INSTALLATION

7
8

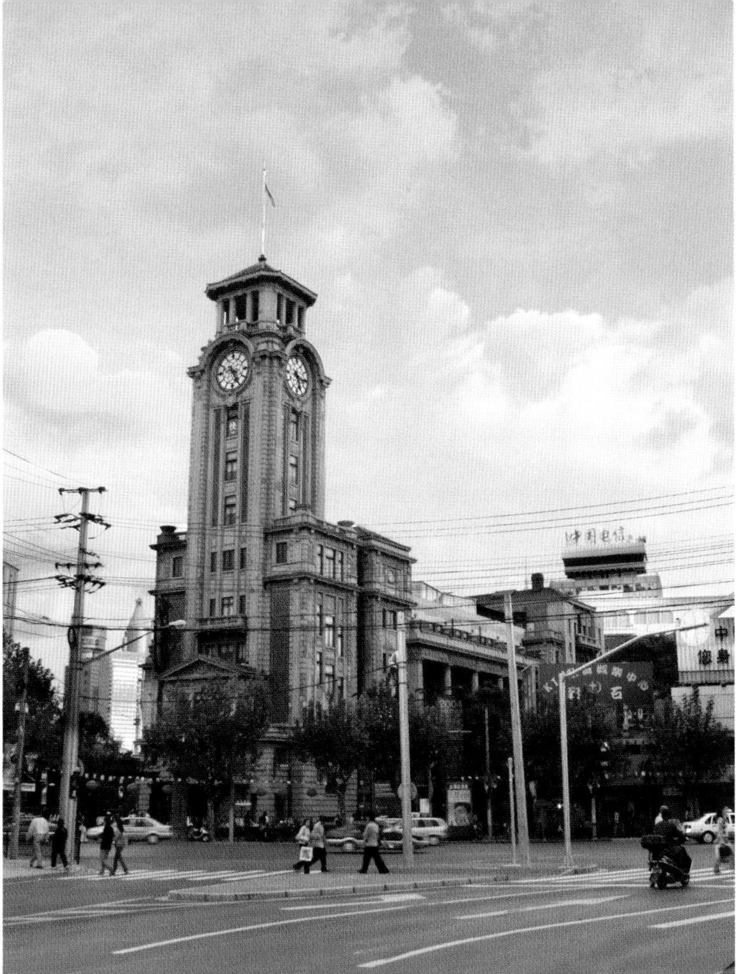

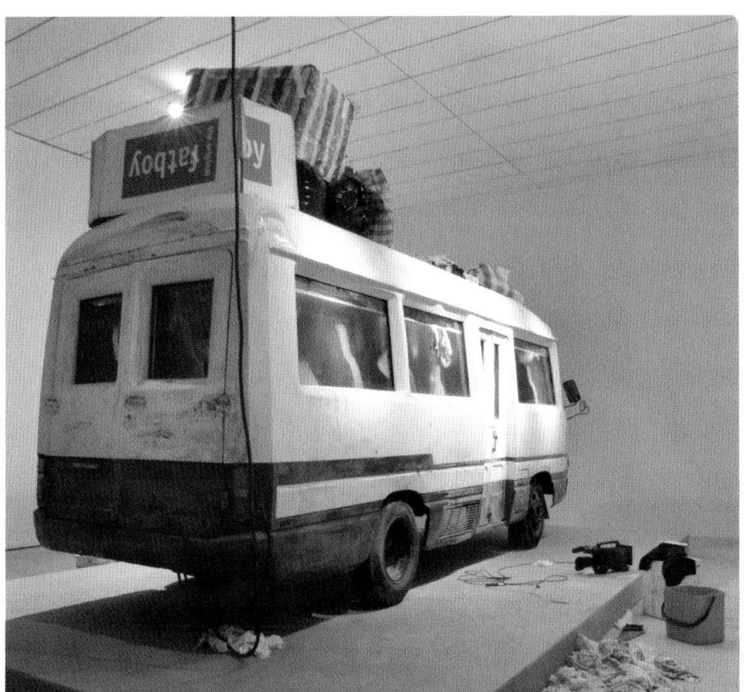

EXHIBITIONS

SELECTED SOLO EXHIBITIONS

2009
Seeing One's Own Eyes
ShanghART,
Shanghai, China

2006
8848-1.86: Xu Zhen Solo Exhibition,
Museum Boijmans Van Beuningen,
Rotterdam, The Netherlands

2002
Careful, Don't Get Dirty,
Galerie Waldburger,
Berlin, Germany

SELECTED GROUP EXHIBITIONS

2008
Avant-Garde China: Twenty Years of Chinese Contemporary Art,
The National Art Center, Tokyo /
The National Museum of Art, Osaka /
Aichi Prefectural Museum of Art,
Nagoya, Japan

2008
Mellow Fever,
Galerie des Galeries,
Paris, France

2007
Performa 07: The 2nd Biennial of New Visual Art Performance,
New York, U.S.

2007
China: Facing Reality,
Museum Moderner Kunst Stiftung Ludwig,
Vienna, Austria

2007
China Power Station: Part II,
Astrup Fearnley Museum of Modern Art,
Oslo, Norway

2007
The Real Thing: Contemporary Art from China,
Tate Liverpool,
Liverpool, U.K.

2001
49th Venice Biennale: Plateau of Humankind,
Venice, Italy

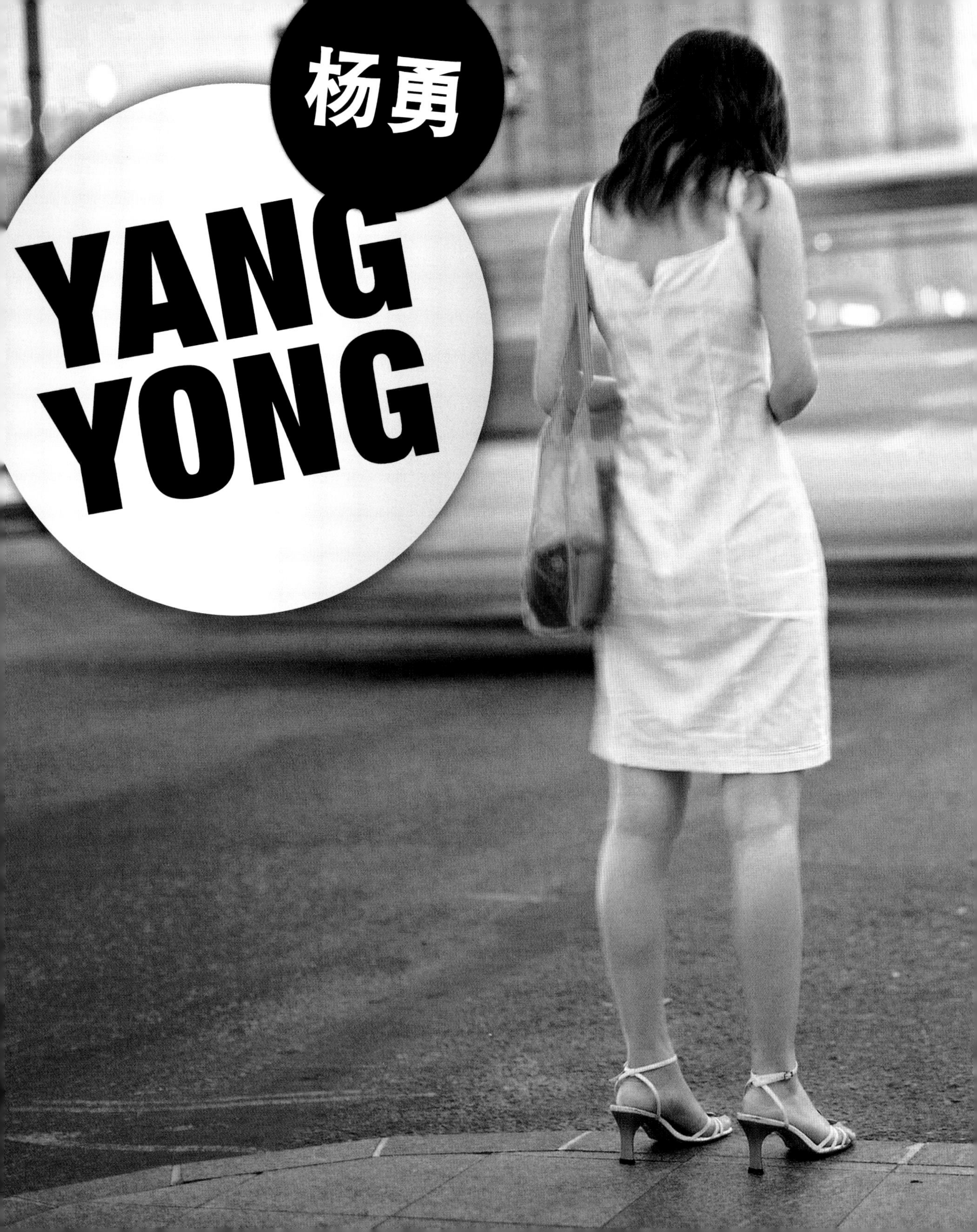
杨勇
YANG
YONG

NAME

YANG YONG

BORN IN

1975, SICHUAN PROVINCE

LIVES IN

SHENZHEN

STUDY

SICHUAN INSTITUTE OF FINE ARTS, CHONGQING

MEDIA

INSTALLATION, PAINTING, PHOTOGRAPHY

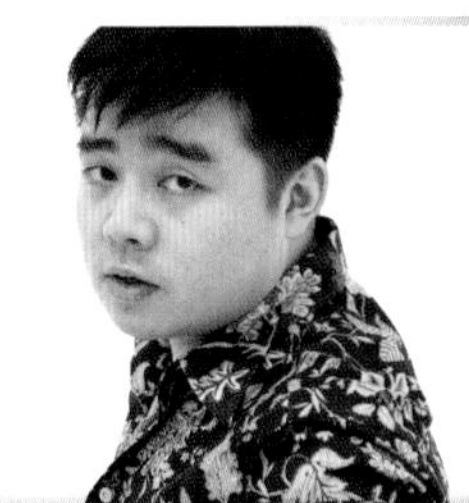

AN ARCHIVE OF NARRATIVES WITHOUT A PLOT

Yang Yong's photographic oeuvre lives from visual repetition, from the systematic recording of moments. These moments appear to be authentic snapshots but are actually to a great extent arranged by the artist, taken from scenes he staged with his friends. The effect is one that resembles film stills; a film without a plot, without heroines, without movement, but with a series of images full of strange-looking locations with reoccurring characters. These stills constitute the narrative of Yang Yong's city, Shenzhen.

Originally from Sichuan Province, Yang has been living in Shenzhen for ten years. This synthetic metropolis in the Pearl River Delta – built overnight from a fishing village – has captured his interest and plays a decisive role in the formation of his personal style. Shenzhen is not only a young city but also a city of young people who come from all over China. Living in China's earliest special economic zone known for an unrestricted Western-style capitalism, this youth forms a kind of "special social zone." Yang's creative imagination is in particular linked to those elements of this "social zone" who are most receptive to the fancy city life and its temptations, and who are thus most fragile: young country girls and women trying their luck in the southern Chinese metropolis. One of his earliest works, *Women are Beautiful, Always and Forever* (1999), a series of color prints, portraits these girls who often earn their living as prostitutes. Yang's approach is prosaic, showing them still naïve, unaffected, and mainly sincerely gazing straight into the camera. He does not want to question their social environment nor their status but rather tries to define a kind of visual language reflecting the triviality of the urban reality. "This is the reality of China. I don't care if a woman is a prostitute or not. I'm just trying to show how people really live."[1]

As the narrative of Yang Yong's city goes on, his protagonists change locations and attitude. Yang starts to choose a variety of settings, ranging from apartments and bathrooms to passageways, tunnels, public toilets, street scenes, shopping malls, airports, and construction sites, reflecting the multiple facets of city life. Yet he shows these common locations in a somehow strange and murky light that makes them appear mundane and alien at the same time. The images of his series *The Cruel Diary of Youth* (1999–2001), *City Lights* (1999–2002), *The Cruel Daily of Youth* (2003), and *Yang Yong's City – Anonymous Still* (2004/2005) glow with bright colors from inside; light seems to shine through them. It is therefore logical that Yang uses light boxes, large semitransparent material, and projections as supports for his images.

Maybe the change in attitude of Yang's protagonists, which is evident in his later works, is linked to their growing desires and need to fill in the void of their never-to-be-fulfilled aspirations. His girls have become fashionable, lascivious, erotic. In most of the artist's recent works they do not directly face the camera. Yang shows them from the back, preoccupied with mundane activities. They are seldom communicative and there is nearly no communication between viewer and image. Even though one can imagine the energy and sensuality of these young women, they seem sterile; even though Yang Yong records moments of their life, there is not much life in his images. They are rather still lifes, expressing void and futility.

While Yang Yong records his direct personal environment through photography, he started to record more general impressions and thoughts related to international events and historical developments through painting. Here he reveals his background as a graduate in oil painting from the Sichuan Fine Arts Academy. Similar to his photos, his series of oil paintings entitled *International Passage* records particular moments , too. A further similarity is the strange use of light, the choice of a singular and somehow strange perspective that makes the represented common object, location, or event appear unfamiliar and alien. For a recent solo exhibition Yang created an ensemble of paintings and painted objects entitled *International Passage – The World is Yours* (2007–8). Alluding to a scene in Brian De Palma's film *Scarface* (1983), as the exhibition title does, the ambience created by the artist appears as a recreation of that ultimate dream to make the world one's own. Pictures (depictions) and images (mental images) that actually construct the world and shape the social environment and identity play a crucial role in the process of appropriation and occupation/generation of space. In this regard the ambience designed by Yang recalls the concept of the "pictorial turn"[2] and his ensemble of pictures actually represents part of the canon of images constituting the new symbolic order of contemporary Chinese culture.

Yang's photos and paintings are highly metaphorical. His women wear the insignia of the new Chinese society: fashionable dresses, make-up, and fancy accessories, such as the omnipresent cell phones; but the fact that they are well equipped and conform to the general trend does not make them any happier, does not make their life more tangible, nor their narratives more real. Yang Yong's oeuvre thus constitutes a kind of visual canon of the new China, an archive of distilled images from her changing society. Seriality and visual repetition in his work underline this aspect. Here, as well as in his understanding of photography not as an aesthetic distance from reality but as reality itself, he is referring to Nan Goldin. Nevertheless, Yang's archive shows the ambiguity of the real, the imaginary narratives of Chinese youth that have no plot.

By Martina Köppel-Yang

1 Jonathan Napack, "Yang Yong and the Four Elephants," in *Art News Online*, March 2000.

2 See W.J.T. Mitchell, *Picture Theory: Essays on Verbal and Visual Representation* (Chicago, 1994), p. 11. An earlier version appeared as "The Pictorial Turn," *Artforum* XXX (March 1992), pp. 89–94.

1

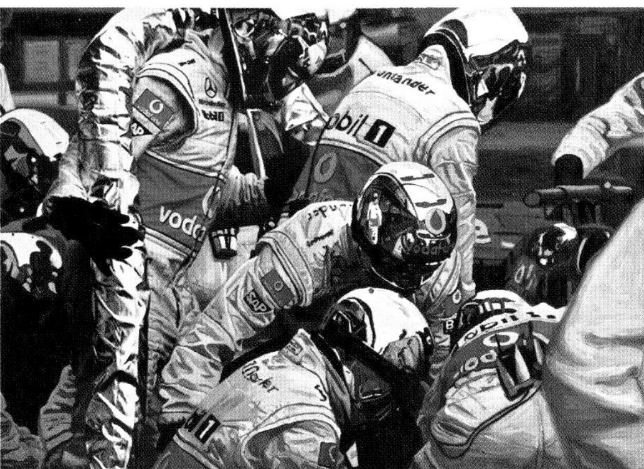

ONLINE CHAT WITH EDITORS

5/13/08 • AFTERNOON

[15:35:59] Remembering your childhood, what was your favorite childhood toy?

[15:37:20] I really loved color pens and also riding the tricycle.

[15:38:17] Could you name the sentence your parents said to you most often?

[15:42:01] In my childhood, they often told me to study hard. Now they ask me whether I have thought about having a baby. But right now I have no plans to found a family, because I'm too busy.

[15:43:54] Then we want to ask you about love. Do you believe in true love?

[15:45:18] Yes. For me it means a real feeling and I've experienced true love.

[15:46:29] How do you try to maintain your health in your everyday life?

[15:48:42] Through listening to music and swimming I try to relieve worries which occur at work and in everyday life.

[15:49:09] What is your recent wish?

[15:51:57] My latest wish occurred as a result of yesterday's happenings. I hope my countrymen in Sichuan can get over the negative influences of the heavy earthquake (5/12/08, 2:27 p.m.). My hometown is also in Sichuan Province, and I am very lucky that none of my family got hurt by it.

[15:52:46] If you could define your ideal living environment, what would it look like?

[15:54:11] There should be freedom and efficiency in the sense of efficient working. This is very important, as you can save a lot of time which can be used to daydream.

[15:56:40] Which type of media provides you most of your inspiration?

[15:58:13] First of all, it comes from real life, which is my most important inspiration. Secondly, it comes from media.

[15:59:52] What do you like/dislike about being an artist?

[16:01:08] There's nothing to like or dislike. I just use art to express my attitude towards the world.

[16:03:41] How would you say you communicate with the audience through your art?

[16:04:53] Well, they can sink into my works, and then discover their inwardness.

[16:06:11] You were born in 1975. Which five words would you use to describe your generation?

[16:08:31] I would say: luck, loneliness, confusion, and freedom. Only four words. Is this okay?

[16:09:10] Sure. Last question. If the whole world would listen to you for fifteen seconds, what would you say?

[16:11:28] Fight for the great adventure and conquest the peak in your heart!

1 VELOCITY-LIMIT EDITION • 2009 • OIL ON PHOTO • 210 x 300 CM

2 INTERNATIONAL PASSAGE / THE WORLD IS YOURS • 2008 • INSTALLATION

3 INTERNATIONAL PASSAGE / THE WORLD IS YOURS NO. 23 • 2008 • PAINTING INSTALLATION • 38 x 160 x 90 CM

2
3

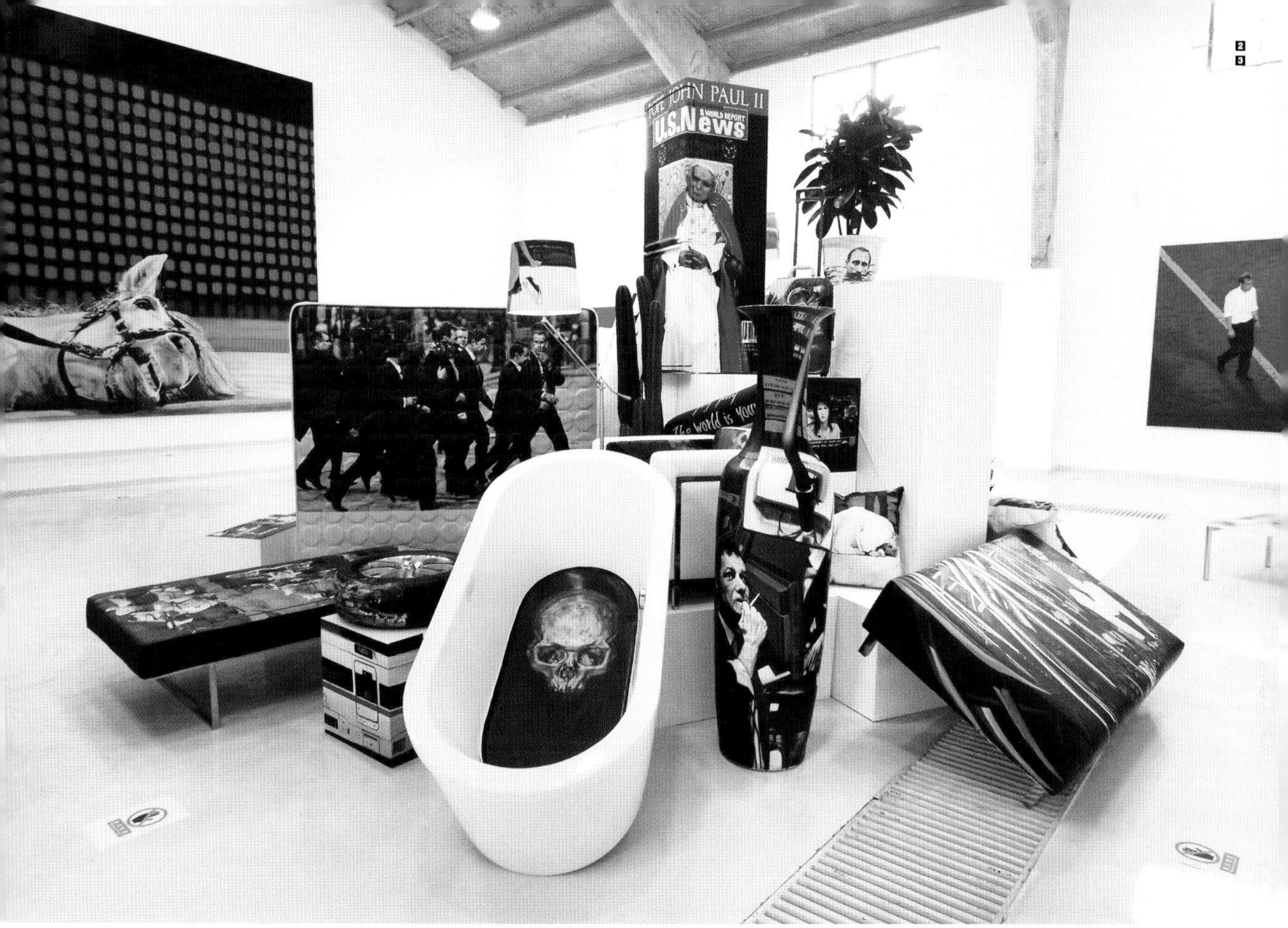

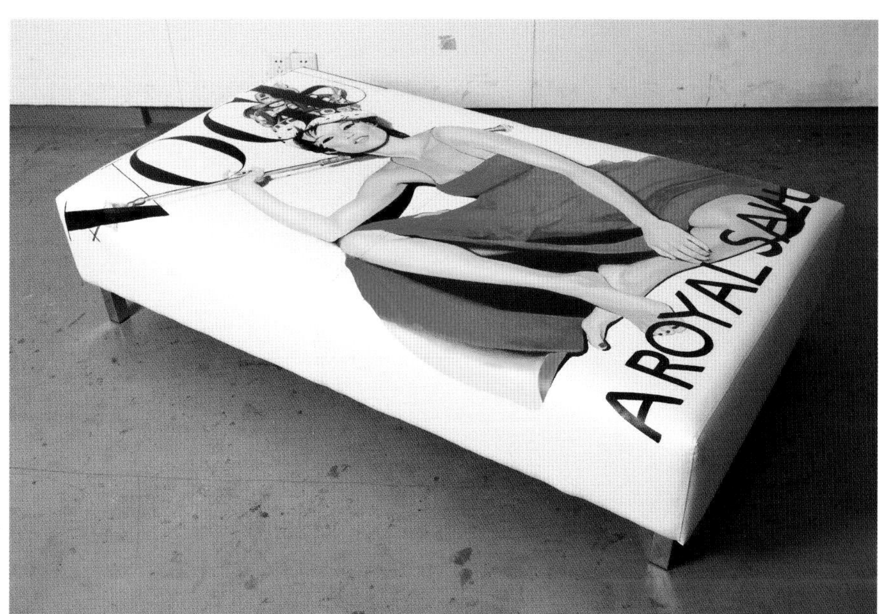

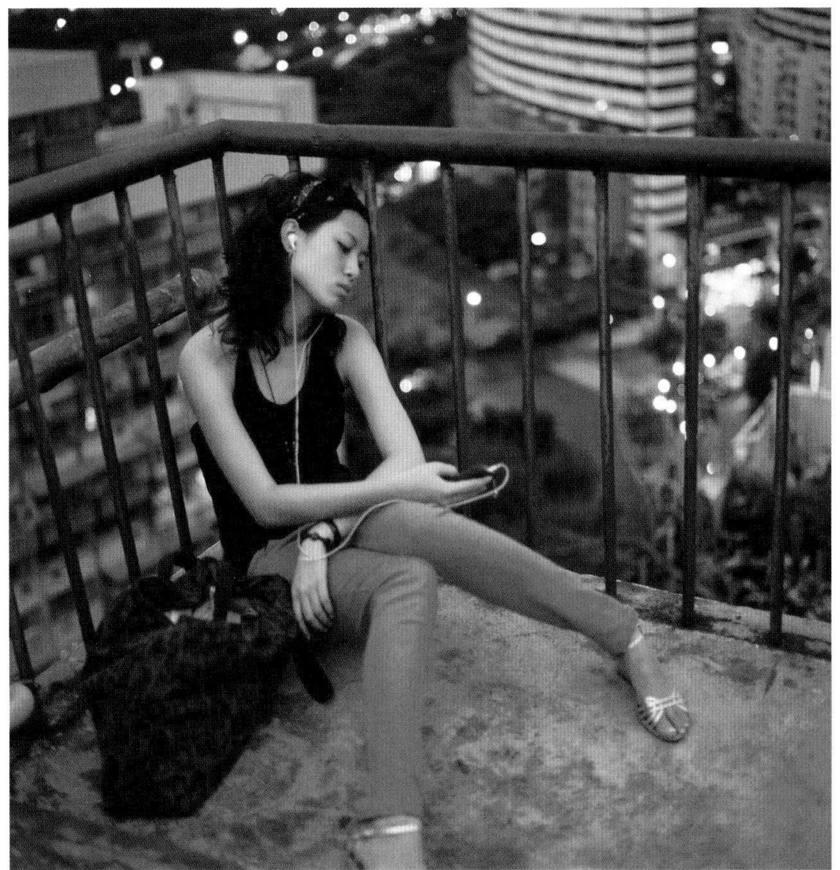

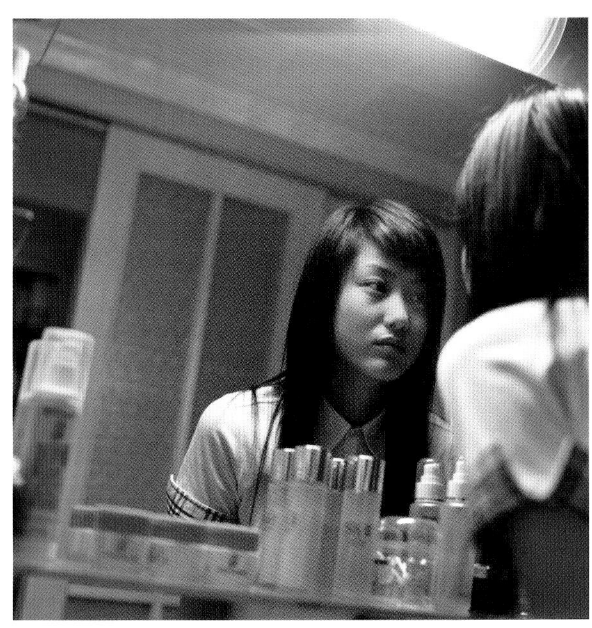

6

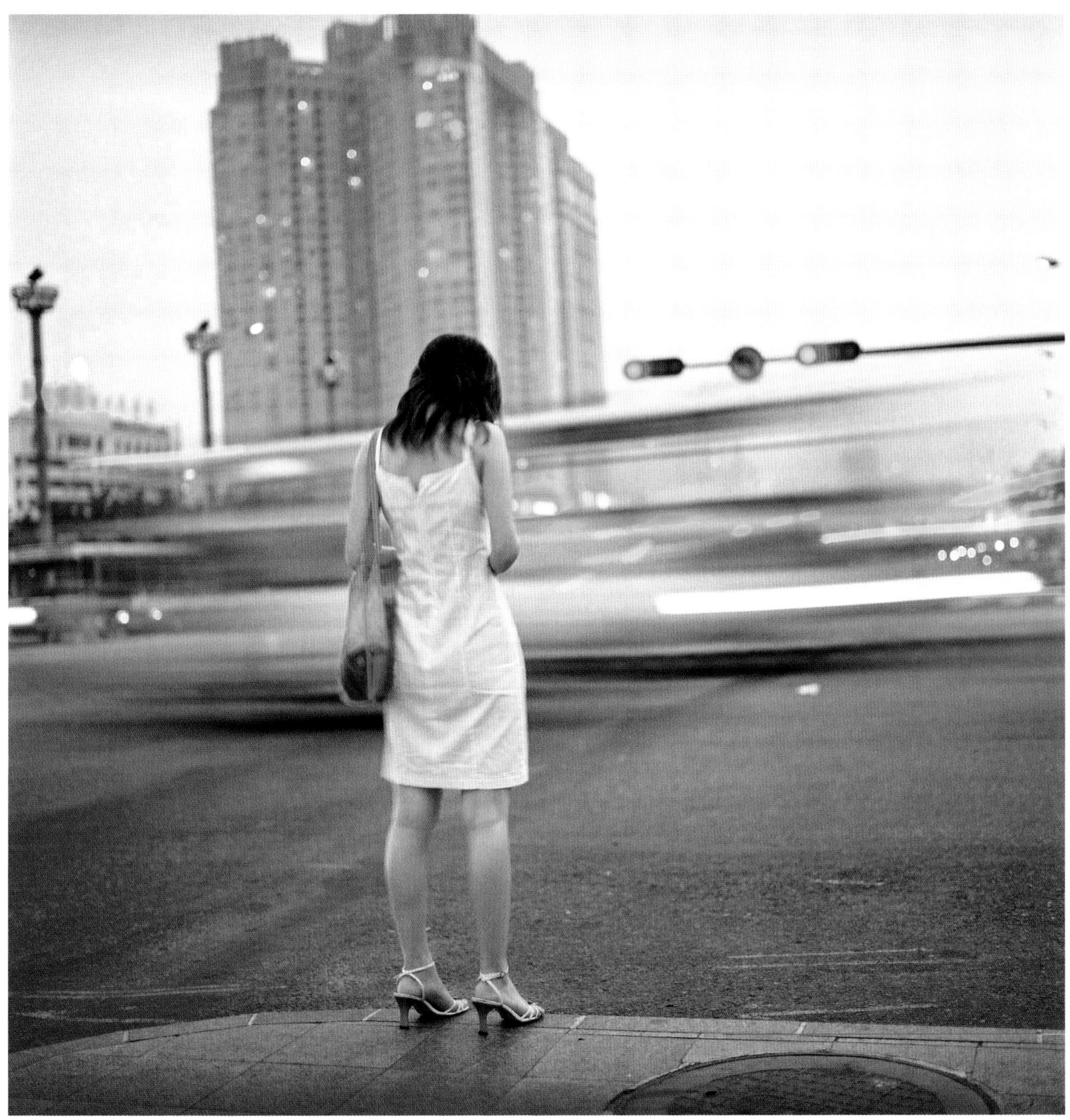

4 ANONYMOUS STILL • 2005 • C-PRINT • 120 x 120 CM

5 THE CRUEL DIARY OF YOUTH • 2003 • C-PRINT • 120 x 120 CM

6 ANONYMOUS STILL • 2004 • C-PRINT • 120 x 120 CM

7

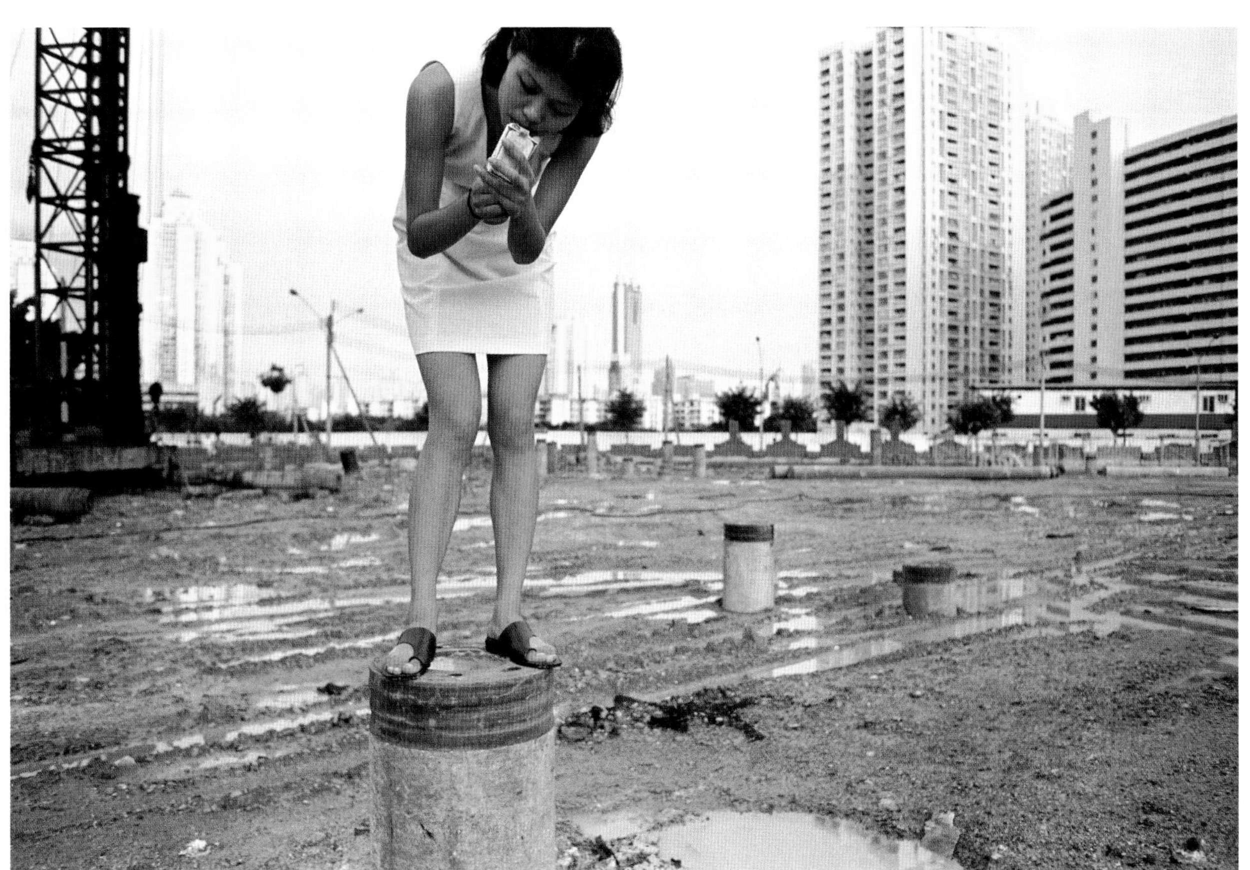

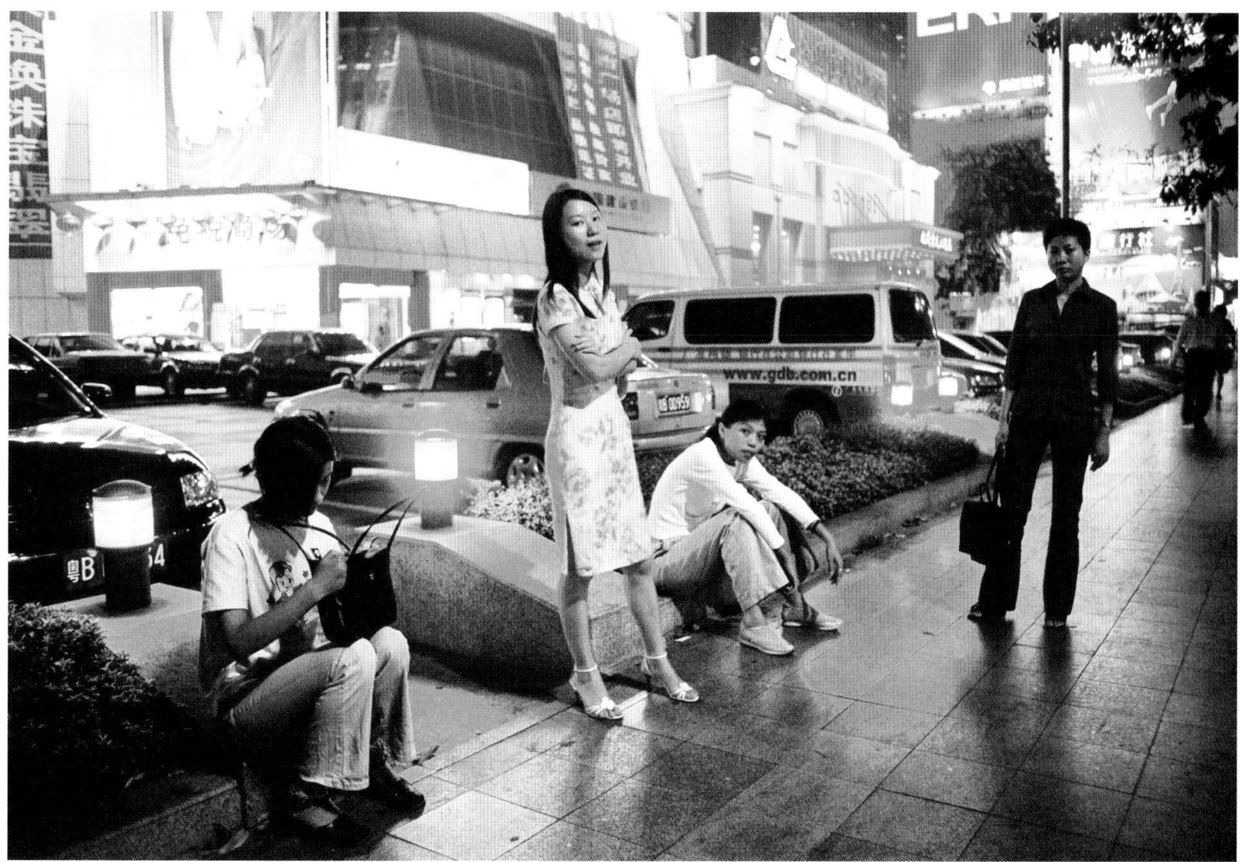

7 THE CRUEL DIARY OF YOUTH – THE DUSK OF GODS • 2000 • C-PRINT • 80 x 120 CM

8 SLEETING SHADOW • 2002 • C-PRINT • 80 x 120 CM

9
10

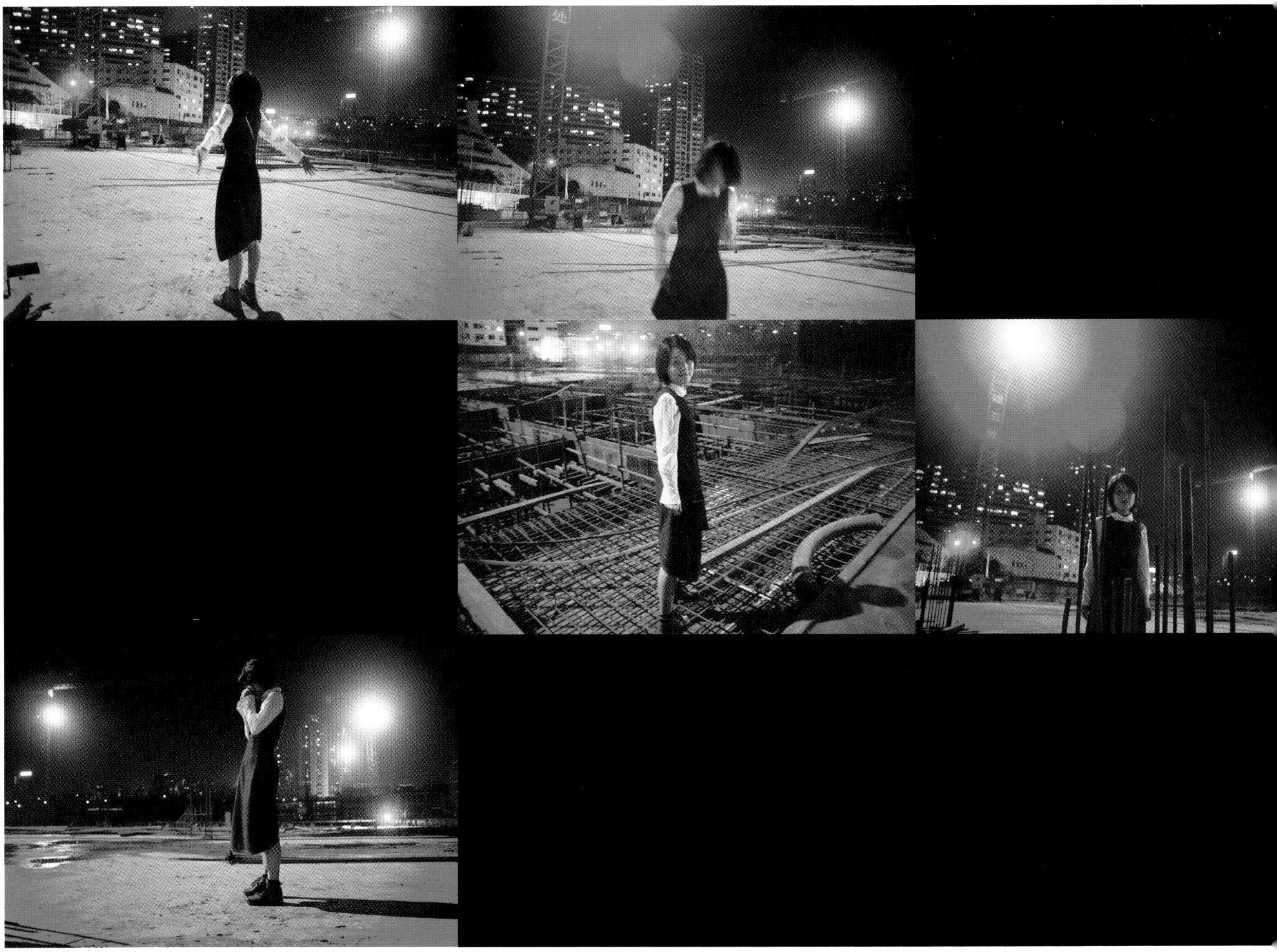

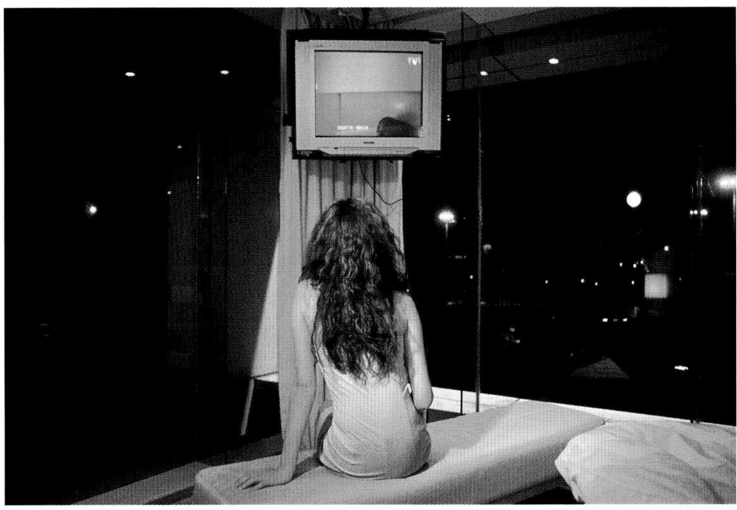

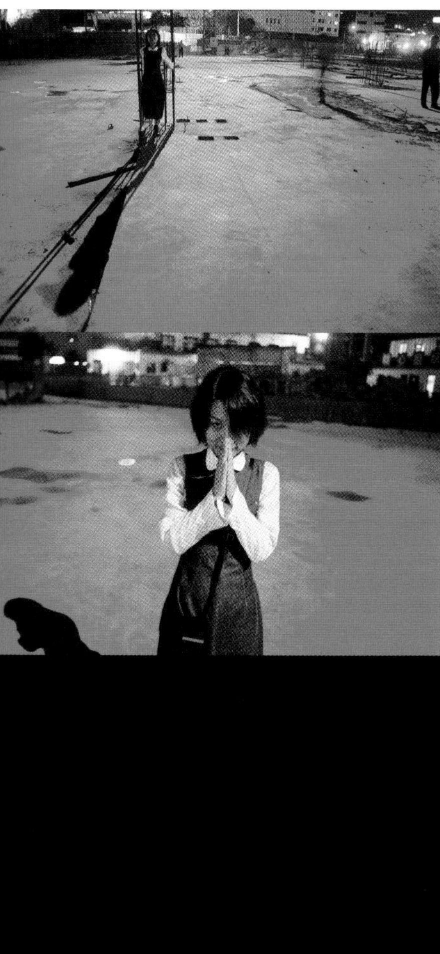

9 CITY LIGHTS • 1999 • C-PRINT • 120 x 240 CM

10 ORECTIC HOTEL • 2003 • C-PRINT • 80 x 120 CM

EXHIBITIONS

SELECTED SOLO EXHIBITIONS

2008
The World is Yours / International Passage,
Tang Contemporary Art,
Beijing, China

2008
Eleven Times a Lady,
Libreria Borges Institute for
Contemporary Art,
Guangzhou, China

2004
City Myths:
Recent Photographs by Yang Yong,
Goedhuis Contemporary,
New York, U.S.

2002
From China: Personal Plan of Yang Yong,
Art Design Institute Linz,
Linz, Austria

SELECTED GROUP EXHIBITIONS

2009
Open Vision
National Gallery,
Prague, Czech Republic

2008
Guangzhou Station:
Review of Chinese Contemporary Art,
Guangdong Museum of Art,
Guangzhou, China

2006
Between Past and Future,
Haus der Kulturen der Welt,
Berlin, Germany

2006
China,
Museum Boijmans van Beuningen,
Rotterdam, The Netherlands

2006
AllLookSame?,
Fondazione Sandretto Re Rebaudengo,
Turin, Italy

2005
The 2nd Guangzhou Triennial,
Guangdong Museum of Art,
Guangzhou, China

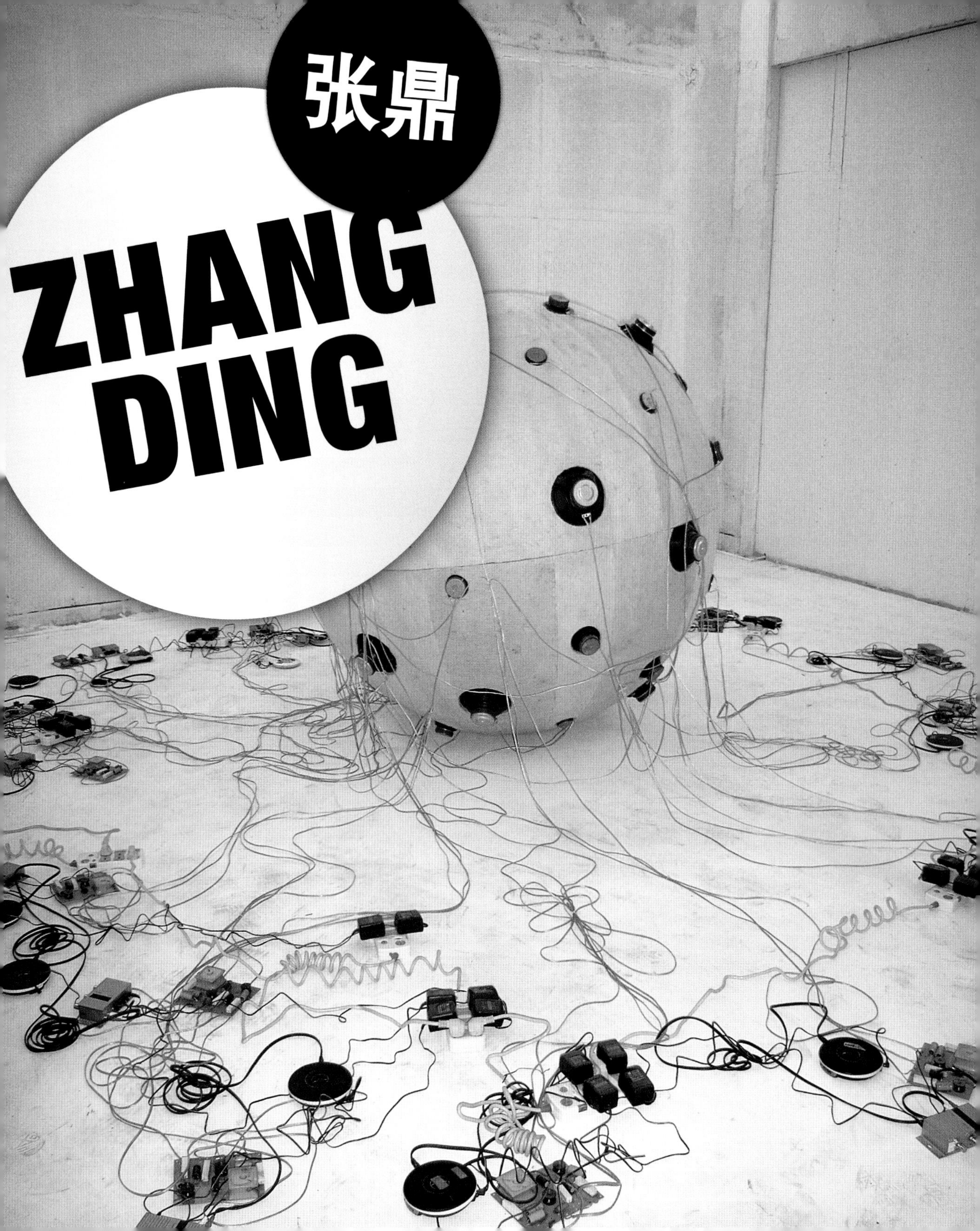
张鼎
ZHANG
DING

NAME
ZHANG DING
BORN IN
1980, GANSU PROVINCE
LIVES IN
SHANGHAI
STUDY
CHINA ACADEMY OF ART, HANGZHOU
MEDIA
INSTALLATION, PERFORMANCE, PHOTOGRAPHY, VIDEO

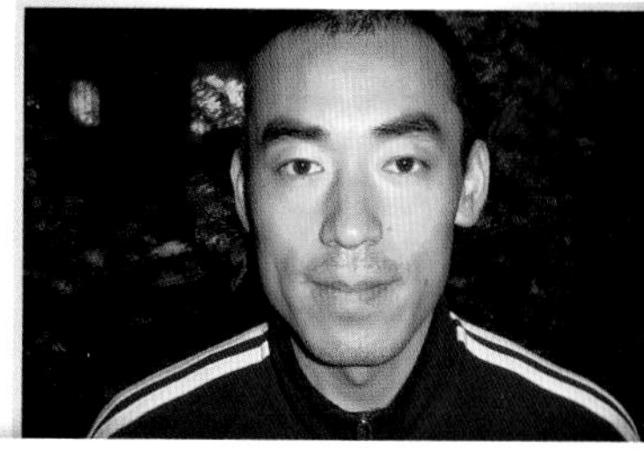

LISTENING TO THOSE WHO CANNOT SPEAK

Zhang Ding, born in 1980, is a native of Lanzhou in the northwestern Chinese province of Gansu. After graduating from the Oil Painting Department of Northwest University for Nationalities in 2003, he studied New Media Art in the Chinese Academy of Art. He made a conscious decision to turn towards creative work in new media such as installations, video, and photography. Zhang Ding's works possess a powerful awareness of reality, but this is not to say that they are concerned with close-up perspectives of the mainstream condition and dominant social trends. He rather involves himself with the "edges" of the isolated, excluded, and alienated, signaling from a distance a downcast substrata of existential reality that does not cooperate with mainstream consciousness. Zhang's works present this dispirited reality through missing persons notices of big cities, abandoned children's playgrounds, muffled city soundscapes, or elderly homosexual transvestites. As an artist of the younger generation, Zhang Ding's concept of art focuses on arranging threads of creativity on top of a microscopic, personal narrative, gradually establishing the sober perspective and language patterns of an observer. In the tiniest imperceptible places, he uncovers, gathers, and manifests the focal points of society's sicknesses. He is in no hurry to give a diagnosis, but instead aims to uncover the wounds; he is always ready to listen.

Lanzhou, Zhang Ding's home, was an important town on the ancient silk route. Today it is a city of turbulence and rampant organized crime but also a center where many ethnicities coexist; its residents are hot-tempered and filled with instability and volatility. This melting pot is precisely what attracted the artist to choose the city as a key subject and background in his works. After Zhang Ding moved to Shanghai, he continued focusing on topics of city life. Out of a newcomer's perspective, he observed his new living conditions. For *Big City* (2004), Zhang Ding photographed various types of missing persons notices in railway and bus stations as well as the subway entrances of Shanghai. It is here that the city's floating population is at its most concentrated. The common feature of these notices was that the missing person in each case was a migrant worker who had come to Shanghai hoping to make ends meet. These rootless people are swept along by fate; their transient identities effectively invisible to the city make it unlikely to find clues to their whereabouts when they are lost, let alone for anyone to be concerned about them. These frail individual lives are lowly and powerless in the face of the vast, complex mechanisms by which the city operates, and this type of collective sinking or disappearance makes them even harder to seek out. Consequently, Zhang Ding's works display a concern with the inescapability and absence of choice inherent in fate and hardship.

Lanzhou is an ethnic minority region that is home to large numbers of Muslims, and it is therefore no surprise that issues of ethnicity can also be seen in Zhang Ding's work. However, Zhang Ding does not use ethnic issues as a springboard for any particular position or declaration; what he is concerned with is the resulting personal and collective relationships brought about by these issues. In collective situations, the individual is shifted into a primeval, unconscious state, and so collective action often takes barbaric forms such as riots or even rebellions. The installation *N kilometers towards the West* (2006) is a riot of collected sounds. Various types of sound ricochet around inside a giant ball, which is covered with wool blankets. These sounds, gathered from everyday life on a late spring day in Gansu, are transmitted back inside via dozens of megaphones connected to the ball, forming an expanding yet sealed soundscape of noise. In *The 57th Ethny* (2005), the artist interprets concepts of race and ethnicity formation and extinction, while *My Photographs* (2006), in which Zhang Ding combines pornographic images downloaded from the Internet with fictional interviews, hones in on the same themes but transposes them into a witty cocktail.

In 2005, Zhang Ding began his *Pry* series of works, which explores topics including survival, destiny, and reality. This series will include a total of seven videos out of which four are already completed; the subjects are elderly homosexual transvestites, Muslim youth, living Buddhas, and a male fortune-teller. Each of these represent both typicality and difference – in the sense of gender, religion, and politics – but they also share certain forms of innate, predestined properties in their fates which leave them wavering, resigned, resolute, or powerless to choose. Recognition of one's innate destiny and identity is more often than not an unconscious process, but it nevertheless includes an obvious degree of self-consciousness. In this sense they are self-aware, self-determining individuals. Zhang Ding's creative intention remained understated during the filming process as he strove to avoid prompting or directing the subjects of the films, instead allowing them to tell their own stories until they said everything they had to say. The documentary nature of the films is reinforced by their presentation in installation form. Photographs hung over wooden cabinets appear more like photographic seals bearing witness to the reality behind the work. For *Drawers* (2006), Zhang Ding used a similar installation. Looking into the drawers of timeworn commodes, one can see many light boxes, picturing commodities of daily life and snapshots of various scenarios. The drawer functions like a container, which can receive but also release fragments of life. The artist calls this "assemblies of reality."

In most of Zhang Ding's works collective self-reflection and deconstruction serve as his topics. Coherently examined, all of his works reflect the intensity and complexity of the social reality, and we shouldn't concentrate too much on the surface and outer appearance, but primarily reflect on their context.

By Azure (Wei) Wu

1

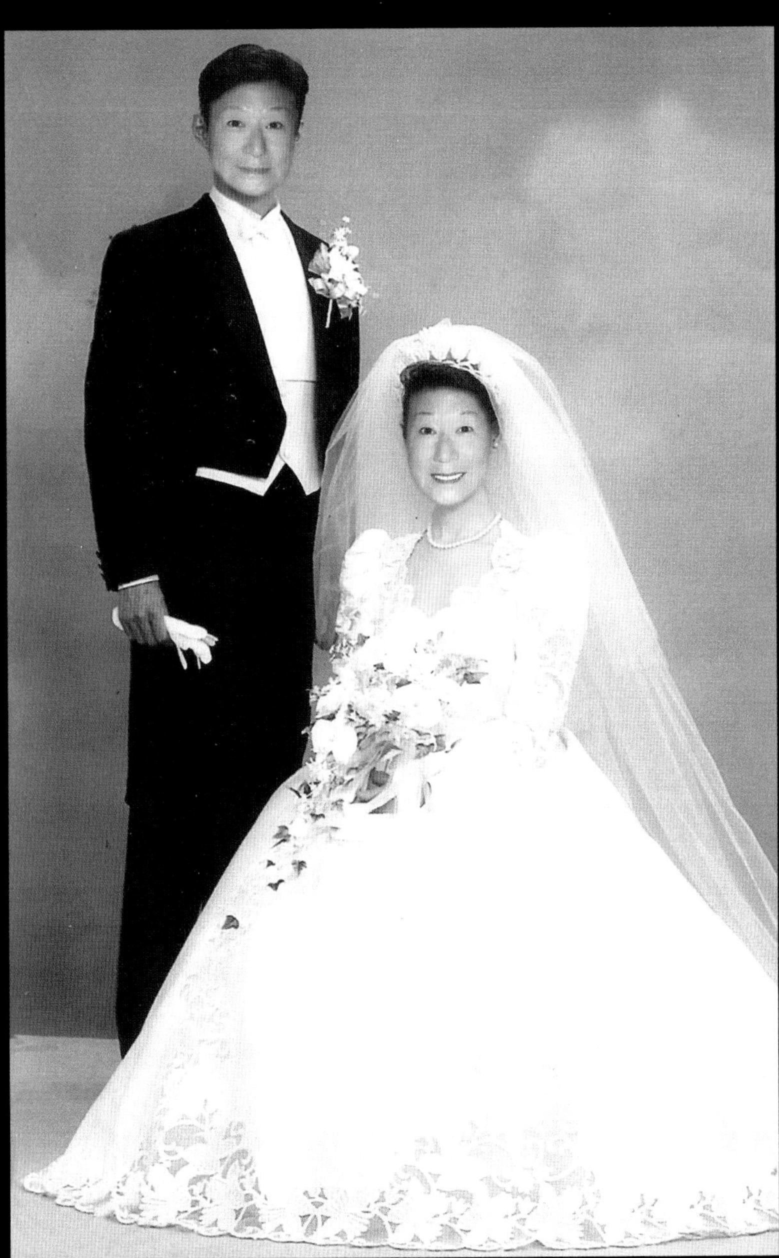

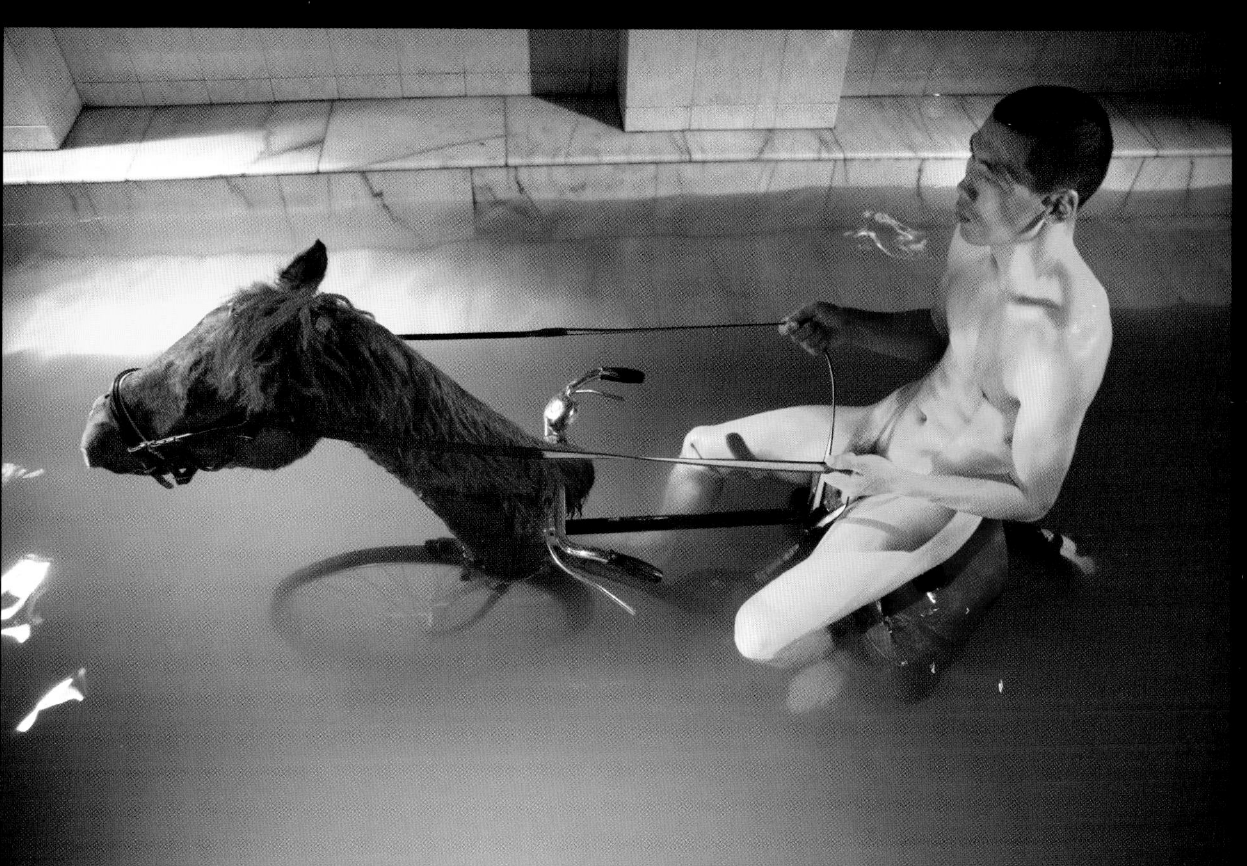

1 SONG MO (PRY SERIES) • 2005 • VIDEO • 20'

2 BIG TIME • 2007 • VIDEO • 14'

3

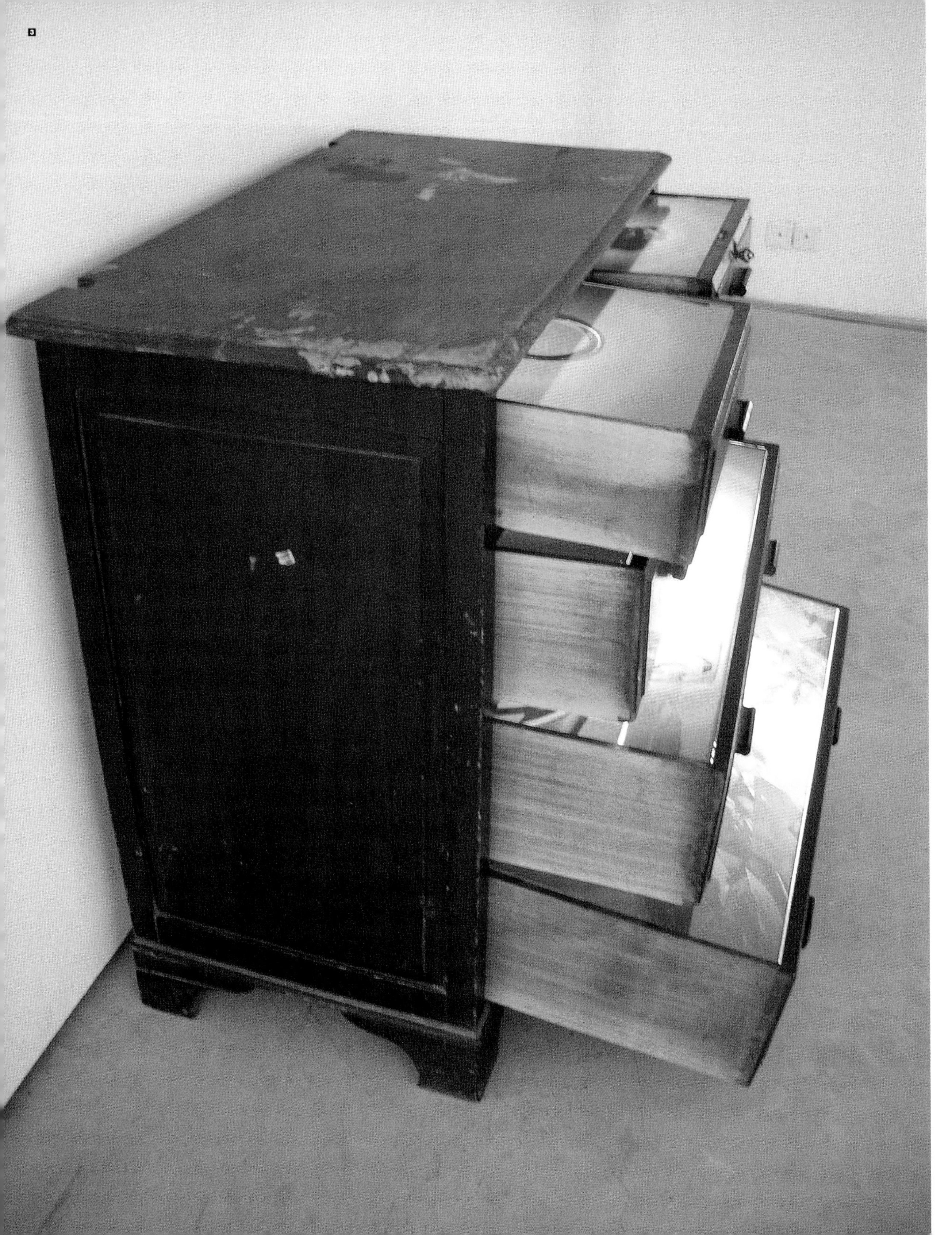

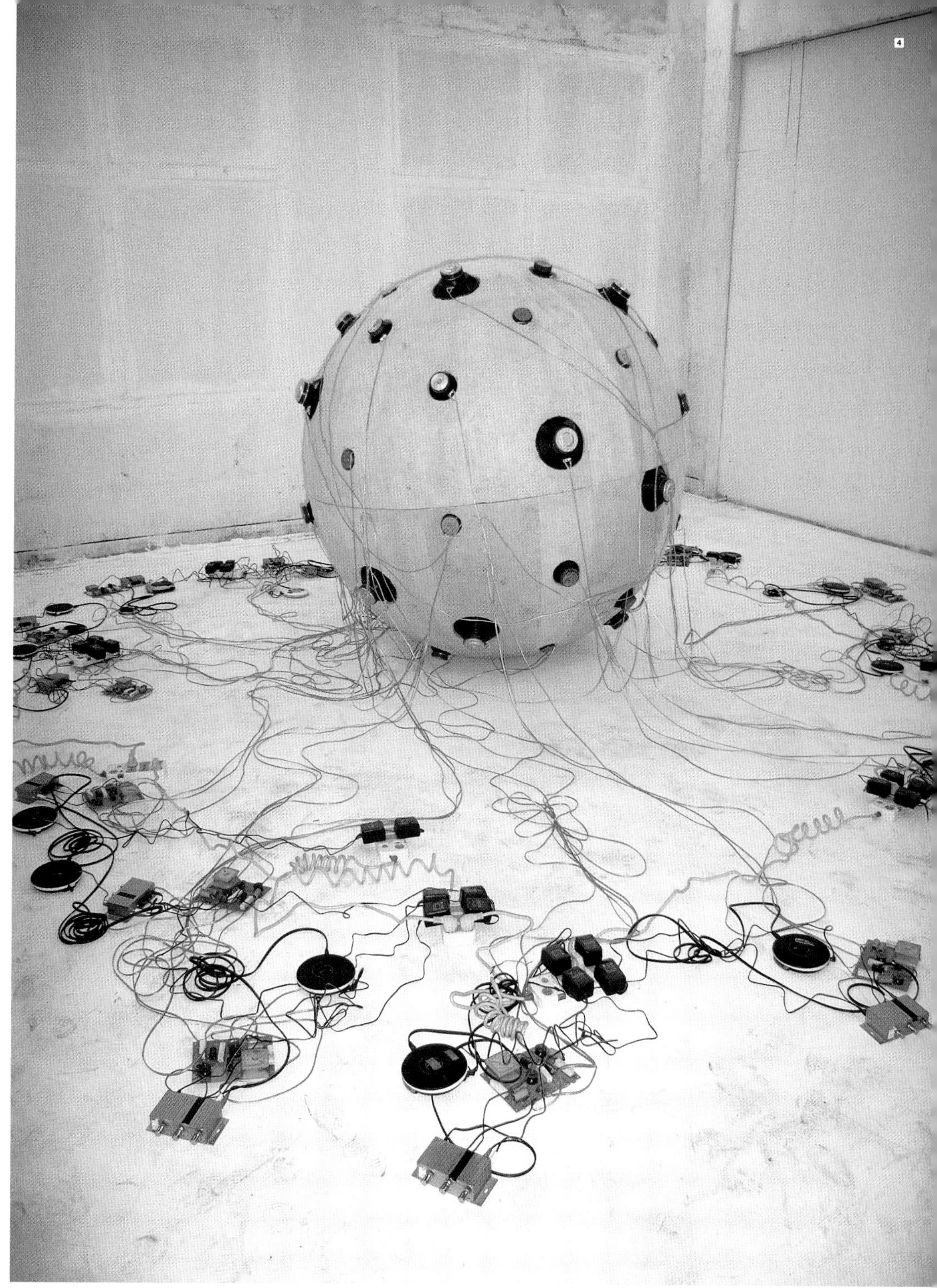

3 DRAWERS • 2006 • INSTALLATION: FURNITURE, LIGHT BOXES • SIZE VARIES

4 N KILOMETERS TOWARDS THE WEST • 2006 • SOUND INSTALLATION • 165 CM DIAMETER

5

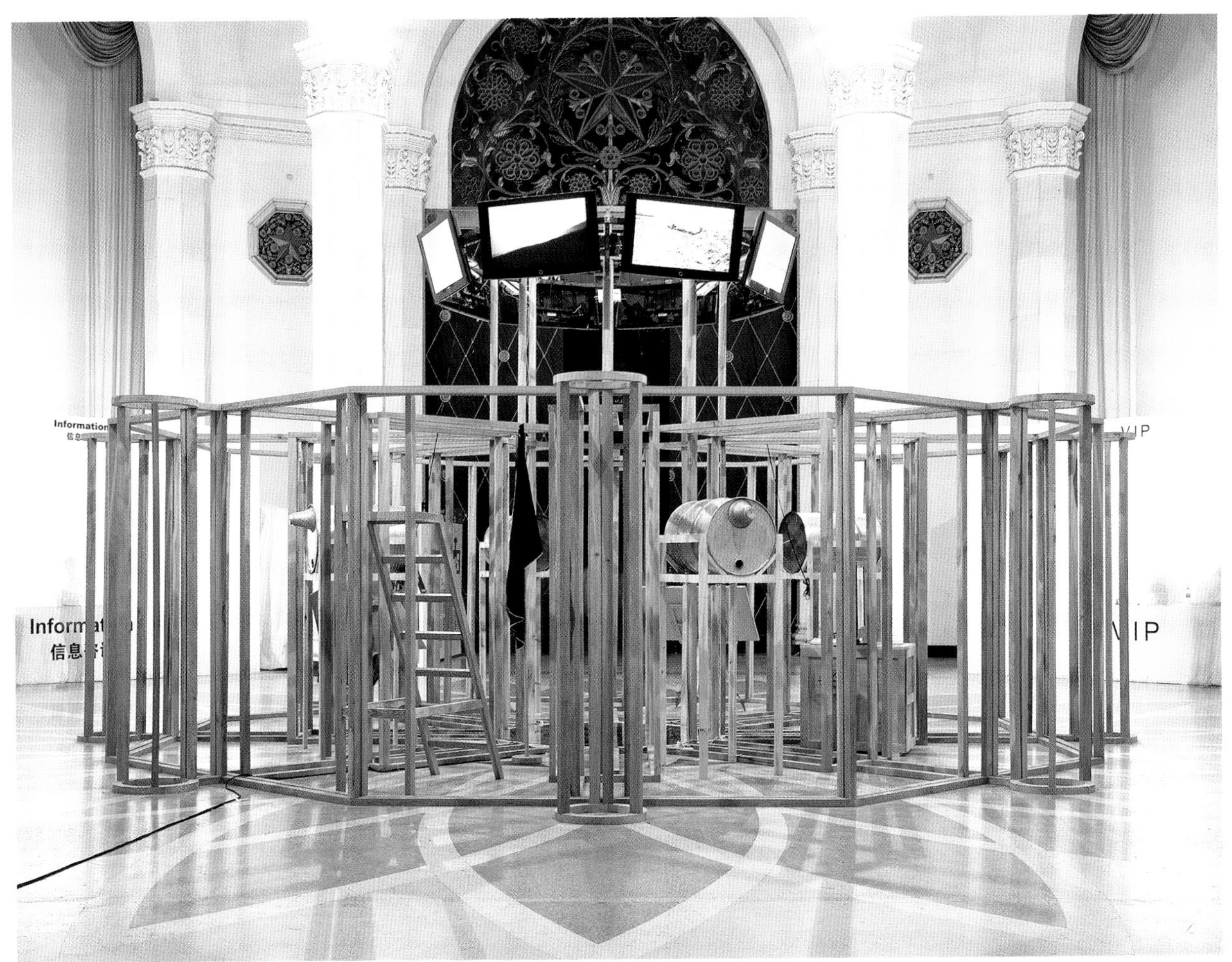

5 THE DREAM OF YABULAI • 2008 • WOOD CONSTRUCTION,
9-CHANNEL VIDEO INSTALLATION • 385 × 972 × 972 CM

6 THEIR COMMON AMUSEMENT PARK • 2006 • C-PRINT • 57.6 × 43.3 CM

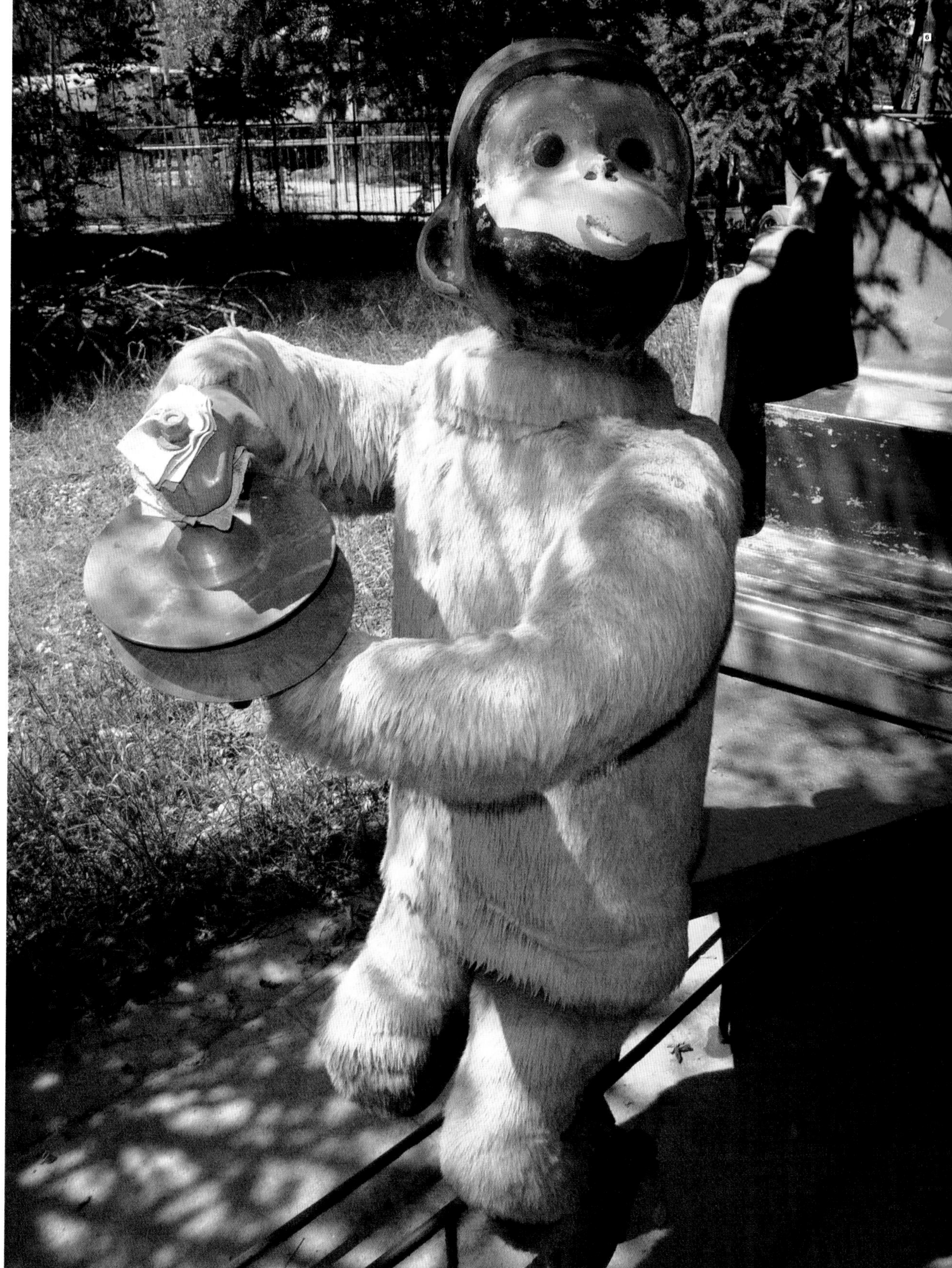

6

7
8

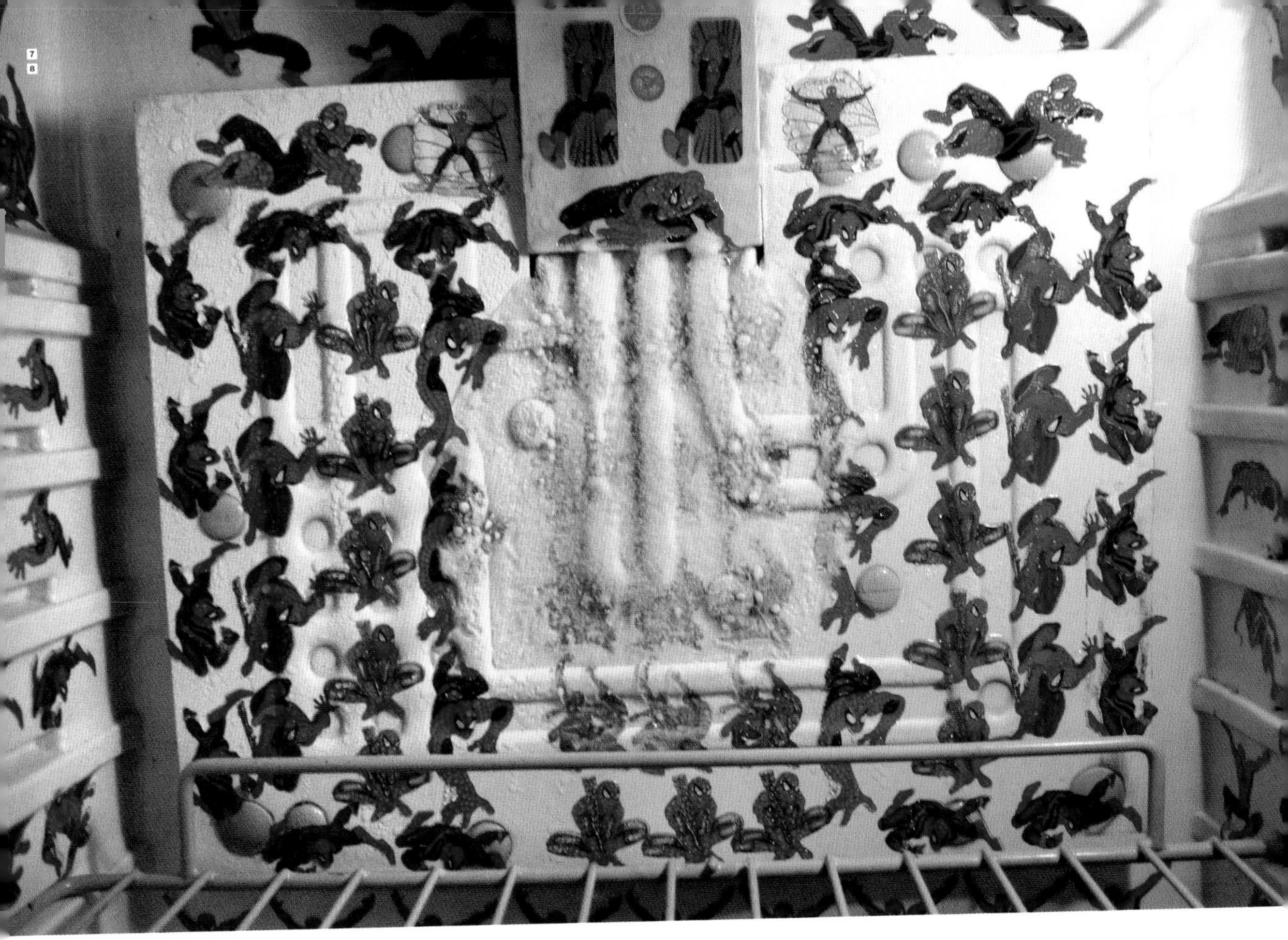

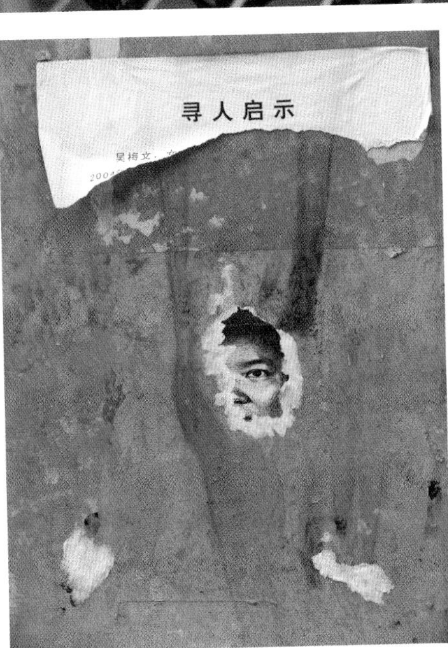

7 HEROISM IS MAFIOSIC BY NATURE • 2005 • INSTALLATION

8 BIG CITY • 2004 • C-PRINT • 101 x 76 CM

QUESTIONNAIRE

5/3/08 • SHANGHAI

WHAT WAS YOUR FAVORITE CHILDHOOD TOY?

Handmade toys.

WHAT DID YOUR PARENTS SAY TO YOU MOST OFTEN?

"What have you been doing recently?"

HOW DO YOU TRY TO STAY HEALTHY IN YOUR EVERYDAY LIFE?

I don't care much about my health.

WHAT HAVE YOU BEEN WISHING FOR MOST RECENTLY?

To go driving to new places with my car.

DO YOU BELIEVE IN TRUE LOVE?

Yes!

WHAT DOES YOUR IDEAL LIVING ENVIRONMENT LOOK LIKE?

To be able to share good times with good friends.

FROM WHICH TYPE OF MEDIA DO YOU DERIVE MOST OF YOUR INSPIRATION?

I get inspiration from traveling and backpacking.

WHAT DO YOU LIKE/DISLIKE ABOUT BEING AN ARTIST?

The feeling of being an artist.

HOW DO YOU COMMUNICATE WITH THE AUDIENCE IN YOUR ART?

Through creating an atmosphere that suits my works.

IF YOU HAD FIVE WORDS TO DESCRIBE YOUR GENERATION, WHAT WOULD THEY BE?

Extroverted, lovable, selfish, bored, and lost.

IF THE WHOLE WORLD WOULD LISTEN TO YOU FOR FIFTEEN SECONDS, WHAT WOULD YOU SAY?

"Hi guys, how are you?"

EXHIBITIONS

SELECTED SOLO EXHIBITIONS

2009
Law,
ShanghArt,
Beijing, China

2008
Wind,
Krinzinger Projekte,
Vienna, Austria

2007
N Kilometers Towards the West,
ShanghART F-Space,
Shanghai, China

SELECTED GROUP EXHIBITIONS

2008
Building Code Violations II,
Long March Space,
Beijing, China

2007
China Power Station: Part II,
Astrup Fearnley Museum of Modern Art,
Oslo, Norway

2007
Artissima Cinema, Shanghype!: Portrait of the City from Dawn to Dusk,
Mirafiori Motor Village,
Turin, Italy

2006
CineCity: The Brighton Film Festival,
Brighton, U.K.

2006
Restless: Photography and New Media,
MoCA,
Shanghai, China

2005
The 2nd Guangzhou Triennial: Self Organisation-BizART,
Xinyi International Club,
Guangzhou, China

2004
Dial 62761232,
BizArt Art Center,
Shanghai, China

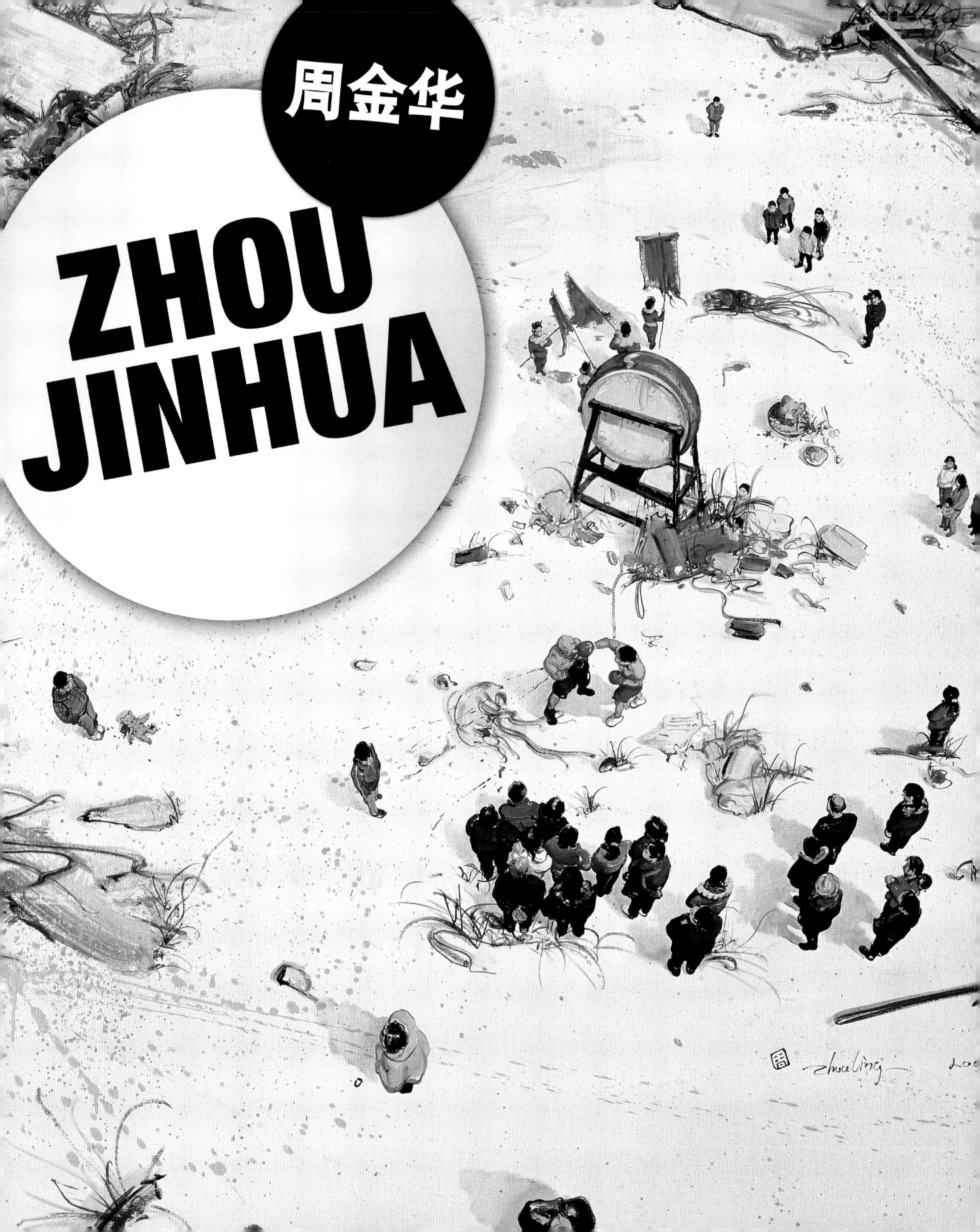
周金华
ZHOU
JINHUA

NAME
ZHOU JINHUA
BORN IN
1978, DEYANG
LIVES IN
BEIJING
STUDY
SICHUAN INSTITUTE OF FINE ARTS, CHONGQING
MEDIA
PAINTING

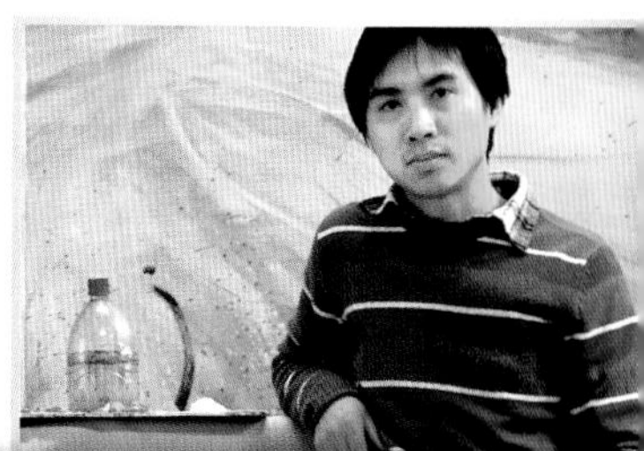

IN THE DISTANCE, SO NEAR

Beijing artist Zhou Jinhua feels deeply connected to the people he observes and paints from a more or less considerable distance. "The bird's-eye view I adopt for my pictures is not a position of power for me – I need distance from the event in order to understand what's happening there."

The artist identifies himself as a pessimist; his mood: melancholy. His life experiences don't exactly incline him to a feeling of confidence, especially since he moved from Sichuan to Beijing. He is aware of the contradictory situation in which he lives: on the one hand availing himself of the advantages of the metropolis, and on the other realizing that the rapid modernization of the city comes at a cost. His works allow for this ambivalence, conveying the double standard and ostensible harmlessness of the reality that surrounds him in the varied play of near and far.

From afar, Zhou Jinhua's works – often in large format – have a contemplative effect. For the flat and largely unformed backgrounds, the artist chooses a predominantly friendly palette, such as lilac, mint, egg yolk yellow, or ochre. It is only when one stares closely at a detail that the scene's sometimes apocalyptical dimensions become clear. What, for example, is going on in the *Spotty-Series* (2005)? A filthy, oily film flows over portions of the canvas. Between the people who perambulate alone or in groups and a clearly unmotivated manner across the pictorial space, red spots appear again and again. Blood? *Freedom of Travel* (2007) presents an exceptionally macabre scenario: a seemingly endless row of waiting people of which the first sink down and are dragged off over the floor, their wrists bound, in the direction of a luxuriant batch of flowers. Their suitcases pile up between uniformed characters armed with bludgeons. Off to the side lovers are amusing themselves. Where does this travel lead to?

In the early phases of his artistic career, Zhou Jinhua photographed various scenes of bridges or high-rises. But the results left him dissatisfied. Since the completion of his studies he has been painting his miniature people in oil on canvas. "Painting gives me the freedom to choose which perspective I will take, how much I want to empathize with a single person, or if I should focus my observation on humanity in general."

Zhou Jinhua's tenor is deeply molded by traditional Chinese art, literature, and philosophy. The open spaces in his pictures clearly indicate a reverence for traditional landscape painting. These spaces, so particular to the "Mountain and River Painting" scrolls (Chinese: *shan shui hua*) still highly valued today, offer the viewer a place to reflect. The lack of a single perspective, too, owes itself to the guiding maxims of the Chinese masters – that no one particular perspective should dominate the picture. It is the task of art to mirror ideas that are valid beyond the moment. *The Recluse* (2006), however, exposes a highly conceited and trivial take on religion. Leaning on the aesthetic of traditional Chinese landscape painting, little details of the composition point to the illusory nature of the country idyll: electrical cables run into the hermitage and urbanite clothing hangs on a drying line, while the weekend Buddhists in monks' robes sit on the floor.

As a matter of course borrowings from Confucius or Lao-tzu flow into Zhou Jinhua's ponderings and shape the values of his own life. "Confucius says one must grapple with both the positive and negative sides of life, and may not permanently withdraw oneself from society." The viewer can reproduce the artist's inner deliberation with his own eyes, going from picture to picture and allowing himself to be drawn in as if looking through a telephoto lens. Only one who takes the time to honor the pictures' details, with its central theme and many subsidiary scenarios, will understand the full story.

Sometimes it's an abstract idea that initiates a composition, sometimes an observation which Zhou Jinhua has captured in a photograph, sometimes it's an article or picture in a newspaper. The sources of inspiration are no longer recognizable in the work itself. His stock of themes is simply inexhaustible: fantastical end-time scenarios in which people go on a pilgrimage to a glowing cleft in the earth (*Outing*, 2006), or where the beggarly remains of a ship in a desert landscape proffer little hope to the people stranded there (*Sinking Ship*, 2006); the absurd disparity between a totally desolate neighborhood and an undamaged statue of Mao towering into the sky (*After the Storm 2*, 2007); the parody of pseudo-nature-loving urbanites in *The Long Weekend* (2006). One of his newest pictures makes an exception by alluding directly to a concrete experience based on international headlines. It shows the last house of a settlement in the southern Chinese city of Chongqing that has fallen victim to China's rampant modernization madness. For weeks, a lone occupant resisted eviction and refused to leave his house. This picture is also notable for the ink wash- or watercolor-like appearance with which Zhou Jinhua forms the mid- and background. It clearly documents a compositional redefining of the image plane.

In *Tragedy* (2006), Zhou Jinhua refers to one of his favorite Western artists Pieter Bruegel. Despite the artist's strong leanings toward his own tradition, the miniature-packed and grotesquely overcrowded environments common to both artists allow one to draw parallels between the painter of the Dutch Renaissance and the Chinese artist of the present. And yet another thing binds the two: to this day, art history has trouble fitting Bruegel into any established genre or category.

By Ulrike Münter

1

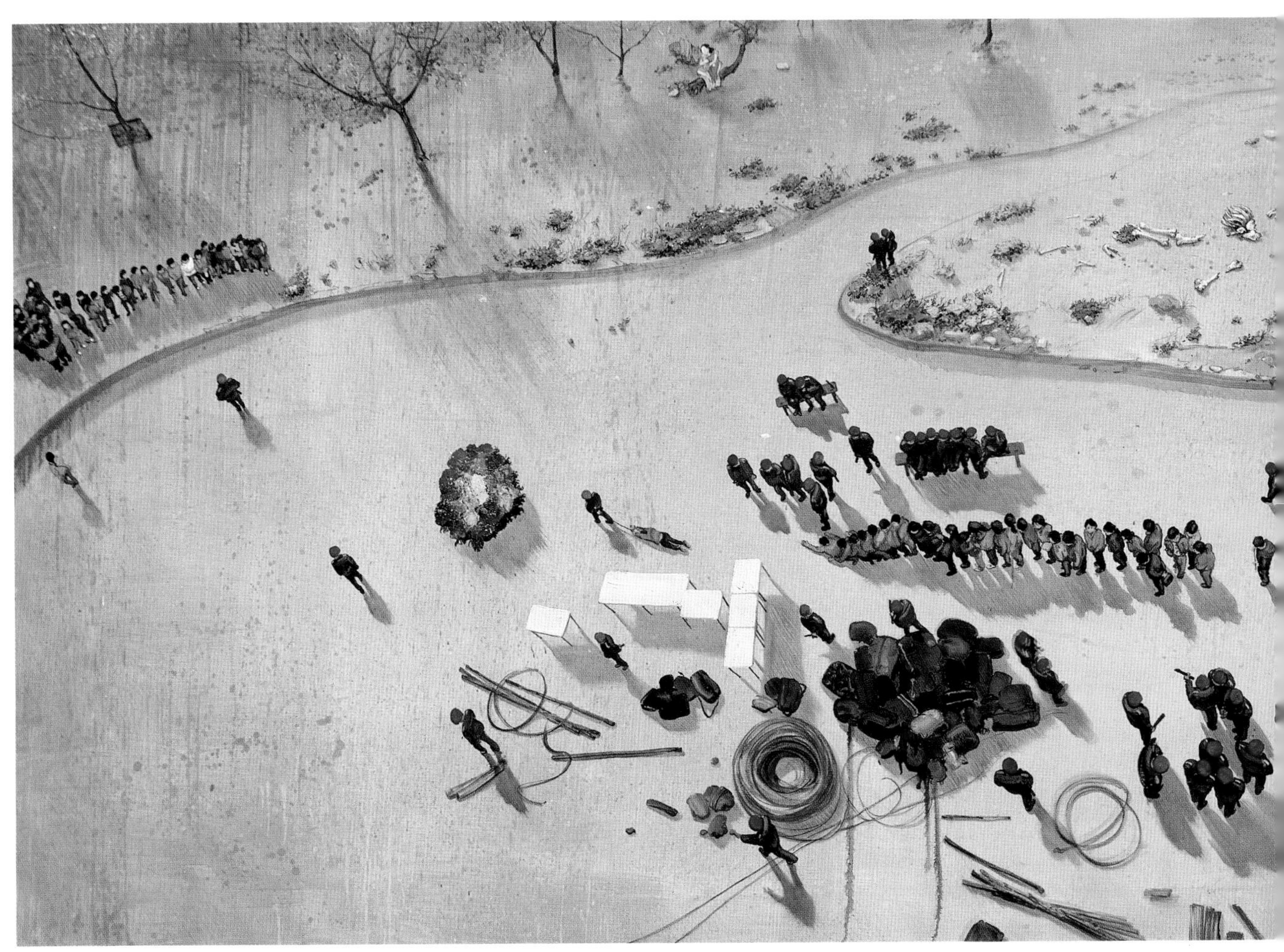

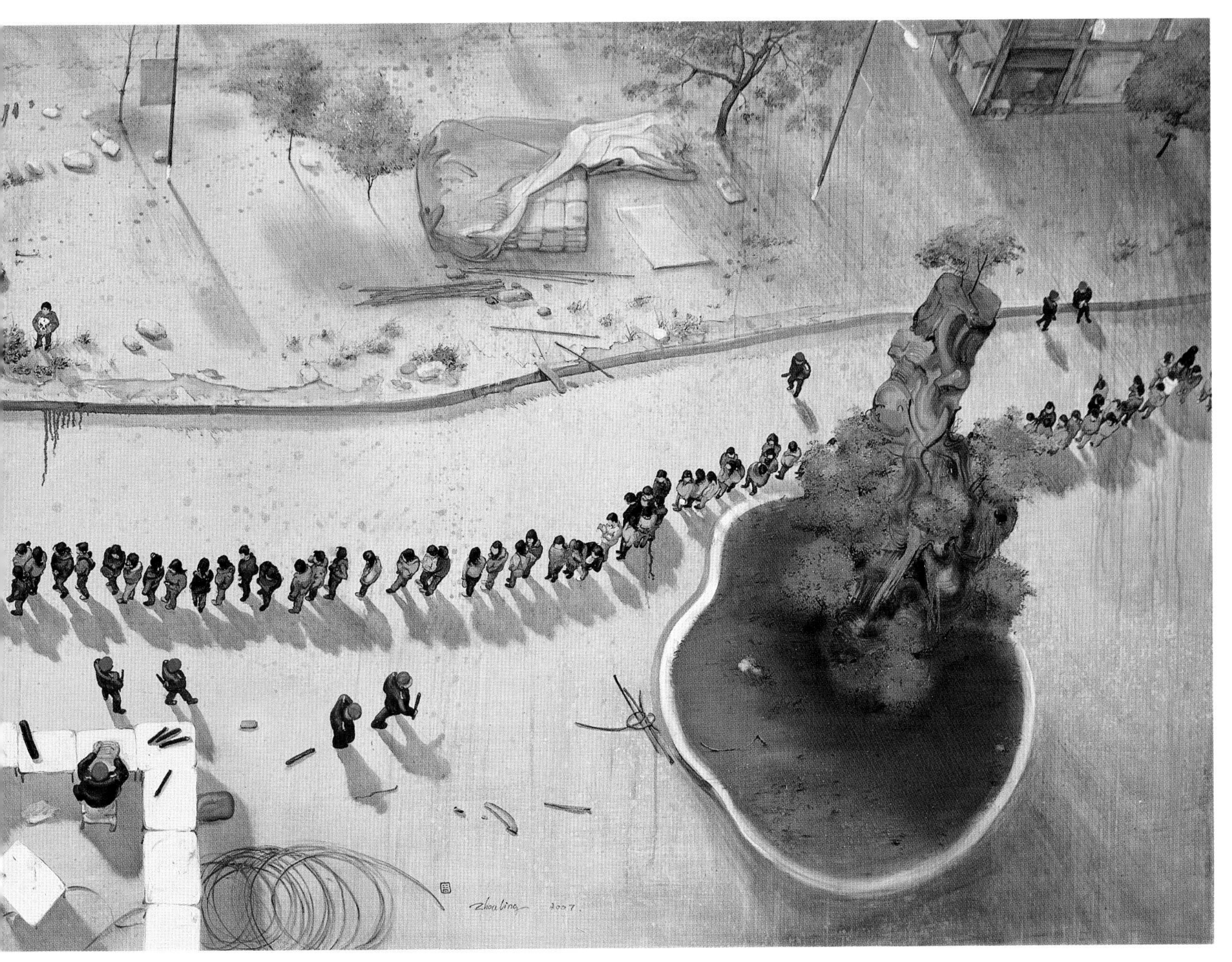

1 FREEDOM OF TRAVEL • 2007 • OIL ON CANVAS • 150 x 400 CM

2

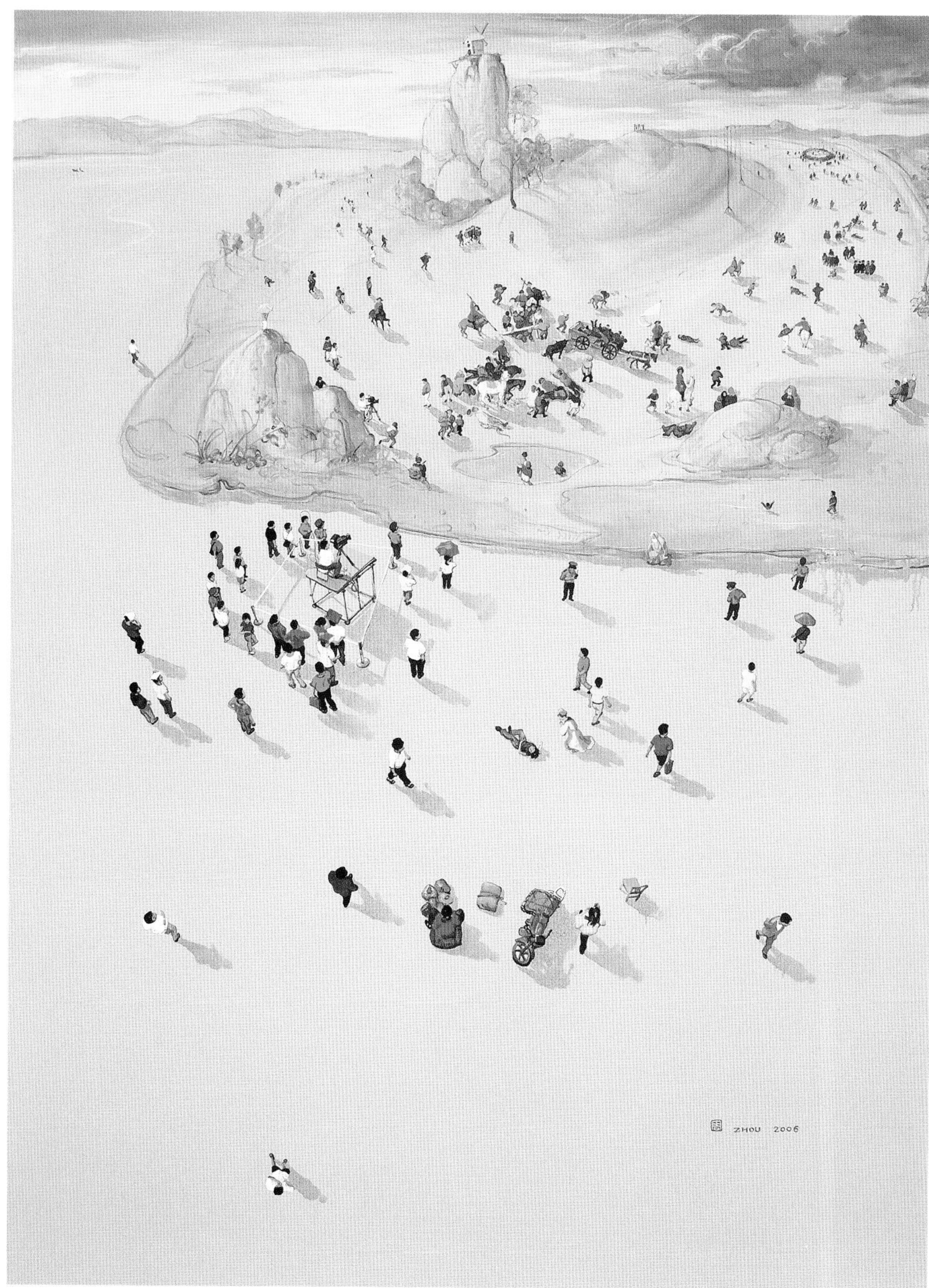

2 TRAGEDY • 2006 • OIL ON CANVAS • 200 x 150 CM

3 AFTER THE STORM NO. 2 • 2007 • OIL ON CANVAS • 180 x 150 CM

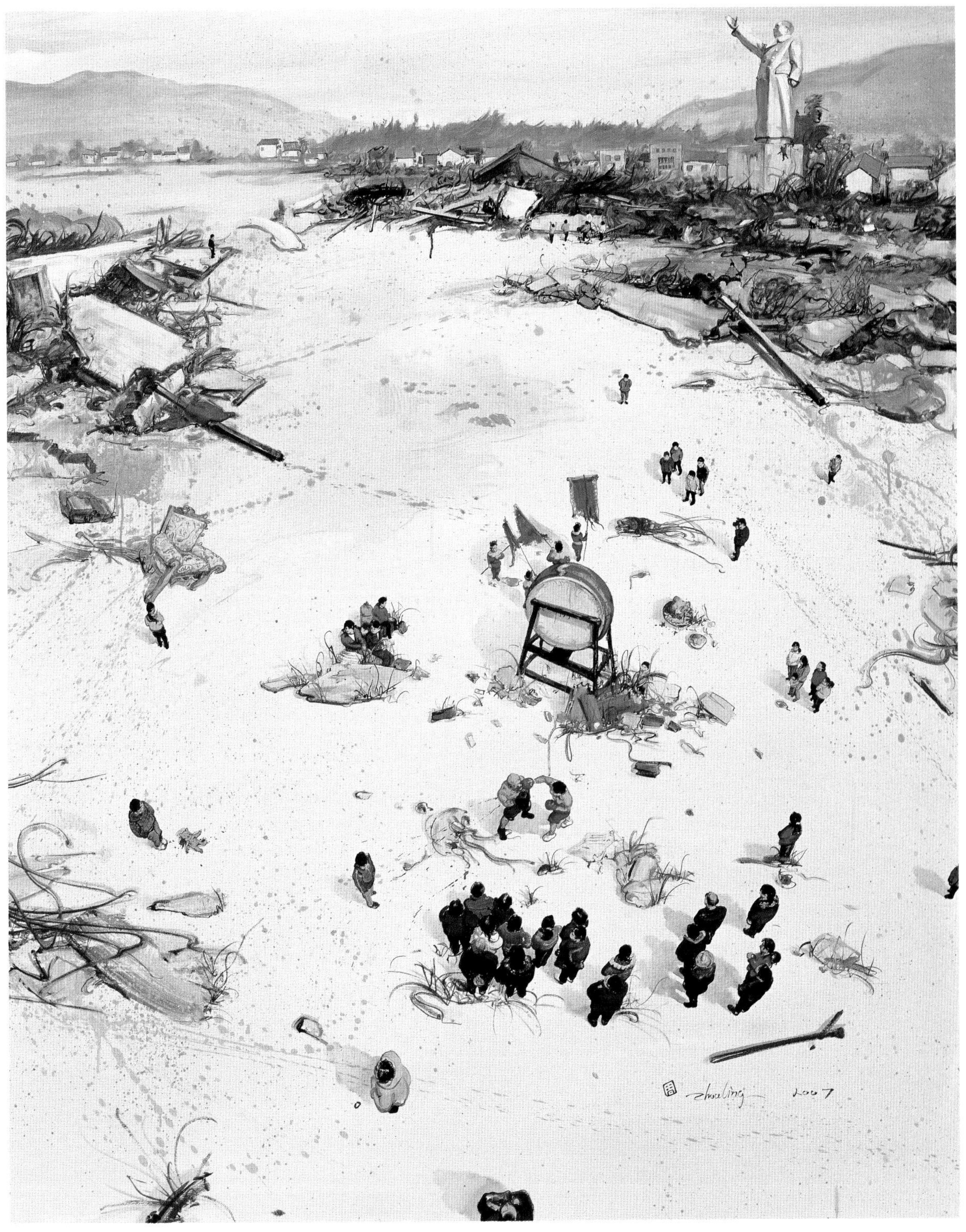

4

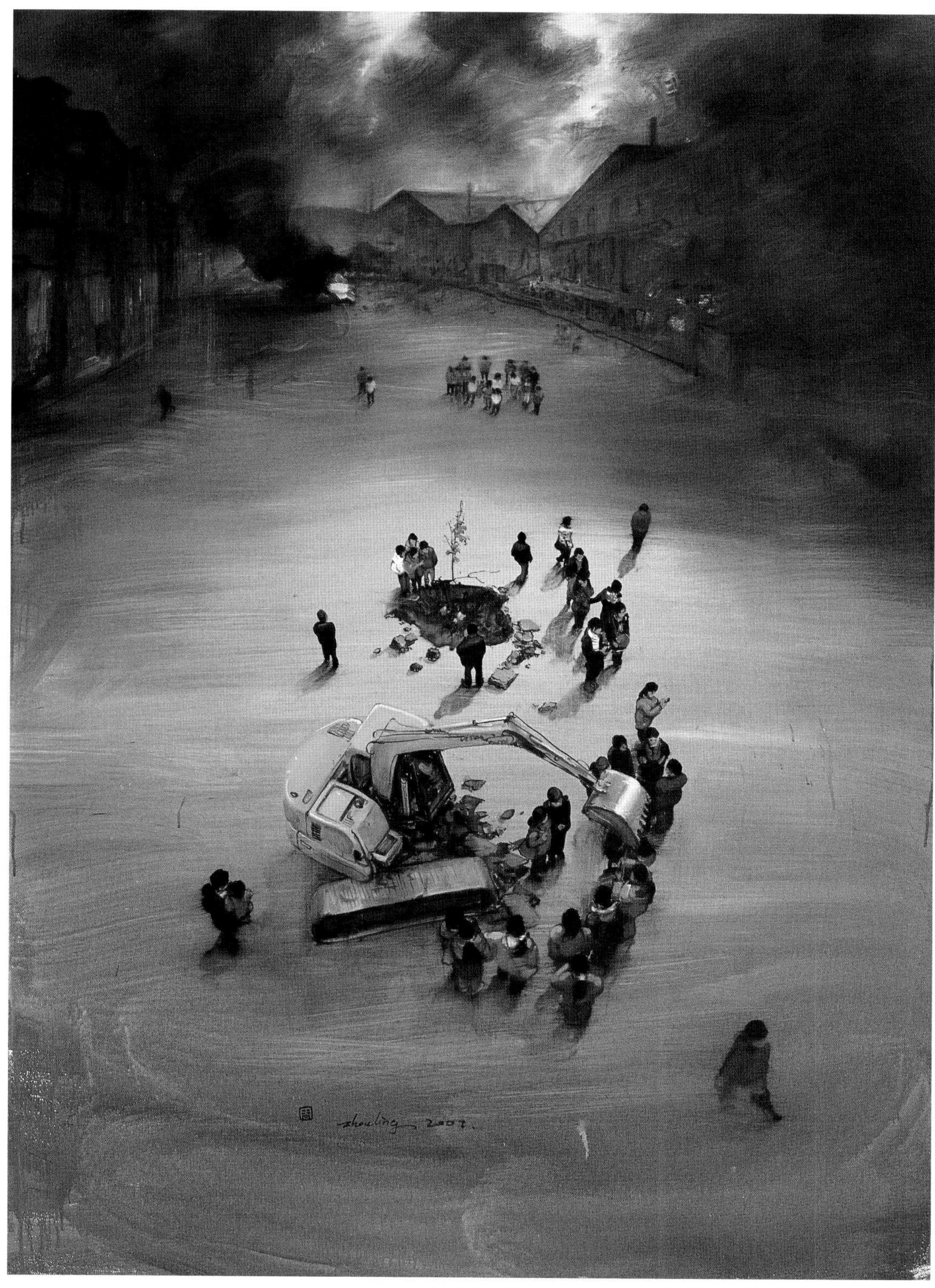

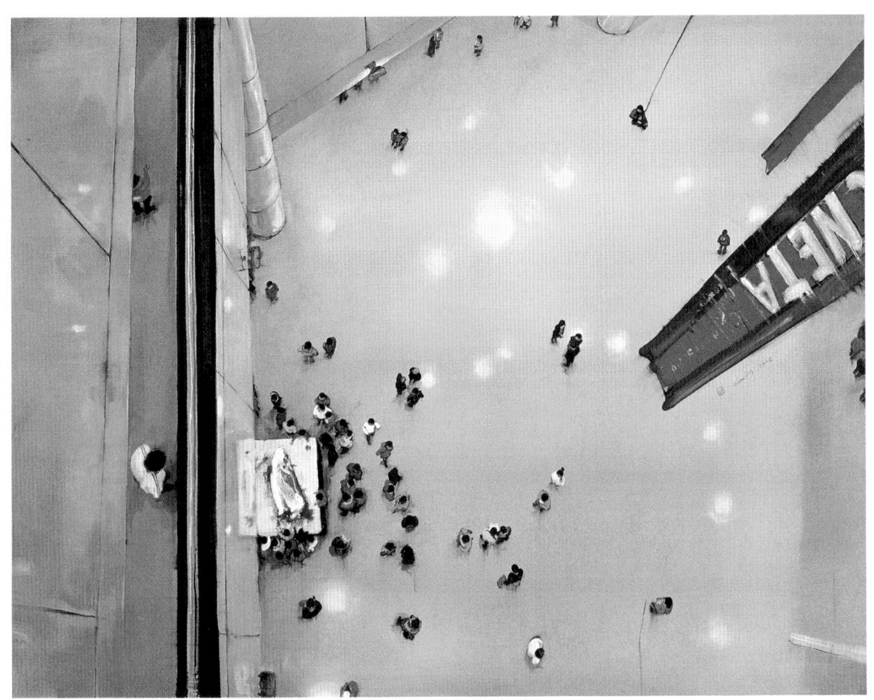

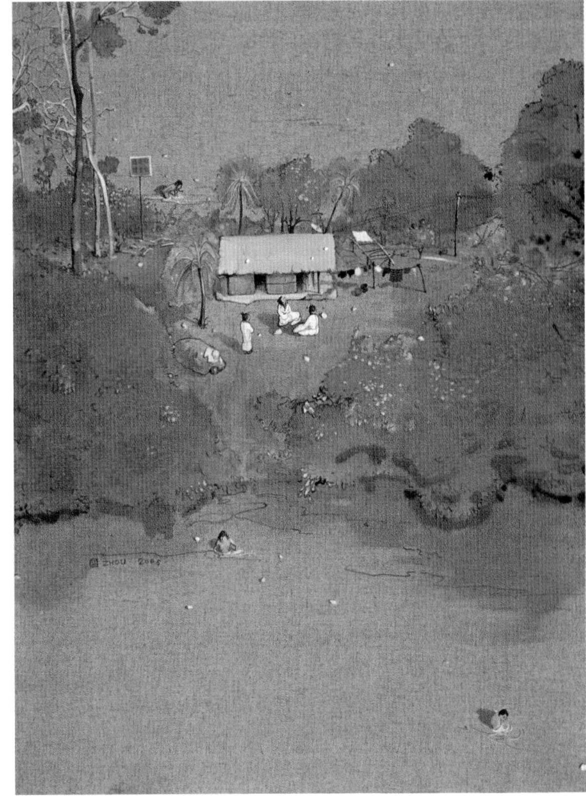

4 AT THE END IT IS ALL THE SAME NO. 4 • 2007 • OIL ON CANVAS • 145 x 110 CM

5 RESPLENDENCE NO. 2 • 2008 • OIL AND ACRYLICS ON CANVAS • 145 x 190 CM

6 THE RECLUSE • 2006 • OIL ON CANVAS • 70 x 60 CM

7

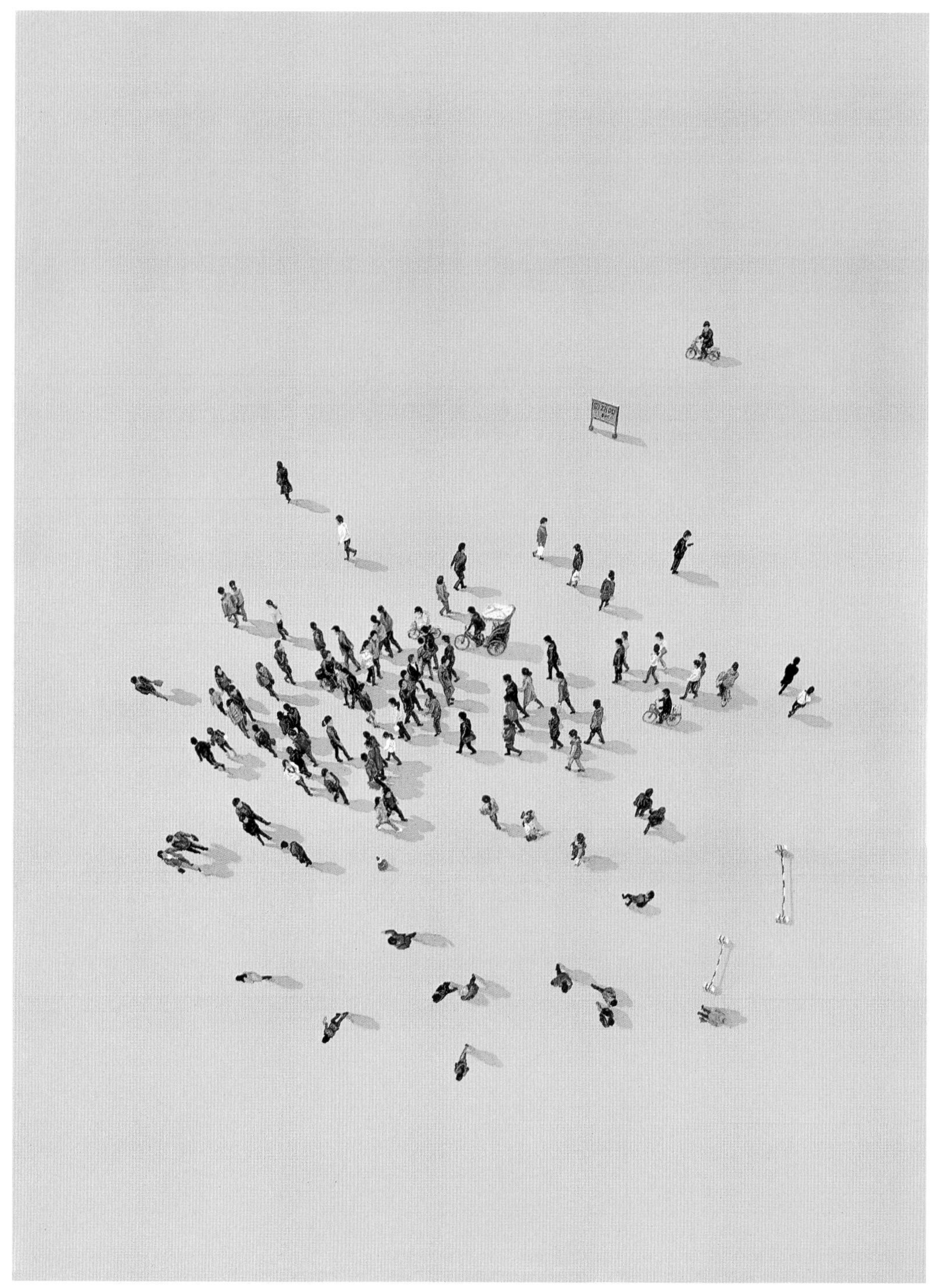

7 WE SERIES NO. 7 • 2005 • OIL ON CANVAS • 145 x 110 CM

8 SPOTTY SERIES NO. 1 • 2005 • OIL ON CANVAS • 30 x 30 CM

8

FACE-TO-FACE INTERVIEW WITH EDITORS

4/29/08 • AFTERNOON • CAFE IN 798 IN BEIJING

EDITORS *Do you still remember what was your favorite childhood toy?* **ZHOU JINHUA** A toy pistol. **EDITORS** *What sentence did your parents say to you most often?* **ZHOU JINHUA** They always requested that I should rest more and pay close attention to my health.

EDITORS *We know that you are always very busy working. How do you try nowadays to maintain your health in your everyday life?* **ZHOU JINHUA** I try to maintain a healthy diet; for example, not eat too much meat and not to drink alcohol. **EDITORS** *And do you also practice any sports?* **ZHOU JINHUA** When I lived in Chongqing, I used to go running at the sports field of our university campus. After moving to Beijing, I stopped exercising. Although I was a member of a fitness center here, I gave up after I went two or three times, because I didn't have enough time to go.

EDITORS *Do you have any recent wish?* **ZHOU JINHUA** Let me think ... I hope to be able to travel to other provinces within China; for example, the Bashang grassland between Beijing and Inner Mongolia. **EDITORS** *And do you believe in true love?* **ZHOU JINHUA** Yes, I definitely do.

EDITORS *What does your ideal living environment look like?* **ZHOU JINHUA** For me, a clean environment is very important. Last year I visited a small town in Denmark, which I enjoyed a lot. The local environment was very natural, and what is most important to me is the living conditions were very good. In China, the environment in provinces such as Yunnan and Tibet is probably the best; however, these provinces also have limited traffic and communication facilities. There is often a trade-off between the level of development and environmental problems. **EDITORS** *Could you name which type of media provides you most of your inspiration?* **ZHOU JINHUA** I guess I get most of my ideas out of novels and magazines. In addition, I also do some photography and many of the photos I take also provide me with some inspiration.

EDITORS *What do you like about being an artist?* **ZHOU JINHUA** I like the simplicity and truthfulness. **EDITORS** *And is there something you do not like?* **ZHOU JINHUA** I dislike the complexity, dishonesty, and indirectness.

EDITORS *How can you communicate with the audience through your art?* **ZHOU JINHUA** There are many ways: through the color, the lines, the settings and atmosphere, and of course, through the topic itself and what's happening in the painting.

EDITORS *This year you turn thirty. Could you name five words to describe your generation?* **ZHOU JINHUA** I would say, luck, confusion, pressure, responsibility, and uncertainty.

EDITORS *If the whole world could listen to you for fifteen seconds, what would you say?* **ZHOU JINHUA** "I hope the world will become a better place!"

EXHIBITIONS

SELECTED SOLO EXHIBITIONS

2009
Alles war in Ordnung, bis das Unerwartete geschah, Kunstverein Konstanz, Konstanz, Germany

2008
Constancy. Inconstancy, Gallery Beijing Space, Beijing, China

2007
The Observer, Schoeni Gallery, Hong Kong, China

SELECTED GROUP EXHIBITIONS

2007
Your View, My Story, Pferdeställe des alten Postfuhramtes, Berlin, Germany

2007
Starting from the Southwest, Guangdong Museum of Art, Guangzhou, China

2007
Generation Süss-Sauer: Chinas neue Künstler, Mannheimer Kunstverein, Mannheim, Germany

2007
Visual Experiences, National Art Museum of China, Beijing, China

2005
Southern life, Kunming Loft, Kunming, China

2004
Track: Sino-Korean Art Exhibition, Chongqing, China

2003
National Outstanding Graduates Oil Painting Exhibition, He Xiangning Art Museum, Shenzhen, China

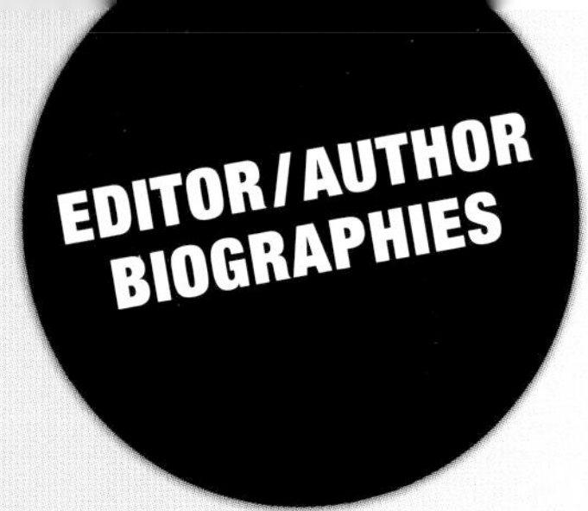

EDITORS

CHRISTOPH NOE

After finishing his studies in business administration and history at the University of Mannheim and the University of Strathclyde, Glasgow, Christoph Noe has been working for a number of years as a strategic management consultant in Europe and Asia. Based in Beijing and Berlin, in 2005 Christoph Noe founded THE MINISTRY OF ART, following his passion for contemporary Chinese art. THE MINISTRY OF ART acts as a platform to promote young Chinese artists by, for example, facilitating and curating exhibition projects. Specializing on the Post-70s generation of artists, Christoph Noe has lectured frequently on this topic.

CORDELIA NOE

Cordelia Noe is a graduate of social sciences and intercultural communication from Ludwig-Maximilians-University, Munich. After initially gaining experience in the field of Western art, she became fascinated by the variety and happenings in the Chinese art scene, bringing her to co-found THE MINISTRY OF ART. Specialized on Chinese artists of the Post-70s generation, Cordelia Noe works as a curator for various exhibition projects and also serves as an advisor for private and public collections as well as corporate art programs.

XENIA PIËCH

Xenia Piëch is a Beijing-based specialist in the field of contemporary Chinese art. She is a Sinologist and art historian by training, having received her education at the School of Oriental and African Studies (SOAS), University of London, and the Institute of Fine Arts, New York University. Since 2002 she has been writing for various English- and German-language art publications and has authored a number of catalogue essays. Beginning in 2004, Xenia Piëch has been the China Desk Editor for *ArtAsiaPacific* and has also give a number of lectures on Chinese contemporary art, including at the Rietberg Museum (Switzerland), the UBS Arts Forum, and the World Economic Forum.

AUTHORS

JAMES CHAU

James Chau is one of China's leading television presenters, anchoring the news and current affairs for the English-language state channel, CCTV-9. He has covered headline news from the Asian Tsunami to the 9/11 attacks and writes a monthly guest column for a Hong Kong-based architecture journal. He has interviewed a range of figures in the arts including Daniel Libeskind, Jimmy Choo, Lord Snowdon, and most recently Olivia Newton-John. Born in London and a graduate of Cambridge University, James Chau was chosen by Google and the United Nations as one of its "Young Leaders" in 2008 for his ongoing work on HIV/AIDS.

HUANG DU

Huang Du was born in 1965, Shaanxi Province, China. He works as senior curator at Beijing Today Art Museum and was appointed chief curator of the 3rd Nanjing Triennial 2008, China. A graduate in Art History from the Central Academy of Fine Arts in 1988, Huang Du studied at Bologna University, Italy in 1991–92. He worked as editor for *Meishu (Art Monthly)* in Beijing from 1988 to 2001 and got his Ph.D. at the Central Academy of Fine Arts in 2004. He has written articles on contemporary art for numerous magazines and contributed to various catalogues. Huang Du curated and co-curated numerous important exhibitions such as *Chinese Pavilion of the 50th Venice Biennale 2003*, *Thermocline of Art: New Asian Waves*, ZKM Center for Art and Media Karlsruhe, Germany, 2007, and *The First Today's Documents 2007*, Beijing Today Art Museum.

DIRK JEHMLICH

Dirk Jehmlich is co-founder and General Manager of China's first trend research agency, Trendbüro Asia-Pacific in Beijng, a branch of the well-established German consultancy Trendbüro. He gained intense insight into Asian consumer culture as well as into emerging social trends during various research projects. He is a consultant to many Fortune 500 companies specializing in trend-based branding and strategic trend management. Possessing a background in marketing and economics in Europe, Asia, and the United States, Dirk Jehmlich also worked as promoter and DJ during which time he established a network of trailblazers across the world.

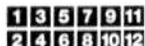

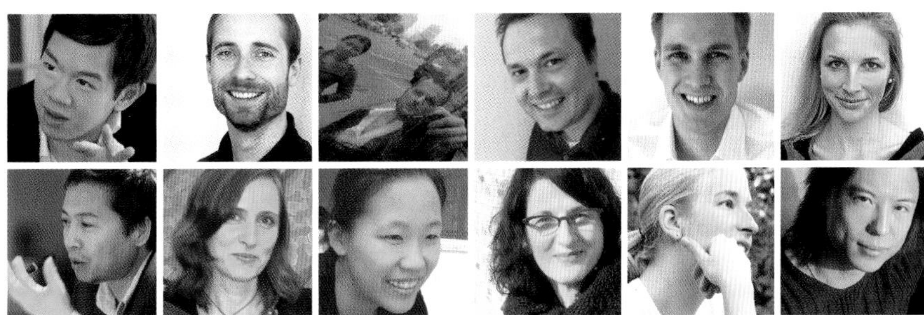

MARTINA KÖPPEL-YANG

Martina Köppel-Yang is an independent art historian and curator with a Ph.D. in East Asian Art History and Sinology from the University of Heidelberg. She studied in Heidelberg, Beijing, and Paris and has been involved in contemporary Chinese art since her time as a student at the Central Fine Arts Academy in Beijing in the mid-1980s. She has written extensively on the subject and is a member of the editorial boards of, for example, *Yishu: Journal for Contemporary Chinese Art*, and *Red Flag Collection*, a compilation of contemporary Chinese artists, Map Book Publishers, Hong Kong. She also created Mühlgasse 40, Centre for Contemporary Chinese Art, together with her husband Yang Jiechang.

NAUDIA LOU

Born in Beijing in the early 80s, Naudia Lou moved to the U.S. in her youth. After graduating with a degree in economics and psychology, her strong ties with China drew her back. Naudia has a strong interest in developing countries and different cultures, and currently researches and writes about various issues involving development in China including trade and e-commerce. She is currently working with Christian Taeubert on a photography book called *Beijing Full-Throttle*. The photos document Beijing as it undergoes rapid development during the pre-Olympic era.

CAROL (YINGHUA) LU

Carol Yinghua Lu is an independent curator and art writer based in Beijing. She is the co-editor of *Art & Investment* and *Contemporary Art & Investment* magazines, and a frequent contributor to a number of international art magazines such as *Frieze, Contemporary,* and *Today Art*. As a graduate of the Critical Studies program at the Malmö Art Academy, Lund University, Sweden, she was the China researcher for the Asia Art Archive from 2005 to 2007. Her curatorial work includes *The Temperament of Detail* at The Red Mansion Foundation, London; *Foreign Objects* at the Project Space of Kunsthalle Wien, Vienna; two curatorial projects in ARCO'06 and ARCO'07, Madrid; and *Community of Taste*, the inaugural exhibition of the Iberia Center for Contemporary Art, Beijing. She also served as the art consultant for the Olympic Museum Lausanne on a major exhibition about China.

JOHN MILLICHAP

John Millichap has lived in China for thirteen years. From 1995 to 1999 he was an editor for *Asian Art News* and *World Sculpture News* magazines in Hong Kong. He has contributed to numerous international magazines and newspapers on contemporary Asian art and culture. In 2005, he founded the independent publishing house 3030 Press and edited its debut title, *3030: New Photography in China*. John Millichap also curated the exhibition *New Photography in China*, which was presented at the Beijing International Art Fair 2007 as well as at the Hong Kong City Festival 2008, and co-presented the seminar "Contemporary China Through The Lens" at the Hong Kong City Festival 2008.

ULRIKE MÜNTER

Based in Berlin, Ulrike Münter works as an art historian and freelance art critic focusing on Chinese contemporary art. Since 2002, she visits China frequently for research purposes and to conduct interviews. Her texts on contemporary Chinese art have been published in a number of publications, including *artnet.net, Eikon, Kunstzeitung, Informationsdienst Kunst, Kunstjahr, The Asia Pacific Times, Capital, NZZ, and Die Tageszeitung (taz)*. In relation to "art and culture from China," Ulrike Münter has collaborated with a number of artists, galleries, and art institutions.

ROCK (SHI HAI LONG)

Rock is a pioneer in the Beijing fitness scene, having worked in the field of fitness and as a private trainer since 2000. He has given private lessons and conducted classes in a number of major sport clubs in Beijing. Having a strong background in martial arts and Kung Fu, he is specialized in Body Combat classes, though is enthusiastic about being an instructor for spinning and—the latest fitness trend in China—"Zumba" dance classes. His career includes the title "Mr. Fitness Beijing," which he was awarded in 2004.

1 James Chau **2** Huang Du **3** Dirk Jehmlich **4** Martina Köppel-Yang
5 Naudia Lou and Christian Taeubert **6** Carol (Yinghua) Lu
7 John Millichap **8** Ulrike Münter **9** Christoph Noe **10** Xenia Piëch
11 Cordelia Noe **12** Rock (Shi Hai Long)

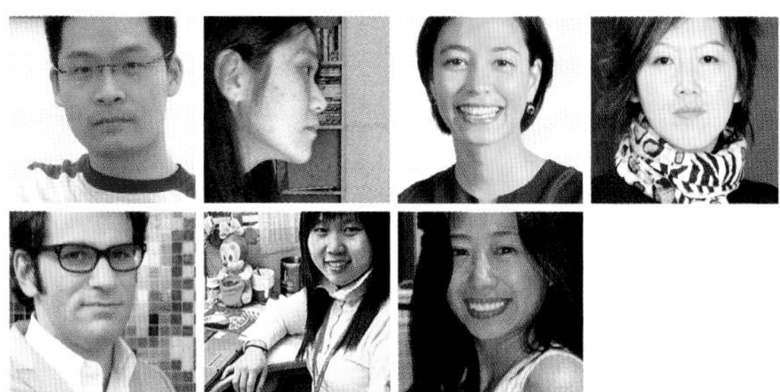

AUTHORS

SONG YI

Song Yi was born in 1983 in Chengdu, Sichuan Province, China. A graduate of the Sichuan Academy of Fine Arts printmaking department in 2006, he now works in and lives in Beijing. Currently, Song Yi works as an editor of *Art & Investment* and *Contemporary Art & Investment* magazines, and has published a number of articles on young Chinese artists.

CHRISTIAN TAEUBERT

Christian Taeubert, born in Germany in 1972, is a designer and architect. He settled down in Beijing in 2005 after working in Los Angeles, Vienna, and London. Christian's writing and design work reflect the idea that no observation is made only by the observer and that no design is impartial. He is currently working with Naudia Lou on a photography book called *Beijing Full-Throttle*. The photos document Beijing as it undergoes rapid development during the pre-Olympic era.

PHILIP TINARI

Philip Tinari is a writer and curator based in Beijing. He directs the editorial studio Office for Discourse Engineering, and serves as Contributing Editor of *Artforum* and China Advisor to Art Basel. He has written, edited, and translated numerous books and essays on the contemporary Chinese art scene, and his articles have appeared in various publications, including *Artforum, Parkett, The Wall Street Journal*, and *The New York Times Magazine*. He has also contributed to a number of museum catalogues, including for the Guggenheim, Serpentine Gallery, and MMK Frankfurt. Philip Tinari holds an A.M. in East Asian studies from Harvard University, 2005, and was a Fulbright Fellow at Peking University from 2001 until 2002. He has lectured at the China Institute in America, New York, and the China Art Academy, Hangzhou, and consults frequently for international arts organizations on their projects in China.

AZURE (WEI) WU

Azure Wu, born in 1981, works as an art critic and curator based in Shanghai. From 2004 to 2006, Azure Wu worked at Shanghai Duolun Museum of Modern Art and Zhu Qizhan Art Museum, Shanghai. Since 2007, she works as an editor at *Art China Magazine* and also is a frequent contributor to numerous publications on contemporary Chinese art, such as *artforum.com.cn, Time Out Shanghai*, and *Vision*. Azure Wu has not only written on the Chinese art scene, but has also reviewed the work of Western artists.

XIA JUAN

Having graduated from the Department of Journalism at Nanjing Normal University, Xia Juan gained experience working with important Chinese magazines, such as *Nanfang Ren Wu (Southern People's Weekly)*, and the weekly newspaper *The Economic Observer*. Since 2007, she works at an Internet start-up.

PAULINE J. YAO

Pauline J. Yao is an independent curator and writer based in Beijing and San Francisco. She received her M.A. in East Asian Languages and Civilizations from the University of Chicago, and from 2000 to 2006 held the post of Assistant Curator of Chinese Art at the Asian Art Museum and was Senior Lecturer at California College of Arts in San Francisco. Yao serves on the editorial board of *Yishu: Journal of Contemporary Chinese Art* and *Contemporary Art & Investment*, and her writings have appeared in *Yishu, Flash Art, Contemporary Art & Investment* (Chinese), *ArtAsiaPacific*, and *Art Papers*. She is the 2007 inaugural recipient of the Contemporary Chinese Art Critic Award.

MIAO YU

Miao Yu, born in 1974, is a Ph.D. candidate in Art History at McGill University, Montreal, and doctoral fellow at the Social Science and Humanities Research Council of Canada. She is currently researching her dissertation on the images of urban destruction and urban waste in Chinese contemporary art since the 1990s. Writing in both English and Chinese, Miao Yu is a frequent contributor to *Art World, Contemporary*, and *Urban China*, and lives in Beijing.

ZHONG YU (LILY)

Zhong Yu, born in 1976, works as editor-in-chief for *Parents* magazine, a publication of the Gruner + Jahr publishing house in Beijing. During her more than seven years experience with the magazine, she not only enjoys witnessing the growing up of the featured children, but also the development of the young parents. According to Zhong Yu, her current position provides her with the chance to find out more about the topics that mean the most to all of us: love, happiness, and family values.

13 Song Yi **14** Philip Tinari **15** Azure (Wei) Wu **16** Xia Juan
17 Pauline J. Yao **18** Miao Yu **19** Zhong Yu

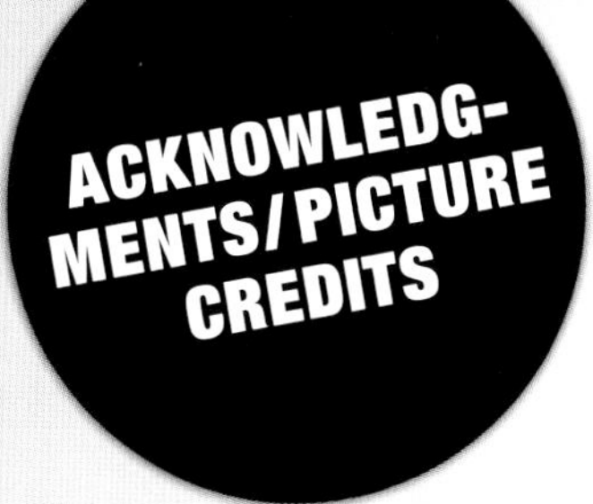

ACKNOWLEDGMENTS

WE WOULD LIKE TO THANK ALL THE ARTISTS, THEIR GALLERIES AND ASSISTANTS FOR THE TIME AND EFFORT IN PROVIDING IMAGES AND INFORMATION.

SPECIAL THANKS TO

Alexia Dehaene
Li Xuehui
Zhang Xiaomo
Boers-Li Gallery, Beijing
F2 Gallery, Beijing
Lombard Freid Projects, New York
Max Protetch Gallery, New York
ShanghART, Shanghai
Tang Gallery, Beijing
Vitamin Creative Space, Guangzhou

PICTURE CREDITS

Cover Courtesy of the artists
Birdhead pp. 12, 18, 24, 38–47: Courtesy of the artists and ShanghART
Cao Fei pp. 33, 50 above, 53–55: Courtesy of the artist and Lombard-Freid Projects, New York
pp. 48, 50 below, 51, 52: Courtesy of the artist and Vitamin Creative Space
Chen Ke pp. 56–64: Courtesy of the artist
Chen Qiulin pp. 66, 73: Courtesy of the artist and Max Protetch
pp. 68–72, 74 right: Courtesy of the artist
p. 74 left: Courtesy of the artist and Long March Space
Chi Peng pp. 29, 76–85: Courtesy of the artist
Gong Jian pp. 86–95: Courtesy of the artist, Boers-Li Gallery, and Fine Arts Literature Center
Han Yajuan pp. 26, 96, 98, 99 top, 100 right, 101: Courtesy of BTAP
p. 99 bottom: Courtesy of Olyvia Oriental
p. 100 left: Courtesy of Willem Kerseboom Gallery
pp. 102/103: Courtesy of the artist
Li Hui pp. 104–113: Courtesy of the artist
Li Jikai pp. 114–122: Courtesy of the artist
Li Qing pp. 13, 14, 124–132: Courtesy of the artist and F2 Gallery
p. 133: Courtesy of the artist
Li Yu / Liu Bo pp. 134–141: Courtesy of the artists
Liang Yue pp. 12, 30, 142–148: Courtesy of the artist and ShanghART
Liu Ding pp. 150, 154–158: Courtesy of the artist
pp. 152, 153: Courtesy of the artist and L.A. Gallery, Frankfurt
Liu Ren pp. 160–169: Courtesy of the artist, Paris-Beijing Photo Gallery, and Ooi Botos Gallery
Liu Weijian pp. 12, 20, 170–177: Courtesy of the artist and ShanghART
Ma Yanhong pp. 178–187: Courtesy of the artist
Qiu Xiaofei pp. 16, 188–196: Courtesy of the artist
Ta Men pp. 16, 198–205: Courtesy of the artists
Tang Maohong pp. 206–213: Courtesy of the artist and ShanghART
Wang Guangle pp. 214–218, 220–223: Courtesy of the artist
p. 219: Courtesy of Beijing Commune
Wei Jia pp. 224–233: Courtesy of the artist
Wen Ling pp. 22, 234–242: Courtesy of the artist
Wu Junyong pp. 244–253: Courtesy of the artist
Xu Zhen pp. 34, 254–261: Courtesy of the artist and ShanghART
Yang Yong pp. 264, 266, 268–271: Courtesy of the artist
pp. 262, 265, 267: Tang Gallery
Zhang Ding pp. 272–280: Courtesy of the artist and ShanghART
Zhou Jinhua pp. 282–291: Courtesy of the artist

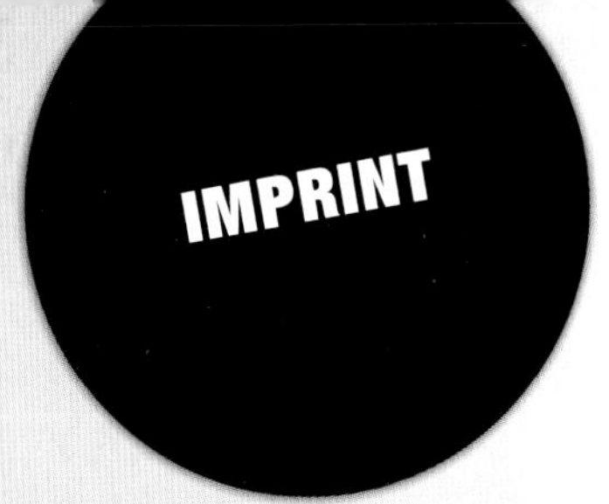

FRONT COVER: TA MEN, LOST HEAVEN NO.2, 2008-2009, OIL ON CANVAS, 380 X 1000 CM

PRESTEL VERLAG
Königinstrasse 9
80539 Munich
Tel. +49 (0)89 24 29 08 - 300
Fax +49 (0)89 24 29 08 - 335
www.prestel.de

PRESTEL PUBLISHING LTD.
4 Bloomsbury Place
London WC1A 2QA
Tel. +44 (0)20 7323 - 5004
Fax +44 (0)20 7636 - 8004

PRESTEL PUBLISHING
900 Broadway, Suite 603
New York, NY 10003
Tel. +1 (212) 995 - 2720
Fax +1 (212) 995 - 2733
www.prestel.com

The Library of Congress Control Number: 2010928279
Library of Congress Control Number is available; British Library Cataloguing-in-Publication Data: a catalogue record for this book is available from the British Library; Deutsche Nationalbibliothek holds a record of this publication in the Deutsche Nationalbibliografie; detailed bibliographical data can be found under: http://dnb.d-nb.de

Prestel books are available worldwide. Please contact your nearest bookseller or one of the above addresses for information concerning your local distributor.

Project management Anita Dahlinger
Copyediting Jonathan Fox, Barcelona
Production Simone Zeeb
Art direction Cilly Klotz
Design and layout: SOFAROBOTNIK, Augsburg & Munich
Origination Repro Ludwig, Zell am See
Printing and Binding Printer Trento srl, Trento

Printed in Italy.

ISBN 978-3-7913-5060-8

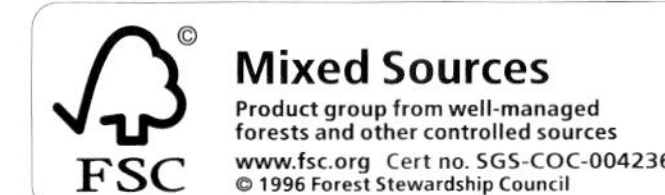